HB 139 ECO.

ECONOMIC DECISION-MAKING: GAMES, ECONOMETRICS AND OPTIMISATION

Contributions in Honour of Jacques H. Drèze

ECONOMIC DECISION-MAKING: GAMES, ECONOMETRICS AND OPTIMISATION

Contributions in Honour of Jacques H. Drèze

Edited by

J.J. GABSZEWICZ, *CORE*
J.-F. RICHARD, *Duke University*
L.A. WOLSEY, *CORE*

1990

NORTH-HOLLAND
Amsterdam-New York-Oxford-Tokyo

ELSEVIER SCIENCE PUBLISHERS B.V.
Sara Burgerhartstraat 25
P.O. Box 1991, 1000 BZ Amsterdam
The Netherlands

Distributors for the United States and Canada
ELSEVIER SCIENCE PUBLISHING COMPANY INC.
655 Avenue of the Americas
New York, N.Y. 10010, U.S.A.

ISBN North-Holland 0 444 88422 X

Library of Congress Cataloging-in-Publication Data

Economic decision-making : games, econometrics, and optimisation :
  contributions in honour of Jacques H. Drèze / edited by J.J.
  Gabszewicz, J.F. Richard, L.A. Wolsey.
      p.   cm.
   Includes bibliographical references.
   ISBN 0-444-88422-X (U.S.)
   1. Econometrics. 2. Decision-making. 3. Game theory.
  4. Mathematical optimization. 5. Drèze, Jacques H.   I. Drèze,
  Jacques H. II. Gabszewicz, Jean Jaskold. III. Richard, Jean
  François. IV. Wolsey, Laurence A.
  HB139.E34   1990
  330'.01'5195--dc20   90-32284
                                                            CIP

PRINTED IN THE NETHERLANDS

PREFACE

In his 1970 Presidential address to the Econometric Society entitled "Econometrics and Decision Theory", Jacques Drèze outlined the potential interaction of economic theory, econometrics and optimisation. To quote: *"My theme will be that we should now regard as a realistic challenge the formal analysis of decision problems in economics, resting on a specification of ends and means firmly rooted in economic theory, incorporating a probabilistic treatment of econometric information, and making use of the possibilities offered by mathematical programming techniques to compute optimal policies."*
Among the many excited by this perception, those having contact with Jacques Drèze either directly, or initially through the three CORE seminars in Mathematical Economics, Econometrics and Mathematical Programming, have been able to observe the advances, failures, and modifications in that vision. Though few have the breadth to measure the progress made on this wide front, all of us can marvel at many of the developments of the last twenty years in several of which Drèze has played an active role.

This collection of papers is an expression of friendship for Jacques Drèze. The editors found unconditional support in the idea of assembling such a collection. Clearly Jacques Drèze has left on those who have been at CORE over the last twenty years a lasting impression that goes way beyond mere scientific recognition but more deeply reflects his exceptional human qualities and friendship. There are many who would have liked to contribute but have been deprived of this opportunity by space or time constraints. We can only hope that this will give him pleasure and thank the contributors for their efforts.

Such a collection cannot do justice to his vision. He is one of the rare people with the breadth of knowledge and interest to digest all these contributions. For the ordinary mortal we hope these papers give an insight into some of the progress that has been made, new topics that have caught the imagination, and how numerous researchers in each of the areas have been marked by Jacques' insights, guidance and example. Jacques has contributed in numerous areas. To cite just a few: in economics there are papers in the Microeconomic Theory of Uncertainty, Consumption,

Production, Investments, Markets, Theory of the Second Best, General Equilibrium Theory, Worker Management Theory, Public Finance and International Trade, in econometrics there are important papers in Bayesian Econometrics, and Decision Theory, and in Optimisation there is a beautiful paper on a warehouse model under uncertainty.

In this collection we have chosen to group the papers into (I) Economics and Game Theory, (II) Econometrics and (III) Optimisation, reflecting his vision and the three areas which have led us to meet Jacques at CORE. The papers in Part I can be roughly classified as falling in the areas of Equilibrium Theory, Industrial Economics and Game Theory. Those in Part II are in demand and policy related models and Bayesian econometrics, while the papers in Part III concern linear, stochastic and integer programming. The introduction that follows contains a more detailed overview of the collection.

Quoting again the final words of his address: "*Those who will extend the work in this area . . . are sure to learn a great deal from looking at real life problems; and I will make the modest promise that it will be a lot of fun.*" To finish we can only reiterate the pleasure the contributors and editors have derived from knowing and talking to Jacques, and we look forward to much fun in the future.

J.J. Gabszewicz, Louvain-la-Neuve
J.-F. Richard, Durham
L.A. Wolsey, Louvain-la-Neuve

LIST OF CONTRIBUTORS

Ronny Aboudi, *University of Miami*

Dennis J. Aigner, *University of California, Irvine*

Claude d'Aspremont, *CORE, Université Catholique de Louvain*

Robert J. Aumann, *The Hebrew University of Jerusalem*

Anton P. Barten, *Tilburg University, and CORE, Université Catholique de Louvain*

Luc Bauwens, *GREQE, Ecole des Hautes Etudes en Sciences Sociales, Marseille*

Robin Boadway, *Queen's University, Kingston*

Paul Champsaur, *Direction de la Prévision, Paris*

Parkash Chander, *Indian Statistical Institute, New Delhi*

Bernard Cornet, *Université de Paris I Panthéon-Sorbonne and Laboratoire d'Econométrie de l'Ecole Polytechnique, Paris*

James M. Dickey, *University of Minnesota, Minneapolis*

Herman K. van Dijk, *Erasmus University Rotterdam*

Jean-Pierre Florens, *GREMAQ, Université des Sciences Sociales, Toulouse*

Louis-André Gérard-Varet, *GREQE, Ecole des Hautes Etudes en Sciences Sociales, Marseille*

Louis Gevers, *Facultés Universitaires Notre-Dame de la Paix, Namur, and CORE, Université Catholique de Louvain*

Victor Ginsburgh, *Université Libre de Bruxelles, and CORE, Université Catholique de Louvain*

Stephen M. Goldfeld, *Princeton University*

Joseph Greenberg, *University of Haifa*

Ronald M. Harstad, *Virginia Commonwealth University, Richmond*

Robert Jordan, *GREQE, Université d'Aix-Marseille II*

Alan P. Kirman, *European University Institute, Florence*

Frank Lad, *University of Canterbury, Christchurch*

Jean-Paul Lambert, *Facultés Universitaires Saint-Louis, Bruxelles, and CORE, Université Catholique de Louvain*

Gilbert Laporte, *Ecole des Hautes Etudes Commerciales de Montréal*

François Louveaux, *Facultés Universitaires Notre-Dame de la Paix, Namur*

Maurice Marchand, *CORE and IAG, Université Catholique de Louvain*

Jean-François Mertens, *CORE, Université Catholique de Louvain*

Michel Mouchart, *CORE and IAG, Université Catholique de Louvain*

Benoît Mulkay, *Facultés Universitaires Saint-Louis, Bruxelles*

George L. Nemhauser, *Georgia Institute of Technology, Atlanta*

Damien Neven, *INSEAD, Fontainebleau*

Pierre Pestieau, *Université de Liège, and CORE, Université Catholique de Louvain*

Louis Phlips, *European University Institute, Florence*

Richard E. Quandt, *Princeton University*

Jean-Marie Rolin, *CORE and PROB, Université Catholique de Louvain*

Cornelus Roos, *Delft University of Technology*

Peter Schönfeld, *Universität Bonn*

Henri Sneessens, *Département de Sciences Economiques, Université Catholique de Louvain, and Faculté Libre de Sciences Economiques, Lille*

Jacques-François Thisse, *CORE, Université Catholique de Louvain*

Henry Tulkens, *CORE, Université Catholique de Louvain, and Facultés Universitaires Saint-Louis, Bruxelles*

Jean-Philippe Vial, *Université de Genève*

Roger J.-B. Wets, *University of California, Davis*

Laurence A. Wolsey, *CORE, Université Catholique de Louvain*

CONTENTS

INTRODUCTION

Economics and game theory

The papers in economics and game theory are grouped into the following subgroups. The three first papers deal with equilibrium theory while the fourth and the fifth are related, respectively, to decision theory under uncertainty and employment in the public sector. The next two papers touch issues in investment theory while the two papers, the one by Harstad and Phlips, and the other by Neven and Thisse provide theoretical developments in Industrial Economics. Finally, the last three papers address to important questions in game theory.

Chapter 1. In their paper, Champsaur and Cornet define a non-tâtonnement exchange process, using the framework of a pure exchange economy. At each period t, the consumers participate in a so-called "marginal" exchange economy in which, starting from their initial endowments, they can perform infinitesimal trades at a price vector which is determined competitively: the resulting allocation $x(t)$ and the price vector $p(t)$ which clears the infinitesimal trades at period t are a competitive equilibrium in this marginal economy; through this process initial endowments are modified. The authors show that the resulting exchange process converges to a Pareto-optimal allocation x^* of the initial exchange economy and the trajectory $p(t)$ converges to the price system p^* which sustains the Pareto optimum x^*.

Chapter 2. The paper by Chander and Tulkens discusses whether MDP quantity guided spanning processes for pure exchange economies can be shown to converge from the initial endowments to an allocation in the core of the economy. Such a process is exhibited which has this property, at least in the case of economies in which agents have quasi linear utilities. The process is of the nature of a "non-tâtonnement", in the sense that it

Economic Decision-Making: Games, Econometrics and Optimisation
Edited by J.J. Gabszewicz, J.-F. Richard and L.A. Wolsey
© *Elsevier Science Publishers B.V., 1990*

involves files. With those prices, the core allocation to which the process converges is also a competitive equilibrium.

Chapter 3. The paper of Gérard-Varet, Jordan and Kirman presents a model which provides a basis for a satisfactory treatment of short-run disequilibria with quantity rationing. The framework is a stochastic version of the three-market Benassy–Drèze–Malinvaud model. A genuinely dynamic structure is introduced since production today is only for sale tomorrow and consumers may only spend today past earnings. Expectations about rationing are taken as formed on the basis of observations about the present state of disequilibrium of the markets and the horizon problem is solved by assuming that the agents' forecasting capacity is more limited than their economic lives. A temporary equilibrium is given by associating with a wage-price pair a vector of quantity signals, under the condition that agents' reactions generate a state of the economy consistent with these signals. Existence and stability of temporary equilibria are studied, and the structure of the set of these equilibria is considered, giving insights into long-term price adjustments.

Chapter 4. In decision theory under risk one can contrast the approach of von Neumann and Morgenstern, axiomatizing directly a preference relation on a set of lotteries, to a Bernoullian approach deriving first a cardinal utility based on the comparisons of riskless outcome differences, and then extending it to risky prospects. In their paper d'Aspremont and Gevers follow a Bernoullian approach to the theory of decision under uncertainty, and this is to be contrasted to Savage's approach to expected utility. They use results obtained in the framework of social choice theory to weaken the usual continuity conditions and analyse the consequences of introducing various assumptions of invariance and neutrality, which are new in an individual decision-theoretic context.

Chapter 5. The paper by Boadway, Marchand and Pestieau addresses the question of appropriate rules for public sector hiring policy in the context of models in which unemployment is generated through wages being set too high endogenously: such wages are called efficiency wages. There are two reasons evoked for explaining why wages are set above their market clearing level: the shirking and turnover costs. According to the shirking model, high wages inducing unemployment are used to discipline workers; according to the turnover model, high wages reduce the attractiveness to quit and thus save the turnover costs to the firm. A public sector is introduced by the authors into these models, with shirking or turnover costs also present in the public sector. Optimal wage and employment policies are then derived for the public sector in the absence and presence of wage subsidies. In both models, the shadow wage differs from the market wage, but it may be either higher or lower depending on the parameters of the problem. However, once wage subsidies are allowed as a policy instrument, the case for an active employment policy vanishes in the turnover case, but not in the shirking case.

Chapter 6. The paper by Ginsburgh and Sneessens considers the problem raised by investment subsidies to firms, and their impact in shifting investment forward in time and in promoting welfare. To this end, they construct a two-sector overlapping generations model where consumers live for two periods, both consumers and firms have perfect foresight, and prices and wages are perfectly flexible, so that the economy is always at full-employment. The structural shock is represented by an unanticipated permanent change in consumers' preferences. This change induces firms to scrap part of their capital stock in one sector and to invest in the other. Because adjustment costs make capital imperfectly mobile across sectors, this structural change implies a loss of welfare for the generations living at the moment of the shock. The question is whether the scrapping and investment rates generated by the market are optimal, or whether there is room for government intervention.

It is shown by means of a numerical example that investment subsidies alone cannot improve each generation's welfare. This result can be achieved however if the government combines its investment incentives with an appropriate system of compensatory transfers from future to current generations.

Chapter 7. Lambert and Mulkay explore in their paper the investment behaviour of firms in a disequilibrium context. Their intention is to examine the effects of alternative policy instruments when their longer run impact is taken into consideration. This is not done in existing empirical disequilibrium models which are essentially short-term models treating key variables — like price and investment — as exogenous. To realize this objective, the authors build a model based on a stochastic rationing of firms, induced by the fact that firms face uncertain future demand: then, the expected constraint on the level of demand is a stochastic variable for the firm. First, they have a theoretical section, in which the firm decides jointly on its optimal capacity and optimal technical coefficients: the authors conclude that profitability is a prime long-run determinant of desired capacity. Then an empirical application conducted on the Belgian manufacturing sector supports the hypothesis that an important role is played by profitability as a long-run determinant of investment behaviour.

Chapter 8. Harstad and Phlips propose a model of a futures market for an exhaustible resource, based on an industry with a duopolistic structure. When the commodity traded on a futures market is produced in a concentrated industry, the producers can manipulate the market value of futures contracts at maturity since they control the time path of production. The authors build a two-stage noncooperative game, based on particular price setting and allocation determining rules in futures activity, embodying three players, the duopolists, one of whom is risk-averse, and a single risk-neutral speculator. All three hold inconsistent prior beliefs about the level of final demand for the resource. The situation is analyzed as a two-stage noncooperative game with inconsistent incomplete information. The authors show that in a subgame perfect equilibrium of this game, there remain mutually beneficial trades of futures contracts which are not realized, leading to a suboptimal, inefficient volume of futures trading.

Chapter 9. Two products are vertically (resp. horizontally) differentiated when, sold at the same price, all consumers (resp. not all consumers) prefer to buy one product rather than the other. In the product differentiation literature, price competition under horizontal and vertical product differentiation have so far been analyzed separately. In contrast, Neven and Thisse study a duopoly model encompassing simultaneously horizontal and vertical differentiation. The authors seek subgame perfect Nash equilibria in a game where firms choose, first, the horizontal (variety) and the vertical (quality) characteristics of their product and, then, compete in prices. They show that, whatever the products' characteristics, a price equilibrium exists. In the product selection stage, firms choose maximum differentiation along one of the characteristics and minimum differentiation along the other. When the quality range is broad enough relative to the variety range, firms choose the same variety but maximise differentiation in quality. Otherwise, they both choose the maximum quality but maximise their difference in terms of variety.

Chapter 10. The intuitive basis for Nash's concept of strategic equilibrium in noncooperative games has received considerable attention. A justification for its use which has been proposed is that Nash equilibria represent "self-enforcing agreements": a preplay agreement to play a particular tuple of strategies will be kept if, and only if, it is a Nash equilibrium. By means of an example, Aumann throws some doubts on this assertion by showing that a nonenforceable preplay agreement may have no effect on removing the players' doubts about the choice of a particular strategy by his opponent. This is not true for all games, and an agreement to play an equilibrium is often self-enforcing (as in the "battle of the sexes"). In conclusion, Aumann shows that a nonbinding agreement can affect the outcome of a game if the information that such an agreement conveys is that each player wants the other to keep it.

Chapter 11. Greenberg has recently proposed a theory of social situations which applies to social environments in which it is impossible to impose a course of action on the individuals, while such a course of action can be recommended to them and each is then free to accept or reject the proposal. The theory has then been applied to games, and representing games as "situations", it turns out that this approach yields several of the better known game-theoretic solution concepts. In the present paper, Greenberg describes the main concepts of this theory, and states the main results which are obtained when the theory is applied to games in extensive form.

Chapter 12. In two different applications of game theory one needs approximations of $[0, 1]$-valued functions by $\{0, 1\}$-valued ones, namely in the Shapley value theorem of nonatomic games, for approximating an "ideal coalition" by a real coalition, and in the problem of approximating mixed strategies by pure strategies. Two existing approximation theorems, one by Aumann and the other by Dvoretzky, Wald and Wolfowitz, are strengthened in the paper proposed by Mertens. The strengthening requires only finite additivity and allows to deal with games which are not uniform limits of functions of finitely many measures.

Econometrics

The six papers in econometrics are organized into two subgroups. The first three papers analyse demand and policy related issues: rationing models with endogenous rationing, appliance specific components of household electricity consumption and Allais coefficients in the context of demand systems. The last three papers address specifically Bayesian issues: invariance, conditional prevision and limited information analysis.

Chapter 13. Goldfeld and Quandt analyse a class of rationing models in which rationing behavior emerges as an optimal strategy on the part of a policy maker, and discuss the econometric implications of such models. The formal model is that of a financial authority which lends to a regulated sector. The policy maker sets an interest rate, which in turn influences the demand for loans, and decides upon a volume of loans. A quadratic loss function is assumed. A "simplified" version of the model assumes that the policy maker first sets the interest rate, then observes the demand for loans and finally chooses the volume of loans. An "expected loss" version of the model assumes instead that interest rate and volume of loans are set jointly.

Various estimation techniques are proposed and evaluated by means of a simulation experiment. These techniques are then applied to a model of the Federal Home Loan Bank Board which provides loans to Saving and Loan Associations.

Chapter 14. The paper by Aigner and Schönfeld addresses the issue of decomposing the total electricity consumption of a household into appliance-specific components. Conditional Demand Analysis (CDA) aims at exploring the differences in appliance ownership patterns among households for that purpose. Lack of heterogeneity of appliance ownership does, however, mitigate CDA's ability to estimate specific appliance contribution with sufficient accuracy. The authors discuss the augmentation of the CDA approach by direct metering of major appliances and specifically address the problem of optimal experimental design of the metering experimentation in the context of a two-appliance model. A numerical illustration is provided. The authors also propose a combined analysis-of-covariance and error components model which provides a general framework for modelling end-use electricity demand.

Chapter 15. Barten discusses the relationship between estimable coefficients of regular and inverse demand systems and the so-called Allais coefficients. The latter are meant to measure complementarity, substitution or independence between commodities. Relative to other measures, the Allais coefficients offer the advantage that they are invariant under monotone transformations of the utility function and, hence, that they characterize intrinsic properties of the underlying preference ordering. Barten specifically discusses the relationships between the matrix of Allais coefficients and the Slutsky matrix (regular systems) or the Antonelli matrix (inverse systems). Separability of preferences is easily characterized in terms of the Allais coefficients and shifts in the preference ordering can be accommodated for. An application is provided to a nine equation regular demand system for food, estimated for Belgium.

Chapter 16. Florens, Mouchart and Rolin propose an extension of the standard concept of invariant measures to the conditional case and apply it to three problems of importance to Bayesian statisticians. Firstly, invariance arguments naturally lead to the construction of a so called "noninformative" prior distribution. Secondly, invariance may serve to provide a characterization of the notion of mutual sufficiency, which is central to a Bayesian treatment of invariance parameters, without recourse to extensive calculations. Thirdly invariance arguments play a central role in the derivation of sufficient conditions for the almost sure convergence of the posterior expectation of a given function of the parameters. The paper includes an exposition of the relevant statistical tools and considers prior measures instead of prior probabilities, thereby considerably extending the use of invariance arguments.

Chapter 17. Lad and Dickey offer an operational definition for a notion of conditional prevision when the conditioning quantity is not merely an event but an arbitrary general quantity. The relevance of their concept is illustrated by means of a simple currency exchange model where the stakes and future prices are labeled in either of two currencies and the future rate of exchange is unknown. Numerical solutions to this simple problem serve to illustrate the nature of the problem. The basic mathematical requirement of coherent conditional prevision is that of linearity relative to the object quantity (but non-linearity relative to the conditioning quantity). Two important related issues are emphasized. Previsions must be evaluated in terms of some "constant" units of net yields; conditional previsions are not logically related to temporal learning.

Chapter 18. Bauwens and van Dijk provide a systematic discussion of Bayesian Limited Information techniques in the context of (incomplete) Simultaneous Equation Models. Three different reparametrisations of the model are considered and conditions are given under which a "non-informative" prior distribution is invariant under the three representations. Posterior densities are derived for the structural parameters of interest and, in the context of a single structural equation, conditions are given under which that density is a so-called ratio-form poly-t density. These results are then used to provide insight on the issues of overidentification and exogeneity. It is also shown that the use of "non-informative" prior distributions in the context of an underidentified model may generate sharp explosive posterior distributions for some of the coefficients.

Optimisation

The five papers in optimisation touch on four different fields of interest: polyhedra and their structure, new linear programming algorithms and their relation to classical nonlinear programming approaches, stochastic programming, and finally integer and combinatorial optimisation.

Chapter 19. The paper of Wets contains simple, constructive proofs of three famous theorems about polyhedra. The first is Weyl's Theorem that any convex cone obtained as a nonnegative combination of a finite set of vectors is the intersection of a finite number of halfspaces. From this he demonstrates Farkas' lemma giving a necessary and sufficient condition for a system of linear inequalities to be nonempty, which is the fundamental result behind the duality theory of linear programming, and the Minkowski's theorem that is the converse of Weyl's theorem.

Chapter 20. The hottest topic in optimisation over the last five years has been the area of so-called interior point methods for linear programming. The computational success of algorithms based on these ideas indicates that in certain circumstances such algorithms can outperform the simplex method. The paper of Roos and Vial describes an adaptation of the classical logarithmic barrier method that leads to a polynomial algorithm for linear programming. The idea of several algorithms that have been shown to be polynomial is to follow a trajectory of points (centres, or minima of the barrier function) parametrised by the penalty term in the barrier function. The algorithms progress by making small decreases in the penalty parameter, and take correspondingly small steps along the trajectory. However making such small steps does not lead to a good algorithm in practice.

The originality of this paper is to show that the algorithm is still polynomial if one makes much larger reductions in the barrier parameter. The iterative step may then lead one away from the trajectory, but it is then proposed to fix the value of the penalty parameter and make a series of "long" projected Newton steps to get back into the vicinity of the trajectory. This leads to a practical algorithm with good theoretical properties.

Chapter 21. Solving practical routing problems is very difficult even when all the demands are known in advance. When the data is uncertain at the moment routing decisions are made, the vehicle may find itself with insufficient capacity at some stage during its trip. The vehicle then has to return to the depot to unload the material it has picked up on route, before heading to the next client on its tour. Such problems are thus doubly difficult because of their stochastic nature.

Laporte and Louveaux make a first step towards tackling such problems by presenting formulations capable of giving upper and lower bounds on the optimal vehicle utilisation and routing costs. Such bounds could potentially be used to judge the quality of a given routing plan. Two different formulations are presented, the difference being the moment at which the demand information becomes available. In one case the driver only discovers the real demand on arriving at a client. If he has insufficient capacity he must return to the depot to unload and then return to the client to continue his tour. In the second case he receives the information just before starting his tour, so he will return to the depot directly rather than visit a client whose demand he cannot handle. Then after unloading he can continue on to that client and pursue his tour.

Chapter 22. Most interesting or practical integer or combinatorial optimisation problems are known to be hard to solve. However much progress has been made in the last ten years in tackling certain classes of problems by studying the structure of the polyhedra that are obtained by looking at the convex hull of the feasible solutions. These polyhedra are given implicitly, and the difficulty is to find an approximation by linear inequalities.

Aboudi and Nemhauser take this approach to tackle an assignment problem having side constraints of the type "x is assigned to y if and only if u is assigned to v". The problem arose in timetabling for a university where certain classes run over several periods, so x and u correspond to the assignment of a class to two consecutive periods and y and v to the allocation of a room to two successive periods. A family of valid inequalities is developed to approximate the convex hull, and then a heuristic separation algorithm is given which permits the inequalities to be generated as cutting planes. This is because in practice one is only looking for a good approximation in the neighbourhood of the optimal solution. Some encouraging computational experience is reported.

Chapter 23. Machine scheduling is one area in which it is often easy to find fairly good feasible solutions and thus upper bounds on the optimal objective value, such as the minimum of the maximum completion time. However it is typically very difficult to find good lower bounds. Therefore this also is a natural area in which to look for a good linear inequality description, namely integer or mixed integer programming formulations which could provide strong lower bounds. So far there has been relatively little success in this direction.

Recently, however, Queyranne and Wang made some progress in formulating single machine problems with precedence constraints. Wolsey suggests alternative formulations using additional variables that are shown to be at least as strong, and have the advantage that they can be handled by standard mathematical programming systems. Results are reported for a problem with thirty jobs.

PART I

ECONOMICS AND GAME THEORY

Chapter 1

WALRASIAN EXCHANGE PROCESSES

Paul CHAMPSAUR

Direction de la Prévision, Paris, France

Bernard CORNET

Université de Paris I Panthéon-Sorbonne and Laboratoire d'Econométrie de l'Ecole Polytechnique, Paris, France

1. Introduction

The study of exchange processes without recontract was extensively studied in the early sixties by Negishi (1961), Uzawa (1962), Hahn (1962), Hahn and Negishi (1962) and Morishima (1962). These papers are surveyed in Chapter 13 of Arrow and Hahn's book *"General Competitive Analysis"*. This question was reexamined by Smale (1975) who mainly weakened the assumptions made in the previous papers that the "economic process satisfies some ordinary differential equation". Finally, in the study of dynamic exchange processes, Tulkens and Zamir (1979) also exhibit exchange processes with a different rule of price adjustment.

Our paper is very much in the spirit of the previous ones in the sense that we analyze non-tâtonnement processes for which trading out of equilibrium is allowed. Our treatment, however, is fundamentally different from the previous work since a Walrasian exchange process is determined endogenously at each time t by a competitive mechanism, the solution of which determines the infinitesimal trades $(d/dt)x_1(t), \ldots, (d/dt)x_m(t)$ of the different consumers and the associated (common) price system $p(t)$ at which the infinitesimal trades are made. This provides a solution to the question raised by Arrow and Hahn (1971, p. 325) of "how prices come to change in the absence of an auctioneer".

Economic Decision-Making: Games, Econometrics and Optimisation
Edited by J.J. Gabszewicz, J.-F. Richard and L.A. Wolsey
© *Elsevier Science Publishers B.V., 1990*

Consider a pure exchange economy with l commodities and m consumers. A Walrasian exchange process is a path which associates, to each time t, an allocation $x(t) = (x_1(t), \dots, x_m(t))$ and a price system $p(t)$ such that the infinitesimal trade $(d/dt)x(t) = (d/dt)x_1(t), \dots, (d/dt)x_m(t))$ and the price system $p(t)$ are Walras equilibria of the marginal economy $\mathscr{E}'(t)$ defined as follows. The economy $\mathscr{E}'(t)$ has the same numbers of commodities and consumers as the original economy $\mathscr{E}$ but, in $\mathscr{E}'(t)$, each consumer i is maximizing his (her) marginal utility $(d/dt)u_i(x_i(t))$ subject to his (her) ("marginal") budget constraint $p(t) \cdot (d/dt)x_i(t) = 0$, on his (her) ("marginal") consumption set, which will be precisely defined later.

We can now state our main result which asserts that, under standard assumptions, of differentiability, strict convexity and monotonicity of the preferences, Walrasian exchange processes are price adjustment processes in the sense that the following conditions are satisfied: (i) the allocation $x(t) = (x_1(t), \dots, x_m(t))$ is attainable for every t, (ii) the utility of each consumer is non-decreasing along the process, (iii) exchange takes place at the current price system $p(t)$, that is, $p(t) \cdot (d/dt)x_i(t) = 0$ for every i, and (iv) when $t \to +\infty$, $x(t)$ converges to a Pareto optimum x^* and $p(t)$ converges to the price system p^* which sustains x^*.

2. The model and the result

We consider a pure exchange economy with positive finite numbers l, of commodities and m, of consumers. The preferences of each consumer are represented by a utility function $u_i : X_i \to \mathbb{R}$, where X_i, a subset of $\mathbb{R}^l$, denotes his (her) consumption set. We denote by $\omega_i \in \mathbb{R}^l$ the vector of initial endowments of the consumer i. If $x = (x_h)$, $y = (y_h)$ are vectors in $\mathbb{R}^l$, we let $x \cdot y = \sum_{h=1}^{l} x_h y_h$ be the scalar product of $\mathbb{R}^l$ and $\|x\| = (x \cdot x)^{1/2}$ be the Euclidean norm. The notation $x \geq y$ (resp. $x \gg y$) means $x_h \geq y_h$ (resp. $x_h > y_h$) for every h; we let $\mathbb{R}^l_+ = \{x \in \mathbb{R}^l | x \geq 0\}$ and $\mathbb{R}^l_{++} = \{x \in \mathbb{R}^l | x \gg 0\}$.

In this paper we make the following basic assumption.

Assumption C. For every $i = 1, \dots, m$, (i) $X_i = \mathbb{R}^l_{++}$ and $\omega_i \in \mathbb{R}^l_{++}$; (ii) u_i is twice continuously differentiable, quasi-concave,[1] strongly differentiably monotone (i.e., $\nabla u_i(x_i) \gg 0$ for every x_i), and satisfies the following boundary condition: the set $u_i^{-1}(c)$ is closed in $\mathbb{R}^l$ for every real number c.[2]

---

[1] I.e., for every real number c, the set $\{x \in X_i | u_i(x) \geq c\}$ is convex.
[2] Here, $\nabla u_i(x) = ((\partial u_i/\partial x_1)(x), \dots, (\partial u_i/\partial x_l)(x))$ denotes the gradient vector of u_i at x.

We now recall some definitions. An allocation $x = (x_1, \ldots, x_m)$ is an element of the set $(\mathbb{R}_{++}^l)^m$. An attainable allocation is an element of the set

$$A = \left\{ x = (x_1, \ldots, x_m) \in (\mathbb{R}_{++}^l)^m \,\middle|\, \sum_{i=1}^m x_i = \sum_{i=1}^m \omega_i \right\}.$$

A Pareto optimum is an attainable allocation $x^* = (x_1^*, \ldots, x_m^*)$ such that there exists no attainable allocation $x = (x_1, \ldots, x_m)$ satisfying $u_i(x_i) \geq u_i(x_i^*)$ for every i and $u_j(x_j) > u_j(x_j^*)$ for some j. The following lemma gives a characterization of Pareto optima which will be useful in the following (see Smale, 1976; Cornet, 1988; for the proof).

For every i, and every $x_i \gg 0$, we let

$$g_i(x_i) = \nabla u_i(x_i) / \|\nabla u_i(x_i)\|.$$

Lemma 2.1. *Let* $x = (x_1, \ldots, x_m) \in (\mathbb{R}_{++}^l)^m$. *Under Assumption C the two following conditions are equivalent*:

(i) *x is a Pareto optimum*;

(ii) $g_1(x_1) = \cdots = g_m(x_m)$. □

2.1. The local game

We now define formally the local game, the solutions of which will be candidates for the infinitesimal trade $(\dot{x}_1(t), \ldots, \dot{x}_m(t))$ and the associated price system $p(t)$ at the allocation $x(t) = (x_1(t), \ldots, x_m(t))$. In the following we omit the reference to time t.

Let $\delta = (\delta_1, \ldots, \delta_m) \in (\mathbb{R}_{++}^l)^m$ be a fixed parameter and let $x = (x_1, \ldots, x_m)$ be a given allocation. We say that $(v_1^*, \ldots, v_m^*, p^*) \in (\mathbb{R}^l)^{m+1}$ is a *marginal Walrasian equilibrium at x* if it satisfies the two following conditions:

(a) For every i, v_i^* maximizes $g_i(x_i) \cdot v_i$ over the set

$$\{v_i \in \mathbb{R}^l \,|\, v_i \geq -\delta_i \text{ and } p^* \cdot v_i \leq 0\}.$$

(b) $\sum_{i=1}^m v_i^* = 0$.

We notice that the monotone assumption on the preference (that is, $g_i(x_i) \gg 0$) implies that $p^* \gg 0$.

Remark 2.1. We recall that the solution v_i^* is a candidate for the direction of move $(d/dt)x_i(t)$ of the consumer i at time $t > 0$. Thus at time $t > 0$,

$$g_i(x_i(t)) \cdot \dot{x}_i(t) = [1/\|\nabla u_i(x_i(t))\|]\nabla u_i(x_i(t)) \cdot \dot{x}_i(t)$$

$$= [1/\|\nabla u_i(x_i(t))\|]\frac{d}{dt} u_i(x_i(t)).$$

In words, the consumer i is maximizing his (her) marginal utility $(d/dt)u_i(x_i(t))$ at $x_i(t)$ (up to the multiplication by a positive scalar).

Remark 2.2. To justify the term "Walrasian" in the above definition we make the following change of variable: $w_i = v_i + \delta_i$ ($i = 1, \ldots, m$) and we notice that $(v_1^*, \ldots, v_m^*, p^*)$ is a marginal Walrasian equilibrium if and only if $(w_1^*, \ldots, w_m^*, p^*)$ satisfies the two following conditions:

(a') For every i, w_i^* maximizes $g_i(x_i) \cdot w_i$ over the set

$$\{w_i \in \mathbb{R}_+^l \mid p \cdot w_i \leq p \cdot \delta_i\}.$$

(b') $\sum_{i=1}^m w_i^* = \sum_{i=1}^m \delta_i$.

Thus, $(w_1^*, \ldots, w_m^*, p^*)$ is a Walras equilibrium of the (linear) pure exchange economy having l commodities and m consumers, with consumption sets $X_i = \mathbb{R}_+^l$, with utility functions, the linear functions $w_i \to g_i(x_i) \cdot w_i$, and with initial endowments the vectors $\delta_i \in \mathbb{R}_{++}^l$. Hence, from Debreu (1959), we deduce that there exist marginal Walrasian equilibria at every allocation x.

The signification (and the role) of the "initial endowment" δ_i is not so clear on economic grounds. From a technical point of view, it guarantees that the "marginal budget set" $\{w_i \in \mathbb{R}_+^l \mid p \cdot w_i \leq p \cdot \delta_i\}$ is compact.

2.2. Walrasian exchange processes

Let $\delta = (\delta_1, \ldots, \delta_m) \in (\mathbb{R}_{++}^l)^m$ be a fixed parameter. For every allocation $x = (x_1, \ldots, x_m)$ we denote by $\mathrm{MWE}(x)$ the set of marginal Walrasian equilibria at x and we define the sets $M(x)$ of marginal quantity equilibria and $P(x)$ of marginal price equilibria as follows:

$$M(x) = \{(v_1, \ldots, v_m) \in \mathbb{R}^{lm} \mid \exists p \in \mathbb{R}^l : (v_1, \ldots, v_m, p) \in \mathrm{MWE}(x)\},$$

$$P(x) = \{p \in \mathbb{R}^l \mid \|p\| = 1, \exists v \in \mathbb{R}^{lm} : (v, p) \in \mathrm{MWE}(x)\}.$$

Then a *Walrasian exchange curve* is a solution[3] $x(\cdot) : [0, +\infty) \to (\mathbb{R}_{++}^l)^m$ of the multivalued differential equation

$$\dot{x}(t) \in M(x(t)), \quad x(0) = (\omega_1, \ldots, \omega_m). \tag{MWP}$$

We now present our main result.

---

[3] In the sense that, for every $T > 0$, the function $x(\cdot)$ is Lipschitzian on $[0, T]$ (that is, there exists $k_T > 0$ such that $\|x(t_1) - x(t_2)\| \leq k_T |t_1 - t_2|$ for every t_1, t_2 in $[0, T]$), hence admits almost everywhere on $[0, +\infty)$ a derivative $\dot{x}(t)$ which satisfies $\dot{x}(t) \in M(x(t))$ for almost every $t \in [0, +\infty)$ and $x(0) = (\omega_1, \ldots, \omega_m)$.

Theorem 2.1. *Under Assumption* C *the following holds.*

(a) *There exists a Walrasian exchange curve* $x(\cdot)$ *and the correspondence* $t \to P(x(t))$ *reduces to a continuous mapping, denoted by* $p(\cdot)$ *in the following.*

Furthermore, every Walrasian exchange curve $x(\cdot)$ *satisfies the three following conditions:*

    (i) *for every* $t > 0$, $x(t)$ *is an attainable allocation;*

    (ii) *the function* $t \to u_i(x_i(t))$ *is nondecreasing for every* i;

    (iii) *for every* i, $p(t) \cdot \dot{x}_i(t) = 0$ *for almost every* $t > 0$.

(b) *Assume in addition that, for every* i, *the function* u_i *is strictly quasi-concave.*[4] *Then every Walrasian exchange curve* $x(\cdot)$ *converges to a Pareto optimum* x^* *when* $t \to +\infty$.

Furthermore, when $t \to +\infty$, $p(t)$ *converges to the price vector* p^* *which sustains the Pareto optimum* $x^* = (x_1^*, \ldots, x_m^*)$, *that is,* $p^* = g_1(x_1^*) = \cdots = g_m(x_m^*)$.[5]

The proof of the theorem is given in the next section.

3. Proof of Theorem 2.1

We prepare the proof of Theorem 2.1 with several lemmas. The first one guarantees the uniqueness of the price component of the marginal Walrasian equilibria, up to the multiplication by a positive scalar.

Lemma 3.1. *Under Assumption* C, *for every allocation* $x \in (\mathbb{R}_{++}^l)^m$, *the set* $P(x)$ *contains one and only one element.* $\square$

The lemma is a direct consequence of the result stated and proved in the Appendix.

Lemma 3.2. *Under Assumption* C, *the correspondence* $x \to P(x)$, *from* $(\mathbb{R}_{++}^l)^m$ *to* $\mathbb{R}^l$ *reduces to a continuous mapping and the correspondence* $x \to M(x)$, *from* $(\mathbb{R}_{++}^l)^m$ *to* $\mathbb{R}^{lm}$, *is an upper hemicontinuous correspondence with nonempty, convex, compact values.*

---

[4] In the sense that, for every x_1, x_2 in $\mathbb{R}_{++}^l$ such that $x_1 \neq x_2$, $u_i(x_1) \geq u_i(x_2)$ implies $u_i(tx_1 + (1-t)x_2) > u_i(x_2)$ for every $t \in (0, 1)$.

[5] Without the strict quasi-concavity assumption on the u_i, the following weaker result holds. Every limit point of a Walrasian exchange curve is a Pareto optimum.

Proof. We first notice that an element $(v_1, \ldots, v_m, p) \in \mathbb{R}^{l(m+1)}$ is a marginal Walrasian equilibrium if and only if it satisfies the following systems of equalities and inequalities:

$$p \geqslant 0,$$

$$\sum_{i=1}^{m} v_i = 0,$$

$$v_i \geq -\delta_i \quad \text{and} \quad p \cdot v_i \leq 0 \qquad \text{for every } i,$$

$$g_i(x_i) \cdot v_i \geq \alpha_i(x_i, p) \qquad \text{for every } i,$$

where $\alpha_i(x_i, p) = \max\{g_i(x_i) \cdot v \mid v \geq -\delta_i \text{ and } p \cdot v \leq 0\}$.

We first notice that, for every i, the function $\alpha_i : \mathbb{R}^l_{++} \times \mathbb{R}^l_{++} \to \mathbb{R}$ is continuous (cf. the maximum theorem in Berge, 1966). Hence the correspondence $x \to \mathrm{MWE}(x)$ has a closed graph in $(\mathbb{R}^l_{++})^m \times \mathbb{R}^{lm} \times \mathbb{R}^l_{++}$. Since the two correspondences $x \to M(x)$ and $x \to P(x)$ are bounded, we deduce that they are upper hemicontinuous. But the second correspondence is single-valued (Lemma 3.1), hence it reduces to a continuous mapping. Finally, the uniqueness property of the price component also implies that, for every x, the set $M(x)$ (that is the set of solutions $(v_1, \ldots, v_m)$ of the above system for the unique vector $p \in P(x)$) is convex compact and nonempty. $\square$

We now can give the proof of the first part of the theorem.

Proof of Theorem 2.1(a). Since the correspondence $x \to M(x)$ is upper hemicontinuous, with nonempty, convex, compact values (Lemma 3.2), the multivalued differential equation (MWP) has a (local) solution $x(\cdot):[0, T] \to (\mathbb{R}^l_{++})^m$, for some $T > 0$ (Castaing and Valadier, 1969; Cellina, 1969, 1970; Aubin and Cellina, 1984).

To show that this solution can be extended to $[0, +\infty)$, it suffices to check that every (local) solution $x(\cdot):[0, T] \to (\mathbb{R}^l_{++})^m$ of (MWP) remains in a compact subset of $\mathbb{R}^{lm}$ (cf., for example, Hirsh and Smale, 1974, in the single-valued case and their proof carries over to the multivalued case). Indeed, for almost every $t > 0$, there exists $p(t)$ such that $(\dot{x}_1(t), \ldots, \dot{x}_m(t), p(t))$ is a marginal Walrasian equilibrium at $x(t)$.

Hence:

$$\sum_{i=1}^{m} \dot{x}_i(t) = 0,$$

$$\frac{\mathrm{d}}{\mathrm{d}t} u_i(x_i(t)) = \nabla u_i(x_i(t)) \cdot \dot{x}_i(t) = \|\nabla u_i(x_i(t))\| g_i(x_i(t)) \cdot \dot{x}_i(t)$$

$$\geq \|\nabla u_i(x_i(t))\| g_i(x_i(t)) \cdot 0 = 0.$$

This implies that, for every i, the function $t \to u_i(x_i(t))$ is nondecreasing and that, for every t, $\sum_{i=1}^{m} x_i(t) = \sum_{i=1}^{m} x_i(0) = \sum_{i=1}^{m} \omega_i$. Thus, the solution $x(\cdot)$ remains in the set $A(w)$ of attainable allocations which are preferred or indifferent to the initial situation by every consumer, that is

$$A(\omega) = \{(x_1, \ldots, x_m) \in A \mid u_i(x_i) \geq u_i(\omega_i) \text{ for every } i\}.$$

The set $A(\omega)$ is clearly bounded; it is closed in $\mathbb{R}^{lm}$ by Assumption C. Hence $A(\omega)$ is compact.

From Lemma 3.2, the correspondence $p(\cdot)$, from $[0, +\infty)$ to $\mathbb{R}^l$, defined by $p(t) = P(x(t))$, reduces to a continuous mapping. We have shown above that (i) for every t, $x(t)$ is an attainable allocation and (ii) the function $t \to u_i(x_i(t))$ is nondecreasing for every i. Finally, the last condition (iii) is also a consequence of the fact that, for almost every t, $(\dot{x}_1(t)), \ldots, \dot{x}_m(t)), p(t))$ is a marginal Walrasian equilibrium, which implies that

$$p(t) \cdot \dot{x}_i(t) = 0 \quad \text{for every } i. \qquad \square$$

We prepare the second part of the proof of the theorem with a last lemma.

Lemma 3.3. *We make Assumption* C *and we let* $x = (x_1, \ldots, x_m)$ *be an allocation.*

(a) *The following holds*:

$$g_i(x_i) \cdot v_i \geq 0 \quad \text{for every } i \text{ and every } v = (v_1, \ldots, v_m) \in M(x).$$

(b) *The following four conditions are equivalent*:
  (i) x *is a Pareto optimum*;
  (ii) $g_1(x_1) = \cdots = g_m(x_m)$;
  (iii) $0 \in M(x)$;
  (iv) $g_i(x_i) \cdot v_i = 0$ *for every* i *and every* $v = (v_1, \ldots, v_m) \in M(x)$.

Proof. (a) Let $v = (v_1, \ldots, v_m) \in M(x)$. Then, for every i, $g_i(x_i) \cdot v_i \geq g_i(x_i) \cdot 0 = 0$.

(b) The equivalence between the two first conditions (i) and (ii) is a consequence of Lemma 2.1.

(ii)$\Rightarrow$(iii) Let $p = g_1(x_1)$, then one easily checks that $(0, \ldots, 0, p)$ is a marginal Walrasian equilibrium.

(iii)$\Rightarrow$(iv) Let $v = (v_1, \ldots, v_m) \in M(x)$. Since $0 \in M(x)$ we deduce that, for every i, $g_i(x_i) \cdot 0 \geq g_i(x_i) \cdot v_i$. This inequality, together with (a), imply that $g_i(x_i) \cdot v_i = 0$.

(iv)$\Rightarrow$(ii) Let $v = (v_1, \ldots, v_m) \in M(x)$ and let p be an associated equilibrium price vector such that $\|p\| = 1$. From the duality theorem of Linear Programming one deduces that, for every i,

$$0 = g_i(x_i) \cdot v_i = \max\{g_i(x_i) \cdot w \,|\, p \cdot w \le 0 \text{ and } w \ge -\delta_i\}$$
$$= -g_i(x_i) \cdot \delta_i + p \cdot \delta_i \sup\{g_{ih}(x_i)/p_h \,|\, h = 1, \ldots, l\}.$$

Consequently, for every i,

$$p_h \ge [p \cdot \delta_i / g_i(x_i) \cdot \delta_i] g_{ih}(x_i) \quad \text{for every } h.$$

Recalling that the vectors p and $g_i(x_i)$ $(i = 1, \ldots, m)$ are both of norm 1, the proof will be complete if we show that the above inequalities are, in fact, equalities for every h. Indeed, suppose on the contrary that the above inequality is strict for some h; multiplying each inequality by δ_{ih} and summing up, one gets

$$p \cdot \delta_i > [p \cdot \delta_i / g_i(x_i) \cdot \delta_i] g_i(x_i) \cdot \delta_i,$$

a contradiction. $\square$

We now end the proof of the theorem.

Proof of Theorem 2.1(b). We define the function $V : (\mathbb{R}^l_{++})^m \to \mathbb{R}$ as follows:

$$V(x) = \sum_{i=1}^{m} u_i(x_i) \quad \text{for every } x = (x_1, \ldots, x_m).$$

Then, for every solution $x(\,\cdot\,) : [0, +\infty) \to (\mathbb{R}^l_{++})^m$ of the multivalued differential equation (MWP), one has, for almost every $t > 0$,

$$\frac{d}{dt} V(x(t)) = \sum_{i=1}^{m} \|\nabla u_i(x_i(t))\| g_i(x_i(t)) \cdot \dot{x}_i(t).$$

Consequently, from Lemma 3.3,

$$\frac{d}{dt} V(x(t)) > 0 \quad \text{if } 0 \notin M(x(t)),$$

$$\frac{d}{dt} V(x(t)) = 0 \quad \text{if } 0 \in M(x(t)).$$

Thus $V(\,\cdot\,)$ is a Lyapunov function and from Champsaur, Drèze and Henry (1977), we deduce that every limit point[6] x^* of the solution $x(\,\cdot\,)$ satisfies $0 \in M(x^*)$, hence x^* is a Pareto optimum by Lemma 3.3(b).

---

[6] An element $x^* \in \mathbb{R}^{lm}$ is a limit point of $x(\,\cdot\,)$ if there exists a sequence $(t^\nu) \subset [0, +\infty)$ converging to $+\infty$ and such that $x^* = \lim_\nu x(t^\nu)$.

We now prove that, when $t \to +\infty$, $x(t)$ converges to some element $x^* \in \mathbb{R}^{lm}$. Since the solution remains in a compact set (the set $A(\omega)$), it suffices to show that $x(\cdot)$ has a unique limit point. Suppose on the contrary that $x(\cdot)$ has two different limit points x^* and x^{**}. The strict quasi-concavity of u_i implies that, for every i, $u_i(\frac{1}{2}x_i^* + \frac{1}{2}x_i^{**}] > u_i(x_i^*)$, which contradicts the fact that x^* is a Pareto optimum.

We end the proof by showing that, when $t \to +\infty$, $p(t) \to g_1(x_1^*)$ $(=g_2(x_2^*) = \cdots = g_m(x_m^*)$ by Lemma 3.3(b) since x^* is a Pareto optimum). Recalling that $p(t) = P(x(t))$ and that the correspondence $x \to P(x)$ reduces to a continuous mapping (Lemma 3.2), at the limit when $t \to +\infty$, $p(t) \to p^* = P(x^*)$. From above, we know that $0 \in M(x^*)$ and that $g_1(x_1^*) = \cdots = g_m(x_m^*)$. One easily checks that $(0, \ldots, 0, g_1(x_1^*))$ is a marginal Walrasian equilibrium at x^* or, equivalently, that $g_1(x_1^*) \in P(x^*)$. But the set $P(x^*)$ contains a unique element (Lemma 3.1), hence $p^* = g_1(x_1^*)$. □

Appendix

Consider the *linear* exchange economy $\mathscr{L}$ with l commodities and m consumers, with consumption sets $\mathbb{R}_+^l$, with initial endowment $e_i \in \mathbb{R}^l$ and with *linear* utility function $u_i : \mathbb{R}_+^l \to \mathbb{R}$ defined by $u_i(x_i) = a_i \cdot x_i$ for some given vector $a_i \in \mathbb{R}^l$.

Lemma A.1. *Assume that $e_i \gg 0$ and $a_i \gg 0$ for every i. Then the price component of the Walras equilibria of $\mathscr{L}$ belongs to $\mathbb{R}_{++}^l$ and is uniquely defined, up to the multiplication by a positive scalar, that is, if $(x_1, \ldots, x_m, p)$ and $(y_1, \ldots, y_m, q)$ are two Walras equilibria of $\mathscr{L}$, then $p = tq$ for some real number $t > 0$.*

Proof. Let $(x_1, \ldots, x_m, p)$ be a Walras equilibrium of $\mathscr{L}$, the proof that $p \gg 0$ is standard.

For every i and every $p \gg 0$ we let

$$v_i(p) = \max a_i \cdot x_i,$$

$$p \cdot x_i \leq p \cdot e_i,$$

$$x_i \geq 0.$$

Then from the duality theorem of Linear Programming (cf., for example, Gale, 1960), we deduce that, for every i and every $p \gg 0$, one has

$$v_i(p) = \min \lambda_i p \cdot e_i = p \cdot e_i \max\{a_{ih}/p_h \mid h = 1, \ldots, l\},$$

$$\lambda_i p_h \geq a_{ih},$$

$$\lambda_i \geq 0.$$

We now suppose that there are two Walras equilibria $(x_1, \ldots, x_m, p)$ and $(y_1, \ldots, y_m, q)$ of $\mathcal{L}$ such that, for every $t > 0$, $p \neq tq$. We have shown above that p and q belong to $\mathbb{R}^l_{++}$ and we define the vector $r \in \mathbb{R}^l_{++}$ by

$$r_h = \sqrt{p_h q_h} \quad \text{for every } h = 1, \ldots, l.$$

We claim that, for every i,

$$\tfrac{1}{2} v_i(p) + \tfrac{1}{2} v_i(q) > v_i(r).$$

We prove the claim as follows. Since the arithmetic mean is greater than or equal to the geometric mean (and the equality holds only when the two numbers are equal) one deduces that, for every h,

$$\frac{1}{2} \frac{p_j e_{ij}}{p_h} + \frac{1}{2} \frac{q_j e_{ij}}{q_h} \geq \sqrt{\frac{p_j e_{ij}}{p_h}} \sqrt{\frac{q_j e_{ij}}{q_h}} = \frac{r_j e_{ij}}{r_h} \quad \text{for every } j.$$

Furthermore, one of the above inequalities is strict for some j. Indeed, suppose on the contrary that the equality holds for every j, then $p_j e_{ij}/p_h = q_j e_{ij}/q_h$ for every j. Recalling that $e_{ij} > 0$ for every j, one deduces that $p = (p_h/q_h)q$, which contradicts the assumption that $p \neq tq$ for every $t > 0$.

Summing up (over j) the above inequalities, one deduces that $\tfrac{1}{2}[p \cdot e_i/p_h + q \cdot e_i/q_h] > r \cdot e_i/r_h$ for every h. Multiplying each inequality by $a_{ih} > 0$, and taking the supremum over h, one ends the proof of the claim.

Since $(x_1, \ldots, x_m, p)$ and $(y_1, \ldots, y_m, q)$ are two Walras equilibria of $\mathcal{L}$, one deduces that, for every i, $a_i \cdot x_i = v_i(p)$ and $a_i \cdot y_i = v_i(q)$. Consequently, from the above claim,

$$a_i \cdot \tfrac{1}{2}[x_i + y_i] = \tfrac{1}{2} v_i(p) + \tfrac{1}{2} v_i(q) > v_i(r) \quad \text{for every } i.$$

Hence

$$r \cdot \tfrac{1}{2}[x_i + y_i] > r \cdot e_i \quad \text{for every } i.$$

Summing up these inequalities, and recalling that $\sum_{i=1}^{m} x_i = \sum_{i=1}^{m} y_i = \sum_{i=1}^{m} e_i$ one gets

$$r \cdot \left[\frac{1}{2} \sum_{i=1}^{m} e_i + \frac{1}{2} \sum_{i=1}^{m} e_i \right] > r \cdot \sum_{i=1}^{m} e_i,$$

a contradiction. This ends the proof of the lemma. $\quad \square$

References

Arrow, K. and F.H. Hahn (1971) *General Competitive Analysis.* San Francisco: Holden-Day.

Aubin, J.-P. and A. Cellina (1984) *Differential Inclusions.* Berlin: Springer.

Berge, C. (1966) *Espaces Topologiques, Fonctions Multivoques.* Paris: Dunod.

Castaing, C. and M. Valadier (1969) 'Equations différentielles multivoques dans les espaces localement convexes', *Revue Française Informatique et Recherche Opérationnelle*, 16:3–16.

Cellina, A. (1970) 'Multivalued differential equations and ordinary differential equation', *SIAM Journal of Applied Mathematics*, 18:533–538.

Cellina, A. (1971) 'The role of approximation in the theory of multivalued mappings', in: Kuhn and Szego, eds., *Differential Games and Related Topics.* Amsterdam: North-Holland.

Champsaur, P. (1976) 'Neutrality of planning procedures in an economy with public goods', *Review of Economic Studies*, 43:293–300.

Champsaur, P., J. Drèze and C. Henry (1977) 'Stability theorems with economic applications', *Econometrica*, 45:273–294.

Cornet, B. (1983) 'Neutrality of planning procedures', *Journal of Mathematical Economics*, 11:141–160.

Cornet, B. (1988) 'Accessibility of Pareto optima', Working Paper, Université Paris 1.

Cornet, B. (1990) 'Linear exchange economics', Working Paper, Université Paris 1.

Debreu, G. (1959) *Theory of Value.* New York: John Wiley.

Gale, D. (1960) *The Theory of Linear Economic Models.* New York: Academic Press.

Hirsh, M. and S. Smale (1974) *Differential Equations, Dynamical Systems and Linear Algebra.* New York: Academic Press.

Smale, S. (1976) 'Exchange processes with price adjustment', *Journal of Mathematical Economics*, 3:211–216.

Tulkens, H. and S. Zamir (1979) 'Surplus-sharing local games in dynamic exchange processes', *Review of Economic Studies*, 46:305–313.

Chapter 2

EXCHANGE PROCESSES, THE CORE AND COMPETITIVE ALLOCATIONS

Parkash CHANDER

Indian Statistical Institute, New Delhi, India

Henry TULKENS

CORE, Université Catholique de Louvain, Louvain-la-Neuve, Belgium, and Facultés Universitaires Saint-Louis, Bruxelles, Belgium

1. Introduction

Most of the theory of the core of pure exchange economies has been developed in a context of "positive" analysis, i.e., with the aim of providing an additional logical support to the descriptive concept of competitive equilibrium: by showing that the latter belongs to the core, a virtue of "group rationality" is attached to the equilibrium concept, and thereby increases its explicative power.

By contrast, informationally decentralized processes that converge to a Pareto optimum or a competitive equilibrium have been formulated in the literature both from a "positive" as well as from a "normative" point of view. However, little seems to have been done in this regard with respect

This paper was written in part during a stay of the first author at CORE in 1988, and for another part during a visit of the second author at Laboratoire d'Econométrie, Ecole Polytechnique, Paris, in 1989. Both authors are very grateful to these institutions for their hospitality, and to Bernard Cornet, Claude Henry, Jean-Marc Bonnisseau and Cheng Zhong Qin for valuable discussions.

Economic Decision-Making: Games, Econometrics and Optimisation
Edited by J.J. Gabszewicz, J.-F. Richard and L.A. Wolsey
© *Elsevier Science Publishers B.V., 1990*

to the core concept. One reason for this might be that the basic issue of existence had to be cleared up first, before any dynamic analysis could be developed. But this issue has by now been fairly well resolved, especially thanks to the path breaking work of Scarf (1967), where he established sufficient conditions for the non-emptiness of the core of an economy which are completely independent of the equilibrium concept. This time may therefore be an appropriate one for considering dynamic approaches to the core.

For this purpose, informationally decentralized processes that converge to an individually rational Pareto efficient (IRPE) allocation provide a natural starting point. Core allocations are indeed a subset of the individually rational Pareto efficient allocations.

There are several such processes, though. To name only a few, let us mention here

(i) barter processes such as Uzawa's (1962);

(ii) non-tâtonnement processes such as Hahn's and Negishi's (see Negishi, 1962), Smale's (1976) and Champsaur's and Cornet's (Chapter 1).

(iii) arbitrage processes as proposed by Allais (1967, Parts IV–VI) and discussed in English in Malinvaud (1972, pp. 155–169);

(iv) stochastic decentralized resource allocation processes such as Green's (1974) and Hurwicz, Radner and Reiter's (1975); and finally

(v) MDP-type[1] quantity guided planning processes, first applied to pure exchange economies by Malinvaud (1968, pp. 34–35; 1972, pp. 190–193) and further developed by Ledyard (1974), Tulkens and Zamir (1979) and d'Aspremont and Tulkens (1980).

For at least one class of these processes namely the "MDP-type processes", a neutrality property established by Champsaur (1976)[2] implies that they can determine *any* IRPE allocation, thus also core allocations. However, Champsaur's result is in the qualitative form of an existence

---

[1] The use of these initials, which refer to Malinvaud, Drèze and de la Vallée Poussin, was first made in Champsaur (1976), and became classical since then. Actually, Drèze and de la Vallée Poussin's contribution to the field is not really on pure exchange, but rather through their path breaking paper (1971) on public goods. However the gradient structure of their model, exhibited in d'Aspremont and Tulkens (1980), is of the same formal nature as the private goods processes we are dealing with here. This explains the established usage of ranking the latter in the "MDP" category.

[2] This was for economies with public goods (see Cornet, 1983, for various generalisations).

theorem, rather constructive; in other words, it does not allow one to know which values of the relevant parameters in the MDP process make it converge to the core.

The purpose of this paper is precisely to exhibit an MDP-type process for which it can be shown that it converges from the initial endowments to an allocation in the core, at least for a certain class of economies.

This convergence property has some game theoretic interest in itself. Very few dynamic approaches to solution concepts are available in the game theory literature (Stearns, 1968; Billera, 1972; Kalai, Maschler and Owen, 1973). As far as the core concept is concerned, we are aware of only one contribution so far, by Shiao and Wang (1974) for games with transferable utilities. However, these approaches are more in the manner of computational algorithms without any consideration for informational decentralization.

From the economic theoretic viewpoint, it is also of interest to point out here that our process is of the nature of a "non-tâtonnement" process, i.e., it implies the possibility of trades away from equilibrium. It also involves prices, and with those prices, the core allocation to which it is shown to converge appears to be a competitive equilibrium. We thus exhibit here, for the class of economies we are considering in Section 4, a non-tâtonnement process with a stronger property than has usually been obtained for such processes. Lastly, our process also illustrates and somewhat qualifies a theorem of Jordan (1987) according to which any process converging to a competitive equilibrium must necessarily involve information about first and second derivatives of the utility functions: the process we propose does involve such information for usual exchange economies, but second order information appears to be unnecessary for the special class of economies for which we here show convergence.

Our exposition is structured as follows. After defining the economy and exchange processes in Section 2, we introduce in Section 3 the notion of replicable exchange processes, and we prove the general proposition that any process which is replicable and converges to the core must necessarily converge to a competitive allocation. Next, we turn in Section 4 to the specific MDP-type process we propose. We observe that it is replicable, and then show that with the prices it involves, it converges to a competitive equilibrium, hence to the core, for the class of economies with quasi-linear utility functions. We conclude with some general remarks, suggested by our results, on Jordan's theorem as well as on the compatibility between the notions of equilibrium and non-tâtonnement.

2. The economy and exchange processes

2.1. The economy

Consider a pure exchange economy $e = \{(X_i, u_i(x_i), w_i) \mid i \in N\}$, where N is the set of agents (indexed $i = 1, \ldots, n$; $n = |N|$), $X_i \subseteq \mathbb{R}^l_+$ denotes i's consumption set (of which $x_i = (x_{i1}, \ldots, x_{ij}, \ldots, x_{il})$ is a typical element) and $\mathbb{R}^l_+$ is the l-dimensional commodity space, commodities being indexed by $j = 1, \ldots, l$; $u_i(x_i)$ is the utility function of agent i, defined on X_i, and $w_i = (w_{i1}, \ldots, w_{ij}, \ldots, w_{il}) \in \mathbb{R}^l_+$ his initial endowment of commodities. An economy will be denoted by $e = (e^1, e^2, \ldots, e^n)$, where $e^i = (X_i, u_i(x_i), w_i)$ are the characteristics of agent i.

In this and the following Section 3, we make the following assumptions on the economy:

(A1) $\forall i \in N$, $X_i = \mathbb{R}^l_+ \backslash \partial \mathbb{R}^l_+$ where for any set S in any Euclidean space, ∂S denotes the boundary of S.

(A2) $\forall i \in N$, $w_i \in X_i$.

(A3) $\forall i \in N$, $u_i(x_i)$ is strictly quasi-concave and defined on X_i; $u_i(x_i)$ is twice continuously differentiable, and such that $\partial u_i / \partial x_{ij} > 0$, $j = 1, \ldots, l$, $\forall x_i \in X_i$.

(A4) $\forall i \in N$, and for any sequence x_i^k, $k = 1, 2, \ldots$, in X_i, if $x_{ij}^k \to 0$ for some j, then $u_i(x_i^k) \to -\infty$.

These assumptions are standard ones, with (A4) being made to avoid boundary problems and obtain below differential equations systems with classical properties. In Section 4, a more restrictive set of assumptions will be made.

For this economy, an *allocation* is a vector $x = (x_1, \ldots, x_n) \in \mathbb{R}^{nl}_+$ such that $x_i \in X_i$ $\forall i \in N$. An allocation is *feasible* if $\sum_{i \in N} x_{ij} = \sum_{i \in N} w_{ij}$ for each j; let X denote the set of feasible allocations.

An *individually rational Pareto efficient* (IRPE) *allocation* is a feasible allocation x such that $u_i(x_i) \ge u_i(w_i)$ for all $i \in N$, and there exists no alternative feasible allocation y for which $u_i(yi) \ge u_i(x_i)$ for all i and $u_i(y_i) > u_i(x_i)$ for at least some i. A *core allocation* is a feasible allocation x such that there exists no subset $S \subseteq N$ and no vector

$$x^S \stackrel{\text{def}}{=} (x_1^S, \ldots, x_i^S, \ldots, x_s^S) \in \underset{i \in S}{\times} X_i$$

satisfying $\sum_{i \in S} x_{ij}^S \le \sum_{i \in S} w_{ij}$ $\forall j$, for which $u_i(x_i^S) \ge u_i(x_i)$ $\forall i \in S$, and $u_i(x_i^S) > u_i(x_i)$ for at least some $i \in S$.

A *competitive equilibrium* is a feasible allocation x and a price vector $p = (p_1, \ldots, p_l) \in \mathbb{R}^l_+$ such that for all i, x_i maximizes $u_i(x_i)$ subject to

$px_i \leq pw_i$. A *competitive allocation* is the allocation component of a competitive equilibrium.

It is well known that under the assumptions made above (in fact, even under much weaker ones), every competitive equilibrium is a core allocation. As the reverse is not true in general for economies with a finite number of agents, we call *competitive core allocations* those allocations in the core which are also competitive allocations for some price vector.

2.2. Exchange processes

An exchange process is intuitively described as a sequence over time in the space of feasible states of an economy; it associates to each point in time an allocation of the economy's resources.

Formally, it can be defined as follows. For some economy $e = (e_1, \ldots, e_n)$, consider any feasible allocation $x = (x_1, \ldots, x_n)$. Let $m^i = f^i(e^i, x)$ be the control message of agent i, where the function f^i, called i's *response function*, describes the rule used by agent i to select a control message depending only on his own characteristics and the current state of the economy. Let also $dx = \alpha(m^1, \ldots, m^m; x)$ be a rule according to which the state of the economy is modified, as a function of the messages expressed by its agents; the function α is called an *adjustment rule*. For the economy e, an *exchange process* is then defined as the pair

$$(f, \alpha) = [f(e, \cdot), \alpha(f(e, \cdot))],$$

where $f(e, \cdot)$ denotes the vector of functions $f^i(e^i, x)$, $i = 1, \ldots, n$, defined for any feasible state x, and $\alpha(f(e, \cdot))$ is the autonomous system of differential[3] equations

$$\dot{x} = \alpha(f^1(e^1, x), \ldots, f^n(e^n, x), x). \tag{1}$$

A path of the exchange process (f, α) is a solution to (1), i.e., a vector-valued function $x(t):[0, +\infty) \to \mathbb{R}^{nl}$ such that the derivative dx/dt exists and satisfies the above differential equation. An *equilibrium of the process* is a value x of its solution such that in (1) $\dot{x} = 0$.

An example of an exchange process, that belongs to the class of "MDP-type" processes described in the introduction, is provided by Ledyard (1974) and, independently, by Tulkens and Zamir (1979, Section 5-3), a process

---

[3] In this paper, we limit ourselves to continuous time processes. As usual, a dot over a time dependent variable denotes the operator d/dt.

that the latter authors call "Marshallian". To describe it, let $t \in [0, +\infty)$ be the time variable and let $x(t) \in \mathbb{R}^{nl}_+$ be the allocation at time t. Define

$$\pi_{ij}(x_i(t)) = \frac{\partial u_i / \partial x_{ij}}{\partial u_i / \partial x_{i1}} \bigg|_{x_i(t)} \quad \forall i \in N, \; j = 2, \ldots, l,$$

the marginal rate of substitution of agent i between commodities j and 1, evaluated at point $x_i(t)$ (we write only π_{ij} when no confusion can arise as to the point where derivatives are evaluated and when the time argument is immaterial); define also $\bar{\pi}_j = (1/n) \sum_{i \in N} \pi_{ij}, j = 2, \ldots, l$. Then the process reads as follows:

Marshallian process:

$$x_i(0) = w_i \quad \forall i, \tag{2}$$

$$\dot{x}_{ij} = \pi_{ij} - \bar{\pi}_{ij} \quad \forall j \neq 1, \forall i, \tag{3}$$

$$\dot{x}_{i1} = -\sum_{j \neq 1} \bar{\pi}_j \dot{x}_{ij} \quad \forall i. \tag{4}$$

Here, at every $t \geq 0$ and for each $i \in N$, the response function f^i associates with $(e^i, x(t))$ the vector $(\pi_{i2}, \ldots, \pi_{il})$, and the adjustment rule α, in its differential form (1), reads

$$\alpha(f(e, x), x) = [(-\bar{\pi}(\pi_1 - \bar{\pi}), \pi_1 - \bar{\pi}), \ldots, (-\bar{\pi}(\pi_i - \bar{\pi}), \pi_i - \bar{\pi}),$$
$$\ldots, (-\bar{\pi}(\pi_n - \bar{\pi}), \pi_n - \bar{\pi})],$$

where $\pi_i = (\pi_{i2}, \ldots, \pi_{il})$ and $\bar{\pi} = (\bar{\pi}_2, \ldots, \bar{\pi}_l)$.

It is shown in the just quoted papers that under assumptions identical to, or weaker than (A1)-(A4), the process (2)-(4) has at least one solution, which converges from any feasible initial state (here assumed to be defined by the individual endowments) to some IRPE allocation.

Another important property of this process is individual monotonicity, i.e., the fact that, at every point $x(t)$ along any solution, the general expression

$$\frac{du_i(x_i(t))}{dt} = \sum_{j=1}^{l} \frac{\partial u_i}{\partial x_{ij}} \dot{x}_{ij} = \frac{\partial u_i}{\partial x_{i1}} \left(\dot{x}_{i1} + \sum_{j \neq 1} \pi_{ij} \dot{x}_{ij} \right)$$

takes on the non-negative value

$$\frac{du_i(x_i(t))}{dt} = \frac{\partial u_i}{\partial x_{i1}} \left[\sum_{j \neq 1} (\pi_{ij} - \bar{\pi}_j) \dot{x}_{ij} \right] = \frac{\partial u_i}{\partial x_{i1}} \left[\sum_{j \neq 1} (\pi_{ij} - \bar{\pi}_j)^2 \right] \quad \forall i,$$

with $\sum_{i \in N} du_i / dt > 0$, unless $x(t)$ is an equilibrium point of the process, in which case all terms in this sum are equal to zero.

3. Replicable exchange processes

For the process just presented, Tulkens and Zamir (1979) establish that the monotonicity property is in fact stronger than in other previously proposed ones. Indeed, they show that the reallocations specified by (3)–(4) belong to the core of local games defined at each point $x(t)$ of the solution. One thus can say that the Marshallian process enjoys "coalitional strategic monotonicity".

What does this stronger monotonicity imply for global convergence? Although one can easily show that the above process converges to a *proper* subset of the IRPE allocations, the question whether it would always converge to an allocation in the core of the economy was settled in the negative by means of a numerical counter example. See Tulkens and Zamir (1979, footnote 8; 1976; for details).

We can provide here a logical argument for this result, based on a property of the concept of "replicable exchange process" that we presently introduce.

An exchange process is said to be *replicable* if

$$\dot{x}^{(s)} = \alpha(f(e^{(s)}, x^{(s)}); x^{(s)}),$$

where $e^{(s)}$, $x^{(s)}$ and $\dot{x}^{(s)}$ are s-fold replicas of e, x and $\dot{x}$, respectively, in the manner of Debreu and Scarf (1963), i.e., $e^{(s)} = (e, e, \ldots, e)$, $x^{(s)} = (x, x, \ldots, x)$ and $\dot{x}^{(s)} = (\dot{x}, \ldots, \dot{x})$, s times each. This means the functions f and α are such that for each individual of each type i, the path of the process is not affected by replications of the economy.

A property of replicable exchange processes useful for our purposes is the following.

Proposition 1. *If a replicable exchange process always converges to a core allocation, then it must always converge to a competitive core allocation.*

Proof. For an economy e, let x be the core allocation to which the process converges, and for any s-fold replica of e, $e^{(s)}$, $s = 1, 2, \ldots$, let $x^{(s)}$ be the allocation to which the s-fold replicated process converges. Since the process is replicable, one has for every $s \geq 1$,

$$x_i^{(s)} = x_i \quad \forall i, \tag{5}$$

and since the process always converges to a core allocation, $x^{(s)}$ belongs to the core of $e^{(s)}$, also for every s.

Now, by Debreu and Scarf's (1963) theorem, every allocation in the core of an s-replicated economy is also a competitive allocation for this economy, when s is large enough. Thus, for s large enough, $x^{(s)}$ must be a competitive allocation. But in view of (5), this property is in fact true for every s, as well as for x itself. $\square$

Upon noticing that the Marshallian process (2)–(4) is a replicable one, since

$$\bar{\pi}_j = \frac{1}{n} \sum_{i \in N} \pi_{ij} = \frac{1}{ns} \left(\sum_{i \in N} s\pi_{ij} \right)$$

for any $s \geq 1$, it is now clear that it can converge to the core only if it does also converge to a competitive equilibrium.

In Subsection 4.1 below, we shall present arguments suggesting that such a property is unlikely to hold. These arguments are related to the rôle that prices play in this process. At another level, Jordan (1987) also provides arguments pointing in the same direction. Indeed, Theorem 3.6 in his paper states that any adjustment process that makes all regular competitive equilibria at least locally stable must use control messages at least as large as those of the Newton method. As argued by Jordan, it can be seen from his theorem that any exchange process which always converges to a competitive allocation must use as control messages the first and second derivatives of the utility function at the current allocation. Now, second derivatives play no rôle in the Marshallian process.

We can derive three general conclusions by a combined use of Proposition 1 and of the result of Jordan:

(a) The quest for an exchange process converging to the core necessarily amounts to a quest for a process converging to a competitive allocation, if the process is restricted to be a replicable one.

(b) a contrario, any exchange process that converges to non-competitive core allocations (for economies with a finite number of agents) must be a non-replicable one.

(c) any replicable process converging to an allocation in the core of an exchange economy will necessarily involve information about first and second derivatives of the utility functions.[4]

---

[4] Notice that in the case of an economy with public goods, none of these conclusions hold, due to the non-equivalence between Lindahl equilibria and the core. Indeed, Chander (1988) exhibits a process which involves information only about the first derivatives of utility functions and which always converges to the core, but not necessarily to a Lindahl equilibrium. This brings to light an important qualitative difference between processes for private and public good economies.

With conclusion (a), the study of convergence to the core by means of purely quantity-guided processes of the MDP-type might seem to lose some of its interest, as these processes involve no prices in their usual formulations. In the case of the Marshallian process, however, this same conclusion does in fact suggest, together with conclusions (b) and (c), a direction of further search, that we shall explore in the following section.

4. An example of an exchange process converging to a competitive core allocation

4.1. Formulation of the process

It emerges from the preceding considerations that for converging to a core allocation, any replicable exchange process will necessarily have "competitive" properties, i.e., it must involve prices in an essential way.

Now prices do play a rôle in many of the processes listed in the introduction, most prominently so, of course, in non-tâtonnement processes. Even within the class of purely quantity guided MDP-type processes, it was observed by Tulkens and Zamir (1979) that the Marshallian process does also involve prices:[5] indeed eq. (4) specifies that for each commodity $j \neq 1$, the local net trade $\dot{x}_{ij}$ of each agent i takes place against commodity 1 at a rate $\bar{\pi}_j$ which is the same for all traders. At each time t along the solution, the mean $\bar{\pi}_j$ thus serves as common exchange ratio.

Why is it, then, that none of these processes converges to a competitive equilibrium? Apart from the second order information requirements implied by Jordan's result recalled above, we think that the answer lies in the fact that in these processes, all the functions that prices have in the competitive mechanism are not completely taken into account.

Besides market clearing (i.e., ensuring feasible allocations), the balancing of the individual budgets is one of these functions. At an equilibrium, this is expressed by the conditions

$$\sum_j p_j(x_{ij} - w_{ij}) = 0 \quad \forall i. \tag{6}$$

Along the trajectory of most non-tâtonnement processes, this is also specified by expressions of the form

$$\sum_j p_j(t)\dot{x}_{ij}(t) = 0 \quad \forall i, \tag{7}$$

[5] This is in fact the reason why these authors called the process "Marshallian", alluding to Book 5, Chapter 3, Section 6 and Appendix H of Marshall (1920).

which ensure a zero value of the individual "local" net trades occurring at time t, at the prices $p(t)$ prevailing then. By local net trades, we mean here net trades with respect to the current holdings of commodities, i.e., with respect to $x_i(t)$. Note that (7) is also satisfied by the process (2)-(4), with the prices $p_j(t) = \bar{\pi}_j(t)$, as was pointed out in Tulkens and Zamir (1979, pp. 311-312).

But equalities (7) do by no means ensure that at the same time t, another series of conditions are satisfied, which are of the form

$$\sum_j p_j(t)(x_{ij}(t) - w_{ij}) = 0 \quad \forall i. \tag{8}$$

These amount to requiring that the values of the individual net trades with respect to the initial endowments, naturally called now "global" net trades, be also zero. As these conditions should be met at the final allocation for a competitive equilibrium to be achieved, it might be a good strategy to impose them at each step of the exchange process.

Formally, we thus propose to reformulate the exchange process in such a way that its solution satisfies (8) at each point in time. In differential form, this reads

$$\sum_j p_j(t)\dot{x}_{ij}(t) + \sum_j \dot{p}_j(t)(x_{ij}(t) - w_{ij}) = 0,$$

or equivalently

$$\dot{x}_{i1} = -\sum_{j \neq 1} p_j(t)\dot{x}_{ij}(t) - \sum_{j \neq 1} \dot{p}_j(t)(x_{ij}(t) - w_{ij}) \quad \forall i. \tag{9}$$

As in the Marshallian process (2)-(4), the local exchanges of each commodity $j \neq i$ against commodity 1 (used as numéraire) do take place at prices $p_j(t) = \bar{\pi}_j(t)$, we can now consider introducing in it the restriction (9) expressed in terms of these particular prices. This leads us to formulate the following new process, to which we give a name justified by its property subsequently demonstrated.

Competitive exchange process:

$$x_i(0) = w_i \quad \forall i, \tag{10}$$

$$\dot{x}_{ij} = \pi_{ij} - \bar{\pi}_j \quad \forall j \neq 1, \ \forall i, \tag{11}$$

$$\dot{x}_{i1} = -\sum_{j \neq 1} \bar{\pi}_j \dot{x}_{ij} - \sum_{j \neq 1} \dot{\bar{\pi}}_j (x_{ij} - w_{ij}) \quad \forall i. \tag{12}$$

This simply amounts to adding a transfer term for commodity 1 in equation (4) of the Marshallian process. Notice also that in accordance with Jordan

(1987) use is made of first and second derivatives of utility functions, since

$$\dot{\bar{\pi}}_j = \frac{1}{n} \sum_{i \in N} \dot{\pi}_{ij} = \frac{1}{n} \sum_{i \in N} \sum_{k=1}^{l} \frac{\partial \pi_{ij}}{\partial x_{ik}} \dot{x}_{ik}$$

$$= \frac{1}{n} \sum_{i \in N} \sum_{k=1}^{l} (\pi_{ijk} - \pi_{ij}\pi_{i1k})\dot{x}_{ik}, \quad j = 2, \ldots, l,$$

where

$$\pi_{ijk} \overset{\text{def}}{=} \frac{\partial^2 u_i}{\partial x_{ij}\partial x_{ik}} \left(\frac{\partial u_i}{\partial x_{i1}}\right)^{-1}, \quad j, k = 1, \ldots, l.$$

For the exchange process (10)-(12), the individual response functions are

$$f^i(e^i, x) = (w_i, \pi_i, \dot{\pi}_i), \quad i = 1, \ldots, n,$$

and the adjustment rule reads

$$\alpha(f(e, x); x) = [-\bar{\pi}(\pi_i - \bar{\pi}) - \dot{\bar{\pi}}(x_i - w_i), (\pi_i - \bar{\pi})].$$

Clearly, the process is replicable, and it determines a feasible reallocation at each point of time, since by (10) it starts at such an allocation, and for every $t \geq 0$,

$$\sum_i \dot{x}_{ij}(t) = 0, \quad j = 2, \ldots, l,$$

and

$$\sum_i \dot{x}_{i1}(t) = - \sum_{j \neq 1} \bar{\pi}_j \sum_i \dot{x}_{ij}(t) - \sum_{j \neq 1} \dot{\bar{\pi}}_j \sum_i (x_{ij}(t) - w_{ij}) = 0,$$

because $\sum_i (x_{ij}(t) - w_{ij}) = 0$ for $j = 2, \ldots, l$.

The direction of adjustment for the process (10)-(12) in comparison with that of process (2)-(4) is illustrated diagrammatically in Figure 1. Points A and B are the reallocations under processes (2)-(4) and (10)-(12), respectively. Both points involve the same amounts of good 2, but different amounts of good 1.

Finally, an equilibrium of the process, i.e., a value x of its solution (if one exists) such that $\dot{x}(x) = 0$, is a competitive equilibrium of the economy, for the price vector $p = (p_1, \ldots, p_j, \ldots, p_l)$ equal to $(1, \bar{\pi}_2(x), \ldots, \bar{\pi}_j(x), \ldots, \bar{\pi}_l(x))$. This property is a direct consequence of the feasibility of x at every t and of the fact that, at an equilibrium of the process, $\forall i \in N$, $\pi_{ij}(x_i) = \bar{\pi}_j(x)$ for every $j \neq 1$, combined with Proposition 2 in Malinvaud (1972, p. 32), according to which marginal equalities are sufficient to determine the individual equilibrium of each consumer.

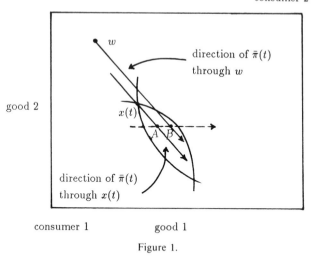

Figure 1.

Thus if the process (10)–(12) has a solution that converges to an equilibrium, it converges to a competitive core allocation.

4.2. The monotonicity issue

Does the system of differential equations (10)–(12) have a solution, and does it converge to a competitive equilibrium? For MDP-type processes in general, properties of existence and convergence of a solution usually rest on monotonicity, as defined towards the end of Section 2 above.

For the present process, it turns out that, at any point t along a solution, if one exists, one has

$$\sum_{i \in N} \frac{\mathrm{d}u_i(x_i(t))}{\mathrm{d}t} = \sum_{i \in N} \frac{\partial u_i(t)}{\partial x_{i1}} \left\{ \sum_{j \neq 1} [(\pi_{ij}(t) - \bar{\pi}_j(t))^2 - \dot{\bar{\pi}}_j(t)(x_{ij}(t) - w_{ij})] \right\}.$$

(13)

If $x(t)$ is not an equilibrium of the process, the first term in the square bracket is unambiguously positive, but the second one may apparently be of either sign; this prevents monotonicity to be established, either individually (i.e. $\mathrm{d}u_i/\mathrm{d}t > 0$ for each $i \in N$) or collectively (i.e., $\sum_i \mathrm{d}u_i/\mathrm{d}t > 0$). Notice however that collective monotonicity does hold if for each $i \in N$,

$$\partial u_i / \partial x_{i1} = 1 \quad \forall x_i \in X_i.$$

(14)

Indeed, (13) then becomes

$$\sum_{i \in N} \frac{du_i}{dt} = \sum_{i \in N} \sum_{j \neq 1} (\pi_{ij} - \bar{\pi}_j)^2 - \sum_{i \in N} \sum_{j \neq 1} \dot{\bar{\pi}}_j (x_{ij}(t) - w_{ij}) > 0 \qquad (15)$$

(unless $x(t)$ is an equilibrium of the process), where the second double sum term on the right is equal to zero at every t since it can be rewritten as

$$\sum_{j \neq 1} \dot{\bar{\pi}}_j \sum_{i \in N} (x_{ij}(t) - w_{ij})$$

and $x(t)$ has been shown to be determined by the process, at every t, as a feasible allocation.

Existence and convergence of a solution for the process (10)-(12) is thus more likely to be established if we restrict ourselves to a class of utility functions satisfying (14), i.e., a narrower one than the class of functions implied by our assumption (A3). This is provided by the class of so-called quasi-linear utility functions (see, e.g., Varian, 1984, pp. 278-284), for general properties; Green and Laffont, 1979, for typical applications in economic theory), which are also often used in game theory (see, e.g., Shapley and Shubik, 1975).

4.3. Suitable assumptions for economies with quasi-linear utilities

The restriction of (A3) to quasi-linear utility functions has implications, however, for other characteristics of the economy that we have assumed in (A1)-(A4). Indeed, linearity is incompatible with assumption (A4) as far as commodity 1 is concerned. Moreover boundary problems that assumption (A4) was meant to avoid, are likely to occur for commodity 1.

To circumvent these two difficulties, we now substitute for (A1), (A3) and (A4) the following alternative assumptions:

(A1') $\forall i \in N$, $X_i = \mathbb{R} \times (\mathbb{R}_+^{l-1} \setminus \partial \mathbb{R}_+^{l-1})$.

(A3') $\forall i \in N$, $u_i(x_i)$ is defined on X_i as $u_i(x_i) = x_{i1} + v_i(x_{i2}, \ldots, x_{il})$ where $v_i(\cdot)$ is strictly quasi-concave, twice continuously differentiable and such that $\partial v_i / \partial x_{ij} > 0$, $j = 2, \ldots, l$.

(A4') $\forall i \in N$, and for every sequence x_i^k, $k = 1, 2, \ldots$, in X_i, if $x_{ij}^k \to 0$ for some $j \neq 1$, then $v_i(x_{i2}^k, \ldots, x_{il}^k) \to -\infty$.

Quasi-linear utilities are defined by the functions $u_i(x_i)$ stated in (A3'). With theses functions, notice that the marginal rates of substitution $\pi_{ij}(x_i)$ are identical to the marginal utilities $\partial u_i(x_i)/\partial x_{ij}$, and are independent of x_{i1}. (A4') is here assumed for the same reason that (A4) was assumed earlier, that is, to avoid boundary problems and thus to have continuous differential equations with classical properties. However, the variables relating to commodity 1 are no longer covered by (A4'). This explains the introduction of assumption (A1'), which differs from (A1) by extending the individual consumption sets to allow for negative amounts of this commodity. This is fairly common practice in the game theoretic literature on market games, and is rationalized as describing situations where agents are allowed to borrow from one another.

For pure exchange economies satisfying (A1'), (A2), (A3') and (A4'), it is known (see Varian, 1984) that a competitive equilibrium always exists, and is unique. Moreover, for individual endowments in commodity 1 that are positive and large enough (this amounts to a strengthening of (A2), all agents hold positive amounts of commodity 1 at the competitive allocation.

4.4. Properties of the competitive exchange process, for economies with quasi-linear utilities

For the process (10)–(12), defined for an economy satisfying (A1'), (A2), (A3') and (A4'), we can now establish existence and uniqueness of a solution, as well as convergence to the competitive equilibrium.

Proposition 2. *Under assumptions* (A1'), (A2), (A3') *and* (A4'), *there exists for the system of differential equations* (10)–(12) *a unique solution* $x(t; x(0))$, *defined over the interval* $[0, +\infty)$; *this solution converges to the competitive equilibrium.*

Proof. Notice first that, although it is formulated in terms of variables in an $n \times l$-dimensional space, the process does actually take place in a manifold of dimension $n \times (l-1)$. Indeed as it is constructed in such a way that the individual budget constraints (8) be always satisfied, one has that at every t both $\dot{x}_{i1}(t)$ in (12) and $x_{i1}(t)$ along any solution are entirely determined by the $n \times (l-1)$-dimensional vector $x^-(t) = (x_1^-(t), \ldots, x_i^-(t), \ldots, x_n^-(t))$, where $x_i^-(t) = (x_{i2}(t), \ldots, x_{il}(t))$, $i = 1, \ldots, n$. As a result, the differential equation system (10)–(12) is really governed by equation (11) only, and it is sufficient to establish existence and other properties of a solution for a function $x^- : \mathbb{R}_+ \to \mathbb{R}_+^{n(l-1)}$, $t \to x^-(t; x(0))$.

In this setting, we can use the method of proof already used in d'Aspremont and Tulkens (1980, Proposition 1), which we transpose compactly as follows:

(i) *Existence and uniqueness.*

(i)(a) Consider the function

$$L(x^-(t)) \overset{\text{def}}{=} \sum_{i \in N} v_i(x_{i2}(t), \ldots, x_{il}(t)). \tag{16}$$

Along any solution of (11), if one exists, this function is increasing since (recall that $\partial v_i / \partial x_{ij} = \pi_{ij}$, $j \neq 1$, under (A3'))

$$\frac{d}{dt} L(x^-(t)) = \sum_{i \in N} \sum_{j \neq 1} \frac{\partial v_i}{\partial x_{ij}} \dot{x}_{ij} = \sum_{j \neq 1} \sum_i \pi_{ij}(\pi_{ij} - \bar{\pi}_j)$$

$$= \sum_{j \neq 1} \sum_i (\pi_{ij} - \bar{\pi}_j)^2 > 0, \tag{17}$$

unless $x^-(t)$ is an equilibrium of the process. Now, assumption (A4') can be used to show that for any sequence $(x^-)^k$, $k = 1, 2, \ldots$, in the compact set

$$X_i^-(x^-(0)) = \left\{ x^- \mid \sum_{i \in N} x_{ij} = \sum_i w_{ij}, j = 2, \ldots, l; L(x^-) \geq L(x^-(0)) \right\},$$

one must have $\lim_{k \to \infty} (x_{ij})^k > 0$ for any i and $j \neq 1$. Hence, if a solution exists, it must be such that for every $t \in [0, +\infty)$, $x^-(t) \in \mathbb{R}_+^{n(l-1)} \backslash \partial \mathbb{R}_+^{n(l-1)}$, i.e., it never reaches the boundaries of the relevant commodity space.

(i)(b) Moreover, any solution has been shown in Section 4.1 to be such that $\sum_i x_{ij}(t) = \sum_i w_{ij}, j = 2, \ldots, l, t \in [0, +\infty)$. Together with (1.1), this implies that any solution remains in a compact subset of the feasible allocations.

(i)(c) In view of (A3'), each one of the functions $v_i(x_{i2}, \ldots, x_{il})$ are twice continuously differentiable on $\mathbb{R}_+^{l-1}$; hence their first and second derivatives are bounded, which implies that their first derivatives are locally Lipschitz. This in turn implies that the right hand side of (11) is locally Lipschitz in $\mathbb{R}_+^{n(l-1)}$. Hence, there exists for (11) a unique solution $x^-(t; x(0))$ on some interval in $\mathbb{R}_+$ which cannot be continued on the right.

(i)(d) As the solution $x^-(t; x(0))$ maps into a compact set of $\mathbb{R}_+^{n(l-1)}$, with $x_{ij}(t) > 0$ $\forall i, j = 2, \ldots, l, \forall t$, the interval for which the solution exists must be $[0, +\infty)$.

(ii) *Convergence.*

(ii)(a) Quasi-stability, i.e., that any accumulation point of the solution be an equilibrium of the process, follows as a corollary to Theorem 6.1 of Champsaur, Drèze and Henry (1977), from the Lipschitz property of the process, and from the fact that the function $L(x^-(t))$ defined in (16) satisfies the definition of a Lyapounov function. $L(x^-(t))$ is indeed continuous, defined on a compact set and monotonically non-decreasing unless $x^-(t)$ is an equilibrium of the process, where $L(x^-(t))$ is constant; hence, $\lim_{t \to \infty} L(x^-(t))$ exists.

(ii)(b) Stability, i.e., uniqueness of the accumulation point of the solution, follows from the fact that an equilibrium of the process is a competitive equilibrium of the economy, and that the latter is unique with quasi-linear utilities. □

5. Concluding remarks

From the argument presented at the beginning of the proof of Proposition 2, it appears that eqs. (12) play no rôle in the convergence of process (10)-(12). As these equations are the only ones containing second derivatives of the utility functions, we have identified here a special class of economies for which, contrary to Jordan's (1987) general theorem, a process can be exhibited that converges to a competitive equilibrium without requiring such information.

As to the non-tâtonnement character of our process, let us recall the following comment of Smale (1976, p. 113): "A Walrasian price equilibrium in a pure exchange economy depends on the trader's endowments. Thus if one allows a real passage of time, say, for actual exchange to take place, and several such, this initial endowment becomes lost in the reshuffle. Thus if one allows this kind of time passage ("non-tâtonnement") one must replace the Walrasian price equilibrium by a different notion of price equilibrium". This suggests that the notions of non-tâtonnement and competitive equilibrium might be incompatible.

In this paper, we do in fact show the opposite, but only for the special case of economies with quasi-linear utility functions. A characteristic of these being the absence of income effects, our result indicates that these effects may be at the source of the suggested incompatibility. However, a general proof of impossibility remains to be formulated for Smale's statement to receive its full scope.

References

Allais, M. (1967) 'Les conditions de l'efficacité dans l'économie', *IV° Seminario Internazionale, Rapallo, Centro Studi e Richerche sui Problemi Economico-Sociali (CESE)*. Milan.

d'Aspremont, C. and H. Tulkens (1980) 'Commodity exchanges as gradient processes', *Econometrica*, 48(2):387-399.

Billera, L.J. (1972) 'Global stability in *n*-person games', *Transactions of the American Mathematical Society*, 172:45-56.

Champsaur, P. (1976) 'Neutrality of planning procedures in an economy with public goods', *Review of Economic Studies*, 43(2):293-300.

Champsaur, P., J. Drèze and C. Henry (1977) 'Stability theorems with economic applications', *Econometrica*, 45(2):273-294.

Chander, P. (1988) 'Incentives and a process converging to the core of a public goods economy', Caltech Social Sciences Working Paper 677. Pasadena, CA: California Institute of Technology.

Cornet, B. (1983) 'Neutrality of planning procedures', *Journal of Mathematical Economics*, 11(2):141-160.

Debreu, G. and H. Scarf (1963) 'A limit theorem on the core of an economy', *International Economic Review*, 4(3):235-246.

Drèze, J.H. and D. de la Vallée Poussin (1971) 'A tâtonnement process for public goods', *Review of Economic Studies*, 37(2):133-150.

Green, J. (1974) 'The stability of Edgeworth's recontracting process', *Econometrica*, 42(1):21-34.

Green, J. and J.J. Laffont (1971) *Incentives in Public Decision Making*. Amsterdam: North-Holland.

Hurwicz, L., R. Radner and S. Reiter (1975) 'A stochastic decentralized resource allocation process, Part I', *Econometrica*, 43(2):187-223. 'Part II', *Econometrica*, 43(3):363-395.

Jordan, J.S. (1987). The informational requirements of local stability in decentralized allocation mechanisms', in: T. Groves, R. Radner and S. Reiter, eds., *Information, Incentives and Economic Mechanisms: Essays in Honour of Leonid Hurwicz*. Oxford: Blackwell; and Minneapolis, MN: University of Minnesota Press, pp. 183-212.

Kalai, G., M. Maschler and G. Owen (1975) 'Asymptotic stability and other properties of trajectories and transfer sequences leading to the bargaining sets', *International Journal of Game Theory*, 4(4):193-213.

Ledyard, J.O. (1974) 'Decentralized disequilibrium trading and price formation', Discussion Paper No. 68. Evanston, IL: The Center for Mathematical Studies in Economics and Management Science, Northwestern University.

Malinvaud, E. (1968) 'Notes sur l'étude des procédures de planification', *Canadian Journal of Economics/Revue Canadienne d'Economique*, 1(1):16-36.

Malinvaud, E. (1972) *Lectures in Microeconomic Theory*. Amsterdam: North-Holland.

Marshall, A. (1920) *Principles of Economics*. London: Macmillan, 8th ed. (Reprinted 1962.)

Negishi, T. (1962) 'The stability of competitive economy: A survey article', *Econometrica*, 30(4):635-669.

Scarf, M. (1967) 'The core of an *n*-person game', *Econometrica*, 35(1):50-69.

Shapley, L. and M. Shubik (1975) 'Competitive outcomes in the cores of market games', *International Journal of Game Theory*, 4(4):229-237.

Shiao, L. and Y. Wang (1974) 'A dynamic theory for the core', IBM Research Memorandum, RC 4687 (# 20891). Yorktown Heights, NY: IBM Thomas J. Watson Research Centre.

Smale, S. (1976) 'Exchange processes with price adjustment', *Journal of Mathematical Economics*, 3(3):1211-1266.

Stearns, R.E. (1968) 'Convergent transfer schemes for *n*-person games', *Transactions of American Mathematical Society*, 134:449-456.

Tulkens, H. and S. Zamir (1976) 'Local games in dynamic exchange processes', CORE Discussion Paper No. 7606. Louvain-la-Neuve: Université Catholique de Louvain.

Tulkens, H. and S. Zamir (1979) 'Surplus-sharing local games in dynamic exchange processes', *Review of Economic Studies*, 46(2):305-313.

Uzawa, H. (1962) 'On the stability of Edgeworth's barter process', *International Economic Review*, 3(2):218-232.

Varian, H. (1984) *Microeconomic Analysis*. New York: Norton, 2nd ed.

Chapter 3

A MODEL OF TEMPORARY EQUILIBRIA WITH STOCHASTIC QUANTITY RATIONING

Louis-André GÉRARD-VARET

GREQE, Ecole des Hautes Etudes en Sciences Sociales, Marseille, France

Robert JORDAN

GREQE, Université d'Aix-Marseille II, Aix-Marseille, France

Alan P. KIRMAN

Institut Universitaire Européen, Florence, Italy

Introduction

The name of Jacques Drèze is associated along with those of Benassy (1982) and Malinvaud (1977) with one of the more important recent theoretical developments in the field of macro economics that of the study of fixed price equilibrium. This field, which curiously enough has engaged almost exclusively the attention of European economists since the early work of Barro and Grossman (1971) is founded, as is so much of the work of Drèze, on a simple and undeniable empirical fact, namely that in many situations prices which do not clear markets prevail.

On such markets quantity rationing must occur and Drèze (1975) proved the existence of an equilibrium with rationing and later with Müller (Drèze

Research financed under a contract with Commissariat Général du Plan, Paris, "Méthodes et Instruments de la Planification". We wish to thank J.P. Benassy, V. Böhm, J. Drèze, J.P. Florens, R. Kast, C. Nilsson, G. Weinrich and Y. Younès for their helpful comments. We are of course responsible for any remaining errors.

Economic Decision-Making: Games, Econometrics and Optimisation
Edited by J.J. Gabszewicz, J.-F. Richard and L.A. Wolsey
© *Elsevier Science Publishers B.V., 1990*

and Müller, 1980) went on to discuss the optimality of rationing schemes. Already at this point he was discussing prices which were subject to inequality rather than equality constraints which implies some possible flexibility as in the case of downwardly rigid wages for example.

Our purpose in this paper is to pursue this work in the natural direction that in which prices do adjust slowly in the longer term but where immediate discrepancies are resolved by quantity rationing.

This is clearly the idea that lies at the heart of all the work in this area and an approach has already been made by Malinvaud (1977) and Blad and Kirman (1985) but in models which, for different reasons, left much to be desired.

We work within the by now standard three market framework but we develop a model which meets a certain number of basic requirements for a satisfactory dynamic treatment.

(1) The behaviour of the individuals should be fully specified and their decisions should be intertemporal.

(2) The model should be really dynamic in the sense that today's decisions have consequences for the real state of the economy tomorrow.

(3) The equilibria discussed should have a certain compatibility with the expectations of the individuals.

(4) The model should be such that there is a clear and explicit definition of the difference between what individuals desire conceptually and what they obtain effectively. This difference then provides the basis for the dynamics of prices and wages.

Our model meets these criteria. In the first section we develop the model and specify the behaviour of the individual firms and households. Time plays an explicit role in that:

  (i) individuals can spend today only what they earned yesterday;

  (ii) firms can sell today only what they produced yesterday;

  (iii) firms can hold inventories from one period to the next.

The individual households or firms maximise utility or profit over an infinite horizon. To avoid arbitrarily complicated calculations we assume that the individual expects parameters to change from one period to the next but after that assumes them to be constant. This is formally the same as assuming that from some n periods onwards they assume that these parameters remain constant. This captures the idea that while individuals have no fixed horizon they are only able to forecast for a limited period, an assumption which does not seem unrealistic!

Individuals are faced with rationing in disequilibria and anticipate rationing in the future. This rationing is stochastic, corresponding to the idea that households visit firms at random, and thus that the quantities that may be bought or sold are uncertain at the outset. Then after visits either firms may be left with stocks on their hands or households may be left unsatisfied. On the labour market either there will be unemployment or there will be firms unable to hire their desired quantity of labour. Markets are thus "orderly" but what each individual buys or sells is random. This type of rationing gives rise to a clear definition of the excess demand for, or offer of, labour and of goods, avoids the difficulties of "manipulation" and provides a basis for the adjustments of prices and wages.

In the second section we define the different types of rationed temporary equilibria under stochastic quantity rationing. These equilibria are *rational* in the sense that the signals perceived by the agents give rise to behaviour on their part which yields states of the market consistent with those signals.

After proving the existence of a Walrasian equilibrium we emphasise Keynesian Unemployment equilibria. We then characterise the set of equilibria and show which configurations of multiple equilibria can occur. In particular we see that Keynesian equilibria can occur at Walrasian prices.

Some of the elements of our model have been developed by other authors, Benassy (1982) in particular who examined the role of different types of rationing, Böhm (1981) and Honkapohja and Ito (1980) examined the problem of stock adjustment whilst Weinrich (1984) looked at measures of disequilibrium. The juxtaposition of these elements together with intertemporal decision making and dynamic interdependence provides a complete and manageable model. However even this simple model seems to present considerable difficulty for the analysis of its dynamics.

1. The model

We consider a three good economy — labour, one produced good and money — with a set F of firms, a set H of households and a public sector. Individual firms maximise their expected discounted profit over an infinite horizon; individual households behave accordingly in terms of their expected utility. We assume discrete time. At each date $t \geq 0$, the economy is described by market signals which are the nominal wage rate w_t the price of the produced good p_t and quantity signals R_t^c and R_t^z giving the ratio of aggregate supply to aggregate demand on the produced good and labour market respectively. At the beginning of every period $t \geq 0$, individual money holdings by households M_{ht} and inventories held by firms S_{ft} are given. There is also given a stationary volume G of autonomous public expenditure.

At date $t = 0$, the agents observe current price signals denoted (w, p) which are fixed. For these signals and for all future dates $t \geq 1$, they have stationary point expectations denoted $(\hat{w}, \hat{p})$. Quantity signals at date $t = 0$, denoted R^c and R^z, are the solution of an equilibrium at fixed prices with stochastic quantity rationing where expectations about the current state of the market are fulfilled. The agents' "effective demands" are based upon R^c and R^z since the probability distributions on the level of transactions depend on those signals. Clearly, individual behaviour is conditional upon all future expected states of the market. In the same way as for prices, we assume for quantities a stationarity property which holds for every future date $t \geq 1$ either with respect to the signals themselves or with respect to their probability distributions if these signals are considered as random variables.

Our description of agents' future expectations introduces "partial myopia". This simplification is a compromise which solves the horizon problem without involving the solution of a highly complex dynamic programming problem. Furthermore it is perhaps not unreasonable to consider that forecasting horizons are short relative to economic lives. In particular it should be observed that it would make no formal difference to assume that agents forecast up to n periods ahead and then consider that things remain stationary from then on. This approach should be contrasted with the "pessimistic" hypothesis adopted by Malinvaud (1977) and which, except for Neary and Stiglitz (1983), has hardly been questioned. The interaction between expectations as to the future and current behaviour is nevertheless central to the whole of Keynesian analysis.

1.1. Firms behaviour

Take any date $t \geq 0$: the level of inventories of firm f resulting from past events is S_{ft} and the supply on the good market is $\mathscr{S}_t \stackrel{\text{def}}{=} \sum_{f \in F} S_{ft}$. For any possible total demand $\mathscr{D}_t$, the market coefficient of supply rationing is: $r_t^Q \stackrel{\text{def}}{=} \text{Min}\{1, 1/R_t^c\}$, where $R_t^c \stackrel{\text{def}}{=} \mathscr{S}_t / \mathscr{D}_t$.

We see the level of sales of firm f at date t as a random variable $\tilde{Q}_{ft}$ determined by

$$\tilde{Q}_{ft} = \text{Min}\{\tilde{D}_{ft}, S_{ft}\}$$

where $\tilde{D}_{ft}$ is a random variable describing the demand with which the firm is faced. The distribution of $\tilde{D}_{ft}$ assumed to be the same for each firm is derived as follows. Each household visits a firm chosen at random. It purchases what it desires: if it is not fully satisfied it moves on to a new firm chosen at random. This process continues until either all households are satisfied or all firms have sold all their stocks. From the point of view of firm f, the density function of $\tilde{D}_{ft}$ (resp., cumulative), conditional on r_t^Q is denoted $\phi(\cdot | r_t^Q)$ (resp., $\Phi(\cdot | r_t^Q)$). Notice that by construction whenever $r_t^Q = 1$ (namely $R_t^c \leq 1$), firms are sure to sell all their current stocks, i.e., $\Phi(S_{ft} | 1) = 0$. This can be seen as an "efficiency" or orderly market condition.

Given a value of the coefficient r_t^Q the expected sales of firm f holding inventories S_{ft} are

$$E[\tilde{Q}_{ft} | S_{ft}, r_t^Q] \stackrel{\text{def}}{=} \int_0^{S_{ft}} \tilde{D}_{ft} \phi(D_{ft} | r_t^Q) \, dD_{ft} + [1 - \Phi(S_{ft} | r_t^Q)] S_{ft}.$$

The individual coefficient of rationing on the good market that the firm expects to face is now

$$\rho_{ft}^Q = E[\tilde{Q}_{ft} | S_{ft}, r_t^Q] / S_{ft}.$$

By construction ρ_{ft}^Q is rational. When $r_t^Q = 1$, it is necessarily the case that $\rho_{ft}^Q = 1$. However, when $r_t^Q < 1$, ρ_{ft}^Q is greater (resp., less than) r_t^Q if S_{ft} is less than (resp., greater than) $\mathscr{S}_t / F$.

At date $t \geq 0$ firm f demands Z_{ft} units of labour. Let $r_t^z \stackrel{\text{def}}{=} \mathrm{Min}\{1, R_t^z\}$ be the market coefficient of demand rationing on the labour market. The effective employment of firm f for period t is a random variable $\tilde{Z}_{ft}$. It is a function of Z_{ft} and its distribution conditional on r_t^z, is given by

$$\tilde{Z}_{ft} = \begin{cases} Z_{ft} & \text{with probability } \gamma_f r_t^z, \\ \alpha_{ft} Z_{ft} & \text{with probability } 1 - \gamma_f r_t^z, \end{cases} \tag{1}$$

with

$$\gamma_f \in [0, 1], \quad \alpha_{ft} \stackrel{\text{def}}{=} \frac{r_t^z - \gamma_f r_t^z}{1 - \gamma_f r_t^z}, \quad r_t^z \stackrel{\text{def}}{=} \mathrm{Min}\{1, R_t^z\}.$$

In such a rationing scheme[1] γ_f is a subjective parameter describing the "agent's perception of the market". Clearly the expected level of employment is

$$E[\tilde{Z}_{ft}] = \gamma_f r_t^z Z_{ft} + (1 - \gamma_f r_t^z) \alpha_{ft} Z_{ft} = r_t^z Z_{ft}.$$

This is a rationality condition: the firm expects rationing in a proportion which is on average consistent with the state of the market. Also if $r_t^z = 1$

---

[1] We could have proceeded in the same way as we did for firms on the good market. But this would have unduly complicated the analysis. So we have adopted a standard approach (see Green, 1980; Weinrich, 1984).

(i.e., $R_t^z \geq 1$) then $\alpha_{ft} = 1$ and the random variable $\tilde{Z}_{ft}$ degenerates to the point Z_{ft}, which again can be seen as an "efficiency" or orderly market condition.

The production at date $t \geq 0$ is available only at date $t+1$. Production takes place under constant returns to scale and $\lambda_f > 0$ is the stationary labour productivity of firm f. The level of inventories expected by firm f at date t for date $t+1$ is

$$\tilde{S}_{ft+1} = \lambda_f \tilde{Z}_{ft} + S_{ft} - \tilde{Q}_{ft}.$$ (2)

As soon as labour is available and demand is realised, then stocks for date $t+1$ are known.

From now on we consider the behaviour of one particular firm and to simplify matters we omit the subscript f.

At date $t = 0$, the firm, having current stocks S, considers as given *current* market signals w/p, r^z and r^Q. For future periods, i.e., $t \geq 1$, the firm expects price signals to be stationary at the level $\hat{w}/\hat{p}$. Forecasted quantity signals are treated differently. The rationing coefficient on the good market r_t^Q, $t \geq 1$, is for the firm a random variable having a stationary distribution denoted ν; when for the rationing on the labour market (given by (1)), the firm has a stationary point expectation denoted $\hat{r}^z$. This lack of symmetry in the treatment of the two future quantity signals may be justified by arguing that the firm perceives "less uncertainty" on the labour market than on the good market. Nevertheless, what follows can be extended with some technicalities to a symmetric treatment of quantity expectations on the two markets.

At date $t = 0$, given the level S of inventories at that date, given current market signals and stationary expectations about future market signals, the firm maximises the expected value of discounted profits,

$$E\left[\sum_{t=0}^{\infty} \delta^t \left(\tilde{Q}_t - \frac{w_t}{p_t} \tilde{Z}_t \right) \right],$$

under constraint (2) for each $t \geq 0$; where $\delta \in \,]0, 1[$ is an exogenous discount factor. This program gives, for each date $t \geq 0$, the optimal level of employment Z_t^* as a function of all exogenous variables. However for our purpose, only the current level of employment at date $t = 0$, denoted Z^*, is relevant. Under the assumption of stationary expected future market signals, optimal levels of employment are implicitly given by the "value" of the level of inventories at date $t = 1$. Thus, we can divide the optimisation problem into two parts: first determine the "value" of a given level of inventories at date $t = 1$, second determine, given that value, optimal current employment.

We treat first the problem for date $t = 1$ onwards. At date $t = 1$ the firm's maximisation program is:

$$\underset{Z_t > 0}{\text{Max}} \quad E\left[\sum_{t=1} \delta^t \left(\tilde{Q}_t - \frac{\hat{w}}{\hat{p}}\tilde{Z}_t\right)\right]$$

s.t. $\tilde{S}_{t+1} = \lambda \tilde{Z}_t + S_t - \tilde{Q}_t, \quad t \geq 1.$

This dynamic optimisation problem is solved using Bellman's equation (Bellman, 1957, p. 11) which gives the "value" of inventories S_1 held at date $t = 1$:

$$V(S_1)$$

$$\stackrel{\text{def}}{=} \underset{Z_1 > 0}{\text{Max}}\left\{(1 - \gamma \hat{r}^z)\left(\int_0^1 \int_0^{S_1} [\tilde{D}_1 + \delta V(\lambda \hat{\alpha} Z_1 + S_1 - \tilde{D}_1)]\phi(D_1 \mid r_1^Q)\,\mathrm{d}D_1\right.\right.$$

$$+ [1 - \Phi(S_1 \mid r_1^Q)][S_1 + \delta V(\lambda \hat{\alpha} Z_1)]\nu(r_1^Q)\,\mathrm{d}r_1^Q$$

$$\left. + \left[1 - \int_0^1 \nu(r_1^Q)\,\mathrm{d}r_1^Q\right][S_1 + \delta V(\lambda \hat{\alpha} Z_1)]\right)$$

$$+ \gamma \hat{r}^z \left(\int_0^1 \int_0^{S_1} [\tilde{D}_1 + \delta V(\lambda Z_1 + S_1 - \tilde{D}_1)]\phi(D_1 \mid r_1^Q)\,\mathrm{d}D_1\right.$$

$$+ [1 - \Phi(S_1 \mid r_1^Q)][S_1 + \delta V(\lambda Z_1)]\nu(r_1^Q)\,\mathrm{d}r_1^Q$$

$$\left.\left. + \left[1 - \int_0^1 \nu(r_1^Q)\,\mathrm{d}r_1^Q\right][S_1 + \delta V(\lambda Z_1)]\right) - \frac{\hat{w}}{\hat{p}}\hat{r}^z Z_1\right\}.$$

By a well-known argument (Bellman, 1957, p. 21), V is concave in S_1; moreover using an argument similar to Abel's (1985, pp. 288–289), V is *strictly concave*. There is a unique maximum at $Z_1^* > 0$ and in a neighbourhood of this point V is twice continuously differentiable. The first order condition at $Z_1^* > 0$ is

$$(1 - \gamma \hat{r}^z)\hat{\alpha}\left(\int_0^1 \int_0^{S_1} V'(\lambda \hat{\alpha} Z_1^* + S_1 - \tilde{D}_1)\phi(D_1 \mid r_1^Q)\,\mathrm{d}D_1\right.$$

$$+ [1 - \phi(S_1 \mid r_1^Q)]V'(\lambda \hat{\alpha} Z_1^*)\nu(r_1^Q)\,\mathrm{d}r_1^Q$$

$$\left. + \left[1 - \int_0^1 \nu(r_1^Q)\,\mathrm{d}r_1^Q\right][S_1 + \delta V'(\lambda \hat{\alpha} Z_1^*)]\right)$$

$$+ \gamma \hat{r}^z \left(\int_0^1 \int_0^{S_1} V'(\lambda Z_1^* + S_1 - \tilde{D}_1) \phi(D_1 | r_1^Q) \, dD_1 \right.$$

$$+ [1 - \phi(S_1 | r_1^Q)] V'(\lambda Z_1^*) \nu(r_1^Q) \, dr_1^Q$$

$$+ \left. \left[1 - \int_0^1 \nu(r_1^Q) \, dr_1^Q \right] [S_1 + \delta V'(\lambda Z_1^*)] \right) - \frac{\hat{w}\hat{r}^z}{\lambda \delta \hat{p}} = 0. \qquad (3)$$

Condition (3) gives Z_1^* as a continuously differentiable function of S_1 and $\hat{w}/\hat{p}$,

$$Z_1^* = \hat{\xi}^z(\underset{(-)}{S_1}, \underset{(-)}{w/\hat{p}}),$$

with $\hat{r}^z$ and ν considered as parameters. The signs of the effects are computed easily.

At $Z_1^* > 0$, the value of S_1 given $\hat{w}/\hat{p}$ (and all expectations) is denoted $V^*(S_1, \hat{w}/\hat{p})$ and such that $\partial^2 V^*/\partial S_1^2 < 0$. Let us go back to date $t = 0$. Maximising the expected discounted profit over the whole horizon becomes equivalent to maximise the current expected profit plus the expected value of inventories carried to the next period, namely

$$E \left[\tilde{Q} - \frac{w}{p} \tilde{Z} \right] + \delta E \left[V^* \left(\lambda \tilde{Z} + S - \tilde{Q}, \frac{\hat{w}}{\hat{p}} \right) \right]$$

$$= (1 - \gamma r^z) \int_0^S \left[\tilde{D} + \delta V^* \left(\lambda \alpha Z + S - \tilde{D}, \frac{\hat{w}}{\hat{p}} \right) \right] \phi(D | r^Q) \, dD$$

$$+ [1 - \Phi(S | r^Q)] \left[S + \delta V^* \left(\lambda \alpha Z + S - \tilde{D}, \frac{\hat{w}}{\hat{p}} \right) \right]$$

$$+ \gamma r^z \int_0^S \left[\tilde{D} + \delta V^* \left(\lambda Z + S - \tilde{D}, \frac{\hat{w}}{\hat{p}} \right) \right] \phi(D | r^Q) \, dD$$

$$+ [1 - \Phi(S | r^Q)] \left[S + \delta V^* \left(\lambda Z, \frac{\hat{w}}{\hat{p}} \right) \right] - \frac{w}{p} r^z Z.$$

This objective, as a function of Z is the sum of a concave and of a strictly concave function and thus is strictly concave in Z. The first order condition for a maximum at $Z^* > 0$ is

$$(1 - \gamma) r^z \int_0^S \frac{\partial V^*}{\partial S_1} \left(\lambda \alpha Z^* + S - \tilde{D}, \frac{\hat{w}}{\hat{p}} \right) \phi(D | r^Q) \, dD$$

$$+ [1 - \Phi(S | r^Q)] \frac{\partial V^*}{\partial S_1} \left(\lambda \alpha Z^*, \frac{\hat{w}}{\hat{p}} \right)$$

$$+ \gamma r^z \int_0^S \frac{\partial V^*}{\partial S_1} \left(\lambda Z^* + S - \tilde{D}, \frac{\hat{w}}{\hat{p}} \right) \phi(D \,|\, r^Q)\, dD$$

$$+ [1 - \Phi(S \,|\, r^Q)] \frac{\partial V^*}{\partial S_1} \left(\lambda Z^*, \frac{\hat{w}}{\hat{p}} \right) = 0. \tag{4}$$

It gives Z^* as a continuously differentiable function of all the relevant exogenous variables,

$$Z^* = \xi^z(\,\underset{(-)}{S}\,,\, \underset{(-)}{w/p},\, \underset{(+)}{\hat{w}/\hat{p}},\, \underset{(-)}{r^z}\,,\, \underset{(+)}{r^Q}\,). \tag{5}$$

Static comparative properties justifying the sign of the effects are easily obtained. The only difficult point concerns $\partial \xi^z / \partial r^Q$. In order to conclude that this effect is positive we have to assume that today's expected sales increase when r^Q increases:

$$\frac{\partial}{\partial r^Q} E[\tilde{Q} \,|\, S, r^Q] > 0. \tag{6}$$

Such a property is obtained for instance when the random variable which gives the demand with which a firm is faced is given by $\tilde{D} = E[\tilde{D} \,|\, r^Q] + \varepsilon$ with $(\partial / \partial r^Q) E[\tilde{D} \,|\, r^Q] > 0$ and where ε is a "white noise".

1.2. The households behaviour

Consider now one particular household whose index is omitted for simplicity. At each date, the household offers one unit of labour and consumes $C_t > 0$ units of the produced goods. Its money holding at the beginning of period t M_t, after payment of taxes and receipts of profits defines an upperbound on its consumption. The utility of consumption at date t is given by a $\mathscr{C}^2$ function U such that:

$$U' > 0 \quad \text{and} \quad U'' < 0, \tag{7a}$$

$$U'(C_t) \to \infty \text{ as } C_t \to 0 \quad \text{and} \quad U'(C_t) \to 0 \text{ as } C_t \to \infty. \tag{7b}$$

The agent spends during period t the income earned during period $t-1$. Money endowments at the beginning of period $t+1$ depend upon effective employment and effective consumption during period t which at date t are random. Once these two random variables are realised taxes are paid, profits distributed and the result is M_{t+1}.

From the point of view of an agent effective employment is given by

$$\tilde{L}_t = \begin{cases} 0 & \text{with probability } \theta_t, \\ 1 & \text{with probability } 1 - \theta_t, \end{cases}$$

where $\theta_t \overset{\text{def}}{=} \text{Max}\{0, 1 - 1/R_t^z\}$ is the rate of unemployment at date t. At that date, the effective consumption of period t, as a function of the agents demand for good C_t, is

$$\tilde{C}_t = \begin{cases} C_t & \text{with probability } \mu_t r_t^c, \\ \beta_t C_t & \text{with probability } 1 - \mu_t r_t^c, \end{cases} \tag{8}$$

where $\beta_t \overset{\text{def}}{=} (r_t^c - \mu_t r_t^c)/(1 - \mu_t r_t^c)$, with $\mu_t \in [0, 1]$ and $r_t^c \overset{\text{def}}{=} \text{Min}\{1, R_t^c\}$.

It should be noted that the rationing scheme for the consumers on the good market is not symmetric with that of firms on the same market. Firstly, we have to think of this scheme as "perceived" by the household, μ_t being the parameter which gives the agent's view of the scheme. The fact that the consumer's perception does not necessarily coincide with a full description of reality requires defining β as above to guarantee rationality, namely

$$E(\tilde{C}_t) = \beta_t C_t \mu_t r_t^c + C_t (1 - \mu_t r_t^c) = r_t^c C_t.$$

Secondly, we must take account of the fact that firms will be faced with the following situation: either initially they can supply the demand with which they are faced, in which case their consumers are satisfied; or they are faced with an excess demand, in which case we suppose that they split their supply amongst their clients. Thus, we describe here the perception that a consumer has of entering queues at a given position when visiting firms at random. From this point of view μ_t gives a "relative mean position" of the household in all possible queues. With many such queues, his expected level of transactions is $r_t^c C_t$.

Real money holdings expected by the agent at date t for date $t + 1$ are

$$\tilde{M}_{t+1}/p_{t+1} = (M_t + w_t \tilde{L}_t - p_t \tilde{C}_t)/p_{t+1}. \tag{9}$$

Clearly, given that we have $Z_t = L_t$ and $C_t + G = Q_t$, and that money demand is given by (9), the money market is always in equilibrium.

Now the behaviour of the household at date $t = 0$ is described by the maximisation of discounted expected utility over an infinite horizon under the relevant constraints

$$\text{Max} \quad E\left[\sum_{t=0}^{\infty} \delta^t U(C_t) \right]$$

$$\text{s.t.} \quad C_t \leq M_t/p_t, \quad t \geq 0,$$

$$\text{constraint (9)}, \quad t \geq 1,$$

where $\delta \in]0, 1[$ is an exogenous discount factor (which is the same for every agent).

In order to solve this program we consider a household which, at date $t = 0$, has current nominal money holdings M and takes as given current market signals w/p, θ and r^c. For future periods, i.e., $t \geq 1$, the household expects, as do the firms, price signals to be stationary at the level $\hat{w}/\hat{p}$. Quantity signals are forecasted on a point expectation basis and expectations are, for $t \geq 1$, stationary at the level $\hat{\theta}$ and $\hat{r}^c$. Now the program gives, for each date $t \geq 0$, the optimal level of consumption C_t^* as a function of all exogenous variables. However, for our purpose, only current consumption at date $t = 0$, denoted C^*, is relevant. Given our assumption of stationary expected future market signals, the optimal level of future consumptions $(C_t^*)_{t \geq 1}$ are implicitly given by the "value" of real money holdings at date $t = 1$. Thus, we may divide the general optimisation problem into two parts: first determine the "value" of given real money holdings $M_1/\hat{p}$ at date $t = 1$; second, given that value, determine optimal consumption C^* at date $t = 0$.

Let us consider first the behaviour of the household at date $t = 1$. Using Bellman's equation, the value of expected real money holdings at that date is given by

$$
V\left(\frac{M_1}{\hat{p}}\right) \stackrel{\text{def}}{=} \underset{0 \leq C_1 \leq M_1/\hat{p}}{\text{Max}} \left\{ (1 - \mu\hat{r}^c) \left[U(\hat{\beta}C_1) + \delta\hat{\theta}V\left(\frac{M_1}{\hat{p}} - \hat{\beta}C_1\right) \right. \right.
$$
$$
\left. + \delta(1 - \hat{\theta})V\left(\frac{M_1}{\hat{p}} + \frac{\hat{w}}{\hat{p}} - \hat{\beta}C_1\right) \right]
$$
$$
+ \mu\hat{r}^c \left[U(C_1) + \delta\hat{\theta}V\left(\frac{M_1}{\hat{p}} - C_1\right) \right.
$$
$$
\left. \left. + \delta(1 - \hat{\theta})V\left(\frac{M_1}{\hat{p}} + \frac{\hat{w}}{\hat{p}} - C_1\right) \right] \right\}.
$$

The first order condition for a maximum at $C_1^* \in]0, M_1/\hat{p}[$ is

$$
(1 - \mu\hat{r}^c)\hat{\beta} \left\{ U'(\hat{\beta}C_1^*) - \delta \left[\hat{\theta}V'\left(\frac{M_1}{\hat{p}} - \hat{\beta}C_1^*\right) \right. \right.
$$
$$
\left. \left. + (1 - \hat{\theta})V'\left(\frac{M_1}{\hat{p}} + \frac{\hat{w}}{\hat{p}} - \hat{\beta}C_1^*\right) \right] \right\}
$$
$$
+ \mu\hat{r}^c \left\{ U'(C_1^*) - \delta \left[\hat{\theta}V'\left(\frac{M_1}{\hat{p}} - C_1^*\right) + (1 - \hat{\theta})V'\left(\frac{M_1}{\hat{p}} + \frac{\hat{w}}{\hat{p}} - C_1^*\right) \right] \right\} = 0.
$$

$$
(10)
$$

By a standard argument (see Bellman, 1957, p. 20) V is concave, and since U is strictly concave, the second order condition is strictly satisfied:

$$(1 - \mu \hat{r}^c) \hat{\beta}^2 \left\{ U''(\hat{\beta} C_1^*) + \delta \left[\hat{\theta} V'' \left(\frac{M_1}{\hat{p}} - \beta C_1^* \right) \right.\right.$$

$$\left.\left. + (1 - \hat{\theta}) V'' \left(\frac{M_1}{\hat{p}} + \frac{\hat{w}}{\hat{p}} - \hat{\beta} C_1^* \right) \right] \right\}$$

$$+ \mu \hat{r}^c \left\{ U''(C_1^*) + \delta \left[\hat{\theta} V'' \left(\frac{M_1}{\hat{p}} - C_1^* \right) \right.\right.$$

$$\left.\left. + (1 - \hat{\theta}) V'' \left(\frac{M_1}{\hat{p}} + \frac{\hat{w}}{\hat{p}} - C_1^* \right) \right] \right\} < 0.$$

We show that only a unique interior solution is possible.

Let us show first that we cannot have a maximum at $C_1^* = 0$. Assume that at some date $\tau \geq 1$, $C_\tau^* = 0$; since $U'(C)$ goes to infinity when C goes to zero, the agent may always increase his expected utility by transferring one unit of money to period τ, making consumption in that period positive. Thus, a sequence of optimal choices $(C_t^*)_{t \geq 1}$ must be strictly positive. Furthermore the increase of value associated with a finite positive variation in the money holding is always finite since the marginal value of money holding at date τ must be proportional to the variation of utility in the period from which the money comes and this is finite. Then for $t = 1$, we have

$$U'(0) - \delta \left[\hat{\theta} V' \left(\frac{M_1}{\hat{p}} \right) + (1 - \hat{\theta}) V' \left(\frac{M_1}{\hat{p}} + \frac{\hat{w}}{\hat{p}} \right) \right] > 0.$$

Let us see now that we cannot have a maximum at $C_1^* = M_1/\hat{p}$. If it was the case we would have

$$V \left(\frac{M_1}{\hat{p}} \right) = (1 - \mu \hat{r}^c) \left\{ U \left(\hat{\beta} \frac{M_1}{\hat{p}} \right) + \delta \left[\hat{\theta} V \left((1 - \hat{\beta}) \frac{M_1}{\hat{p}} \right) \right.\right.$$

$$\left.\left. + (1 - \hat{\theta}) V \left((1 - \hat{\beta}) \frac{M_1}{\hat{p}} + \frac{\hat{w}}{\hat{p}} \right) \right] \right\}$$

$$+ \mu \hat{r}^c \left\{ U \left(\frac{M_1}{\hat{p}} \right) + \delta \left[\hat{\theta} V(0) + (1 - \hat{\theta}) V \left(\frac{\hat{w}}{\hat{p}} \right) \right] \right\}. \tag{11}$$

In a boundary solution, it is necessarily the case that

$$(1 - \mu \hat{r}^c)\hat{\beta} \left\{ U'\left(\hat{\beta}\frac{M_1}{\hat{p}}\right) - \delta\left[\hat{\theta}V'\left((1-\hat{\beta})\frac{M_1}{\hat{p}}\right)\right.\right.$$
$$\left.\left. + (1-\hat{\theta})V'\left((1-\hat{\beta})\frac{M_1}{\hat{p}}+\frac{\hat{w}}{\hat{p}}\right)\right]\right\}$$
$$+ \mu\hat{r}^c \left\{ U'\left(\frac{M_1}{\hat{p}}\right) - \delta\left[\hat{\theta}V'(0) + (1-\hat{\theta})V'\left(\frac{\hat{w}}{\hat{p}}\right)\right]\right\} \geq 0. \quad (12)$$

Differentiating (11) with respect to $M_1/\hat{p}$ gives

$$V'\left(\frac{M_1}{\hat{p}}\right) = (1 - \mu\hat{r}^c) \left\{ \hat{\beta}U'\left(\hat{\beta}\frac{M_1}{\hat{p}}\right) + \delta(1-\hat{\beta})\left[\hat{\theta}V'\left((1-\hat{\beta})\frac{M_1}{\hat{p}}\right)\right.\right.$$
$$\left.\left. + (1-\hat{\theta})V'\left((1-\hat{\beta})\frac{M_1}{\hat{p}}+\frac{\hat{w}}{\hat{p}}\right)\right]\right\} + \mu\hat{r}^c U'\left(\frac{M_1}{\hat{p}}\right).$$

Consider an interior solution at $C_1 = M_1/\hat{p}$. Taking (12) as an equality and substituting into the definition of $V'(M_1/\hat{p})$ gives

$$V'\left(\frac{M_1}{\hat{p}}\right) = \frac{(1-\mu r^c)\hat{\beta}U'(\hat{\beta}(M_1/\hat{p})) + \mu r^c U'(M_1/\hat{p})}{\hat{\beta}}$$
$$- \frac{1-\hat{\beta}}{\hat{\beta}}\delta\left[\hat{\theta}V(0) + (1-\hat{\theta})V'\left(\frac{\hat{w}}{\hat{p}}\right)\right]$$

and then

$$V'\left(\frac{M_1}{\hat{p}}\right) = \frac{1}{\hat{\beta}}E\left[U'(\tilde{C})\,\Big|\,C_1^* = \frac{M_1}{\hat{p}}\right] + \text{const.}$$

We see immediately that $V'(\ )$ behaves like $U'(\ )$ when the level of consumption goes to zero. More precisely we can calculate, letting $M_1/\hat{p}$ go to zero, the marginal value of real balances,

$$V'(0) = \frac{U'(0)}{\hat{\beta} + (1-\hat{\beta})\delta\hat{\theta}} - \frac{(1-\beta)\delta(1-\hat{\theta})}{\hat{\beta} + (1-\hat{\beta})\delta\hat{\theta}}V'\left(\frac{\hat{w}}{\hat{p}}\right),$$

and for any finite real wage V' goes to infinity when the real balance goes to zero. Hence for any positive real balance,

$$(1 - \mu\hat{r}^c)\hat{\beta}\left\{ U'\left(\beta\frac{M_1}{\hat{p}}\right) - \delta\left[\hat{\theta}V'\left((1-\hat{\beta})\frac{M_1}{\hat{p}}\right)\right.\right.$$
$$\left.\left. + (1-\theta)V'\left((1-\hat{\beta})\frac{M_1}{\hat{p}}+\frac{\hat{w}}{\hat{p}}\right)\right]\right\}$$

$$+ \mu \hat{r}^c \left\{ U' \left(\frac{M_1}{\hat{p}} \right) - \delta \left[\hat{\theta} V'(0) + (1 - \hat{\theta}) V' \left(\frac{\hat{w}}{\hat{p}} \right) \right] \right\} < 0.$$

which contradicts the fact that $M_1/\hat{p}$ is a solution to the consumer optimization program. Of course, any $C_1 > M_1/\hat{p}$ is no longer a solution either.

By the concavity of V and the strict concavity of U we have a unique strictly interior solution C_1^* which depends continuously on the parameters $\hat{w}/\hat{p}$, $M_1/\hat{p}$, $\hat{r}^c$ and $\hat{\theta}$: $C_1^* = \hat{\xi}^c(M_1/\hat{p}, \hat{w}/\hat{p}, \hat{r}^c, \hat{\theta})$. In the following, we shall neglect the dependence upon the quantity parameters and focus only on $M_1/\hat{p}$.

Now, we can define the value of money holdings at date $t = 1$:

$$V \left(\frac{M_1}{\hat{p}} \right) = (1 - \mu \hat{r}^c) \left\{ U \left(\hat{\beta} \hat{\xi}^c \left(\frac{M_1}{\hat{p}}, \cdot \right) \right) + \delta \left[\hat{\theta} V \left(\frac{M_1}{\hat{p}} - \hat{\beta} \hat{\xi}^c \left(\frac{M_1}{\hat{p}}, \cdot \right) \right) \right. \right.$$

$$\left. + (1 - \hat{\theta}) V \left(\frac{M_1}{\hat{p}} + \frac{\hat{w}}{\hat{p}} - \hat{\beta} \hat{\xi}^c \left(\frac{M_1}{\hat{p}}, \cdot \right) \right) \right] \right\}$$

$$+ \mu \hat{r}^c \left\{ U \left(\hat{\xi}^c \left(\frac{M_1}{\hat{p}}, \cdot \right) \right) + \delta \left[\hat{\theta} V \left(\frac{M_1}{\hat{p}} - \hat{\xi}^c \left(\frac{M_1}{\hat{p}}, \cdot \right) \right) \right. \right.$$

$$\left. \left. + (1 - \hat{\theta}) V \left(\frac{M_1}{\hat{p}} + \frac{\hat{w}}{\hat{p}} - \hat{\xi}^c \left(\frac{M_1}{\hat{p}}, \cdot \right) \right) \right] \right\}. \quad (13)$$

Differentiating with respect to $M_1/\hat{p}$ and using the first order condition gives

$$V' \left(\frac{M_1}{\hat{p}} \right) = (1 - \mu r^c) \hat{\beta} U' \left(\hat{\beta} \hat{\xi}^c \left(\frac{M_1}{\hat{p}}, \cdot \right) \right) + \mu \hat{r}^c U' \left(\hat{\xi}^c \left(\frac{M_1}{\hat{p}}, \cdot \right) \right)$$

$$= E \left[U'(\tilde{C}_1) \, \middle| \, C_1 = \hat{\xi}^c \left(\frac{M_1}{\hat{p}}, \cdot \right) \right],$$

which allows us to write

$$V \left(\frac{M_1}{\hat{p}} \right) = \mathcal{V}_1 \left(\frac{M_1}{\hat{p}}, \frac{\hat{w}}{\hat{p}}, \cdot \right)$$

such that

$$\frac{\partial \mathcal{V}_1}{\partial (M_1/\hat{p})} = V'(M_1/\hat{p}).$$

We have also

$$\frac{\partial^2 \mathcal{V}_1}{\partial (M_1/\hat{p})^2} = \frac{\partial \hat{\xi}^c}{\partial (M_1/\hat{p})} \left[(1 - \mu r^c) \hat{\beta}^2 U'' \left(\hat{\beta} \hat{\xi}^c \left(\frac{M_1}{\hat{p}}, \cdot \right) \right) \right.$$

$$+ \mu r^c U'' \left(\hat{\xi}^c \left(\frac{M_1}{\hat{p}}, \cdot \right) \right) \Bigg] < 0,$$

since $\partial \hat{\xi}^c / \partial (M_1/\hat{p}) > 0$ by the concavity of V and the strict concavity of U; and

$$\frac{\partial^2 \mathcal{V}_1}{\partial (M_1/\hat{p}) \, \partial (\hat{w}/\hat{p})}$$

$$= \frac{\partial \hat{\xi}^c}{\partial (\hat{w}/\hat{p})} \left[(1 - \mu r^c) \hat{\beta}^2 U'' \left(\beta \hat{\xi}^c \left(\cdot, \frac{\hat{w}}{\hat{p}} \right) \right) + \mu r^c U'' \left(\hat{\xi}^c \left(\frac{\hat{w}}{\hat{p}}, \cdot \right) \right) \right] < 0,$$

since $\partial \xi^c / \partial (\hat{w}/\hat{p}) > 0$ by the concavity of V and the strict concavity of U. The function $\mathcal{V}_1$ is then strictly concave in $M_1/\hat{p}$.

Let us consider now the problem at date $t = 0$ with M denoting the initial money holding. Maximisation of expected utility for this period to infinity is equivalent to maximising

$$\mathcal{V} \left(C, \frac{M}{p}, \frac{w}{p}, \frac{p}{\hat{p}}, \frac{\hat{w}}{\hat{p}}, \theta, r^c \right) = EU(\tilde{C}) + \delta E \mathcal{V}_1 \left(\frac{M + w\tilde{L} - p\tilde{C}}{\hat{p}}, \frac{\hat{w}}{\hat{p}}, \cdot \right)$$

with respect to $C \in [0, M/p]$. We have

$$\mathcal{V}(C, \cdot) = (1 - \mu r^c) \left\{ U(\beta C) + \delta \left[\theta \mathcal{V}_1 \left(\frac{M - pC}{\hat{p}}, \frac{\hat{w}}{\hat{p}}, \cdot \right) \right. \right.$$

$$\left. + (1 - \theta) \mathcal{V}_1 \left(\frac{M + w - pC}{\hat{p}}, \frac{\hat{w}}{\hat{p}}, \cdot \right) \right] \Bigg\}$$

$$+ \mu r^c \left\{ U(C) + \left[\theta \mathcal{V}_1 \left(\frac{M - pC}{\hat{p}}, \frac{\hat{w}}{\hat{p}}, \cdot \right) \right. \right.$$

$$\left. + (1 - \theta) \mathcal{V}_1 \left(\frac{M + w - pC}{\hat{p}}, \frac{\hat{w}}{\hat{p}}, \cdot \right) \right] \Bigg\}.$$

The first order condition for a maximum at C^* is

$$\frac{\partial \mathcal{V}}{\partial C} = (1 - \mu r^c) \beta \left\{ U'(\beta C^*) - \delta \frac{p}{\hat{p}} \left[\theta \frac{\partial \mathcal{V}_1}{\partial (M_1/\hat{p})} \left(\frac{M - p\beta C^*}{\hat{p}}, \frac{\hat{w}}{\hat{p}}, \cdot \right) \right. \right.$$

$$\left. + (1 - \theta) \frac{\partial \mathcal{V}_1}{\partial (M_1/\hat{p})} \left(\frac{M + w - p\beta C^*}{\hat{p}}, \frac{\hat{w}}{\hat{p}}, \cdot \right) \right] \Bigg\}$$

$$+ \mu r^c \left\{ U'(C^*) - \delta \frac{p}{\hat{p}} \left[\theta \frac{\partial \mathcal{V}_1}{\partial (M_1/\hat{p})} \left(\frac{M - pC^*}{\hat{p}}, \frac{\hat{w}}{\hat{p}}, \cdot \right) \right. \right.$$

$$\left. + (1 - \hat{\theta}) \frac{\partial \mathcal{V}_1}{\partial (M_1/\hat{p})} \left(\frac{M + w - pC^*}{\hat{p}}, \frac{\hat{w}}{\hat{p}}, \cdot \right) \right] \Bigg\} = 0. \quad (14)$$

The second order condition is satisfied since $\mathcal{V}_1$ and U are strictly concave and for $t \geq 1$ we have a unique interior solution $0 < C^* < M/p$ that varies continuously with the parameters of $\mathcal{V}(\ )$,

$$C^* = \xi^c(M/p, w/p, p/\hat{p}, \hat{w}/\hat{p}, \ \theta \ , \ r^c \ ). \qquad (15)$$
$$(+) \quad \ (+) \quad \ ? \quad \ (+) \quad (-) \quad (-)$$

The sign of the effects is a matter of calculation.

2. Temporary equilibria with stochastic quantity rationing

In this section we will define and describe the characteristics of the various types of temporary equilibria with stochastic rationing. We are dealing with temporary equilibria in the sense that prices wages and quantity rationing solve the market problem today. There is nevertheless a complicated inter-dependence between today's market signals and agents expectations as to the future. Our notation of equilibrium is based upon a rationality condition which requires that conditionally on market signals agents take actions which generate situations consistent with those signals.

2.1. Effective excess demand correspondence and Walrasian temporary equilibrium

Let $\sigma = ((M_h)_{h \in H}, (S_f)_{f \in F})$ be the current holdings of money by households and inventories by firms and G be an exogenous level of government expenditures. Given *current* price signals $\pi = (w, p)$ *expected* future price signals $\hat{\pi} = (\hat{w}, \hat{p})$, identical for all agents, are assumed to be given by a rule $\hat{\pi} = \psi(\pi)$. It summarizes the notion that the agents have about how future prices are formed on the basis of current disequilibrium and about how such disequilibrium depends upon current prices.[2] The relationship between expected future quantity and price signals remains here behind the scene: only price signals are relevant to define all expectations and we do not worry either about a possible relationship between future and current quantity signals $R = (R^c, R^z)$.

Consider a state (π, R) of market signals and a state (σ, G) of exogenous variables. *The aggregate demand of the goods and the labour markets are,*

_____

[2] As it will become clear later this implicitly requires that there is, at given current prices, a "selection" among different temporary equilibria.

respectively,

$$\xi^c(\pi, R, \sigma) \stackrel{\text{def}}{=} \sum_{h \in H} \xi_h^c \left(\frac{M_h}{p}, \frac{w}{p}, \frac{\psi_w(w, p)}{\psi_p(w, p)}, \frac{p}{\psi_p(w, p)}, \right.$$

$$\left. \text{Max}\left\{0, 1 - \frac{1}{R^z}\right\}, \text{Min}\{1, R^c\} \right) \tag{16}$$

and

$$\xi^z(\pi, R, \sigma) \stackrel{\text{def}}{=} \sum_{f \in F} \xi_f^z \left(S_f, \frac{w}{p}, \frac{\psi_w(w, p)}{\psi_p(w, p)}, \text{Min}\{1, R^z\}, \text{Min}\left\{1, \frac{1}{R^c}\right\} \right) \tag{17}$$

where ξ_h^c and ξ_f^z are individual demands given by (15) and (5).

We also define *effective excess demand on the goods and the labour markets*:

$$\varepsilon^c(\pi, R, \sigma, G) \stackrel{\text{def}}{=} R^c[\xi^c(\pi, R, \sigma) + G] - \mathscr{S}, \tag{18}$$

$$\varepsilon^z(\pi, R, \sigma, G) \stackrel{\text{def}}{=} R^z \xi^z(\pi, R, \sigma) - H, \tag{19}$$

and we denote: $\varepsilon(\pi, R, \sigma, G) = (\varepsilon^c(\pi, R, \sigma, G), \varepsilon^z(\pi, R, \sigma, G))$.

In this section we shall consider the particular case of a *Walrasian temporary equilibrium with stochastic quantity rationing*, which, given σ and G, is characterized by a pair of price signals $\pi^* = (w^*, p^*) \in \mathring{\mathbb{R}}_+^2$ such that

$$\varepsilon(\pi^*, 1, 1, \sigma, G) = 0.$$

From now on we shall make the following two assumptions:

(A1) The vector of exogenous variables (σ, G) is such that

$$G < \mathscr{S}, \quad \mathscr{S} \stackrel{\text{def}}{=} \sum_{f \in F} S_f.$$

(A2) Price expectations satisfy the property that there exist $\underline{k} > 0$ and $\bar{k} > \underline{k}$ such that

$$\underline{k} \le \lim_{p \to 0} \psi_p(w, p) \quad \text{and} \quad \lim_{p \to \infty} \psi_p(p, w) \le \bar{k}, \quad w \ge 0.$$

We give in the Appendix the proof of the following theorem.

Theorem 1. *Under* (A1) *and* (A2), *given a state* (σ, G) *of exogenous variables, there exists a Walrasian temporary equilibrium with stochastic quantity rationing* $\pi^* = (w^*, p^*)$, $0 < w^* < \infty$, $0 < p^* < \infty$.

Let $D_\pi \varepsilon(\pi, 1, 1, \sigma, G)$ be the Jacobian matrix of the Walrasian excess demand (i.e., for $R = (1, 1)$) given (σ, G) at prices $\pi = (w, p)$. From now on we shall restrict ourselves to a Walrasian temporary equilibrium π^* satisfying the following assumption (where $|\cdot|$ stands for determinant of $\cdot$):

(A3) $|D_\pi \varepsilon(\pi^*, 1, 1, \sigma, G)| \neq 0$, i.e., the equilibrium is locally unique.

2.2. Non-Walrasian equilibria

Let σ be a given state of individual holdings and G a given level of government expenditures satisfying (A1). A *non-Walrasian temporary equilibrium with stochastic quantity rationing* is a pair of current quantity signals $R = (R^c, R^z) \in [0, \mathcal{S}/G] \times \mathbb{R}_+$ which, for a given pair of current price signals $\pi = (w, p) \in \Pi$, is such that

$$\varepsilon(\pi, R) = 0. \tag{20}$$

Note that for given σ and G, Π is bounded above and below, since not all prices and wages are consistent with the existence of a Walrasian or non-Walrasian equilibrium. Although Π and all our arguments depend on σ and G, we take them as given throughout this section and thus omit them from our notation.

A *Keynesian unemployment* temporary equilibrium with stochastic quantity rationing is a non-Walrasian equilibrium which is given by a pair of quantity signals:

$$R_K = (R_K^c, R_K^z) \quad \text{such that } R_K^c \geq 1,\ R_K^z \geq 1.$$

A *classical unemployment* temporary equilibrium is a non-Walrasian equilibrium:

$$R_C = (R_C^c, R_C^z) \quad \text{such that } 0 < R_C^c \leq 1,\ R_C^z \geq 1.$$

An *under-consumption* equilibrium is a non-Walrasian equilibrium:

$$R_U = (R_U^c, R_U^z) \quad \text{such that } R_U^c \geq 1,\ 0 < R_U^z \leq 1.$$

A *repressed inflation equilibrium* is a non-Walrasian equilibrium:

$$R_I = (R_I^c, R_I^z) \quad \text{such that } 0 < R_I^c \leq 1,\ 0 \leq R_I^z \leq 1.$$

Let us start with Keynesian equilibria.

2.2.1. Keynesian equilibrium

Consider the quantity $\tilde{R}^z \geq 1$ defined by letting: for every $\pi \in \Pi$ and $R^c \geq 1$,

$$\varepsilon^z(\pi, R^c, \tilde{R}^z) = 0. \tag{21}$$

We clearly have $\varepsilon^z(\pi, 1, \tilde{R}^z) = 0$ and, when it exists, $\tilde{R}^z$ is a function of $\pi \in \Pi$, denoted $\tilde{R}^z = \tilde{\mathcal{R}}^z(\pi)$, giving the ratio of effective supply to effective demand for labour when firms perceive no rationing on the markets. Symmetrically, we have $\tilde{R}^c \geq 1$ such that for every $\pi \in \Pi$ and $R^z \leq 1$,

$$\varepsilon^c(\pi, \tilde{R}^c, R^z) = 0. \tag{22}$$

It is such that $\varepsilon^c(\pi, \tilde{R}^c, 1) = 0$ and, when it exists, is a function of $\pi \in \Pi$, denoted $\tilde{R}^c = \tilde{\mathcal{R}}^c(\pi)$, giving the ratio of effective supply to effective demand for goods when households perceive no rationing on the markets.

Let $\bar{R}^z \geq 1$ be such that for every $\pi \in \Pi$,

$$\varepsilon^c(\pi, 1, \bar{R}^z) = 0. \tag{23}$$

Whenever it exists it is a function[3] $\bar{R}^z = \bar{\mathcal{R}}^z(\pi)$ giving for prices $\pi \in \Pi$ the ratio of effective supply to effective demand for labour at which effective excess demand of goods vanishes without demand rationing. When, for $\pi \in \Pi$ and $R^c \geq 1$, there is no $\bar{R}^z \geq 1$ solving (23), this implies

$$\varepsilon^c(\pi, R^c, R^z) < 0, \quad 0 \leq R^z < 1.$$

Consider finally $\bar{R}^c \geq 1$ such that

$$\varepsilon^z(\pi, \bar{R}^c, 1) = 0, \quad \pi \in \Pi. \tag{24}$$

Again, whenever it exists it is a function[4] $\bar{R}^c = \bar{\mathcal{R}}^c(\pi)$ which associates with prices $\pi \in \Pi$ the ratio of effective supply to demand for goods at which effective excess demand of labour vanishes without demand rationing. When for $\pi \in \Pi$, and $R^z \geq 1$, there is no $\bar{R}^c \geq 1$ solving (24), which implies

$$\varepsilon^z(\pi, R^c, R^z) < 0, \quad 0 \leq R^c \leq \mathcal{S}/G.$$

Figures 1 and 2 illustrate these definitions. As is easily seen, for every $\pi \in \Pi$, we have $\tilde{R}^z(\pi) \leq 1$ iff $\bar{R}^c(\pi) \geq 1$ and $\tilde{R}^c(\pi) \leq 1$ iff $\bar{R}^z(\pi) \geq 1$.

Let us define two sets:

$$\mathcal{K} \stackrel{\text{def}}{=} (R = (R^c, R^z); 1 \leq R^c < \mathcal{S}/G, R^z \geq 1\}$$

and

$$\Pi_K \stackrel{\text{def}}{=} \{\pi = (w, p) \in \Pi;$$

$$\tilde{\mathcal{R}}^z(\pi) \geq \text{Max}(1, \bar{\mathcal{R}}^z(\pi)) \text{ or } \tilde{\mathcal{R}}^c(\pi) \geq \text{Max}(1, \bar{\mathcal{R}}^c(\pi))\}.$$

---

[3] Whenever defined, $\bar{\mathcal{R}}^z(\pi)$ is uniquely given by (23), since for every h, $\partial \xi_h^c / \partial \theta < 0$.
[4] Whenever defined, $\bar{\mathcal{R}}^c(\pi)$ is uniquely given by (24), since for every f, $\partial \xi_f^z / \partial r^Q < 0$.

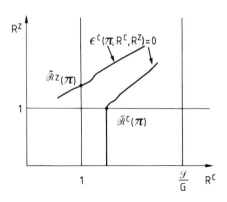

Figure 1.

Let us assume

(A4) $\lim_{R^z \to \infty} \xi^c(\pi, R^c, R^z) > 0$, $\pi \in \Pi$, $R^c \geq 1$;

(A5) $\lim_{R^c \to \mathcal{S}/G} \xi^z(\pi, R^c, R^z) > 0$, $\pi \in \Pi$, $R^z > 1$.

Clearly from these boundary conditions we get

$$\lim_{R^z \to \infty} \frac{\mathcal{S}}{\xi^c(\pi, R^c, R^z) + G} < \frac{\mathcal{S}}{G}, \quad R^c \geq 1,$$

and

$$\lim_{R^c \to \mathcal{S}/G} \frac{H}{\xi^c(\pi, R^c, R^z)} < \infty, \quad R^z \geq 1.$$

We thus have an existence theorem, which proof is given in the Appendix.

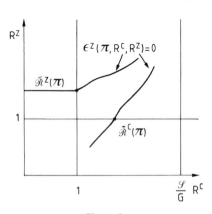

Figure 2.

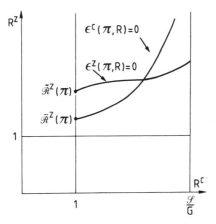

Figure 3.

Theorem 2. *Under assumptions* (A1), (A4) *and* (A5), *for every* $\pi \in \Pi_K$ *there exists a Keynesian temporary equilibrium* $R_K \in \mathcal{R}$.

The intuition behind the proof of Theorem 2 (see the Appendix) is given by Figures 3 and 4 which illustrate the two cases in which there is existence of a Keynesian equilibrium.

It is convenient to give local stability properties of non-Walrasian equilibria in terms of *normalized excess supply functions*, namely

$$\zeta(\pi, R) = (\zeta^c(\pi, R), \zeta^z(\pi, R)) \tag{25}$$

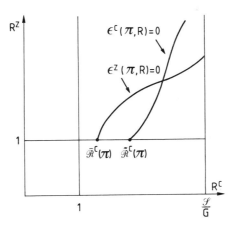

Figure 4.

where

$$\zeta^c(\pi, R) = -\frac{R^c}{\mathcal{S}}\,\varepsilon^c(\pi, R) \quad \text{and} \quad \zeta^z(\pi, R) = -\frac{R^z}{H}\,\varepsilon^z(\pi, R).$$

The Jacobian matrix of ζ at a Keynesian equilibrium $(\pi_K, R_K) \in \Pi_K \times \mathcal{R}$ is

$$D_R\zeta(\pi_K, R_K) = \begin{bmatrix} -1 & -\dfrac{R_K^c}{R_K^z}\,e_{R^z}^c \\[2ex] -\dfrac{R_K^z}{R_K^c}\,e_{R^c}^z & -1 \end{bmatrix} \tag{26}$$

where $e_{R^c}^z$ (resp., $e_{R^z}^c$) is the elasticity of global labour demand (resp., global goods demand) with respect to the rationing of good supply (resp., the rationing of labour supply). Clearly the trace of $D_R\zeta(\pi_K, R_K)$ is negative and its determinant is given by

$$|D_R\zeta(\pi_K, R_K)| = 1 - e_{R^c}^z e_{R^z}^c.$$

By the Routh–Hurwitz condition a Keynesian equilibrium (π_K, R_K) is *locally stable* iff $1 - e_{R^c}^z e_{R^z}^c > 0$.

2.2.2. Other non-Walrasian equilibria

Classical unemployment, under-consumption and repressed inflation[5] equilibria can be studied as we just did for Keynesian unemployment. For that matter, subspaces of the spaces of quantity-signals and price-signals are required, namely

$$\mathcal{C} = \{R = (R^c, R^z); \; 0 \le R^c \le 1, \; R^z \ge 1\},$$

$$\mathcal{U} = \{R = (R^c, R^z); \; R^c \ge 1, \; 0 < R^z \le 1\},$$

$$\mathcal{I} = \{R = (R^c, R^z); \; 0 < R^c \le 1, \; 0 < R^z \le 1\},$$

$$\Pi_C = \{\pi = (w, p) \in \Pi; \; \bar{\mathcal{R}}^z(\pi) \ge \tilde{\mathcal{R}}^z(\pi) \ge 1\},$$

$$\Pi_U = \{\pi = (w, p) \in \Pi; \; \bar{\mathcal{R}}^c(\pi) \ge \tilde{\mathcal{R}}^c(\pi) \ge 1\},$$

$$\Pi_I = \{\pi = (w, p) \in \Pi; \; \tilde{\mathcal{R}}^c(\pi) \le 1, \; \tilde{\mathcal{R}}^z(\pi) \le 1\}.$$

We also need two more boundary conditions, namely

---

[5] It is easy to see that $\bar{\mathcal{R}}^z$ gives the equilibrium values of R^z for those values of π to which are associated classical unemployment situations (see (21)), when $\bar{\mathcal{R}}^c$ (see (22)) gives the equilibrium values of R^c for values of π to which are associated under consumption equilibria.

(A6) $\lim_{R^c \to 0} \xi^c(\pi, R^c, R^z) < \infty$, $\pi \in \Pi$, $R^z \geq 1$;

(A7) $\lim_{R^z \to 0} \xi^z(\pi, R^c, R^z) < \infty$, $\pi \in \Pi$, $R^c \geq 1$;

which give that

$$\lim_{R^c \to 0} \varepsilon^c(\pi, R^c, R^z) < 0, \quad R^z \geq 1,$$

and

$$\lim_{R^z \to 0} \varepsilon^z(\pi, R^c, R^z) < 0, \quad R^z \geq 1.$$

This allows us to prove the following.

Theorem 3. *Under assumptions* (A6) *and* (A7), *for every* $\pi \in \Pi_C$ (*resp.*, $\pi \in \Pi_U$ *or* $\pi \in \Pi_I$) *there exists a classical unemployment equilibrium* $R_C \in \mathscr{C}$ (*resp.*, *an under-consumption equilibrium* $R_U \in \mathscr{U}$ *or a repressed-inflation equilibrium* $R_I \in \mathscr{I}$). $\square$

We omit the proof of the theorem which is quite straightforward (for more details see Gérard-Varet, Jordan and Kirman, (1986).

Local stability properties are also interesting. They are obtained by studying the Jacobian matrix $D_R \zeta(\cdot)$ of the normalized excess supply functions ζ at the relevant equilibrium. At a classical unemployment equilibrium $(\pi_C, R_C) \in \Pi_C \times \mathscr{C}$ we have

$$\text{Trace } D_R \zeta(\pi_C, R_C) < 0 \text{ and } |D_R \zeta(\pi_C, R_C)| > 0 \quad \text{iff} \quad 1 + \theta^c_{R^c} > 0$$

where $\theta^c_{R^c}$ is the elasticity of the global demand for the good with respect to demand rationing on the good market. At an under-consumption equilibrium $(\pi_U, R_U) \in \Pi_U \times \mathscr{U}$ observing that $\text{Trace } D_R \zeta(\pi_U, R_U) < 0$, local stability is obtained iff $|D_R \zeta(\pi_U, R_U)| = 1 + \theta^z_{R^z} > 0$ where $\theta^z_{R^z}$ stands for the elasticity of the global demand of labour with respect to the rationing it faces. When both conditions $1 + \theta^c_{R^c} > 0$ and $1 + \theta^z_{R^z} > 0$ hold together a repressed-inflation equilibrium $(\pi_I, R_I) \in \Pi_I \times \mathscr{I}$ is also locally stable.

2.3. Structure of the set of equilibria

As before, σ, G and $\hat{R}$, which are given, will be omitted from the notation. Let E be the *equilibrium correspondence* from Π to $[0, \mathscr{S}/G] \times \mathbb{R}_+$ defined by letting

$$E(\pi) \stackrel{\text{def}}{=} \{R \in [0, \mathscr{S}/G] \times \mathbb{R}; \varepsilon(\pi, R) = 0\}, \quad \pi \in \Pi.$$

In this section we prove that there is "generically" an odd number of temporary equilibria with stochastic quantity rationing. As corollaries, we obtain a characterisation of possible configurations of multiple equilibria.

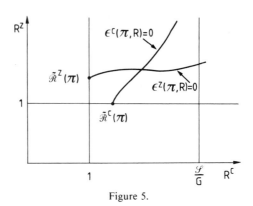

Figure 5.

Let us introduce the covering $\{\Pi_i ; i = 1, 2, 3, 4\}$ of Π defined by

$$\Pi_1 \stackrel{\text{def}}{=} \{\pi \in \Pi; \tilde{\mathcal{R}}^c(\pi) \le 1, \tilde{\mathcal{R}}^z(\pi) \le 1\},$$

$$\Pi_2 \stackrel{\text{def}}{=} \{\pi \in \Pi; \tilde{\mathcal{R}}^c(\pi) \ge 1, \tilde{\mathcal{R}}^z(\pi) \le 1\},$$

$$\Pi_3 \stackrel{\text{def}}{=} \{\pi \in \Pi; \tilde{\mathcal{R}}^c(\pi) \le 1, \tilde{\mathcal{R}}^z(\pi) \ge 1\},$$

$$\Pi_4 \stackrel{\text{def}}{=} \{\pi \in \Pi; \tilde{\mathcal{R}}^c(\pi) \ge 1, \tilde{\mathcal{R}}^z(\pi) \ge 1\},$$

where $\tilde{\mathcal{R}}^c$ and $\tilde{\mathcal{R}}^z$ are given by (21) and (22). Clearly, a Walrasian equilibrium is $E^{-1}(1, 1) = \bigcap_{i=1}^{4} \Pi_i$. Furthermore, by assumption (A3) for every $i = 1$ to 4, Π_i contains a set which has positive Lebesgue measure. We also observe the following relations all easily obtained from the definitions:

$$\Pi_1 = \Pi_I, \qquad \Pi_4 \subset \Pi_K, \qquad \Pi_U \subset \Pi_2 \quad \text{and} \quad \Pi_C \subset \Pi_3.$$

The second of these inclusions is illustrated by Figure 5.

As a corollary of the inclusion $\Pi_4 \subset \Pi_K$, we have (using Theorem 2) the easy conclusion that the set of pairs of prices Π_K for which there exists a Keynesian equilibrium has positive Lebesgue measure. For classical under-employment and under-consumption equilibria, since one only has $\Pi_C \subset \Pi_3$ and $\Pi_U \subset \Pi_2$, there is no such straightforward argument. However, the following theorem provides the conclusion.

Theorem 4. *Assume* (A1), (A2), (A3) *and* (A6) (*resp.* (A7). *There exists a neighbourhood* $\mathcal{V}(\pi^*)$ *of the Walrasian equilibrium* π^* *such that for every* $\pi \subset \Pi_C \cap \mathcal{V}(\pi^*)$ (*resp.,* $\pi \subset \Pi_U \cap \mathcal{V}(\pi^*)$) *one may find* $\varepsilon > 0$, *such that the ball* $B(\pi, \varepsilon)$ *of centre* π *and radius* ε, *is included in* Π_C (*resp., in* Π_U).

Proof. Under (A1), (A2) and (A3) there exists a Walrasian temporary equilibrium π^* which is locally unique and under (A6), $\Pi_C \neq \emptyset$ (resp. (A7), $\Pi_U \neq \emptyset$). Thus one may find a neighbourhood $\mathcal{V}(\pi^*)$ such that $\mathcal{V}(\pi^*) \cap \Pi_C \neq \emptyset$ (resp., $\mathcal{V}(\pi^*) \cap \Pi_U \neq \emptyset$). It is sufficient to show that there exists

$$\pi \in \mathcal{V}(\pi^*) \cap \Pi_C \quad \text{such that} \quad \bar{\mathcal{R}}^z(\pi) > \tilde{\mathcal{R}}^z(\pi) > 1$$

(resp., $\pi \in \mathcal{V}(\pi^*) \cap \Pi_U$ such that $\bar{\mathcal{R}}^c(\pi) > \tilde{\mathcal{R}}^c(\pi) > 1$). We have

$$\left.\frac{dw}{dp}\right|_{\tilde{R}^z = 1} = \frac{\partial\varepsilon^z(\pi^*, 1, 1)/\partial p}{\partial\varepsilon^z(\pi^*, 1, 1)/\partial w} = \left.\frac{dw}{dp}\right|_{\bar{R}^c = 1}$$

and

$$\left.\frac{dw}{dp}\right|_{\tilde{R}^z = 1} = \left.\frac{dw}{dp}\right|_{\tilde{R}^c = 1} = -\frac{\partial\varepsilon^c(\pi^*, 1, 1)/\partial p}{\partial\varepsilon^c(\pi^*, 1, 1)/\partial w}.$$

Every π in $\mathcal{V}(\pi^*) \cap \Pi_C$ (resp., in $\mathcal{V}(\pi^*) \cap \Pi_U$) such that $\bar{\mathcal{R}}^z(\pi) = \tilde{\mathcal{R}}^z(\pi) \geq 1$ (resp., $\bar{\mathcal{R}}^c(\pi) = \tilde{\mathcal{R}}^c(\pi) \geq 1$) satisfies $\varepsilon^c(\pi, 1, \tilde{\mathcal{R}}^z(\pi)) = 0$ (resp., $\varepsilon^z(\pi, \mathcal{R}^c(\pi), 1) = 0$). Thus

$$\left.\frac{dw}{dp}\right|_{\tilde{R}^z = \bar{R}^z} = -\left(H\frac{\partial\varepsilon^c}{\partial p} - \frac{\partial\varepsilon^c}{\partial R^z}\frac{\partial\varepsilon^z}{\partial p} \right) \Big/ \left(H\frac{\partial\varepsilon^c}{\partial w} - \frac{\partial\varepsilon^c}{\partial R^z}\frac{\partial\varepsilon^z}{\partial w} \right)$$

$$\left(\text{resp.,} \left.\frac{dw}{dp}\right|_{\tilde{R}^c = \bar{R}^c} = -\left(\mathcal{G}\frac{\partial\varepsilon^z}{\partial p} - \frac{\partial\varepsilon^z}{\partial R^c}\frac{\partial\varepsilon^c}{\partial p} \right) \Big/ \left(\mathcal{G}\frac{\partial\varepsilon^z}{\partial w} - \frac{\partial\varepsilon^z}{\partial R^c}\frac{\partial\varepsilon^c}{\partial w} \right) \right)$$

and every such π is in the interior of Π_2 (resp., of Π_1).

Only π^* satisfies simultaneously $\tilde{R}^c \leq 1$ and $\bar{R}^z = \tilde{R}^z \geq 1$ (resp., $\tilde{R}^z \leq 1$ and $\bar{R}^c = \tilde{R}^c \geq 1$). Now the conclusion follows from the observation that

$$|D_\pi\varepsilon(\pi^*, 1, 1)| \neq 0$$

$$\Rightarrow \left.\frac{dw}{dp}\right|_{\tilde{R}^z = 1} \neq \left.\frac{dw}{dp}\right|_{\bar{R}^z = 1} \quad \left(\text{resp.,} \left.\frac{dw}{dp}\right|_{\tilde{R}^c = 1} \neq \left.\frac{dw}{dp}\right|_{\bar{R}^c = 1} \right)$$

$$\Rightarrow \left.\frac{dw}{dp}\right|_{\tilde{R}^z = \bar{R}^z} \neq \left.\frac{dw}{dp}\right|_{\tilde{R}^z = 1} \quad \left(\text{resp.,} \left.\frac{dw}{dp}\right|_{\tilde{R}^c = \bar{R}^c} \neq \left.\frac{dw}{dp}\right|_{\tilde{R}^c = 1} \right). \quad \square$$

We now discuss the structure of the set of equilibria. Let us assume (A1) and (A4), and define

$$R_+^z \stackrel{\text{def}}{=} \max_{\{\pi \in \Pi; \tilde{\mathcal{R}}^z(\pi) \geq 1\}} \lim_{R^c \to \mathcal{S}/G} \left[H \Big/ \sum_{f \in F} \xi_f^z\left(\frac{w}{p}, \frac{\psi_w(w, p)}{\psi_p(w, p)}, 1, \frac{1}{R^c} \right) \right].$$

We have $1 < R_+^z < \infty$. Letting $\Omega \stackrel{\text{def}}{=} [0, \mathcal{S}/G] \times [0, R_+^z]$, under assumptions (A1) and (A4) we have

$$\forall \pi \in \Pi, \quad E(\pi) \subset \Omega.$$

Consider now, at any $\pi \in \Pi$, the continuous vector field $\zeta(\pi, \cdot): \Omega \to \mathbb{R}^2$ generated by normalised excess supply functions (see (25)). Under assumptions (A4) to (A7), the vector field points in on the boundary of Ω. Next, we introduce one more assumption:

(A8) $|D_R\zeta(\pi, R)| \neq 0$, wherever $D_R\zeta(\pi, \cdot)$ is defined for every $\pi \in \Pi$. By standard results — see Sard's theorem — this assumption only rules out "exceptional" cases, in the sense of having zero Lebesgue measure.

By the Poincaré–Hopf index theorem, whenever assumption (A8) holds the number of equilibria is odd. The set in Π for which (A8) holds is of Lebesgue measure one, giving:

Theorem 5. *Under assumptions* (A1) *and* (A4)–(A8), *there exists a set Q in Π of Lebesgue measure* 1 *such that for every $\pi \in Q$, $\#E(\pi)$ is odd.* $\square$

Consider now the set

$$(\Pi_K \cup \Pi_C) = (\Pi_4 \cup \Pi_3) = \{\pi \in \Pi; \, \tilde{\mathcal{R}}^z(\pi) \geq 1\}.$$

For every π in this set, we have

$$E(\pi) \cap (\mathcal{I} \cup \mathcal{U}) = \emptyset.$$

Thus, except on a null set in $\Pi_K \cup \Pi_C$,

$\#E(\pi) \cap (\mathcal{K} \cup \mathcal{C})$ is odd,

i.e., there exists "generically" an odd number of under-employment equilibria. Figure 6 illustrates a "generic" case, when Figure 7 illustrates a "non-generic" case.[6]

Similar observations are easily made with respect to $\mathcal{K} \cup \mathcal{U}$ or $\mathcal{K} \cup \mathcal{I}$.

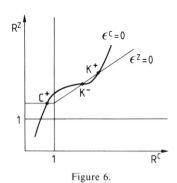

Figure 6.

---

[6] The superscript $+$ $(-)$ designates a stable (unstable) equilibrium, the superscript $\circ$ an equilibrium which is stable and unstable (two equilibria coinciding).

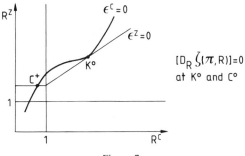

Figure 7.

For a vector π^* which is a Walrasian equilibrium, we have

$$E(\pi^*) \cap \overset{\circ}{C} = \emptyset, \qquad E(\pi^*) \cap \overset{\circ}{U} = \emptyset,$$

$\#E(\pi^*) \cap \mathcal{K}$ is an odd number ≥ 1, $\#E(\pi^*) \cap \mathcal{J}$ is an odd number ≥ 1, and $E(\pi^*) \cap (\mathcal{K} \cup \mathcal{J}) = (1, 1)$ (as in Figure 8, where at $W^+ = (\pi^*, R), |D_R\zeta(\pi^*, R)| > 0, R \in \mathcal{V}(1, 1) \cap (\mathcal{J} \cup \mathcal{K}))$. This is true except for some π^* for which, given a neighbourhood $\mathcal{V}(1, 1)$ of $(1, 1)$,

$$|D_R\zeta(\pi^*, R)| > 0 \quad \text{for } R \in \mathcal{V}(1, 1) \cap \mathcal{J},$$

and

$$|D_R\zeta(\pi^*, R)| < 0 \quad \text{for } R \in \mathcal{V}(1, 1) \cap \mathcal{K},$$

as illustrated by Figure 10. For π such that $\tilde{\mathcal{R}}^z(\pi) = \bar{\mathcal{R}}^z(\pi)$ there exists a Walrasian equilibrium but at those prices a Keynesian equilibrium is not

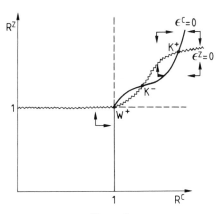

Figure 8.

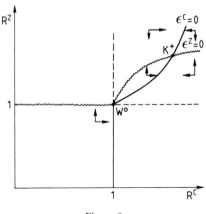

Figure 9.

at all ruled out. It is then possible to observe the configuration of multiple equilibria illustrated above.

In Figure 9 the Walrasian equilibrium W^o is locally stable with respect to the inflationary quantity adjustment process and unstable in the Keynesian. The absence of symmetry of the unstability property is due to the specification of our model where the labour supply is exogenously given. Introducing consumers decreasing marginal utility for leisure would lead to a situation where the loci of $\varepsilon^c = 0$ and $\varepsilon^z = 0$ in the (R^c, R^z) space are upward sloped. It would then be possible to observe the case where the

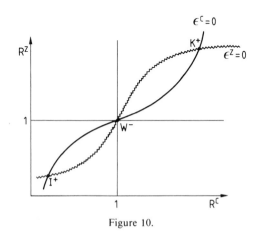

Figure 10.

Walrasian equilibrium is totally unstable in the quantity adjustment process as depicted in Figure 10.

Conclusion

We have specified and rigorously defined a model with temporary stochastically rationed equilibria, in which the effective excess demand is a good measure of the size of "disequilibrium" that remains as long as prices are constant. This model can be used to try to study the long run evolution of the economy, which consists in the price movements governed by effective excess demands and the dynamics of stocks. This last point raises the difficult question of the distribution of inventories between firms and of money between households. In order to simplify the study it is convenient to consider the case of representative agents and then to neglect the influence of the distribution of stocks on aggregate effective excess demands. In this sense the attempt is closely linked to macroeconomic tradition.

The main departure from the usual issues in this domain is the possible existence of cyclical behaviour of the system. It is associated with the existence of multiple fixed price equilibria and/or to the role of quantity adjustment parameters which interfere with the price adjustment when the differential equations describing the motion are not linear. The first case can be studied in the context of "catastrophe theory" proposed by Thom (1972) and applied to general equilibrium theory by Balasko (1977) and to the study of business cycles by Varian (1979). The second is to be regarded from the point of view of bifurcation theory in a dynamical system used for example by Torre (1977), again in the case of business cycle.

The problem of the dynamic evolution of our model is then the problem of the evolution of a three dimensional system of differential equations. The multiplicity of equilibria means that stability considerations must be confined to the local case. Bifurcations and cycles will certainly occur but the problem with an analysis of this type is that existing techniques permit us to say rather little in terms of formal propositions.

Appendix

Proof of Theorem 1. (i) For every $w \ge 0$,

$$\lim_{p \to \infty} \varepsilon^c(w, p, 1, 1, \sigma, G) < 0 \quad \text{and} \quad \lim_{p \to 0} \varepsilon^c(w, p, 1, 1, \sigma, G) = \infty.$$

Assume $R^c = R^z = 1$. Without rationing on the current markets the behaviour of household $h \in H$ is given by

$$C_h^* = \xi_h^c \left(\frac{M_h}{p}, \frac{w}{p}, \frac{\psi_w(w, p)}{\psi_p(w, p)}, \frac{p}{\psi_p(w, p)}, 0, 1 \right)$$

$$\text{s.t.} \quad 0 \le C_h^* \le M_h/p \tag{27}$$

and according to (14),

$$U'(C_h^*) - \frac{p}{\psi_p(p, w)} \delta E \left[U' \left(\hat{\xi}_h^c \left(\frac{M_h + w - pC_h^*}{\psi_p(p, w)}, \frac{\psi_w(p, w)}{\psi_p(p, w)}, \cdot \right) \right) \right] = 0. \tag{28}$$

Condition (27) implies that $\lim_{p \to \infty} \xi^c(\cdot) = 0$. On the other hand, for any $w \ge 0$, using assumption (28) and condition (27),

$$\lim_{p \to 0} [(M_h + w - pC_h^*)/\psi_p(p, w)] \quad \text{and} \quad \lim_{p \to 0} [\psi_w(p, w)/\psi_p(p, w)]$$

are both positive and finite. Thus we have $\hat{\xi}_h^c(\cdot) > 0$ and $U'(\hat{\xi}_h^c(\cdot)) < \infty$. Since (again with (A2)), $\lim_{p \to 0} [p/\psi_p(p, w)] = 0$, it must be the case that $E[U'(\xi_h^c(\cdot))]$ goes to infinity when p goes to 0, which implies $\lim_{p \to 0} \xi_h^c(\cdot) = \infty$. Thus, using (16) and (18) we have, for every $w \ge 0$, $\lim_{p \to \infty} \varepsilon^c(w, p, 1, 1, \sigma, G) = G - \mathscr{S} < 0$ with (A1) and $\lim_{p \to 0} \varepsilon^c(w, p, 1, 1, \sigma, G) = \infty$.

(ii) For every $p > 0$,

$$\lim_{w \to \infty} \varepsilon^z(w, p, 1, 1, \sigma, G) < 0 \quad \text{and} \quad \lim_{w \to 0} \varepsilon^z(w, p, 1, 1, \sigma, G) = \infty.$$

Assume $R^c = R^z = 1$. Without rationing on the current markets the behaviour of firm $f \in F$ is given by

$$Z_f^* = \zeta_f^z \left(S_f, \frac{w}{p}, \frac{\psi_w(w, p)}{\psi_p(w, p)}, 1, 1 \right),$$

satisfying

$$pV^* \left(\lambda Z_f^*, \frac{\psi_w(w, p)}{\psi_p(w, p)} \right) \le \psi_p(w, p) \lambda Z_f^*, \tag{29}$$

$$pS_f - wZ_f^* + \delta p V^* \left(\lambda Z_f^*, \frac{\psi_w(w, p)}{\psi_p(w, p)} \right) \ge pS_f \tag{30}$$

and (according to (4)),

$$\frac{\partial V^*}{\partial S_{f1}}\left(\lambda Z_f^*, \frac{\psi_w(w,p)}{\psi_p(w,p)}\right) = \frac{w}{\delta \lambda p}. \tag{31}$$

From (29) and (30) we get

$$Z_f^*(\delta \lambda \psi_p(p,w) - w) \geq 0.$$

Since $\lim_{w \to \infty}(\delta \lambda \psi_p(p,w) - w) < 0$, for any $p > 0$, we conclude that $\lim_{w \to \infty} \xi_f^z(\cdot) = 0$. On the other hand, we have in condition (31),

$$\frac{\partial}{\partial S_{f1}} V^*\left(\lambda Z_f^*, \frac{\psi_w(w,p)}{\psi_p(w,p)}\right)$$

$$= 1 - \int_0^1 \Phi(\lambda Z_f^*; r_1^Q)\nu(r_1^Q)\,dr_1^Q$$

$$+ \int_0^1 \int_0^{Z_f^*} V'\left(\lambda \hat{\xi}_f^z\left(\lambda Z_f^*, \frac{\psi_w(w,p)}{\psi_p(w,p)} + \lambda Z_f^* - \tilde{D}_{f1}\right)\right)$$

$$\times \phi(D_{f1}|r_1^Q)\,dD_{f1}\nu(r_1^Q)\,dr_1^Q.$$

Since, for every $p > 0$ it must be the case that $\lim_{w \to 0}(\partial V^*/\partial S_{f1}) = 0$, we will have $1 - \Phi(\lambda Z_f^*, r_1^Q) = 0$. Since $\lim_{S \to \infty} \Phi(S_f; r_1^Q) = 1$, we conclude that $\lim_{w \to 0} \xi_f^z(\cdot) = \infty$. Thus using (17) and (19), we have for every $p > 0$, $\lim_{w \to 0} \varepsilon^z(w, p, 1, 1, \sigma, G) = -H < 0$ and $\lim_{w \to 0} \varepsilon^z(w, p, 1, 1, \sigma, G) = \infty$.

(iii) Using (i) and the continuity of ε^c, one may select bounds $\underline{p} > 0$ and $\bar{p} > \underline{p}$ such that whatever may be $w \geq 0$, we have

$$\varepsilon^c(w, p, 1, 1, \sigma, G) > 0 \quad \text{for } p \leq \underline{p}$$

and

$$\varepsilon^c(w, p, 1, 1, \sigma, G) < 0 \quad \text{for } p \geq \bar{p}.$$

By (ii) and by continuity of ε^z, one may also select bounds $\underline{w} > 0$ and $\bar{w} > \underline{w}$ such that whatever may be $p > 0$ we have

$$\varepsilon^z(w, p, 1, 1, \sigma, G) > 0 \quad \text{for } w \leq \underline{w}$$

and

$$\varepsilon^z(w, p, 1, 1, \sigma, G) < 0 \quad \text{for } w \geq \bar{w}.$$

Let $\Pi \stackrel{\text{def}}{=} [\underline{w}, \bar{w}] \times [\underline{p}, \bar{p}]$, which is a compact connected orientable surface in $\mathbb{R}^2$. The excess demand $\varepsilon(\cdot, 1, 1, \sigma, G)$ is a continuous vector field on Π which, by (i) and (ii) points in on the boundary of π. Thus there exists a critical point $\pi^* \in \Pi$ of $\varepsilon(\cdot, 1, 1, \sigma, G)$ which is a Walrasian equilibrium. $\square$

Proof of Theorem 2. (i) Take $\pi \in \Pi_K$ and assume first that $\bar{\mathscr{R}}^z$ is well defined, given by (23), and such that $\bar{\mathscr{R}}^z(\pi) \geq 1$, i.e., $\tilde{\mathscr{R}}^c(\pi) \leq 1$. Define $\Gamma(\cdot, \pi)$ from $\mathbb{R}$ to $\mathbb{R}$ by letting

$$\Gamma(R^c, \pi) \stackrel{\text{def}}{=} H/\xi^z(\pi, R^c, 1).$$

We have $\partial \Gamma/\partial R^c > 0$ and $\lim_{R^c \to 1} \Gamma(R^c, \pi) = \tilde{\mathscr{R}}^z(\pi) \geq 1$. Thus if $R^c \geq 1$, $\Gamma(R^c, \pi) \geq 1$ and $\varepsilon^z(\pi, R^c, \Gamma(R^c, \pi)) = 0$. It remains to be shown that there exists $R_K^c \in [1, \mathscr{S}/G[\text{s.t. } \varepsilon^c(\pi, R_K^c, \Gamma(R_K^c, \pi)) = 0$.

(a) We have

$$\lim_{R^c \to 1} \varepsilon^c(\pi, R^c, \Gamma(R^c, \pi)) = \varepsilon^c(\pi, 1, \tilde{\mathscr{R}}^z(\pi)).$$

Since $\partial \varepsilon^c/\partial R^z < 0$, $\tilde{\mathscr{R}}^z(\pi) \geq \bar{\mathscr{R}}^z(\pi)$, using (23) we conclude that

$$\varepsilon^c(\pi, 1, \tilde{\mathscr{R}}^z(\pi)) \leq \varepsilon^c(\pi, 1, \bar{\mathscr{R}}^z(\pi)) = 0,$$

giving

$$\lim_{R^c \to 1} \varepsilon^c(\pi, R^c, \Gamma(R^c, \pi)) \leq 0.$$

(b) We also have

$$\lim_{R^c \to \mathscr{S}/G} \varepsilon^c(\pi, R^c, \Gamma(\pi, R^c)) = \frac{\mathscr{S}}{G}\left[\xi^c\left(\pi, 1, \Gamma\left(\pi, \frac{\mathscr{S}}{G}\right)\right) + G\right] - \mathscr{S}$$

$$= \frac{\mathscr{S}}{G}\xi^c\left(\pi, 1, \Gamma\left(\pi, \frac{\mathscr{S}}{G}\right)\right) > 0,$$

since with (A5), $\Gamma(\pi, \mathscr{S}/G) > 0$.

The conclusion follows from (a) and (b) by continuity of ε^c. The equilibrium is given by R_K^c and $R_K^z = \Gamma(\pi, R_K^c)$.

(ii) Given $\pi \in \Pi_K$, assume now that $\bar{\mathscr{R}}^z(\pi)$ is not defined. Thus we must have $\tilde{\mathscr{R}}^c(\pi) \geq 1$. One must now show that for $\pi \in \Pi$ such that $\tilde{\mathscr{R}}^c(\pi) \geq \bar{\mathscr{R}}^c(\pi)$, there exists $R_K \in \mathscr{K}$ for which $\varepsilon(\pi, R_K) = 0$. Define $\Omega(\cdot, \pi)$ from $\mathbb{R}$ to $\mathbb{R}$ by letting

$$\Omega(R^z, \pi) \stackrel{\text{def}}{=} \mathscr{S}/\xi^c(\pi, 1, R^z) + G.$$

We have $\partial \Omega/\partial R^z > 0$ and $\lim_{R^z \to 1} \Omega(R^z, \pi) = \tilde{\mathscr{R}}^c(\pi) \geq 1$. Thus if $R^z \geq 1$, $\Omega(R^z, \pi) \geq 1$ and $\varepsilon^c(\pi, \Omega(R^z, \pi), R^z) = 0$. It remains to be shown that there exists $R_K^z \geq 1$ such that $\varepsilon^z(\pi, \Omega(R_K^z, \pi), R_K^z) = 0$.

(a) We have

$$\lim_{R^c \to 1} \varepsilon^z(\pi, \Omega(\pi, R^z), R^z) = \varepsilon^z(\pi, \tilde{\mathscr{R}}^c(\pi), 1).$$

Since $\partial \varepsilon^z/\partial R^c < 0$, $\bar{\mathscr{R}}^c(\pi) \leq \tilde{\mathscr{R}}^c(\pi)$, using (24), we conclude that

$$\varepsilon^z(\pi, \tilde{\mathscr{R}}^c(\pi), 1) \leq \varepsilon^z(\pi, \bar{\mathscr{R}}^c(\pi), 1) = 0,$$

giving

$$\lim_{R^z \to 1} \varepsilon^z(\pi, \Omega(\pi, R^z), R^z) \leq 0.$$

(b) We also have

$$\lim_{R^z \to 0} \varepsilon^z(\pi, \Omega(\pi, R^z), R^z) = \infty,$$

since with (A4), $\lim_{R^z \to 0} \Omega(\pi, R^z) < \mathscr{S}/G$, and with (A5), $\xi^z(\pi, R^c, R^z) > 0$, $R^c \leq \mathscr{S}/G$, $R^z \geq 1$.
The conclusion follows from (a) and (b) by continuity of ε^z. The equilibrium is given by R_K^z and $R_K^c = \Omega(\pi, R_K^z)$. $\square$

References

Abel, A. (1985) 'Inventories, stock-outs and production smoothing', *Review of Economic Studies*, 52:283-293.
Balasko, Y. (1977) 'Economie et théorie des catastrophes', *Cahiers du Séminaire d'Econométrie*, Editions du CNRS.
Barro, R.J. and H.I. Grossman (1971) 'A general disequilibrium model of income and employment', *American Economic Review*, 61:82-93.
Barro, R.J. and H.I. Grossman (1976) *Money Employment and Inflation*. New York: Cambridge University Press.
Bellman, R. (1957) *Dynamic Programming*. Princeton: Princeton University Press.
Benassy, J.P. (1982) *The Economics of Market Disequilibrium*. New York: Academic Press.
Blad, M.C. and A.P. Kirman (1985) 'Dynamique du déséquilibre à long terme', *Revue d'Economie Politique*.
Böhm, V. (1981) 'Inventories and money balances in a dynamic model with rationing', CARESS Working Paper.
Drèze, J. (1975) 'Existence of an exchange equilibrium under price rigidities', *International Economic Review*, 16(2):301-320.
Drèze, J. and H. Müller (1980) 'Optimality properties of rationing schemes', *Journal of Economic Theory*, 23(2):131-149.
Gérard-Varet, L.A., R. Jordan and A.P. Kirman (1986) 'Towards disequilibrium dynamics. A model of temporary equilibria with stochastic quantity rationing', SEEDS DP 46.
Green, J. (1980) 'On the theory of effective demand', *Economic Journal*, 90:341-353.
Honkapohja, S. and T. Ito (1980) 'Inventory dynamics in a simple disequilibrium macro model', *Scandinavian Journal of Economics*, 82:184-198.
Malinvaud, E. (1977) *Theory of Unemployment Reconsidered*. New York: Basil Blackwell.
Malinvaud, E. (1980) *Profitability and Unemployment*. Cambridge: Cambridge University Press.
Neary, P. and J.F. Stiglitz (1983) 'Toward a reconstruction of Keynesian economics: expectation and constrained equilibria', *Quarterly Journal of Economics*, 392:198-228.
Thom, R. (1972) *Stabilité Structurelle et Morphogénèse*. Reading, MA: Benjamin.
Torre, V. (1977) 'Existence of limit cycles and control in a complete Keynesian system by theory of bifurcations', *Econometrica*, 45:1457-1466.
Varian, H. (1979) 'Catastrophe theory and the business cycles', *Economic Inquiry*, 17:14-28.
Weinrich, G. (1982) 'On the theory of effective demand under stochastic rationing', Discussion Paper, University of Mannheim.
Weinrich, G. (1984) 'On the size of disequilibrium in an equilibrium with quantity rationing', CORE Discussion Paper 8418, Université Catholique de Louvain, Louvain-la-Neuve.

Chapter 4

INVARIANCE, NEUTRALITY AND WEAKLY CONTINUOUS EXPECTED UTILITY

Claude d'ASPREMONT

CORE, Université Catholique de Louvain, Louvain-la-Neuve, Belgium

Louis GEVERS

Facultés Universitaires Notre-Dame de la Paix, Namur, Belgium, and CORE, Université Catholique de Louvain, Louvain-la-Neuve, Belgium

Introduction

One can think of many choice situations the outcome of which depends not only on the decision maker, but also on a host of circumstances that escape his control and that can be thought of as exogenous. Given an exhaustive list of uncontrolled states of the world together with a set of potential outcomes, a decision under uncertainty is best understood as a list of outcomes, each of them being associated with a particular state of the world.

This paper is concerned with preference orderings of decisions under uncertainty and their utility representations. Hence it should be seen as an alternative to Savage (1954) expected utility theory, dealing with the comparisons of "acts" (or uncertain decisions) and not as an alternative to the von Neumann–Morgenstern (1944) theory dealing with the comparisons of "lotteries" (or risky prospects objectively determined as probability distributions over the set of potential outcomes). Moreover, as a decision theory under uncertainty, our contribution will be mostly in the Bernoulli (1738) tradition. We shall start from the construction of a cardinal preference on a set of deterministic outcomes and then use it to compare uncertain

Economic-Decision Making: Games, Econometrics and Optimisation
Edited by J.J. Gabszewicz, J.-F. Richard and L.A. Wolsey
© *Elsevier Science Publishers B.V., 1990*

decisions, unlike Savage who axiomatizes immediately a preference relation amongst acts. This is, under uncertainty, the analogue of a decision theory under risk starting from a Bernoullian utility function based on the comparisons of riskless outcome differences and then deriving the expected utility criterion to evaluate risky prospects, as opposed to the direct approach of von Neumann and Morgenstern who axiomatize immediately a preference relation amongst lotteries.[1]

From Savage's days, the scope of expected utility theory was both extended and questioned. Drèze (1987) extended the theory to cover state-dependent preferences and cases where decisions affect the likelihood of events; more recently, Aumann (1987) provided an illuminating reinterpretation of the concept of state of the world, to include the choice of action by all the players in a game. He further demonstrated the profound connexion between Bayesian rationality, expected utility maximization, and the concept of correlated equilibrium. In Aumann's approach the relative likelihood of events becomes fully endogenous. On the other hand, actual randomization of strategies is not used: what matters are the subjective beliefs of each player.

Thus, expected utility has assumed an increasing role in game theory, while game theory has become more and more important in many parts of economics.

These developments did not prevent empiricists to accumulate more and more telling experimental evidence clashing with expected utility theory. The reader is referred to the lucid survey by Machina (1987) and the recent book by Fishburn (1988).

In the present juncture, we believe that it could be useful to reconsider some axiomatic treatments of expected utility. We shall start with a pedagogic approach of expected utility proper, akin to the "homiletic" presentation by Blackorby, Davidson and Donaldson (1977). Next we shall weaken our continuity axiom and turn to what we call weakly continuous expected utility representations, that is preferences whose continuous approximation agrees with expected utility.

Our study draws upon two strands of literature that are often kept apart from the Savage approach to expected utility, viz. measurement theory and social choice theory.

Social choice theory starts where the measurement of individual welfare stops and then attempts to base social evaluation on various conditions of collective rationality and equity requirements. The possible methods of

---

[1] See for example Fishburn (1988, Chapter 1).

social evaluation, though, depend crucially on the type of individual welfare measures which are available, that is depend on what Sen (1970) calls the available "informational basis". This is expressed by various invariance conditions specifying the interpersonal comparability and measurability of individual welfare. It is far from easy to decide, on a priori ethical or practical grounds, which form of invariance principle should be adopted. Hence social choice theorists have been much concerned with the tradeoffs among the many versions of invariance one can think of and other principles that may be relevant for collective decisions. Now it is well-known that the formal apparatus of social choice theory can be reinterpreted in the theory of individual decision under uncertainty and, hence, the invariance conditions can be given an "intrapersonal" interpretation. This we shall do in the following. Moreover we shall attempt to give a measurement-theoretic foundation to some invariance conditions. As well emphasized by Krantz, Luce, Suppes and Tversky (1971, Chapter 1) in their remarkable presentation of the main "fundamental system of properties" leading to numerical measurement: "only a few basic procedures are known for assigning numbers to objects or events on the basis of qualitative observations of attributes". Of the three basic procedures they quote — ordinal comparisons, counting of units and solving inequalities — we shall mostly retain the second: our procedure will be close to the use of "standard sequences" constructed by replication of a single unit.

In the next section, after proving an expected utility theorem based on a first invariance-neutrality assumption and on continuity, we shall adopt the Bernoullian approach, weaken continuity and strengthen invariance-neutrality, to get a weakly continuous expected utility criterion. In Section 3, we shall modify again the invariance-neutrality assumption and get alternative decision criteria. All proofs are gathered in an appendix after the concluding section.

1. Invariance-neutrality axioms and weakly continuous expected utility

In this paper we shall rely on Savage's formulation of a decision problem under uncertainty. An individual is confronted with a set $S = \{1, 2, \ldots, s, \ldots\}$ of possible "states of the world" and with a set $\mathscr{X} = \{x, y, z, \ldots\}$ of possible "consequences", a connected separable topological space. He has to choose an "act", or decision, that is a function f associating a consequence $x = f_s$ in $\mathscr{X}$ to every possible state s in S. This choice is to be seen as an expression of a preference relation R on the set $\mathscr{X}^S = \{f, g, h, k, \ldots\}$ of all possible acts.

By this we mean that R is a transitive and complete binary relation on $\mathscr{X}^S$: if, for any f, g, h in $\mathscr{X}^S$, $f R g$ and $g R h$, then $f R h$; for any f, g in $\mathscr{X}^S$, either $f R g$ or $g R f$. The corresponding indifference relation is denoted I and strict preference is denoted P. Also we maintain throughout an independence or *separability assumption* on R with respect to any "event" S_0 (a subset of S) and all acts f, g, ..., having a common consequence pattern on the complementary event, that is $f = g$ on S_0^c (or $f(s) = g(s)$, all $s \notin S_0$).

Separability (SE). For every $S_0 \subset S$ and on all acts f, g, f', g' in $\mathscr{X}^S$ such that $f = g$ on S_0^c, $f' = g'$ on S_0^c, there is a preference ordering $R(S_0)$ satisfying

$$f\ R(S_0)\ g\ \Leftrightarrow\ f\ R\ g\ \Leftrightarrow\ f'\ R(S_0)\ g'$$

whenever $f = f'$, $g = g'$ on S_0.

We identify R and $R(S)$. Moreover, we shall say that, for any x, y in $\mathscr{X}$ and any s in S, $x R(\{s\}) y$ whenever $f R(\{s\}) g$ for any f, g in $\mathscr{X}^S$ with $f_s = x$, $g_s = y$ and $f = g$ on $S \backslash \{s\}$.

We impose moreover that the ordering of consequences be state-independent:

State by State Uniformity (SSU). For any states s, t in S and any consequences x, y in $\mathscr{X}$,

$$x\ R(\{s\})\ y\ \Leftrightarrow\ x\ R(\{t\})\ y.$$

We shall assume that the set of states is finite (in Savage, 1954, S has to be infinite). However we shall take it to be sufficiently diverse in the sense that it does not contain too many *null states*, that is states s_0 such that $f I g$ whenever $f = g$ on $S \backslash \{s_0\}$.

State Diversity (SD). S is finite but includes at least three distinct nonnull states.

Also, as described in the introduction, we reconsider Savage's theory from a Bernoullian viewpoint, by assuming a notion of preference on consequence differences. We define a complete binary relation D on $\mathscr{X} \times \mathscr{X}$ and denote by E the corresponding symmetric relation, i.e.,

$$(x, y)\ E\ (x', y')\ \Leftrightarrow\ (x, y)\ D\ (x', y')\ \text{and}\ (x', y')\ D\ (x, y).$$

For D to become meaningful, it has to be given more structure. We shall

	s	t	$\{s, t\}^c$
f	x	y	z
g	y	x	z

Figure 1.

follow two alternative paths. One of them is Bernoullian and introspective in character. The other one, which we follow first, is more directly operational. It relies on the notion of equally likely states. Two distinct states s, t are said to be *equally likely* if, for any x, y, z in $\mathscr{X}$ and f, g in $\mathscr{X}^S$, such that $f_s = x$, $f_t = y$, $g_s = y$, $g_t = x$ and $f = g = z$ on $\{s, t\}^c$, as shown in Figure 1, then $f I g$.

We then have the additional assumption establishing the consistency of the two preference relations R and D.

R and D consistency (RDC). There are at least two equally likely nonnull states s and t such that, for all x, y, x', y' and z in $\mathscr{X}$ and f, g in $\mathscr{X}^S$ satisfying $f_s = x$, $f_t = y'$, $g_s = y$, $g_t = x'$ and $f = g = z$ in $\{s, t\}^c$ (see Figure 2),

$$(x, y) \ D \ (x', y') \quad \Leftrightarrow \quad f \ R \ g.$$

In some sense this assumption gives an operational anchoring to the relation between R and D based on the notion of equally likely states. As such D is an intermediate construct which does not constrain R, except for the existence of two equally likely states. It would be embarrassing though to have D depending on the choice of a particular pair of equally likely states, when several are available. The following assumption eliminates this source of confusion. But it goes further: it is a parsimony assumption concerning the information needed to choose among two decisions. It can be compared to some conditions in the social choice literature: independence of irrelevant alternatives or neutrality, together with a scale-invariance

	s	t	$\{s, t\}^c$
f	x	y'	z
g	y	x'	z

Figure 2.

property[2] (invariance of social evaluation with respect to common translation of individual utilities). Although there, these are conditions concerning
interpersonal comparability, and here we have only an intra-personal comparability condition. This condition tells us that to compare any two acts,
we should only look at the revealed relation between the gains associated
with changes in consequences. Any other two acts revealing equivalent gains
should be ordered in the same way. The nature of outcomes is not important.
Only the structure of gains as revealed by relation D (or the associated
equivalence relation E) should matter.

Difference-Scale Neutrality (DSN). For any f, g, h, k in $\mathcal{X}^S$, if, for some t
and all s in S,

$$(f_t, f_s) \ E \ (h_t, h_s) \quad \text{and} \quad (f_t, g_s) \ E \ (h_t, k_s),$$

then

$$f \ R \ g \quad \Leftrightarrow \quad h \ R \ k.$$

The first theorem we shall prove relies heavily on a strong continuity
assumption and the theorem of Debreu (1959). This continuity assumption
can be stated:

Continuity of R (CR). The sets $\{g \in \mathcal{X}^S : g \ R f\}$ and $\{g \in \mathcal{X}^S : f \ R \ g\}$ are closed
for every $f \in \mathcal{X}^S$.

Theorem 1. *Suppose that R is a continuous (CR), separable (SE) and state
by state uniform (SSU) preference ordering on the set $\mathcal{X}^S$, with S containing
at least three nonnull states, of which at least two are equally likely. Suppose
that D, the binary relation on $\mathcal{X} \times \mathcal{X}$ consistent with R (RDC), satisfies
Difference-Scale Neutrality (DSN). Then, there exists a real-valued con-
tinuous function u defined on $\mathcal{X}$ and nonnegative numbers $\{p_s : s \in S\}$ such
that $p_s = 0$ iff s is null, $p_s = p_t$ iff s and t are equally likely, $\sum_{s \in S} p_s = 1$ and:
$f R g \Leftrightarrow \sum_{s \in S} p_s u(f_s) \geq \sum_{s \in S} p_s u(g_s)$ for any f, g in $\mathcal{X}^S$. The function u is unique
up to a positive affine transformation, i.e. v satisfies the same relation iff
$v \equiv \alpha + \beta u$, for some reals α and $\beta > 0$.*

This theorem gives a characterization of the set of orderings that are
adequately represented by the expected utility criterion. The proof is given
in the appendix.

---

[2] For definitions and references, see d'Aspremont (1985).

	S_0	S_1	$(S_0 \cup S_1)^c$
f	x	z	y
g	z	x	y

Figure 3.

We want to stress that the weights used to compute the mathematical expectations have an operational interpretation: they measure the implicit relative likelihood of events. Once we recognize that $R(\{s\})$ is the same for all $s \in S$ under the assumptions of Theorem 1, we can easily define event S_0 as more likely than event S_1 (assuming $S_0 \cap S_1 = \emptyset$), whenever there exist $x, y, z \in \mathcal{X}$ such that $x\, P(\{s\})\, z$ and for any f, g such that $f = x$, $g = z$ on S_0, $f = z$, $g = x$ on S_1 and $f = g = y$ on $(S_0 \cup S_1)^c$, as shown in Figure 3, and we have $f\, P(S_0 \cup S_1)\, g$.

And indeed, by Theorem 1, $\sum_{s \in S_0} p_s \geq \sum_{s \in S_1} p_s$ whenever S_0 is more likely than S_1. In other words, the likelihood relation on events is represented by the probabilities $\{p_s : s \in S\}$: They can be interpreted as subjective probabilities. Similarly, the function u, representing $R(\{s\})$ for all s, may also be used to represent the difference relation D. That is for any x, y, x', y' in $\mathcal{X}$, $(x, y)\, D\, (x', y')$ iff $u(x) - u(y) \geq u(x') - u(y')$. Thus Theorem 1 gives interesting insights into relation D. Let us summarize them under the following heading:

Bernoullian Preference (BP). D is a complete transitive relation on $\mathcal{X} \times \mathcal{X}$ satisfying $\forall x, y, z, x' \in \mathcal{X}$,

$$(x, y)\ D\ (x', x') \ \Leftrightarrow \ x\ R(\{s\})\ y \qquad \forall x \in S,$$

$$(x, y)\ D\ (x', z) \ \Leftrightarrow \ (x, x')\ D\ (y, z),$$

and moreover D is continuous: $\{(x, y) \in \mathcal{X} \times \mathcal{X} : (x, y)\, D\, (x', z)\}$ and $\{(x, y) \in \mathcal{X} \times \mathcal{X} : (x', z)\, D\, (x, y)\}$ are closed sets.

Disregarding the requirement of operational consistency between R and D that we based on equally likely states, we shall next take as a primitive our description of Bernoullian Preference. The weaker continuity assumption that is an element of BP allows us to drop the direct requirement that R be continuous and to characterize a family of preference relations the continuous approximation of which agrees with expected utility.

To obtain these results, we shall find expedient to simplify the structure of $R(\{s\})$ and to strengthen somewhat our other axioms.

We wish to avail ourselves of the simple axiomatic treatment of cardinal utility presented by Shapley (1975).[3] One could interpret $\mathscr{X}$ as being an already given numerical scale defined on some set of outcomes and axiomatized following well-known methods (see Debreu, 1959). As in Shapley (1975), we take $\mathscr{X} = X$ a nonempty convex subset of the real line. Also let us turn to $R(\{s\})$ and impose a condition subsuming SSU that we call:

State by State Monotonicity (SSM). For every $s \in S$, any $f, g \in X^S$ such that $f = g$ on $\{s\}^c$,

$$f\ R(\{s\})\ g \quad \Leftrightarrow \quad f_s \geq g_s.$$

Under BP and SSM, Shapley proved[4] in this framework the existence of a "cardinal utility" u on X such that, for any x, y, x', y' in X,

$$u(x) - u(y) \geq u(x') - u(y') \quad \Leftrightarrow \quad (x, y)\ D\ (x', y').$$

Our proofs rely on the ordering induced by R on the image set $[u(X)]^S$. This cardinal utility is far from unique and we would like the orderings induced by R on the respective image sets to be consistent. Let us observe that condition SSM, together with the separability of R implies a strong Pareto principle that is often used in social choice theory. However, for our purpose, this is not enough and we need to strengthen the invariance neutrality assumption: DSN requires neutrality together with invariance of R with respect to a common change of origin of u; we now add invariance of R with respect to a common change of unit. As we wish to keep an operational character to the condition, from a measurement point of view, we shall limit these changes and base them on the notion of a repeated addition of identical gains, much in the spirit of the "standard sequences" used in measurement theory (see Krantz et al., 1971). Consider any positive integer m. If, for any sequence of $m + 1$ consequences $x_0, x_1, x_2, \ldots, x_m$ and any w, x, y, z in X, we have

$$(w, x)\ E\ (x_0, x_m)$$

and

$$(y, z)\ E\ (x_0, x_1)\ E\ (x_1, x_2)\ E\ \cdots\ E\ (x_{m-1}, x_m),$$

---

[3] Our results could be extended by generalizing Shapley (1975) or taking some other characterization of preference intensities such as Suppes and Winet (1955).

[4] Shapley actually uses a weaker continuity requirement.

then we shall write $(w, x)\ E^m\ (y, z)$ and say that the difference (w, x) is equivalent to the m-replication of (y, z). Of course, we identify E and E^1. Then we assume:

Interval-Scale Neutrality (ISN). For any f, g, h, k in X^S, if for some $m \in \mathbb{N}_+$, some t and all s in S,

$$(f_t, f_s)\ E^m\ (h_t, h_s) \quad \text{and} \quad (f_t, g_s)\ E^m\ (h_t, k_s),$$

then

$$f\ R\ g \quad \Leftrightarrow \quad h\ R\ k.$$

Clearly, this condition is stronger than DSN: it suffices to fix $m = 1$ to obtain DSN.

Notice that, for any u, a cardinal representation of D that can be shown to exist under conditions BP and SSM, we are interested in the relation R^* induced by R on the utility space $\mathbb{R}^S$. As shown in the appendix (Proposition 1), under ISN, R^* is a well-defined ordering. Hence what is relevant for comparing decisions is only the associated welfare as measured in utility. Different acts leading to different consequences but the same utility level should be ordered in the same way (this property is called "welfarism" in the social choice literature). Finally, we need to strengthen the "diversity" of X. First we say that a state s is *dominated* if, for some state $t \in S$, $f P(\{s, t\})\ g$ whenever $(f_t, g_t)\ D\ (x, x)$ and not $(g_t, f_t)\ D\ (x, x)$ for some $x \in X$ (i.e., $f_t > g_t$). Letting W denote the set of states that are not dominated, we require:

Strong Diversity (SDV). $|W| \geq 3$.

Second we want our decision criterion to be sensitive to the relative likelihood of events. In particular, we want to exclude a situation where for some s, $t \in S$, and for some x, y, $z \in X$, with $y > x$, for all f, $g \in X^S$, $f P g$ whenever $f_t = x$ and $g_t = y$, $f_s = z + \varepsilon$ and $g_s = z - \varepsilon$ with ε an arbitrarily small positive number (see Figure 4), and $f = g$ on $\{s, t\}^c$.

	$\{s\}$	$\{t\}$
f	$z + \varepsilon$	x
g	$z - \varepsilon$	y

Figure 4.

If the situation we just described occurs, we shall say that state s locally dominates state t. Our assumption is:

Freedom from Local Domination (FLD). No state in W locally dominates another state in W.

We then get:

Theorem 2. *Consider R, a separable (SE) and state by state monotone (SSM) preference ordering defined on the convex interval X^S. Suppose we have at least three undominated states (SDV), no locally dominated state within W (FLD) and there exists a continuous Bernoullian Preference D (BP) for which R meets the Interval-Scale Neutrality (ISN) condition. Then there exists a real-valued continuous function u defined on X and nonnegative numbers $\{p_s : s \in S\}$ such that $p_s > 0$ iff $s \in W$, $\sum_{s \in S} p_s = 1$ and, for any $f, g \in X^S$,*

$$\sum_{s \in S} p_s u(f_s) > \sum_{s \in S} p_s u(g_s) \quad \Rightarrow \quad f \, P \, g.$$

Function u is unique up to a positive affine transformation. The proof of the theorem is given in appendix and is an adaptation of Deschamps and Gevers (1977, 1978). In fact we could get a stronger version of the theorem since we could replace FLD by a weaker assumption: it is enough to exclude the "leximin" and the "leximax" criterion which are respectively the lexicographic extensions of the "maximin" and the "maximax" criteria. Also notice that we only get a weakly continuous expected utility criterion: if two acts have the same expected utility it does not follow that they should be indifferent.

2. Weakening invariance-neutrality

In this last section, we would like to see how the preceding result is affected by the modification of the invariance-neutrality axiom ISN. By analogy to results in social choice theory we know that if we reduce the scope of invariance — or in other words if we give a more precise informational basis — then many other decision criteria may become available. To confirm this statement it is enough to weaken the ISN axiom and to require that every advantage or gain be assessed with respect to a single base consequence that is the same for every choice problem. There are several ways of formalizing this requirement. For simplicity, we assume here that there exists a worst consequence $x_0 \in X$ and that x_0 is universally used for difference comparisons.

Existence of a least desirable consequence (LDC). There exists $x_0 \in X$ such that for all $x \in X$, $x \geq x_0$.

Ratio-Scale Neutrality (RSN). For any f, g, h, k in X^S, if for some $m \in \mathbb{N}_+$ and all $s \in S$,

$$(x_0, f_s) \ E^m \ (x_0, h_s) \quad \text{and} \quad (x_0, g_s) \ E^m \ (x_0, k_s),$$

then

$$f \ R \ g \quad \Leftrightarrow \quad h \ R \ k.$$

The following theorem, using RSN in place of ISN, opens up many other weakly continuous representations of R. These are generalized means of some order r.

Theorem 3. *Consider R, a separable (SE) and state by state monotone (SSM) preference ordering defined on the convex interval X^S. Suppose there are at least three undominated states (SDV), no locally dominated state within W (FLD), there exists a least desirable consequence x_0 (LDC), and there exists a continuous Bernoullian Preference D (BP) for which R meets the Ratio-Scale-Neutrality (RSN) condition. Then there exists a positive-valued continuous function u defined on $X_0 = X \backslash \{x_0\}$, nonnegative numbers $\{p_s : s \in S\}$ summing to 1, with $p_s > 0$ if and only if $s \in W$, and some number r such that*

$$\left[\sum_{s \in S} p_s (u(f_s))^r \right]^{1/r} > \left[\sum_{s \in S} p_s (u(g_s))^r \right]^{1/r} \quad \Rightarrow \quad f \ P \ g, \qquad r \neq 0,$$

$$\prod_{s \in S} [u(f_s)]^{p_s} > \prod_{s \in S} [u(g_s)]^{p_s} \quad \Rightarrow \quad f \ P \ g, \qquad r = 0,$$

for any f, $g \in X_0^S$. The function u is unique up to a positive linear transformation, i.e. v satisfies the same relations if and only if $v(\cdot) \equiv \beta u(\cdot)$, for some $\beta > 0$.

The proof is a variant of the preceding theorem and uses a result of Blackorby and Donaldson (1982), based on Eichhorn (1973) and Aczél (1966).

3. Conclusion

Relying on invariance-neutrality assumptions may be more operational in the context of individual decision-making under uncertainty than in the context of social welfare evaluation. In the former case, they are based on intrapersonal comparisons and they reduce the decision maker's computational burden by having him judge what is best in a binary choice problem with help of information that is restricted to the possible consequences involved. Also they can be more easily expressed in measurement theoretic terms. However, the individual decision criteria we have arrived at are still subject to criticisms usually addressed to Expected Utility Theory. In particular, they all subsume separability.

Appendix 1. Proof of Theorem 1

Since R is continuous and separable and there are at least three nonnull states, the classical theorem of Debreu (1959) says that there exists, for every s, a continuous real-valued function such that, for all f, g in the product space $\mathcal{X}^S$,

$$f \ R \ g \quad \Leftrightarrow \quad \sum_s u_s(f_s) \geq \sum_s u_s(g_s).$$

Suppose next that state 1 and state 2 are nonnull and equally likely, and let us consider $R(\{1, 2\})$. By definition, $\forall x$, $x' \in \mathcal{H}$, $u_1(x) + u_2(x') = u_1(x') + u_2(x)$. Hence, $u_1(x) - u_1(x') = u_2(x) - u_2(x')$ and we must have $u_1(\cdot) = u_2(\cdot) + \Delta$ where Δ is some constant.

Therefore, there exist u and v such that $R(\{1, 2, 3\})$ may be represented by $\frac{1}{2}u(f_1) + \frac{1}{2}u(f_2) + v(f_3)$.

Moreover, because D is consistent with $R(\{1, 2, 3\})$, we note that, $\forall x$, x', z, $z' \in \mathcal{X}$, $(x, x') \ E \ (z, z')$ iff $\frac{1}{2}u(x) + \frac{1}{2}u(z') = \frac{1}{2}u(x') + \frac{1}{2}u(z)$, i.e., iff $u(x) - u(x') = u(z) - u(z')$.

We are now in position to prove that there exists two numbers α, β such that $\forall x \in X$, $v(x) = \alpha + \beta u(x)$. If state 3 is null, we must obviously set $\beta = 0$. If state 3 is nonnull, β should be positive in due of SSU.

Suppose that there were no such α, β. Then by continuity[5] we can find distinct consequences x, y and z in some open subset of $\mathcal{X}$ such that $u(x) - u(y) = u(y) - u(z) = \delta$ whereas $v(x) - v(y) \neq v(y) - v(z)$ and $\max\{|\delta|, |v(x) - v(y)|, |v(y) - v(z)|\}$ is as small as we please (resp., such that the similar relations hold with u and v permuted). Without loss of generality, suppose $v(x) - v(y) > v(y) - v(z)$. Since $\mathcal{X}$ is connected, its continuous

---

[5] And using the fact that $v(\cdot) = \alpha + \beta u(\cdot)$ for some reals α and β, whenever $u(x) - u(y) = u(y) - u(z) \Leftrightarrow v(x) - v(y) = v(y) - v(z)$ for all distinct x, y, z in $\mathcal{X}$.

	$\{1,2\}$	$\{3\}$	$S\backslash\{1,2,3\}$
f	x'	z	z
g	w'	y	z
h	z'	y	y
k	y'	x	y

Figure 5.

image is connected. Hence we can find some r_1 and r_2 in $u(\mathcal{X})$, such that $r_1 + \delta$ and $r_2 + \delta$ still be in $u(\mathcal{X})$ and

$$v(x) - v(y) > r_1 - r_2 \geq v(y) - v(z).$$

Taking $x' \in u^{-1}(r_1)$, $w' \in u^{-1}(r_2)$, $z' \in u^{-1}(r_1 + \delta)$ and $y' \in u^{-1}(r_2 + \delta)$, we get

$$u(z') - u(y') = u(x') - u(w') = r_1 - r_2,$$

and also

$$u(x') + v(z) \geq u(w') + v(y),$$

$$u(y') + v(x) > u(z') + v(y).$$

Now consider f, g, h and k in $\mathcal{X}^S$ as given by Figure 5.

Hence, $f R g$ and $k P h$.

On the other hand, consider the matrix of utility values that can be obtained from Figure 5 and function u. By construction, we have $\forall s \in S$, $u(h_s) = u(f_s) + \delta$ and $u(k_s) = u(g_s) + \delta$, and we can apply the difference scale neutrality assumption, so that $f R g$ iff $h R k$, contrary to our previous finding.

If $v(x) - v(y) < v(y) - v(z)$ (resp., if u and v are permuted), an analogous argument applies.

In conclusion, $R(\{1,2,3\})$ has an expected utility representation. The same ideas may be used to encompass successively all other states in S. All null states will be assigned a zero weight. All equally likely states will receive the same weight. Finally all positive weights (by SSU) can be normalized so that their sum equals 1. $\quad\square$

Appendix 2. Proofs of Theorems 2 and 3

Since the proofs of Theorems 2 and 3 are similar (in Theorem 3, ISN is replaced by RSN), we shall give them in parallel.

First recall the following:

Cardinal Utility Theorem (Shapley, 1975). *Under BP and SSM, there exists a set $[u]$ of continuous real-valued functions defined on X such that*: $\forall u \in [u]$, $\forall x, x', z, z' \in X$,

$$u(x) - u(x') \geq u(z) - u(z') \quad \textit{iff} \quad (x, x') \; D \; (z, z')$$

and any v, v' in $[u]$ are related by a positive affine transformation. $\square$

Given $u^* \in [u]$ we may define the set of positive affine transformations of u^*, with rational scaling coefficient. Formally let

$$A(u^*) = \{u \in [u]: \exists \alpha \in \mathbb{R}, \beta \in Q_+ \text{ such that } u(\cdot) \equiv \alpha + \beta u^*(\cdot)\}.$$

Similarly, for every utility function in $[u]$ associating zero value with the least desirable consequence in X we define the set of its positive linear transformations with rational coefficient. Let
$X_0 = X \backslash \{x_0\}$, where x_0 stands for the least desirable consequence (see LDC);
$[u]_+^0 = \{u \in [u]: u(x_0) = 0\}$;
$A_+^0(u^*) = \{u \in [u]_+^0: \exists \beta \in Q_+ \text{ such that } u(\cdot) \equiv \beta u^*(\cdot)\}$, where $u^* \in [u]_+^0$.
Observe that $u \in A(u^*)$ (resp. $u \in A_+^0(u^*)$) implies $u^* \in A(u)$ (resp. $u^* \in A_+^0(u)$). Also we let, for all $f \in X^S$ and $u \in [u]$,

$$u(f) = (u(f_1), u(f_2), \ldots, u(f_s)),$$

$$u(X) = \{r \in \mathbb{R}: \exists x \in X \text{ such that } u(x) = r\},$$

$$\mathbb{R}_+^S = \{v \in \mathbb{R}^S: \forall s \in S, v_s \geq 0\}, \qquad \mathbb{R}_{++}^S = \{v \in \mathbb{R}^S: \forall s \in S, v_s > 0\}.$$

Then:

Lemma 1 (welfarism). *Let R be an ordering on X^S satisfying BP and SSM.*
(a) *If ISN holds then, for any $u^* \in [u]$, $\bigcup_{u \in A(u^*)} \{[u(X)]^S\} = \mathbb{R}^S$ and there exists an ordering R^* of $\mathbb{R}^S$ such that $\forall f, g \in X^S$, $\forall a, b \in \mathbb{R}^S$, $f R g$ iff $\exists u \in A(u^*)$ for which $a = u(f)$, $b = u(g)$ and $a R^* b$.*
(b) *If RSN and LDC hold then, for any $u^* \in [u]_+^0$, $\bigcup_{u \in A_+^0(u^*)} \{[u(X)]^S\} = \mathbb{R}_+^S$ and there exists an ordering R^* of $\mathbb{R}_+^S$ such that for any $f, g \in X^S$, $\forall a, b \in \mathbb{R}_+^S$, $f R g$ iff $\exists u \in A_+^0(u^*)$ for which $a = u(f)$ and $b = u(g)$ and $a R^* b$.*

Proof. Let us show the first part of (b), $\bigcup_{u \in A_+^0(u^*)} \{[u(X)]^S\} = \mathbb{R}_+^S$. Take any $a \in \mathbb{R}_+^S$. Since, by BP, SSM and LDC, $u^*(X)$ is the positive half line or an interval $[0, r]$ (or $[0, r)$) for some $r > 0$, there is some $\bar{x} \in X$, $\bar{x} > x_0$, and some $\beta \in Q_+$ such that $a_1, a_2, \ldots, a_s$ all belong to the interval $(0, \beta u^*(\bar{x}))$. Hence $a \in [\beta u^*(X)]^S$. To show the first part of (a), $\bigcup_{u \in A(u^*)} \{[u(X)]^S\} = \mathbb{R}^S$, we can proceed similarly.

Now it is clear that R induces an ordering R^* on $[u^*(X)]^S$ as well as an ordering R_u on $[u(X)]^S$ for any $u \in [u]$ (resp., $[u]^0_+$). It remains to show that all these orderings agree in both cases (a) and (b). We give the argument for case (a). Consider any $u, u' \in A(u^*)$, any $a, b \in \mathbb{R}^S$ and any $f, g, f', g' \in X^S$ such that

$$a = u(f) = u'(f'), \qquad b = u(g) = u'(g').$$

We want to show that $f R g$ iff $f' R g'$.

By definition of $A(u^*)$, there is a positive rational β such that: $\forall s \in S$,

$$u'(f'_1) - u'(f'_s) = \beta(u(f'_1) - u(f'_s)) = u(f_1) - u(f_s),$$

$$u'(f'_1) - u'(g'_s) = \beta(u(f'_1) - u(g'_s)) = u(f_1) - u(g_s).$$

If β (or $1/\beta$) is an integer, ISN applies immediately because u is continuous.

If β is the ratio of two integers λ and μ, we can write $\beta = (1/\mu)/(1/\lambda)$, so that the last equalities become

$$\frac{1}{\mu}(u(f'_1) - u(f'_s)) = \frac{1}{\lambda}(u(f_1) - u(f_s)),$$

$$\frac{1}{\mu}(u(f'_1) - u(g'_s)) = \frac{1}{\lambda}(u(f_1) - u(g_s)).$$

Because u is continuous, we can discover $h, k \in X^S$ such that $\forall s \in S$,

$$\frac{1}{\lambda}(u(f_1) - u(f_s)) = (u(h_1) - u(h_s)),$$

$$\frac{1}{\lambda}(u(f_1) - u(g_s)) = (u(h_1) - u(k_s)),$$

and we apply ISN twice. $\square$

Our next task is to study some properties of R^*. A very useful property is the following: $\forall a, a', b, b' \in \mathbb{R}^S$, *if there exist two reals α, β with β a positive rational such that $\forall s \in S$,*

$$a_s = \alpha + \beta b_s, \qquad a'_s = \alpha + \beta b'_s,$$

then $a R^* a'$ iff $b R^* b'$.

We call this property *quasi-co-cardinality* (QCC*), for lack of a better word. If this property is satisfied only for $\alpha = 0$, then we call it *quasi-ratio-scale invariance* (QRI*).

Lemma 2. *Let R be an ordering on X^S satisfying BP and SSM.*
  (a) *If ISN holds, then $\forall u^* \in [u]$, the ordering R^* on $\mathbb{R}^S$ satisfies quasi-co-cardinality.*
  (b) *If RSN and LDC hold, then, $\forall u^* \in [u]_+^0$, the ordering R^* on $\mathbb{R}_+^S$ satisfies quasi-ratio-scale invariance.*

Proof. Choose any a, $b \in \mathbb{R}^S$ such that $a\, R^*\, b$. Then there exists $u \in A(u^*)$ and f, $g \in X^S$ such that $a = u(f)$, $b = u(g)$ and $a\, R^*\, b$ iff $f\, R\, g$. Consider next any $\alpha \in \mathbb{R}$, any $\beta \in Q_+$ and any a', $b' \in \mathbb{R}^S$ such that $\forall s \in S$, $a_s' = \alpha + \beta a_s$, $b_s' = \alpha + \beta b_s$. Then there exist $u' \in A(u^*)$ such that $a' = u'(f)$ and $b' = u'(g)$ and, by Lemma 1, $a'\, R^*\, b'$ iff $f\, R\, g$ iff $a\, R^*\, b$.
  This proves case (a). The proof of case (b) is similar. $\square$

We are now ready to adapt some results of Deschamps and Gevers (1977, 1978).
  Suppose S is partitioned in two subsets M and H. Let γ be any fixed vector of $\mathbb{R}^H$. Any subspace B is said associated with M if it satisfies the following definition: $B = \{a: \forall s \in H, a_s = \gamma_s\}$ where a is taken (and γ fixed) in $\mathbb{R}^S$ or in $\mathbb{R}_{++}^S$ as the case may be (ISN or RSN). This will be clear from the context.
  Furthermore, $\forall a, b, a', b' \in \mathbb{R}^S$, we shall say that (a, b) is similar to (a', b') with respect to M (in short: $(a, b)\, \sigma_M\, (a', b')$) if B and B' are two subspaces associated with M, $a, b \in B$, $a', b' \in B'$ and $\forall s \in M$, $a_s = a_s'$ whereas $b_s = b_s'$.
  If R is separable, it should be clear that R^* enjoys an induced separability property (SE*): $\forall a, b, a', b' \in \mathbb{R}^S$, $a\, R^*\, b$ iff $a'\, R^*\, b'$ whenever there exists $M \subset S$ such that $(a, b)\, \sigma_M\, (a', b')$.
  We show next that if R displays properties SE and SSM, then R^* meets a strong dominance condition called strong Pareto (SP*) in the social choice literature: $\forall a, b \in \mathbb{R}^S$, $a\, R^*\, b$ if $\forall s \in S$, $a_s \geq b_s$; and if, moreover, $a_t > b_t$ for some $t \in S$, $a\, P^*\, b$.

Lemma 3. *R^* meets SP* if R satisfies SE, BP, SSM and either ISN or RSN and LDC.*

Proof. We write this proof for ISN, the other case requiring only trivial changes. Consider first any $a, b \in \mathbb{R}^S$ such that for some $t \in S$, $a_t \geq b_t$ (resp.

$a_t > b_t$), whereas $\forall s \in S \setminus \{t\}$, $a_s = b_s$. Then there exist $g, f \in X^S$ such that $g_t \geq f_t$ (resp. $g_t > f_t$) and $\forall s \in S \setminus \{t\}$, $g_s = f_s$ and there exist $u \in A(u^*)$ such that $a = u(g)$, $b = u(f)$, and, by SSM, $g \, R f$ (resp. $g \, P f$), so that, by Lemma 1, $a \, R^* \, b$ (resp. $a \, P^* \, b$).

Now, suppose SP* holds true for every subspace B' associated with some $M \subset S$. Then, it is easy to see that it holds also true for all subspaces associated with $M \cup \{s\}$, assuming $s \notin M$, $s \in S$. Indeed, take any subspace B associated with $M \cup \{s\}$, any $a, b \in B$ such that $\forall h \in M \cup \{s\}$, $a_h \geq b_h$. Now consider $c \in B$ such that $c_s = b_s$ and $\forall h \in M$, $c_h = a_h$. By our assumption we get $c \, R^* \, b$. By construction, we have $a \, R^* \, c$. By transitivity, $a \, R^* \, b$. This argument extends easily to strict preference. $\square$

In the sequel, we shall find convenient to abbreviate our notation. Given $M \subset S$, and any B associated with M, $\forall a, b \in B$, we write $a \geq_B b$ (resp. $a \gg_B b$) if $\forall s \in M$, $a_s \geq b_s$ (resp. $a_s > b_s$).

Our next task is to define a continuous approximation of R^* and to study its properties.

Given any $M \subset S$, any subspace B associated with M, any $b \in B$, we define the following subsets of B:

$$C_b^B = \{a \in B, \exists (a') \subset B, a' \to a, \forall t, a^t \, R^* \, b\},$$

$$C_B^b = \{a \in B, \exists (a') \subset B, a' \to a, \forall t, b \, P^* \, a'\},$$

$$C(b, B) = C_b^B \cap C_B^b.$$

Let us remark that, $\forall a, b \in B$ such that $a \, R^* \, b$, we get $a \in C_b^B$; on the other hand, if a and b are such that $a \in C_b^B \setminus C(b, B)$, we get $a \, P^* \, b$. Indeed, suppose on the contrary that $b \, R^* \, a$. Then, by SP* and transitivity of R^*, $a \in C_B^b$, which contradicts our assumption. If SE* holds true we also note that $C(b, B)$ is not empty.

In the sequel, the binary relation defined by $a \in C_b^B$ will be treated as the relevant continuous approximation of R^*. The latter is not necessarily continuous, so that it is generally inconsistent with a utility representation. The former relation inherits interesting properties from R^* and it can be represented by an expected utility formula in case ISN holds.

Let us observe first that, $\forall a \in B$, $a \in C_a^B$ (reflexivity). Moreover, $\forall a, b \in B$, $a \in C_b^B$ (if $a \, R^* \, b$) or $b \in C_a^B$ (if $b \, R^* \, a$) (completeness). Furthermore, our binary relation is continuous by construction.

In order to derive other useful properties, we shall quote two lemmata by Deschamps and Gevers (1978). For easy reference we have retained the original numbering.

Lemma 4. *If R^* satisfies SP^*, $\forall M \subset S$, $\forall B$ associated with M, $\forall a$, b, $c \in B$ such that $a\, R^*\, b\, P^*\, c$ and $\forall i \in M$, $a_i > c_i$, there exists a unique α, $0 \leq \alpha \leq 1$, such that $\alpha a + (1 - \alpha)c \in C(b, B)$.*
  Moreover, if $0 \leq \beta < \alpha$ (resp., $\alpha < \beta \leq 1$), $\beta a + (1 - \beta)c \in C_B^b \backslash C(b, B)$ (resp., $C_b^B \backslash C(b, B)$). $\square$

Remark 4.1.

$C_b^B = \{a' \in B, a' \geq_B a, a \in C(b, B)\}$,

$C_b^B \backslash C(b, B) = \{a' \in B, a' \gg_B a, a \in C(b, B)\}$.

Proof of Remark. Given any arbitrary $b' \in B$, we can draw a straight line through b' connecting the region of B that is Pareto superior to any b with the region that is Pareto inferior to b. In particular, b' may be any point of C_b^B.

Remark 4.2.

$C_B^b = \{a' \in B, a \geq_B a', a \in C(b, B)\}$,

$C_B^b \backslash C(b, B) = \{a' \in B, a \gg_B a', a \in C(b, B)\}$.

Remark 4.3. For every $b \in B$, there is a unique point of the diagonal of B that is an element of $C(b, B)$ if R^* satisfies SE^*.

Lemma 5. *For every $M \subset S$, $\forall B$ associated with M, $\forall a$, b, $c \in B$, $a\, P^*\, c$ if $a \in C_b^B \backslash C(b, B)$ and $c \in C_B^b \backslash C(b, B)$.* $\square$

Lemma 6. *If R^* satisfies SE^*, SP^* and either QCC^* or QRI^*, then $\forall M \subset S$, $\forall B$ associated with M, $\forall a$, $b \in B$, $C(a, B) = C(b, B)$ whenever $a \in C(b, B)$.*

Proof. Assume R^* satisfies QRI^* together with SE^* and SP^*; then, $\forall M \subseteq S$, $\forall B$ associated with M, $\forall a$, $b \in B$, $a \in C(b, B)$ implies $C(b, B) \subseteq C(a, B)$. Suppose not: $\exists c \in B$, such that $c \in C(b, B)$ and $c \notin C(a, B)$. Consider the line $\{v = \lambda c, \lambda \in \mathbb{R}_{++}\}$. By Lemma 4, there exists a unique $\lambda^* \in \mathbb{R}_{++}$ such that

$$\lambda^* c \in C(a, B).$$

Suppose $\lambda^* > 1$ and consider $\lambda^* > \lambda^0 > \hat{\lambda} > 1$. By Lemma 4, $\hat{\lambda} a \in C_a^B \backslash C(a, B)$, $\lambda^0 c \in C_B^a \backslash C(a, B)$. By Lemma 5, $(\hat{\lambda} a)\, P^*\, (\lambda^0 c)$, and, $\forall n \in Q_+$, $((\hat{\lambda}/n)a)\, P^*\, ((\lambda^0/n)c)$, by QRI^*. Choose in particular n such that $\lambda^0/n > 1 > \hat{\lambda}/n$. On the other hand, by assumption $\{a, c\} \subset C(b, B)$. Then,

$((\lambda^0/n)c) \in C_b^B \backslash C(b, B)$ by Lemma 4, and $((\hat{\lambda}/n)a) \in C_B^b \backslash C(b, B)$ by Lemma 4. Thus, by Lemma 5, $((\lambda^0/n)c) \, P^* \, ((\hat{\lambda}/n)a)$ and we have a contradiction. Had we assumed $\lambda^* < 1$, we would also be facing a contradiction. We conclude that $a \in C(b, B) \Rightarrow C(b, B) \subseteq C(a, B)$ and therefore, $b \in C(a, B)$, so that $C(a, B) \subseteq C(b, B)$.

In the case where QCC* is satisfied, the proof is given in Deschamps and Gevers (1978). □

Lemma 7 (Transitivity). *If R^* satisfies SE^*, SP^* and either QCC^* or QRI^*, then $\forall M \subseteq S$, $\forall B$ associated with M, $\forall a, b \in B$, $C_a^B \subseteq C_b^B$ whenever $a \in C_b^B$.*

Proof. If $a \in C(b, B)$, then $C(a, B) = C(b, B)$ by Lemma 6, and $C_a^B = C_b^B$ by Remark 4.1.

If $a \in C_b^B \backslash C(b, B)$, $C(a, B) \subset C_b^B \backslash C(b, B)$ because $C(a, B)$ must be disjoint of $C(b, B)$ by Lemma 6 and because there is no hole in $C(a, B)$ or $C(b, B)$ by Lemma 4.

In view of Remark 4.1, we get then $C_a^B \subset C_b^B \backslash C(b, B)$. □

If R^* is quasi-co-cardinal (QCC*), our continuous approximation of R^* also satisfies a property called co-cardinality in the social choice literature. Similarly, if R^* satisfies QRI*, its continuous approximation is homothetic.

Lemma 8. *Suppose R^* satisfies SP^* and SE^*; $\forall M \subseteq S$, $\forall B$ associated with M, $\forall a, b, a', b' \in B$, $a' \in C_a^B$ iff $b' \in C_b^B$ whenever*

(a) *there exist two real numbers α, β (with $\beta > 0$) such that $\forall s \in M$, $b_s = \alpha + \beta a_s$, $b'_s = \alpha + \beta a'_s$ and R^* enjoys the quasi-co-cardinality (QCC^*) property*;

(b) *there exists a positive real number β such that $\forall s \in M$, $b_s = \beta a_s$, $b'_s = \beta a'_s$ and R^* enjoys the quasi-ratio-scale invariance (QRI^*) property.*

Proof. Case (a). Suppose first $M = S$, so that $B = \mathbb{R}^S$. Choose any $a, b, a', b' \in B$ satisfying the restriction expressed under (a). Consider next two sequences $(\alpha'), (\beta')$ where $(\alpha') \subset \mathbb{R}$, $(\beta') \subset Q_+$, $\beta' \to \beta$. Suppose $a' \in C_a^B$. Then there exists $(a') \subset B$, $a' \to a'$, $\forall t, a'R^*a$ and by QCC*, $\forall t, (\alpha' + \beta'a') \, R^* \, (\alpha' + \beta'a)$. Let us choose $\alpha' = \alpha + \max_{s \in M} \{(\beta - \beta')a_s\}$. Then, by construction, $\alpha' \to \alpha$, and by SP*, $\forall t, (\alpha' + \beta'a) \, R^* \, (\alpha + \beta a)$, so that, by transitivity, $(\alpha' + \beta'a') \, R^* \, (\alpha + \beta a) = b$. Moreover, $(\alpha' + \beta'a') \to (\alpha + \beta a') = b'$. In conclusion, $b' \in C_b^B$. If $M \subset S$, the same result holds by SE*.

Case (b) is proved analogously, by choosing a sequence (β') such that $\beta' \to \beta$, and $\forall t, \beta' > \beta$. □

We have observed that R^* satisfies both the strong Pareto property (SP*) and separability (SE*). This does not extend to its continuous approximation without further restrictions. This is the role of the "Freedom from local domination" assumption (FLD), which is prepared by the next lemma.

Lemma 9. *Suppose SP* holds true. For any $M \subseteq S, \forall B$ associated with M, if there exist $v \in M$, and $a, c \in B$ such that*

$$a_v = c_v \quad and \quad \forall s \in M, \ s \neq v, \ a_s > c_s,$$

whereas the set $\{a' \in B, a'_v = a_v, \forall s \in M \backslash \{v\}, \ a_s \geq a'_s \geq c_s\}$ is a subset of $C(b, B)$ for some $b \in B$, then state v dominates locally every other state of M.

Proof. Define $a^*, c^* \in B$ as follows:

$$a^*_v = a_v - \varepsilon, \qquad c^*_v = a_v + \varepsilon,$$

$a_t > a^*_t > c^*_t > c_t$, for some $t \in M \backslash \{v\}$, and $a_s > a^*_s = c^*_s > c_s, \forall s \in M \backslash \{v, t\}$. For every $\varepsilon > 0$, we observe that $a^* \in C^b_B \backslash C(b, B)$ (Remark 4.2) and $c^* \in C^B_b \backslash C(b, B)$ (Remark 4.1). By Lemma 5, $c^* \ P^* \ a^*$ for every $\varepsilon > 0$ such that $a^* \in B$ and we conclude that state v dominates state t locally. Because the same reasoning may be applied to every state of $M \backslash \{v\}$, we conclude that state v dominates locally every other state of M. $\square$

Our next task is to study the separability of our continuous approximation of R. This property requires two things:

(i) $\forall M \subseteq S, \forall B, B' \subset \mathbb{R}^S$ (resp., $\mathbb{R}^S_{++}$) associated with $M, \forall b \in B, \forall b' \in B'$, with $b_s = b'_s \ \forall s \in M, \ \forall a, c \in C(b, B), \ \exists a', c' \in C(b', B')$ such that $(a, c) \sigma_M (a', c')$; this is an obvious implication of the separability of R^*.

(ii) $\forall M \subseteq S, \forall v \in S, \forall B$ associated with $M, \forall B^*$ associated with $M \backslash \{s\}$ and such that $B^* \subset B, \forall b \in B^*, C(b, B^*) = C(b, B) \cap B^*$.

We want to show that this property holds under SP*, SE* and QCC* (resp. QRI*) unless there exists one state that is locally dominated by another.

Lemma 10. *Suppose R^* satisfies SP*, SE* and QCC* (resp. QRI*); either $\forall M \subseteq S, \ \forall v \in S, \ \forall B$ associated with $M, \forall B^* \subset B$ associated with $M \backslash \{v\}, \forall b \in B^*$, either $C(b, B^*) = C(b, B) \cap B^*$ or every state in $M \backslash \{v\}$ is locally dominated by state v.*

Proof. Suppose $\exists b \in \mathbb{R}^S$ (resp. $\mathbb{R}^S_{++}$), $\exists M \subseteq S$, $\exists v \in M$, $\exists B$ associated with M, $\exists B^* \subset B$ associated with $M\backslash\{v\}$ such that $C(b, B^*) \neq C(b, B) \cap B^*$. By definition, we must always have $C(b, B^*) \subseteq C(b, B) \cap B^*$. Our new assumption implies $C(b, B^*) \subset C(b, B) \cap B^*$. In view of Remark 4.3 in conjunction with Lemma 6, there must then be at least two distinct elements a and c along the diagonal of B^* such that $a \in C(b, B)$, $c \in C(b, B)$ and $c \notin C(a, B^*)$. W.l.o.g. we assume $a \gg_{B^*} c$. By Remarks 4.1 and 4.2, we notice that the set

$$\{a' \in B^*, a \geq_{B^*} a' \geq_{B^*} c\} \subset C(b, B).$$

There remains to apply Lemma 9. □

Lemma 11 (Extended Strong Pareto Principle). *Let W^* be the set of states that are not dominated locally. Suppose R^* satisfies SP*, SE* and QCC* (or QRI*). For every $M \subseteq W^*$, $\forall B$ associated with M, $\forall a, c \in B$ such that $\exists t \in M$ for which $a_t > c_t$ and $\forall s \in M\backslash\{t\}$, $a_s \geq c_s$, we must have $a \in C^B_c$ and $c \notin C^B_a$.*

Proof. By SP* we get $a P^* c$ and hence $a \in C^B_c$ and $c \in C^a_B$. We want to show that $c \notin C(a, B) = C^a_B \cap C^B_a$. If $a \gg_B c$, we apply Remark 4.2. In the other cases, we can single out one state v such that $a_v = c_v$ and collect all states t such that $a_t > c_t$, and consider the subset $N \subseteq M$ made up of v together with the latter states. We further consider $B^* \subset B$ associated with N and such that a and $c \in B^*$. Since we are dealing with $N \subseteq W^*$ we can apply Lemma 10 and state that $C(a, B^*) = C(a, B) \cap B^*$. Assume now that $c \in C(a, B)$. Then $c \in C(a, B^*)$ and by Remarks 4.1 and 4.2, and Lemma 6, we are in position to apply Lemma 9 and to recognize that $c \in C(a, B)$ leads to a contradiction. □

We finally get:

Proof of Theorem 2. By Deschamps and Gevers (1977), any ordering defined on $\mathbb{R}^S$ has a (two-way) expected utility representation if it is continuous, separable and satisfies both the cocardinality and strong Pareto requirements, and if, moreover, the number of undominated states is at least three. We apply this theorem to our continuous approximation of R^* for every B associated to the set of states that are free from local domination, which is assumed coextensive with W. The implication of $a \in C(b, B)$ for R^* is ambiguous, whereas we can guarantee that $a P^* b$ if $a \in C^B_b \backslash C(b, B)$. Hence, we have a one-way or weakly continuous expected utility representation.

In order to extend the theorem to the whole space, it is sufficient to apply Lemmas E and F of Deschamps and Gevers (1977). □

Proof of Theorem 3. By Blackorby and Donaldson (1982, Corollary 2.1), any ordering defined on $\mathbb{R}^{S}_{++}$ which is continuous, separable, satisfies ratio-scale comparability and the strong Pareto condition, and admits at least three undominated states can be represented by a mean of order r. We apply this theorem to our continuous approximation of R^* for every B associated with W. The rest follows as in the preceding proof. □

References

Aczél, J. (1966) *Lectures on Functional Equations and their Applications.* New York: Academic Press.

d'Aspremont, Cl. (1985) 'Axioms for social welfare orderings', in: L. Hurwicz, D. Schmeidler and H. Sonnenschein, eds., *Social Goals and Social Organization.* Cambridge: Cambridge University Press.

Aumann, R.J. (1987) 'Correlated equilibrium as an expression of Bayesian rationality', *Econometrica,* 55:1-18.

Bernoulli, D. (1738) 'Specimen theoriae novae de mensura sortis', translated in: *Econometrica,* 1954:23-36.

Blackorby, C., R. Davidson and D. Donaldson (1977) 'A homiletic exposition of the expected utility hypothesis', *Economica,* 44:351-358.

Blackorby, C. and D. Donaldson (1982) 'Ratio-scale and translation-scale full interpersonal comparability without domain restrictions: Admissible social-evaluation functions', *International Economic Review,* 23:249-268.

Debreu, G. (1959) 'Topological methods in cardinal utility theory' in: K.J. Arrow, S. Karlin and P. Suppes, eds., *Mathematical Methods in the Social Sciences.* Stanford, CA: Stanford University Press, pp. 16-26.

Deschamps, R. and L. Gevers (1977) 'Separability, risk-bearing and social welfare judgements', *European Economic Review,* 10:77-94.

Deschamps, R. and L. Gevers (1978) 'Leximin and utilitarian rules: A joint characterization', *Journal of Economic Theory,* 17:143-163.

Drèze, J.H. (1987) 'Decision theory with moral hazard and state-dependent preferences', in: *Essays on Economic Decisions under Uncertainty.* Cambridge: Cambridge University Press, pp. 23-89.

Eichhorn, W. (1973) 'Characterization of the CES production functions by quasi-linearity', in: W. Eichhorn, R. Henn, O. Spitz and R. Shephard, eds., *Production Theory.* Berlin: Springer, pp. 21-33.

Fishburn, P.C. (1988) *Nonlinear Preference and Utility Theory.* Wheatsheaf Books Ltd.

Krantz, D.H., R.D. Luce, P. Suppes and A. Tversky (1971) *Foundations of Measurement.* New York: Academic Press.

Machina, M. (1987) *The Journal of Economic Perspectives,* 1:121-154.

Neumann, J. von and O. Morgenstern (1944) *Theory of Games and Economic Behavior.* Princeton, NJ: Princeton University Press.

Savage, L.J. (1954) *The Foundations of Statistics.* New York: Wiley.

Shapley, L.S. (1975) 'Cardinal utility representations from intensity comparisons', Report R-1683-PR. Santa Monica, CA: The Rand Corporation.

Suppes, P. and M. Winet (1955) 'An axiomatization of utility based on the notion of utility differences', *Management Science,* 1:259-270.

Chapter 5

OPTIMAL PUBLIC SECTOR EMPLOYMENT POLICY WITH ENDOGENOUS INVOLUNTARY UNEMPLOYMENT

Robin BOADWAY

Queen's University, Kingston, Ont., Canada

Maurice MARCHAND

IAG and CORE, Université Catholique de Louvain, Louvain-la-Neuve, Belgium

Pierre PESTIEAU

Université de Liège, Liège, Belgium, and CORE, Université Catholique de Louvain, Louvain-la-Neuve, Belgium

1. Introduction

The question of appropriate rules for public sector hiring policy in the presence of unemployment has been prominent in the literature on cost-benefit analysis. Most of the results to date have been derived in the context of fixed-wage models of unemployment. Perhaps the best known of these are the analyses of shadow wage rates in developing countries by Little and Mirrlees (1968) and by Dasgupta, Marglin and Sen (1972), further summarized in Sen (1972). The models used there simply postulate a fixed wage above the market clearing level in the industrial sector and a subsistence wage in the rural sector and analyze the consequences for project evaluation. Abstracting from other issues, such as the effect of hiring on savings and

We would like to thank Helmuth Cremer for helpful comments on an earlier version.

Economic Decision-Making: Games, Econometrics and Optimisation
Edited by J.J. Gabszewicz, J.-F. Richard and L.A. Wolsey
© *Elsevier Science Publishers B.V., 1990*

income distribution, the conventional result here is a shadow wage for industrial projects below the market wage.

A related area of analysis incorporates a labour market equilibrating mechanism which induces involuntary unemployment into a model incorporating the fixed-wage assumption. Two studies of this sort are Harberger (1971) and Harris and Todaro (1970). Shadow wages derived in the context of this model will, under certain conditions, equal market wages, and will in any case be much closer to market wages than under the earlier models.[1] Thus, in these models, the case for using public hiring partly to address unemployment is weak or non-existent.

These models rely on exogenously-fixed wages to generate unemployment and hence have been dubbed naive. There is now a considerable literature on labour markets which generate unemployment through wages being set too high endogenously, so-called *efficiency wages*.[2] The basic idea of these models (which goes back at least to Stiglitz, 1974, and Solow, 1979) is that wages are positively correlated with productivity at the firm level. The purpose of this paper is to investigate the role for public sector hiring and wage policies in models of efficiency wage.

There are various reasons for wages to be positively correlated with productivity. The two most prominent ones are shirking and turnover costs, and our analysis will concentrate on these two. According to the shirking model, high wages which induce unemployment are necessary to discipline workers not to shirk, since the possibility of being unemployed increases the cost of being caught shirking.[3] In the turnover model, high wages reduce the attractiveness of turnover and save turnover costs to the firm.[4] In either case, the wage is set above the market clearing level with the consequence that unemployment is induced.

The main concern of efficiency wage models has been positive analysis (see, e.g., Carmichael, 1987). They aim to provide a coherent explanation of why firms may find it unprofitable to cut wages in the presence of involuntary unemployment. With few exceptions (one being Shapiro and Stiglitz, 1984), the normative policy implications are not addressed. Normative concerns raise the issue of whether full employment is a relevant policy objective, and, if so, what instruments ought to be used to pursue it. The

---

[1] In Harberger's version of the model, where the wages in the urban and rural sectors are given, the shadow wage is precisely the market wage. More generally, as discussed in Boadway and Bruce (1984), the shadow wage will be less than the market wage when, as in Harris and Todaro, there is diminishing marginal product of labour.

[2] A good survey may be found in Akerlof and Yellen (1986).

[3] See Shapiro and Stiglitz (1984) and Bulow and Summers (1986).

[4] See Stiglitz (1974) and Salop (1979).

standard policy instrument used in these models is the wage subsidy to increase employment. In a recent survey, Johnson and Layard (1986) analyze the effect of an employment subsidy in a labour turnover model. They compare a per capita subsidy to a proportional wage subsidy and show that the latter has no effect on unemployment while the former decreases it. This result is quite intuitive and robust. A proportional subsidy affects equally the firm's marginal cost from raising its relative wage and the marginal benefit of reduced turnover costs. By contrast, a per capita subsidy just reduces the marginal benefit of quitting. In their paper on shirking, Shapiro and Stiglitz (1984) show that a subsidy on wages is also desirable to boost employment. Yet, as non-shirking is incompatible with full employment, even a very large subsidy cannot fully eradicate unemployment. Note that these results are consistent with those found in naive fixed price models, in which employment subsidies are also desirable.

Another policy instrument which could also be contemplated concerns unemployment compensation. In naive models, an increase in unemployment compensation generates employment; wages and prices are assumed to be fixed, while aggregate demand is stimulated by that increase. In the shirking and labour turnover versions of the efficiency wage models, firms will have to raise their wages following an increase in unemployment compensation so as to induce workers not to shirk or quit. This results in higher unemployment. The appropriate policy could be to decrease unemployment compensation.

With the exception of Stiglitz (1974), public employment policy has not been envisioned in the efficiency wage literature as a policy instrument, whereas it is widely discussed in the naive fixed-wage models. Even Stiglitz' treatment is aimed at unemployment in developing countries. On the basis of a labour turnover model, he shows that a national output maximizing government is unlikely to restore full employment even though it controls both employment and wages in the public sector. In other words, full employment would be too costly to be implemented. This raises the question of the relevant objective function. Shapiro and Stiglitz as well as Bulow and Summers (1986) study the subsidy that maximizes total economic surplus. Doing so, they assume implicitly that all individuals are treated identically towards employment. In this paper, we adopt the same approach; that is, we focus on efficiency considerations and assume away all equity aspects.

Before proceeding further, two remarks are in order. They concern the objections raised towards the relevancy of efficiency wage models and what is meant by public employment policy. Efficiency wage theory in general and in its various versions has been subject to a range of critiques which are nicely summarized in Carmichael (1987). We are well aware of them, but note that all unemployment theories have their limits and among them the efficiency wage theory stands up quite well. It does not explain all kinds of unemployment, but bears some relevance for cases where factors such as shirking or turnover costs play an important role. Further, the gist of this paper is rather to illustrate the extreme sensitivity of public employment policy to the specification of the unemployment model selected. That sensitivity is obvious when shifting from the naive fixed-wage models to the efficiency wage models and also when going from one to another version of these latter models. Even within the same version, whether there is free entry or not and whether a wage subsidy is available or not can make a difference.

Throughout the paper we analyze the case for active public sector employment policy in an economy experiencing a lasting spell of unemployment jointly with wages higher than their market clearing levels. By active, we mean that public firms will adopt an employment and wage policy which is different from that which would be adopted by private sector firms in the same circumstances.

2. Public employment policy in the shirking model

2.1. The Shapiro–Stiglitz model

The basic model we use to illustrate shirking is similar to that of Shapiro and Stiglitz (1984), though with a public sector added, and with the possibility of free entry in the private sector. There are other variants of the shirking model which could be used, and they would yield qualitatively similar results.[5] The economy consists of a single sector of n identical firms each of which selects a wage rate[6] w and a level of employment L. There are S identical workers who can choose either to supply an exogenously fixed amount of effort e or to shirk and provide zero effort. When shirking, their

---

[5] For example, we could use a two-sector model, or dual labour market model, as in Bulow and Summers (1986). Also, we could allow for shirking to be a continuous variable rather than simply a shirking-no shirking choice.

[6] In a more general version, firms might also be allowed to select a wage rate (e.g., unemployment insurance) to be paid to layed-off workers. We ignore that possibility here. Note that while Shapiro and Stiglitz assume an exogenously-given number of firms, one of the things we investigate is the consequences of free entry for their results and public employment policy.

productivity is zero. Their utility function is linear in income and effort so $u(w, e) = w - e$. Information is imperfect and those shirking will be caught with a probability p. If caught, they are fired and enter the unemployment pool. In addition to being fired for shirking, workers also face an exogenous separation (quit) probability q. Once unemployed, workers are rehired randomly with π being the instantaneous rate of rehiring.

Workers can be in one of three states — employed and shirking, employed and not shirking, and unemployed. Each of these states has a discounted present value of utility associated with it: V_E^S, V_E^N, and V_U, respectively. Shapiro and Stiglitz show that the following relationships must exist among them:

$$rV_E^S = w + (q + p)(V_U - V_E^S), \tag{1}$$

$$rV_E^N = w - e + q(V_U - V_E^N), \tag{2}$$

$$rV_U = \pi(V_E^N - V_U), \tag{3}$$

where r is the interest rate.[7] These equations are all like asset equilibrium equations. They state that the "rate of return" to being in a particular state equals the flow income from being in that state plus the expected capital gain. Note that the only decision workers take here is the decision whether or not to shirk.

The labour market is in equilibrium when the wage and employment levels set by each employer are the best for it, given that other employers behave the same. As Shapiro and Stiglitz show, the wage will be set so as just to induce no shirking by the workers. That is, $V_E^N \geq V_E^S$, or, from (1) and (2),

$$w \geq rV_U + (r + q + p)e/p. \tag{4}$$

This is the so-called no-shirking condition (NSC) that guarantees that workers will not shirk. Eliminating V_U from (4) using (2) and (3) gives

$$w \geq e + (r + q + \pi)e/p. \tag{5}$$

This version of the NSC determines the wage that must be set by the firm. Note that $\pi = qnL/(S - nL)$, which follows from the equality of flows into and out of the unemployment pool in the steady state. Then, (5) alone

---

[7] Equations (1) and (2) take V_U as given and derive the value to the worker of shirking or not shirking, given that he is employed. For the shirking case, over a small interval of time $[0, t]$, $V_E^S = wt + (1 - rt)[(q + p)tV_U + (1 - (q + p)t)V_E^S]$. Solving for V_E^S and taking limits as t approaches 0 yields (1). A similar derivation holds for (2). The third equation is derived in an analogous way and holds in equilibrium when workers do not shirk.

guarantees unemployment since with full employment $\pi = \infty$. Firms will select w to satisfy (5) with equality in equilibrium.

Output is produced according to a concave production function $F(L)$. Firms' hiring policy will be to set $w = F'(L)$. Using this, and the fact that $\pi = qnL/(S - nL)$, we can write the labour market equilibrium condition as

$$F'(L) = e + [qS/(S - nL) + r]e/p. \tag{6}$$

This equation determines L as a function of the exogenous variables to the problem (e, q, N, r, p and n). We refer to this fixed-n case as the *no-entry case*.

With free entry, n becomes endogenous. We assume that each firm has a fixed cost K and that all firms are identical. The number of firms is determined by the zero profit condition:

$$F(L) - wL - K = 0.$$

This condition, together with (6), determines n and L in terms of the remaining exogenous variables. We refer to this as the *free-entry case*.

2.2. Public employment policy in the no-entry case

Our purpose is to amend this single-sector model by adding a public sector and to investigate labour policy in the public sector. The results we obtain depend upon the assumptions we make about the detection and separation probabilities in the two sectors (p and q). Workers are always assumed to be identical, and the unemployment pools are homogeneous.

Using the subscripts 1 and 2 to denote private and public sectors respectively, the addition of public sector employment changes the instantaneous hiring rate in each sector to

$$\pi_1 = \frac{q_1 nL_1}{S - nL_1 - L_2}, \qquad \pi_2 = \frac{q_2 L_2}{S - nL_1 - L_2}, \tag{7}$$

where π_1 is the rate of hiring in the private sector and π_2 is the rate of hiring in the public sector. Workers are assumed to take the first job offered to them, whether in the public or the private sector. It can be shown that this will be the case if the following conditions hold:[8]

$$w_2 - e \geq (w_1 - e)\pi_1/(\pi_1 + q_1 + r), \qquad w_1 - e \geq (w_2 - e)\pi_2/(\pi_2 + q_2 + r).$$

---

[8] If unemployed individuals accept any offered job, their expected lifetime utility is given by V_U in equation (19) below. They will do so if their utility is larger than that reached by accepting only jobs in either the private sector or the public sector. If they accept only jobs in the private sector, their expected lifetime utility would be $\pi_1(w_1 - e)/(r + \pi_1 + q_1)$. This can be proved by using (1), (2) and (3) with the appropriate subscripts and the NSC condition with equality ($V_E^S = V_E^N$). It is lower than V_U iff the first of the two following conditions is satisfied. Likewise for the second condition.

We assume these conditions apply. We consider first the case in which p and q are identical across sectors, and then allow them to differ.

In the first case in which $q_1 = q_2$, the economy-wide hiring rate can be expressed as

$$\pi = \frac{q(nL_1 + L_2)}{S - nL_1 - L_2}.\tag{8}$$

The same NSC applies in the public and private sectors, and both sectors offer the same wage w.[9] Labour market equilibrium becomes simply

$$F'(L_1) = e + [qS/(S - nL_1 - L_2) + r]e/p.\tag{9}$$

This generates an equilibrium L_1 which depends on the exogenous variables and public sector employment L_2. In particular, differentiation of (9) yields

$$\frac{\partial nL_1}{\partial L_2} = \left[\frac{F''}{n} - \frac{q}{p}\frac{eS}{U^2}\right]^{-1}\frac{q}{p}\frac{eS}{U^2} \equiv -\alpha,\tag{10}$$

where U denotes the number of unemployed $(S - nL_1 - L_2)$. From (10), $0 < \alpha \le 1$ with the equality applying when $F'' = 0$. Thus, increases in public employment reduce private employment and generally increase w.

This result can be given a simple geometric interpretation. Figure 1 depicts an equilibrium allocation of L_1 as the intersection of a marginal product

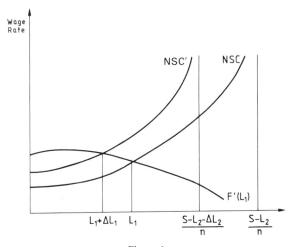

Figure 1.

[9] The proof is sketched in footnote 12 that the public sector will offer no higher wage than that required to satisfy the NSC. That implies, in this context, that the public sector wage will be w, the same as in the private sector.

of labour curve $F'(L_1)$ and the NSC curve. The latter is the right hand side of (9). An increase in L_2 shifts the NSC curve horizontally to the left by $\Delta L_2/n$ since L_2 and nL_1 enter symmetrically in the NSC. This causes aggregate private sector employment to fall by less than ΔL_2 as long as $F'(L_1)$ is downward sloping. In the special case of $F''(L_1) = 0$, $\Delta L_1 = -\Delta L_2/n$, or $\alpha = -1$.

Optimal public sector behaviour in this model involves maximizing total output net of the costs of effort.[10] Letting $G(L_2)$ be the production technology in the public sector, the planner's problem is to maximize social welfare denoted by Ω:

$$\underset{L_2}{\text{Max}} \quad \Omega = nF[L_1(L_2)] + G(L_2) - e(nL_1(L_2) + L_2). \tag{11}$$

The first-order condition is:

$$-(F' - e)\alpha + (G' - e) = 0 \quad \text{or} \quad G' = \alpha w + (1 - \alpha)e. \tag{12}$$

Since $w > e$ and $0 < \alpha \le 1$, this implies that

$$e < G' \le w, \tag{13}$$

with the equality applying when $F'' = 0$. Thus, if $F'' < 0$, the public sector will encourage employment overall by hiring labour beyond the point at which its wage equals the marginal product. This is consistent with the Shapiro–Stiglitz finding that employment is inefficiently low in the private sector and therefore should be encouraged. They consider a per capita wage subsidy as a policy instrument. We return to that below.

Equivalently, we can derive a shadow wage in this model by evaluating the perturbation in total net output from a change in L_2 starting from an arbitrary equilibrium. From (11),

$$\partial\Omega/\partial L_2 = -(F' - e)\alpha + G' - e = G' - \alpha w - (1 - \alpha)e.$$

A project evaluator in the public sector could proceed by costing labour inputs at the shadow wage $\alpha w + (1 - \alpha)e$. This has the conventional intuitive interpretation that the shadow wage is a weighted average of the opportunity cost of attracting labour from the private sector (w) and from unemployment (e) where the weights are the proportions in which additional hiring comes from these two sources.

---

[10] We ignore complications that will arise if the public firm is producing public goods. The benefit of public sector employment is evaluated as the market value of output it produces.

The analysis is somewhat more complicated when public firms differ from private firms in p and q. In this case, NSC equations analogous to (4) will apply to each sector and will be

$$w_1 \geq rV_U + (r + q_1 + p_1)e/p_1, \qquad w_2 \geq rV_U + (r + q_2 + p_2)e/p_2. \tag{14}$$

It can be readily shown that these conditions apply with equality.[11] This immediately gives the following relationship between w_1 and w_2:

$$w_2 = w_1 + e[(r + q_2)/p_2 - (r + q_1)/p_1]. \tag{15}$$

When workers take the first jobs offered, (2) and (3) become:

$$rV_{E_1}^N = w_1 - e + q_1(V_U - V_{E_1}^N), \tag{16}$$

$$rV_{E_2}^N = w_2 - e + q_2(V_U - V_{E_2}^N), \tag{17}$$

$$rV_U = \pi_1(V_{E_1}^N - V_U) + \pi_2(V_{E_2}^N - V_U). \tag{18}$$

Solving for V_U yields

$$V_U = \frac{\pi_1(w_1 - e)(r + q_2) + \pi_2(w_2 - e)(r + q_1)}{r(r + q_1)(r + q_2) + \pi_1 r(r + q_2) + \pi_2 r(r + q_1)}. \tag{19}$$

Substituting this into the NSC for the private sector in (14) and using (15) and (7), we obtain

$$w_1 = F'(L_1) = e\left[\frac{r + q_1}{p_1} + 1 + \frac{q_1 nL_1}{p_1(S - nL_1 - L_2)} + \frac{q_2 L_2}{p_2(S - nL_1 - L_2)}\right]. \tag{20}$$

This is the labour market equilibrium condition in this economy. It determines L_1 in terms of the exogenous parameters and public employment L_2. Total differentiation yields

$$n\frac{\partial L_1}{\partial L_2} = \frac{q_2 e/(p_2 U) + e\pi_1/(p_1 U) + e\pi_2/(p_2 U)}{F''/n - q_1 e/(p_1 U) - e\pi_1/(p_1 U) - e\pi_2/(p_2 U)} \equiv -\alpha. \tag{21}$$

In this case, $\alpha > 0$; but $\alpha \gtrless 1$ depending on parameter values. In particular, $\alpha > 1$ iff $q_2/p_2 > -F''U/(ne) + q_1/p_1$. For example, if q_2/p_2 is large enough relative to q_1/p_1, it is possible for $\alpha > 1$, that is, for public hiring actually to increase unemployment. Note that if $q_1/p_1 = q_2/p_2$, the results for this case reduce to those for the previous case given by (10). Thus, absolute

---

[11] The main lines of the proof of this are as follows. We first substitute (19) into the first equation of the NSC conditions (14), which is satisfied with equality by the private firms. This gives w_1 as a function of w_2. Differentiating this function totally with respect to w_2 allows one to prove that dL_1/dw_2 is negative. So, $d\Omega/dw_2 = n[F'(L_1) - e]\,dL_1/dw_2 < 0$, and it is socially optimal to satisfy the second condition in (14) with equality.

differences in q_i and p_i only matter in so far as they affect the relative values of q_i/p_i across the two sectors.

Optimization in this model involves solving the same problem (11) as before, but now with the altered relationship between nL_1 and L_2. As before,

$$G' = \alpha F' + (1 - \alpha)e = \alpha w_1 + (1 - \alpha)e.$$

In this case, $e < G' \gtreqless w_1$ with $G' \gtreqless w_1$ as $\alpha \gtreqless 1$. Equivalently, the shadow wage is now $\alpha w_1 + (1 - \alpha)e$ at any arbitrary equilibrium. This will be $\gtreqless w_1$ as $\alpha \gtreqless 1$. Thus, the relationship between the marginal product in the public sector and the private sector wage depends upon whether α is greater than or less than one; that is, whether public hiring increases or decreases aggregate employment, $nL_1 + L_2$. Given (15), it is also the case that w_2 can be greater than or less than w_1. Thus, we cannot say *a priori* whether or not public firms should hire beyond the point at which its wage equals its marginal product.

2.3. Public employment policy with free entry

The above results were derived within the confines of the Shapiro-Stiglitz model where the number of firms in the private sector are given and there are no fixed costs. In this context, pure profits would be generated whenever $F'' < 0$. It is useful to see how the results stand up when the profits are competed away by free entry. As mentioned earlier, we suppose each firm has a fixed cost of operation K.[12] The number of firms is determined endogenously by the zero profit condition:

$$F(L_1) - w_1 L_1 - K = 0. \tag{22}$$

Market equilibrium now consists of two conditions. In the case in which q and p are identical across sectors and the NSC applies, these conditions are given by (9) and (22). These equations simultaneously determine n and L_1 in terms of the exogenous parameters and L_2. A comparative static analysis yields

$$\frac{\partial L_1}{\partial L_2} = 0, \qquad \frac{\partial n}{\partial L_2} = -\frac{1}{L_1}, \qquad \frac{\partial(nL_1 + L_2)}{\partial L_2} = 0. \tag{23}$$

That is, a change in public employment has no effect on either the number of workers per firm or on total employment. It merely reduces the number of firms in the private sector.

---

[12] This formulation for the free entry case is similar to that used by Salop (1979).

The optimal level of public employment is obtained as the solution to the following problem:

$$\underset{L_2}{\text{Max}} \quad \Omega = n(L_2)F(L_1)+G(L_2)-e(n(L_2)L_1+L_2)-n(L_2)K. \tag{24}$$

The first-order conditions give, using (22) and (23),

$$G' = F' = w. \tag{25}$$

A differential analysis confirms that the shadow wage for public project evaluation is the market wage w. Therefore, the existence of free entry removes the need for using public employment as a policy instrument when q and p are the same across sectors.

Things are again somewhat more complicated when q and p differ between the public and private sectors. In this case, the labour market equilibrium conditions become (20) and (22). Comparative static analysis yields $\partial L_1/\partial L_2 = 0$ and

$$\frac{\partial(nL_1)}{\partial L_2} = L_1 \frac{\partial n}{\partial L_2} \equiv -\beta, \tag{26}$$

where

$$\beta \equiv \left[\frac{q_2}{p_2 U}+\frac{q_1 n L_1}{p_1 U^2}+\frac{q_2 L_2}{p_2 U^2}\right]\Big/\left[\frac{q_1}{p_1 U}+\frac{q_1 n L_1}{p_1 U^2}+\frac{q_2 L_2}{p_2 U^2}\right]. \tag{27}$$

Notice that β is equivalent to α with the term involving the F'' absent. Analogously, note that $\beta \gtreqless 1$ as $(q_2/p_2) \gtreqless (q_1/p_1)$. Therefore, $\partial(nL_1 + L_2)/\partial L_2 \gtreqless 0$ as $(q_1/p_1) \gtreqless (q_2/p_2)$. Conventional wisdom would be that $q_1 > q_2$ and $p_1 > p_2$. In this case, the effect on total employment of an increase in L_2 is ambiguous in sign.

Solving problem (24) for this case, using (22) and (26), yields

$$G' = \beta F'+(1-\beta)e = \beta w_1+(1-\beta)e. \tag{28}$$

Therefore,

$$G' \gtreqless w_1 \quad \text{as} \quad (q_2/p_2) \gtreqless (q_1/p_1).$$

Again, it is the relative sizes of the ratios q_i/p_i that are relevant. A differential analysis yields the shadow wage in this case to be $\beta w_1 + (1-\beta)e$, a weighted average of w_1 and e. The existence of free entry in this case also apparently reduces the case for public employment. An interesting point to note here, as well as in the no-entry case is that in the weighted-average formula the public sector does not use its own wage w_2 for (small) project evaluation.

Instead, it uses the private sector wage w_1. Its own wage is used independently for other purposes. The two wages are related via (15) which indicates that $w_2 \gtrless w_1$ as $(r + q_2)/p_2 \gtrless (r + q_1)/p_1$. Thus, similar circumstances that call for restricting public employment, $(q_2/p_2) > (q_1/p_1)$, also tend to raise the public sector wage vis-a-vis that in the private sector. That is all that can be said.

2.4. Social optimality in the presence of per capita wage subsidies

We have so far investigated the use of public employment (and public sector wages) as a policy instrument when no other instruments are used. Shapiro and Stiglitz (1984) in their welfare analysis considered the use of wage subsidies in a model with no entry and argued that as long as $F'' < 0$, per capita wage subsidies could increase social welfare.

This result can be shown in our no-entry model with no public sector. Shapiro and Stiglitz characterize a social optimum as the solution to the following problem:

$$\underset{L}{\text{Max}} \qquad \Omega = nF(L) - nK - neL$$

$$\text{subject to} \quad [F(L) - K]/L - e[1 + qS/(S - nL) + r] \geq 0. \qquad (29)$$

Notice that the constraint that labour receives its average product net of fixed costs (recalling that $w = e[1 + qS/(S - nL) + r]$) effectively restricts the total amount of wage subsidy not to exceed the rents of the firm. Assuming that $F'(S/n) > e$ (implying that without imperfect information, full employment would be optimal), Ω is monotonically increasing in L for any $L \leq S/n$. Since the right hand side of the constraint approaches $-\infty$ as nL approaches S, the constraint must ultimately bind. At the market equilibrium, (9) applies and, assuming pure profits exist, $[F(L) - K]/L > F'(L)$. Therefore, the constraint is not binding and social welfare can be enhanced by increasing L. Let s be the per capita wage subsidy. The optimal subsidy is the one which makes $F'(L) + s = [F(L) - K]/L$. Thus, the subsidy is equal to rents per capita. It does not eliminate unemployment.

The optimal and market solutions are illustrated in Figure 2. The market equilibrium is at A where the NSC and $F'(L)$ curves intersect. The Shapiro-Stiglitz optimum occurs at B where the NSC intersects the $[F(L) - K]/L$ curve. The subsidy supporting this optimum is shown as s.

It is interesting to extend the Shapiro–Stiglitz notion of social optimality to the free-entry case. In this case, entry ensures that $[F(L) - K]/L = F'(L)$ by (22) so the optimal employment per firm is achieved. In Figure 2, entry

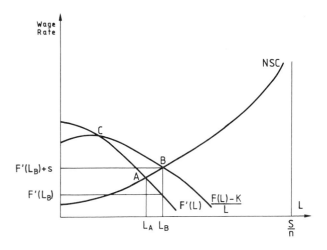

Figure 2.

occurs until the NSC intersects both the $F'(L)$ and the $[F(L)-K]/L$ curves simultaneously. This is shown as the point C. The only issue is whether or not the number of firms is optimal. To show that it is, differentiate Ω with respect to n to obtain

$$\frac{d\Omega}{dn} = [F(L)-K-eL] + n[F'(L)-e]\frac{dL}{dn}$$

where, using (29),

$$\frac{dL}{dn} = \frac{eqSL/(pU^2)}{F'(L)/L-[F(L)-K]/L^2-eqSn/(pU^2)} = -\frac{L}{n}.$$

Therefore, $d\Omega/dn = 0$ and the number of firms, as well as the number of workers per firm, is optimal. Thus, free entry generates social optimality in the Shapiro–Stiglitz sense, and there appears to be no role for public employment or subsidy policy.

However, these results on optimality are contingent on the implicit assumption made by Shapiro and Stiglitz that wage subsidies be financed out of taxes on rents. That is, the total wage bill for a firm inclusive of the subsidy is limited to total output net of fixed costs in the private sector (i.e., constraint (29) which is also found in Shapiro and Stiglitz). Suppose, however, that we allow wage subsidies to be financed by general lump-sum taxes. We find then that wage subsidies can improve social welfare in both the no-entry and the free-entry cases. Furthermore, we obtain the following general results:

(i) Welfare is monotonically increasing in wage subsidies financed by lump-sum taxes. Thus, there is no internal solution to the optimal wage subsidy problem; the subsidy should be indefinitely large.[13]

(ii) The existence of wage subsidies of whatever (finite) magnitude has no bearing on the form of the rules for optimal public employment and wages. The earlier analysis continues to apply in the presence of wage subsidies.

To see this, consider the simple case in which q and p are the same across sectors and there is a fixed number of firms. The firm sets the marginal product of labour to the net-of-subsidy wage ($w - s$), and the labour market equilibrium condition (9) becomes

$$F'(L_1) = e + (qS/(S - nL_1 - L_2) + r)e/p - s. \qquad (30)$$

This equation determines L_1 as a function of both L_2 and s where $\partial L_1/\partial L_2$ is given by (10) and

$$n\frac{\partial L_1}{\partial s} = -\left[F'' - \frac{q}{p}\frac{eS}{U^2}\right]^{-1}. \qquad (31)$$

Note that $n\partial L_1/\partial s > 0$ is independent of whether $F'' = 0$ or <0. The optimization problem (11) is amended to

$$\underset{L_2, s}{\text{Max}} \quad \Omega = nF[L_1(L_2, s)] + g(L_2) - e(nL_1(L_2, s) + L_2).$$

The first-order conditions on L_2 yield (12) and (13) as before, demonstrating point (ii) above. The condition on s is

$$(F' - e)\partial L_1/\partial s = 0. \qquad (32)$$

Since $F' > e$ for all values of $L_1 \leq N$, eq. (32) has no internal solution. The subsidy should be indefinitely large. Furthermore, if one imposes arbitrary limits on the size of the wage subsidy, the policy rules on L_2 are unaffected.

This result can be seen in the above figures. The subsidy drives a wedge between the wage received by the workers on the NSC curve and the wage used for hiring decisions on the marginal productivity curve. As the NSC curve is asymptotically vertical, the subsidy should be increased indefinitely, unless there is some institutionally-imposed limit on it.

---

[13] Note that Shapiro and Stiglitz obtained a finite optimal subsidy by implicitly restricting subsidies to those that could be financed out of the rents in the private sector. Their optimal subsidy is therefore identically equal to the difference between the average and marginal products of labour.

The same results go through in the more general models considered earlier — those with q and p differing across the two sectors, and those with free entry. For example, consider the case in which q and p differ and there is free entry. The equilibrium conditions are now the zero profit condition (22) and the labour market equilibrium:

$$F'(L_1) = e\left[\frac{r+q_1}{p_1} + 1 + \frac{q_1 n L_1}{p_1 U} + \frac{q_2 L_2}{p_2 U}\right] - s. \tag{33}$$

Comparative static analysis of this two-equation system yields $\partial L_1/\partial L_2 = 0$ and $L_1 \partial n/\partial L_2 = -\beta$ as before, and now $\partial L_1/\partial s = 0$ and

$$\frac{\partial n}{\partial s} = \left[\frac{eq_1 n L_1}{p_1 U^2} + \frac{eq_1 L_1}{p_1 U} + \frac{eq_2 L_2}{p_2 U^2}\right]^{-1} L_1^{-1} > 0. \tag{34}$$

Solving the analogue of (24) for this case yields (28) as before as well as

$$(F'-e)\partial n/\partial s = 0. \tag{35}$$

Since $(F'-e) > 0$ and $\partial n/\partial s > 0$, this problem has no internal solution; an indefinitely large wage subsidy is called for. This illustrates the general result for this case. It is a simple matter of taxonomic calculation to show that the same results apply for the other possible cases.

This concludes our analysis of public employment policy in the shirking version of the efficiency wage model. We have derived optimal rules for public employment and have shown that the case for using public employment as an instrument for increasing aggregate employment depends on whether or not there is free entry in the private sector, and whether or not q and p differ between sectors. Free entry reduces the case for public employment stimulation. The higher is q_1/p_1 relative to q_2/p_2, the greater is the case for public employment. The possible existence of wage subsidies as an additional instrument has no qualitative effect on the public employment decision rules. We turn now to the turnover version of the efficiency wage model.

3. Public employment policy in the turnover model

3.1. The Salop model

In the turnover model, as in the shirking model, productivity is positively correlated with the wage rate, and firms exploit that relationship in their wage-setting policies. However, here the source of that relationship differs considerably. Whereas in the shirking model a higher wage increases the penalty on workers found shirking and thereby induces less shirking, in the turnover model a higher wage reduces the incentive for workers to quit and allows the firms to economize on turnover costs. In other words, the quit parameter q used above is made endogenous. The consequence of all firms using wage policy in this manner can be to induce an equilibrium wage rate in excess of the full employment wage, causing involuntary unemployment.

The essence of the turnover model is captured in the stylized version of Salop (1979). We use this version in both a free-entry and no-entry framework as the basis for our analysis of public employment policy.[14] In the Salop model, firms take as given the amount of "tightness" in the labour market and set their own wage accordingly to obtain the profit-maximizing level of turnover. Consider first the behaviour of a typical firm in such a model. Following Salop, let z be an index of labour market tightness, treated as parametric by the firm. It can be interpreted as the average of economy-wide wages adjusted by the probability of getting a job, and perhaps also adjusted for non-pecuniary utility differentials. If the wage w is offered by this firm, the firm's quit rate q is assumed to depend upon its own wage relative to labour market tightness z. Thus, let $q = Q(w/z)$, where $Q' < 0$ and $Q'' > 0$. Total employment of the firm is denoted L, and N is the number of new hires. The firm's output depends upon L according to a concave production function $F(L)$. Turnover costs are an increasing concave function of new hires, $T(N)$. The firm's hires N will equal its quits qL, or,

$$N = Q(w/z)L. \tag{36}$$

The firm also faces a fixed cost K.

Normalizing output prices to unity, the firm's problem is

$$\underset{L,w}{\text{Max}} \quad F(L) - wL - T[Q(w/z)L] - K, \tag{37}$$

where we have used (36) in the turnover cost function $T(N)$. The first-order conditions for this problem yield

$$F'(L) = w + Q(w/z)T'(N), \tag{38}$$

$$L = -T'(N)Q'(w/z)L/z. \tag{39}$$

The first of these indicates that hiring should go to the point at which the marginal product equals the wage plus the cost of the induced flow of

---

[14] Again, as with the shirking model, there are other versions of the turnover model, such as in Stiglitz (1974). They differ in detail but not in substance.

turnover associated with one more worker. The second says that the cost of increasing the wage (i.e., L) equals the benefit of reduced turnover costs, where $Q'L/z$ is the fall in turnover resulting from an increase in w. These two first-order conditions together with (36) implicitly determine L, w and N as functions of z, which is exogenous to the firm.

It can be shown by conventional comparative static analysis that the following properties apply

$$L = L(z), \qquad L' < 0, \tag{40}$$

$$w/z = W(z), \qquad W' < 0, \tag{41}$$

$$N = N(z), \qquad N' \gtreqless 0 \quad \text{as} \quad -F'' \gtreqless -T'Q''Qw/(Q'L). \tag{42}$$

Following Salop, we assume that the absolute value of $F''(L)$ is small enough such that $N'(z) < 0$.

The variable z is determined in the labour market as a whole. Assuming that all firms have the same technology and are symmetric in non-pecuniary benefits relative to worker's preferences, all firms will offer the same wage w in equilibrium and the degree of market tightness z will be given by the probability-adjusted wage rate:

$$z = \pi w, \tag{43}$$

where π is the instantaneous rate of being hired from the pool of unemployed. The pool of unemployed consists of the involuntarily unemployed. Salop also included the frictionally unemployed in the pool. Frictional unemployment is not accounted for in the present formulation since we have chosen to treat time as a continuous variable. This simplifies the analysis without making any qualitative difference to the results. The number of involuntarily unemployed is the difference between the total supply of labour, S, assumed to be fixed, and the total number employed in equilibrium, $nL(z)$. Making S an increasing function of z, as in Salop, would make no qualitative difference to the analysis. Thus, the probability of being hired from the unemployed pool is:

$$\pi(z) = \frac{nN(z)}{S - nL(z)}, \tag{44}$$

where $d\pi/dz < 0$. From (43) and (41), $\pi = 1/W(z)$. Therefore, from (44), the equilibrium value of z must satisfy

$$\frac{1}{W(z)} = \frac{nN(z)}{S - nL(z)}. \tag{45}$$

Two cases can be distinguished here, as in the shirking model — the no-entry case and the free-entry case. In the no-entry case, n is predetermined. Equation (45) can then be solved for z. Depending on the parameters of the model, the equilibrium can either be one of full employment ($\pi = 1$) or involuntary unemployment ($\pi < 1$).[15] The case of interest for us is that of unemployment. Full employment can be ruled out formally by postulating that $\lim_{w/z \to 0} Q(w/z) = \infty$.

In the free-entry case, entry (or exit) will occur until the following zero profit condition is satisfied:

$$F[L(z)] - zW(z)L(z) - T[N(z)] - K = 0. \tag{46}$$

Together, (45) and (46) can be solved for n and z.[16] Furthermore, inspection of (46) indicates that it alone determines z, independent of, say, the supply of labour S. Given z from (46), (45) determines n. Thus, a change in the supply of labour has no effect on the labour market tightness z, but will affect the number of firms n. Given z, the firms will set the same wage w (by (41)) and the market will yield the same value of π (since $\pi = z/w$).

The social optimum in this model is the allocation which maximizes social output given by

$$\Omega = n[F(L) - T(qL) - K - eL],$$

where the quit rate q is now defined implicitly by

$$q \equiv Q(1/\pi) = Q[(S - nL)/nqL].$$

Differentiating the latter totally with respect to nL yields

$$\frac{dq}{d(nL)} = -\frac{SQ'}{q(nL)^2}(1+\eta)^{-1}, \tag{47}$$

where η is the elasticity of the quit function Q (i.e., $\eta \equiv \pi^{-1}Q'/q < 0$). It can be shown that stability of the quit function in q requires tht $\eta > -1$.[17] We assume that to be the case. Therefore, $dq/d(nL) > 0$.

---

[15] This may be contrasted with the shirking model, where unemployment must exist in equilibrium.

[16] Salop demonstrates that the equilibrium must be unique.

[17] To see this, the quit function can be converted into a dynamic relationship in the following manner: $q_{t+1} = Q((S - nL)/(nq_t L))$. Stability in this relationship requires that $dQ/dq < 1$. Differentiating the function $Q(\cdot)$ yields $(d/dq)Q((S-nL)/(nqL)) = -Q'((S-nL)/(nqL)^2)nL = -(1/\pi q)Q' = -\eta < 1$.

Consider first the market equilibrium in the no-entry case. To determine whether it is socially optimal, first differentiate Ω with respect to L to obtain

$$\frac{\partial \Omega}{\partial L} = n[F'(L) - T'(q - nL\ dq/dnL) - e].$$

Using the first order conditions (38) and (39), this becomes

$$\frac{\partial \Omega}{\partial L} = n\left[w - e + \pi w \frac{L}{Q'} \frac{dq}{dnL}\right].$$

Substituting from (47), we obtain

$$\frac{\partial \Omega}{\partial L} = n\left[-e - w\frac{nL - (S - nL)\eta}{1 + \eta}\right]. \tag{48}$$

Therefore, since $0 > \eta > -1$, $\partial \Omega / \partial L < 0$. Social welfare could be increased by reducing L starting at the market equilibrium.

In the free-entry case, the same expression for $\partial \Omega / \partial L$ applies. Furthermore, at the market equilibrium,

$$\frac{\partial \Omega}{\partial n} = F(L) - eL - T - K - nT'L^2 \frac{dq}{dnL}$$

$$= L\left[w - e - T'nL\frac{dq}{dnL}\right] = \frac{L}{n}\frac{\partial \Omega}{\partial L}. \tag{49}$$

Therefore, since $\partial \Omega / \partial L < 0$, $\partial \Omega / \partial n < 0$. There is apparently some room for employment policy in the turnover model.

3.2. Public employment policy in the Salop model

Introducing a public firm into the model affects the labour market equilibrium condition (45). Public employment policy alters the equilibrium values of z in the no entry case and n in the free entry case, and thereby influences firm behaviour. The degree of market tightness must be redefined to be

$$z = \pi_1 w_1 + \pi_2 w_2 \tag{50}$$

where subscripts 1 and 2 refer to the private and public sectors respectively.[18]

---

[18] Here we assume for simplicity that it is only expected wages that workers care about. In a more general treatment, there may also be non-pecuniary differences between the two sectors.

The probabilities of employment in the two sectors are now given by

$$\pi_1 = \frac{nN(z)}{S - nL_1(z) - L_2},$$ (51)

$$\pi_2 = \frac{Q_2(w_2/z)L_2}{S - nL_1(z) - L_2}.$$ (52)

This assumes that new hirings are drawn randomly from the total pool of the voluntary unemployed, and that workers accept the first job offered. The public sector quit function $Q_2(\cdot)$ has the same properties as the private sector one, but need not be identical.

To determine how the public sector employment policy affects labour market conditions, first rearrange (50) to yield

$$\frac{w_1}{z} = \frac{1}{\pi_1} - \frac{\pi_2}{\pi_1}\frac{w_2}{z}.$$

For the typical private firm, $w_1/z = W(z)$ defined by (44). Therefore, using (51) and (52), this condition can be written as

$$W(z) = \frac{S - nL(z) - L_2[1 + Q_2(w_2/z)]}{nN(z)}.$$ (53)

In the no-entry case, (53) determines z as a function of n, L_2 and w_2. Notice that the public employment policy terms enter in the numerator like a shift in the supply of labour to the private sector. Total differentiation of (53), holding n constant, yields the following result:

$$\frac{\partial z}{\partial L_2} = -\frac{1 + q_2 w_2/z}{D} > 0,$$ (54)

$$\frac{\partial z}{\partial w_2} = -\frac{q_2 L_2/z}{D} > 0,$$ (55)

where

$$D \equiv n(NW' + WN') + nL_1' - (Q_2' + q_2)w_2^2 L_2/z^3 < 0.$$

These results are intuitive. Increases in public sector employment and in the public sector wage both increase labour market tightness. This, in turn, reduces private sector employment L_1 and new hirings N by (40) and (42).

In the free-entry case, z is determined uniquely by the zero profit condition (46). In this case, n is determined by (53). Total differentiation, holding z constant, yields

$$\frac{\partial n}{\partial L_2} = -\frac{(1 + q_2 w_2/z)}{L_1 + NW} < 0, \tag{56}$$

$$\frac{\partial n}{\partial w_2} = -\frac{q_2(1 + \eta_2)L_2/z}{L_1 + NW} < 0 \quad \text{as } \eta_2 > -1, \tag{57}$$

where $\eta_2 \equiv w_2 Q_2'/(z q_2)$ is the elasticity of the public sector quit function. Thus, increasing public sector employment crowds out private firms as in the shirking model. However, increasing the public sector wage decreases the number of firms only if the public sector quit function, like the private sector one, has an elasticity which exceeds -1.

Given these effects of public policy on labour markets, we can now investigate optimal public policy, beginning with the no-entry case.

(i) *No-entry case.* Optimal public employment policy is the solution to the following problem:

$$\underset{L_2, w_2}{\text{Max}} \quad \Omega = nF[L_1(z)] - nT_1[Q_1(W(z))L_1(z)]$$

$$- nK + G(L_2) - T_2[Q_2(w_2/z)L_2] - e(nL_1(z) + L_2), \tag{58}$$

where e is the disutility of work and $G(L_2)$ is the public sector production function as before, and z is a function of L_2 and w_2. The first-order conditions may be written as

$$G' - T_2'q_2 - e + (F' - T_1'q - e)nL_2'\frac{\partial z}{\partial L_2}$$

$$- nT_1'Q_1'W'L_1\frac{\partial z}{\partial L_2} + T_2'Q_2'\frac{w_2}{z^2}L_2\frac{\partial z}{\partial L_2} = 0, \tag{59}$$

$$(F' - T_1'q - e)nL_1'\frac{\partial z}{\partial w_2} nT_1'Q_1'W'L_1\frac{\partial z}{\partial w_2}$$

$$- T_2'Q_2'\frac{L_2}{z}\left(1 - \frac{w_2}{z}\frac{\partial z}{\partial w_2}\right) = 0. \tag{60}$$

Consider (59) first. It can be rewritten in the following intuitive way, using $w_1 = F' - T_1'q$ by (38),

$$G' - T_2'q_2 = \alpha w_1 + (1 - \alpha)e + nT_1'L_1\frac{\partial q_1}{\partial L_2} + T_2'L_2\frac{\partial q_2}{\partial L_2}, \tag{61}$$

where $\alpha = -nL_1' \, \partial z/\partial L_2$ is the reduction in private sector employment from an increase in L_2, analogous to before. The latter two terms represent the increase in turnover costs in the private and public sectors respectively from an increase in L_2. Since these terms are positive, a necessary condition for $(G' - T_2'q_2) < w_1$ (that is, for active public employment policy) is that $\alpha < 1$. Unfortunately, in contrast to the shirking model, that is not sufficient. Depending on the relative magnitudes of the induced employment effect (α) and the induced turnover, the net marginal product of labour in the public sector could be $>$ or $< w_1$.[19]

Public sector employment policy also involves a choice of wage rate w_2. From eq. (60) we derive

$$(w_1 - e)nL_1' \, \partial z/\partial w_2 - nT_1' \, \partial N/\partial w_2 - T_2' \, \partial q_2/\partial w_2 = 0. \tag{62}$$

The first term, which is negative, is the efficiency cost of the fall in private sector employment induced by an increase in w_2. The second and third terms involve the change in turnover costs when w_2 is changed. There is no apparent relationship between w_2 and w_1 (unlike in the shirking model). Notice that if there were no spillover effects between the public and private sectors, the first two terms in (62) would vanish and the public sector wage w_2 would be chosen as high as possible.

(ii) *Free-entry case.* With free entry, z is determined uniquely by the free entry condition (46), and n is a function of L_2 and w_2. The problem (58) again applies but with z given and n endogenous. Using (46), the first-order conditions reduce to

$$G' - T_2'q_2 = \alpha w_1 + (1 - \alpha)e, \tag{63}$$

$$T_2'Q_2'L_2/z = (w_1 - e)L_1 \, \partial n/\partial w_2, \tag{64}$$

where $\alpha \equiv -L_1 \, \partial n/\partial L_2 = (1 + q_2 w_2/z)/(1 + q_1 w_1/z)$ from (56). Thus, if $\alpha < 1$, so that an increase in L_2 increases total employment, $G' - T_2'q_2 < w_1$ and the public sector should hire labour beyond the point at which the net marginal product equals the private sector wage. On the other hand, if $\alpha > 1$, which is quite possible, the public sector will restrict employment. This is an intuitive result. The wage in the public sector is also a free choice variable. By (64), it is set such that the gain from reduced turnover equals the loss from reduced employment in the public sector. Again, the relation between the sizes of w_2 and w_1 is ambiguous.

---

[19] A shadow wage analysis confirms this. Using the same methodology as before, the shadow wage to be used for project evaluation is $\alpha w + (1 - \alpha)e + nT_1'L_1 \, \partial q_1/\partial L_2 + T_2'L_2 \, \partial q_2/\partial L_2$.

3.3. The possibility of wage subsidies

Consider first the case in which there is no public firm and let s be the subsidy per worker. In the no-entry case, the private firm's problem is:

$$\underset{L,w}{\text{Max}} \quad \Omega = F(L) - (w - s)L - T[Q(w/z)L] - K. \tag{65}$$

This yields the following first order conditions:

$$T'Q' = -z, \tag{66}$$

$$F' - w + s - T'q = 0. \tag{67}$$

As earlier, the effect of a change in L on social welfare is given by

$$\partial\Omega/\partial L = n[F' - e - T'(q + nL \, dq/dnL)]$$

$$= n[w - s - e - T'nL \, dq/dnL] \quad \text{(using (67))}, \tag{68}$$

where dq/dnL is given by (47). From (68), we conclude that the optimal subsidy is given by

$$s^* = w - e - T'nL \, dq/dnL = -e - w\frac{nL - (S - nL)\eta}{1 + \eta} \quad \text{(using (47))}.$$

Therefore, since $0 > \eta > -1$, the per capita subsidy is negative. That is, employment should be taxed. Introducing a per worker subsidy equal to $-s^*$ will take the economy to a "first best" allocation; that is, first best given the turnover constraint. The fact that a wage tax is needed clearly comes from the increase in turnover costs that a rise in L causes to other firms. This externality cost is not accounted for by the private firms.

Analogous reasoning in the free-entry case yields an optimal subsidy which again yields the first best values of L and n. Note the contrast here with the shirking model where the optimal allocation did not exist, and an indefinitely high subsidy is called for.

Since s^* allows one to reach the first best allocation, there is no room for an active role by the public firm. Provided that the public firm is in all respects identical to private firms, it should adopt the same employment and wage policies as the private firms. L_2 and w_2 are indeed chosen independently of each other. (For private firms, the (negative) subsidy disconnects the wage paid to workers from that used to make employment decisions.)

4. Conclusion

Public employment policy as a way to enhance employment has been widely studied within the setting of naive models of wage rigidity, namely models which impose such rigidity without attempting to explain it. In these models, wages are fixed at a higher level than that which clears the labour market and hence unemployment results. Public employment policy is generally shown to be effective at reducing unemployment.

In this paper, we wanted to verify whether this policy implication holds in models in which the gap between current wages and market clearing wages is accounted for by the "efficiency wage" hypothesis that workers' productivity is a function of the wage paid. There are a variety of such models which differ markedly depending on how productivity depends on wages. We chose two versions: that based on labour turnover — the lower the wage, the higher the rate of labour turnover the cost of which is incurred by the firm; and that based on shirking — higher wages induce workers not to shirk which is costly to the firm.

For either of these efficiency wage models, we have looked at the effect of public employment with and without free entry in the private sector, and with and without a wage subsidy as an additional policy instrument. Note that in the context of naive models of wage rigidity, a subsidy equal to the gap between the current and the Walrasian wage would restore full employment without further need for public employment. The qualitative results obtained for the efficiency wage as compared with naive models are summarized in Table 1.

This table, as well as the specific results derived in the paper, show that optimal public employment policies differ decisively depending on the

Table 1
Is there a case for public employment policy?

Setting	Naive model	Efficiency wage models	
		Shirking	Labour turnover
No entry	yes[a]	yes[b]	yes[b]
Free entry	yes[a]	yes, but weaker[b]	yes[b]
Wage subsidy possible	no[c]	yes[b]	no[d]

[a] Shadow wage generally below private sector wage.
[b] Shadow wage below or above private sector wage depending on the parameters.
[c] Subsidy achieves first-best employment without involuntary unemployment.
[d] Identical to [c] except that there remains (efficient) involuntary unemployment.

model chosen: naive or efficiency wage models, and among the latter, shirking or labour turnover models. We believe that in terms of relevancy and realism, wage efficiency models are superior. It is thus clear that the case for active expansion of public employment in case of unemployment cannot be taken for granted. For particular values of the model parameters, shadow wages to be used by the public sector can indeed be higher than the market wage.

Which of the two efficiency wage models apply more to the real world is an empirical question which has not yet received a satisfactory answer. It is likely that both models apply to different sectors of the economy, in which case a synthetic public sector employment and wage policy should be derived.

One of the obvious limitations of this paper, as, in fact, of the whole efficiency wage literature, is the neglect of equity considerations. To a certain extent, this limitation is particularly crucial here since our analysis is not just positive but also normative. To avoid equity considerations, we have treated all individuals identically from an expected income point of view. However, unemployment affects different persons in different ways and an equity analysis would take these into account. Take the example of a wage subsidy in practice. We have shown that this would increase efficiency wages as well as the level of employment. However, if the subsidy is financed through lump-sum taxation, unemployed persons are likely to lose in the process even though the number of them decreases. To avoid that, one would need a tax system differentiating the employed from the unemployed. The incorporating of equity considerations is worthy of future research.

References

Akerlof, G.A. and J. Yellen (1986) *Efficiency Wage Models of the Labor Market*. New York: Cambridge University Press.
Boadway, R.W. and N. Bruce (1984) *Welfare Economics*. Oxford: Blackwell.
Bulow, J.I. and L.H. Summers (1986) 'A theory of dual labor markets with application to industrial policy, discrimination, and Keynesian unemployment', *Journal of Labor Economics*, 4(3):376–414.
Carmichael, H.L. (1987) 'Efficiency wage models of unemployment: a survey', Queen's University, Kingston, mimeo.
Dasgupta, P., S.A. Marglin and A.K. Sen (1972) *Guidelines for Project Evaluation*. New York: UNIDO.
Harberger, A.C. (1971) 'On measuring the social opportunity cost of labour', *International Labour Review*, 103:559–579.
Harris, J.R. and M.P. Todaro (1970) 'Migration, unemployment and development: a two-sector analysis', *American Economic Review*, 60:136–142.

Johnson, G.E. and P.R.G. Layard (1986) 'The natural rate of unemployment: explanation and policy', in: O.C. Ashenfelter and R. Layard, eds., Handbook of Labor Economics, Volume II. Amsterdam: North-Holland, pp. 921–999.
Little, I.M.D. and J.A. Mirrless (1968) Manual of Industrial Project Analysis in Developing Countries. Paris: OCDE.
Salop, S.C. (1979) 'A model of the natural rate of unemployment', American Economic Review, 69:117–125.
Sen, A.K. (1972) 'Control areas and accounting prices: an approach to economic evaluation', Economic Journal, 82:486–501.
Shapiro, C. and J.E. Stiglitz (1984) 'Unemployment equilibrium as a worker discipline device', American Economic Review, 74:433–444.
Solow, R. (1979) 'Another possible source of wage stickiness', Journal of Macroeconomics, 1:79–82.
Stiglitz, J.E. (1974) 'Wage determination and unemployment in L.D.C.s: the labor turnover model', Quarterly Journal of Economics, 88:194–227.

Chapter 6

STRUCTURAL SHOCKS AND INVESTMENT SUBSIDIES IN AN OVERLAPPING GENERATIONS MODEL WITH PERFECT FORESIGHT

Victor GINSBURGH

Université Libre de Bruxelles, Bruxelles, Belgium, and CORE,
Université Catholique de Louvain, Louvain-la-Neuve, Belgium

Henri SNEESSENS

Département de Sciences Economiques, Université Catholique de Louvain,
Louvain-la-Neuve, Belgium, and Faculté Libre de Sciences Economiques, Lille, France

1. Introduction

In most countries, and especially in Europe, the post-1974 recession has been accompanied by deep structural changes resulting from the collapse of traditionally important sectors like steel and textiles. This evolution was probably the outcome of several factors (raw materials' price changes, increased competition from newly industrialized countries, exogenous changes in habits and in production technologies, etc.). As a consequence, European economies were characterized by huge excess capacities in declining sectors and by capacity shortages in expanding sectors. At the same time, investment rates were abnormally low. This has raised concern about

We are grateful to C. Blackorby and P. Pestieau for comments on a previous version. We also benefitted from discussions with H. Polemarchakis and J. Waelbroeck. The first author acknowledges support from Action de Recherches Concertées under contract 84–89/65 as well as from Fonds National de la Recherche Scientifique. The work of the second author is part of a project on structural adjustments financed by Fonds de Développement Scientifique; it was also partially supported by GREQE, Ecole des Hautes Etudes en Sciences Sociales, Marseille, France.

Economic Decision-Making: Games, Econometrics and Optimisation
Edited by J.J. Gabszewicz, J.-F. Richard and L.A. Wolsey
© *Elsevier Science Publishers B.V., 1990*

the appropriate way to stimulate capital formation and accelerate the return to full-employment. The issue was taken up in one of the reports prepared by the Macroeconomic Policy Group of the Center for European Policy Studies (CEPS). We quote (see Modigliani et al., 1987, pp. 28-29):

"Given our previous discussion, we must ensure that the requisite savings emerge to finance the construction of new capacity. (· · ·) Incentives to investment in the form of tax provisions and subsidies have apparently proved to be not very effective in stimulating investment. In addition, they have the serious drawback of encouraging substitution of labor with capital at the time when labour is abundant and capital is presumably scarce. So we see little use in trying more of that medicine *except for an investment tax credit of relatively short duration. In this case the dominant effect of such a measure is the desirable one of shifting investment forward in time.* (· · ·) What has to be stressed, in the context of our proposed strategy, is that financial support by governments seems to go to a large extent to the protection of unproductive capacity at old firms in sectors facing declining demand, to the detriment of the creation of new firms and of capital formation in sectors facing high demand". (Emphasis is ours).

The objective of this paper is not to analyze the various factors responsible for the structural changes just mentioned nor their impact on unemployment, but rather to consider again in that context the issue raised by investment subsidies, and more specifically their role in shifting investment forward in time and in promoting welfare. To this end, we have constructed a two-sector overlapping generations model where consumers live for two periods. Every young generation inelastically supplies its labor force, consumes and saves; every old generation finances its consumption with the savings of the previous period and does not leave bequests to its descendants. At variance with consumers, firms optimize over an infinite horizon. All agents are endowed with perfect foresight, and prices and wages are perfectly flexible, so that the economy is always at full-employment. Since we are mostly interested by the transition to the stationary state, we have to solve the model numerically.

In this setting, the structural shock is represented by an unanticipated permanent change in consumers' preferences, which shifts consumption from good 2 to good 1.[1] This change induces firms to scrap part of their capital stock in sector 2 and to invest in sector 1. Because adjustment costs make capital imperfectly mobile across sectors, the shock implies a loss of

---

[1] This shift can be interpreted as the consequence of the emergence of newly industrialized countries in sectors like the textile or the steel industry. We could also have considered a shock on the supply side and interpret it as the consequence of the oil crisis.

welfare for the two generations living at the moment of the shock. As time goes on and investment takes place, the distribution of capital across sectors is adjusted and progressively reaches its new equilibrium value, while consumers' welfare increases again and eventually returns to normal.

The question that we consider is whether the scrapping and the investment rates so generated are "optimal", or whether government intervention can improve every generation's welfare with respect to "laisser faire". We look at the effects of an investment subsidy that decreases the adjustment costs borne by firms, without changing the equilibrium capital intensity. In this way, we avoid the usual criticisms against government intervention (see the above quotation). We show that investment subsidies financed by consumption taxes are not sufficient to improve each generation's welfare. Such subsidies are successful in speeding up the adjustment of production capacities to their new equilibrium values, at the expense of the two generations living at the moment of the shock. Through its effect on financial markets, the subsidy works like a transfer from current to future generations and worsens the problem created by the structural change. We then show that it is possible to improve every generation's welfare, provided that the government combines investment incentives with compensatory transfers from future to current generations. In our case, these transfers imply a temporary public deficit, later compensated by a surplus, and produce a temporary and substantial increase in the interest rate. Because of the subsidy, the net effect on investment remains positive.

The use of overlapping generations models to analyze the intertemporal effects of fiscal policy is not new (see, for instance, Auerbach and Kotlikoff, 1987, from which many of our specifications are inspired). The novelty[2] of our paper lies in the analysis of structural shocks and in the explicit distinction between two sectors, where Auerbach and Kotlikoff have only one. The paper is organized as follows. The model is set up and its stationary equilibrium is analyzed in Section 2. Section 3 describes the dynamic effects of the structural shock, which provides the reference path used in Section 4 to measure the effects of alternative government policies. We end up in Section 5 with a few concluding remarks.

2. The model

We consider a closed economy with three types of agents: firms, consumers

---

[2] The recent paper by Davies, Whalley and Hamilton (1989) came known to us after our paper was almost completed.

and the government. There are four markets: two goods, labor and a financial asset. Labor is thus homogeneous across sectors and the financial assets sold by firms (to finance their investment) and by the government (to finance its deficit) are perfect substitutes. There is no uncertainty. Consumers live for two periods. They work only when young and inelastically supply their labor. Their second period consumption is entirely financed by the net (after taxes and transfers) income accrued from their savings. We first describe each agent's behavior, and next turn to the market demand and supply functions and the equilibrium conditions.

2.1. Firms' behavior

The technology is represented by a Cobb–Douglas function with constant returns to scale and two inputs, labor and capital (L and K). The parameters of the production function are the same for the two sectors:

$$Y_{it} = (K_{it})^{\varepsilon}(L_{it})^{1-\varepsilon}, \quad i = 1, 2. \tag{2.1}$$

We set ε to 0.25. Firms behave competitively and adjust labor costlessly. Since labor is homogeneous and perfectly mobile, the wage rate must be the same in the two sectors. Firms will hire labor up to the point where the marginal productivity is equal to the real wage rate (W in sector 1, W/P_2 in sector 2).

Each firm maximizes its profits subject to its technology; this leads to the following demand functions for labor:

$$L_{1t} = K_{1t}\left[\frac{1-\varepsilon}{W_t}\right]^{1/\varepsilon}, \qquad L_{2t} = K_{2t}\left[\frac{1-\varepsilon}{W_t/P_{2t}}\right]^{1/\varepsilon}.$$

The capital stocks of the two firms, K_1 and K_2 consist of good 1 only and depreciate at a rate $d = 0.20$.[3] As in the q-theory of investment, we assume that changing the capital stocks generates (quadratic) adjustment costs:

$$C(\Delta K_{it}) = \left[1 + \frac{(1-z_{it})b_{it}}{2}\frac{\Delta K_{it}}{K_{it}}\right]\Delta K_{it}, \quad i = 1, 2;$$

---

[3] This is admittedly a much too low value for a model where one period of time represents thirty years. It would seem more realistic to assume that the capital stock is completely depreciated within the period and set d equal to 1. This however would preclude the analysis of the consequences of imperfect capital mobility across sectors after a structural shock in a simple two period overlapping generations model.

this implies the following marginal cost function:

$$C'(\Delta K_{it}) = 1 + (1 - z_{it})b_{it}\frac{\Delta K_{it}}{K_{it}}, \quad i = 1, 2,$$ (2.2)

where b_{it} represents the adjustment costs parameter and z_{it} the subsidy rate. The optimal investment rate in each sector is such that the marginal cost of investment defined in (2.2) (which takes into account the subsidy rate) is equal to the price of existing capital goods Q_{it}. The adjustment cost parameter b_{it} is defined in the same way for the two sectors and is smaller for capital accumulation than for capital scrapping:

$$b_{it} = 2 \quad \text{if } \Delta K_{it} > 0 \quad \text{and} \quad b_{it} = 5 \quad \text{if } \Delta K_{it} < 0.$$

z_{it} represents the share of the total adjustment costs borne by the government. The total investment subsidy to sector i at time t is, by definition, equal to

$$IS_{it} = z_{it}b_{it}\frac{\Delta K_{it}}{K_{it}}\Delta K_{it}, \quad i = 1, 2.$$ (2.3)

Because only adjustment costs are subsidized, this type of government intervention does not affect the stationary value of the capital stock, though it speeds up the adjustment process to a new equilibrium value.

Demand for investment is given by

$$I_{it} = \left[1 + b_{it}\frac{\Delta K_{it}}{K_{it}}\right]\Delta K_{it} + dK_{it}, \quad i = 1, 2,$$

where net investment ΔK_{it} is defined by the marginal condition

$$\Delta K_{it} = \frac{1}{b_{it}(1 - z_{it})}(Q_{it} - 1)K_{it}, \quad i = 1, 2,$$

as in the q-theory of investment. It can be shown that $Q_{it} = 1$ at the stationary state, so that $\Delta K_{it} = 0$.

2.2. Consumers' behavior

Consumers born at time t maximize the following two-period utility function:

$$U = \frac{1}{1 - 1/\gamma}\left[(U_t^y)^{1 - 1/\gamma} + \frac{1}{1 + \delta}(U_{t+1}^o)^{1 - 1/\gamma}\right]$$ (2.4a)

where U^y and U^o represent the utility when young and old respectively. Utility is thus assumed to be additive over time, with a constant intertemporal elasticity of substitution γ and a rate of time preference δ. γ is set at 0.25. With individuals living only for two periods, one period of time represents something like twenty-five or thirty years; in this perspective, a discount rate δ equal to 1 seems a reasonable value.

The within-period utility is itself a CES function of the quantities consumed of each good, with an elasticity of substitution between goods equal to ρ; in the following expressions, C stands for consumption (the upper index y or o refers to young and old consumers, the lower index 1 or 2 to good 1 or 2):

$$U^y_t = [(C^y_{1t})^{1-1/\rho} + \alpha(C^y_{2t})^{1-1/\rho}]^{1/(1-1/\rho)} \tag{2.4b}$$

and

$$U^o_{t+1} = [(C^o_{1,t+1})^{1-1/\rho} + \alpha(C^o_{2,t+1})^{1-1/\rho}]^{1/(1-1/\rho)}. \tag{2.4c}$$

ρ is set equal to 0.8; α which represents the intensity of consumers' preferences for good 2 relative to good 1 is initially set to 1 (both goods receive the same weight). Leisure is not an argument of the utility function: consumers' labor supply is independent of the wage rate. We assume that every generation of consumers works only when young and retires when old. Units of labor are chosen in such a way that the supply of labor is equal to 1.

The intertemporal budget constraint of the consumer reads

$$(1 + T_t)[C^y_{1t} + P_{2t}C^y_{2t}] + \frac{1 + T_{t+1}}{1 + R_{t+1}}[C^o_{1,t+1} + P_{2,t+1}C^o_{2,t+1}]$$

$$= W_t + \mathrm{TR}^y_t + \frac{\mathrm{TR}^o_{t+1}}{1 + R_{t+1}}. \tag{2.5}$$

The price of good 1 is normalized to one in every period; P_2 is the price of good 2 and W stands for the wage income received by the young. R_{t+1} represents the real interest rate (in terms of goods 1) between period t and period $t + 1$. Government transfers received when young and old are denoted by TR^y and TR^o respectively, while T represents the consumption tax rate.

Demands of (young y and old o) consumers on both markets (1 and 2) are obtained as the solution of maximizing (2.4) subject to (2.5). This leads to

$$C^y_{1t} = \frac{1}{1 + T_t} \beta_t (1 - \sigma_t)\left(W_t + \mathrm{TR}^y_t + \frac{1}{1 + R_{t+1}} \mathrm{TR}^o_{t+1}\right),$$

$$C^o_{1t} = \frac{1}{1 + T_t} \beta_t (\mathrm{WW}_t + \mathrm{TR}^o_t),$$

and

$$C_{2t}^y = \frac{1}{(1+T_t)P_{2t}}(1-\beta_t)(1-\sigma_t)\left(W_t + TR_t^y + \frac{1}{1+R_{t+1}}TR_{t+1}^o\right),$$

$$C_{2t}^o = \frac{1}{(1+T_t)P_{2t}}(1-\beta_t)(WW_t + TR_t^o),$$

for young and old consumers on both markets 1 and 2. In these expressions, β stands for the marginal propensity to spend on good 1, σ is the marginal propensity to save out of current and future income and WW represents the financial wealth of each old generation with

$$\beta_t = [1 + \alpha^\rho(P_{2t})^{1-\rho}]^{-1} \le 1,$$

$$\sigma_t = \left[1 + \left[(1+R_{t+1})\frac{1+T_t}{1+T_{t+1}}\right]^{(1-\gamma)}(1+\delta)^\gamma\left(\frac{\beta_{t+1}}{\beta_t}\right)^{(1-\gamma)/(1-\rho)}\right]^{-1} \le 1,$$

and

$$WW_t = Q_{1t}K_{1t} + Q_{2t}K_{2t} + D_t + (\varepsilon Y_{1t} - dK_{1t}) + (\varepsilon P_{2t}Y_{2t} - dK_{2t}) + R_tD_t.$$

$$(2.6)$$

Note that, given the parameter values which have been chosen, σ is a decreasing function of the interest rate. In WW the first three terms represent the market value of old consumers' financial assets (including public debt D); the next two terms stand for dividends paid out by firms in both sectors; the last one represents interest payments on the public debt.

2.3. Government behavior

The government collects consumption taxes (IT) and issues bonds ($D_{t+1} - D_t$); the proceeds are distributed to consumers under the form of (positive or negative) lump sum transfers (TR) and interest payments (R_tD_t) on the outstanding debt, while firms collect investment subsidies (IS) — see eq. (2.11).

2.4. Market equilibrium conditions

On the *markets for good 1 and 2*, the equilibrium conditions state that demand (left-hand side) is equal to supply (right-hand side):

$$C_{1t}^y + C_{1t}^o + I_{1t} + I_{2t} = Y_{1t},$$
$$(2.7)$$

$$C_{2t}^y + C_{2t}^o = Y_{2t},$$
$$(2.8)$$

where Y_{it} is defined by (2.1).

Likewise, on the *labor market* demand is equal to supply (normalized to 1):

$$L_{1t} + L_{2t} = 1. \tag{2.9}$$

Finally, since bonds issued by the government and shares issued by the firms in each sector are perfect substitutes, there is only one equilibrium condition on the *market for assets*, which reads

$$Q_{1t}K_{1,t+1} + Q_{2t}K_{2,t+1} + D_{t+1} = \sigma_t \left[W_t + \text{TR}_t^y + \frac{\text{TR}_{t+1}^o}{1 + R_{t+1}} \right] - \frac{\text{TR}_{t+1}^o}{1 + R_{t+1}}; \tag{2.10}$$

the left-hand side represents demand (defined as the value of assets issued by the firms in the two sectors and the government) while the right-hand side represents supply (the savings of the young generation, defined as the difference between its total expenditure and its current income). The stocks of assets are defined by

$$K_{i,t+1} = K_{it} + \Delta K_{it}, \quad i = 1, 2,$$

and

$$D_{t+1} = D_t + \text{TR}_t^y + \text{TR}_t^o + \text{IS}_{1t} + \text{IS}_{2t} + R_t D_t - \text{IT}_t. \tag{2.11}$$

By Walras's law, (2.7) will always be satisfied, and the price on the market for good 1 is set to 1 by normalization; (2.8) defines P_2, the price of good 2; (2.9) defines W, the wage rate and (2.10) the interest rate R_{t+1}. We assume that agents have perfect foresight, except for the structural shock to be considered later on, which is unanticipated. With this assumption, the relationship between the prices of shares (Q_{1t} and Q_{2t}) and the interest rate R_{t+1} is simply

$$Q_{1t} = (1 + R_{t+1})^{-1} \left[Q_{1,t+1} + \left(\varepsilon \frac{Y_{1,t+1}}{K_{1,t+1}} - d \right) \right]$$

and

$$Q_{2t} = (1 + R_{t+1})^{-1} \left[Q_{2,t+1} + \left(\varepsilon \frac{P_{2,t+1} Y_{2,t+1}}{K_{2,t+1}} - d \right) \right].$$

The stationary values of P_2, Q_1 and Q_2 can be shown to be equal to 1, no matter the values of the parameters.

3. The consequences of a structural shock

We now consider the consequences of an *unanticipated* structural shock, which takes the form of an unanticipated change in the preference parameter α. For generations born before time $t = 1$, the preference parameter α is equal to 1, i.e., goods 1 and 2 have the same weight in the utility function. For generations born at time $t = 1$ and afterwards, α is set to 0.5, which implies a substantial increase in the relative preference for good 1 and will induce a reallocation of capital from sector 2 to sector 1.

The idea is thus to (numerically) examine the transition path from the "old" stationary state (i.e. with $\alpha = 1$) to the "new" one ($\alpha = 0.5$); this can be done by solving[4] the set of equations described in Section 2. We first consider the case where the government plays no role ($D_t = \mathrm{IT}_t = \mathrm{IS}_{it} = \mathrm{TR}_t^y = \mathrm{TR}_t^o = 0$ for all t) and postpone to the next section the analysis of the effects of government transfers and subsidies.

The main consequences of the structural shock in the absence of government intervention are illustrated in Figures 1 to 3. Figure 1 describes the deviations of the price of shares and of good 2 from their stationary state values (equal to 1) during the first ten periods following the shock. The lower demand for good 2 produces a temporary fall of its price, which reaches a maximum of 11% one period after the shock. At the same time,

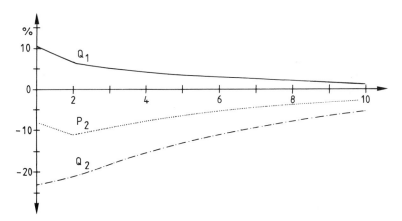

Figure 1. Goods and share prices (deviations from stationary state values, in percentage points).

[4] To compute these values, we assumed that the adjustment process to the new stationary state was completed after 40 periods, which proved to be more than what was actually needed for the economy to stabilize.

there are substantial capital gains (10% in period 1) on the equities issued by sector 1, and substantial capital losses (over 20%) on the equities issued by sector 2. These changes in equity prices stimulate investment in sector 1 and capital scrapping in sector 2. As the allocation of capital progressively approaches its new stationary value, the price of good 2 increases again, and the price of shares in each sector returns to normal.

Figure 2 shows that this adjustment process implies a temporary increase in the interest rate[5] and, consequently, a temporary decrease in the real wage rate (not shown). The value of the interest rate at time $t = 1$ is not given in Figure 2, because it is different for the two assets. This is the result of the unanticipated capital gains and losses: the interest rate on shares issued by sector 1 is equal to 1.08 at time $t = 1$, while it is only 0.48 for sector 2. From time $t = 2$ onwards, there is no new unanticipated shock and both interest rates are again equal.

Figure 3 shows the progressive adjustment of the capital stocks in the two sectors. The capital stock in sector 2 is initially 37% larger than its new equilibrium value; after ten periods, the excess capacity in sector 2 is brought down to 6.5%. A similar but opposite adjustment is observed for sector 1. There is initially a capital shortage of some 20%, reduced to 3% after ten periods. More than half the adjustment is realized after five periods.[6] Figure

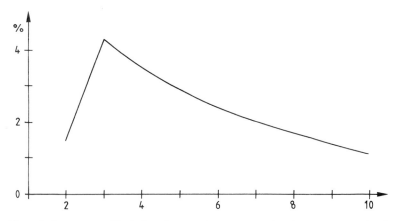

Figure 2. Interest rate (deviations from stationary state value, in percentage points).

[5] Note that the stationary state value of the interest rate remains almost unchanged at 0.73 before and after the shock.

[6] This may seem too slow an adjustment process. The speed of adjustment would be faster with a larger depreciation rate. We explained above (see footnote 1) why we chose a depreciation rate of only 20%.

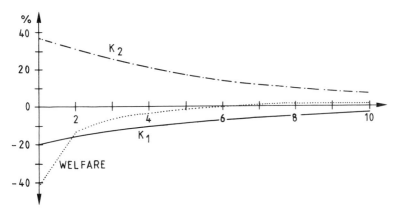

Figure 3. Capital stocks and welfare (deviations from new stationary state values, in percentage points).

3 also reproduces the welfare of each generation of consumers, compared to what it would be in the stationary state. The figure is constructed so that the welfare reported for time t refers to the old generation living during that period. The unanticipated change in preferences implies a substantial loss of welfare for the old living at the time of the shock. This is the result of the huge capital loss experienced by the holders of sector 2 equities, which is not compensated by the capital gains on sector 1 equities. Taking all that into account, the (unexpected) loss of financial wealth for the old generation living at time $t = 1$ is equal to 5%. Although there is no unexpected financial loss for the subsequent generations, their welfare remains abnormally low for some time. It progressively returns to normal as the process of capital reallocation goes on. Note the slight overshooting after time $t = 6$.

4. The effects of transfers and investment subsidies

The aim of this section is to examine how government intervention modifies the adjustment path of the economy after a structural shock of the type described in Section 3. We are especially interested in the effect of government intervention on welfare. We compare two types of policies:

In *policy 1*, the government subsidizes investment by paying to the firms 20% of the adjustment cost when investment is positive (that is, $z_{it} = 0.20$ when $\Delta K_{it} > 0$, and $z_{it} = 0$ otherwise). These subsidies are financed period by period by a consumption tax and the government budget is always in equilibrium.

In *policy 2*, investment subsidies are paid in period 1 by issuing bonds while consumption taxes are levied afterwards. The public debt is reabsorbed at time $t = 2$ by levying lump-sum taxes on the young generation. This policy is accompanied by transfers from younger to older generations; that is, in every period, the old generation receives an amount equal to 10% of the discrepancy between the current value of its financial wealth and what this financial wealth would be in a stationary state. Given that the structural shock creates substantial financial losses for the older generation living at time $t = 1$, this policy essentially amounts to transferring money from future to current generations.

Both policies leave the stationary state unchanged, affecting only the transition path; the way they are set up ensures that both subsidies and transfers are progressively phased out. The consequences are illustrated in Figures 4 to 7, where the variables are measured with reference to the situation without government intervention described in the previous section. We consider each policy in turn.

4.1. Policy 1: Investment subsidies without transfers

Investment subsidies financed by consumption taxes have the effect of speeding up capital accumulation in sector 1 (Figure 4) and of slowing

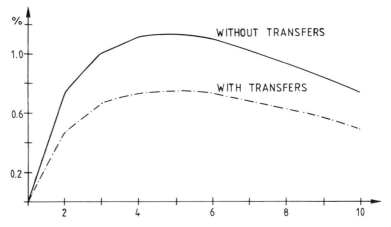

Figure 4. Effect of investment subsidy on capital accumulation in sector 1 (deviations from reference path in %).

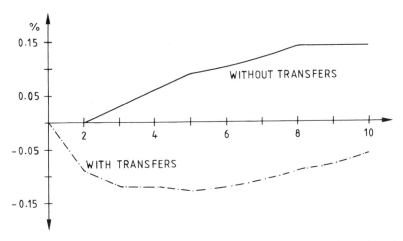

Figure 5. Effect of investment subsidy on capital scrapping in sector 2 (deviations from reference path in %).

down capital scrapping in sector 2 (Figure 5). They also have a negative impact on the interest rate,[7] at least after period 2 (Figure 6). As time goes on, the capital stocks and the interest rate move back to the same stationary state as in the reference case. This looks like the sort of result one may

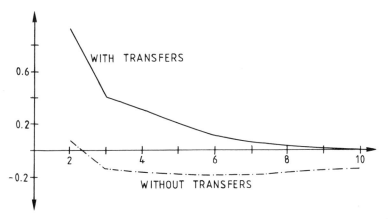

Figure 6. Effect of investment subsidy on the interest rate (deviations from reference path in percentage points).

[7] As indicated before, the (ex post) period 1 interest rate is not reported because it differs widely for sector 1 and sector 2 equities.

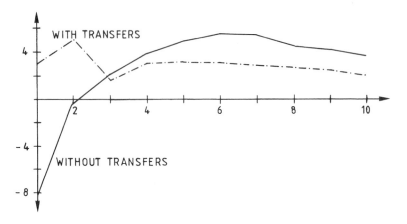

Figure 7. Effect of investment subsidy on welfare (deviations from reference path).

desire. Figure 7 shows however that this increased investment effort is done at the expense of the old generation living and holding the assets at the moment of the shock. Their welfare is substantially lower than what it would have been in the absence of government intervention. This is because the investment subsidy has a negative impact on the price of sector 1 equities and increases the financial losses of the old from 4.9 to 5.2%. The increased investment effort is obviously to the advantage of future generations who inherit a larger capital stock in both sectors. The investment subsidy succeeds in shifting investment forward in time but, from the consumer's point of view, it works like a transfer from current to future generations. Given that the generations living at the moment of the shock (time $t = 1$) are those which are mostly hit by the shock, this seems a very undesirable result, and suggests that it might be useful to supplement the investment subsidies by a policy aiming at transferring from future to current generations part of the benefits derived from investment. This is precisely what the type 2 policy does.

4.2. Policy 2: Investment subsidies with transfers

Policy 2 is less demanding for the generations living at time $t = 1$ because of the systematic transfers described above and also because investment subsidies in period 1 are financed by a larger government debt, rather than by consumption taxes. The effects of this combination of subsidies and transfers are clear. Compared to the case without government intervention, there is faster capital accumulation in sector 1 (Figure 4) and faster capital scrapping in sector 2 (Figure 5). There is also a strong positive impact on the interest rate (Figure 6), due to government borrowing in period 1. In the longer run, the capital stocks and the interest rate return to the same stationary state values as in the reference case. When this is compared to the effects of policy 1, one observes that the impulse given to investment in the expanding sector is weaker, but that the adjustment in the declining sector is much faster. In terms of welfare, Figure 7 shows that, compared to policy 1, policy 2 has the advantage of being beneficial to all, and not only to future generations. The figure also makes it clear that policy 2 "transfers" welfare from future to current generations.[8]

5. Concluding remarks

We have shown that the welfare deteriorating consequences of a structural shock can be alleviated with investment subsidies that shift investment forward in time without affecting the equilibrium capital stocks. We have also shown that such a policy should preferably be accompanied by transfers from future to current generations, so that the benefits of the increased investment effort can be shared by all. It is thus possible that a right mix of investment subsidies and intergenerational transfers improves the welfare of every generation on the transition path to the equilibrium. It is worth emphasizing that, in every policy experiment, the policies were designed so as to obtain the same stationary equilibrium. There is no doubt that our results crucially depend on the way we have modelled the economy. The problem is not so much the value of the parameters chosen in our example, but rather the representation of the behavior of agents. Our results would probably change if we were to assume that each generation takes into account its descendants' welfare as well as its own, or if we postulated a single representative consumer with infinite horizon. The approach taken here seemed, to us at least, more appropriate.

The model can of course be sophisticated in many useful ways. A most interesting research direction would be to introduce labor mobility costs in the same way as capital adjustment costs. It may seem odd (especially to European economists) to discuss the effects of structural shocks in a model where there is no sales constraints and no unemployment. Erlich, Ginsburgh

---

[8] It may be useful here to remind the reader that policy 2 is "uniformly" better than the reference solution without government intervention.

and Van der Heyden (1987) conclude their analysis (based on a two-period computable general equilibrium model with 24 sectors) by writing that: "In the short run, real wage policies can only do very little to alleviate the burden of unemployment. They however have strong effects in the medium and in the long run, provided that they are supported by fairly large capacity increases". In other words, there may be more than simple real wage problems behind Europe's unemployment; real wage policies should be accompanied by policies promoting an adequate allocation of production capacities across sectors. Two-sector overlapping generations models seem a natural framework to investigate further this sort of question.

References

Auerbach, A.J. and L.J. Kotlikoff (1987) *Dynamic Fiscal Policy*. Cambridge: Cambridge University Press.
Davies, J., J. Whalley and B. Hamilton (1989) 'Capital income taxation in a two-commodity life cycle model', *Journal of Public Economics*, 39:109–126.
Erlich, S., V. Ginsburgh and L. Van der Heyden (1987) 'Where do real wage policies lead Belgium', *European Economic Review*, 31:1369–1383.
Modigliani, F., M. Monti, J.H. Drèze, H. Giersch and R. Layard (1987) 'Reducing unemployment in Europe: the role of capital formation', in: R. Layard and L. Calmfors, eds., *The Fight Against Unemployment*. Cambridge, MA: MIT Press.

Chapter 7

INVESTMENT IN A DISEQUILIBRIUM MODEL OR DOES PROFITABILITY REALLY MATTER?

Jean-Paul LAMBERT

*Facultés Universitaires Saint-Louis, Bruxelles, Belgium, and CORE,
Université Catholique de Louvain, Louvain-la-Neuve, Belgium*

Benoît MULKAY

Facultés Universitaires Saint-Louis, Bruxelles, Belgium

1. Introduction

Existing empirical disequilibrium models (Sneessens, 1981; Artus, Laroque and Michel, 1984; Kooiman and Kloek, 1985; Lambert, 1988; to cite some of them) are, in their present state, essentially short-term models due to their treating some key variables like prices/wages and investment as exogenous. This feature does not at all invalidate these models as useful instruments for policy analysis: indeed they proved highly valuable for examining some crucial issues, like the extent of Keynesian vs. classical vs. frictional unemployment to take only one example. However, in order to

We wish to thank participants of seminars at CORE, the Commission of the European Communities, the 6th International Symposium on Forecasting, Paris, and the 1st European Economic Association Congress, Vienna, for helpful comments and suggestions. Victor Ginsburgh offered comments which helped improve the presentation and which are therefore gratefully acknowledged, without however involving him in any remaining error or short-comings.

Financial support of the Commissariat Général du Plan, France and the Commission of the European Communities is gratefully acknowledged. The second author has also benefited from a fellowship of the College Interuniversitaire du Management (CIM), Brussels.

Economic Decision-Making: Games, Econometrics and Optimisation
Edited by J.J. Gabszewicz, J.-F. Richard and L.A. Wolsey
© *Elsevier Science Publishers B.V., 1990*

qualify as fully operational instruments for policy analysis these models clearly need to be extended to be able to capture longer run effects of alternative policies. Let us illustrate this point by looking at a particular but important issue. A majority of the above mentioned studies (and other similar ones) pointed towards a major share of present unemployment to be of a "classical" nature, i.e., to be caused by insufficient profitable (at prevailing price and cost conditions) equipment. Such a diagnosis implies that only some share of total unemployment (called the "Keynesian" share) could be relatively rapidly and easily (in the absence of any other constraint like an external or budget constraint) alleviated through reflationary policies. But this is clearly for the short term. In the longer term, the "potential employment" ceiling (level of employment corresponding to the full use of all profitable equipment) is itself crucially dependent on the investment response to the particular policy chosen, which may not be obvious a priori. Imagine indeed the case of a wage increase intended to stimulate internal demand: such a policy, no doubt, exerts a positive effect on investment via the well-known accelerator mechanism but also a negative effect through reduced profitability perceptions induced by the wage increase. What is the ultimate sign of the resulting long-term multiplier effect? What are the respective dynamics of the two opposed influences? The appropriateness of the policy depends of course on the precise answer given to these questions. More generally, any policy intended to tackle the unemployment problem at the root has to be assessed according to its longer run influence on the level of (profitable) equipment.

Endogenizing investment behaviour within disequilibrium models hence appears as a necessary step in the development of models designed to study most adequately disequilibrium phenomena, like unemployment.

This could be done very easily by simply incorporating conventional investment specifications within existing disequilibrium models but such a practice is clearly unsatisfactory since the treatment of investment would be at odds with the rest of the model. What is needed is an explicit (and of course appropriate) account of the rationing context.

There have been, to date, a few attempts, conducted in a partial equilibrium setting, to study investment in a disequilibrium context (see, for example, Artus and Muet, 1984; Gérard and Vanden Berghe, 1984; Mulkay, 1983).

Despite some important differences (see Lambert, 1987, for a critical discussion), all these studies adopt basically the same approach which may be roughly described as follows: aggregate investment is computed as a weighted sum of investment performed by firms situated in the various regimes. All firms are assumed to compute their optimal capital stock taking into account constraints which vary according to the ruling regime. To concentrate here on the two most relevant regimes, "Keynesian firms" are assumed to consider only a known, *deterministic* sales constraint while "classical firms" do not even consider the possibility of any constraint at all when determining their optimal capital stock, which implies a necessary hypothesis of decreasing returns to scale in order to get a finite solution. Such an approach seems to us open to criticism for two main reasons. The first one concerns the treatment of perceived rationing as deterministic: while perhaps acceptable for the analysis of shorter-run behaviour (like short-term production and employment decisions) it is, in our view, no more acceptable for analyzing decisions involving the longer term and incorporating some degree of irreversibility — like investment decisions — where *uncertainty* surely ought to enter the picture. The second criticism of the approach just described concerns its unrealistic treatment of firms finding themselves in a classical situation: they are assumed to invest without having to bother at all about future demand! This is simply conflicting with factual observation: in the "real world", firms facing a situation of excess demand (for their products) on fast growing markets try to assess (with any unavoidable degree of imprecision) the growth potential of the market and then decide on their investments conditionally on the market share that they fixed to themselves as a reasonable objective.

So here also, a (somewhat) uncertain future demand has to be considered. The conclusion of this short discussion is clear: the appropriate framework for examining investment behaviour of firms is a *stochastic rationing context*, whatever the present (and necessarily temporary) situation of the firms. Firms of course may differ from each other as regards the level of their present — and expected future — demand with respect to their present capacity and, if available, statistical information on such discrepancies might profitably be exploited in the estimation; but such a heterogeneity among firms does not stand against stochastic rationing being the appropriate framework, valid for all firms, to examine investment behaviour.

Such an approach has been suggested, and sketched, by Malinvaud (1983, 1987) (see also Nickell, 1978, Chapter 5, for a prior suggestion along this direction). It has been adopted by Artus (1985) who analyses, in an intertemporal optimization setting, the decisions of the firm confronted to an uncertain future demand. The dynamic approach is no doubt, from a theoretical point of view, more attractive than the static model proposed initially by Malinvaud; however, the empirical results obtained by Artus (1985) suggest that adopting the static model does not entail a significant distortion of reality, at least for the problems of interest here[1] (refer to the observation by Malinvaud, 1987, on this point). In view of this prior evidence, and since we want to refine the analysis in some respects while still keeping the problem tractable, we opt here for the static model. Besides some other interesting features, the main difference between Artus' work and ours lies in the fact that our investment model is not estimated in isolation but simultaneously within a complete (fix-price) disequilibrium model. This strategy is not only meant to help improve the efficiency of estimation (since taking account of the multiple cross-equations restrictions) but presents the additional considerable advantage of enabling us to use (in the estimation) the appropriate measure of some crucial unobservable variables (like the demand for goods, a crucial determinant of desired capacity and a non-observable variable in a disequilibrium context).

The plan of the paper is as follows: the theoretical model is developed in the next section where testable specifications are derived while the estimation results are presented in Section 3 together with a discussion of their policy implications. A conclusive section summarizes the main lessons to be drawn from this work and sketches some suggestions for future research.

2. The theoretical model

Let us describe the problem facing our investor and be more specific about some of its assumed characteristics before going to formalization and derivation of optimal choices.

A first remark concerns the static character of the analysis developed in this theoretical section. Investment decisions should in full rigor and generality be analyzed as an intertemporal optimization problem with due account for all future prices/costs and all future expected constraints. This is bound to lead to a very complicated model with virtually no chance of ending up with tractable specifications. We chose instead to adopt a static framework where prices/costs and expected constraints may be interpreted as reflecting average medium-term expectations. The main argument in support of such

---

[1] Unlike the model of this paper, Artus (1985) develops an intertemporal model which is then linearized either around the steady growth solution or the steady state solution. This latter formulation may be shown to be analogous to the one adopted here, provided an appropriate definition of the capital usage cost is adopted. In this respect, it may be interesting to note that, according to the empirical results obtained by Artus, the "steady growth model" does not perform better than the "steady state model".

a simplifying strategy comes from the ability of the resulting model to successfully explore the basic implications of stochastic rationing on investment decision, as will be shown below. Such a practice moreover is backed by a now firmly established tradition in empirically oriented research, going from Jorgenson's approach — where a dynamic problem was converted into a static one through the user cost of capital device — to the latest papers mentioned above.[2]

The problem of the investor may now be described as follows: at the start of the (unique) period, the investor has to decide on his optimal capital stock K^* taking into account (future) prices and costs (assumed to be known with certainty) and expected constraints on the level of demand for his output Y^d.

As argued in the introductory section, the level of this constraint is most realistically assumed not to be known with certainty, so Y^d is a stochastic variable distributed according to a density function $g(Y^d)$. Such a function receives the following interpretation (see Malinvaud, 1983): the demand Y^d, which is still uncertain at the time when investment has to be decided on, will subsequently materialize at some level (consider it as representing the average level of demand during the equipment's life span) and $g(Y^d)$ then represents the investor's subjective probability distribution as to the occurrence of demand. Demand for goods Y^d is the only source of uncertainty introduced in this model: future prices and costs are predetermined variables assumed to be known for sure and the firm does not anticipate any constraint on the availability of labour.[3]

One has to pay attention to an important aspect of the investor's decision, namely the character of irreversibility stemming from the very limited substitution possibilities (between factors), once equipment has been installed. Indeed, while the investor may choose among a broad set of different production techniques when deciding on his optimal investments, i.e., *before* installation of physical equipment, he has to stick to the chosen technique for running current operations, once equipment has been installed. This is the well known "putty–clay" property of productive operations where a distinction is introduced between the *ex-ante* (or long-term) *production function* describing the broad substitution possibilities offering themselves

---

[2] See however, Michel (1986) who explores the implications of future quantity constraints for the computation of the user cost of capital.

[3] This latter assumption does not seem too restrictive in our situation of huge unemployment. It is moreover somewhat supported by the conclusions of the available empirical studies (as those mentioned in the Introduction) which failed generally to detect any significant influence of labour constraints on investment behaviour.

when deciding on investment and the *ex-post* (or short-term) production function describing the limited (or even non-existent) substitution possibilities once physical capital has been installed.

Our production model will also exhibit this "putty-clay property" with a CES and a Leontieff being adopted respectively for the ex-ante and the ex-post production function.[4]

Adopting the following notation:

K^*: optimal stock of capital to be installed;

Y^*: optimal production capacity;

L^*: amount of labour corresponding to the full use of the optimal capacity Y^*;

Y: effective production level ($Y \le Y^*$);

L: amount of labour needed to get the level of production Y ($L \le L^*$);

the choice of the optimal stock of capital K^* and the optimal production technique — expressed by technical coefficients like L^*/Y^* — will thus be made along a CES production function; once a specific technique has been embodied into physical capital, it has to be used for subsequent current operations, i.e., $L/Y = L^*/Y^*$ for example.

Assuming the firm to be risk-neutral, it will choose K^*, L^* and Y^* so as to maximize expected profit, which writes down

$$\underset{K^*, L^*, Y^*}{\text{Max}} \; E(\pi) = E(pY - wL - cK^*) \tag{2.1}$$

subject to the following constraints:

$$Y^* = \gamma[\delta(e^{\gamma_L T}L^*)^{-\rho} + (1-\delta)(e^{\gamma_K T}K^*)^{-\rho}]^{-1/\rho}, \tag{2.2}$$

$$L/Y = L^*/Y^*, \tag{2.3}$$

$$Y^d \sim g(Y^d), \tag{2.4}$$

$$Y = \min(Y^d, Y^*), \tag{2.5}$$

where

π = profit,

p = product price,

w = nominal wage rate,

c = user cost of capital,

---

[4] The "putty-clay" property is most often associated with vintage production functions, but it is not a logical necessity. The production framework adopted here exhibits indeed this desirable property without being of the vintage type. This approach has been first initiated in Sneessens (1981) and Lubrano and Sneessens (1984) and further developed in Lambert (1988) who also discusses (in Chapter 2) the problems arising from aggregation.

γ_L, γ_K = factor augmenting technical progress for labour and capital respectively,

T = time trend term,

E is the expectation operator.

Equations (2.2) and (2.3) express respectively the ex-ante production function and the ex-post production function. Notice the constant return to scale assumption, less restrictive than decreasing returns to scale assumed in previous works. (2.4) reminds us that demand Y^d is a stochastic variable distributed according to a density function g. Equation (2.5) expresses the fact that the investment decision is assumed to be taken and capital installed prior to the occurrence of the uncertain demand, so that once demand has materialized at some level Y^d it will be completely satisfied only to the extent that Y^d is lower or equal to Y^* since, by definition, production cannot be pushed beyond full productive capacity Y^*.

The investor's problem may be rewritten as

$$\underset{K^*,L^*,Y^*}{\text{Max}} \left[p - w \frac{L^*}{Y^*} \right] E(Y) - cK^*$$

$$+ \Lambda \{ Y^* - \gamma [\delta (e^{\gamma_L T} L^*)^{-\rho} + (1-\delta)(e^{\gamma_K T} K^*)^{-\rho}]^{-1/\rho} \} \qquad (2.6)$$

with the constraints (2.4) and (2.5) integrated within the expression of $E(Y)$ as

$$E(Y) = \int_0^{Y^*} Y^d g(Y^d) \, dY^d + Y^* \int_{Y^*}^{\infty} g(Y^d) \, dY^d.$$

The computation of the first order conditions requires the derivation of $E(Y)$ which, by using Leibniz's rule, is readily shown to yield

$$\frac{\partial}{\partial Y^*} E(Y) = \int_{Y^*}^{\infty} g(Y^d) \, dY^d = \text{Prob}(Y^d > Y^*).$$

Using this result and adopting the symbol $\mathscr{L}$ for the Lagrangian, one easily obtains the system of first order conditions:

$$\frac{\partial \mathscr{L}}{\partial K^*} = -c - \Lambda \frac{Y^*}{K^*} \frac{(1-\delta)(e^{\gamma_K T} K^*)^{-\rho}}{[\delta(e^{\gamma_L T} L^*)^{-\rho} + (1-\delta)(e^{\gamma_K T} K^*)^{-\rho}]} = 0, \qquad (2.7)$$

$$\frac{\partial \mathscr{L}}{\partial L^*} = -w \frac{E(Y)}{Y^*} - \Lambda \frac{Y^*}{L^*} \frac{\delta(e^{\gamma_L T} L^*)^{-\rho}}{[\delta(e^{\gamma_L T} L^*)^{-\rho} + (1-\delta)(e^{\gamma_K T} K^*)^{-\rho}]} = 0, \qquad (2.8)$$

$$\frac{\partial \mathscr{L}}{\partial Y^*} = \frac{wL^* E(Y)}{(Y^*)^2} + \left[p - w \frac{L^*}{Y^*} \right] \text{Prob}(Y^d > Y^*) + \Lambda = 0. \qquad (2.9)$$

Let us first derive the optimal technical coefficients. Dividing expression (2.8) by expression (2.7) and taking logarithms, one gets

$$\ln\left(\frac{K^*}{L^*}\right) = \text{const.} + (1-\sigma)(\gamma_L - \gamma_K)T + \sigma \ln\left(\frac{w}{c}\right) + \sigma \ln\left(\frac{E(Y)}{Y^*}\right)$$

where $\sigma = 1/(1+\rho)$ is the elasticity of substitution of the ex-ante production function. Designating the degree of utilization of capacity ($\stackrel{\text{def}}{=} Y/Y^*$) by the symbol DUC, the above equation may be rewritten as

$$\ln\left(\frac{K^*}{L^*}\right) = \text{const.} + (1-\sigma)(\gamma_L - \gamma_K)T + \sigma \ln\left[\frac{w}{c}E(\text{DUC})\right]. \qquad (2.10)$$

The optimal capital-labour ratio is seen to depend, as usual, on the factor augmenting technical progress and on the relative factor costs but a novel element is introduced via the factor $E(\text{DUC})$ in the last term of (2.10). This factor is clearly linked with the uncertainty of demand Y^d. Indeed, in a world with deterministic — instead of stochastic — rationing, i.e., with a known demand constraint Y^d, the optimal level of capacity (at least with non-decreasing returns to scale) will be $Y^* = Y^d$ and $E(\text{DUC}) = Y^d/Y^* = 1$. As soon as demand uncertainty is brought into the picture, $E(\text{DUC})$ becomes strictly lower than one, which introduces a bias towards more labour intensive techniques than in the pure certainty case. Everything happens as if demand uncertainty resulted in making the cost of capital more expensive since the cost $c/E(\text{DUC}) > c$ has now to be considered instead of c. This may be easily explained with our assumptions: once installed, total capital cost cK^* has to be fully supported, whatever the level of production, while labour has been assumed to be fully adjustable since $L = (L^*/Y^*)Y \le L^*$ by virtue of our Leontieff short-run production function. Of course, the distinction between fully-adjustable labour and unadjustable capital is probably overemphasized in this theoretical model when compared to the "real world" where a number of considerations tend sometimes to transform labour into a "quasi-fixed" factor. Such a distinction, even if somewhat exaggerated, is nevertheless useful at this stage since it allows to highlight a main effect of demand uncertainty on the choice of techniques.

The derivation of tractable specifications for the other technical ratios (capital/output and labour/output ratios) may be performed in a similar way. Let us first investigate the meaning of the Lagrangian multiplier Λ. Multiplying expressions (2.7) and (2.8) respectively by K^* and L^*, adding them up and dividing the sum by Y^*, we get, after some manipulations,

$$\Lambda = -\left[\frac{wE(L)+cK^*}{E(Y)}\right]\frac{E(Y)}{Y^*}. \tag{2.11}$$

The first factor in the right-hand side represents the unit production cost at the "average" or "normal" level of operation.

Referring to it shortly as the average production cost, we may write

$$\Lambda = -(\text{average production cost}) \cdot E(\text{DUC})$$

where $E(\text{DUC})$ departs from 1 only in case of demand uncertainty. If we make the usual assumption that, in the long run, prices are set equal to a constant mark-up over long-run average costs, we may substitute an expression proportional to $-p \cdot E(\text{DUC})$ for Λ.

Doing so with expression (2.7) yields, after some manipulation and taking logarithms,

$$\ln\left(\frac{Y^*}{K^*}\right) = \text{const.} + (1-\sigma)\gamma_K T + \sigma \ln\left[\frac{c}{p}\frac{1}{E(\text{DUC})}\right]. \tag{2.12}$$

Similarly, (2.8) yields

$$\ln\left(\frac{Y^*}{L^*}\right) = \text{const.} + (1-\sigma)\gamma_L T + \sigma \ln\left(\frac{w}{p}\right). \tag{2.13}$$

These expressions look familiar except for the presence of the term $E(\text{DUC})$ in (2.12): one verifies that the user cost of the (unadjustable) capital has to be amended to account for uncertainty while the prices of the (adjustable) labour and output remain unaffected.

Expressions (2.10), (2.12) and (2.13) yielding optimal values for the technical coefficients could be derived from the two first order conditions (2.7) and (2.8) but the third condition (2.9) has not yet been used.

Substituting expression (2.11) for Λ in (2.9), one obtains readily that Y^* has to satisfy

$$\text{Prob}(Y^d > Y^*) = \frac{cK^*}{pY^* - wL^*} = \frac{cK^*}{\pi^* + cK^*} \tag{2.14}$$

with $\pi^* \overset{\text{def}}{=} pY^* - wL^* - cK^*$ being the profit which would be obtained if operating at full capacity.[5]

---

[5] Expression (2.14) is formally identical to the one obtained in the well-known problem of the newspapers boy who has to manage optimally his stock of newspapers. We thank Jacques H. Drèze for bringing this to our attention.

In order to end up with a useful specification for the optimal capacity Y^*, one has to provide an analytical expression for $\text{Prob}(Y^d > Y^*)$ which implies choosing a specific density function $g(Y^d)$ for the subjective distribution of (future) demand. The problem of course is to find a density function which does not conflict with current knowledge about the shape of demand expectations while at the same time conducting to tractable specifications.

The lognormal distribution may be shown to satisfy both criteria. Indeed, as far as the first point is concerned, it conforms to the available evidence dealing with business survey results and identifying demand uncertainty to be multiplicative instead of additive (see, for example, Waelbroeck-Rocha, 1984).

Lognormality amounts indeed to the following assumption:

$$\ln Y^d = \bar{y}^d + \varepsilon^d \quad \text{with } \varepsilon^d \sim N(0, \sigma^2_{\varepsilon^d}).$$

The median of the distribution of Y^d is equal to $\exp(\bar{y}^d)$ and the mean $E(Y^d)$ is equal to $\exp(\bar{y}^d + \frac{1}{2}\sigma^2_{\varepsilon^d})$. One has thus $\bar{y}^d = \ln E(Y^d) - \frac{1}{2}\sigma^2_{\varepsilon^d}$. Since the distribution of $\ln Y^d$ is normal, it may be approximated by a logistic distribution having the same mean $\bar{y}^d = \ln E(Y^d) - \frac{1}{2}\sigma^2_{\varepsilon^d}$ and the same variance $\sigma^2_{\varepsilon^d}$. In this case

$$\text{Prob}(Y^d > Y^*) = \text{Prob}(\ln Y^d > \ln Y^*)$$

$$= 1 - \text{Prob}(\ln Y^d \le \ln Y^*)$$

$$= 1 - \left\{ 1 + \exp\left[\frac{\ln E(Y^d) - \frac{1}{2}\sigma^2_{\varepsilon^d} - \ln Y^*}{(\sqrt{3}/\pi)\sigma_{\varepsilon^d}} \right] \right\}^{-1}$$

$$= 1 - \left\{ 1 + b_* \left[\frac{E(Y^d)}{Y^*} \right]^{\rho_*} \right\}^{-1}$$

where

$$b_* = \exp\left[-\frac{\pi\sigma_{\varepsilon^d}}{2\sqrt{3}} \right] \quad \text{and} \quad \rho_* = \frac{\pi}{\sqrt{3}} \frac{1}{\sigma_{\varepsilon^d}}.$$

Finally,

$$\text{Prob}(Y^d > Y^*) = \left\{ 1 + b_*^{-1} \left[\frac{E(Y^d)}{Y^*} \right]^{-\rho_*} \right\}^{-1}.$$

Substituting this expression into equation (2.14) yields, after some manipulation,

$$\ln Y^* = \frac{1}{\rho_*} \ln b_* + \ln E(Y^d) + \frac{1}{\rho^*} \ln\left(\frac{\pi^*}{cK^*}\right)$$

which may be rewritten as

$$\ln Y^* = \text{const.} + \ln E(Y^d) + \sigma_K \ln\left(\frac{\pi^*}{cK^*}\right) \tag{2.15}$$

where the constant equals $-\frac{1}{2}\sigma_{\varepsilon^d}^2$ and $\sigma_K = 1/\rho^* = (\sqrt{3}/\pi)\sigma_{\varepsilon^d}$ is a direct measure of the degree of uncertainty about Y^d.[6]

The investor's optimization program thus boils down to determining optimal capacity Y^* as a simple loglinear function of expected demand $E(Y^d)$ and the profitability indicator $\pi^*/(cK^*)$. The presence of demand prospects as a main determinant of capacity is of course not surprising: it is in line with a long tradition of "accelerator models" of all types. This is however not the case for profitability, which here comes out as another prime determinant of desired capacity (and hence of investment behaviour) and which is most generally absent from theoretical work. Of course, profits (past and present) are often included among explanatory variables in empirical work about investment but are then supposed to capture the more transitory effects of (possible) financial constraints on the pace of investment; such a role is radically different from the one played by our profitability indicator which comes out as a fundamental long-run determinant, on par with demand expectations.

However, since a theoretically unveiled effect may turn out to be empirically of minor significance, empirical testing will have to be the final judge of the practical relevance of profitability considerations. This point will be handled in the next section. Let us come back to equation (2.15) and develop a few remarks.

First, the long run elasticity of optimal capacity Y^* with respect to demand expectations $E(Y^d)$ is equal to unity, which seems sensible in view of the implications for the steady growth properties of the model.

Second, our profitability indicator $\pi^*/(cK^*)$, equal to "profit at full capacity" divided by total capital cost, may be shown to be closely linked to Tobin's q, as already suggested by Malinvaud (1983). Indeed, Tobin's q

---

[6] Indeed, the standard deviation of the lognormally distributed variable Y^d is equal to $\sigma_{Y^d} = \exp(\bar{y}^d)\{\exp(\sigma_{\varepsilon^d}^2)[\exp(\sigma_{\varepsilon^d}^2) - 1]\}^{1/2} = \cdots = E(Y^d)\{\exp(\sigma_{\varepsilon^d}^2) - 1\}^{1/2}$. For the relevant range of values of σ_{ε^d}, $\exp(\sigma_{\varepsilon^d}^2) \simeq 1 + \sigma_{\varepsilon^d}^2$, so that $\sigma_{Y^d} \simeq E(Y^d)\sigma_{\varepsilon^d}$ and hence $\sigma_{\varepsilon^d} \simeq \sigma_{Y^d}/E(Y^d)$ is a direct measure of the degree of uncertainty about Y^d.

being defined as the market value of the firm (equal to the present value of expected net returns in the case of perfect market valuation) divided by the value of capital, its transposition in a static framework would imply (see Malinvaud, 1983)

$$q \overset{\text{def}}{=} \frac{pE(Y) - wE(L)}{cK^*}.$$

Simple computation then permits to verify that

$$\frac{\pi^*}{cK^*} = \frac{q}{E(\text{DUC})} - 1.$$

The final specification proposed for estimation will however be much more elaborate than is usual in the literature concerned with the empirical testing of the q theory.[7]

Our third remark concerns the influence of profitability on investment decisions: since the parameter σ_K is by definition always positive, increased profitability unambiguously leads to higher optimal capacity and hence — other things being equal — higher investment. Such a result of course corresponds to intuition and, as said above, empirical testing will have to be the final judge of the practical significance of such an effect. Equation (2.15) also informs us about the relative position of optimal capacity Y^* with respect to parameters governing the position of the uncertain demand. It may readily be verified that Y^* will be higher (lower) than the median of Y^d if the profitability indicator is greater (lower) than unity. This result is quite general and in no way linked to the particular distribution adopted for Y^d since it simply corresponds to the first order optimality condition (2.14). In addition, Y^* is seen to be higher than $E(Y^d)$ when "profitability at full capacity" exceeds a critical level defined as $\exp[(\pi/2\sqrt{3})\sigma_{\varepsilon^d}]$ (approximately equivalent, for the relevant range of parameter values, to $1 + \pi\sigma_{\varepsilon^d}/2\sqrt{3}$) but this result is of course dependent on the lognormality assumption for Y^d. Actually, the closest proxy for our "profitability at full capacity" indicator computed from available statistical information (see the appendix for precise data definition) suggests profitability to have stayed persistently below such a critical level (except perhaps for some isolated years at the start of the observation period).

A fourth series of comments concerns the influence of demand uncertainty on optimal capacity and hence on "capital widening" investment decisions.

---

[7] Actually, our profitability indicator π^*/cK^* is not really an exogenous variable like prices or demand expectations. It will however be treated as such in the remainder of this paper in view of the strong appeal presented by our approach for studying the crucial issue of the role played by profitability in investment decisions.

Let us first notice that uncertainty plays a role here although our firms were assumed to be risk-neutral: indeed, in the absence of any (demand) uncertainty, σ_{ε^d} boils down to zero and Y^* becomes equal to $E(Y^d) = Y^d$ which may be significantly different from the optimal Y^* under uncertainty. A natural question to ask now is: what is the effect on optimal capacity of an increase in uncertainty? Remembering that the standard deviation $\sigma_{\varepsilon^d} \cong \sigma_{Y^d}/E(Y^d)$ (see footnote 3) and defining an increase in uncertainty as a mean-preserving spread of Y^d, this amounts to compute the sign of $(dY^*/d\sigma_{\varepsilon^d})|_{dE(Y^d)=0}$.

From equation (2.15), one gets easily

$$\frac{d \ln Y^*}{d\sigma_{\varepsilon^d}}\bigg|_{dE(Y^d)=0} = -\sigma_{\varepsilon^d} + \frac{\sqrt{3}}{\pi} \ln\left(\frac{\pi^*}{ck^*}\right)$$

so that

$$\frac{d Y^*}{d\sigma_{\varepsilon^d}}\bigg|_{dE(Y^d)=0} = Y^* \left\{ \frac{\sqrt{3}}{\pi} \ln\left(\frac{\pi^*}{cK^*}\right) - \sigma_{\varepsilon^d} \right\},$$

the sign of which depends on $\pi^*/(cK^*)$ being larger or smaller than $\exp[(\pi/\sqrt{3})\sigma_{\varepsilon^d}]$. So, if "profitability" (as perceived by the firms) happens to be "low" (i.e., $< 1 + (\pi/\sqrt{3})\sigma_{\varepsilon^d}$), increased demand uncertainty will induce risk-neutral firms to reduce capacity while the converse is true in the case of a "high" profitability. Hence, uncertainty does not appear to exert a theoretically definite effect (see, for example, Nickell, 1978, Chapter 5 for a similar undeterminacy result in a slightly different setup). However, in view of the historical profitability records reported above, uncertainty is most likely to have exerted, throughout the period, a quite depressing effect on desired capacities.[8] This effect of uncertainty corresponds to intuition and is moreover supported by casual information coming from specific business surveys.

3. Estimation results

The empirical analysis of investment behaviour in a stochastic rationing context will thus rely on the following specifications derived from the

---

[8] Assume a firm holding a diversified portfolio of activities, characterized by different profitabilities ranging from "low" to "high". An evolution of the overall conditions towards greater uncertainty would, according to our model, result in a restructuring process aiming at enhanced specialization in the most profitable activities. The model might hence perhaps have some relevance for explaining the extensive restructuring in which major firms seem to be engaged since the mid-seventies.

theoretical model:

$$\ln Y^* = \text{const.} + \ln E(Y^d) + \sigma_K \ln \left(\frac{\pi^*}{cK^*} \right)$$ (2.15)

and

$$\ln k^* \overset{\text{def}}{=} \ln \left(\frac{K^*}{Y^*} \right) = \text{const.} - (1-\sigma)\gamma_K T + \sigma \ln \left[\frac{p}{c} E(\text{DUC}) \right].$$ (2.12)

The optimal capital stock K^* thus obtains as

$$\ln K^* = \ln k^* + \ln Y^*.$$

This is a purely static specification which, for obvious reasons, may not simply be transposed as such for the empirical application. Adjustment costs of all sorts, delivery lags, ..., etc., prevent an immediate adjustment of the actual capital stock K towards its optimal value K^*; aggregate technical coefficients only adjust slowly to their new optimal values through a progressive process of scrapping of obsolete equipments and replacement by more efficient ones; finally, the expectations about (future) demand, profitability, relative prices are not only based on current observation but are formed by integrating all available information, including past observations.

Adopting a stochastic difference equation formulation, a most general dynamic specification will be used:

$$\ln k_t = \text{const.} + \Phi_k(L) \ln k_t^*$$

$$+ \Phi_Y(L) \ln Y_t^d + \sigma_K \Phi_\pi(L) \ln \left(\frac{\pi^*}{cK^*} \right)_t + \Phi_\varepsilon(L)\varepsilon_t$$ (3.1)

where $\Phi_k(L)$, $\Phi_Y(L)$, $\Phi_\pi(L)$ and $\Phi_\varepsilon(L)$ represent (possibly different) rational lag functions and ε_t is the stochastic disturbance term.

The rational lag functions $\Phi_i(L)$ ($i = k, Y, \pi, \varepsilon$) are assumed to have a common structure

$$\Phi_i(L) = \frac{\delta_{0i} + \delta_{1i}L + \delta_{2i}L^2}{1 - \delta_3 L}$$

with the additional constraint $\delta_{0i} + \delta_{1i} + \delta_{2i} + \delta_3 = 1$ and the parameter δ_3 being identical for all $\Phi_i(L)$. Imposing moreover $\delta_{0\varepsilon} = 1$ and $\delta_{1\varepsilon} = \delta_{2\varepsilon} = 0$ allows to multiply both sides of equation (3.1) by the factor $(1 - \delta_3 L)$ in order to end up with a highly tractable (from an estimation point of view) stochastic difference equation, with $\Delta \ln K_t$ as the dependent variable.

Equation (3.1) makes clear that net investment is determined by relative prices, demand prospects and profitability considerations, each of these factors being allowed to exert its effects with different dynamics. Relative prices (including exogenous technical progress) pertains to what is known as "capital deepening" while the other two factors are behind the "capital widening" process. The most relevant aspects of investment behaviour are thus captured in this model.

Before presenting and commenting on estimation results, a few remarks on the final specification are in order.

The capital user cost c to be considered for the determination of k^* is generally specified as

$$c_t = p_{1t}[i_t^e + \delta]$$

where

p_{1t} = price of investment goods,
i_t^e = anticipated real rate of interest,
δ = depreciation rate of capital equipment.

The variable i_t^e is to be understood as the average — taken over the whole equipment's life horizon — real interest rate, as perceived at time t by investors. If the time horizon to be considered is sufficiently large, these real interest rate expectations are likely to fluctuate only very slowly so as to be hardly distinguishable (empirically) from a constant. This happens to be the case here: various attempts to get a sensible specification for i_t^e (as the observed nominal long-run interest rate minus a weighted average of current and past inflation rates) proved unsuccessful so that we had to assume i_t^e to be constant implying the capital user cost c_t to be proportional to the price of investment goods p_{1t}. (See, for example, Sneessens and Drèze, 1986, for a similar finding.)

The factor $E(DUC)$ present in the last term of k_t^* to amend somewhat the relative cost of capital (see discussion in Section 2) has simply been approximated by observed DUC in the empirical estimation.

The profitability indicator $\pi^*/(cK^*)$ is not readily available as such in published statistics since it is defined as the ratio of the profits *which would be obtained at full capacity* to the total cost of installed capital. However, remembering our assumption about the firm's short-run production function and combining its implication with recorded profitability ratios allows us to construct a suitable proxy of our theoretical indicator $\pi^*/(cK^*)$ (refer to the Data Appendix for further details.)

Let us comment briefly on the estimation strategy. Estimation was performed on annual data (1965-1984) referring to the Belgian manufacturing sector. Equation (3.1) was estimated jointly within a complete fix-price disequilibrium model of the Belgian manufacturing sector. (See Lambert, 1988, for an extensive presentation of this model.) The resulting model is a 6 equations (not counting the identities) model which was estimated by a FIML method. This way of proceeding offers many advantages. First, it allows to substitute an appropriate estimate (or, more properly, an appropriate specification) for the unobservable demand for goods Y^d, which has anyway — and quite understandably in a disequilibrium model — to be considered elsewhere in the model. (See Lambert, 1987, for a critical comment of the usual practice of substituting the observable variable Y for the unobservable Y^d.) Second, it allows a much more efficient estimation by taking into account cross-equations restrictions for the parameters: this is especially the case for the parameters of the long-run production function (involved in the term k^* in (3.1)) and some dynamic parameters (those of $\Phi_k(L)$ to be precise) which show up also in other equations of the model. A last and most obvious advantage of our estimation strategy is to take account of simultaneity in the estimation.

Estimation results will now be presented with a particular emphasis on policy implications.

First, the two parameters directly linked with the (ex-ante) long-run production function, namely the elasticity of substitution σ and the capital-augmenting technical progress γ_K. One gets (with asymptotic standard errors in parentheses),

$$\sigma = 0.679 \quad \text{and} \quad \gamma_K = 0.029.$$
$$\quad (0.044) \qquad\qquad (0.004)$$

These results deserve no comment, except to mention that their estimation has benefited from the increase in efficiency due to the use of cross-equations restrictions and that the additional constraint $\gamma_K = \gamma_L$, namely Hicks' neutral technical change had to be imposed due to multicollinearity problems (arising in another equation).

Remember that uncertainty about (future) demand is the channel through which profitability considerations have been found to play a role in the determination of desired capacities.

The degree of demand uncertainty (see footnote 3) is measured by the parameter σ_K in equation (2.15).

There is no general reason to believe that the degree of demand uncertainty has remained constant through time: quite on the contrary, it is generally believed that demand uncertainty may vary according to business conditions and also that uncertainty might have increased significantly from the mid-seventies on, compared to the previous period. Consequently, we tried various specifications (including of course a simple constant) to be substituted for σ_K in the empirical application. Prior beliefs happen to be comforted by the estimation results.

Indeed, although $\sigma_K = $ const. yields quite satisfactory results (with σ_K significantly different from zero), the best performing specification (on the basis of the maximum likelihood value criterion) was found to be

$$\sigma_{Kt} = 0.053 \ln P_{Gt} - 0.106 \ln P_{Gt-1}$$
$$(0.016) \qquad (0.023)$$

with $\mathscr{L} = 355.6$ (against $\mathscr{L} = 349.3$ for $\sigma_K = $ const.) and an additional constant being non-significant.

The variable P_{Gt} takes values between zero and one and represents the proportion of firms currently in a situation of excess demand; it is an endogenous variable in the context of the complete model (and is treated as such in the estimation) and is provided by the (correctly interpreted) answers to regular business surveys conducted in the manufacturing sector (for an extensive discussion of this source of information and its use in macroeconometric models, refer to Lambert, 1988).

The implications of our estimation results for σ_{Kt} appear more clearly when rewriting σ_{Kt} as

$$\sigma_{Kt} = -0.053 \ln P_{Gt} + 0.106 \, \Delta \ln P_{Gt}.$$
$$(0.011) \qquad (0.023)$$

The first term, always positive (since $0 \le P_{Gt} \le 1$), may be seen as yielding an estimate of the basic level of (demand) uncertainty while the second term would account for shorter-run variations due to changing business conditions. Since the average proportion of firms in excess demand was much higher before than after 1975, this implies an average degree of demand uncertainty significantly lower in the first subperiod than in the second one. Indeed, the average value of σ_{Kt} over the subperiod 1965–1974 is about 0.039 (implying σ_{Y^d} to be about 7% of $E(Y^d)$] and the average value over the subperiod 1976–1984 is about 0.097 (implying $\sigma_{Y^d} \simeq 0.18 \, E(Y^d)$]. Since σ_K also measures the long run effect of profitability, the above results suggest that governments' efforts to enhance profitability may be expected to be more rewarding (in terms of their impact on investment) than if taken twenty years ago.

The three main determinants of net investment identified by our theoretical analysis, namely relative prices (including technical progress), demand prospects and profitability, are found to work their effects with different dynamics. The estimates obtained for the dynamic parameters are presented in Table 1.

Some of these parameters [namely those of $\Phi_k(L)$] appear also in other equations of the model, so that their estimation benefited from the increase in efficiency due to cross-equation restrictions. Remember that some constraints were imposed from the start, namely δ_3 common to all three determinants and $\delta_0 + \delta_1 + \delta_2 + \delta_3 = 1$ to be satisfied for all three rational lag functions. However, the zero restrictions appearing in Table 1 were in some sense "imposed by the data" since not rejected by a likelihood ratio test. The best "summary-statistic" of such dynamic parameters is probably the implied "median lag" which reports on the number of periods necessary for 50% of the total (long-run) effect to have been exerted (or, alternatively, half of the total adjustment to have been completed).

This delay is equal to some 2.3 years for the adjustment of the aggregate capital-output ratio to changing relative prices, some 3.7 years for the reaction of desired capacities to changing demand prospects and some 2.1 years for the reaction to changing profitability conditions. It is noteworthy that desired capacities seem to react significantly faster to profitability considerations than to demand developments.[9]

Table 1
Estimates of the dynamic parameters

	$\Phi_k(L)$ Relative prices	$\Phi_Y(L)$ Demand prospects	$\Phi_\pi(L)$ Profitability
δ_0	0.261 (0.02)	0	0.304 (0.05)
δ_1	0	0.170 (0.02)	−0.043 (0.037)
δ_2	0	0.091 (0.02)	0
δ_3	0.739 (0.02)	0.739 (0.02)	0.739 (0.02)

[9] As far as comparison is warranted, our estimated median lags are in line with previous findings on Belgian data (see, for example, Sneessens and Drèze, 1986, who estimate a median lag of about 2.2 years for the adjustment of the aggregate technical coefficients; and the MARIBEL model, 1984, of the Belgian Planning Bureau where net investment is found to react to demand changes with a median lag of about 5.2 years). Comparison is more difficult for profitability since profitability, when present, does not play the role of a fundamental long-run determinant, like in our paper.

Apart from identifying (theoretically and statistically) profitability as a long-run determinant of investment behaviour, it might be interesting to try to assess the actual relative importance of profitability developments when compared to the other main determinants.

This will now be done from two different points of view. Consider first the results presented in Table 2.

The figures reported in the first three rows represent the estimated total effect (converted into yearly growth rate of the capital stock) of the evolutions effectively recorded during successive subperiods. Each row concerns the contribution of one fundamental determinant of net investment: changes in relative prices $(\Delta \ln k^*)$, in demand $(\Delta \ln Y^d)$ and in profitability $(\Delta \sigma_K \ln(\pi^*/(cK^*)))$ successively. For example, the evolution of demand Y^d recorded during the subperiod 1965–1969 is responsible for a long-run effect (which develops itself only progressively, thus also during the succeeding subperiods) estimated to be about 5.62% when converted into yearly growth rates. The last row is simply the sum of the first three rows $(\Delta \ln K^* \overset{\text{def}}{=} \Delta \ln k^* + \Delta \ln Y^d + \Delta \sigma_K \ln(\pi^*/(cK^*)))$ from the static equations (2.12) and (2.15)).

These results suggest the following. First, relative price developments have always exerted a negative effect on net investment: this is so only because of the capital (and labour) saving technical progress which is also included under the heading "relative prices" (see equation (2.12)). Second, the recession of the mid-seventies really appears as an event partitioning the whole observation period into two very different subperiods: before 1975, demand developments were by far the most prominent determinant of the long-run evolution of net investment with profitability counting almost as nothing; after 1975, things change dramatically in the sense that profitability developments exert a long-run influence which is at par with demand (if not stronger, like in 1975–1979). Such results might perhaps help to explain why empirical studies conducted on data covering up to the late

Table 2
Long-run effects on the investment rate caused by the evolution of its
fundamental determinants

	1965–1969	1970–1974	1975–1979	1980–1984	1965–1984
Relative prices	−0.13	−3.12	−2.52	−1.18	−1.74
Demand	5.62	6.54	0.80	1.51	3.62
Profitability	0.05	−0.15	−2.17	1.00	−0.31
Total	5.54	3.27	−3.88	1.33	1.57

seventies were most unsuccessful to identify profitability as a prime long-run determinant. Since the total (long-run) effects computed in Table 2 take some time to materialize, it is crucial to take into account the most recent observations to catch the "profitability effect".

Another way of assessing the relative importance of profitability is to compute, for each year, the effective contribution of each prime determinant of the estimated investment rate. This may be done in the following way.

Starting from equation (3.1) and reexpressing it in first differences, one gets (disregarding the stochastic disturbance term),

$$\Delta \ln K_t = \sum_{i=0}^{\infty} \phi_{ki} \Delta \ln k^*_{t-i} + \sum_{i=0}^{\infty} \phi_{Yi} \Delta \ln Y^d_{t-i}$$

$$+ \sum_{i=0}^{\infty} \phi_{\pi i} \Delta \sigma_{Kt-i} \ln \left(\frac{\pi^*}{cK^*} \right)_{t-i} .$$

The weights ϕ_j $(j = k, Y, \pi)$ sum up to one and may be easily computed from the dynamic parameter estimates reported in Table 1. Since the sample size is limited, we have to consider computing finite sums instead of the infinite sums of the above equation. This is however not such a serious limitation once we notice that the first ten weights sum up to a number already close to 1 (0.95 for $\sum_{i=0}^{9} \phi_{ki}$ and for $\sum_{i=0}^{9} \phi_{\pi i}$ and 0.93 for $\sum_{i=0}^{9} \phi_{Yi}$). Considering only the first ten terms of each infinite sum should hence be sufficient to get an appropriate picture of the respective contribution of each determinant to the observed investment rate.

One may thus write

$$\Delta \ln K_t \simeq \Delta \ln \hat{K}_t \stackrel{\text{def}}{=} \sum_{i=0}^{9} \phi_{ki} \Delta \ln k^*_{t-i} + \sum_{i=0}^{9} \phi_{Yi} \Delta \ln Y^d_{t-i}$$

$$+ \sum_{i=0}^{9} \phi_{\pi i} \Delta \sigma_{Kt-i} \ln \left(\frac{\pi^*}{cK^*} \right)_{t-i} ,$$

the discrepancy between observed $\Delta \ln K_t$ and computed $\Delta \ln \hat{K}_t$ being due both to the truncation of the infinite sums when computing $\Delta \ln \hat{K}_t$ and to the existence of estimation residuals. The results of the computations are presented in Figure 1 for the years 1975–1984.

The time pattern of the respective contributions to the growth rate of capital is quite remarkable. The contribution of demand has always been positive but has decreased steadily in importance. The same is true, but with the opposite sign, for the contribution of relative prices so that both influences in some sense "cancel out". This leaves room for profitability

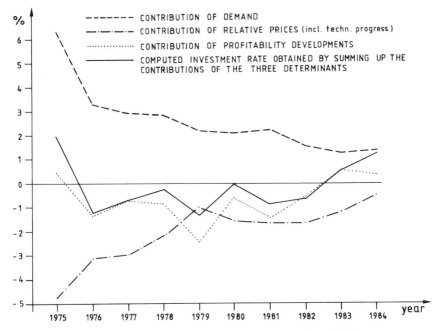

Figure 1. Contribution of each determinant to the actual evolution of the investment rate.

(multiplied by demand uncertainty) to exert a major influence on net investment as is most apparent in Figure 1. Restoring profitability has been presented as a top priority of the policies pursued by Belgian governments since 1981. Judging from the results summarized in Figure 1, such an emphasis on profitability does not seem to be misplaced.

4. Conclusion

To go beyond the necessary — but insufficient — diagnosis of the present disequilibria affecting most European economies, one has to develop models apt to capture the longer-term effects of present disequilibria. This is an unavoidable step in view of exploring ways of settling our economies on more desirable dynamic paths.

The study of investment behaviour in a disequilibrium context has of course to be given the highest priority. The present paper is a contribution to this study. Unlike earlier attempts, we chose to analyze investment behaviour within a stochastic rationing context since we feel that uncertainty surely ought to enter the picture when dealing with decisions incorporating such a high degree of irreversibility. Our theoretical analysis (inspired by Malinvaud, 1983) ended up with the identification of profitability as a fundamental long-run determinant of investment behaviour. This result, which should constitute no surprise for practitioners, is however quite uncommon in theoretical studies dealing with investment. However, since a theoretically identified effect may turn out to be empirically insignificant, confrontation with the data has to be the final judge of the relevance of this "profitability effect". The available empirical evidence reported in the preceding section seems to support the hypothesis of a not insignificant profitability effect, particularly in recent years. If such a conclusion happened to be supported by subsequent studies, the message would be clear: yes, demand keeps the crucial role in the determination of desired capacity but profitability too matters, all the more since the future looks more uncertain (refer to the theoretical discussion in Section 2). Moreover, since the ultimate objective is to increase the number of (profitable) jobs, restoring profitability should be conducted without favouring capital at the expense of labour. In this respect, "neutral" policies (like reducing taxation on profit) or "labour friendly" policies (like marginal employment subsidies or reductions in employers' social security contributions) should be preferred to "capital friendly" policies (like investment tax credits), when the choice is available between various policies with equivalent profitability — and budgetary — implications.

If the role of profitability is to be taken seriously, it should however be kept in mind that its effect is very nonlinear (consider our equation (2.15) and refer to Malinvaud, 1987, for a theoretical analysis of this non-linearity): this entails that boosting profitability is characterized by decreasing returns (i.e., it is much more effective if starting from a deteriorated position than from an already satisfactory position). Hence, while urgently needed at the time of their implementation (the early eighties), the convergent set or "profitability restoring policies" conducted for a few years throughout Europe might at some time have to hand over to more traditional expansionary policies.

Many avenues offer themselves for future research: developing a truly dynamic theoretical model, incorporating risk aversion for firms, departing from the fix-price assumption by considering downward sloping demand curves, etc. Another possible direction of research might stem from the recognition that, while stochastic demand rationing is thought to be the appropriate theoretical framework common to all firms whatever their present regime (see discussion in Section 1), individual firms are likely to differ severely from each other in their perception of optimal compared to installed capacity. Since extraneous information is sometimes available on such a heterogeneity, it should be profitably exploited in the estimation, in the spirit of Lambert (1988). This calls for the development of the appropriate methodology.

Data appendix

The data are annual time series covering the period 1963–1984. Except for the profitability indicator $\pi^*/(cK^*)$ which is discussed in detail below, they are standard statistics which do not deserve further mention than definition and source.

P: Deflator of value added of the manufacturing sector (source: National Accounts).

P_I: Price index of investment goods (source: National Accounts).

Y: Value added in the manufacturing sector (billions of 1975 Belgian Francs; source: National Accounts).

K: Capital stock in the manufacturing sector (billions of 1975, Belgian Francs; source; Bureau du Plan, Brussels).

DUC: Degree of utilization of production capacity in the manufacturing sector (source: Banque Nationale de Belgique).

P_G: Proportion of firms in excess demand (on their goods market) in the manufacturing sector (source: Banque Nationale de Belgique).

$\pi^*/(cK^*)$: Profitability at full capacity in the manufacturing sector.

As explained in the text, no ready-made statistic is available on this theoretical profitability indicator since it pertains to profitability at full capacity which is of course never directly observed. A suitable proxy may however be devised making use of the short-term production function assumed in the text. Indeed, remember the definition of π^* as profits at full capacity

$$\pi^* \stackrel{\text{def}}{=} pY^* - wL^* - cK^*$$

where Y^* and L^* represent respectively output and employment at full capacity and K^* is the corresponding total (installed) capital stock. Profit at any level of operation below full capacity would be defined as $\pi \stackrel{\text{def}}{=} pY - wL - cK^*$ since the total cost of capital cK^* had anyway to be supported. Remembering our assumption of a Leontieff-type short-run production function, we have $L/Y = L^*/Y^*$ (eq. (2.3)), which combined with the definition of DUC (degree of utilization of capacity) as DUC $\stackrel{\text{def}}{=} Y/Y^*$, yields

$$\pi^* = (pY - wL)/\text{DUC} - cK^*$$

so that

$$\frac{\pi^*}{cK^*} = \frac{1}{\text{DUC}} \left\{ \frac{pY - wL}{cK^*} \right\} - 1.$$

Remembering our definition of c as

$$c = p_1 [i_{\text{real}}^e + \delta],$$

$\pi^*/(cK^*)$ may finally be computed as

$$\frac{\pi^*}{cK^*} = \frac{1}{\text{DUC}} \left\{ \left(\frac{pY - wL}{p_1 K^*} \right) \frac{1}{[i_{\text{real}}^e + \delta]} \right\} - 1.$$

The quantity $(pY - wL)/(p_1 K^*)$ is the gross operating surplus as a percentage of the value of installed capital. Such a statistic is available from the MARIBEL data bank constructed by the Belgian Planning Bureau. DUC is readily available from regular business surveys conducted by the Belgian National Bank and $(i_{\text{real}}^e + \delta)$ has been assumed to be constant (and equal to 0.15) to be consistent with the empirical findings exposed in the text. The evolution of the resulting profitability indicator is illustrated in Figure 2.

Figure 2. "Profitability at full capacity" $\pi^*/(cK^*)$ in the Belgian manufacturing sector, 1960–1984.

References

Artus, P. (1985) 'Inventory investment, investment and employment with uncertain demand', *Empirical Economics*, 10:177-200.

Artus, P., G. Laroque and G. Michel (1984) 'Estimation of a quarterly macroeconomic model with quantity rationing', *Econometrica*, 52:1387-1414.

Artus, P. and P.A. Muet (1984) 'Investment, output and labor constraints, and financial constraints: the estimation of a model with several regimes', *Recherches Economiques de Louvain*, 50(1-2):25-44.

Gérard, M. and C. Vanden Berghe (1984) 'Econometric analysis of sectoral investment in Belgium (1956-1982)', *Recherches Economiques de Louvain*, 50(1-2):89-118.

Kooiman, P. and T. Kloek (1985) 'An empirical two-market disequilibrium model for Dutch manufacturing', *European Economic Review*, 29:323-354.

Lambert, J.-P. (1987) 'Conflicting specifications for investment functions in rationing models: a reconciliation', *Recherches Economiques de Louvain*, 53(2):135-145.

Lambert, J.-P. (1988) *Disequilibrium Macroeconomic Models: Theory and Estimation of Rationing Models Using Business Survey Data.* Cambridge: Cambridge University Press.

Lubrano, M. and H.R. Sneessens (1984) 'Un modèle de production CES-Leontieff pour l'industrie française', *Annales de l'INSEE*, 54:3-30.

Malinvaud, E. (1983) 'Profitability and investment facing uncertain demand', Working Paper INSEE No. 8303.

Malinvaud, E. (1987) 'Capital productif, incertitudes et profitabilité', *Annales d'Economie et de Statistique*, 5:1-36.

'MARIBEL: model for analysis and rapid investigation of the Belgian economy', (1984) Brussels: Bureau du Plan.

Michel, Ph. (1986) 'Dynamique de l'accumulation du capital en présence de contraintes de débouchés', *Annales d'Economie et de Statistique*, 2:117-145.

Mulkay, B. (1983) 'Fonctions d'investissement néoclassiques dans un modèle macroéconomique avec rationnement', *Recherches Economiques de Louvain*, 49(3):247-276.

Nickell, S. (1978) *The Investment Decisions of Firms.* Cambridge: Cambridge University Press.

Sneessens, H.R. (1981) *Theory and Estimation of Macroeconomic Rationing Models.* Berlin: Springer.

Sneessens, H.R. and J.H. Drèze (1986) 'A discussion of Belgian unemployment, combining traditional concepts and disequilibrium econometrics', *Economica*, 53:89-119.

Waelbroeck-Rocha, E. (1984) 'Price and quantity decisions under demand uncertainty', Ph.D. Dissertation, Brussels, Université Libre de Bruxelles.

Chapter 8

PERFECT EQUILIBRIA OF SPECULATIVE FUTURES MARKETS

Ronald M. HARSTAD

Virginia Commonwealth University, Richmond, VA, USA

Louis PHLIPS

European University Institute, Florence, Italy

1. Introduction

Barriers to investing in futures markets are negligible. This may be the reason why futures markets are typically modeled as perfectly competitive. The underlying industry which produces the commodity traded on a futures market, however, is often heavily concentrated, for at least some stages of the production process.[1] A producer with oligopolistic influence upon the time path of production, and thus upon the market value of futures contracts a maturity, is never a negligible actor in the futures market; purely competitive models cannot capture his rational futures contracting activity. Behaviour ascribed to non-producing speculators in competitive models becomes myopic, even perilous, when the other party to a futures contract they sign subsequently acts to alter the cash price, i.e., the spot price at maturity (as a direct result of signing the contract).

This paper was begun while the authors were visiting the Centre for Interdisciplinary Research, Bielefeld, West Germany. We are grateful for the Center's support, and for helpful comments from Tiziano Brianza, Eric van Damme, Jean-François Richard and Reinhard Selten.
[1] A few independent actors have substantially influenced production and prices in such exhaustible resource markets as copper, tin and petroleum. Intermediate stages of the production and distribution process appear oligopolistic for some agricultural products traded on futures markets.

Economic Decision-Making: Games, Econometrics and Optimisation
Edited by J.J. Gabszewicz, J.-F. Richard and L.A. Wolsey
© *Elsevier Science Publishers B.V., 1990*

When speculators and producers view futures prices and cash prices as immutable, a model of their individual behaviour need not take into account institutional procedures by which prices are determined on futures markets. The particular price-setting (or, more generally, allocation-reaching) rules being used may nonetheless play a key role in describing the strategic behaviour of actors with nonnegligible influence on prices.

A third sense in which the standard approaches to futures market modeling may be limiting their scope is a tendency to focus on futures contracts as a means of hedging against price risk in the spot market at maturity.[2] Upon casual observation, we are inclined to model the bulk of futures transactions as purely speculative, with any relation to hedging of underlying stocks secondary.[3] In essence, many futures contracts seem to be bets about the level of the spot price at maturity, with each party undaunted by the willingness of the other to accept the bet.

We offer an alternative model of a futures market for an exhaustible resource, based on an underlying oligopolistic industry structure. It features a stylized set of price-determining rules, and agents who knowingly hold divergent beliefs about the economic value of the resource at maturity. As our purpose is demonstrative, the model is in many directions simple, almost stark. Nonetheless, complex interplay arises among contractual behaviour, rules, and anticipation of behaviour to follow.

With an underlying oligopoly, inefficient allocation of resources attained in subgame-perfect equilibrium may have been anticipated. The nature of the inefficiency is insufficient volume of futures market activity; we discuss its relation to incentives facing market-making institutions who determine the trading rules.

The futures market examined here is streamlined by having one type of contract, which technically states that, in return for a mutually agreeable, certain payment, the seller will provide the buyer with an agreed quantity of the resource at the one and only maturity date (which we call period 2). However, the contract in fact specifies that, once the cash price at maturity becomes known, the buyer pays the seller the contracted futures price minus the cash price (be this difference positive or negative). Thus futures positions

---

[2] Several models and extensive references are in Anderson (1984).

[3] Transactors' positions are closed out day-by-day, including at maturity, via adjustments to balances in margin accounts. Delivery at maturity is almost unheard of in futures markets.

are not constrained by the total amount of the resource available; nor are they subject to any budget constraints.[4]

The model enriches this simple futures market with explicit attention to the institutional rules by which such futures markets as the London Metal Exchange operate. A stylized version of their "open cry" auction, with its incentives for consummating trades just before the closing bell, is built in Sections 2 and 3 below.

Attention is focused on the economic impact of rules which have one party to a contract, the offeror, determine a price and a maximum quantity, and then have the other party, the acceptor, determine the actual quantity exchanged. Thus, the offeror fixes the price, the acceptor fixes the quantity. This is the source of inefficient subgame-perfect equilibrium allocations, because it puts the offeror in a temporary monopoly position.

The resource-extracting industry is presented in simplest form, a Cournot (quantity-setting) duopoly. We will refer to the actors as producers $\mathscr{A}$ and $\mathscr{B}$, but abstract from all production decisions except the choice to influence profitability of futures contracts. That is, each producer will have an exogenously determined stock of resources, and all producers simultaneously decide how much of their stock to supply prior to maturity (period 1), the remainder being supplied at maturity (period 2). This decision is made after the futures market closes, but before revelation of the uncertain level of final demand for the resource.

No explicit role is given to brokers; we limit our futures market analysis to the two producers $\mathscr{A}$ and $\mathscr{B}$, one of whom must be risk-averse, and a single, risk-neutral speculator $\mathscr{S}$.[5] These three hold inconsistent prior beliefs about the level of final demand for the resource. These beliefs are common

---

[4] Any budget constraint in the model would likely be more severe than budget constraints seen in futures markets, except when a crash is fresh in memory. It is more illuminating to derive finite volumes of futures trades between producers and speculators from producers' manipulative opportunities.

[5] Many speculators competing in the terms of trade offered to the two producers on the futures market would primarily serve to enhance the producers' manipulative opportunities. The already cumbersome notation needed to keep track of contract offers and acceptances would explode in complexity with the added speculators. If competition between speculators sufficiently reduced the level of profit expected from trading a given volume of contracts, and a speculator did not know whether he was trading with a producer (and what net short position that producer has attained in other futures contracts), subgame-perfect equilibrium futures trading might collapse with many speculators. None of the analysis depends on the single speculator being risk-neutral. The model can only accommodate two risk-neutral actors if exactly one of them is a producer with a nonzero initial resource stock; otherwise futures positions become infinite.

knowledge. The situation is thus analyzed as a two-stage noncooperative game with inconsistent incomplete information.[6] The futures game is positive-sum (in terms of expected profit) whenever positions taken in the futures market are sufficiently small relative to differences in the prior beliefs.

2. The game

In the futures market, an *offer* is a specification of (i) whether the offeror is suggesting that he *buys* (in the jargon of futures markets, he "goes *long*") or *sells* ("goes *short*"), (ii) a *price* quotation, and (iii) a *maximum quantity*, in units of some "standard contract" as specified by the market-maker. An *acceptance* is a specification of (i) which offer is being accepted, and (ii) the *quantity* (the *position*) being accepted. An acceptance is constrained to be at most the maximum quantity offered, less any quantity of the same offer already accepted by another player. A *rejection* can be thought of as the special case where the accepted position is zero.

The game proceeds as follows.

Step 1. The futures market opens. Simultaneously, each player publicly and irrevocably announces one offer to buy and one offer to sell, each with a price and a maximum quantity.[7]

Step 2. Nature chooses a commitment order, a permutation of ($\mathscr{A}, \mathscr{B}, \mathscr{S}$), each drawn with equal probability.

Step 3. The player designated *first* in the commitment order irrevocably accepts or rejects each of the four offers made by another player.

Step 4. The player designated *second* in the commitment order irrevocably accepts or rejects each of the four offers made by another player.

Step 5. The player designated *third* in the commitment order irrevocably accepts or rejects each of the four offers made by another player. The futures market then *closes.*[8]

---

[6] Selten (1982, Sections B.9–B.13), formalizes noncooperative games with inconsistent incomplete information. See van Damme (1987) for a definition and discussion of the restriction to subgame-perfect equilibria.

[7] It will always be possible to announce one of these offers at a price guaranteeing rejection.

[8] Intermediate steps before or after Step 2 could have been added, where players may irrevocably accept offers made by other players, but rejections during these intermediate steps would be tentative. Such steps would not alter the set of subgame-perfect equilibria. An alternative set of rules would have the players simultaneously make irrevocable acceptances or rejections just before the futures market closes. This would yield at least a 3-parameter family of subgame-perfect equilibria, with little qualitative features in common. Since this is not a signaling game, further refinements would not notably reduce the set of equilibria. Equilibrium selection theory (Harsanyi and Selten, 1988) would obtain a unique outcome, but a cooperative element would be de facto introduced, and all relationships between trading rules and behaviour would disappear.

Step 6. The *extraction subgame* occurs: producers $\mathscr{A}$ and $\mathscr{B}$ simultaneously decide what fraction of their exogenous stock of the resource to supply before maturity of the futures contracts. Technically, this ends the game.

Step 7. The aggregate level of final demand for the resource (both before and at maturity) is revealed. Together with the decisions made in Step 6, this determines the spot price at maturity.

The payoff to each player is the certainty equivalent level of profit; notation to specify payoff functions is introduced in the next section.

3. Formalisms

The analysis requires notational conventions that keep track of the identity of the player suggesting a contract, the player accepting, and the direction of flow (which player goes short), all while striving for coherence. The cash market will have a uniform price at each date, represented by p_t, $t = 1, 2$. A superscripted price is a futures price (sometimes called a "forward" price), as suggested by the agent shown, i.e., p^a is the price at which $\mathscr{A}$ offers to buy futures, to go long. The convention of superscripting the offeror is maintained throughout.

Typestyle distinguishes short sales from long sales, in a manner that is hopefully mnemonic. $\mathscr{A}$ offers to buy at price $\boldsymbol{p}^a$ (bold typeface for "buy"), and to sell at price p^a (soft typeface for "sell"). Each offer combines a price with a maximum position (quantity), as in $(\boldsymbol{p}^s, \boldsymbol{f}^s)$, (p^s, f^s), $\mathscr{S}$'s offers to go long and short, respectively. Since typestyle indicates the direction of a trade, all positions are nonnegative numbers.

Players accepting contracts are identified throughout by subscripts. The amount of offer $(\boldsymbol{p}^s, \boldsymbol{f}^s)$ which $\mathscr{A}$ accepts is represented as $\boldsymbol{f}_a^s$, which is a long position for $\mathscr{S}$, and thus a short position for $\mathscr{A}$. Correspondingly, (p^s, f_a^s) is the agreed terms where $\mathscr{S}$ set the price, $\mathscr{A}$ determined the position, and $\mathscr{A}$ goes long. For example, $\mathscr{B}$ offers to go short in (p^b, f^b), $f_a^b \leq f^b$ is the extent to which $\mathscr{A}$ agrees to accommodate by going long. $\mathscr{B}$'s revenue on this contract is then $p^b f_a^b$.

The six offers announced allow up to twelve contracts to be formed (each player can accept at most four offers). Positions on different contracts cancel each other (but not in revenue effects, unless prices match), so payoffs depend upon net short positions, which are:

$$\mathbb{A} := f_b^a + f_s^a - \boldsymbol{f}_b^a - \boldsymbol{f}_s^a + \boldsymbol{f}_a^b - f_a^b + \boldsymbol{f}_a^s - f_a^s,$$
$$\mathbb{B} := f_a^b + f_s^b - \boldsymbol{f}_a^b - \boldsymbol{f}_s^b + \boldsymbol{f}_b^a - f_b^a + \boldsymbol{f}_b^s - f_b^s$$

and

$$\mathbb{S} := f_a^s + f_b^s - f_a^s - f_b^s + f_s^a - f_s^a + f_s^b - f_s^b.$$

A position which enters positively in net short position also enters positively in net revenue on the futures market, which is:

$$R^a := p^a(f_b^a + f_s^a) - p^a(f_b^a + f_s^a) + p^b f_a^b - p^b f_a^b + p^s f_a^s - p^s f_a^s,$$

$$R^b := p^b(f_a^b + f_s^b) - p^b(f_a^b + f_s^b) + p^a f_b^a - p^a f_b^a + p^s f_b^s - p^s f_b^s$$

and

$$R^s := p^s(f_a^s + f_b^s) - p^s(f_a^s + f_b^s) + p^a f_s^a - p^a f_s^a + p^b f_s^b - p^b f_s^b.$$

The two producers have exogenous initial stocks of the resource s_{a0} and s_{b0}, these levels are common knowledge. Producer $i = \mathscr{A}, \mathscr{B}$ extracts and sells q_{i1} units of resource in the single cash market that occurs prior to maturity of futures contracts, and extracts and sells

$$q_{i2} = s_{i0} - q_{i1}, \quad i = \mathscr{A}, \mathscr{B}, \tag{1}$$

units in the single cash market at maturity. For simplicity, both extraction costs and the rate of interest are zero.

Each cash market will exhibit the same instantaneous inverse market demand curve:

$$p_t(q_{at} + q_{bt}) = \frac{\alpha}{\beta} - \frac{q_{at} + q_{bt}}{\beta}, \quad t = 1, 2, \tag{2}$$

where $\alpha > 0$ is unknown, and $\beta > 0$ is common knowledge.[9] Let

$$\hat{p} = \frac{\alpha}{\beta} - \frac{s_{a0} + s_{b0}}{2\beta};$$

$\hat{p}$ is the price that would prevail in both cash markets in Cournot equilibrium, were there no futures market activity by producers. As such, $\hat{p}$ is a natural benchmark. It is more convenient to express uncertainty in terms of $\hat{p}$ than α; this will be done throughout. Each player will have expectations (i.e., prior beliefs) about $\hat{p}$.

---

[9] This formulation simplifies by omitting any speculative demand for stocks. Were speculative demand included, it would act as a multiplier effect on the manipulative possibilities producers have in this model.

Finally, the payoff functions can be specified. For each player, payoff is the certainty equivalent level of profit:

$$C^a = E_a[p_2(q_{a2} + q_{b2})](q_{a2} - \mathbb{A}) + p_1(q_{a1} + q_{b1})q_{a1} + R^a - \tfrac{1}{2}K_a(s_{a0} - \mathbb{A})^2,$$

$$C^b = E_b[p_2(q_{a2} + q_{b2})](q_{b2} - \mathbb{B}) + p_1(q_{a1} + q_{b1})q_{b1} + R^b - \tfrac{1}{2}K_b(s_{b0} - \mathbb{B})^2,$$

$$C^s = R^s - E_s[p_2(q_{a2} + q_{b2})]\mathbb{S}, \tag{3}$$

where E_i is the expectation operator for $i = \mathscr{A}, \mathscr{B}, \mathscr{S}$, and $K_a \geq 0$ and $K_b \geq 0$ are coefficients of constant absolute risk aversion, with one of K_a, K_b positive.[10] We have simplified notation by assuming the variance of each player's expectation is 1.[11] $\mathscr{S}$ is only active in the futures market; for $\mathscr{A}$ and $\mathscr{B}$, the payoffs relating only to the futures market are $R^a - E_a[p_2]\mathbb{A}$ and $R^b - E_b[p_2]\mathbb{B}$. Of course, $\mathbb{A} + \mathbb{B} + \mathbb{S} = 0 = R^a + R^b + R^s$. However, differences in expectations can make the futures market a positive-sum game.

4. Behaviour in the extraction subgame

Let net short positions $\mathbb{A}$ and $\mathbb{B}$ be given, positive or negative. The unique Cournot equilibrium which results in the extraction subgame is found by simultaneous maximization of C^a in q_{a1} and C^b in q_{b1} (with q_{i2} eliminated by (1)), subject to[12]

$$0 \leq q_{i1} \leq s_{i0}, \quad i = \mathscr{A}, \mathscr{B}. \tag{4}$$

The extraction equilibrium function $Q: \mathbb{R}^2 \mapsto [0, s_{a0}] \times [0, s_{b0}]$ is defined by

$$C^a(Q_a(\mathbb{A}, \mathbb{B}), Q_b(\mathbb{A}, \mathbb{B}), \mathbb{A}, R^a)$$
$$\geq C^a(z, Q_b(\mathbb{A}, \mathbb{B}), \mathbb{A}, R^a) \quad \forall z \in [0, s_{a0}],$$

and

$$C^b(Q_b(\mathbb{A}, \mathbb{B}), Q_a(\mathbb{A}, \mathbb{B}), \mathbb{B}, R^b)$$
$$\geq C^b(z, Q_a(\mathbb{A}, \mathbb{B}), \mathbb{B}, R^b) \quad \forall z \in [0, s_{b0}].$$

---

[10] This treatment of constant absolute risk aversion follows Newbury and Stiglitz (1981).

[11] In this model, no behavioural separation of risk aversion and variance in expectations is possible.

[12] The "path strategies" that arise in Reinganum and Stokey (1985) do not arise in subgame-perfect equilibrium here, unless stocks are made endogenous, or at least a third extraction period (post-maturity) is added. Each producer's marginal revenue is a declining function of the rival's extraction, which is sufficient for equilibrium to exist (Novshek, 1985).

When an interior maximum (w.r.t. (4)) occurs, the first-order condition is

$$\alpha - 2q_{i1} - q_{j1} = \alpha - 2q_{i2} - q_{j2} + \mathbb{S}$$

$$= \beta\eta_i \quad \text{for } \mathbb{I} = \mathbb{A}, \mathbb{B}, \; i = \mathcal{A}, \mathcal{B}, \; j = \{\mathcal{A}, \mathcal{B}\}\backslash\{i\}, \tag{5}$$

where the η_i's are Lagrangian Multipliers.
The solution to (5) is:[13]

$$q_{a1} = \tfrac{1}{2}s_{a0} + \tfrac{1}{6}\mathbb{B} - \tfrac{1}{3}\mathbb{A}, \qquad q_{a2} = \tfrac{1}{2}s_{a0} - \tfrac{1}{6}\mathbb{B} + \tfrac{1}{3}\mathbb{A},$$
$$q_{b1} = \tfrac{1}{2}s_{b0} + \tfrac{1}{6}\mathbb{A} - \tfrac{1}{3}\mathbb{B}, \qquad q_{b2} = \tfrac{1}{2}s_{b0} - \tfrac{1}{6}\mathbb{A} + \tfrac{1}{3}\mathbb{B}, \tag{6}$$

which sum to total extraction rates

$$q_1 = \tfrac{1}{2}(s_{a0} + s_{b0}) + \tfrac{1}{6}\mathbb{S}, \qquad q_2 = \tfrac{1}{2}(s_{a0} + s_{b0}) - \tfrac{1}{6}\mathbb{S}.$$

Each producer adjusts the amount of resource extracted prior to maturity for the futures market position he had taken, and partially counteracts the adjustment his rival makes. If $\mathbb{A} > 0$ and $\mathbb{B} < 2\mathbb{A}$, then $\mathcal{A}$ has taken a net short position, which he makes more profitable by shifting extraction from pre-maturity supply to at-maturity supply, driving down the value of the futures positions he has sold.

Equation (6) yields equilibrium cash market prices

$$p_1 = \hat{p} + \theta(\mathbb{A} + \mathbb{B}), \qquad p_2 = \hat{p} - \theta(\mathbb{A} + \mathbb{B}), \tag{7}$$

where $\theta = 1/(6\beta) > 0$, to simplify a recurrent term in expressions.[14] A higher θ indicates a steeper final demand for the resource. In a world of increasing spot prices — with a positive real interest rate — (7) means that a combined net short position of producers reduces the variability of spot prices.[15] Final demanders of the resource gain from this process, obtaining a larger gain (in present value) of consumer surplus in the cash market with a price below $\hat{p}$ than the loss in surplus suffered in the other cash market.

A critical aspect of the extraction equilibrium function Q is its independence from expectations[16] If a producer expected different intercepts α_t of

---

[13] Equations (6) characterize the extraction subgame equilibrium whenever they satisfy (4). Otherwise, the rival's net short position is replaced by that fraction of his net short position to which the rival responds, before reaching the constraint (4); in this case, one extraction rate depends upon both stocks.

[14] When the extraction equilibrium is not interior to (4), still $\mathbb{S} < 0 \Leftrightarrow p_1 > \hat{p}$.

[15] However, comparison with a monopolist with initial stock $s_{a0} + s_{b0}$ and net short position $\mathbb{A} + \mathbb{B}$ would further reduce spot price variability: the coefficient θ in (7) would be replaced by 1.5θ (Brianza, Phlips and Richard, 1987).

[16] This independence allows applying the subgame-perfect equilibrium concept to a game of inconsistent incomplete information. For further discussion, see Phlips and Harstad (1990).

the final demand curve in cash markets at different dates t, the time path of extraction would be affected; but the extent to which extraction is shifted into the period in which futures contracts mature, from pre-maturity cash markets, does not depend upon the producer's beliefs about the general level of final resource demand. In particular, this separates futures game behaviour from extraction subgame behaviour to the extent that a trading partner of a producer on the futures market need not know the producer's expectations in order to predict the extent to which he will shift extraction in reaction to a contract signed.[17]

5. Accounting for equilibrium in the subgame

The game tree is common knowledge; all players can calculate the function Q that will characterize behaviour in the extraction subgame for any $\mathbb{A}$, $\mathbb{B}$ determined in the futures market. Let the mean expectations of $\hat{p}$ for $\mathscr{A}$, $\mathscr{B}$, $\mathscr{S}$ be $\hat{p}_a$, $\hat{p}_b$, $\hat{p}_s$.[18] Focusing on subgame-perfect equilibria by incorporating (6) into the payoffs yields:[19]

$$\pi^a = R^a + \hat{p}_a(s_{a0} - \mathbb{A}) + \tfrac{1}{3}\theta\mathbb{S}^2 - \tfrac{1}{2}K_a(s_{a0} - \mathbb{A})^2,$$

$$\pi^b = R^b + \hat{p}_b(s_{b0} - \mathbb{B}) + \tfrac{1}{3}\theta\mathbb{S}^2 - \tfrac{1}{2}K_b(s_{b0} - \mathbb{B})^2, \tag{8}$$

$$\pi^s = R^s - \hat{p}_s\mathbb{S} - \theta\mathbb{S}^2.$$

Comparing (8) and (3) indicates that a speculator trading with a producer, should he fail to take into account the producer's market power in the cash market, would be neglecting a quadratic term with negative coefficient in

---

[17] It is important, however, for a trading partner to know how far from binding constraint (4) is.

[18] Note that differences in beliefs are not the result of differences in information; no player updates his beliefs upon learning that rivals have different beliefs. Thus, these are pure differences in *opinion* in the terminology of Varian (1989). Notice also that inconsistent prior beliefs avoid the impossibility theorems for speculative trading in rational expectations equilibrium (e.g., Kreps, 1977; Tirole, 1982; Milgrom and Stokey, 1982). Null hypotheses that give rational expectations wide latitude nonetheless fail to organize data on prices in metals futures markets (cf., MacDonald and Taylor, 1988; Hall and Taylor, 1988, and references therein).

[19] The model has multi-stage Nash equilibria which we ignore because they fail to be subgame-perfect. To wit, they involve threats by a producer to punish deviations from the equilibrium path in the futures market via altering his extraction policy to harm both himself and the player being threatened. Since the futures market is closed before the producers can commit themselves to extraction plans, such threats are not credible, and such equilibria are not sensible.

an otherwise linear payoff function![20] The producer need not have any market power in the futures market per se for this concern to be serious. A producer choosing to be inactive in the futures market nonetheless profits from its existence. That is, if $\mathbb{A} = 0 \neq \mathbb{B}$, then $\mathbb{S} = -\mathbb{B}$, and $\mathcal{A}$ attains a benefit in the quadratic term in (8). This benefit results from $\mathcal{B}$ shifting extraction from a higher-priced to a lower-priced period (so $\mathcal{B}$ can enhance profitability of his futures contracts), and $\mathcal{A}$ having a profitable opportunity to counteract this shift.

Finally, the futures game specified by payoffs (8) will yield purely speculative trades. To be precise, the alterations to (8) that would result from trivializing the extraction subgame by setting $s_{a0} = s_{b0} = 0$ would still yield a positive-sum game, whenever futures positions were sufficiently small relative to differences in beliefs.[21]

6. Futures market behaviour

Subgame-perfect equilibrium behaviour involves best responses at every node of the game tree, so best responses must be specified backwards from the end of the game. Step 6 was treated in Section 4 above. To handle acceptance behaviour, let the set of permutations of the ordered triple $(\mathcal{A}, \mathcal{B}, \mathcal{S})$ be Ω, and an arbitrary element be $(3, 4, 5)$, and designate vectors of offered prices $P := (p^a, p^a, p^b, p^b, p^s, p^s)$ and maximum quantities $F := (f^a, f^a, f^b, f^b, f^s, f^s)$. Each π^i, $i = \mathcal{A}, \mathcal{B}, \mathcal{S}$, is treated as a real-valued function with arguments: P, the four acceptances by i, and the eight other acceptances. The constraint that an acceptance cannot be more than the currently available amount is specified by feasible sets:

$$\Delta_5 := [0, f^3 - f_4^3] \times [0, f^3 - f_4^3] \times [0, f^4 - f_3^4] \times [0, f^4 - f_3^4],$$

$$\Delta_4 := [0, f^3] \times [0, f^3] \times [0, f^5 - f_3^5] \times [0, f^5 - f_3^5],$$

$$\Delta_3 := [0, f^4] \times [0, f^4] \times [0, f^5] \times [0, f^5].$$

To characterize Step 5 behaviour, let $v_5 := (f_5^3, f_5^3, f_5^4, f_5^4)$, the vector of acceptances. The history of acceptances up to Step 5 is

$$h_5 := (f_3^4, f_3^4, f_3^5, f_3^5, f_4^3, f_4^3, f_4^5, f_4^5).$$

---

[20] In the much lengthier payoff functions when (4) is binding, the quadratic term involving $\mathbb{S}$ stops increasing, as speculator–producer trading continues, at the level where (4) became binding. If the producer is risk-averse, however, equilibrium positions will still be finite. One producer being risk-averse makes gains from producer–producer trades quadratic, hence these positions are also finite in equilibrium.

[21] For finite trading in equilibrium, there would have to be at most one risk-neutral player.

The best response function $V_5 : \mathbb{R}^{14}_+ \mapsto \Delta_5$ is defined by

$$\pi^5(P, V_5(P, h_5), h_5) \geq \pi^5(P, v_5, h_5) \quad \forall v_5 \in \Delta_5. \tag{9}$$

V_5 is the restriction onto Δ_5 of a linear function. When the offer most profitable to 5 is (p^3, f^3), V_5 takes the form $Y + Z^{-1} p^3$, with Y reflecting $\hat{p}_5$ and 5's net short position on trades already completed, Z reflecting θ and K_i.[22]

To characterize Step 4 behaviour, let $u_4 := (f_4^3, f_4^3, f_4^5, f_4^5)$, the vector of acceptances. The history of acceptances up to Step 4 is

$$g_4 := (f_3^4, f_3^4, f_3^5, f_3^5).$$

The best response function $U_4 : \mathbb{R}^{10}_+ \mapsto \Delta_4$ is defined by

$$\pi^4(P, U_4(P, g_4), g_4, V_5[P, g_4, U_4(P, g_4)])$$
$$\geq \pi^4[P, u_4, g_4, V_5(P, g_4, u_4)] \quad \forall u_4 \in \Delta_4. \tag{10}$$

So player 4 incorporates the value of 5's best response function, for each decision 4 might make, in the right-hand side of (10). The left-hand side of (10) is his equilibrium payoff, given P, g_4. U_4 is a complicated, piecewise linear function, with slopes and intercepts similar to V_5 in cases when V_5 does not react locally to U_4, and marginal insensitivity to prices in some cases where the partial derivative of V_5 with respect to u_4 is 1 or -1.

To characterize Step 3 behaviour, let $t_3 := (f_3^3, f_3^3, f_3^5, f_3^5)$, the vector of acceptances. The best response function $T_3 : \mathbb{R}^6_+ \mapsto \Delta_3$ is defined by

$$\pi^3[P, T_3(P), U_4[P, T_3(P)], V_5(P, T_3(P), U_4[P, T_3(P)])]$$
$$\geq \pi^3(P, t_3, U_4(P, t_3), V_5[P, t_3, U_4(P, t_3)]) \quad \forall t_3 \in \Delta_3. \tag{11}$$

So player 3 incorporates the value of 4's best response function, for each decision 3 might make, and the value of 5's best response to 4's best response, for each decision 3 might make, in the right-hand side of (11). The left-hand side of (11) is his equilibrium payoff, given P. T_3 is a quite complicated, piecewise linear function.

In Step 2, each permutation (i, j, k) in $\Omega = \{(\mathscr{A}, \mathscr{B}, \mathscr{S}), \ldots, (\mathscr{S}, \mathscr{B}, \mathscr{A})\}$ occurs with probability $\frac{1}{6}$. Thus, the expected payoff given (P, Q), for player

---

[22] When $5 = \mathscr{S}$, $Z = 2\theta$; if 5 is a producer accepting the other producer's offer, $Z = K_5$; otherwise, $Z = K_5 - \frac{2}{3}\theta$, if this is positive (if not, an interior acceptance does not occur). If $f_5^3 = f^3 - f_4^3$, this is now figured into the intercept term for f_5^3's linear equation. The sign of Z is reversed throughout if 5 chooses to accept offers to sell (in equilibrium, he does not accept both offers of one other player during Step 5).

$l = \mathcal{A}, \mathcal{B}, \mathcal{S}$, is a function $G^l: \mathbb{R}_+^{12} \mapsto \mathbb{R}$ defined by

$$G^l(P, Q) := \tfrac{1}{6} \sum_{(i,j,k) \in \Omega} \pi^l[P, T_i(P), U_j[P, T_i(P)],$$

$$V_k(P, T_i(P), U_j[P, T_i(P)])].$$

This definition has best response behaviour at each step incorporated as history in the following steps.[23]

During Step 1, offers

$$(p^a, \boldsymbol{p}^a, p^b, \boldsymbol{p}^b, p^s, \boldsymbol{p}^s, f^a, \boldsymbol{f}^a, f^b, \boldsymbol{f}^b, f^s, \boldsymbol{f}^s)$$

satisfy subgame perfection if:

$$G^a(p^a, \boldsymbol{p}^a, p^b, \boldsymbol{p}^b, p^s, \boldsymbol{p}^s, f^a, \boldsymbol{f}^a, f^b, \boldsymbol{f}^b, f^s, \boldsymbol{f}^s)$$
$$\geq G^a(p, \boldsymbol{p}, p^b, \boldsymbol{p}^b, p^s, \boldsymbol{p}^s, f, \boldsymbol{f}, f^b, \boldsymbol{f}^b, f^s, \boldsymbol{f}^s)$$
$$\forall (p, \boldsymbol{p}, f, \boldsymbol{f}) \geq 0,$$
$$G^b(p^a, \boldsymbol{p}^a, p^b, \boldsymbol{p}^b, p^s, \boldsymbol{p}^s, f^a, \boldsymbol{f}^a, f^b, \boldsymbol{f}^b, f^s, \boldsymbol{f}^s)$$
$$\geq G^b(p^a, \boldsymbol{p}^a, p, \boldsymbol{p}, p^s, \boldsymbol{p}^s, f^a, \boldsymbol{f}^a, f, \boldsymbol{f}, f^s, \boldsymbol{f}^s)$$
$$\forall (p, \boldsymbol{p}, f, \boldsymbol{f}) \geq 0,$$
$$G^s(p^a, \boldsymbol{p}^a, p^b, \boldsymbol{p}^b, p^s, \boldsymbol{p}^s, f^a, \boldsymbol{f}^a, f^b, \boldsymbol{f}^b, f^s, \boldsymbol{f}^s)$$
$$\geq G^s(p^a, \boldsymbol{p}^a, p^b, \boldsymbol{p}^b, p, \boldsymbol{p}, f^a, \boldsymbol{f}^a, f^b, \boldsymbol{f}^b, f, \boldsymbol{f})$$
$$\forall (p, \boldsymbol{p}, f, \boldsymbol{f}) \geq 0. \tag{12}$$

The next section discusses implications of (12).

7. Subgame-perfect offers

All subgame-perfect contracts have the offeror fixing the price, and later the acceptor fixing the quantity. The basic considerations involved in payoff-maximizing offers can be illustrated graphically. Figure 1 will aid in seeing how prices to be announced are determined by anticipating the quantities that would be accepted for different prices which could be announced, and in seeing what calculations guide the choice of trading partner to focus on in determining an announcement. In subgame-perfect equilibrium, changing the maximum quantity announced will affect quantities accepted only if the constraint that no more can be accepted than is available should happen to be binding. Thus, Figure 1 will only indicate lower bounds for the maximum quantity that should be announced.

---

[23] F affects G^h via restrictions on the range of T_i, U_j and V_k.

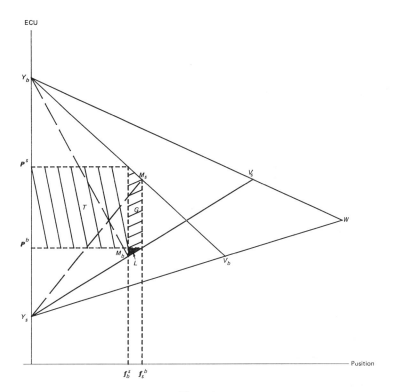

Figure 1.

To reach a relatively simple diagrammatic analysis, initially one of the players is ignored. For convenience, focus on the two contracts f_b^s and f_s^b where $\mathscr{S}$ sells to $\mathscr{B}$, assuming no gains from trade could result from $\mathscr{B}$ selling to $\mathscr{S}$. Naturally, the price p^s at which $\mathscr{S}$ announces he would like to sell will exceed the price p^b at which $\mathscr{B}$ announces he would like to buy.

Because each prefers his own announced price, in commitment orders where $\mathscr{S}$ accepts before $\mathscr{B}$, $\mathscr{S}$ will set $f_s^b = 0$. Similarly, in the remaining commitment orders, $\mathscr{B}$ will set $f_b^s = 0$, knowing that $\mathscr{S}$ in a later step will accept $\mathscr{B}$'s price p^b rather than forego all gains from trade with $\mathscr{B}$. (We continue to ignore $\mathscr{A}$ for the moment.)

With the quantity of $\mathscr{S}$'s futures sales to $\mathscr{B}$ on the horizontal axis in Figure 1, and the price shown vertically, we can create an analogue to an Edgeworth box diagram: any (quantity, price) vector inside the "lens" $Y_s Y_b W$ represents a mutually beneficial trade. Differences in beliefs, size of hedgable stocks, and net positions on contracts with $\mathscr{A}$ determine the intercepts Y_s and Y_b. When $\mathscr{B}$ is determining the quantity f_b^s after $f_s^b = 0$, $\mathscr{B}$ maximizes his payoff by setting f_b^s for any p^s halfway across from 0 to $Y_b W$, that is, along the line $Y_b V_b$. Similarly, if f_b^s has been set at zero, $\mathscr{S}$ will choose to respond to p^b by setting f_s^b along $Y_s V_s$, which bisects the angle $Y_b Y_s W$.

Note. Let $(\mathbb{S}\backslash f_b^s)$ denote $\mathscr{S}$'s net short position under the assumption $f_b^s = 0$, with $(\mathbb{S}\backslash f_s^b)$, $(\mathbb{B}\backslash f_b^s)$, $(\mathbb{B}\backslash f_b^a)$ analogous incomplete net short positions. Assuming the only contract between $\mathscr{B}$ and $\mathscr{S}$ is f_s^b, $Y_s = -(\mathbb{S}\backslash f_s^b) - \hat{p}_s/2\theta$, which may be positive or negative (the horizontal axis need not imply a zero price, though the lens is bounded below by zero prices and quantities). The slope of $Y_s W$ is $(4\theta)^{-1}$; this and the intercept are obtained by solving $\pi_s - \pi_s|_{f_s^b = f_b^s = 0} = 0$.

Assuming the only contract between $\mathscr{B}$ and $\mathscr{S}$ is f_b^s,

$$Y_b = (\hat{p}_b + \tfrac{2}{3}\theta(\mathbb{S}\backslash f_b^s) + K_b[s_{b0} - (\mathbb{B}\backslash f_b^s)])/(K_b - \tfrac{2}{3}\theta),$$

assuming the denominator is positive (otherwise, f_b^s will be either 0 or $f^s - f_a^s$). The slope of $Y_b W$ is $-(2K_b - \tfrac{4}{3}\theta)^{-1}$; this and the intercept are obtained by solving $\pi_b - \pi_b|_{f_s^b = f_b^s = 0} = 0$. If, instead, we were focusing on f_b^a and f_b^a, Y_b would be

$$\hat{p}_b/K_b - (s_{b0} - (\mathbb{B}\backslash f_b^a)),$$

and $Y_b W$ would have slope $(2K_b)^{-1}$. Analogous results would be obtained for $\mathscr{A}$.

Now consider what price $\mathscr{S}$ should announce. The price he sets will be relevent when he will get to set $f_s^b = 0$ before $\mathscr{B}$ determines f_b^s. Assuming this, he should act like a monopolist. That is, he draws a "marginal revenue" line $Y_b M_b$, and sets price p^s so that $\mathscr{B}$ will later choose to set f_b^s equal to the quantity where $Y_b M_b$ reaches $Y_s V_s$ ($\mathscr{S}$'s "marginal cost"), as shown.

In the reverse situation, $\mathscr{B}$ should act like a monopsonist, drawing line $Y_s M_b$, and setting price p^b so that $\mathscr{S}$ will later choose to set f_s^b equal to the quantity where $Y_s M_s$ reaches $Y_b V_b$, as shown.

How large is the payoff difference to $\mathscr{S}$ that results from trading with $\mathscr{B}$ on his own terms rather than (p^b, f_s^b)? This payoff difference is the area of the rectangle T, the transfer amount, less the area of the triangle L, $\mathscr{S}$'s share of the efficiency loss between f_b^s and f_s^b. The payoff difference to $\mathscr{B}$ between his own terms and $\mathscr{S}$'s terms is the sum of the areas of the rectangle T and the trapezoid G ($\mathscr{B}$'s share of the efficiency gain). Thus, the player with the steeper V_i function (cf. (9)) will have more at stake in the determination of terms of trade.

While a number of complicated issues arise, principally with determining the intercepts for diagrams like Figure 1, the central theme of the Step 1 decisions is a comparison of the amounts at stake for each contract. That is, $\mathscr{S}$ determines (p^s, f^s) essentially by calculating whether more payoff difference is at stake in (p^s, f_b^s) versus (p^b, f_s^b) than in (p^s, f_a^s) versus (p^a, f_s^a), each weighted by the number of commitment orders for which he could dictate his terms to the rival in question.

8. Efficiency

Proposition. *Given divergent prior beliefs, in subgame-perfect equilibrium, due to the rule which has one party to a contract fixing the price and the other determining the quantity, there remain volume-enhancing, mutually beneficial trades of futures contracts.*

Remark. The proof is straightforward; Pareto-efficiency so constrains contracts as to give some party a profitable opportunity to have offered to buy at a lower, or sell at a higher price, reducing volume in the process.

Proof of the proposition. Suppose, contrary to the proposition, that there exists a set of parameters with $\hat{p}_a$, $\hat{p}_b$, $\hat{p}_s$ all distinct, and an associated subgame-perfect equilibrium behaviour which yields a Pareto-efficient outcome, in that no mutually beneficial trades remain. Hence, no mutually beneficial trades may remain for the pattern of acceptances occurring in any commitment order. Thus, in an arbitrary commitment order $\omega \in \Omega$, for each pair of players $i, j \in \{\mathscr{A}, \mathscr{B}, \mathscr{S}\}$, the following property must be satisfied (perhaps by relabelling): (†): {j has accepted a contract offered by i, at precisely the same net position that i would have chosen at that price, had i been the one accepting}. Under these circumstances, it would be inconsistent with equilibrium for i to prefer to trade with j at the terms j offered rather than at i's own terms. So j offered either identical or less favourable terms to i. Across commitment orders, there are 18 pairs constraining an offer by one of the pair to satisfy (†). As only 6 offers are made, either (i) every offer must be accepted and satisfy (†) in at least 3 commitment orders, or (ii) some offer (††) must be accepted and satisfy (†) in at least 4 commitment orders. Option (i) constrains some i, j pair to offer each other identical prices and maximum quantities sufficient to reach a Pareto-efficient outcome; so i can gain by announcing the same maximum quantity at a price slightly more favourable to him, as in the commitment orders where i follows j, he cannot be worse off, since j is by presumption offering him his original terms. Thus, option (i) yields a contradiction to the presumed equilibrium, in the direction of reduced volume of futures contracts for those commitment orders where j accepts i's terms. Option (ii) is similarly inconsistent with equilibrium, as the player i offering (††) has available to him sufficiently favourable terms in the remaining two commitment orders to be able to alter (††) backward along the steepest V_j accepting it, attaining a higher payoff. □

If our stylized version of trading rules on futures markets is capturing some essentials of rules and incentives in actual futures markets, such as the London Metal Exchange, then the proposition calls for a more careful look at the incentives facing the market-makers who determine which rules are to be employed. Market-makers have not been introduced explicitly in this model, nor have commissions. Both sides to each trade in subgame-perfect equilibrium, however, would be willing to pay some positive commission to a market-maker and still accept the trades consummated.[24] A market-maker looking to maximize commissions via maximizing total futures contract volume would be expected to investigate whether an alternative set of trading rules could be found which would attain the higher Pareto-efficient trading volume. In fact, such a set of rules may exist: Phlips and Harstad (1990) find that subgame-perfect equilibria reach Pareto-efficient volume when any trader accepting a contract must accept the full maximum quantity offered, that is, when a potential acceptor must simply say "yes" or "no", not "I'll take 100 of that". (All other rules unchanged.)

If such "all-or-nothing" rules were used, in subgame-perfect equilibrium any contract acceptor obtains just enough profit to induce him to agree; it is the appropriation of all gains from trade (in excess of this minimum) that leads to the contract's offeror to announce a Pareto-efficient position. If commissions were introduced, they would figure into the minimum profit level allowed an acceptor. Averaging across commitment orders, all three players would expect positive profits, but every contract that generates a commission for the market-maker would require the signature of a party nearly indifferent to signing. This uneven distribution of profit, on a contract-by-contract basis, may likely impose some notable cost or disutility upon

---

[24] A nonzero marginal commission would, naturally, reduce total volume of contracts, but may not affect equilibrium net short positions.

the market-maker, which would explain why market-makers appear to prefer using rules more like those we have studied in this paper, even at the expense of a reduced commissionable trading volume. If the model were extended to allow for some uncertainty about trading partners' prior beliefs, it is possible that expected trading volume would be higher when trades by design have not-too-uneven profit splits (because the acceptor determines the quantity traded), than when the offeror attempts a total profit appropriation. Extending the model in this direction would take us hopelessly far afield.

9. Concluding remarks on uniform prices

It is customary in models of futures markets to impose a uniform price upon all trades in one market period of futures contracts with a common maturity date. Most models then proceed to ask whether this one price is an unbiased predictor of the spot price at maturity.

When differences in opinion are the source of gains from purely speculative trade on futures markets, market participants are not looking to "the" futures price to aggregate or provide information about the spot price at maturity; they are not about to modify their beliefs upon learning that "the market" has different beliefs.

Only with some violence can the contract data observed on futures markets be fitted into a uniform price model. Although simple in many respects, our model nonetheless produces a diversity of prices, which seems entirely natural. It is even possible to find parameters for which a subgame-perfect equilibrium outcome involves multiple prices on contracts between the same trading pair.

Unlike capital asset pricing models currently in vogue, no efficient markets assumption is employed, and equilibrium outcomes are inefficient. The root of suboptimal volume of futures activity is not the small number of participants, but must be traced to the procedure wherein a trader can accept a part of the quantity offered for sale or purchase, at the offered price, without having to accept the entire offer. However, only an oligopolistic and game-theoretic model can allow analysis of such impacts of trading rules upon outcomes.

Finally, in a very real sense, a uniform price on a futures market would itself be a source of inefficiency. Whatever the volume of trade that occurs at a uniform price, there remain gains from further trade, for almost any pair of traders, which can be reached only by discarding the uniform price.

Except for pathological parameter sets, subgame-perfect equilibrium outcomes in this model involve at least one contract between each pair of traders, such that expected profit to each trader on that contract (given inconsistent prior beliefs) is bounded above zero. Thus, at least one trader will be both buying and selling, viewing both as profitable. This realistic feature is only possible when a uniform price rule is discarded.

References

Anderson, R.W. (1984) *The Industrial Organization of Futures Markets.* Lexington, MA: Lexington Books.

Brianza, T., L. Phlips and J.-F. Richard (1987) 'Futures markets, speculation and monopoly', CORE Discussion Paper 8725, Louvain-la-Neuve.

Damme, E. van (1987) *Stability and Perfection of Nash Equilibria.* Berlin: Springer.

Hall, S.G. and M.P. Taylor (1988) 'Modelling risk premia in commodity forward prices: some evidence from the London metal exchange', Economics Division Discussion Paper, Bank of England, London.

Harsanyi, J.C. and R. Selten (1988) *A General Theory of Equilibrium Selection in Games.* Cambridge, MA: M.I.T. Press.

Kreps, D. (1977) 'A note on 'fulfilled expectations' equilibria'', *Journal of Economic Theory*, 14:32-43.

MacDonald, R. and M.P. Taylor (1988) 'Testing rational expectations and efficiency in the London metal exchange', *Oxford Bulletin of Economics and Statistics*, 50:41-52.

Milgrom, P.R. and N.L. Stokey (1982) 'Information, trade and common knowledge', *Journal of Economic Theory*, 26:17-27.

Newbury, D.M. and J.E. Stiglitz (1981) *The Theory of Commodity Price Stabilisation: A Study in the Economics of Risk.* Oxford: Clarendon Press.

Novshek, W. (1985) 'On the existence of Cournot equilibrium', *Review of Economic Studies*, 52:85-98.

Phlips, L. and R.M. Harstad (1990) 'Interaction between resource extraction and futures markets: a game-theoretic analysis', in: R. Selten, ed., *Game Equilibrium Models.* Heidelberg: Springer.

Reinganum, J.F. and N.L. Stokey (1985) 'Oligopoly extraction of a common property natural resource: the importance of the period of commitment in dynamic games', *International Economic Review*, 26:161-173.

Selten, R. (1982) 'Einführung in die Theorie der Spiele mit unvollständiger Information', in: *Information in der Wirtschaft, Schriften des Vereins für Sozialpolitik, Gesellschaft für Wirtschafts- und Sozialwissenschaften (N.F. Band 126).* Berlin: Duncker & Humbolt, pp. 81-147.

Tirole, J. (1982) 'On the possibility of speculation under rational expectations', *Econometrica*, 24:74-81.

Varian, H.R. (1989) 'Differences in opinion in financial markets', in: C. Stone, ed., *Financial Risk: Theory, Evidence and Implications.* Amsterdam: Kluwer Academic Publishers.

Chapter 9

ON QUALITY AND VARIETY COMPETITION

Damien NEVEN

INSEAD, Fontainebleau, France

Jacques-François THISSE

CORE, Université Catholique de Louvain, Louvain-la-Neuve, Belgium

1. Introduction

It was Hotelling's (1929) belief that duopoly competition on a one-dimensional market — Main Street — would lead both firms to choose a central location. Indeed, such a location is most favourable in terms of consumers' proximity. Still, as shown by d'Aspremont et al. (1979), price competition destroys the advantage of being centrally located. Similarly, whereas selling a high quality product seems to be a sensible policy, price competition will also induce one duopolist to pick a low quality product (see Shaked and Sutton, 1981). The purpose of this paper is to examine such interplay between price and product competition in the context of an example combining both horizontal and vertical differentiation. Firms are, therefore, allowed to choose to differentiate along one of the characteristics and not necessarily on both.

In the Lancasterian tradition, two models of product differentiation prevail, namely *horizontal* and *vertical*. Two products are *horizontally differentiated* when there is no ranking among consumers based on their

The authors wish to thank J.J. Gabszewicz, E. Gal-Or, D. Henriet, C. Holt, N. Ireland and seminar audiences at Universitat Autonoma de Barcelona and University of Virginia for helpful comments and suggestions. The second author gratefully acknowledges financial support from CIM (Belgium) and INSEAD.

Economic Decision-Making: Games, Econometrics and Optimisation
Edited by J.J. Gabszewicz, J.-F. Richard and L.A. Wolsey

willingness-to-pay for the two products. By contrast, two products are *vertically differentiated* when there exists such a ranking of consumers. Prototypes of the former class of models include Hotelling (1929) and his followers (see, e.g., d'Aspremont et al., 1979; Eaton and Wooders, 1985; Economides, 1989; Neven, 1985; Salop, 1979). The latter class was developed more recently by Gabszewicz and Thisse (1979) and Mussa and Rosen (1978) (see also Gabszewicz and Thisse, 1980; Gabszewicz et al., 1986; Shaked and Sutton, 1983). These various contributions indicate that the nature of competition differs along several lines depending on the type of differentiated products.

Horizontal differentiation is associated with the existence of product *varieties*, while vertical differentiation occurs when products differ according to *quality*. Our purpose is to combine these two types of models. Indeed, casual observation suggests that most products cannot be sorted out into either of these polar cases. Rather, they differ in variety as well as in quality. For example, consumer durables are typically sold under different designs (variety), each offered with various degrees of reliability (quality). To illustrate, consider the market for washing machines; machines are usually offered with either top or front loading of the clothes. This is a matter of design over which consumers might disagree. Both types will still be offered with different degrees of reliability. Presumably, all consumers will also prefer a more reliable machine. The analysis of product and price competition when both dimensions matter is therefore warranted from an empirical perspective. As noted above, such an inquiry is also justified from a theoretical standpoint, competition being affected by the prevailing type of product differentiation.

In this paper, we couple a vertically differentiated characteristics à la Mussa and Rosen with a horizontally differentiated characteristics à la Hotelling. Our model thus encompasses these two popular paradigms of product differentiation. However, it goes beyond a simple addition of the two models: the interplay between quality and variety leads to results which are qualitatively different from those encountered in either of the single characteristics models. To the best of our knowledge, only two recent contributions address this question. First, Ireland (1987) studies only price competition in a model where two products are given. Second, Ginsburgh et al. (1987) consider a model in which, for given varieties, competition occurs in price and quality. Our model differs from those contributions in that firms compete in price, variety and quality.

Following a well-established tradition in this stream of literature, we formulate firms' choices as a two-stage game. In the first stage, both firms choose simultaneously the variety and quality characteristics of their product. In the second stage, they compete in price. We have thus chosen to model the decisions on product variety and quality as being simultaneous because production will often require the joint specification of these characteristics.

Our results include the following. First, a price equilibrium exists in our duopoly model for any product configuration. Second, two types of equilibrium obtain at the product selection stage: (i) when the quality range is sufficiently large relative to the variety range, then in equilibrium both firms select a pair of products which are maximally differentiated along the vertical characteristics but minimally differentiated along the horizontal characteristics. (ii) If the variety range is wide enough compared to the quality range, in equilibrium firms choose products which are minimally differentiated along the vertical characteristics but maximally differentiated along the horizontal characteristics. Interestingly, there is an overlap in the ranges of parameters for which these equilibria occur.

The paper is organised as follows. We present the model in Section 2. As usual, we solve the model by backwards induction. Hence, Section 3 deals with the price competition stage of the game. Some comparative statics is performed in Section 4. In Section 5, we then analyse firms' product selection, contingent on the equilibrium prices. Some concluding remarks are provided in Section 6.

2. The model

Assume there is an industry in which products can be defined along two characteristics, namely variety (y) and quality (q). The range of potential varieties is represented by the $[0, 1]$ interval.[1] Consumers do not rank the product varieties in the same way and, accordingly, this first characteristic corresponds to some horizontal differentiation. The range of potential qualities is represented by the interval $[q, \bar{q}]$ and all consumers prefer a high quality to a low quality. This second characteristic then portrays vertical differentiation. On the whole, each product i is thus characterised by its variety, y_i, and its quality, q_i, with $(y_i, q_i) \in [0, 1] \times [q, \bar{q}]$.

Consumer preferences vary along two dimensions. First, each consumer has a "most preferred" variety, say x, with $x \in [0, 1]$. Second, each consumer

---

[1] The unit interval is selected, without loss of generality, by an adequate choice of the length unit.

has a quality valuation, say θ, with $\theta \in [0, 1]$.[2] A consumer of type (x, θ) derives the following (indirect) utility from buying one unit of product i:

$$U(y_i, q_i; x, \theta) = R + \theta q_i - (x - y_i)^2 - P_i, \tag{1}$$

where P_i denotes the price of product i and R is a positive constant. We suppose that consumers buy at most one unit of the differentiated commodity. They will select the product for which utility (1) is higher. We also assume that R is large enough for all consumers to find a product for which their utility is positive (in equilibrium). Finally, consumers as represented by the parameters (x, θ) are supposed to be uniformly distributed over the unit square, with a total mass equal to one. These assumptions enable us to describe a product's aggregate demand as the measure of a subset of $[0, 1] \times [0, 1]$.

We consider two single product firms $(i = 1, 2)$, operating with zero marginal cost of production. Without loss of generality, we label the firm with the higher quality as firm 2, i.e., $q_2 \geq q_1$, and assume that $y_2 \geq y_1$. The opposite situation in which $y_1 \geq y_2$ can be dealt with in a symmetric way, by rotating the parameter space $[0, 1] \times [q, \bar{q}]$ around the axis $y = 0$ and making an appropriate change of variables.

Given (1), we can derive the set of consumers who are just indifferent between products 1 and 2. For any consumer type $x \in [0, 1]$, the marginal consumer in terms of θ who is indifferent between the two products is written as

$$\bar{\theta}(x) = \frac{(P_2 - P_1) + (y_2^2 - y_1^2) - 2(y_2 - y_1)x}{q_2 - q_1}. \tag{2}$$

The set of consumers, given by the unit square, is partitioned in two groups as illustrated in Figure 1. For any $x \in [0, 1]$, the consumers in the interval $[0, \bar{\theta}(x)]$ purchase product 1 while those for whom $\theta \in]\bar{\theta}(x), 1]$ buy product 2. We also observe that $\bar{\theta}(x)$ is a linear and nonincreasing function of x. That is to say that consumers with a high valuation of quality will be attracted more easily by the (high quality) product 2 and the more so, the less attractive is product 1 (as compared to product 2) in terms of variety. An increase in P_1 (decrease in P_2) will have the effect of shifting down $\bar{\theta}(x)$, thereby reducing demand for product 1.[3]

---

[2] The unit interval can be chosen, without loss of generality, by an adequate choice of the quality unit.

[3] It is worth noting that the present model encompasses two popular paradigms of differentiation: (i) By setting $y_1 = y_2$, $\bar{\theta}(x)$ becomes a horizontal segment and the model reduces to a duopoly à la Mussa and Rosen (as analysed by Gabszewicz and Thisse, 1988); (ii) If $q_1 = q_2$, $\bar{\theta}(x)$ is a vertical segment and our formulation boiled down to Hotelling's model with quadratic transport costs.

FIRM 2'S MARKET AREA

FIRM 1'S MARKET AREA

Figure 1.

In order to derive the aggregate demand for product 1, say D_1, we have to integrate the function $\theta(x)$ over $[0, 1]$. According to the position of the θ-line, we obtain three main cases. First, if P_1 is "high", the θ-line crosses the bottom and left sides of the unit square and gives rise to the segment D_1^1 of firm 1's demand (see (6)).

Second, for "intermediate" values of P_1, the θ-line while shifting up will cross either the vertical sides or the horizontal sides of the unit square. The former case will occur when the absolute value of the slope of the θ-line is smaller than one. This situation is characterised by the fact that the quality difference dominates the difference in variety. It will be referred to as a situation of *vertical dominance*. Formally, $|\partial\bar{\theta}/\partial x| < 1$ is equivalent to

$$2(y_2 - y_1) < q_2 - q_1. \tag{3}$$

The latter case arises when the absolute value of the θ-line is greater than 1, i.e.,

$$q_2 - q_1 < 2(y_2 - y_1). \tag{4}$$

This situation will be referred to as a situation of *horizontal dominance*. Clearly, if

$$q_2 - q_1 = 2(y_2 - y_1), \tag{5}$$

the θ-line is parallel to the negative diagonal of the unit square and neither vertical nor horizontal differentiation dominates. Whether (3), (4) or (5) holds, the corresponding segment of D_1 is denoted D_1^{11} (see (7) and (8)).

Third, and last, for "small" values of P_1, $\theta(x)$ now crosses the top and right sides of the unit square and yields the segment D_1^{III} (see (9)).

The demand D_1 is described in detail in Appendix 1. The results can be summarised as follows:

$$D_1^I = \frac{[(\bar{P}_2 - P_1) + (y_2^2 - y_1^2)]^2}{4(y_2 - y_1)(q_2 - q_1)} \tag{6}$$

when $P_1' \equiv \bar{P}_2 + (y_2^2 - y_1^2) \geq P_1 \geq P_1''$;

$$D_1^{II} = \frac{(\bar{P}_2 - P_1) + (y_2^2 - y_1^2)}{q_2 - q_1} - \frac{y_2 - y_1}{q_2 - q_1} \tag{7}$$

if vertical dominance prevails and

$$P_1'' \equiv \bar{P}_2 + (y_2^2 - y_1^2) - 2(y_2 - y_1) \geq P_1 \geq P_1''' \equiv \bar{P}_2 + (y_2^2 - y_1^2) - (q_2 - q_1),$$

or

$$D_1^{II} = \frac{(\bar{P}_2 - P_1) + (y_2^2 - y_1^2)}{2(y_2 - y_1)} - \frac{q_2 - q_1}{4(y_2 - y_1)} \tag{8}$$

if horizontal dominance prevails and

$$\hat{P}_1'' \equiv \bar{P}_2 + (y_2^2 - y_1^2) - (q_2 - q_1) \geq P_1 \geq \hat{P}_1''' \equiv \bar{P}_2 + (y_2^2 - y_1^2) - 2(y_2 - y_1);[4]$$

$$D_1^{III} = [4(y_2 - y_1)(q_2 - q_1)]^{-1}[2(q_2 - q_1)((\bar{P}_2 - P_1) + (y_2^2 - y_1^2)) - (q_2 - q_1)^2$$
$$- ((\bar{P}_2 - P_1) + (y_2^2 - y_1^2) - 2(y_2 - y_1))^2], \quad (9)$$

when $\hat{P}_1''' \geq P_1 \geq \hat{P}_1'''' \equiv \bar{P}_2 + (y_2^2 - y_1^2) - (q_2 - q_1) - 2(y_2 - y_1)$. The domains of parameters (y_1, y_2, q_1, q_2) corresponding to the above four price domains are denoted respectively R_1, R_{II}', R_{II}'' and R_{III}.

It is readily verified that at each kink (P_1'' and P_1''') demand is continuous. A typical example of D_1 is depicted in Figure 2.

To sum up, the demand for firm 1 is in general composed of *three* segments. The expressions for demand in the first and third segments are independent of whether horizontal or vertical dominance prevails. The domain of parameters for which these expressions apply, however, depends on the type of dominance. With respect to the intermediate segment, the expression of demand (and the domain of parameters) is affected by the type of dominance. Finally, notice that D_1^I is strictly convex, D_1^{II} linear and D_1^{III} strictly concave. This sequence can be explained as follows. In the domain R_1, demand is strictly convex because the θ-line while shifting up generates a

---

[4] If (5) is satisfied, then $D_1^{II} = 0$ so that D_1^I and D_1^{III} are directly connected.

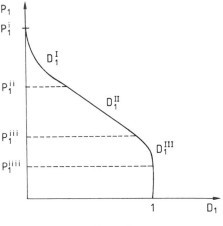

Figure 2.

longer and longer upper frontier of the firm's market area. In the intermediate domain (R_{II} or R_{II}), the segment is linear because the θ-line is straight and intersects two parallel sides of the unit square. Finally in R_{III}, demand is strictly concave for the same reason, mutatis mutandis, as to why demand is strictly convex in R_I.

The aggregate demand for product 2 can be directly computed since consumers never abstain from buying: $D_2 = 1 - D_1$. The various segments of D_2 can be derived along the lines of the analysis performed above for D_1 (leading to a partition of the price segment $[P_2''', P_2']$ akin to (A.1)-(A.4) (see Appendix 1), in which P_1 and P_2 are permuted). The shape of D_2 is identical to that of D_1, mutatis mutandis.

We can now turn to the analysis of the second stage price equilibrium.

3. Price equilibrium

For each pair of products, the profit function of firm i ($i = 1, 2$) is defined as $\Pi_i(P_i, P_j) = P_i D_i(P_i, P_j)$ for $j \neq i$.

First, we shall prove that an equilibrium exists.

Proposition 1. *For any pair of products* (y_1, q_1) *and* (y_2, q_2), *there exists a price equilibrium in the corresponding subgame.*

Proof. Consider the profit function Π_1 when vertical dominance prevails. On the interval $[P_1''', P_1'']$, the demand D_1 is concave and decreasing which implies that Π_1 is concave in P_1. By contrast, D_1 is strictly convex on $[P_1'', P_1']$. However, it is straightforward to show that $\partial^3 \Pi_1/\partial P_1^3 > 0$, so that $\partial \Pi_1/\partial P_1$ is strictly convex in P_1. Since the left hand side derivative of Π_1 is negative at P_1', $\partial \Pi_1/\partial P_1 = 0$ has at most one solution in $[P_1'', P_1']$. Furthermore, at P_1'' (as given by (A.2)), it is easy to check that $(\partial \Pi_1/\partial P_1)|_-$, using (6), and $(\partial \Pi_1/\partial P_1)|_+$ are both equal to $(3(y_2 - y_1) - (y_2^2 - y_1^2) - \bar{P}_2)/(q_2 - q_1)$. Accordingly, the sign of $\partial \Pi_1/\partial P_1$ is the same on both sides of P_1''.

Combining this result with the fact that Π_1 is concave on $[P_1''', P_1'']$ and zero outside of $[P_1''', P_1']$, we obtain that Π_1 has a unique maximum w.r.t. P_1 and therefore is quasi-concave in P_1.

The above argument can be repeated, mutatis mutandis, under horizontal dominance and for Π_2, under both types of dominance. As the profit functions are continuous, it follows that an equilibrium exists. □

We now determine the equilibrium prices as a function of the product characteristics. This leads us to distinguish between six types of equilibria, namely three under vertical dominance and three under horizontal dominance. For each kind of dominance, we have the following types of equilibria. *Case 1*: The equilibrium occurs on the linear segments of both D_1 and D_2. *Case 2*: The equilibrium occurs on the strictly convex segment of D_1 and the strictly concave segment of D_2. *Case 3*: The equilibrium occurs on the strictly concave segment of D_1 and the strictly convex segment of D_2.

We shall analyse each case in turn and determine the region of parameters for which the equilibrium prices indeed fall on the corresponding segments. In each case, vertical and horizontal dominance are dealt with sequentially.

Case 1. (i) *Vertical dominance.* We seek an equilibrium on the linear segment of D_1 and D_2. The appropriate expressions for demand are thus D_1^{II} as given by (7) and $D_2^{II} = 1 - D_1^{II}$. The first order conditions for maximisation of the corresponding profit functions have a single solution given by

$$P_1^* = \frac{(q_2 - q_1) + (y_2^2 - y_1^2) - (y_2 - y_1)}{3}, \tag{10}$$

$$P_2^* = \frac{2(q_2 - q_1) - (y_2^2 - y_1^2) + (y_2 - y_1)}{3}. \tag{11}$$

As a price equilibrium exists and the FOC's are necessary, these prices are the equilibrium prices, provided that they belong to the intervals for which demand is indeed given by $D_1 = D_1^{II}$ and $D_2 = 1 - D_1^{II}$. This is

$$P_1^* \in [P_1'''(P_2^*), P_1''(P_2^*)] \quad \text{and} \quad P_2^* \in [P_2'''(P_1^*), P_2''(P_1^*)].$$

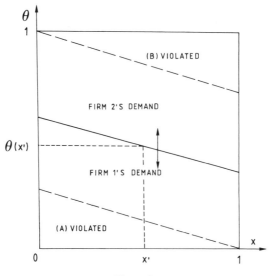

Figure 3.

First, $P_1^* \leq P_1''(P_2^*)$ (as given by (A.2)) is satisfied if and only if

(A) $(y_2 - y_1)(4 - (y_1 + y_2)) \leq q_2 - q_1$.

Second, $P_1^* \geq P_1'''(P_2^*)$ (as given by (A.3)) is satisfied if and only if

(B) $(y_2 - y_1)(2 + (y_1 + y_2)) \leq 2(q_2 - q_1)$.

Similarly, some simple computations show that $P_2^* \in [P_2'''(P_1^*), P_2''(P_1^*)]$ if and only if both conditions (A) and (B) are satisfied. As a result, (10) and (11) define the unique price equilibrium for the parameter region defined by conditions (A) and (B), i.e., region R_{11}'.

The heavy line in Figure 3 illustrates the typical split of the market between the two firms, which will be encountered when the products' characteristics satisfy conditions (A) and (B).

(ii) *Horizontal dominance.* We now consider the linear segment of the demand functions, with the assumption that horizontal dominance prevails. Hence, D_1^{11} is now given by (8) and $D_2^{11} = 1 - D_1^{11}$. As before, solving the FOC's yields a unique pair of prices given by

$$P_1^{**} = \frac{4(y_2 - y_1) + 2(y_2^2 - y_1^2) - (q_2 - q_1)}{6}, \qquad (12)$$

$$P_2^{**} = \frac{8(y_2 - y_1) - 2(y_2^2 - y_1^2) + (q_2 - q_1)}{6}. \qquad (13)$$

Again, as an equilibrium exists and FOC's are necessary, these prices are equilibrium prices, provided they belong to the appropriate intervals, i.e.,

$$P_1^{**} \in [\hat{P}_1'''(P_2^{**}), \hat{P}_1''(P_2^{**})] \quad \text{and} \quad P_2^{**} \in [\hat{P}_2'''(P_1^{**}), \hat{P}_2''(P_1^{**})].$$

The conditions $P_1^{**} \le \hat{P}_1''(P_2^{**})$ and $P_1^{**} \ge \hat{P}_1'''(P_2^{**})$ are met respectively if and only if

(C) $(y_2 - y_1)(2 + (y_1 + y_2)) \ge 2(q_2 - q_1),$

and

(D) $(y_2 - y_1)(4 - (y_1 + y_2)) \ge q_2 - q_1.$

Similarly, the restrictions on P_2^{**} lead to the same conditions as (C) and (D). Hence, (12) and (13) provide the unique price equilibrium for the parameter region R_{11}'', defined by (C) and (D).

The heavy line in Figure 4 represents a typical boundary between the firms' market when both conditions (C) and (D) are met.

Notice that condition (D) (resp. (C)) is the reverse of condition (A) (resp. (B)). This accords with intuition; for example, condition (A) will be violated when firm 1 has a variety which is not favourably positioned, under vertical dominance. This will correspond, under horizontal dominance, to a competitive advantage for firm 2 and hence a large market share for this firm. In turn, a large market share for firm 2 will obtain when condition (D) is

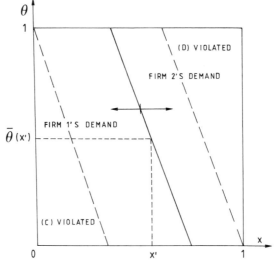

Figure 4.

satisfied. A similar reasoning can be held with respect to conditions (B) and (C).

Case 2. (i) *Vertical dominance.* In this case, the demand faced by firm 1 (on the strictly convex segment), D_1^1, is given by (6), while the demand for firm 2 is $D_2^1 = 1 - D_1^1$. In terms of the parameter region, we have that (A) fails (i.e., $P_1^* > P_1''(P_2^*)$) and (B) holds.

Some simple manipulations using the FOC's show that there exists a unique pair of candidate prices given by

$$\tilde{P}_1 = \tfrac{1}{8}(y_2^2 - y_1^2) + \tfrac{1}{8}[(y_2^2 - y_1^2)^2 + 16(y_2 - y_1)(q_2 - q_1)]^{1/2}, \tag{14}$$

$$\tilde{P}_2 = -\tfrac{5}{8}(y_2^2 - y_1^2) + \tfrac{3}{8}[(y_2^2 - y_1^2)^2 + 16(y_2 - y_1)(q_2 - q_1)]^{1/2}. \tag{15}$$

As a price equilibrium exists, it follows that (14) and (15) is the unique pair of equilibrium prices, provided they fall in the appropriate region. That is

$$\tilde{P}_1 \in [P_1''(\tilde{P}_2), P_1'(\tilde{P}_2)] \quad \text{and} \quad \tilde{P}_2 \in [P_2''''(\tilde{P}_1), P_2'''(\tilde{P}_1)].$$

It is straightforward to check that $\tilde{P}_1 < P_1'(\tilde{P}_2)$ and $\tilde{P}_2 > P_2''''(\tilde{P}_1)$ are always true. The other two inequalities are met if and only if condition (A) fails. Hence, (14) and (15) describe the equilibrium prices when (A) does not hold.

Notice that when condition (A) is met as an equality, $\tilde{P}_1 = P_1^*$ and $\tilde{P}_2 = P_2^*$, which means that equilibrium prices vary continuously when parameters change between R_1 and R_{11}'.

(ii) *Horizontal dominance.* In this case, the functional form of the demands is not affected by the type of dominance, so that the demand expressions just used still apply. With respect to parameters, condition (C) is not met (i.e., $P_1^{**} > \hat{P}_1(P_2^{**})$). The expressions of the equilibrium prices are still given by (14) and (15). However, the region of parameters for which these prices are valid is now different and corresponds to condition (C) (instead of (A)) being violated.

As before, $P_1^{**} = \tilde{P}_1$, $P_2^{**} = \tilde{P}_2$, when condition (C) is just met. Again, equilibrium prices change continuously when parameters move between R_1 and R_{11}''.

Case 3. Vertical (horizontal) dominance. The demand faced by firm 1, D_1^{111} is now given by (9), with as usual, $D_2^{111} = 1 - D_1^{111}$. In terms of parameters, we have that condition (B) in case of vertical dominance, and condition (D) in case of horizontal dominance, are violated.

The FOC's yield a system of two quadratic equations (which are the same under both types of dominance) for which we have not been able to determine a solution. However, as we shall see later, it will not preclude us from solving for the first stage of the game.

4. Comparative statics

Before turning to the analysis of the first stage we proceed with a few comments on the equilibrium prices derived in Case 1. We restrict ourselves to the only case which yields the most striking results. First, notice that under vertical dominance we have $P_2^* > P_1^*$. Hence, the high quality product is always sold at a premium. By contrast, under horizontal dominance it is not always true that $P_2^{**} > P_1^{**}$. *The low quality product might very well be sold a higher price than the high quality product*, if it can secure a large market share by enjoying a better location than the high quality product along the horizontal characteristics.

We now undertake some comparative statics on the equilibrium which is summarised in Tables 1 and 2.

First, we observe that equilibrium prices under vertical (resp. horizontal) dominance behave with respect to quality (resp. variety) parameters in the

Table 1
Comparative statics under vertical dominance

	$y_1 < \frac{1}{2},\ y_2 < \frac{1}{2}$	$y_1 < \frac{1}{2},\ y_2 > \frac{1}{2}$	$y_1 > \frac{1}{2},\ y_2 > \frac{1}{2}$
$\dfrac{\partial P_1^*}{\partial y_1}$	≥ 0	≥ 0	< 0
$\dfrac{\partial P_1^*}{\partial y_2}$	≤ 0	> 0	> 0
$\dfrac{\partial P_2^*}{\partial y_1}$	< 0	< 0	≥ 0
$\dfrac{\partial P_2^*}{\partial y_2}$	> 0	≤ 0	≤ 0

$$\frac{\partial P_1^*}{\partial q_1} < 0, \qquad \frac{\partial P_1^*}{\partial q_2} > 0, \qquad \frac{\partial P_2^*}{\partial q_1} < 0, \qquad \frac{\partial P_2^*}{\partial q_2} > 0$$

Table 2
Comparative statics under horizontal dominance

$$\frac{\partial P_1^{**}}{\partial q_1} > 0, \qquad \frac{\partial P_1^{**}}{\partial q_2} < 0, \qquad \frac{\partial P_2^{**}}{\partial q_1} < 0, \qquad \frac{\partial P_2^{**}}{\partial q_2} > 0$$

$$\frac{\partial P_1^{**}}{\partial y_1} < 0, \qquad \frac{\partial P_1^{**}}{\partial y_2} > 0, \qquad \frac{\partial P_2^{**}}{\partial y_1} < 0, \qquad \frac{\partial P_2^{**}}{\partial y_2} > 0$$

same way as they would in a model with vertical (horizontal) differentiation only (see Gabszewicz and Thisse, 1988; resp. Neven, 1985). Second, with respect to changes in the "dominated" characteristics, one finds non-standard effects (which are underlined in the above tables); under vertical dominance, prices may *increase* as varieties get *closer*. Under horizontal dominance, the price of the low quality product always *increases* if the quality difference *is reduced*.[5]

These unusual comparative statics results can be explained as follows. Consider, first, the case of vertical dominance (Table 1). The more surprising result is $\partial P_1^* / \partial y_1 > 0$, when $y_1 < \frac{1}{2}$. Using (2), (10) and (11), we can show that firm 1's demand increases with y_1. This increase in demand, which leads to an increase in price as y_1 increases, can be said to arise because *the price competition effect is dominated by the advantage of being centrally located.* This is in contrast with pure horizontal models where the former effect always dominates. The price competition effect is here less stringent because firms are already differentiated along the vertical characteristics. The advantage of being centrally located is then stronger. (The above argument applies, mutatis mutandis, to $\partial P_2^* / \partial y_2$.)

Another unusual comparative statics result can be observed in the first and the third columns of Table 1. Specifically, when both firms are located to the left of the market centre, an increase in y_2 leads to a decrease in P_1^*; even though firm 1's location is not affected, the fact that firm 2 moves to the centre renders firm 1's variety relatively less attractive than before. Given that, in addition, firm 1 sells the low quality products, it becomes profitable for that firm competing from an unfavourable position to intensify price competition to attract enough customers.

Similarly, when both firms are located to the right of the market centre, the same effect appears, mutatis mutandis, with respect to an increase in y_1. Indeed, firm 2 increases its price, even though firm 1 gets closer; this firm sells the high quality product and as firm 1 moves, the impact of its relatively unfavourable variety is weakened. As a result, firm 2 will end up in a relatively better position than before, thereby allowing an increase in price.

Let us discuss the case of horizontal dominance (Table 2). Here, the most striking result is $\partial P_1^{**} / \partial q_1 > 0$. In a pure vertical model, competition would lead to a fall in P_1^{**} as q_1 increases, compensating and over the increase in price that one normally expects when quality increases. In the present

---

[5] Those effects clearly show that our model is *not* simply the addition of two one-dimensional models; some interactive effects come into play and generate unusual outcomes.

case, *the competitive effect is weakened because products are already differenti-ated along the horizontal characteristics. As a result, price increases with quality.*

5. Product equilibrium

We now look at product choices, contingent on the equilibrium prices derived in the previous section. The uniqueness of price equilibrium has not been established in the domain of parameters R_{III}. However, as will be seen below, it has no bearing on the product equilibria identified in Propositions 2 and 3.

As a preliminary to the analysis of product equilibria, we describe how changes in each product characteristics affect the equilibrium prices. More specifically, we indicate what kind of price equilibria will be generated by changing y_i and/or q_i. This will enable us to construct the profit functions for the product selection game, by referring to the appropriate equilibrium prices.

At the outset, observe that any move from some point (y'_i, q'_i) to some other point (y''_i, q''_i) can be decomposed into two separate moves, namely $(y'_i, q'_i) \rightarrow (y'_i, q''_i) \rightarrow (y''_i, q''_i)$ (or similarly, $(y'_i, q'_i) \rightarrow (y''_i, q'_i) \rightarrow (y''_i, q''_i)$).

Let us first analyse the effect of changing q_i; starting from given values for y_1, y_2 and $q_2 = q_1$, we gradually increase q_2, up to $\bar{q}$. By so doing, we go through the following sequence:

(a) When $q_2 = q_1$, horizontal dominance and both conditions (C) and (D) are met. In other words, this original parameter configuration lies in the domain R''_{II} and the corresponding equilibrium prices are given by (12) and (13).

(b) Increasing q_2, condition (C) is first violated (and hence condition (B) is met), while horizontal dominance and condition (D) still hold. Accordingly, the domain of parameters is now R_I with horizontal domi-nance, so that the equilibrium prices are given by (14) and (15).

(c) As q_2 is further increased, we reach the region of vertical dominance. Condition (D) is still satisfied (so that (A) is violated). The domain of parameters is R_I with vertical dominance.

(d) Ultimately, an increase in q_2 will lead condition (A) to become satisfied. As (B) is already met, the parameter region is now R'_{II} and the equilibrium prices are given by (10) and (11).

With respect to this sequence of equilibria, the following remarks are in order: first, as noticed above, the equilibrium prices change continuously as one moves across domains of parameters. It follows that the profit functions evaluated at those prices are continuous in product characteristics. Second, the above sequence might be terminated at any step depending on the admissible increase in q_2 (given q_1, y_1, y_2 and $\bar{q}$). Third, the same path occurs if q_1 decreases from the initial configuration $q_1 = q_2$. This is so because all what matters in the above conditions with respect to quality is the quality difference. Last, if $y_1 + y_2 = 2$ (so that both firms sell variety 1), we shift directly from R'_{11} to R''_{11}, without passing through the domain R_1.

Let us now consider an increase in the variety y_2, up to 1, starting from given q_1, q_2 and $y_1 = y_2$:

(a) For this original configuration, conditions (A) and (B) and vertical dominance hold and the domain is R'_{11}.

(b) Increasing y_2, condition (A) is first violated (and hence (D) is met), while vertical dominance and condition (B) are still valid. Accordingly, the domain of parameters is R_1 with vertical dominance.

(c) As y_2 is further increased, we enter the region of horizontal dominance. Condition (B) is still satisfied, so that (C) is violated. Consequently, the domain of parameters is R_1 with horizontal dominance.

(d) Ultimately, an increase in y_2 will bring us in the region where (C) applies and the corresponding domain is R''_{11}.

The four comments stated above, with respect to the sequence of equilibria following a quality change, remain valid, mutatis mutandis, if a variety change is considered.

We now turn to the product selection. Two types of product equilibria may emerge, described in Propositions 2 and 3, respectively. For this purpose, let us define $K_v \equiv (\frac{51}{32})^2$ and $K_h \equiv 2 + \frac{1}{4}\sqrt{63}$.

Proposition 2. *If $(\bar{q} - \underline{q}) \geq K_v$, there exists a product equilibrium given by* $q_1^* = \underline{q}$, $q_2^* = \bar{q}$, $y_1^* = y_2^* = \frac{1}{2}$.

Proposition 3. *If $\bar{q} - \underline{q} \leq K_h$, there exists a product equilibrium given by* $q_1^{**} = q_2^{**} = \bar{q}$, $y_1^{**} = 0$, $y_2^{**} = 1$.

The proofs of these two propositions can be found in Appendix 2.[6]

To sum up, we have identified two types of product equilibrium. If $\bar{q} - \underline{q} \geq K_v$, there exists an equilibrium such that both firms choose the same variety under respectively the lowest and the highest possible quality. Hence, they *minimise* differentiation along the horizontal dimension and *maximise*

---

[6] Notice that the configuration in which firms' indices are permuted are also equilibria.

differentiation along the vertical dimension. The equilibrium outcome is characterised by vertical dominance. If $\bar{q} - q \leq K_h$, there is an equilibrium such that both firms select the top quality but opposite varieties. Hence, they *maximise* differentiation along the horizontal dimension and *minimise* differentiation along the vertical dimension. The equilibrium now features horizontal dominance.

In addition, since $K_h > K_v$ there is a nondegenerate segment $[K_v, K_h]$ in which the two equilibria occur.[7] A question then naturally arises: does one equilibrium Pareto dominate the other in terms of profits? The answer is no. Indeed, firm 1 always prefers the equilibrium with horizontal dominance, while firm 2 always prefers the other. This reflects the asymmetry which arises at the equilibrium under vertical dominance (favourable to firm 2), whereas the equilibrium under horizontal dominance yields a symmetric outcome in terms of profits. It is also easy to verify that the welfare (the sum of profits and consumer surplus) is always higher in the horizontal dominance equilibrium than in the equilibrium of vertical dominance.

Interestingly, it follows (from the proofs of Propositions 2 and 3) that *a product configuration in which firms are maximally differentiated on both dimensions is not an equilibrium.* Such an outcome might, however, accord with intuition, given that it would be most effective in relaxing price competition. It is not an equilibrium because firms have other concerns than relaxing price competition: (i) *firms prefer a central variety and a high quality*, and (ii) *the extent to which a firm can exercise more market power stemming from a favourable position along one characteristic depends on its relative position along the other one.* Hence, when firms are already differentiated along the quality (variety) dimension, price competition is, so to speak, already soft enough and firms select a central variety (a high quality).

Finally, one should point out that we have not been able to establish that the equilibria identified in Propositions 2 and 3 are the only ones (in pure strategies).

6. Conclusion

We have found two product equilibria, such that firms differentiate themselves as much as possible along one characteristics, while selecting the

---

[7] This existence of multiple equilibria in some domain of parameters indicates, once more, that the present model is not simply an addition of two models, one of the horizontal, and the other of the vertical type.

same strategy on the other characteristics. A similar result could be established in a model with two vertical characteristics. This is also reminiscent, in a different context, of a result by de Palma et al. (1985), who show that firms choose to agglomerate at the market centre when their products are perceived as sufficiently heterogeneous (along some other horizontal characteristics). All in all, these results suggest that *firms will have a tendency to select similar strategies with respect to some characteristics, if at the same time they are sufficiently differentiated along the remaining dimensions.* When firms choose similar strategies, they will do so in order to obtain the benefit from selling a high quality product, or to exploit a central location. Accordingly, an outcome where firms differentiate themselves as much as possible along all dimensions, will probably not be an equilibrium.

Our results have admittedly been derived in the context of a very bare model. In this respect, one would normally expect (fixed or variable) production cost to increase with the quality of the product. As a result, firms' incentive to differentiate themselves by increasing quality would be reduced, but presumably not eliminated. With respect to our demand formulation, some recent work by Caplin and Nalebuff (1989) shows that the existence of a price equilibrium will be guaranteed for a wide class of customer distributions. The question remains as to how the product choices will be affected by non-uniform distributions. Following Neven (1986), one could reasonably conjecture that more concentrated customer distributions will lead to less differentiation.

In addition, our comparative statics analysis have revealed unexpected effects of some product characteristics on equilibrium prices. Everything depends on whether horizontal or vertical dominance prevails. In this respect, the difference between variety and quality is indeed particularly noticeable. An important topic for future research will be to analyse whether and how these results can be generalised to a framework encompassing several horizontal and vertical characteristics.

Appendix 1

For any fixed $\bar{P}_2$, define P'_1 as the lowest price for which firm 1 has no demand, i.e., such that $\bar{\theta}(x = 0) = 0$. From (2),

$$P'_1 = \bar{P}_2 + (y_2^2 - y_1^2). \tag{A.1}$$

For any price below P'_1, firm 1 will have a positive demand. Denote $\tilde{x}$ as the intersection point between $\bar{\theta}(x)$ and the bottom side of the unit square, i.e., $\tilde{x}$ is the solution of $\bar{\theta}(x) = 0$. It follows immediately from (2) that

$$\tilde{x} = \frac{\bar{P}_2 - P_1}{2(y_2 - y_1)} + \frac{y_2 + y_1}{2}.$$

For $P_1 < P'_1$ and as long as $\bar{\theta}(x) < 1$, i.e., as long as $\bar{\theta}(x)$ does not reach a corner of the unit square, the demand function can be written as

$$D_1 = D^1_1 = \int_0^{\tilde{x}} \bar{\theta}(x) \, dx = \frac{[(\bar{P}_2 - P_1) + (y_2^2 - y_1^2)]^2}{4(y_2 - y_1)(q_2 - q_1)}.$$

Depending now on the absolute value of its slope, $\bar{\theta}(x)$ will reach the upper left hand corner of the unit square before or after the bottom right hand corner, as P_1 is reduced. Hence, we have to distinguish between the following cases: (i) if $|\partial\bar{\theta}/\partial x| < 1$, $\bar{\theta}(x)$ passes first through $x = 1$, $\theta = 0$, i.e., the bottom right hand corner.

(ii) If $|\partial\bar{\theta}/\partial x| > 1$, $\bar{\theta}(x)$ passes first through $x = 0$, $\theta = 1$, i.e., the upper left hand corner of the unit square.

(iii) If $|\partial\bar{\theta}/\partial x| = 1$, $\bar{\theta}(x)$ passes through both corners at the same time.

We consider the first two cases in turn.

(i) *Vertical dominance.* Denote P''_1 as the price for which $\bar{\theta}(x)$ passes through $x = 1$, $\theta = 0$, i.e.,

$$P''_1 = \bar{P}_2 + (y_2^2 - y_1^2) - 2(y_2 - y_1). \tag{A.2}$$

For $P_1 \in [P''_1, P'_1]$, demand is defined by D^1_1. For $P_1 < P''_1$, demand is given by

$$D^{11}_1 = \int_0^1 \bar{\theta}(x) \, dx = \frac{(\bar{P}_2 - P_1) + (y_2^2 - y_1^2)}{q_2 - q_1} - \frac{y_2 - y_1}{q_2 - q_1}.$$

This formulation of demand will be valid as long as $\bar{\theta}(x)$ does not go through $x = 0$, $\theta = 1$. This will occur for some price P'''_1 such that

$$P'''_1 = \bar{P}_2 + (y_2^2 - y_1^2) - (q_2 - q_1). \tag{A.3}$$

Notice that, given (3), we have that $P'''_1 < P''_1$. Hence, for $P_1 \in [P'''_1, P''_1]$, D_1 is defined by (7).

For $P_1 < P'''_1$, $\bar{\theta}(x)$ intersects both the upper and right sides of the unit square. Denote $\hat{x}$ as the intersection point of $\bar{\theta}(x)$ with the upper side of the unit square, i.e., $\hat{x}$ solves $\bar{\theta}(x) = 1$,

$$\hat{x} = \frac{(\bar{P}_2 - P_1) + (y_2^2 - y_1^2) - (q_2 - q_1)}{2(y_2 - y_1)}.$$

The demand faced by firm 1 is then given by

$$D_1^{\mathrm{III}} = \hat{x} + \int_{\hat{x}}^{1} \bar{\theta}(x)\,\mathrm{d}x$$

$$= [4(y_2 - y_1)(q_2 - q_1)]^{-1}[2(q_2 - q_1)((\bar{P}_2 - P_1) + (y_2^2 - y_1^2)) - q_2 - q_1)^2$$

$$- ((\bar{P}_2 - P_1) + (y_2^2 - y_1^2) - 2(y_2 - y_1))^2].$$

This demand formulation will be valid as long as $\bar{\theta}(1) < 1$, i.e., before $\bar{\theta}(x)$ reaches the upper right hand corner. This will occur for some price $P_1^{\prime\prime\prime\prime}$ such that

$$P_1^{\prime\prime\prime\prime} = \bar{P}_2 + (y_2^2 - y_1^2) - (q_2 - q_1) - 2(y_2 - y_1). \tag{A.4}$$

Hence, for $P_1 \in [P_1^{\prime\prime\prime\prime}, P_1^{\prime\prime\prime}]$, $D_1 = D_1^{\mathrm{III}}$. Finally, for $P_1 < P_1^{\prime\prime\prime\prime}$, firm 1's demand is equal to one.

(ii) *Horizontal dominance.* The lowest price $\hat{P}_1^{\prime\prime}$ for which D_1^{I} is valid is no longer given by (A.2). Indeed, when (4) holds, $\bar{\theta}(x)$ reaches the upper left hand corner of the unit square before the bottom right hand corner. Hence, the relevant expression for $P_1^{\prime\prime}$ is now given by the right hand side of (A.3). For $P_1 < \hat{P}_1^{\prime\prime}$, D_1^{II} is then written as

$$D_1^{\mathrm{II}} = \bar{x} + \int_{\tilde{x}}^{\bar{x}} \bar{\theta}(x)\,\mathrm{d}x,$$

where $\bar{x}$ (resp. $\tilde{x}$) is the intersection point of $\bar{\theta}(x)$ with the upper (resp. lower) side of the unit square. Some simple calculations show that $\bar{x} = \hat{x}$ and $\tilde{x} = \tilde{x}$, so that

$$D_1^{\mathrm{II}} = \frac{(\bar{P}_2 - P_1) + (y_2^2 - y_1^2)}{2(y_2 - y_1)} - \frac{q_2 - q_1}{4(y_2 - y_1)},$$

when horizontal dominance prevails ((4) rather than (3) holds).

With respect to the third segment of demand, the expression given above for D_1^{III} still applies. What is modified, however, is the interval of prices for which this expression holds. $\hat{P}_1^{\prime\prime\prime}$ is not defined by (A.3) anymore but by the right hand side of (A.2). Of course, the fact that in horizontal dominance, $\hat{P}_1^{\prime\prime\prime}$ (resp. $\hat{P}_1^{\prime\prime}$) is defined by the same equality as $P_1^{\prime\prime}$ (resp. $P_1^{\prime\prime\prime}$) in vertical dominance, stems from the reversal of the inequality (3) which defines the two regimes.

Appendix 2

Lemma. *Given any* (y_i, q_i), *there exists no best reply in the interior of region* R_1 *for firm* $j \neq i$.

Proof. Without loss of generality, suppose $q_1 \leq q_2$ and $y_1 \leq y_2$.

(i) Let us start with firm 1 and assume that vertical dominance prevails. Using the equilibrium prices $\tilde{P}_1$ and $\tilde{P}_2$ given by (14) and (15), firm 1's profit function is written as

$$\tilde{\Pi}_1(y_1, q_1, y_2, q_2) = \frac{\{y_2^2 - y_1^2 + [(y_2^2 - y_1^2)^2 + 16(y_2 - y_1)(q_2 - q_1)]^{1/2}\}^{1/3}}{512(y_2 - y_1)(q_2 - q_1)}.$$

Let

$$F \equiv [(y_2^2 - y_1^2)^2 + 16(y_2 - y_1)(q_2 - q_1)]^{1/2}.$$

Taking the first derivative of $\tilde{\Pi}_1$ w.r.t. q_1 yields (up to a positive factor),

$$(y_2 - y_1)\left[(y_2^2 - y_1^2) + F - \frac{24(y_2 - y_1)(q_2 - q_1)}{F}\right].$$

Since condition (A) is violated and vertical dominance holds, it follows that y_1 must be different from y_2. Hence, for the FOC $\partial \tilde{\Pi}_1 / \partial q_1 = 0$ to be satisfied, it must be that

$$(y_2^2 - y_1^2)F - 8(y_2 - y_1)(q_2 - q_1) + (y_2^2 - y_1^2)^2 = 0.$$

Moving the last two terms of this expression to the right-hand side and taking the square of both sides lead, after simplifications, to

$$(y_2^2 - y_1^2)^2 = 32(y_2 - y_1)(q_2 - q_1).$$

As $q_2 - q_1 > 2(y_2 - y_1)$, it follows that

$$(y_2^2 - y_1^2)^2 > 64(y_2 - y_1)^2 \quad \text{or} \quad (y_1 + y_2)^2 > 64,$$

which is impossible. Accordingly, $\partial \Pi_1 / \partial q_1 = 0$ can never be satisfied in the interior of R_1 under vertical dominance.

(ii) Assume now that horizontal dominance prevails. The expression of firm 1's profit is the same as in (i). Since horizontal dominance holds, we must have y_1 different from y_2. Hence, the argument developed in (i) remains valid and leads to

$$(y_2^2 - y_1^2)^2 = 32(y_2 - y_1)(q_2 - q_1).$$

As condition (C) is violated, it follows from this expression that

$$(y_1 + y_2)^2 > 16(y_1 + y_2 + 2),$$

which is never satisfied. We thus reach a contradiction and $\partial \tilde{\Pi}_1 / \partial q_1 = 0$ cannot be verified in the interior of R_1.

(iii) Consider the case of firm 2. The argument presented below applies to both vertical and horizontal dominance. First, given (16), it is straightforward that $\partial \tilde{P}_2 / \partial q_2 > 0$. Second, some simple manipulations show that $\partial D_2(\tilde{P}_1, \tilde{P}_2) / \partial q_2 > 0$ if and only if $((y_2^2 - y_1^2) + F)/(q_2 - q_1)$ is decreasing in q_2. Taking the first derivative of this expression w.r.t. q_2 gives (up to a positive factor),

$$-2(y_2^2 - y_1^2)^2 - 16(y_2 - y_1)(q_2 - q_1) - 2(y_2^2 - y_1^2)F,$$

which is always negative. Consequently, as both $\tilde{P}_2$ and $D_2(\tilde{P}_1, \tilde{P}_2)$ increase with q_2, $\partial \tilde{\Pi}_2 / \partial q_2 = 0$ cannot hold in the interior of R_1. $\square$

Proof of Proposition 2. (i) First, assume that $q_2^* = \bar{q}$, $y_2^* = \frac{1}{2}$ and show that $q_1^* = \underline{q}$, $y_1^* = \frac{1}{2}$ is the best reply for firm 1, provided $(\bar{q} - \underline{q}) \geq K_v$.

- Consider the domain R_{II}'. Firm 1's profit function evaluated at the corresponding price (P_1^*, P_2^*) is then given by

$$\Pi_1^*(y_1, y_2, q_1, q_2) = \frac{[(q_2 - q_1) + (y_2^2 - y_1^2) - (y_2 - y_1)]^2}{9(q_2 - q_1)}. \tag{A.5}$$

The FOC implies that $y_1^* = \frac{1}{2}$ (whatever y_2, q_1, q_2). Since $y_2^* = \frac{1}{2}$, (A.5) reduces to $\frac{1}{9}(q_2 - q_1)$, which is clearly maximised for $q_1 = \underline{q}$. Thus, $q_1^* = \underline{q}$, $y_1^* = \frac{1}{2}$ is a best reply in R_{II}' and the corresponding profit is

$$\Pi_1^* = \frac{1}{9}(\bar{q} - \underline{q}). \tag{A.6}$$

- By the lemma proved above, it turns out that the FOC of the profit function evaluated at $\tilde{P}_1$, $\tilde{P}_2$, with respect to q_1, can never be satisfied in the interior of R_1 (under either horizontal or vertical dominance). Consequently, there is no best reply for firm 1 in this region (the possibility of a best reply on the boundaries is taken up by the analysis performed for R_{II}' and R_{II}'' because the profit functions evaluated at the equilibrium prices are continuous in the characteristics variables).

- Consider R_{II}''. Firm 1's profit evaluated at (P_1^{**}, P_2^{**}) is given by

$$\Pi_1^{**}(y_1, y_2, q_1, q_2) = \frac{[4(y_2 - y_1) + 2(y_2^2 - y_1^2) - (q_2 - q_1)]^2}{72(y_2 - y_1)}. \tag{A.7}$$

Given (A.7), it is clear that Π_1^{**} is maximised with respect to q_1, when $q_1 = q_2^* = \bar{q}$. Then, (A.7) reduces to

$$\Pi_1^{**} = \frac{1}{18}(y_2 - y_1)(y_1 + y_2 + 2)^2, \tag{A.8}$$

in which we have used the fact that $y_2 - y_1 > 0$, which holds in the region of horizontal dominance. The first derivative of (A.8) w.r.t. y_1 leads the expression $y_2 - 3y_1 - 2$ which is always negative. Consequently, whatever y_2 (in particular, $y_2 = y_2^* = \frac{1}{2}$), the best reply in terms of y_1 in R_{11}'' is $y_1 = 0$. Setting $y_1 = 0$, $y_2 = \frac{1}{2}$ in (A.8) gives

$$\Pi_1^{**} = (\tfrac{5}{12})^2. \tag{A.9}$$

This is the maximum profit earned by firm 1 in R_{11}' (given $y_2^* = \frac{1}{2}$, $q_2^* = \bar{q}$). Comparing (A.6) and (A.9), we see that $\Pi_1^* \geq \Pi_1^{**}$ if and only if $\bar{q} - \underline{q} \geq (\frac{5}{4})^2$, which is satisfied since $K_v \geq (\frac{5}{4})^2$.

(ii) Suppose now that $q_1^* = \underline{q}$, $y_1^* = \frac{1}{2}$ and show that $q_2^* = \bar{q}$, $y_2^* = \frac{1}{2}$ is firm 2's best reply.

– In the domain R_{11}', a reasoning similar to the one held above for firm 1 yields the maximum profit of firm 2 in this region:

$$\Pi_2^* = \tfrac{4}{9}(\bar{q} - \underline{q}).$$

– The above lemma is again used to show that there is no best reply in the interior of R_1 for firm 2.

– In R_{11}'', the profit of firm 2, evaluated at (P_1^{**}, P_2^{**}) is written as

$$\Pi_2^{**}(y_1, y_2, q_1, q_2) = \frac{[8(y_2 - y_1) + 2(y_2^2 - y_1^2) + (q_2 - q_1)]^2}{72(y_2 - y_1)}. \tag{A.10}$$

Taking the first order derivative of (A.10) w.r.t. y_2 yields an expression whose numerator (the denominator is always >0) is equal to

$$2(y_2 - y_1)[4(2 + y_2) - 4 - (y_1 + y_2)] - (q_2 - q_1). \tag{A.11}$$

In order to stay in R_{11}', condition (C) has to be satisfied. Accordingly, the upper bound on $q_2 - q_1$ is given by (C), met as an equality. Replacing $q_2 - q_1$ in (A.11) by this upper bound, and knowing that $y_2 - y_1 > 0$ by the definition of horizontal domination, it is readily checked that $(A.11) > 0$, as long as (C) holds. Consequently, the best reply of firm 2 in terms of y_2 is $y_2 = 1$.

By inspection of (A.10), it is clear that the best reply of firm 2 in terms of q_2 is the maximum admissible value of q_2. Since condition (C) is the first one to be violated as q_2 increases, the maximum admissible value of q_2 is such that (C) is just met, i.e.,

$$q_2 = \underline{q} + \tfrac{1}{2}(y_2 - y_1)(2 + (y_1 + y_2)).$$

Introducing $y_2 = 1$ and the above value of q_2 in (A.10) gives

$$\Pi_2^{**} = (\tfrac{17}{16})^2.$$

Since $\Pi_2^* = \tfrac{4}{9}(\bar{q} - \underline{q})$, it follows that $\Pi_2^* \geq \Pi_2^{**}$ if and only if

$$\bar{q} - \underline{q} \geq \tfrac{9}{4}(\tfrac{17}{16})^2,$$

which holds by assumption. Consequently, $q_2^* = \bar{q}$ and $y_2^* = \frac{1}{2}$ is the best reply of firm 2, given that $q_1^* = \underline{q}$ and $y_1 = \frac{1}{2}$. $\square$

Proof of Proposition 3. (i) First, assume that $q_2^{**} = \bar{q}$, $y_2^{**} = 1$ and show that $q_1^{**} = \bar{q}$, $y_1^{**} = 0$ is the best reply for firm 1, provided that $\bar{q} - \underline{q} \leq K_h$.
- Consider the domain R_{11}''. Firm 1's profit evaluated at the corresponding prices (P_1^{**}, P_2^{**}) is given by (A.7). It is immediate by inspection of this equation that firm 1's best reply in terms of q_1 is $q_1 = q_2^{**} = \bar{q}$. Setting q_1 to this value, (A.7) reduces to (A.8). Taking up the analysis performed above in terms of y_1 in R_{11}'', it follows that firm 1's best reply is $y_1 = 0$. Setting $y_1^{**} = 0$, $y_2^{**} = 1$ in (A.8) yields $\Pi_1^{**} = \frac{1}{2}$.
- The lemma proved above suffices to eliminate the possibility of best replies for firm 1 in the interior of R_1.
- Consider R_{11}'. Firm 1's profit is then given by (A.5). Using $q_2^{**} = \bar{q}$ and $y_2^{**} = 1$, it is readily verified that the more stringent condition for (y_1, q_1) to be in R_{11}' is given by (A) which is here equal to

$$(1 - y_1)(3 - y_1) \leq \bar{q} - q_1. \tag{A.12}$$

Taking the first derivative of (A.5) w.r.t. q_1 shows that Π_1 is decreasing in q_1 since (A.12) holds. Hence, the best reply in terms of q_1 is $q_1^{**} = \underline{q}$ whatever y_1. Replacing in (A.5) yields

$$\Pi_1 = \frac{[\bar{q} - \underline{q} + y_1(1 - y_1)]^2}{9(\bar{q} - \underline{q})} \tag{A.13}$$

which is maximized at $y_1^{**} = \frac{1}{2}$ (assuming that (A.12) is satisfied for $y_1^{**} = \frac{1}{2}$ and $q_1^{**} = \underline{q}$). We then obtain

$$\Pi_1^* = \frac{[\bar{q} - \underline{q} + \frac{1}{4}] - 2}{9(\bar{q} - \underline{q})}. \tag{A.14}$$

Comparing this value with Π_1^{**}, it follows that $\Pi_1^* \leq \Pi_1^{**}$ if and only if $\bar{q} - \underline{q} \leq K_h$ and $\bar{q} - \underline{q} < \frac{5}{4}$, the best reply in terms of y_1 is no longer $y_1^{**} = \frac{1}{2}$ since (A.12) is violated. In other words, (A.12) becomes binging. Clearly, y_1^{**} is now the solution of $y_1^2 - 4y_1 + 3 - (\bar{q} - \underline{q}) = 0$ which is smaller than 1, i.e., $y_1^{**} = 2 - \sqrt{1 + \frac{1}{4}(\bar{q} - \underline{q})}$. This yields for Π_1 a value smaller than (A.14).

(ii) Next, assume that $q_1^{**} = \bar{q}$, $y_1^{**} = 0$ and show that $q_2^{**} = \bar{q}$, $y_2^{**} = 1$ is firm 2's best reply.
- Consider R_{11}''. The profit function of firm 2 in this domain can be expressed as firm 1's profit, i.e., (A.7), in which y_i is replaced by z_i, with

$z_i = 1 - y_j$, $i \neq j$ (the decision variables of firm 2 are then z_1 and q_1):

$$\Pi_2^{**}(z_1, q_1) = \frac{[8(z_2 - z_1) + 2(z_2^2 - z_1^2) - (q_2 - q_1)]^2}{72(z_2 - z_1)}, \qquad (A.15)$$

with $z_1 \leq z_2$, $q_1 \leq q_2$, $z_2 = 1$ and $q_2 = \bar{q}$. In view of (A.15), it is always profitable for firm 2 to set $q_1 = \bar{q}$. Setting $q_2 = \bar{q}$ in (A.15), simplifying by $z_2 - z_1$ and taking the first order derivative w.r.t. z_1 yield the expression $z_2 - 3z_1 - 2$, which is always negative. Hence, firm 2's best reply in terms of z_1 is $z_1 = 0$ or, equivalently, $y_2 = 1$. As a best response to $q_1^{**} = \bar{q}$, $y_1^{**} = 0$, firm 2 will thus set $q_2^{**} = \bar{q}$, $y_2^{**} = 1$.

– The above lemma is again sufficient to rule out firm 2's best replies in the interior of R_I.

– Consider the domain R_{II}'. Using the same change of variable as above in (A.5), one obtains that firm 2's profit is equal to

$$\Pi_2^{**}(z_1, q_1) = \frac{[(q_2 - q_1) + (z_2^2 - z_1^2) - (z_2 - z_1)]^2}{9(q_1 - q_2)}.$$

Setting $z_2 = 1$, $q_2 = \bar{q}$, it can be shown that $q_1 = \underline{q}$ is the best reply of firm 2, whatever z_1. The corresponding profits are given by (A.13). The same profit comparison (between Π_2^{**} and Π_2^{*}) as for firm 1 can then be made. It shows that $\Pi_2^{*} \leq \Pi_2^{**}$ if and only if $\bar{q} - \underline{q} \leq K_h$. $\square$

References

d'Aspremont, C., J.J. Gabszewicz and J.-F. Thisse (1979) 'On Hotelling's stability in competition', *Econometrica*, 47:1045–1050.

Caplin, A.S. and B.J. Nabeluff (1989) 'Aggregation and imperfect competition: on the existence of equilibrium', Princeton University, Princeton, NJ, mimeo.

Eaton, B.C. and M.H. Wooders (1985) 'Sophisticated entry in a model of spatial competition', *Rand Journal of Economics*, 16:282–297.

Economides, N. (1989) 'Symmetric equilibrium existence and optimality in a differentiated product market', *Journal of Economic Theory*, 47:178–194.

Gabszewicz, J.J., A. Shaked, J. Sutton and J.-F. Thisse (1986) 'Segmenting the market: the monopolist's optimal product mix', *Journal of Economic Theory*, 39:273–289.

Gabszewicz, J.J. and J.-F. Thisse (1979) 'Price competition, quality and income disparities', *Journal of Economic Theory*, 20:340–359.

Gabszewicz, J.J. and J.-F. Thisse (1980) 'Entry (and exit) in a differentiated industry', *Journal of Economic Theory*, 22:327–338.

Gabszewicz, J.J. and J.-F. Thisse (1988) 'Competitive discriminatory pricing', in: G. Feiwel, ed., *Economics of Imperfect Competition and Employment: Joan Robinson and Beyond*. London: Macmillan, pp. 387–406.

Ginsburgh, V., B.W. MacLeod and S. Weber (1987) 'Price discrimination and product line rivalry', CEME Discussion Paper 8717, Université Libre de Bruxelles, Brussels.

Hotelling, H. (1929) 'Stability in competition', *Economic Journal*, 39:41-57.
Ireland, N. (1987) *Product Differentiation and Non-price Competition.* Oxford: Basil Blackwell.
Mussa, M. and S. Rosen (1978) 'Monopoly and product quality', *Journal of Economic Theory*, 18:301-317.
Neven, D. (1985) 'Two stage (perfect) equilibrium in Hotelling's model', *Journal of Industrial Economics*, 33:317-325.
Neven, D. (1986) 'On Hotelling's competition with non-uniform customer distributions', *Economics Letters*, 21:121-126.
Palma, A. de, V. Ginsburgh, Y.Y. Papageorgiou and J.-F. Thisse (1985) 'The principle of minimum differentiation holds under sufficient heterogeneity', *Econometrica*, 53:767-781.
Salop, S. (1979) 'Monopolistic competition with outside goods', *Bell Journal of Economics*, 10:141-156.
Shaked, A. and J. Sutton (1981) 'Relaxing price competition through product differentiation', *Review of Economic Studies*, 49:3-13.
Shaked, A. and J. Sutton (1983) 'Natural oligopolies', *Econometrica*, 1469-1483.

Chapter 10

NASH EQUILIBRIA ARE NOT SELF-ENFORCING

Robert J. AUMANN

The Hebrew University of Jerusalem, Jerusalem, Israel

1. Introduction

The intuitive basis for Nash's (1951) concept of strategic equilibrium in non-cooperative games has recently received considerable attention. A rationale that has been suggested is that Nash equilibria represent "self-enforcing agreements"; that a pre-play agreement to play a certain strategy tuple will be kept if and only if it is a Nash equilibrium. Several years ago we came across an example that throws doubt on this contention. The example has been cited in various contexts (e.g., Harsanyi and Selten, 1988; Farrell, 1988), but has not heretofore been discussed on its own merits.

Section 2 contains the main example, with an informal discussion. Sections 3 and 4 discuss two other examples, and how they differ from the main one. Section 5 contains a more carefully formulated — though still verbal — argument. Some scenarios for the main example, including one taken from the international relations literature, will be discussed in Section 6. Section 7 summarizes the main points.

2. Example

The game of Figure 1 has two pure Nash equilibria, (c, c) and (d, d). In the absence of pre-play communication, each one has something going for

Research partially supported by NSF grant IRI-8814953 at the Institute for Mathematical Studies in the Social Sciences (Economics), Stanford University, Stanford, CA, USA.

Economic Decision-Making: Games, Econometrics and Optimisation
Edited by J.J. Gabszewicz, J.-F. Richard and L.A. Wolsey

	c	d
c	9, 9	0, 8
d	8, 0	7, 7

Figure 1.

it; (c, c) is Pareto-dominant, but (d, d) is much safer.[1] Indeed, since the players cannot communicate, the row player (Alice) may well be uncertain that the column player (Bob) will play c; she might therefore wish to play d, which *assures* her 7, whereas with c she may get nothing. Moreover, if she takes into account that Bob may reason in the same way, she is all the more likely to play d; this makes it still more likely that Bob, too, will play d, and so on. We do not, however, assert that reasonable players *must* play d; only that they *may* do so, that d is not unreasonable or foolish. And for the time being, we assert this only when there is no pre-play communication.

Let us now change the scenario by permitting pre-play communication. On the face of it, it seems that the players can then "agree" to play (c, c); though the agreement is not enforceable, it removes each player's doubt about the other one playing c.

But does it indeed remove this doubt? Suppose that Alice is a careful, prudent person, and in the absence of an agreement, would play d. Suppose now that the players agree on (c, c), and each retires to his "corner" in order actually to make a choice. Alice is about to choose c, when she says to herself: "Wait; I have a few minutes; let me think this over. Suppose that Bob doesn't trust me, and so will play d in spite of our agreement. Then he would still want *me* to play c, because that way he will get 8 rather than 7. And of course, also if he does play c, it is better for him that I play c. Thus he wants me to play c no matter what. So he wants the agreement to play (c, c) in any case; it doesn't bind him, and might increase the chances of my playing c. That doesn't imply that he will necessarily play d, but he may; since he wants the agreement no matter what he plays, the agreement conveys no information about his play. In fact, he may well have signed it without giving any thought as to how actually to play. Since he can reason in the same way about me, neither one of us gets any information from the agreement; it is as if there were no agreement. So I will choose now what I would have chosen without an agreement, namely d."

[1] Technically, (d, d) is *risk dominant* (Harsanyi and Selten, 1988).

Figure 2.

Of course, it may be that Alice is not careful and prudent, but impulsive and optimistic,[2] and likes to think that Bob also is. She may then choose c even without an agreement; and so, also with one. We are not saying that rational players will never play c, but only that *agreeing* to do so won't lead them to *do* it. A player might play either c or d, whether or not he has agreed to (c, c); the agreement has no effect, one way or the other. In such circumstances, the agreement should not be called self-enforcing.

3. The battle of the sexes

The above reasoning is not universal; an agreement to play an equilibrium often *is* self-enforcing. Consider, for example, the familiar "battle of the sexes" (Figure 2). Without pre-play communication, the players will be hard put to choose between b (ballet) and f (fight). But if they agree, say, to (b, b), then here they *are* motivated to keep the agreement.

To explain why, consider again how Alice might reason. It is not that she takes the agreement as a direct signal that Bob will keep it. Rather, like in the previous section, she realizes that by signing the agreement, Bob is signalling that he wants *her* to keep it. But unlike in the previous section, here the fact that he wants her to keep it implies that he intends to keep it himself.[3] So for her, too, it is worthwhile to keep it. Similarly for him. *This* agreement *is* self-enforcing.

4. Another example

After reading an early draft of this paper, Professor David Kreps asked if in the game of Figure 3, which is ordinally equivalent to that of Figure 1,

---

[2] Though still rational!
[3] If Bob plays b, then he would prefer her to play b; if he plays f, he would prefer her to play f. In the previous section, he would prefer her to play c no matter what he does.

	c	d
c	100, 100	0, 8
d	8, 0	7, 7

Figure 3.

(c, c) should not be considered a self-enforcing agreement. The question had us stumped for a while. But actually, the answer is straightforward: Indeed, (c, c) is not self-enforcing, even here. It does look better than in Figure 1; not because an agreement to play it is self-enforcing, but because it will almost surely be played even without an agreement.[4] An agreement to play it does not improve its chances further. As before, both players will sign the agreement gladly, whether or not they keep it; it therefore conveys no information.

5. Discussion

To say that a game is non-cooperative means that there is no external mechanism available for the enforcement of agreements. Thus when the time comes to choose an action, the players are assumed to act on the basis of the existing incentives. Therefore an agreement is effective only if it changes the incentives that obtain in the absence of the agreement.

Incentives can be changed by changing either the payoffs or the information of the players. The agreements being discussed here do not change the payoffs; the payoffs for any particular strategy tuple remain the same, whether or not it violates the "agreement". To be effective, therefore, an agreement must change the players' information; specifically, their information about how the others will play.

Information about an event E is acquired by observing a parameter that depends on whether or not E obtains. If the parameter does not really depend on E — has the same value whether or not E obtains — then observing it yields no information about E.

In the games of Figures 1 and 3, Alice is interested in knowing what Bob will play; we may take E to be the event "Bob will play c". The parameter she observes is whether or not he "agrees" to (c, c). But this parameter is

---

[4] Here (c, c) is risk-dominant (cf. Footnote 1).

the same no matter what Bob plays; it is always to his advantage to agree to (c, c). Therefore the agreement yields no information about what he will really play. Since the agreement is important only for the information it yields, and yields no information, it is as if it had not been made.

6. Scenarios for the main example

The game of Figure 1 is sometimes called the "stag hunt".[5] Two men agree to hunt a stag. To succeed, they must go along separate paths, giving the task their undivided attention. On the way, each has the opportunity to abandon the stag hunt and hunt rabbits instead. If he does so the number of rabbits be bags increases if the other continues to hunt the stag. Both would prefer it if both hunted the stag, since it is more valuable than a bag of rabbits. But each fears that each mistrusts the other, that the mistrust breeds more mistrust, and so on.

In the international relations literature, the game has been called the "security dilemma" (Jarvis, 1978). Two countries between which there is tension are each considering the development of a new, expensive weapons system. Each is best off if neither has the system, but would be at a serious disadvantage if only the other had it. Can either side afford not to develop the system?

Some closely related games played a role[6] in the controversy about NTU values between Roth (1980, 1986) and Aumann (1985, 1986). There, each of the two players may be offered a deal by an outside party; if both refuse, they can make a better deal with each other, but each fears that the other will close with the outside party before they get a chance to talk with each other.

7. Summary

A non-binding agreement can affect the outcome of a game only if it conveys information about what the players will do. Directly, the information that such an agreement conveys is not that the players will keep it (since it is not binding), but that each wants the other to keep it. In the battle of the sexes (Figure 2), an agreement to play (b, b), say, conveys the information

---

[5] We have not succeeded in hunting this story down to its source.
[6] See Aumann (1985, Sections 5 and 6, pp. 670–673).

that each player prefers the other to play b; this implies that each will play b himself, and so the agreement is self-enforcing. But in the games of Figures 1 and 3, each player *always* prefers the other to play c, no matter what he himself plays. Therefore an agreement to play (c, c) conveys no information about what the players will do, and cannot be considered self-enforcing.

References

Aumann, R.J. (1985) 'On the non-transferable utility value: A comment on the Roth–Shafer examples', *Econometrica*, 53:667–677.
Aumann, R.J. (1986) 'Rejoinder', *Econometrica*, 54:985–989.
Farrell, J. (1988) 'Communication, coordination, and Nash equilibrium', *Economics Letters*, 27:209–214.
Harsanyi, J.C. and R. Selten (1988) *A General Theory of Equilibrium Selection in Games*. Cambridge and London: MIT Press.
Jervis, R. (1978) 'Cooperation under the security dilemma', *World Politics*, 30:167–214.
Nash, J.F. (1951) 'Non-cooperative games', *Annals of Mathematics*, 54:286–295.
Roth, A. (1980) 'Values for games without side payments: Some difficulties with current concepts', *Econometrica*, 48:457–465.
Roth, A. (1985) 'On the non-transferable utility value: A reply to Aumann', *Econometrica*, 54:981–984.

Chapter 11

THE THEORY OF SOCIAL SITUATIONS: ILLUSTRATED BY AND APPLIED TO EXTENSIVE FORM GAMES

Joseph GREENBERG

University of Haifa, Haifa, Israel

1. Introduction

Two of the most prominent, fulfilling, and joyful "events" in my "academic career" are meeting and working with Professor Jacques Drèze and embarking on the theory of social situations (Greenberg, 1989). It gives me, therefore, great pleasure to contribute to Jacques' Festschrift a (brief and partial) overview of this theory.[1]

The theory of social situations is a new and integrative approach, in the spirit of game theory, to the study of formal models in the social and behavioral sciences. Some important aspects of the proposed approach are closely related to ideas promoted by the founders of game theory, von Neumann and Morgenstern.

The theory of social situations applies to all social environments in which it is impossible to impose a course of action, or an alternative, on the individuals. Rather, a course of action can be recommended, or proposed, to the individuals, who are then free to accept or reject the proposal. (The source of the recommendation is inconsequential. It might be one, some or all of the individuals, or, alternatively, the recommendation can be made by an "outside expert", say, the social scientist. The crucial point to recall

---

[1] Moreover, some of the first basic results were obtained during my, as usual, enjoyable visit to CORE, September 1985.

Economic Decision-Making: Games, Econometrics and Optimisation
Edited by J.J. Gabszewicz, J.-F. Richard and L.A. Wolsey
© *Elsevier Science Publishers, B.V., 1990*

is that the proposer is not a dictator; he[2] has no power to enforce his recommendation.)

In this article I shall outline the basic underlying motivation, and state some of the results that are obtained when the theory is applied to extensive form games (with perfect information and without chance moves). The main purpose of this paper is to acquaint and whet the appetite of the reader to the proposed approach.

The theory of social situations has two main ingredients. First, it offers a *unified way to represent* cooperative and noncooperative social environments, namely, by means of "*situations*". Second, the proposed approach offers a *unified criterion for the recommendations*, namely, that the "*standard of behavior*" (for the given situation) be "*stable*".[3]

Another important merit of the theory of social situations is that it recognizes and accommodates the possibility that a group of individuals may choose to coordinate their actions. (In fact, the proposed theory does not at all distinguish between coalitions and single players.) In contrast, as McKinsey (1952, p. 359) observes:

"... *even if the theory of noncooperative games*[3] *were in a completely satisfactory state, there appear to be difficulties in connection with the reduction of cooperative games to noncooperative games. It is extremely difficult in practice to introduce into the noncooperative games the moves corresponding to negotiations in a way which will reflect all the infinite variety permissible in the cooperative game, and to do this without giving one player an artificial advantage (because of his having the first chance to make an offer, let us say).*"

But, the empirical fact is that our social life is almost entirely conducted within the structure of coalitions. (Individual consumers are households or families, firms are large coalitions of owners of different factors of production, workers are organized into unions, and we organize and govern ourselves in political parties and social clubs.) The theory of social situations overcomes the difficulties mentioned in the above quote, because the notion of situation includes the specification of the opportunities that are available to coalitions, without insisting that an explicit and rigid "process" be given concerning the exact way in which coalitions can form. Thus, for example, we can incorporate tax advantages for married couples without elaborating on the exact way the decision to get married was reached. ... Similarly, majorities can be endowed with (say, veto) power, although the manner in which majorities form remains unspecified.

---

[2] Throughout the paper I use "he" for "she or he", etc.

[3] In contrast, "classical game theory" offers three distinct representations of a social environment, namely, games in extensive form, normal (or strategic) form, and characteristic function (or coalitional) form. Moreover, to each type of game, game theory offers an abundance of solution concepts whose underlying motivations differ considerably.

The application of the theory of social situations to each of the three types of games, that is, representing a "game" as a situation, yields several of the better known game-theoretic solution concepts, such as: the core, the von Neumann and Morgenstern solution for cooperative games, Nash, strong Nash, and coalition proof Nash equilibria for games in normal form, and subgame perfect equilibria for both extensive form and infinitely repeated games (see Sections 8 and 9).

The characterization of these notions as stable recommendations (for the associated situations), sheds new light on and relates these currently disparate notions by pointing out the underlying negotiation processes that lead to them. These conceptual results yield, in turn, new properties of the existing solution concepts. (See, e.g., Theorems 9.2, 9.3 and 9.5.)

The application of the proposed approach to game theory suggests also *new and interesting solution concepts*. It is encouraging that some of these new solution concepts, that naturally emerge from the proposed approach, have been independently suggested, in particular examples and for ad hoc reasons, by other scholars. (See, e.g., the refinements of subgame perfect equilibrium in Examples 8.3–8.5.) Moreover, because of its unifying nature, the theory of social situations enables us to "import" game theoretic solutions from one type of game to another, thereby creating new (analogous) solutions. And, of course, since coalitions are naturally incorporated into the theory, it is also possible to extend "noncooperative" solutions and allow for groups of individuals to coordinate their actions.

As mentioned above, I shall use extensive form games[4] (the next section provides the relevant (and well-known) definitions and notations) to exemplify some of the basic terminology of the theory of social situations. Sections 3 and 4 motivate and provide the definitions of "position" and "situation", and Section 5 describes how a game tree can be represented as a situation. Sections 6 and 7 are devoted to the second ingredient of the proposed approach — the unified solution or equilibrium concept for a situation: Optimistic and conservative stable standards of behavior. The following two sections apply these concepts to the tree situation of Section 5. It turns out, quite unexpectedly, that both the optimistic and the conservative stable standard of behavior for the tree situation refine the notion of subgame perfection. Moreover, the set of subgame perfect equilibria is closely related to the unique maximal conservative stable standard of behavior (for the "tree situation").

---

[4] Throughout this paper, "an extensive form game" means "an extensive form game with perfect information and without chance moves".

2. Extensive form games

Of the three game forms, it is the extensive form, or the game tree, that provides the most detailed description of the actions that are available to the players. I shall argue that (as is the case with the other two game forms) this description is not adequate. On the one hand, it fails to specify, for example, the legal institutions such as whether it is possible for a player to self-commit to his future actions. (It is the answer to this question that lies at the heart of the distinction between Nash and subgame perfect equilibria; see Definitions 2.4 and 2.5.) And, on the other hand, it involves unnecessarily detailed information:

"*The game tree is an extremely useful device for the didactic purposes, but one must often pay a high price for its use, in terms of redundancy. The rules of many games permit the same physical "position" to be reached through various different sequences of moves. Yet in a tree each sequence of moves must lead to a different node. The tree convention forces us to remember the history of the position, whether we want to or not.*" (Shubik, 1984, p. 48.)

Insisting on such a detailed description is not only "wasteful"; it also has serious consequences. Thus, for example, a game in extensive form cannot serve as the framework for analyzing (i) "human rationality", inherent to which is the empirical observation that individuals often ignore (even relevant) information, and, perhaps more importantly, (ii) coalition formation, since it is impossible to provide the complete specifications of the complex sets of messages, verbal inflections, and gestures as sets of moves in a game. Yet all these may figure importantly in face-to-face communication during bargaining.

The theory of social situations overcomes these shortcomings: The existing legal institutions and the precise negotiation process are clearly stated. The notion of situation is sufficiently flexible, allowing to (perceptually) simplify the social environment; and coalition formation is naturally accommodated.

The following definitions and notation will be used throughout the paper.

Definition 2.1. A *directed graph* or *digraph* consists of a nonempty (possibly infinite) set *V*, whose elements are called *vertices* or *nodes*, together with a collection of ordered pairs, *vw*, called *arcs* or *edges*, where *v* and *w* are members of *V*. If *vw* is an arc, then *v* is *adjacent to w* and *w* is *adjacent from v*. The *outdegree* of a vertex *v* is the number of vertices adjacent from it (that is, the number, or cardinality, of arcs beginning at node *v*), and the *indegree* is the number of vertices adjacent to it (that is, the number of arcs ending at node v). A vertex v is a *source* if its indegree is 0 and it is a *sink* if its outdegree is 0.

A *walk*, x, is a sequence of vertices $(v_1, v_2, \ldots)$, where, for all j, $j = 1$, $2, \ldots, v_j$ is adjacent to v_{j+1}. A *finite walk* is a walk $(v_1, v_2, \ldots, v_J)$ where J is a finite number. The *length of the finite walk* $(v_1, v_2, \ldots, v_J)$ is $J - 1$. A walk with all of its nodes distinct is called a *path*. If v and w are vertices in V and there is a finite walk $(v_1, v_2, \ldots, v_J)$, where $v_1 = v$ and $v_J = w$, we say that w is *reachable* from v.

A digraph is *acyclic* if every walk is a path. An acyclic digraph where all its walks (paths) have a finite length that does not exceed a finite integer J, is called a *bounded acyclic digraph*. The *length of a bounded acyclic digraph* is the maximal length of its walks (paths). A *rooted tree* is a digraph with a unique source, called its *root* which has the property that there exists a unique walk (path) from the root to each other vertex. Alternatively, a rooted tree is an acyclic digraph which has exactly one vertex of indegree 0 and all of its other vertices are of indegree 1.

Definition 2.2. *An n-person extensive form game* (with perfect information and without chance moves) is represented by a rooted tree, T, called the *game tree*, that has the following structure:

(E1) The set of nodes, $V(T)$, is partitioned into $n + 1$ sets, $V_0(T)$, $V_1(T)$, $V_2(T), \ldots, V_n(T)$. The length of the unique path which connects the root of T with a vertex $v \in V_i(T)$, $i = 1, 2, \ldots, n$, is finite. The set $V_0(T)$ contains the *terminal nodes*, that is, those nodes whose outdegree is 0.

(E2) Each terminal node, $v \in V_0(T)$, is assigned a *payoff vector* in $\mathbb{R}^N$.

As is well-known, the interpretation of this structure is as follows. For each $i \in N$, $V_i(T)$ is the set of decision nodes of player i. Once $v \in V_i(T)$ is reached, player i has to choose one of the nodes adjacent from v. If a terminal node $v \in V_0(T)$ is reached, then no more choices by the individuals can be made, and player i receives a utility level equal to the ith coordinate of the payoff vector assigned to v.

Let T be a game tree. Denote by $v^*(T)$ the root of T, and by $\Pi(T)$ the set of all paths in the tree T that originate in the root $v^*(T)$ and end in some terminal node in $V_0(T)$. (Since each vertex is fully characterized by the unique path that connects it with the root of the tree, the set $V_0(T)$ can be identified with the set $\Pi(T)$.) By (E2), each path $x \in \Pi(T)$ is assigned a vector, $\mu(x)$, in $\mathbb{R}^N$. The scalar $\mu^i(x)$ is the utility level player i receives if the path x in $\Pi(T)$ is followed. This notation is particularly useful for infinite game trees, where the set of terminal nodes $V_0(T)$ is not defined, but we can assign to each path x (finite or infinite) in $\Pi(T)$ the payoff vector $\mu(x)$ in $\mathbb{R}^N$. Since each vertex $v \in V(T)$ is reachable from $v^*(T)$ by a unique path, we shall extend the domain of the function μ to include all paths in all subtrees, $\tilde{T}$, of T. Thus, for $x \in \Pi(\tilde{T})$, $\mu(x) \equiv \mu(v^*(T), \ldots, v^*(\tilde{T})) = x_1, x_2, x_3, \ldots)$.

For a vertex $v \in V(T)$, denote by $(T \mid v)$ the (sub)tree whose root is v. That is, $\Pi(T \mid v)$ is the set of all paths in T that originate at v and end in some terminal vertex in $V_0(T)$. (Thus, for example, $T = (T \mid v^*(T))$.) It is easily verified that if T is a game tree, that is, if T satisfies (E1)-(E2), then for any $v \in V(T)$, $(T \mid v)$ is also a game tree.

A game tree in which the lengths of all paths do not exceed a finite integer, J, is called a *bounded game tree*, and the *length of a bounded game tree* is the maximal length of its paths. Notice also that there are no restrictions on the cardinality of the set of vertices, $V(T)$, of a bounded game tree. That is, a bounded game tree might contain an infinite number of vertices. A game tree where $V(T)$ contains only a finite number of vertices is called a *finite game tree*. Clearly, every finite game tree is bounded.

The two most important game-theoretic solution concepts for a game tree T are the Nash and subgame perfect equilibria. Both notions make use of the notion of a strategy in a game tree.

Definition 2.3. Let T be a game tree. A (pure) *strategy* (*for player i*) is a function f^i that associates with each node $v \in V_i(T)$ a node w that is adjacent, in T, from v.

Every *strategy profile*, that is, an n-tuple of strategies, $f = (f^1, f^2, \ldots, f^n)$, naturally defines (inductively) a unique path, $\pi(f)$, in $\Pi(T)$: The first vertex in $\pi(f)$ is $v^*(T)$, and the vertex that follows, in $\pi(f)$, a vertex v that belongs to $\pi(f)$ is the vertex w, where $w = f^i(v)$, and i is the (unique) player for whom $v \in V_i(T)$. Therefore, the utility level that player i derives from an n-tuple of strategies, f, is given by

$$h^i(f) \equiv \mu^i(\pi(f)).$$

That is, $h^i(f)$ is the ith coordinate of the payoff vector assigned to the path $\pi(f)$.

Definition 2.4. Let T be a game tree. A *Nash Equilibrium for T* is an n-tuple of strategies $f = (f^1, f^2, \ldots, f^n)$ such that for all $i \in N$, $h^i(f) \geq h^i(g)$ for all g with $g^j = f^j$ for all $j \neq i$, and g^i is a strategy for i. The set of Nash equilibria for T is denoted by $NE(T)$.

Definition 2.5. Let T be a game tree. The strategy profile $f = (f^1, f^2, \ldots, f^n)$ constitutes a (*subgame*) *Perfect Equilibrium for* T if it has the property that for every $v \in V(T)$, the restriction of f to the (sub)tree $(T|v)$, belongs to $\text{NE}(T|v)$. The set of subgame perfect equilibria for T is denoted by $\text{PE}(T)$.

3. Positions

The theory of social situations insists that the social environment be represented as a "situation". The concept of "situation" requires the precise and relevant specification of the alternatives that are available to the individuals. A situation comprises the two notions: "*position*" and "*inducement correspondence*". A position describes "the current state of affairs". It specifies, for the given stage, the set of individuals, the set of all possible outcomes, and the preferences of the individuals over this set of outcomes. Formally:

Definition 3.1. A *position*, G, is a triple $G \equiv (N(G), X(G), \{u^i(G)\}_{i \in N(G)})$, where $N(G)$ is the set of *players*, $X(G)$ is the set of all feasible *outcomes*, and $u^i(G)$ is the *utility function* of player i in position G over the outcomes, that is, $u^i(G): X(G) \to \mathbb{R}$.

The nature of an outcome $x \in X(G)$ is completely arbitrary. An outcome is a feasible alternative; it need not be a "predicted", "reasonable" or "rational" alternative. The set of outcomes describes the feasibility constraints at the particular stage, and not the choices that are likely or should be made. The only requirement is that the domain of the utility functions of the players be the set of outcomes in G, that is, that players in position G be able to evaluate every outcome in $X(G)$.

The fact that an individual's utility function is allowed to depend on the position to which he belongs, is quite important and opens a wide range of applications. Consider, for example, the two positions G and H, where $N(G) = \{1, 2\}$, $N(H) = \{2, 3\}$ and $X(G) = X(H) = \{x, y\}$. Our formulation allows player 2, who is present in both positions, to have in position G preferences over x and y that differ from the preferences he has in H over these same two outcomes. For example, if x means "having dinner", and y stands for "going to the theater", then it is perfectly possible that 2 prefers x to y with 1 but y to x with 3. In this case, $u^2(G)(x) > u^2(G)(y)$ but $u^2(H)(x) < u^2(H)(y)$. Similarly, a consumer may prefer (buying) beer over (buying) milk when he is single, but reverse his choice when he is a parent.

To illustrate the notion of position, consider a game tree T. It seems most natural to associate with T the following position $G(T)$. The set of players in $G(T)$ is the set of players, N. Thus,

$$N(G(T)) \equiv N = \{1, 2, \ldots, n\}.$$

The set of outcomes, $X(G(T))$, in position $G(T)$, is the set of all possible evolvements of the game, that is, the set of all "plays". Thus, $X(G(T))$ consists of all paths in the tree T that originate in the root $v^*(T)$ and end in some terminal node in $V_0(T)$, that is,

$$X(G(T)) \equiv \Pi(T).$$

Since the utility level player i derives from the play x is $\mu^i(x)$, we define $u^i(G(T))$ by: For $x \in X(G(T))$, $u^i(G(T))(x)$ is the ith coordinate of the payoff vector assigned to the path x, that is, for all $i \in N$ and $x \in \Pi(T)$,

$$u^i(G(T))(x) \equiv \mu^i(x).$$

4. Inducement correspondence

Let us now turn to the second building block of the concept of situation — the inducement correspondence. Consider a position G and suppose that outcome $x^* \in X(G)$ is proposed. (Recall that I confine myself to those formal models in which a course of action cannot be imposed, but rather is recommended to the players.) Should player $i \in N(G)$ accept or reject this proposed outcome? In order to answer this question player i must know what are the alternatives that are available to him if he chooses to reject x^*. That is, i must know the set of positions that he can induce from the position G when the outcome x^* is offered. Let $\gamma(\{i\} \mid G, x^*)$ denote this set.[5] Moreover, in order to decide whether or not he wishes to induce a position $H \in \gamma(\{i\} \mid G, x^*)$, player i must be able to anticipate what might happen once H is induced. In particular, he has to know what positions can, in turn, be induced from (the induced) position H.

   The next step is to apply the same reasoning to a group of individuals. It is quite possible that a coalition consisting of several members of society can induce positions that cannot be induced by any single individual. (Passing a bill, for example, requires the consent of a majority of the

---

[5] In many social environments, as is the case with extensive form games, the proposed outcome might, indeed, affect the set of positions a player can induce. It is for this reason that γ is allowed to depend on x^*.

individuals. Similarly, it takes two to get married.) Given a position G and a proposed outcome $x^* \in X(G)$, let $\gamma(S \mid G, x^*)$ denote the set of positions that a coalition,[6] S, $S \subset N(G)$,[7] can induce from G when x^* is proposed. Then, following the same arguments advanced for a single individual, members of S must also know not only the set $\gamma(S \mid G, x^*)$, but also the possible "chain reaction" that might occur should S decide to induce a position $H \in \gamma(S \mid G, x^*)$.

An appropriate description of the social environment or the social interaction is, therefore, given by the following concept of a situation.

Definition 4.1. A *situation* is a pair (γ, Γ), where Γ is a set of positions, and the mapping γ, called *the inducement correspondence*, satisfies the condition that for all $G \in \Gamma$, $S \subset N(G)$, and $x \in X(G)$, $\gamma(S \mid G, x) \subset \Gamma$. (That is, Γ is closed under γ.)

The requirement that Γ is closed under γ guarantees that "the rules of the game" specify what can happen from any (possibly itself an induced) position $G \in \Gamma$, when a feasible outcome $x \in X(G)$ is proposed.

The only requirement imposed on the inducement correspondence, γ, is that the set of players of each position that a coalition S can induce, includes, but need not coincide with, the players in S. Formally,

Assumption 4.2. Let (γ, Γ) be a situation. For all $G \in \Gamma$, $S \subset N(G)$ and $x \in X(G)$, if $H \in \gamma(S \mid G, x)$, then $S \subset N(H)$.

Note that this mild and natural assumption does not rule out the possibility that γ assigns the empty set to some (or even all) coalitions, that is, some coalitions may be unable to induce any position at all. (Think, for example, of the terminal nodes in a game tree.)

5. The tree situation

To illustrate the concept of situation, consider an extensive form game given by the game tree T. Analogous to the position $G(T)$ defined in Section 3, we shall now associate with each subtree $\tilde{T}$ of T a position $G(\tilde{T})$. ($\tilde{T}$ might represent either the original extensive form game or one of its subgames

---

[6] A coalition is a *nonempty* subset of the set of players.
[7] All inclusions in this paper are weak.

$(T|v)$, $v \in V(T)$.) That is,

$$N(G(\tilde{T})) \equiv N = \{1, 2, \ldots, n\}, \qquad X(G(\tilde{T})) \equiv \Pi(\tilde{T}),$$

and, for $i \in N$ and $x \in \Pi(\tilde{T})$,

$$u^i(G(\tilde{T}))(x) \equiv \mu^i(x).$$

Observe that a terminal node $v \in V_0(T)$ defines the position $(N, \{v\}, \{\mu^i(v)\}_{i \in N})$. The *tree situation* (γ, Γ) associated with the game tree T is defined as follows. The set Γ contains all the positions that correspond to subtrees in the original game tree T. That is,

$$\Gamma = \{G(T|v) \mid v \in V(T)\}.$$

Since every vertex $v \in V(T)$ uniquely defines the subtree $(T|v)$, we may simplify the notation and write $G(v)$ for $G(T|v)$. Thus,

$$\Gamma = \{G(v) \mid v \in V(T)\} = \{G(\tilde{T}) \mid \tilde{T} = (T|v), \ v \in V(T)\}.$$

Let us now turn to the definition of the inducement correspondence γ. The rules of the (extensive form) game are such that player i is called upon to make a decision in vertex v, $v \in V(T)$, only if v belongs to the set of vertices assigned to player i by the partition of the set of nodes of the game tree, that is, if and only if $v \in V_i(T)$. In this case, player i can induce all the positions associated with the subtrees that result from the decision he chooses to make, namely, all positions of the form $G(w)$, where the node w is adjacent from v.

Let $G(\tilde{T}) \in \Gamma$ and let $x \in X(G(\tilde{T}))$. As just discussed, if x is followed then player i is called upon to make a choice in each of the vertices that lie along the path x, and, in addition, belong to $V_i(\tilde{T})$. Therefore, when x is proposed in $G(\tilde{T})$, player i can induce all positions $G(w)$ where the node w is adjacent from a node v, which both belongs to $V_i(\tilde{T})$ and lies along the path x. With a slight abuse of notation, the last two conditions imposed on v will be written as $v \in \{x\} \cap V_i(\tilde{T})$. (Note that since $x \in \Pi(\tilde{T})$ we have that $\{x\} \cap V_i(\tilde{T}) = \{x\} \cap V_i(T)$.)

Assuming that coalitions are not allowed to form,[8] (which is the fundamental feature of a "noncooperative game"), the inducement correspondence in the tree situation is given by: For all $i \in N$, $G(\tilde{T}) \in \Gamma$ and $x \in X(G(\tilde{T}))$,

$$\gamma(\{i\} \mid G(\tilde{T}), x) = \{G(w) \mid \exists v \in \{x\} \cap V_i(T)$$
$$\text{such that } w \text{ is adjacent from } v\},$$

$$\gamma(S \mid G(\tilde{T}), x) = \emptyset \quad \text{otherwise.}$$

[8] For the "coalitional tree situation" see Section 8.4 in Greenberg (1990).

The representation of an extensive form game (with perfect information and without chance moves) as a tree situation simplifies the analysis considerably. In particular, it employs the notion of a *path*, rather than the much more complicated, and somewhat artificial, concept of *strategy* (Definition 2.3).

The following specific example might further clarify the notion of (tree) situation.

Example 5.1. Two individuals, 1 and 2, are getting divorced, and have to decide who will raise their only child. The utility level each parent derives from having (or not having, respectively) custody over the child is 100 (respectively, 0) utils. (Side-payments are not allowed.) If the parents agree on who gets custody, the agreement will be implemented. Otherwise, neither gets custody (and the child will go to a boarding school). Suppose that the negotiation process between the parents is such that 1 proposes who gets custody, and 2 can then agree or disagree to the proposal.[9] Let I and U denote the actions of player 1, where I means "I get custody" and U means "You get custody". Similarly, let Y and N denote the actions of player 2, where Y means "I agree to your proposal" and N means "I disagree to your proposal". Figure 1 is the corresponding game tree.

The associated tree situation (γ, Γ) is given by $\Gamma = \{G^1, G^2, \ldots, G^7\}$, corresponding to the seven subtrees $T^1, \ldots, T^7$, where $T^h = (T | v_h)$, $h = 1, 2, \ldots, 7$, that is,

$$V(T^1) \equiv \{v_1, v_2, \ldots, v_7\}, \quad V(T^2) \equiv \{v_2, v_4, v_5\},$$

$$V(T^3) \equiv \{v_3, v_6, v_7\}$$

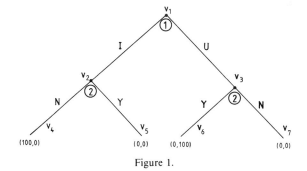

Figure 1.

---

[9] For a less dramatic interpretation of this game, replace the child by an "indivisible object".

and

$$V(T^h) \equiv \{v_h\} \quad \text{for } h = 4, 5, 6, 7.$$

The inducement correspondence γ is given by

$$\gamma(\{1\}\,|\,G^1, x) = \{G^2, G^3\},$$

$$\gamma(\{2\}\,|\,G^1, (v_1, v_2, v_4)) = \gamma(\{2\}\,|\,G^1, (v_1, v_2, v_5)) = \{G^4, G^5\},$$

$$\gamma(\{2\}\,|\,G^1, (v_1, v_3, v_6)) = \gamma(\{2\}\,|\,G^1, (v_1, v_3, v_7)) = \{G^6, G^7\},$$

$$\gamma(\{2\}\,|\,G^2, x) = \{G^4, G^5\}, \qquad \gamma(\{2\}\,|\,G^3, x) = \{G^6, G^7\}$$

and

$$\gamma(S\,|\,G, x) = \emptyset \quad \text{otherwise.}$$

6. Stable standards of behavior

Let $G \in \Gamma$, $x^* \in X(G)$ and $H \in \gamma(S\,|\,G, x^*)$. Should members of S reject x^* and induce H instead? In order to answer this question it is not sufficient for the players to know the set $X(H)$ of potentially feasible outcomes; they must also know the outcomes that are expected to result once position H is induced, namely, "the solution for H". That is, the acceptability of an outcome x^* in $X(G)$ depends on the outcomes that are (predicted to be) accepted in the positions that can be induced from G when x^* is proposed. It is for this important reason that the concept of a standard of behavior is introduced.

Definition 6.1. Let Γ be a collection of positions. A mapping σ that assigns to each position $G \in \Gamma$ a subset, $\sigma(G)$, of $X(G)$, is called a *standard of behavior* (*SB*) *for* Γ. The set $\sigma(G)$ is called *the solution for G* (assigned by σ).

If σ is an SB for Γ, then, according to σ, for every $G \in \Gamma$, outcomes that belong to $X(G)$ but not to $\sigma(G)$ are feasible but will be objected to by some players in $N(G)$. These outcomes, therefore, will never actually be reached.

A situation (γ, Γ) describes the social environment, and the standard of behavior σ for this situation specifies for each position $G \in \Gamma$ the set of outcomes that are "reasonable" or "sensible". By definition, σ can be any arbitrary mapping. But it is clear that "rational" players will not follow a "senseless" standard of behavior. Some restrictions on σ seem necessary if σ is to be adopted. (Recall that players are free to choose to obey or disobey σ). I shall impose only one restriction on the SB σ, namely, that it be "stable".

Let (γ, Γ) be a situation, and let σ be an SB for Γ. If all players adopt the recommendations made by σ, it seems reasonable to stipulate that a group of players, S, will reject an outcome, $x \in X(G)$, if it can induce a position $H \in \gamma(S | G, x)$, whose *solution*, $\sigma(H)$, *benefits all members of S*. (The precise formulation of the emphasized clause is given in the next section.) It is important to note that the rejection of x^* must depend only on those outcomes that belong to $\sigma(H)$, not on the entire set of feasible outcomes, $X(H)$. (Recall that if σ is adopted then outcomes that belong to $X(H) \backslash \sigma(H)$ will never be agreed upon by the players in $N(H)$, and therefore cannot be the basis for "valid objections"). Indeed:

"*If the standard of behavior σ is accepted by the players, then it must impress upon their minds the idea that only outcomes assigned by σ are sound.*" (Von Neumann and Morgenstern, 1947, p. 265, with minor modifications.)

Let (γ, Γ) be a situation, and let σ be an SB for Γ. We shall say that the SB, σ, is *internally stable* for (γ, Γ) if for all $G \in \Gamma$, $x^* \in \sigma(G)$ implies that there exist no coalition $S \subset N(G)$ and position $H \in \gamma(S | G, x^*)$, such that S benefits by rejecting x^* and inducing H, realizing that the solution to H is given by $\sigma(H)$. That is, if σ is internally stable then accepting the SB σ implies the willingness of all players to follow its recommendations.

"*The standard of behavior must be free of inner contradictions: No outcome y conforming with the accepted standard of behavior can be upset by another outcome of the same kind.*" (Von Neumann and Morgenstern, 1947, p. 41, with minor modifications.)

But, in addition to specifying the set of recommended outcomes, a theory, delineated by the SB σ, should also explain why other feasible outcomes are excluded. That is, the SB σ must account, in every position $G \in \Gamma$, not only for elements in $\sigma(G)$ but also for outcomes in $X(G) \backslash \sigma(G)$. There ought to be a reason why an outcome $x \in X(G)$ does not belong to the solution $\sigma(G)$.

I contend that unless the SB σ is arbitrary, then the only reason for excluding $x \in X(G)$ should be that were it included in $\sigma(G)$, the internal stability of the mapping σ would then be violated. This property is called external stability. More specifically, let (γ, Γ) be a situation, and let σ be an SB for Γ. We shall say that the SB σ is *externally stable* if for all $G \in \Gamma$, $x \in X(G) \backslash \sigma(G)$ implies that there exist a coalition $S \subset N(G)$ and a position $H \in \gamma(S | G, x)$, such that S benefits by rejecting x and inducing H, realizing that the solution to H is given by $\sigma(H)$. The appeal of external stability is illustrated by the following quote.

"*If the players have accepted σ as the standard of behavior, then the ability to discredit, with the help of σ, any outcome not assigned by σ, is necessary to maintain their faith in σ*". (Von Neumann and Morgenstern, p. 266, with minor modifications.)

The overall single consistency requirement that I shall impose on the SB is that it be *stable*, that is, that it be both internally and externally stable. Stable standards of behavior are such that:

"*Once they are generally accepted, they overrule everything else and no part of them can be overruled within the limits of the accepted standards. This is clearly how things are in actual social organizations*". (Von Neumann and Morgenstern, 1947, p. 42.)

7. OSSB and CSSB

Although the motivation behind the requirements of internal and external stability is clear, the expression "members of S prefer (the set) $\sigma(H)$ over the outcome $x \in \sigma(G)$", which appears in the definitions of these terms, is ambiguous. The difficulty arises when, as is generally the case, $\sigma(H)$ contains several outcomes, some of which may benefit all members of S while other outcomes in $\sigma(H)$ may make some, or even all, members of S worse off than they are under x. It is by no means evident that these players will then be willing to reject x.

To resolve this difficulty, I shall consider two (extreme) behavioral assumptions: optimistic and conservative. The assumption of optimistic behavior entails that members of S prefer $\sigma(H)$ over $x \in X(G)$ if *there exists* an outcome $y \in \sigma(H)$ that all members of S prefer to x. The opposite extreme assumption is that players behave "conservatively", and S will reject a proposed outcome x in position G, and induce, instead, the position $H \in \gamma(S | G, x)$, only if *all* outcomes in $\sigma(H)$ make all members of S better off.

Definition 7.1. Let σ be an SB for the situation (γ, Γ). The SB σ is *optimistic stable standard of behavior* (*OSSB*) *for* (γ, Γ) if for all $G \in \Gamma, x \in X(G) \backslash \sigma(G)$ if and only if that there exist $S \subset N(G)$, $H \in \gamma(S | G, x)$ and $y \in \sigma(H)$ such that $u^i(H)(y) > u^i(G)(x)$ for all $i \in S$.

If the players behave conservatively, then analogous to Definition 7.1 we have the following:

Definition 7.2. Let σ be an SB for the situation (γ, Γ). The SB σ is *conservative stable standard of behavior* (*CSSB*) *for* (γ, Γ) if for all $G \in \Gamma$, $x \in \sigma(G)$ if and only if that there exist no $S \subset N(G)$ and $H \in \gamma(S | G, x)$ such that $\sigma(H) \neq \emptyset$, and for all $y \in \sigma(H)$, $u^i(H)(y) > u^i(G)(x)$ for all $i \in S$.

Observe that the additional requirement that the induced position H have a nonempty solution is automatically satisfied in Definition 7.1; it is guaranteed by the requirement that there exists $y \in \sigma(H)$. One can interpret $\sigma(H) \neq \emptyset$ to mean that once H is induced, there is no outcome that the players of H might agree upon, that is, H is, according to the SB σ, a "chaotic" position; it contains no "reasonable" outcome. Surely, players who are conservative will avoid such positions.

The notions of ODOM and CDOM, introduced below, provide an alternative and most useful way to define OSSB and CSSB. Let (γ, Γ) be a situation, and let σ be an SB for (γ, Γ). For a position $G \in \Gamma$, define the *optimistic dominion* of G (relative to the SB σ), denoted ODOM(σ, G), by

$$\text{ODOM}(\sigma, G) = \{x \in X(G) | \exists S \subset N(G), H \in \gamma(S | G, x) \text{ and } y \in \sigma(H)$$
$$\text{such that for all } i \in S, u^i(H)(y) > u^i(G)(x)\}.$$

That is, ODOM(σ, G) consists of all outcomes in $X(G)$ which will be rejected by at least one coalition S (whose members behave in an optimistic way). It is easy to see that the following definition coincides with Definition 7.1.

Definition 7.3. Let (γ, Γ) be a situation, and let σ be an SB for (γ, Γ). Then, the SB σ is *optimistic stable* if and only if for all $G \in \Gamma$, $\sigma(G) = X(G) \backslash \text{ODOM}(\sigma, G)$.

Similarly, let (γ, Γ) be a situation, and let σ be an SB for (γ, Γ). For a position $G \in \Gamma$, define the *conservative dominion* of G (relative to the SB σ), denoted CDOM(σ, G), by

$$\text{CDOM}(\sigma, G) = \{x \in X(G) | \exists S \subset N(G) \text{ and } H \in \gamma(S | G, x)$$
$$\text{such that } \sigma(H) \neq \emptyset, \text{ and for all } y \in \sigma(H)$$
$$\text{and } i \in S, u^i(H)(y) > u^i(G)(x)\}.$$

That is, CDOM(σ, G) consists of all outcomes in $X(G)$ which will be rejected by at least one coalition S, (whose members behave conservatively). Again, it is easy to see that the following definition coincides with Definition 7.2.

Definition 7.4. Let (γ, Γ) be a situation, and let σ be an SB for (γ, Γ). Then, the SB σ is *conservative stable* if and only if for all $G \in \Gamma, \sigma(G) = X(G) \backslash \text{CDOM}(\sigma, G)$.

Remark 7.5. At least at first sight, it might appear that when players behave more conservatively they will be more hesitant to reject outcomes that are proposed to them. One may conclude, therefore, that if σ^o and σ^c are OSSB and CSSB, respectively, for a situation (γ, Γ), then for every position $G \in \Gamma, \sigma^o(G)$ is a subset of $\sigma^c(G)$. Such a conclusion is erroneous. It is possible that a situation (γ, Γ) admits a unique OSSB, σ^o, and a unique CSSB, σ^c, having the property that there exists a position $G \in \Gamma$ for which $\sigma^o(G)$ is a strict subset of $\sigma^c(G)$, and there exists another position $H \in \Gamma$ for which $\sigma^c(H)$ is a strict subset of $\sigma^o(H)$. Also, there are situations that admit a CSSB and not an OSSB or vice versa, or that do not admit either OSSB or CSSB. (See Greenberg, 1990. Examples 3.3–3.5 and 5.4.3.) But, for tree situations associated with a finite game tree we have, conforming with our situation, the following result.

Theorem 7.6. *Let T be a game tree with $|V(T)| < \infty$, and let (γ, Γ) be its associated tree situation. Then, there exist a unique OSSB, σ^o, and a unique CSSB, σ^c, for (γ, Γ). Furthermore, both of these SBs are nonempty-valued, and for all $G \in \Gamma, \sigma^o(G) \subset \sigma^c(G)$.*

Proof. Theorem 8.1.4 in Greenberg (1990). $\square$

8. OSSB for the tree situation

As stated in the Introduction, the notions of OSSB and CSSB for tree situations are intimately related to the notion of perfect equilibrium. Since the set of outcomes in a position $G(\tilde{T})$ is the set of paths $\Pi(\tilde{T})$, rather than strategies, it is useful to consider the set of paths in $\Pi(\tilde{T})$ that result from an n-tuple of strategies that is a subgame perfect equilibrium in the game tree $\tilde{T}$. This set will be called the *set of perfect equilibrium paths*, denoted $\text{PEP}(\tilde{T})$. That is,

$$\text{PEP}(\tilde{T}) = \{\pi(f) \mid f \in \text{PE}(\tilde{T})\}.$$

We shall denote by $\text{PEU}(\tilde{T})$ the set of utility payoffs supported by a subgame perfect equilibrium in $\tilde{T}$, that is,

$$\text{PEU}(\tilde{T}) = \{h(f) = \mu(\pi(f)) \in \mathbb{R}^N \mid f \in \text{PE}(\tilde{T})\}.$$

An important result of this section is that in many game trees, including all finite game trees, the OSSB for the associated tree situation leads to an attractive refinement of the notion of subgame perfect equilibrium paths. This unexpected result is quite remarkable because the motivation behind the notion of OSSB is totally unrelated to that which underlies Nash, and, hence, subgame perfect equilibrium.

Let T be a game tree. We shall say that μ is *continuous* if and only if for every $\varepsilon > 0$ there exists an integer κ, such that if the first κ vertices of two paths x and y in $\Pi(T)$ coincide, then for all $i \in N$, $|\mu^i(x) - \mu^i(y)| < \varepsilon$. Intuitively, continuity requires that the difference between the utility levels a player receives from two paths that coincide "long enough" is "negligible". We shall say that the game tree T is a *continuous game tree* if its payoff function μ is continuous. It is evident that all bounded game trees are continuous games.

Theorem 8.1. *Let T be a continuous game tree, and let (γ, Γ) be its associated tree situation. Let σ be an OSSB for (γ, Γ) such that $\sigma(G(\tilde{T})) \neq \emptyset$ for all $G(\tilde{T}) \in \Gamma$. Then, for every $G(\tilde{T}) \in \Gamma$, $\sigma(G(\tilde{T})) \subset \mathrm{PEP}(\tilde{T})$.*

Proof. Theorem 8.3.1 in Greenberg (1990). □

The requirement that the payoffs be continuous is essential for Theorem 8.1 to hold. (See Example 8.2.3 in Greenberg, 1990.) For a tree situation associated with a finite game tree we have the following stronger result.

Corollary 8.2. *Let T be a finite game tree, and let (γ, Γ) be its associated tree situation. Then, there exists a unique OSSB, σ, for (γ, Γ). Moreover, for every $G(\tilde{T}) \in \Gamma$, $\sigma(G(\tilde{T})) \neq \emptyset$ and $\sigma(G(\tilde{T})) \subset \mathrm{PEP}(\tilde{T})$.*

Proof. Theorem 8.3.2 in Greenberg (1990). □

Example 5.1 demonstrates that the inclusion in Corollary 8.2 (and hence in Theorem 8.1) can be strict. That is, there exists a finite game tree T such that the unique OSSB, σ, for the associated tree situation assigns to the position $G(T)$ a *nonempty strict subset* of $\mathrm{PEP}(T)$. Indeed, it is easy to see that in this example,

$$\mathrm{PEP}(T) = \{(v_1, v_2, v_4), (v_1, v_2, v_5), (v_1, v_3, v_6)\},$$

yielding the utility levels,

$$\mathrm{PEU}(T) = \{(100, 0), (0, 0), (0, 100)\}.$$

That is, each of the three possible payoff configurations is supported by some PE. In contrast, the unique OSSB σ for (γ, Γ) satisfies

$$\sigma(G(T)) = \{(v_1, v_2, v_4)\},$$

that is, player 1 proposes that he raises the child and player 2 consents, leading to the unique payoff $(100, 0)$.

It is interesting to note that this rather appealing solution refines other refinements of PEP. Thus, both Selten's (1975) "trembling hand" and Kohlberg and Mertens (1986) "stability" yield, in Example 5.1, the set of the two paths: $\{(v_1, v_2, v_4), (v_1, v_2, v_5)\}$, which strictly includes $\sigma(G(T))$.

The following three examples show that the OSSB for the tree situation (both in bounded and unbounded game trees) yields solutions that were promoted (in the particular cases, and without general theoretical foundations) by other scholars.

Example 8.3. McKelvey and Ordeshook (1988) consider the problem of "retrospective voting", in which candidates cannot commit themselves before the election to adopting particular policies. Specifically, there is a single voter, player 1, who can vote for either candidate 2 or candidate 3. The candidate that player 1 elects becomes the incumbent, and must then choose a policy from the set $\{a, b\}$. After the incumbent chooses a policy, the voter must vote again for the candidate who will be the incumbent in the next period. The voter's preferences are a function only of the policy selected, and he gets a unit of utility every time a is chosen, and 0 every time b is chosen. The candidates get utility only from being elected, obtaining one unit of utility whenever they are elected. This game proceeds a finite number of periods. (Figure 2 depicts the game if it is repeated twice.)

There are many subgame perfect equilibria in this game, because of the following feature of this model. The decision made by the voter affects the utility of the candidate, but not the utility of the voter (except indirectly, insofar as the candidate that is elected by the voter may later adopt a policy more or less favorable to the voter). Similarly, when the candidate adopts a policy, it affects the utility of the voter, but not the utility of the candidate (except insofar as it might affect future decisions by the voter about who to vote for). It is for this reason that, as is easily verified, PEP(T) coincides with $\Pi(T)$. That is, every path in the game tree is supported by a subgame perfect equilibrium. It is interesting to note that in this game neither Selten (1975) "trembling hand" nor Kohlberg and Mertens (1986) "stability" refine subgame perfection.

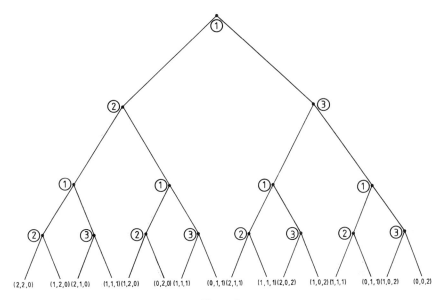

Figure 2.

Clearly, the "plausible" equilibrium is where the voter "rewards" the candidate who chooses the policy a, and "punishes" the candidate who gives him the policy b, thereby inducing the candidate to select the preferred policy, in anticipation of being reelected. These equilibria result in paths for which the voter always gets maximum utility, and the initial incumbent always gets reelected. Quite remarkably, these are precisely the paths assigned by the unique OSSB, σ, for the associated tree situation. More specifically, σ is given by: For positions that correspond to elections, i.e., for $G(v) \in \Gamma \cap V_1(T)$,

$$\sigma(G(v)) = \{(2, a, 2, a, \ldots, 2, a), (3, a, 3, a, \ldots, 3, a)\},^{10}$$

that is, $\sigma(G(v))$ consists of the two paths which yield the voter the maximum utility and the initial incumbent is always reelected. For positions that correspond to candidate i, $i \in \{2, 3\}$ being elected, i.e., for $G(v) \in \Gamma \cap V_i(T)$,

$$\sigma(G(v)) = \{(a, i, a, i, a, \ldots, i, a), (b, i, a, i, a, \ldots, i, a)\},$$

that is, $\sigma(G(v))$ consists of the two paths which, with perhaps the exception of the current period, yield the voter the maximum utility, and, again, the

---

[10] It is, at times, convenient to identify a path with the actions the players take along it.

initial incumbent is always reelected. Winer (1989) shows that this characterization holds also for the discounted infinite case. In particular, the tree
situation associated with the (unbounded) game tree admits a unique OSSB.

The following is another example where the unique OSSB for the tree
situation yields the promoted refinement of subgame perfect equilibrium.

Example 8.4. Consider the "dollar auction game with a budget constraint"
(Shubik, 1971; O'Neil, 1986), where two players bid for an object which is
worth s dollars, $s > 1$. Players bid alternately, and all bids are in integers.
At each round the player who bids can either "give up", or else he has to
(strictly) overbid the last offer. Each player has a budget constraint of b
dollars, $b > s$, which means that no player can bid more than b for the
object. The important feature of this game is that the object is awarded to
the higher bidder, but *both players pay* (to the auctioneer) their final bids.

The multiplicity of equilibria was O'Neil's main concern, and he suggested
to resolve this problem by drawing on "risk-aversion".

"*However, too many possible strategies would result from finding all sequential equilibria, so we find a particular sequential equilibrium that we think is
the most reasonable one. We state a simple rule about players' choice behavior
and regard it as part of the concept of sequential rationality for a dollar
auction: If more than one branch has maximal value, it is assumed that a
rational player will choose the move that involves the smallest bid, including
possibly the bid of zero (that is, dropping out). A player will be risk-averse in
the sense of not venturing money without some positive reason for doing so*".
(O'Neil, 1986, p. 36.)

Quite remarkably the tree situation associated with the dollar auction
game admits a unique OSSB which yields O'Neil's choice of "the most
reasonable" perfect equilibrium. (See Greenberg, 1990, Proposition 8.3.6.)
In particular, at the beginning of the game, player 1 has to bid $1 +
(b-1) \bmod(s-1)$ dollars.[11]

The last (sketch of an) example shows that the refinement offered by the
OSSB is of interest also in unbounded game trees.

Example 8.5. Asheim (1987 and 1988) considered an intergenerational
model where each generation inherits capital stocks from the previous

---

[11] Recall that $s > 1$, and that for two positive integers p and q, $(p) \bmod(q) = m$, where m
is the unique integer which satisfies: $p = kq + m$, $0 \le m < q$, for some integer k.

generation and has to decide on its consumption and on the capital stock it will leave for the next generation. The (subjective) utility function of a generation is additively separable in its consumption and the utility of the next generation. The overall (ethical) welfare function of a generation is equal to the lowest (subjective) utility level of the remaining generations.

This economy can be represented by an infinite game tree where the payoff to each generation is its welfare level. Since zero consumption by all generations is subgame perfect (and can, therefore, serve as a "punishment" for the deviating player), we have that for every subtree $\tilde{T}$, $\mathrm{PEP}(\tilde{T}) = \Pi(\tilde{T})$. Thus, the notion of subgame perfection has no predictive power in this model; it excludes no path in T. In contrast, Asheim shows that there exists a unique OSSB for the corresponding tree situation. This OSSB assigns the unique "time-consistent optimal path" to any position that corresponds to a subgame with strictly positive capital stocks. Thus, this OSSB implies that the present generation chooses the best path among those which later generations will carry out. It is precisely this refinement of PEP which, because of its optimality properties, is promoted in Asheim (1987 and 1988).

9. Conservative stability and subgame perfection

We shall now see that like the optimistic, the other extreme behavioral assumption — conservative, also yields interesting results. The following theorem points out the close relationship between CSSB for the tree situation (γ, Γ) and PEP: In all game trees that possess perfect equilibria, the subgame perfect correspondence σ^P is a CSSB for (γ, Γ), where for $G(\tilde{T}) \in \Gamma$,

$$\sigma^P(G(\tilde{T})) \equiv \mathrm{PEP}(\tilde{T}).$$

Theorem 9.1. *Let T be a game tree and let (γ, Γ) be its associated tree situation. Assume that $\mathrm{PEP}(T) \neq \emptyset$. Define the SB, σ, for (γ, Γ) by: For every subtree $\tilde{T}$ of T, $\sigma(G(\tilde{T})) \equiv \mathrm{PEP}(\tilde{T})$. Then, σ is a CSSB for (γ, Γ).*

Proof. Theorem 8.2.1 in Greenberg (1990). $\square$

This remarkable result can be stated and proved within the paradigm of "classical game theory". It provides a complete and new characterization for, and sheds new light on, the notion of subgame perfect equilibrium:

Theorem 9.2. *Let T be a game tree, and let $x^* \in \Pi(T)$. Then, $x^* \in \mathrm{PEP}(T)$ if and only if x^* satisfies the following condition:*

(C) *For every $i \in N$ and every vertex w adjacent from $v \in V_i(T) \cap \{x^*\}$, there exists $y \in \mathrm{PEP}(T \mid w)$ such that $\mu^i(y) \leq \mu^i(x^*)$.*

Proof. Theorem 8.2.4 in Greenberg (1989). □

The importance of Theorem 9.2, whose proof is quite straightforward, lies in its interpretation. There are fundamental and significant differences between the original definition of PEP and its equivalent formulation as provided in Theorem 9.2. First, and perhaps most important, the deviating individual expects a *correlated retaliation*; in particular, the *other players will not stay put* with their (undefined) strategies. Rather, they will unite and choose a path, from the set of subgame perfect equilibrium paths in the resulting subgame, which will make the deviating player (weakly) worse off than he was under the proposed path. Second, the characterization of PEP in Theorem 9.2 replaces the notion of a *strategy* by the much simpler notion of a *path*. Consequently, a player can deviate *at most once* from a proposed path and generate a new subtree. But in this subtree, the player does accept the paths recommended by its PEP. In contrast, when players are free to choose their strategies, there can be multiple vertices in which deviations occur.

Theorem 9.2 can be instrumental also in establishing new results of interest for a large class of extensive form games, called "*generalized sequential bargaining games*". Assume that a "cake of size 1" is to be divided among n players, provided they reach an agreement on how to divide it. If the n players cannot reach an agreement, then each player receives nothing. Specifically, denote the set of "*possible agreements*" by Δ, that is, $\Delta \equiv \{a \in \mathbb{R}_+^n \mid \sum a_i \leq 1\}$. Events in the bargaining process are confined to times in the set $\{1, 2, \ldots, t, \ldots\}$. When it is player i's turn to make an offer, he has to choose an element in Δ, which represents the way he proposes to divide the cake. Turns are alternated, with player i proposing at times $t = i, i+n, i+2n, i+3n, \ldots$. After a proposal $z \in \Delta$ has been made at time t, the players "vote" sequentially in favor of or against the proposal. If all vote in favor of the proposal (say "yes," denoted by Y), the game ends at time t with player i receiving z^i units of the cake, yielding him the utility level $u^i(z^i, t)$. Otherwise, the game proceeds to time $t+1$ when a new proposal is made.

The only assumptions on the utility functions $u^i(z^i, t)$ that I impose are that for every player $i \in N$, every offer $z \in \Delta$, and any period t,

(A1) $u^i(z^i, 1) = z^i$;

(A2) $(u^1(z^1, t), u^2(z^2, t), \ldots, u^n(z^n, t)) \in \Delta$.

The first assumption states that in the first period the utility function of every player is linear with the amount of cake he receives at that period. Condition (A2) states that the utility level a player attains from any division at any period is always nonnegative, and moreover, the sum of the utility levels attained never exceeds 1. Conditions (A1) and (A2) together imply that any payoff (vector of utility levels) that can be attained by the players at period t, can also be attained in the first period. Observe, however, that (A1) and (A2) do not imply (the commonly employed assumption) that $u^i(z^i, t)$ is (even weakly) monotone decreasing in t.

A special class of utility functions that satisfy the two conditions is the set of functions of the form $u^i(z^i, t) = (\delta^i)^{t-1} z^i$, with δ^i, $\delta^i \in [0, 1]$, being the "future discount factor" of player i. Note that δ^i can assume the value 1, that is, players need not discount the future at all.[12]

Theorem 9.2 together with the particular structure of the game tree, T, that represents a generalized sequential bargaining game allows for the following partial characterization of the payoffs supported by a subgame perfect equilibrium in T.

Theorem 9.3. *Let T be a generalized bargaining game that satisfies* (A1) *and* (A2). *Then* PEU(T) *is a convex set in* $\mathbb{R}^n$.

Proof. See Greenberg (1988) or Greenberg (1990, Theorem 8.2.5). $\square$

If T is a finite game tree, then Theorem 9.1 (or Theorem 9.2) can be strenghthened: In this case the PEP correspondence is the only CSSB for the associated tree situation.

Theorem 9.4. *Let T be a game tree with $|V(T)| < \infty$, and let (γ, Γ) be its associated tree situation. Then, σ^P is the unique CSSB for (γ, Γ).*

Proof. Theorem 8.2.2 in Greenberg (1990). $\square$

An example, due to Benyamin Shitovitz, shows that Theorem 9.3 cannot be extended to unbounded game trees, and that the converse of Theorem 9.3 does not hold. That is, there exists a tree situation whose CSSB is totally unrelated to PEP. More specifically, there exist infinite game trees that

---

[12] The well-known application of Rubinstein (1982) is the special case where $n = 2$ and $\delta^i \in (0, 1)$.

admit two nonempty-valued CSSBs, σ^1 and σ^2, where σ^1 is the PEP correspondence and σ^2 satisfies: For all subtrees $\tilde{T}$, $\sigma^2(G(\tilde{T})) \cap \text{PEP}(\tilde{T}) = \emptyset$. (See Greenberg, 1990, Example 8.2.3.) But, as the following theorem asserts, such cannot be the case if T is a continuous game tree.

Theorem 9.5. Let T be a continuous game tree that admits a subgame perfect equilibrium, and let (γ, Γ) be its associated tree situation. Then, σ^P is the unique maximal[13] nonempty-valued CSSB for (γ, Γ).

Proof. Greenberg and Shitovitz (1990).   □

10. Epilogue

Undoubtedly, the theory of social situations can (and perhaps should) be extended, generalized, and improved. My own beliefs concerning its potential are reflected by the following quote, from a, deservedly, highly esteemed friend and scholar, Jacques Drèze.

"I thus feel tempted to conclude this paper with a note of optimism. But optimism about an exciting subject is too easily wishful. So, to those who will extend the work in this area, I had better refrain from promising success. I will simply offer the modest advice that they are sure to learn a great deal from the proposed approach; and I will make the modest promise that it will be a lot of fun". (Jacques H. Drèze, presidential address at the Second World Congress of the Econometric Society, Cambridge, September 10, 1970, with minor modifications.)

References

Asheim, G. (1987) 'Rawlsian intergenerational justice as a Markov-perfect equilibrium in a resource technology', Norwegian School of Business Administration, mimeo.
Asheim, G. (1988) 'Rawlsian intergenerational justice as a Markov-perfect equilibrium in a resource technology', *Review of Economic Studies*, 55:469–484.
Greenberg, J. (1988) 'Payoffs in generalized bargaining games', *Economics Letters*, 28:33–35.
Greenberg, J. (1990) *The Theory of Social Situations: An Alternative Game-Theoretic Approach.* Cambridge: Cambridge University Press.
Greenberg, J. and B. Shitovitz (1990) 'Conservative stability and subgame perfection', mimeo.

---

[13] With respect to set inclusion.

Kohlberg, E. and J.-F. Mertens (1986) 'On the strategic stability of equilibria', *Econometrica*, 52:1007–1029.

McKelvey, R. and P. Ordeshook (1988) private communication.

Neumann, J. von and O. Morgenstern (1947) *Theory of Games and Economic Behavior.* Princeton, NJ: Princeton University Press.

O'Neil, B. (1986) 'International escalation and the dollar auction', *Journal of Conflict Resolution*, 30:33–50.

Rubinstein, A. (1982) 'Perfect equilibrium in a bargaining model', *Econometrica*, 50:97–110.

Selten, R. (1975) 'Reexamination of the perfectness concept for equilibrium points in extensive games', *International Journal of Game Theory*, 4:25–55.

Shubik, M. (1971) 'The dollar auction game: a paradox in noncooperative behavior and escalation', *Journal of Conflict Resolution*, 15:545–547.

Shubik, M. (1984) *Game Theory in the Social Sciences: Concepts and Solutions.* Cambridge, MA: MIT Press.

Winer, Z. (1989) M.Sc. Thesis, University of Haifa, Israel.

Chapter 12

EXTENSIONS OF GAMES, PURIFICATION OF STRATEGIES, AND LYAPUNOV'S THEOREM

Jean-François MERTENS

CORE, Université Catholique de Louvain, Louvain-la-Neuve, Belgium

Introduction

In at least two different applications in game theory, one needs good approximations of $[0, 1]$-valued functions by $\{0, 1\}$-valued ones: for the Shapley value of non-atomic games, the interpretation being the approximation of an "ideal coalition" by a real coalition, and also for the approximation of mixed strategies by pure strategies (Aumann et al., 1983). This second type of application was already a classical problem in statistical decision theory (existence of non-randomized procedures; Dvoretzky, Wald and Wolfowitz, 1951).

Somewhat more generally, one wants to approximate functions with values in a simplex by functions with values in the extreme points of that simplex: in the second type of application, this means one wants the result to be applicable to problems with more than two actions or decisions, and in the first, this will allow to approximate any finite increasing sequence of ideal coalitions by a similar sequence of real coalitions.

Two types of results are known. The first type deals with exact approximation on a fixed finite set of measures — such are the theorems of Lyapunov and Dvoretzky–Wald–Wolfowitz. Thus, for any measurable function f with values in the simplex $\Delta(A)$, and for any finite set of non-atomic measures μ_i, there exist measurable functions $\tilde{f}$ with values in A, such that $\mu_i(\tilde{f}) = \mu_i(f)$ for all i. We show (Theorem 2.2) that one can in addition dispense in this statement with the requirement of countable additivity (it suffices

Economic Decision-Making: Games, Econometrics and Optimisation
Edited by J.J. Gabszewicz, J.-F. Richard and L.A. Wolsey
© *Elsevier Science Publishers B.V., 1990*

that each μ_i be finitely additive, bounded, and nonatomic), and that f can be uniformly approximated by convex combinations of such functions $\tilde{f}$.

This allows to enlarge the space EXT (cf. Mertens, 1980) of games that have an extension so as to include the whole of $bv'FA$ (and in particular FA itself, and all polynomials in elements of FA), as shown in Section 6 (cf. also Mertens, 1988). Indeed, finite additivity is now allowed, and the uniform approximation by convex combinations allows to deal properly with the atomic parts. As a consequence, the value (cf., e.g., Mertens, 1988) is now a projection of norm 1 onto FA, and is defined on a space that includes all finite games, and much more is gained (cf. loc. cit.).

Along the way, we also obtain an extension to all of FA — the dual of the space of bounded measurable functions on some σ-field — of a classical criterion of weak-compactness in the space of measures: a subset of FA is weakly relatively compact iff any sequence contains a weak*-convergent subsequence (Theorem 2.1) (i.e., a subsequence along which the integral of any bounded measurable function converges).

The second type of known results (Aumann et al., 1983) says essentially that, for any fixed measure Q on the set of nonatomic probabilities ν on the space, f can be approximated by functions $\tilde{f}$ in the sense that $\nu(\tilde{f})$ converges to $\nu(f)$ in measure ($Q(d\nu)$).

Indeed, consider a game with incomplete information, where s is the signal to player I, t that to player II (the set of player I's opponents), $a_{ij}(s, t)$ is the corresponding payoff (vector), with i and j the actions of players I and II. Let s and t be chosen at random with $\nu_t(ds)$ and $Q(dt)$, where each ν_t is nonatomic. Denote by $x_i(s)$ and $y_j(t)$ mixed strategies of both players: the payoff is

$$\int Q(dt) \sum_j y_j(t) \int \sum_i x_i(s) a_{ij}(s, t) \nu_t(ds).$$

Denote by $Q^{ij}(d\mu)$ the distribution of the nonatomic measures (on S) $\mu_t(ds) = a_{ij}(s, t)\nu_t(ds)$. Then if $\int \tilde{x} \, d\mu$ approximates $\int x \, d\mu$ in measure under all measures $Q^{ij}(d\mu)$ (or for $\sum_{ij} Q^{ij}$), the inner integral with $\tilde{x}$ is ε-close (in measure) to the inner integral with x, so that, y being bounded, the payoff with $\tilde{x}$ is uniformly (over y) ε-close to the payoff with x: $\tilde{x}$ is an ε-purification of x.

We show:

(a) that this is really an approximation for some locally convex topology $\mathcal{T}$ on the space of bounded measurable functions — i.e., for a topology of uniform convergence on some class $\mathcal{E}$ of compact, convex, symmetric subsets of the (weak*) dual (the equicontinuous subsets);

(b) that those equicontinuous subsets of the dual (and hence the topology) can be characterised only in terms of the dual as a normed vector space, or as an ordered vector space;

(c) that countable additivity of the non-atomic measure ν_t is superfluous: one can work with the non-atomic elements of the full dual, and obtain in this way a much stronger topology.

Those results imply in particular that one could also define the extension of a game as an extension by continuity for the topology $\mathcal{T}$. As noted at the end of Section 5, the only thing missing to be able to use the full strength of this result is a more direct characterisation of the sets in $\mathcal{E}$: without it, everything still depends on being able to find approximations of the game with specific representations in terms of a distribution on non-atomic measures. But the results of (b) (and (c)) above (cf. Theorem 5.1) suggest there should be such a simple and direct characterisation.

We also show (Theorem 5.2) that the two above approaches for defining the extension of a game are mutually compatible; in particular, no inconsistency could arise (say a lack of linearity or of positivity of the Shapley value) from using one approach in one problem and the other in another. On the contrary, in the restatement of the Lyapunov-Dvoretzky-Wald-Wolfowitz Theorem in the beginning of this introduction, one can further require all functions $\tilde{f}$ to belong to any fixed neighbourhood of f in terms of the $\mathcal{T}$-topology (Theorem 5.2).

Finally, in Section 6, we apply the previous results to the definition of the extension of a game, and we show that the correct definition suggested by Theorem 2.2 already yields the extension for $\mathcal{T}$-continuous games: as far as concerns the extension of games, Theorem 5.2 yields in principle nothing more than Theorem 2.2. But it remains of course true, as observed above, that for practical applications, it would be extremely useful to have a direct characterisation of the class $\mathcal{E}$.

1. Representation of spaces of bounded functions

Recall that an M space is a Banach lattice E such that

$$\|x \vee y\| = \|x\| \vee \|y\|$$

for any two positive elements x and y. We also require it to have a unit e, i.e., a maximal element in the unit ball

$$\|x\| \leq 1 = \|e\| \implies x \leq e.$$

(Observe that those two assumptions imply $\|x\| = \| |x| \|$.)

Alternatively, it may be characterised solely in terms of the algebraic structure as an Archimedean vector lattice, whose positive cone is radial at some point, and which is complete in the Mackey topology $\tau(E, E^*)$, where E^* denotes the order dual (the differences of positive linear functionals). Recall also that those spaces are isometric and lattice isomorphic to $C(X)$, the space of continuous functions on some compact space X, endowed with the supremum norm.

In all cases we are going to consider, the space E will also have a natural multiplication — and be a Banach algebra with unit. This will fix a natural choice for the unit, and thus for the norm. The isomorphism is then also an algebra-isomorphism.

Remark that in this case the algebra structure determines already the order by itself — the positive cone is the cone formed by all squares.

In terms of the algebra structure, one needs

$$\forall f, g, \ \exists x: \quad x^2 = f^2 + g^2;$$

$$\forall y \ \exists \lambda_0 > 0; \ \forall \lambda: \ |\lambda| \leq \lambda_0 \ \exists z: \quad e + \lambda y = z^2;$$

$$\forall x, \ x \neq 0, \ \forall y \ \exists \lambda \geq 0; \ \forall z: \quad \lambda x^2 + z^2 \neq y^2.$$

Observe that X can therefore be identified with the spectrum of E, i.e., the set of all algebra-homomorphisms of E into R (or, if only the order structure is given, the extreme points of the set of positive elements of norm 1 in the dual).

The dual of E can therefore be identified with the space of all regular Borel measures on X.

A positive linear function φ can be defined as non-atomic if, whenever $\varphi = \varphi_1 + \varphi_2$, $\varphi_1 > 0$, $\varphi_2 \geq 0$, φ_1 is not proportional to some algebra-homomorphism (i.e., a 0–1 measure).

E will usually occur as the quotient of a space of bounded functions (continuous functions, Baire measurable functions, Borel measurable functions, universally measurable functions, μ-measurable functions) on some set, modulo some subspace of negligible functions (say, the closure of the functions with finite support; or: the measurable functions that are negligible for all measures in a given class of measures, etc.).

E could also be defined in terms of an abstract Boolean algebra: define first the finite partitions, then the algebra of step functions, then take the completion. This leads to totally disconnected spaces X (the clopen — both closed and open — sets form a basis for a compact topology; or: points are closed and every open covering is refined by a finite open partition). If one had started from a σ-algebra (every increasing sequence has a least upper bound) one would be led to what might be called σ-Stonian spaces: totally disconnected spaces where the closure of an open Baire set is open. The countably additive measures on the σ-algebra correspond then to those measures on X that vanish on every closed Baire set with empty interior. The dual of our M-space is an L-space: a Banach lattice where

$$\| \, |x| + |y| \, \| = \|x\| + \|y\|.$$

The dual of an L-space is an M-space of a special nature: the spectrum X is called Stonian (the closure of an open set is open). The elements of the L-space correspond to those measures on X that vanish on every meager set (subset of a countable union of closed sets with empty interior). Such measures have a clopen support, and a set is negligible iff its intersection with the support is a subset of a closed Baire set with empty interior.

An L_1-space is an L-space with unit: an element e of the positive cone such that any non-zero positive linear functional is strictly positive on e. This amounts to say that e, as a measure on X, has full support: the meager sets are the subsets of closed Baire sets with empty interior, and there exists some regular Borel measure $\mu (= e)$ for which they are the negligible sets. The L_1-space is then $L(\mu)$.

We will be chiefly interested in L-spaces consisting only of non-atomic elements. This means that X is perfect (has no isolated points).

Remark that, on any compact perfect space, there exists a non-atomic probability measure — indeed, the set of probability measures, in the weak* topology, is compact: the set A_n of probability measures having an atom of mass $\geq n^{-1}$ is obviously closed, and by perfectness has no interior point: the Baire category theorem therefore yields the existence of (a dense $\mathscr{G}_\delta$ of) non-atomic probabilities.

Observe finally that any non-atomic Boolean algebra (i.e., $\forall A \neq \emptyset, \exists A_1, A_2 \neq \emptyset: A_1 \cap A_2 = \emptyset, A_1 \cup A_2 = A$) gives rise to a perfect spectrum X.

Similarly, if one starts from some Banach algebra E of bounded functions of a set, and if c_0 denotes the closure of the functions with finite support, then $E/[c_0 \cap E]$ will have perfect spectrum provided $\forall f \in E: f(1-f) = 0$, $\#\{f = 1\} = +\infty \Rightarrow \exists h \in E: \forall \lambda, f(1 - \lambda h) \notin c_0$ which is satisfied in all conceivable applications.

In this case the duality with the space of non-atomic elements of the dual is separating in a strong sense: by the above result on the density of non-atomic probabilities one has

$$\|f\| = \inf\{\alpha \, | \, \{t \, | \, |f(t)| \geq \alpha\} \text{ is finite}\}$$
$$= \sup\{\langle \mu, f \rangle \, | \, \|\mu\| \leq 1, \, \mu \text{ non-atomic}\}.$$

2. The countably additive setup: Some properties of (weakly) σ-Stonian spaces

Definition. A weakly σ-Stonian space is a compact space where any two disjoint open Baire sets have disjoint closures. (The Baire σ-field is the σ-field generated by the continuous real-valued functions.)

For short, we will call totally disconnected spaces S_0-spaces, weakly σ-Stonian spaces S_1-spaces, σ-Stonian spaces S_2-spaces and Stonian spaces S_3-spaces.

Whenever X is compact, we call measures on X the elements of the dual of $C(X)$.

The following lemma gives some elementary properties, and gives equivalent definitions directly in terms of the algebra $C(X)$ or of the Boolean algebra of clopen sets.

Lemma 2.1. (a) $S_3 \Rightarrow S_2 \Rightarrow S_0 \& S_1$.

(b) *A compact X is an S_0-space iff the step functions (i.e., the subspace spanned by $\{f \in C(X) \mid f^2 = f\}$) are dense in $C(X)$.*

(c) *X is an $S_0 \& S_1$-space iff X is compact and for any two increasing sequences of clopen sets U_i and V_i, where $U_i \cap V_i = \emptyset$, there exists a clopen set O such that $\forall i$, $U_i \subseteq O$, $O \cap V_i = \emptyset$.*

(d) *X is an S_1-space (resp. $S_0 \& S_1$) iff X is compact and for any f in $C(X)$, there exists $h \in C(X)$ such that $fh = |f|$ (resp.: and $h^2 = 1$).*

(e) *Let X be an S_1-space, $K \subseteq X$ the support of some measure, $\bar{O} \subseteq X$ the closure of some open Baire set. There exists $f \in C(X)$, with $f \geq I(\bar{O})$, and $f = I(\bar{O})$ on K.*

Proof. Only (e) requires a proof.

Remark first that, if $\mathscr{F} = \{f \in C(X): f \geq I(\bar{O})\}$, then any sequence in $\mathscr{F}$ has a lower bound in $\mathscr{F}$. Indeed, if $V = \bigcup_n \{f_n < 1\}$, V is an open Baire set disjoint from O, so that $\bar{V} \cap \bar{O} = \emptyset$ — by compactness, there exists $f \in C(X)$, $1 \geq f \geq I(\bar{O})$, $f = 0$ on $\bar{V}$: thus $f \leq f_n$ $\forall n$.

Therefore, if μ is any tight probability on X, $\mu(\bar{O}) = \inf_{f \in \mathscr{F}} \mu(f) = \inf_{f_n \in \mathscr{F}} \mu(f_n)$ for some sequence f_n, and if $f \in \mathscr{F}$ satisfies $f \leq f_n$ $\forall n$, we get $\mu(\bar{O}) = \mu(f)$. Thus $\{f > I(\bar{O})\}$ is an open set of measure zero, thus disjoint from the support of μ. $\square$

Proposition 2.1. *Let X be a compact space, and let $\mathscr{B}$ denote a collection of universally measurable sets, closed under finite unions, such that every point* *has a basis of neighborhoods in $\mathcal{B}$. A set H of measures on X is weakly relatively compact if and only if, for any sequence of disjoint sets $B_i \in \mathcal{B}$,*

$$\mu(B_i) \to 0 \quad \text{uniformly on } H.$$

Proof. The criterion is classical for sequences of disjoint open sets O_i, and the necessity of the condition is obvious. Assume therefore there exists a sequence of disjoint open sets O_i that does not converge to zero uniformly on H: replacing the O_i's by a subsequence, there will also exist a sequence $\mu_i \in H$ and can $\varepsilon > 0$ such that, for all i, $\mu_i(O_i) > \varepsilon$ (eventually replacing H by $-H$).

Consider a compact set $K_i \subseteq O_i$ such that $\mu_i(A) > \varepsilon$ for any measurable set A satisfying $K_i \subseteq A \subseteq O_i$ (regularity of μ_i). For any $x \in K_i$, let $B_x \in \mathcal{B}$ be a neighborhood of x contained in O_i. Extract a finite subcovering B_{x_j} from the open covering of K_i by the interiors of the sets B_x, and let $B_i = \bigcup_j B_{x_j} : K_i \subseteq B_i \subseteq O_i, B_i \in \mathcal{B}$, so that $\mu_i(B_i) > \varepsilon$: thus the sufficiency of the condition. □

Theorem 2.1. *Let X be an S_1-space, M the space of all measures on X. Then any weak*-Cauchy sequence in M is weakly convergent, so that a set is weakly relatively compact if and only if it is weak*-relatively strictly semi-compact.*

Proof (following the lines of Grothendieck's proof for the Stonian case).

A weak*-Cauchy sequence (μ_n) is bounded, and therefore by Alaoglu's theorem weak*-convergent — we can further assume w.l.o.g. that it converges weak* to 0.

To show that it is weakly convergent, it is sufficient to show that it is weakly relatively compact: by Proposition 2.1, we have to show that if O_i denotes a sequence of disjoint open Baire sets,

$$\mu_n(\bar{O}_i) \to 0 \quad \text{uniformly in } n.$$

Denote by ρ_n the bounded additive set function defined on every subset I of the integers by

$$\rho_n(I) = \mu_n(\bar{O}_I),$$

where $\bar{O}_I$ denotes the closure of $\bigcup_{i \in I} O_i$. Since I is countable, $\bigcup_{i \in I} O_i$ is an open Baire set, and therefore $I \cap J = \emptyset \Rightarrow \bar{O}_I \cap \bar{O}_J = \emptyset$. Thus the additivity of every ρ_n.

Also $\sup_n \|\rho_n\| \le \sup_n \|\mu_n\| < +\infty$, and finally, by Lemma 2.1(e), the weak convergence to zero of μ_n implies $\rho_n(I) \to 0 \ \forall I \subseteq N$ (considering the support of $\sum_n |\mu_n| 2^{-n}$).

By a lemma of Phillips (1940), every bounded sequence of additive set functions ρ_n on the integers such that $\rho_n(I) \to 0 \; \forall I \subseteq N$ satisfies $\sum_i |\rho_n(i)| \to 0$: it follows immediately that $\mu_n(O_i)$ goes to zero uniformly in n.   □

Remark. This lemma of Phillips is obviously a particular case of Theorem 2.1 (as applied to the Stone-Čech compactification of the integers), because the mapping of a finitely additive set function to its countably additive part is obviously weakly continuous, and because weak convergence and norm convergence are equivalent for sequences in ℓ_1.

Corollary 2.1. *If X is S_1, any convergent sequence is finally constant.*

Proof. Apply Theorem 2.1 to the unit masses at the points of the sequence.   □

Corollary 2.2. *If X is perfect and S_1, every Baire set is perfect, and thus carries some non-atomic probability (if non-empty).*

Proof. Let F be a Baire set, and $x \in F$ isolated in F. Since x has a basis of open Baire neighborhoods, let O be a Baire neighborhood of x such that $O \cap F = \{x\}$: we have $\{x\} = O \cap F$ is a closed Baire set. By compactness, this implies x has a countable basis of neighborhoods O'_n.

Since X is perfect, every O'_n contains some point $x'_n \neq x$. Then the sequence x'_n would converge to x, contradicting Corollary 2.1.

Thus F is perfect. Let μ be any probability carried by F — say the unit mass at some point. Since $\nu(F) = \sup \nu(K)$, where K ranges over all compact Baire subsets of F, it follows that F contains a compact Baire — and thus perfect — subset K. By Section 1, K carries some non-atomic probability.   □

We denote by NA the non-atomic measures on X, by M the Banach space of all measures.

Corollary 2.3. *Assume X is perfect and S_1, $\mathcal{F}$ a separable sub σ-field of the Baire σ-field.*

(a) *Then any (countably additive) measure on $\mathcal{F}$ is the restriction to $\mathcal{F}$ of some $\mu \in$ NA.*

(b) *There exists a continuous mapping φ of X onto a compact metric space I such that $\mathcal{F}$ is the reciprocal image of some separable sub-σ-field of the Borel sets of I. If X is S_0, one can choose $I = \{0, 1\}^\infty$.*

Proof. Let F_i be a sequence of generators of $\mathscr{F}$. Each F_i, being a Baire set, is in the σ-field generated by some sequence f_{ij} of continuous functions — and those can be chosen to be indicators of clopen sets if X is S_0.

Unless X is S_0, let φ_n enumerate all those functions.

If X is S_0, let O_n enumerate all those clopen sets, and define inductively a sequence of clopen partitions π_n and clopen sets U_n, such that π_n is the partition generated by all U_i $(i \le n)$, $\#(\pi_n) = 2^n$, and every set O_n is a union of elements of π_n:

Let $\pi_0 = \{X\}$; for every atom A of π_n, let $k = \inf\{i \mid O_i \cap A \ne \emptyset$ and $A \backslash O_i \ne \emptyset\}$. Let $U_{n+1} \cap A = O_k \cap A$ if $k < \infty$. If $k = \infty$, use instead of O_k an arbitrary clopen subset O of A, such that $O \cap A \ne \emptyset$, $A \backslash O \ne \emptyset$. This defines U_{n+1} everywhere, and π_{n+1} is the partition generated by π_n and U_{n+1}. Finally, let φ_n be the indicator of U_n.

In any case, $\varphi = (\varphi_i)_{i=1}^{\infty}$ is a continuous mapping onto a compact metric space I, satisfying the requirements of (b). (Note that (b) does not use the S_1-hypothesis.)

We now show that any countably additive measure μ on a separable sub σ-field $\mathscr{F}$ of the Borel sets of a compact metric space I can be extended to all Borel sets. There is no loss in assuming μ to be a probability measure. The sequence of generators F_i determines a Borel measurable mapping f of I into $\{0, 1\}^{\infty}$.

If 1 denotes the identity mapping on I, then $\tilde{f} = (f, 1)$ is Borel-measurable and one to one from I into $\{0, 1\}^{\infty} \times I$. Since I is compact metric, it follows that the range of $\tilde{f}$ (i.e., the graph of f) is Borel measurable, and that $\tilde{f}$ is a Borel automorphism between I and $\tilde{f}(I)$. The measure μ can be thought of as being defined on the Borel sets of the analytic set $f(I)$. Since the graph of f is Borel-measurable, it follows that there exists a μ-measurable function g on $f(I)$ into the graph of f — and thus into I — such that $f \circ g$ is the identity of $f(I)$. The measure $\tilde{\mu}$ can be defined on I by $\tilde{\mu}(A) = \mu(g^{-1}(A))$ for any Borel set A in I. Obviously $\tilde{\mu}$ extends μ.

There only remains to show that, if φ denotes a continuous mapping from X onto I, and μ is a (probability) measure on I, then there exists a non-atomic measure ν on X, such that $\mu = \varphi(\nu)$. Decomposing μ into it's atomic and non-atomic parts, one reduces oneself to deal separately with the cases where μ is non-atomic and where μ is a point mass. In the first case μ, as a positive linear functional on a closed subspace of $C(X)$, can (Hahn–Banach) be so extended to the whole of $C(X)$, and thus to a regular Borel measure on X — forcibly non-atomic. If μ is a point mass at $x \in I$, $\varphi^{-1}(x)$ is a closed Baire set in X, and the result follows from Corollary 2.2. $\quad\square$

Corollary 2.4. *Assume X is perfect and S_1.*

(a) *Assume $H \subseteq C(X)$ is $\sigma(C(X), \mathrm{NA})$ relatively semi-compact (every sequence in H has a $\sigma(C(X), \mathrm{NA})$-cluster point in $C(X)$). Then the $\sigma(C(X), M)$-closed convex hull of H is $\sigma(C(X), M)$-compact, and every point in the closure of H is the limit of a $\sigma(C(X), M)$-convergent sequence in H. This statement is still true when $\sigma(C(X), M)$ is replaced by the topology of uniform convergence on weakly $(\sigma(M, M'))$-compact subsets of M.*

(b) *A $\sigma(C(X), \mathrm{NA})$-Cauchy sequence is pointwise convergent, and thus converges uniformly on $\sigma(M, M')$-compact subsets of M.*

(c) *The $\sigma(M, M')$-compact sets are also compact for the topology of uniform convergence on $\sigma(C(X), \mathrm{NA})$-relatively semi-compact sets and on $\sigma(C(X), \mathrm{NA})$-Cauchy sequences.*

Proof. For (a), the result would be well known and follow from compactness of X if we knew H to be $\sigma(C(X), M)$-relatively semi-compact. So assume some sequence $f_i \in H$ has no $\sigma(C(X), M)$-cluster point, and let $f \in C(X)$ be a $\sigma(C(X), \mathrm{NA})$-cluster point. The contradiction follows by applying Corollary 3 to the σ-field generated by f and the f_i's.

(b) also follows from applying Corollary 2.3 to the σ-field generated by the f_i's, and (c) is an immediate corollary of (a) and (b). □

Proposition 2.2 (Lyapunov, Dvoretzky–Wald–Wolfowitz). *Assume X is S_0 & S_1. If $\mu (=(\mu_1, \ldots, \mu_n))$ in any n-tuple in NA, then for any continuous partition of unity $(f_1, \ldots, f_n)$ on X, there exists a clopen partition $(O_1, \ldots, O_n)$ such that $\mu(O_i) = \mu(f_i) \; \forall i$.*

Proof. (In the "countably additive" case, i.e., X σ-Stonian and μ vanishes on closed Baire sets with empty interior, this is the Dvoretzky–Wald–Wolfowitz Theorem. We roughly follow classical lines of proof.)

Decomposing every coordinate of μ into its positive and negative parts, one reduces immediately the problem to the case where each μ_i is a probability.

We first prove that there exists $\forall \delta > 0$ an increasing mapping $t \to O_t$ from $[0, 1]$ to clopen sets such that $\forall i, \forall t, \forall s \neq t$,

$$\left| \ln \frac{\mu_i(O_t) - \mu_i(O_s)}{t - s} \right| \le \delta, \quad O_0 = \emptyset, \quad O_1 = X.$$

Let $\sigma = \sum \mu_i$. X being totally disconnected, the step functions in $\mathcal{I} = \{f \in C(X) \mid 0 \le f \le 1\}$ are dense in $\mathcal{I}$ (Lemma 2.1(b)). Also $\mathcal{I}$ is dense in $\{f \mid f \in L_1(\sigma), 0 \le f \le 1\}$. It follows that, for any σ-measurable set A, its indicator function is approximated in $L_1(\sigma)$ by a step function in $\mathscr{I}$, and therefore also by the indicator of a clopen set: $\forall \varepsilon, \forall A$ σ-measurable, $\exists O$ clopen such that $\sigma(A \triangle O) \le \varepsilon$.

(μ_i) being non-atomic, there exists a measurable set A such that $\mu_i(A) = \frac{1}{2} \forall i$. Let $O_{1/2}$ be a clopen set with $\mu(A \triangle O_{1/2}) \le \varepsilon$. $O_{1/2}$ and its complement are clopen sets of positive μ_i-measure $\forall i$, so we can continue the same argument conditionally on them and construct clopen sets $O_{1/4} \subseteq O_{1/2}$ and $O_{3/4} \supseteq O_{1/2}$ such that $\forall i, |\mu_i(O_{1/4}|O_{1/2}) - \frac{1}{2}| \le \varepsilon^2$ and $|\mu_i(O_{3/4}|O_1 \backslash O_{1/2}) - \frac{1}{2}| \le \varepsilon^2$. Going on in this way (using ε^3 at the third stage, and so on), one gets for every dyadic number t a clopen set O_t, such that $s \le t$ implies $O_s \le O_t$.

Let $u_k = 2^k \max_{i,j} [\mu_i(O_{(j+1)/2^k}) - \mu_i(O_{j/2^k})]$. By construction, we have $u_{k+1} \le (1 + 2\varepsilon^{k+1}) u_k, u_0 = 1$, so that

$$u_k \le \prod_{i=1}^{\infty} (1 + 2\varepsilon^i) \le \exp\left(\frac{2\varepsilon}{1-\varepsilon}\right).$$

And for any two dyadic numbers $s < t$, we have

$$\frac{\mu_i(O_t) - \mu_i(O_s)}{t - s} \le \exp\left(\frac{2\varepsilon}{1-\varepsilon}\right).$$

Similarly, if $v_k = 2^k \min_{i,j} [\mu_i(O_{(j+1)/2^k}) - \mu_i(O_{j/2^k})]$, we have $v_{k+1} \ge (1 - 2\varepsilon^{k+1}) v_k, v_0 = 1$, and therefore

$$v_k \ge \prod_{i=1}^{\infty} (1 - 2\varepsilon^i) \ge \exp\left(-3 \sum_{i=1}^{\infty} \varepsilon^i\right) = \exp\left(\frac{-3\varepsilon}{1-\varepsilon}\right),$$

for ε sufficiently small. Thus we get, for all dyadic numbers $s \ne t$, and for all i,

$$\left| \ln \frac{\mu_i(O_t) - \mu_i(O_s)}{t - s} \right| \le \frac{3\varepsilon}{1-\varepsilon}. \tag{1}$$

For any non dyadic s, $\bigcup_{t<s} O_t$ and $\bigcup_{t>s} (O_1 \backslash O_t)$ are disjoint open Baire sets, so, by Lemma 2.1(c), there exists a clopen set O_s containing the first and disjoint from the second; i.e., $t_1 < s < t_2 \Rightarrow O_{t_1} \subseteq O_s \subseteq O_{t_2}$. So we get an increasing mapping from $[0, 1]$ to clopen sets. By monotonicity, our inequality (1) extends now from dyadic pairs (s, t) to all pairs (s, t).

This proves our first assertion.

Next we prove, by induction on k, that we can have furthermore $\mu_i(O_t) = t \ \forall t, \forall i \le k$.

This is obvious for $k = 1$: get such a mapping O_t with $\frac{1}{2}\delta$ instead of δ, then re-index O_t by $\mu_1(O_t)$.

Assume now $\mu_i(O_t) = t \ \forall t, \forall_i \le k$, and consider $f(t) = \mu_{k+1}(O_t)$. If $\varphi(t) = f(t+\frac{1}{2}) - f(t) - \frac{1}{2}(t \in [0, \frac{1}{2}])$, then $\varphi(0) + \varphi(\frac{1}{2}) = 0$, and φ is continuous, so that, by Rolle's theorem, $\exists t_0 \in [0, \frac{1}{2}]$ such that $f(t_0 + \frac{1}{2}) = f(t_0) + \frac{1}{2}$.

Consider $O = O_{t_0+1/2} \backslash O_{t_0}$: O is clopen, satisfies $\mu_i(O) = \frac{1}{2} \ \forall i \le k+1$, and for other i's

$$\mu_i(O) = \frac{1}{2} \frac{\mu_i(O_{t+1/2}) - \mu_i(O_t)}{t + \frac{1}{2} - t}$$

satisfies therefore $\frac{1}{2} e^{-\delta} \le \mu_i(O) \le \frac{1}{2} e^{\delta}$.

We have shown that one can find a clopen set O such that $\mu_i(O) = \frac{1}{2}$ for $i \le k+1$, $|\mu_i(O) - \frac{1}{2}| \le \varepsilon$ for all other i's. Given this, we can repeat our preliminary construction using all the time such clopen sets, and get an increasing mapping $t \to O_t$ from $[0, 1]$ to clopen sets such that $O_0 = \emptyset$, $O_1 = X$, $\mu_i(O_t) = t$ for $i \le k+1$,

$$\left| \ln \frac{\mu_i(O_t) - \mu_i(O_s)}{t - s} \right| \le \delta$$

$\forall i, \forall t \ne s$.

Thus, by induction, we can get $\mu_i(O_t) = t \ \forall i, \forall t$.

Consider now continuous step functions f_i with $0 = f_0 \le f_1 \le \cdots \le f_{n-1} \le f_n = 1$: there exists a clopen partition π such that every f_i is constant on each element of π.

$\forall C \in \pi$, take U_t an increasing family of clopen sets $\subseteq C$, with $\mu_i(U_t \cap C) = t\mu_i(C) \ \forall t, \forall i$, and let $V_{i,C} = U_{f_i(C)}$. Then $V_i = \bigcup_{C \in \pi} V_{i,C}$ is clopen, and satisfies $\emptyset = V_0 \subseteq V_1 \subseteq \cdots \subseteq V_{n-1} \subseteq V_n = X$, with $\mu_i(V_j) = \mu_i(f_j) \ \forall i, j$.

Denote thus by O_n the set of all partitions of X into n clopen sets; by P_n the set of all continuous partitions of unity on X by n step functions; by $\bar{P}_n$ the set of all partitions of unity on X by n continuous functions.

We have just shown that $\mu(P_n) = \mu(O_n) \ \forall n, \forall \mu$ vector of non-atomic probability measures — and in particular that this set is convex, P_n being so.

We want still to show $\mu(\bar{P}_n) = \mu(P_n) (= \mu(O_n))$.

Let $x \in \mu(\bar{P}_n)$: x is in the closure of the convex set $\mu(P_n)$, so it lies in a face F of this closure: if $x = \mu(f_1, \ldots, f_n)$, $\exists a_{ij}$: $\sum_{i,j} a_{i,j} \mu_i(f_j)$ attains at f its maximum over $\bar{P}_n$. This sum can be written $\int (\sum g_j f_j) \, \mathrm{d}\sigma$, where $\sigma = \sum \mu_i$, and $g_j = \sum_i a_{ij} \, \mathrm{d}\mu_i / \mathrm{d}\sigma$.

The condition for f to be maximal is that σ a.s., $f_i(x) = 0$ on $\{x \mid g_i(x) < \max_j g_j(x)\}$. But $A_i = \{f_i > 0\}$ is an open Baire set, on which a.s. $g_i(x) \ge g_j(x) \ \forall j$. For all i, let A_i^ε be a clopen set with $\{f_i \ge \varepsilon\} \subseteq A_i^\varepsilon \subseteq \{f_i > 0\}$ (the existence of such A_i^ε follows because f_i is continuous and X totally disconnected).

Since $\sum f_i = 1$, we get if $\varepsilon \le n^{-1}, \bigcup_i A_i = X$—let for short $B_i = A_i^{\varepsilon}$: we found a clopen covering B_i, such that on B_i, σ a.s. $g_i(x) \ge g_j(x)$ $\forall j$, and outside $B_i f_i(x) \le \varepsilon$.

Thus we can find a continuous partition of unity by n step functions $\tilde{f}_i$, such that $|\tilde{f}_i - f_i| \le \varepsilon$ everywhere and $\tilde{f}_i = 0$ outside B_i — thus in particular $\tilde{f}_i = 0$ σ a.s. on $\{x \mid g_i(x) < \max g_j(x)\}$. Therefore $\mu(\tilde{f}_i) \in \mu(P_n)$ is in F, and approximates x: x lies in the closure of the (convex set) $\mu(P_n) \cap F$.

The same argument can therefore be repeated (in the hyperplane spanned by F) with this intersection instead of $\mu(P_n)$, and lead to a still lower-dimensional face.

Continuing this argument for lower and lower dimensional faces — or intersections — one gets to intersections of dimension 0, i.e., a single point in $\mu(P_n)$ such that x is in the closure of that singleton: $x \in \mu(P_n)$.

This finishes the proof. $\square$

In fact, we can get the following strengthening:

Denote by S_n the unit simplex of R^n, by C_n the space of all continuous mappings of X into S_n (the continuous partitions of unity), and by E_n the continuous mappings into the extreme points of S_n (the clopen partitions of X).

A bounded, affine mapping φ from C_n to R^k, is called non-atomic if $\forall x \in X$, if O_α denotes the decreasing net of clopen neighborhoods of x, and

$$f_{i,\alpha} = (\underbrace{1 - I_{O_\alpha}, 0, 0, \ldots, 0}_{i \text{ terms}}, I_{O_\alpha}, 0, \ldots, 0) \quad (f_{i,\alpha} \in E_n),$$

then $\forall i \ge 1$,

$$\varphi(f_{i,\alpha}) \to \varphi(1, 0, 0, \ldots, 0).$$

(As will be verified below, those are the mappings φ that can be represented by an $n \times k$ matrix of non-atomic measures on X, $\nu_{i,j}$, with $\varphi^j(f_1, \ldots, f_n) = \sum_{i=1}^{n} \nu_{i,j}(f_i)$.)

Theorem 2.2. *If φ denotes any bounded, affine, non-atomic mapping from C_n to R^k, and $a \in R^k$; then $C_n \cap \varphi^{-1}(a)$ is the closed convex hull of $E_n \cap \varphi^{-1}(a)$ in the uniform topology.*

Proof. Elementary algebra show that any affine mapping φ from C_n to R has a unique linear extension to $\tilde{C}^n$, the vector space of n-tuples of continuous functions f_i on X to R, with constant sum $\sum_{i=1}^{n} f_i$. $\tilde{C}^n$ is obviously isomorphic to $R \times \prod_{i=2}^{n} C(X, R)$, so that φ can be written as $\alpha(\sum_{i=1}^{n} f_i) +$ $\sum_{i=2}^{n} \varphi_i(f_i)$, where φ_i is a linear function on $C(X, R)$. The boundedness of φ on C_n immediately implies that each φ_i is bounded (setting $f_j = 0$ for $j \neq 1, i$), and therefore a measure on X. The non-atomicity hypothesis implies that this measure is non-atomic. If φ is not constant (in this case the theorem would result from Lemma 2.1(b)), one of the non-atomic measures $|\varphi_i|$ has strictly positive total mass, so that by rescaling there exists a non-atomic measure μ of total mass α: we have, using $\varphi_1 = 0$ and denoting by ν_i the non-atomic measure $\varphi_i + \mu$, $\varphi(f, \ldots, f_n) = \sum_i \nu_i(f_i)$.

Therefore our mapping φ can be written as $\varphi_j(f_1, \ldots, f_n) = \sum_{i=1}^{n} \nu_{i,j}(f_i)$ where $\nu_{i,j}$ denotes an $n \times k$ matrix of non-atomic measures on X.

Assume $f \in C_n \cap \varphi^{-1}(a)$, we have to show that f is in the closed convex hull of $E_n \cap \varphi^{-1}(a)$.

Denote by $\mu = (\mu_\ell)$ the vector of all non-atomic measures $\nu_{i,j}$: it will be sufficient to show that f is in the closed convex hull of $\{h \in E_n : \mu(h) = \mu(f)\}$ (μ is a bounded, affine mapping into $R^{n \times (n \times k)}$). If this was not so, we could use the Hahn–Banach theorem to find a bounded linear functional on $[C(X)]^n$, say ρ, that strongly separates f from that set:

$$\rho(f) < \inf\{\rho(h) \mid h \in E_n, \mu(h) = \mu(f)\}.$$

ρ can be written as an n-tuple of measures ρ_i on X:

$$\sum \rho_i(f_i) < \inf\{\sum \rho_i(h_i) \mid h \in E_n, \mu(h) = \mu(f)\}.$$

If we add the non-atomic parts of all ρ_i as additional coordinates to the vector μ, the right-hand member only increases, and the inequality remains due to only the atomic part of the ρ_i's: we can assume the ρ_i's to be purely atomic.

Further, since C_n is bounded, we can approximate (uniformly on C_n) the ρ_i's by ρ_i's with a finite number of atoms, and this will not destroy the strict inequality: we can assume all ρ_i's to be carried by a fixed finite set $\{x_1, x_2, \ldots, x_r\} \subseteq X$: there remains to show that f can, on this finite set, be approximated by convex combinations of elements of $\{h \in E_n : \mu(h) = \mu(f)\}$.

Choose a clopen partition O_i ($i = 1, \ldots, r$) of X, such that $x_i \in O_i$. Replace each coordinate of μ by the vector of its restrictions to every set O_i: it is sufficient to prove the property on each set O_i separately — and thus we are back to the case $r = 1$; i.e., we have to show that, at a fixed point $x_0 \in X, f(x_0)$ is in the convex hull of $\{h(x_0) \mid h \in E_n, \mu(h) = \mu(f)\}$. $f(x_0)$ is some point in S_n, and the $h(x_0)$'s are extreme points: thus we have, for each i, to show that if $f_i(x_0) > 0$, $\exists h \in E_n$, with $\mu(h) = \mu(f)$ and $h_i(x_0) = 1$.

It is sufficient to do the proof for $i = 1$.

To clarify maybe a bit further the situation, we can take an $\varepsilon > 0$ and a clopen neighborhood O of x_0, on which $f_1 \geq \varepsilon$.

Decomposing again μ in the vector of its restrictions to O and to its complement, we are reduced to prove the property separately on those two sets. On the complement of O, Proposition 2.2 gives us immediately the result, and so we are reduced to the case where $f_1 \geq \varepsilon > 0$ everywhere.

We follow now roughly the lines of the proof of Proposition 2.2. To begin with, we can assume that the μ_j's are probability measures.

The result would follow for f_i step functions as in the proof of Proposition 2.2, if we can show that there exists an increasing mapping $t \to O_t$ from $[0, 1]$ to clopen sets, such that $\forall j, \forall t, \mu_j(O_t) = t$, and such that $x_0 \in O_t \ \forall t > 0$.

We know from Proposition 2.2 that there exists a clopen set $O_{1/2}$ with $\mu(O_{1/2}) = \frac{1}{2}$. If $x_0 \notin O_{1/2}$, replace $O_{1/2}$ by its complement. Continue as in Proposition 2.2 the construction of O_t for $t > \frac{1}{2}$. Find also as in Proposition 2.2 a clopen set $O_{1/4} \subseteq O_{1/2}$, such that $\mu(O_{1/4}) = \frac{1}{4}$. If $x_0 \notin O_{1/4}$, replace $O_{1/4}$ by its complement in $O_{1/2}$, and continue as in Proposition 2.2 the construction of O_t for $\frac{1}{4} < t < \frac{1}{2}$. Continuing this process yields the desired mapping.

Thus the result is proved when the f_i's are step functions.

So if the result was not true, we would have $f_1 \geq \varepsilon$ everywhere, and for any $\varphi \in P_n$, such that $\mu(\varphi) = \mu(f)$, $\varphi_1(x_0) = 0$.

Let now $f_0' = \varepsilon$, $f_1' = f_1 - \varepsilon$, $f_i' = f_i$ for $i > 1$. We have a fortiori $\forall \varphi \in P_{n+1}$, such that $\mu(\varphi) = \mu(f')$,

$$\varphi_1(x_0) = 0.$$

Let now $g_i = f_i'/(1 - \varepsilon)$ for $i \geq 1$: we have $g_i \geq 0$, $\sum g_i = 1$, thus $g \in \bar{P}_n$, thus there exist (by Proposition 2.2) $\tilde{g}_i \in E_n$ with $\mu(\tilde{g}_i) = \mu(g_i)$. Let $h_0 = \varepsilon$, $h_i = (1 - \varepsilon)\tilde{g}_i$ for $i \geq 1$: we have $h \in P_{n+1}$, $\mu(h) = \mu(f')$, and $h_0(x_0) = \varepsilon > 0$, thus the contradiction.

This finishes the proof of the theorem. $\square$

It may be worthwhile to state the implication of our result in the more usual language of measure theory:

$(\Omega, \mathcal{B})$ denotes a set endowed with a σ-field $\mathcal{B}$ of subsets (somewhat less than a σ-field would be sufficient).

C_n denotes the set of all $\mathcal{B}$-measurable functions to the unit simplex S_n, and E_n the $\mathcal{B}$-measurable functions to the extreme points of S_n, i.e., the measurable partitions of Ω.

A collection $\mathcal{F} \subseteq \mathcal{B}$ is called a measurable filter if $A, B \in \mathcal{F} \Rightarrow \exists C \in \mathcal{F}, \emptyset \neq C \subseteq A \cap B$.

A measurable ultrafilter is a maximal (by inclusion) measurable filter, i.e., $\mathscr{F}$ satisfies in addition $\forall A \in \mathscr{B} \setminus \mathscr{F}, \exists B \in \mathscr{F}: A \cap B = \emptyset$. Algebraically, a measurable ultrafilter is a maximal collection on non-empty measurable sets, stable under finite intersections.

A measurable filter is ordered by inclusion ($A < B$ iff $A \supseteq B$).

A bounded affine mapping φ from C_n to R^k is called non-atomic if, for any measurable ultrafilter $\mathscr{U}, \forall i \geq 1$,

$$\varphi(\underbrace{1 - I(B), 0, 0, \ldots, 0, I(B), 0, \ldots, 0}_{i \text{ terms}}) \underset{\mathscr{U}}{\to} \varphi(1, 0, 0, 0, 0, \ldots, 0)$$

or, more explicitly, it is sufficient that $\forall i \geq 1, \forall \varepsilon > 0, \forall A \in \mathscr{U}, \exists B \in \mathscr{U}, B \subseteq A$:

$$\left| \varphi(\underbrace{1 - I(B), 0, 0, \ldots, 0, I(B), 0, \ldots, 0}_{i \text{ terms}}) - \varphi(1, 0, 0, \ldots, 0) \right| \leq \varepsilon. \qquad (2)$$

Another equivalent formulation, not involving ultrafilters, is the following: $\forall \varepsilon > 0, \forall i \geq 1$, and for any finite $\mathscr{B}$-measurable partition π, there exists a finer partition π' such that (2) holds $\forall B \in \pi'$. (It is even sufficient to check those conditions separately for each single coordinate of φ.)

Then, for any bounded, non-atomic, affine mapping φ from C^n to R^k, $\forall \varepsilon, \forall f \in C^n, \exists r, \exists \alpha \in S_r, \exists h_i \in E_n: \forall i$,

$$\varphi(h_i) = \varphi(f) \quad \text{and} \quad \sup_\omega \left| f(\omega) - \sum_{i=1}^r \alpha_i h_i(\omega) \right| \leq \varepsilon.$$

3. Integration of measures — measurability of the Hahn decomposition

Here we start moving towards a reinterpretation of the result of Aumann et al. (1983) according to which, if $\mathscr{I}$ denotes the Borel functions f on $[0, 1]$ with values in $[0, 1]$, then the extreme points of $\mathscr{I}$ are dense in $\mathscr{I}$ for the topology of convergence in P-measure of the $\int f \, d\mu$, for all probabilities P on the set NA_1^+ of non-atomic probability measures μ on $[0, 1]$ — where NA_1^+ is endowed with the "cylindrical σ-field", i.e., the coarsest σ-field for which all those functions $\int f \, d\mu$ are measurable.

In this paragraph, we want to establish the tools to dispense with the two restrictions that the underlying measurable space is (isomorphic to) $[0, 1]$ with the Borel sets, and that P is a measure on non-atomic probabilities, instead of on all non-atomic measures. Everything in this paragraph is certainly well-known — and is anyway easy.

We first aim at showing that, in the above model, P is a tight probability (i.e., regular Borel probability measure) when M is endowed with the weak* topology (by the continuous functions on $[0, 1]$).

In this whole paragraph, we use the following notations: K is a compact space, $C(K)$ (resp. $M(K)$) the space of continuous functions on K (resp. tight measures on K). $M(K)$ is endowed with the weak* topology. NA is the space of non-atomic elements of $M(K)$, and $M^+(K)$ (resp. NA^+) the positive cone of $M(K)$ (resp. NA).

Lemma 3.1. NA^+ *is a* G^δ *in* $M^+(K)$.

Proof. The set of measures whose largest atom has mass $\geq n^{-1}$ is closed (i.e., the mass of the largest atom is a u.s.c. function). $\square$

Lemma 3.2. *If K is metrisable, any probability measure on the cylindrical σ-field of $M^+(K)$ is tight.*

(The cylindrical σ-field is the coarsest σ-field for which the integrals of continuous functions are measurable. Tight of course means "a regular Borel probability measure in the weak* topology".)

Proof. $M^+(K)$ is locally compact, metrisable and separable.

$(\{\nu \mid \langle \nu, 1\rangle \leq \langle \mu, 1\rangle + 1\}$ is a compact neighborhood of μ, thus local compactness and σ-compactness. Every compact subset is metrisable, because if f_i is a dense sequence in $C(K)$, the $\langle \mu, f_i\rangle$ separate points. Thus $M^+(K)$ is also metrisable and separable.

The cylindrical σ-field is the σ-field generated by a sequence of continuous functions that separates points (take a dense sequence in $C(K)$): it follows from the Stone–Weierstrass theorem that any continuous function is the limit (uniformly on each compact set) of a sequence of cylindrically measurable functions — and thus is cylindrically measurable.

Because of metrisability and separability, the Borel σ-field coincides with the Baire σ-field (i.e., the σ-field generated by the continuous functions), and therefore with the cylindrical σ-field.

Furthermore, it is well known that any countably additive measure on the Borel sets of such a space is tight (if only because the stated properties imply that $M^+(K)$ is polish). $\square$

It follows from Lemmas 3.1 and 3.2 that we could as well have stated the result of Aumann et al. (1983) by requiring P to be a tight probability on the non-atomic probabilities. In this framework, we want now to dispense with the requirements of metrisability on K and that P be carried by $M^+(K)$.

Lemma 3.3. *The mapping* $H : \mu \to (\mu^+, \mu^-)$ *from* $M(K)$ *to* $M^+(K) \times M^+(K)$ *is universally measurable.*

(I.e., for any tight probability P on $M(K)$, and every $\varepsilon > 0$, there exists a compact set C in $M(K)$, with $P(C) \geq 1 - \varepsilon$, such that the restriction of H to C is continuous.)

Proof. P being tight, there is no loss in assuming P to have compact support. $\forall g \in C^+(K)$, $\langle \mu^+, g \rangle = \sup\{\langle \mu, f \rangle \mid f \in C(K), 0 \leq f \leq g\}$ (either by definition, or, if one uses the set-theoretic definition of μ^+, after a small verification).

Therefore $\langle \mu^+, 1 \rangle$, and similarly $\langle \mu^-, 1 \rangle$, are lower semi-continuous. Thus, they are measurable, and there exists a compact set C with $P(C) \geq 1 - \varepsilon$ such that $\langle \mu^+, 1 \rangle$ and $\langle \mu^-, 1 \rangle$ have continuous restrictions to C.

From now on μ ranges in C.

Now, for any $g \in C(K)$ with $0 \leq g \leq 1$, we have that $\langle \mu^+, g \rangle$ and $\langle \mu^+, 1 - g \rangle$ are lower semi-continuous, and add up to the continuous function $\langle \mu^+, 1 \rangle$: $\langle \mu^+, g \rangle$ is continuous, and this extends by linearity to all $g \in C(K)$. Similarly for $\langle \mu^-, g \rangle$: this means that H is continuous. □

Corollary 3.1. NA *is universally measurable in* $M(K)$.

Proof. $\mathrm{NA} = H^{-1}(\mathrm{NA}^+ \times \mathrm{NA}^+)$, and NA^+ is a $\mathscr{G}_\delta$, thus Borel. □

Lemma 3.4. *Any probability* P *on the cylindrical* σ-*field* (*i.e., the coarsest* σ-*field for which the* $\int f \, d\mu$, *where* f *ranges in* $C(K)$, *are measurable*) *of the unit ball of* $M(K)$ *corresponds uniquely to a tight probability on the unit ball of* $M(K)$.

Proof. By the Stone–Weierstrass theorem, any continuous function on the compact unit ball (Alaoglu's theorem) is cylindrically measurable, so that P corresponds uniquely to a positive linear functional on the space of continuous functions on this compact space. □

Lemma 3.5. *For real valued functions* f *on a topological space* S, *the definition of universal measurability used here* (*cf. Lemma* 3.3) *is equivalent to the more usual definition, that for any tight probability* P *on* S, *there exist two Borel functions* f_1 *and* f_2, *such that* $f_1 \leq f \leq f_2$, *and such that* $P[f_1 < f_2] = 0$.

Proof. The equivalence follows from Lusin's theorem. ☐

Lemma 3.6. *Let S and T be two topological spaces, $f : S \to T$ universally measurable, P a tight probability on S. Then for any universally measurable function g on T to another topological space R, $g \circ f$ is universally measurable from S to R. Further, the set function $f(P)$ defined on T by $\langle f(P), g \rangle = \langle P, g \circ f \rangle$ for all bounded real valued universally measurable g is a tight probability on T.*

Proof. Consider first the case where S is compact and f continuous: $f(S)$ is also compact, and the formula $\langle f(P), g \rangle = \langle P, g \circ f \rangle$ applied to continuous functions g on $f(S)$ defines uniquely a tight probability $f(P)$ on $f(S)$; and thus on T, $f(S)$ being Borel in T.

The equality goes over to all lower semi-continuous g (and $g \circ f$ is lower semi-continuous then) because if f_α is an increasing net of continuous functions, $\sup \int f_\alpha \, d\nu = \int (\sup f_\alpha) \, d\nu$ for any tight probability ν.

Further for all Borel g, $g \circ f$ is Borel and the equality still obtains, since Borel functions can be obtained from differences of lower-semi-continuous g by taking repeated limits of monotone sequences. Finally it also obtains for all universally measurable g, because if Borel functions g_1, g_2 are chosen such that $g_1 \le g \le g_2$ and such that $\int (g_2 - g_1) \, d(f(P)) = 0$, then $\int g \, d(f(P)) = \int g_i \, d(f(P)) = \int (g_i \circ f) \, dP$, so that the $g_i \circ f$ are Borel measurable functions satisfying $g_1 \circ f \le g \circ f \le g_2 \circ f$ and $\int (g_2 \circ f - g_1 \circ f) \, dP = 0$; thus $g \circ f$ is P-measurable, and $\int (g \circ f) \, dP = \int g \, d(f(P))$. Further, P being arbitrary, $g \circ f$ is universally measurable.

Thus our second assertion is established when S is compact and f continuous (and the first when furthermore R stands for the reals).

Now in general, let S_i be an increasing sequence of compact subsets of S, such that the restriction of f to each S_i is continuous, and such that $P(S_i) \to 1$.

If P_i denotes the restriction of P to S_i, then $f(P)$ is the limit of the increasing sequence of tight measures $f(P_i)$ on all universally measurable sets, and therefore $f(P)$ is tight also.

If g is universally measurable from T to R, and S_0 (resp. T_0) is a compact subset of S (resp. T) such that $P(S_0)$ and $[f(P)](T_0)$ are $\ge 1 - \varepsilon$, and such that f (resp. g) has continuous restriction to S_0 (resp. T_0), then $S_0 \cap f^{-1}(T_0)$ is a compact subset of S, with probability $\ge 1 - 2\varepsilon$, such that $g \circ f$ has a continuous restriction to it; thus $g \circ f$ is universally measurable. ☐

Lemma 3.7. *For any bounded universally measurable function f on K, $\langle \mu, f \rangle$ is universally measurable on $M(K)$ and for any tight probability P on a*

bounded subset of $M(K)$, we have $\int \langle \mu, f \rangle \, dP(\mu) = \int f \, d\bar{\mu}_P$, where $\bar{\mu}_P = \int \mu \, dP$
is the tight measure on K, i.e., continuous linear functional on $C(K)$, defined
by using the above equality for all continuous f. In other words, the set function
$\bar{\mu}_P$ defined for any universally measurable set A in K by $\bar{\mu}_P(A) = \int \mu(A) \, dP(\mu)$
is a tight measure on K.

Remark. $\bar{\mu}_P$ is called the barycenter of P.

Proof of Lemma 3.7. Assume first P is carried by $M^+(K)$. We have by
definition $\int \langle \mu, f \rangle \, dP(\mu) = \int f \, d\bar{\mu}$ for $f \in C(K)$.

Therefore, for f lower semi-continuous on K, $\langle \mu, f \rangle$ is lower semi-
continuous on $M^+(K)$ and we keep the equality.

Therefore, if f is bounded Borel on K, $\langle \mu, f \rangle$ is Borel on $M^+(K)$ and we
still keep the equality.

Thus, if f is universally measurable on K, choose f_1, f_2 Borel measurable,
$f_1 \leq f \leq f_2$, such that $\bar{\mu}(f_2 > f_1) = 0$: we have $\int f \, d\bar{\mu} = \int f_i \, d\bar{\mu} = \int \langle \mu, f_i \rangle \, dP(\mu)$
so that $\langle \mu, f_1 \rangle$ and $\langle \mu, f_2 \rangle$ are two Borel functions with the same integral,
and $\langle \mu, f_1 \rangle \leq \langle \mu, f \rangle \leq \langle \mu, f_2 \rangle$: it follows that $\langle \mu, f \rangle$ is P-integrable and that
we keep the equality. This being true for any tight probability P, it follows
that $\langle \mu, f \rangle$ is universally measurable on $M^+(K)$.

In the general case now, we know that the mappings $\mu \to \mu^+$ on $M(K)$
and $\nu \to \langle \nu, f \rangle$ on $M^+(K)$ are universally measurable, so is their composition
$\mu \to \langle \mu^+, f \rangle$ and similarly $\mu \to \langle \bar{\mu}, f \rangle$. Therefore $\mu \to \langle \mu, f \rangle$ is universally
measurable as the difference of two universally measurable functions (the
difference is a continuous — and thus universally measurable — map from
R^2 to R), and $\int \langle \mu, f \rangle \, dP(\mu) = \int \langle \mu^+, f \rangle \, dP(\mu) - \int \langle \bar{\mu}, f \rangle \, dP(\mu)$ for any
bounded universally measurable f and any tight probability P on the unit
ball.

Therefore, if P^+ (resp. P^-) denotes the distribution of μ^+ (resp. μ^-)
under P, we still have

$$\int \langle \mu, f \rangle \, dP(\mu) = \int \langle \nu, f \rangle \, dP^+(\nu) - \int \langle \nu, f \rangle \, dP^-(\nu) = \langle \nu_{P^+}, f \rangle - \langle \nu_{P^-}, f \rangle$$

because (Lemma 3.6) P^+ and P^- are tight probabilities (on a bounded
subset of $M^+(K)$), and because the lemma is already proved on $M^+(K)$.

Thus there exists a tight measure $\mu_P = \nu_{P^+} - \nu_{P^-}$ on K such that, for all
bounded universally measurable f,

$$\int \langle \mu, f \rangle \, dP(\mu) = \langle \mu_P, f \rangle.$$

This finishes the proof of the lemma. $\square$

Remarks. (1) Corollary 3.1 and Lemma 3.4 show that the tight probabilities on bounded subsets of NA could also be defined by saying that they are probabilities on the cylindrical σ-field of a bounded subset of $M(K)$, such that NA has probability 1 for their regular Borel extension.

(2) In Lemmas 3.4–3.7, the term probability can obviously be replaced by "measure", decomposing this into positive and negative parts and rescaling them. (The term "measure" in this paper means bounded measure.)

Corollary 3.2. *For any tight measure P on a bounded subset of* NA, *the barycenter $\bar{\mu}_P$ of P is in* NA.

Proof. $\bar{\mu}_P \in M(K)$ by Lemma 3.7, and by definition $\bar{\mu}_P(\{x\}) = 0 \; \forall x \in K$. $\quad\square$

Corollary 3.3. *For any $\sigma(\mathrm{NA}, C(K))$-compact set C, its $\sigma(\mathrm{NA}, C(K))$-closed convex circled hull is $\sigma(\mathrm{NA}, C(K))$-compact.*

Proof. It is equivalent to show that its weak* closed convex circled hull $\bar{C}$ in $M(K)$ is contained in NA ($\bar{C}$ is weak* compact by Alaoglu's theorem). But $\bar{C}$ is the set of all barycenters of tight measures P on C with $\|P\| \leq 1$, so that the result follows from Corollary 3.2. $\quad\square$

To use the tightness property of measures on NA, we need criteria for $\sigma(\mathrm{NA}, C(K))$-compactness.

Proposition 3.1. (a) *A set C in* NA *is $\sigma(\mathrm{NA}, C(K))$ relatively compact if and only if C is bounded and $\forall \varepsilon > 0, \forall$ finite open covering $(O_i)_{i=1}^n$ of K, $\exists (f_j)_{j=1}^r \in C(K), 0 \leq f_j \leq 1$, such that*
(1) $\forall j \; \exists i : f_j$ *vanishes on the complement of O_i (and $\forall k$, either $f_j = 0$ on O_k or $f_j = 1$ on an open subset of O_k);*
(2) $K = \bigcup_j interior\{f_j = 1\}$; *or*
(2 bis) $\max_j f_j \geq \delta$ *where $\delta > 0$ does not depend on ε;*
(3) $|\langle \mu, f_j \rangle| \leq \varepsilon \; \forall j, \forall \mu \in C$.

(b) *If $C \subseteq \mathrm{NA}^+$, a necessary and sufficient condition is already that $\forall \varepsilon > 0, \exists (O_i)_{i=1}^n$ an open covering of K such that $\mu(O_i) \leq \varepsilon \; \forall \mu \in C, \forall i$.*

(c) *If K is totally disconnected, the open covering in (b) can be taken a clopen partition and the criterion sub (a) becomes:*

$\forall \varepsilon > 0, \forall$ *clopen partition O_i of K, there exists a finer clopen partition $\pi = (U_j)$ of K and π-measurable functions f_j on K with values in $[0, 1]$, such that*
(1) $\forall j$, *if $U_j \subseteq O_i$, then $I(U_j) \leq f_j \leq I(O_i)$;*
(2) $|\langle \mu, f_j \rangle| \leq \varepsilon \; \forall j, \forall \mu \in C$.

Remark. In the case where one has $(\Omega, \mathscr{F})$, a set endowed with a field of subsets, and $C(K)$ is taken as representing the space B of bounded measurable functions on $(\Omega, \mathscr{F})$, K is totally disconnected, and the clopen partitions of K correspond to the finite $\mathscr{F}$-measurable partitions of Ω. Thus the criteria sub (c) give then criteria for weak*-compactness in the non atomic elements of the dual of B, directly in terms of $(\Omega, \mathscr{F})$.

Proof of Proposition 3.1. By Corollary 3.3, it is sufficient to characterize $\sigma(\mathrm{NA}, C(K))$-compact convex circled sets C.

(a) For any $x \in K$, denote by $F = F_x$ the (convex) set of continuous functions on K, with values in $[0, 1]$, that vanish outside of any O_i containing x and on every O_k such that x is not in the closure of O_k and that are equal to 1 on some neighborhood of x. We claim that $\inf_{\mu \in F} \sup_{\mu \in C} |\langle \mu, f \rangle| = 0$. Indeed, C being circled, we have $\sup_{\mu \in C} |\langle \mu, f \rangle| = \sup_{\mu \in C} \langle \mu, f \rangle$. Now C is compact convex, F is convex, and $\langle \mu, f \rangle$ is affine in each variable and continuous on C for each $f \in F$: by the min-max theorem, we have therefore

$$\inf_{f \in F} \sup_{\mu \in C} |\langle \mu, f \rangle| = \sup_{\mu \in C} \inf_{f \in F} \langle \mu, f \rangle.$$

But for each $\mu \in C$, we have by non-atomicity,

$$\inf_{f \in F} \langle \mu, f \rangle \le \inf_{f \in F} \langle \mu^+, f \rangle = \mu^+(\{x\}) = 0.$$

Therefore, $\forall \varepsilon, \forall x \in K, \exists f_x \in F_x$,

$$|\langle \mu, f_x \rangle| < \varepsilon \quad \forall \mu \in C.$$

The necessity of the criterion follows now by extracting a finite open subcovering from the open covering $(U_x)_{x \in K}$ where $U_x = \mathrm{interior}\{f_x = 1\}$.

Assume on the other hand μ is in a set satisfying such a condition, and that μ has an atom at x. Choose ε much smaller than $\delta |\mu(\{x\})|$, and an open neighborhood V of x such that $|\mu|(V \backslash \{x\})$ is much smaller than ε. Consider the open covering $\{O_i\} = \{v, K \backslash \{x\}\} : \exists f_j : f_j(x) \ge \delta$, and thus $f_j = 0$ outside V. Therefore $|\langle \mu, f_j \rangle| \ge \delta |\mu(\{x\})|$ would be larger than ε. Thus the sufficiency of the condition.

(b) When V ranges over the decreasing net of closed neighborhoods of $x \in K$, $\mu(V)$ forms a decreasing net of upper semi-continuous functions on the compact set C, and converges, by non atomicity, pointwise to zero. Therefore, by Dini's theorem, it converges uniformly to zero. The necessity of the condition follows now immediately, and the sufficiency is obvious.

As for (c), remark only that any open covering is refined by some clopen partition, and, for the proof of necessity of (a), restrict further F_x to consist only of step functions. $\quad\square$

Remarks. (1) The open sets in the statement of Proposition 3.1 can be chosen to be members of any base of the topology. In particular, they can be assumed to be open Baire sets.

(2) Since the condition for compactness in NA^+ is so much simpler and stronger than the condition for compactness in NA, there is great advantage in being able to reduce a problem on measures on NA to measures on NA^+.

We end this section by doing this for the topology (on linear functionals on NA) of convergence in measure for any tight measure on NA — as announced in the beginning of the section.

Proposition 3.2. *Denote by F the space of linear functionals on NA of the type $\langle \mu, f \rangle$, where f is a bounded, universally measurable function on K.*

(a) *For any measure P_0 on NA, there exists a probability P_1 on NA_1^+ (the set of probabilities in NA) and a probability P_2 with compact support on NA^+ so that, on F, the topologies of convergence in measure for P_1 and P_2 are equivalent and stronger than for P_0. If P_0 is carried by NA^+, the three are equivalent.*

(b) *On F, the topology of convergence in measure for any measure on NA is equivalent to the topology of convergence in measure for all probabilities with compact support in NA_1^+.*

Remark. The elements of F are universally measurable on NA by Lemma 3.7, so the topologies make sense.

Proof of Proposition 3.2. Replacing P_0 by its absolute value $|P_0|$ and rescaling this does not change the topology of convergence in measure, so we can assume P_0 to be a probability.

Let $Q = H(P_0)$, a tight probability on $NA^+ \times NA^+$ (Lemmas 3.3 and 3.6): for any positive universally measurable function $\varphi(\cdot, \cdot)$ on $NA^+ \times NA^+$, we have $\int \varphi(\mu, \nu) \, dQ(\mu, \nu) = \int \varphi(\mu^+, \mu^-) \, dP_0(\mu)$.

Thus, if f_1, f_2 are bounded universally measurable functions on K,

$$d_0(f_1, f_2) = \int \min(1, |\langle \mu, f_1 - f_2 \rangle|) \, dP_0(\mu)$$

$$\leq \int [\min(1, |\langle \mu^+, f_1 - f_2 \rangle|) + \min(1, |\langle \mu^-, f_1 - f_2 \rangle|)] \, dP_0(\mu)$$

$$= \int \min(1, |\langle \mu, f_1 - f_2 \rangle|) \, dQ(\mu, \nu)$$

$$+ \int \min(1, |\langle \nu, f_1 - f_2 \rangle|) \, dQ(\mu, \nu).$$

Therefore if $\bar{Q}$ denotes the probability on NA^+ which is the average of the distributions under Q of μ and v, we get

$$d_0(f_1, f_2) \le 2 \int \min(1, |\langle \mu, f_1 - f_2 \rangle|) \, \mathrm{d}\bar{Q}(\mu).$$

Thus we are reduced to prove our case when $P_0 \, (= \bar{Q})$ is a probability on NA^+. We can assume without loss of generality that $P_0(\{0\}) = 0$.

The mapping $n : \mu \to n(\mu) = \mu/\langle \mu, 1 \rangle$ is continuous from $\mathrm{NA}^+ \backslash \{0\}$ to NA_1^+, thus measurable.

Let Q_n denote the restriction of P_0 to $\{\mu \in \mathrm{NA}^+ \, | \, 2^{n-1} < \langle \mu, 1 \rangle \le 2^n\}$.

$\langle \mu, f_\alpha \rangle$ converges to $\langle \mu, f \rangle$ in measure (P_0) if and only if it converges in measure $(Q_n) \, \forall n \in Z$. But obviously convergence in measure (Q_n) is equivalent to convergence in measure $[n(Q_n)]$. Thus convergence in probability (P_0) is equivalent to convergence in probability $(n(P_0)) \, (n(P_0) = \sum_{-\infty}^{+\infty} n(Q_n))$. Letting $P_1 = n(P_0)$ the first part of our result is proved.

P_1 being tight on NA_1^+, let C_i denote a sequence of disjoint $\sigma(\mathrm{NA}_1^+, C(K))$-compact sets, such that $P_1(\bigcup_i C_i) = 1$. Choose $1 \ge \varepsilon_i > 0$, $\lim_{i \to \infty} \varepsilon_i = 0$, and denote by $\tilde{\varepsilon}_i$ the multiplication by ε_i in NA.

Obviously $[\{0\} \cup \bigcup_i \tilde{\varepsilon}_i(C_i)] = \bar{C}$ is $\sigma(\mathrm{NA}^+, C(K))$-compact in the unit ball and if Q_i denotes the restriction of P_1 to C_i, convergence in measure (P_1) is equivalent to convergence in measure (Q_i) for all i (this proves (b)), thus to convergence in measure $\tilde{\varepsilon}_i(Q_i)$ for all i, thus to convergence in probability $P_2 = \sum_i \tilde{\varepsilon}_i(Q_i)$. And P_2 has compact support $\bar{C}$, so the proposition is proved. $\quad\square$

4. The topology of convergence in measure on the dual

Lemma 4.1. *Denote by E, F two vector spaces in duality, $\mathcal{K}$ a covering of F by $\sigma(F, E)$ compact, convex, balanced sets such that $K_1, K_2 \in \mathcal{K} \Rightarrow \forall \lambda, \mu, \lambda K_1 + \mu K_2 \in \mathcal{K}$. Let also f be a continuous strictly increasing function on $R_+, f(0) = 0$. Then the following definitions of a vector topology on E are equivalent*:

(1) *0 is in the closure of $A \subseteq E$ iff 0 is in the closed convex hull of $\bar{A} = \{f(|\langle x, \cdot \rangle|) \in C(F) \, | \, x \in A\}$ for the topology of uniform convergence on the elements of $\mathcal{K}$.*

(2) *The sets $O_\mu = \{x : \int f(|\langle x, y \rangle|) \, \mathrm{d}\mu(y) \le 1\}$, where μ ranges over all positive measures on sets in $\mathcal{K}$, form a basis of neighbourhoods of 0.*

Further, whatever be f, this topology coincides on bounded subsets of E with the topology of convergence in measure for any $\mathcal{K}$-tight measure on F.

Proof. For any $K \in \mathcal{K}$, 0 is in the closure in $C(K)$ of the convex hull of $\bar{A}$ iff 0 is in the weak closure in $C(K)$ of this convex hull. This convex hull being $\subseteq C^+(K)$, this will happen if and only if for any positive tight measure μ on K, $\inf\{\langle\mu, \varphi\rangle \,|\, \varphi \in$ convex hull of $\bar{A}\} = 0$. But this is obviously equivalent to $\inf\{\langle\mu, \varphi\rangle \,|\, \varphi \in \bar{A}\} = 0$, i.e., $\inf_{x \in A} \int f(|\langle x, y\rangle|) \,d\mu(y) = 0$.

Obviously the class $\mathcal{V}$ of sets mentioned sub (2) forms a system of neighborhoods of zero for some vector topology on E; the only point really to check is that $U \in \mathcal{V} \Rightarrow \exists V \in \mathcal{V}: V + V \subseteq U$, but this follows from

$$\int f(|\langle x_1 + x_2, y\rangle|) \,d\mu(y) \leq \int f(|\langle x_1, y\rangle| + |\langle x_2, y\rangle|) \,d\mu(y)$$

$$\leq \int [f(|\langle x_1, 2y\rangle|) + f(|\langle x_2, 2y\rangle|) \,d\mu(y)$$

$$= \int f(|\langle x_1, z\rangle|) \,d\mu'(z) + \int f(|\langle x_2, z\rangle|) \,d\mu'(z).$$

Thus there only remains to check that, on bounded subsets of E, this topology coincides with the topology of convergence in measure for any $\mathcal{K}$-tight measure on F.

But, if x_α is a bounded directed set in E, then $f(|\langle x_\alpha, \cdot\rangle|)$ is uniformly bounded on every $K \in \mathcal{K}$, and as we have just shown the convergence to zero of x_α is equivalent to the convergence to zero of $f(|\langle x_\alpha, \cdot\rangle|)$ in μ-measure for every tight measure μ with support in $\mathcal{K}$. But this is obviously equivalent to the same statement when f is the identity, and also equivalent when considering any $\mathcal{K}$-tight positive increase μ (i.e., $\mu(F) = \sup_{K \in \mathcal{K}} \mu(K)$). $\square$

Definition. To avoid the arbitrariness in the choice of f, and since anyway we are going to work mainly on bounded sets of E, we will define $\mathcal{T}$ as the strongest locally convex topology on E that coincides on bounded sets with the topology of convergence in measure for any $\mathcal{K}$-tight measure μ on F.

Lemma 4.2. *Any of the topologies mentioned in Lemma* 4.1 *is weaker than* $\mathcal{T}$.

Proof. It will be sufficient to show that, for any continuous strictly increasing function f on R_+, with $f(0) = 0$, there exists a continuous, convex, strictly increasing function f' on R_+, with $f'(0) = 0$, such that f' defines a finer topology than f, because the topology defined by f' is obviously locally convex.

We first show that $f \leq f_1 + f_2$, where f_2 is continuous, increasing, concave and bounded and f_1 is convex, continuous, increasing, zero in a neighborhood of zero.

Let $\varphi_x(y) = A_x(y - x) + B_x$ such that $\varphi_x(x) = f(x)$, $\varphi_x(\frac{1}{2}x) = 0$, thus $B_x = f(x)$, $A_x(-\frac{1}{2}x) + f(x) = 0 \Rightarrow A_x = (\frac{1}{2}x)f(x)$, thus $\varphi_x(y) = (2y/x - 1)f(x)$, and let $f_1(y) = \sup_{x \geq 1} \varphi_x^+(y)$: then $f_1(y) \leq \sup_{1 \leq x \leq 2y} \varphi_x(y) \leq (2y - 1)f(2y) < +\infty$, and f_1 is convex and continuous, increasing, etc. Further, for $y \geq 1$, $f_1(y) \geq \varphi_y^+(y) = f(y)$, so that $(f - f_1)(y) \leq 0$ for $y \geq 1$. Thus, if f_2 denotes the concavification of $(f - f_1)^+$, f_2 also satisfies all required properties.

Let now $V_{f,\mu} = \{x \mid \int f(|\langle x, y \rangle|) \, d\mu(y) \leq 1\}$. We have

$$V_{f,\mu} \supseteq V_{f_1, 2\mu} \cap V_{f_2, 2\mu} \supseteq V_{f_1, 2\mu} \cap \left\{ x \mid \int |\langle x, y \rangle| \, d\mu(y) \leq f_2^{-1}(1) \right\}$$

by the concavity of f_2 (Jensen's inequality), and therefore $V_{f,\mu} \supseteq V_{f_1, \tilde{\mu}} \cap V_{1, \tilde{\mu}}$, where 1 is the identity mapping and $\tilde{\mu} = 2 \max(1, 1/f_2^{-1}(1))\mu$. Therefore,

$$V_{f,\mu} \supseteq V_{1 + f_1, \tilde{\mu}} \supseteq V_{\alpha f_1(x) + \alpha x, \mu} \quad \text{for some } \alpha > 0.$$

This proves our lemma. Remark however that we could have refined it — replacing among others the identity mapping by some convex function, like x^2 — and get that f' can be assumed to increase slower on some interval $[0, A]$ than any prescribed strictly convex increasing function. In particular, one can assume without loss f' to be differentiable, and its derivative an automorphism of R_+. □

Lemma 4.3. $\mathcal{T}$ *is the strongest locally convex topology on E that coincides on bounded sets with the topology of uniform convergence on the sets $B_\mu \subseteq F$ of the form $B_\mu = \{x \in F \mid \exists \nu \text{ measure on } F, |\nu| \leq \mu, x \text{ is the barycenter of } \nu\}$, where μ ranges over all tight probabilities on sets $K \in \mathcal{K}$.*

Proof. We know that $\mathcal{T}$ is the strongest locally convex topology that coincides on bounded sets with the topology whose neighborhoods of zero are of the form

$$V = \left\{ x \mid \int |\langle x, y \rangle| \, d\mu(y) \leq 1 \right\},$$

where μ is a tight probability on some $K \in \mathcal{K}$.

But $V = \{x \mid \int \langle x, y \rangle f(y) \, d\mu(y) \leq 1 \; \forall f \text{ measurable}, |f| \leq 1\}$ by definition of the L-norm, equality is achieved when $f(y) = \text{sign}\langle x, y \rangle$. This means (Radon-Nikodym theorem) that $V = \{x \mid \langle x, y \rangle \leq 1 \; \forall y \in B_\mu\}$.

Thus the sets B_μ are the polars of the neighborhoods of zero, i.e., the equicontinuous sets. □

Lemma 4.4. *The topology $\mathcal{T}$ is the topology of uniform convergence on the subsets B of F, which are strong limits of sets B_μ (i.e., for every strong neighborhood of zero V in F, there exists μ such that $B \subseteq B_\mu + V$).*

In other words, those sets are the $\mathcal{T}$-equicontinuous subsets of F, i.e., the polars of the $\mathcal{T}$-neighborhoods of zero.

Proof. Since the bounded sets V^0 in E are the polars of the neighborhoods V of O in F with the strong topology, and since the $\mathcal{T}$-equicontinuous sets B in F are the polars of the $\mathcal{T}$-neighborhoods of zero B^0 in E, which are by definition of $\mathcal{T}$ those closed, convex, balanced sets whose intersection with every bounded set V^0 contains the intersection with V^0 of some B_μ^0 (Lemma 4.3), B will be equicontinuous iff $\forall V, \exists \mu : B^0 \cap V^0 \supseteq B_\mu^0 \cap V^0$.

It is a simple exercise with polars to show that this is equivalent with: $\forall V, \exists \mu : B \subseteq B_\mu + V$. (Indeed $(B_\mu + V)^0 \subseteq B_\mu^0 \cap V^0$, so that, if $B_\mu^0 \cap V^0 \subseteq B^0$, then $B \subseteq B_\mu + V$. On the other hand $(B_\mu + V)^0 \supseteq \frac{1}{2}(B_\mu^0 \cap V^0)$ shows that, if $B \subseteq B_\mu + V$, then $(\frac{1}{2}B)^0 \cap V^0 \supseteq B_\mu^0 \cap V^0$, so that $\frac{1}{2}B$, and thus B, is equicontinuous.) $\square$

Consider now the case where E denotes the space of bounded universally measurable functions on some compact space S, and F the space of non atomic, tight measures on S. Denote by $\mathcal{K}_0$ all multiples of closed convex balanced hulls of $\sigma(\text{NA}, C(K))$-compact sets in NA_1^+ and by $\mathcal{K}_1$ all $\sigma(\text{NA}, C(K))$-compact convex balanced sets.

The previous lemmas do not apply as they stand; because neither the sets in $\mathcal{K}_0$ nor those in $\mathcal{K}_1$ are $\sigma(F, E)$-compact.

But the only point that really fails is the equivalence between the two topologies in Lemma 4.1: the first is stronger than the second, because compactness was used to prove the reverse implication. All the rest applies, essentially because Lemma 3.7 allows to integrate elements of E on F, and shows furthermore that barycenters in F are the same when computed on E as when computed on $C(S)$; thus the barycenters of Lemma 4.4 can be thought of as being defined in terms of $C(S)$.

Further, Proposition 3.2 shows that $\mathcal{K}_0$ and $\mathcal{K}_1$ will define the same topology, in fact, it shows that one can use in Lemma 4.4 only those sets B_μ, that arise from some positive measure μ with compact support in NA_1^+. We will therefore still call $\mathcal{T}$ this topology on E.

Remark also that, by Proposition 3.2, $\mathcal{T}$ will be the strongest locally convex topology on E that coincides on bounded sets with the topology of convergence on measure for any tight measure on NA.

We restate our results: let S be a compact space, U_S the space of bounded universally measurable functions on S, NA the space of non-atomic tight measures on S, endowed with the weak*-topology $\sigma(\text{NA}, C(S))$.

Denote by $\mathcal{B}_0$ the class of subsets of NA of the form $B_Q = \{\int \nu \, dP(\nu) \, | \, |P| \le Q\}$ where Q ranges over all positive tight measures with compact support in NA_1^+.

Let $\mathcal{B}_1$ denote the sets B in NA, such that $\inf_Q \sup_{\nu \in B} d(\nu, B_Q) = 0$. Then:

Corollary 4.1. $\mathcal{B}_1$ *is the class of all equicontinuous sets for the strongest locally convex topology on* U_S, *say* $\mathcal{T}$, *that coincides on bounded sets with the topology of convergence in measure for any tight measure on* NA. $\square$

Corollary 4.2. (a) *The closed, convex, balanced hull of any set in* $\mathcal{B}_1$ *is in* $\mathcal{B}_1$, *the union of any two sets in* $\mathcal{B}_1$ *is in* $\mathcal{B}_1$, *as is any scalar multiples of a set in* $\mathcal{B}_1$.

(b) *Any set* $\tilde{B}$ *such that* $\inf_{B \in \mathcal{B}_1} \sup_{\nu \in B} d(\nu, B) = 0$ *is in* $\mathcal{B}_1$. $\square$

Thus from now on we will consider, w.l.o.g., only closed, convex, balanced sets in $\mathcal{B}_1$.

Corollary 4.3. (a) *Any set* B *in* $\mathcal{B}_1$ *is weakly compact* (*i.e., for* $\sigma(\text{NA}, \text{NA}')$ *or* $\sigma(M(S), M'(S))$). *In particular,* $\exists \mu \in \text{NA}_1^+$, *such that* $B \subseteq L_i(\mu)$.

(b) *Any* (*norm-*) *compact, convex balanced set in* NA *is in* $\mathcal{B}_1$.

Proof. (b) follows immediately from the fact that any finite set in NA is contained in some $B \in \mathcal{B}_0$.

(a) Being closed and convex, B is weakly closed, so it is sufficient to show that B is weakly relatively compact.

Approximate B up to ε in norm by some set B_Q. We have to show, for instance, that if O_i is a sequence of disjoint open sets, $\mu(O_i) \to 0$ uniformly on B. But

$$\limsup_{i \to \infty} \sup_{\mu \in B} |\mu(O_i)| \le \varepsilon + \limsup_{i \to \infty} \sup_{\mu \in B_Q} |\mu(O_i)|$$

$$= \varepsilon + \lim_{i \to \infty} \sup_{|f| \le 1} \left| \int \nu(O_i) f(\nu) \, dQ(\nu) \right|$$

$$= \varepsilon + \lim_{i \to \infty} \|\nu(O_i)\| L_{1(Q)} = \varepsilon$$

by the dominated convergence theorem (and by Lemma 3.7). ε being arbitrary, the result follows. $\square$

However, given an M-space E, one could find many compact spaces S such that E can be identified with some subspace of U_S, and each of those would define a different topology $\mathcal{T}$ on E, for which the extreme points of the unit ball would be dense in the unit ball. It is not at all clear whether an optimal such choice exists. The only canonical possibility seems to be to take E as $C(S)$ itself — but such a choice may induce such a strong weak*-topology on NA, that there would remain much less tight measures on NA.

We now aim at removing those difficulties.

Lemma 4.5. *Let S be compact, E a closed algebra of universally measurable functions on S, $C(S) \subseteq E$. NA, the non-atomic elements of the dual of $C(S)$, is identified canonically with the corresponding subspace of $F = E'$, the dual of E. Denote by F_1^+ the set of non-atomic, positive elements of norm 1 in F.*

For any measure Q with compact support on NA_1^+, $\sigma(\mathrm{NA}_1^+, C(S))$, there exists a measure $\tilde{Q}$ with compact support on F_1^+, $\sigma(F, E)$, such that $B_Q = B_{\tilde{Q}}$.

Proof. For each n, denote by π_n a finite covering of S by open (Baire) sets, such that if $K = \{\mu \in \mathrm{NA}_1^+ \,|\, \forall n, \forall O \in \pi_n, \mu(O) \le n^{-1}\}$, then Q is carried by K. Let $\tilde{K} = \{\nu \in F^+ \,|\, \langle \nu, 1\rangle = 1, \forall n, \forall O \in \pi_n, \forall f \in C(S) \ (\subseteq E): f \le I_O \Rightarrow \langle \nu, f\rangle \le n^{-1}\}$.

Remark first that, by its very definition, $\tilde{K}$ is a compact set in F^+, because $C(S) \subseteq E$, and consists of non-atomic elements (by Proposition 3.1) which are of norm 1; thus $\tilde{K}$ is $\sigma(F, E)$-compact in F_1^+, and obviously $K \subseteq \tilde{K}$ under the canonical embedding.

Thus any continuous function on $\tilde{K}$ can, by the Stone–Weierstrass theorem, be uniformly approximated by polynomials in the $\sigma(F, E)$-continuous linear functions, i.e., by linear combinations of expressions $[\langle \mu, \varphi\rangle]^n$, with $n \ge 0$ and $\varphi \in E$.

By Lemma 3.7, those expressions are universally measurable (on K), and therefore any continuous function on $\tilde{K}$ has a universally measurable restriction to K and obviously this restriction is positive if the function is positive, so that we can define $\tilde{Q}$ by $\int f(\mu)\, d\tilde{Q}(\mu) = \int f(\mu)\, dQ(\mu) \forall f \in C(\tilde{K})$, and $\tilde{Q}$ becomes then a positive, tight measure on $\tilde{K}$.

We have

$$B_Q = \left\{ \int \mu f(\mu)\, dQ(\mu) \,\Big|\, |f| \le 1, f \text{ is } \sigma[\mathrm{NA}, C(S)]\text{-measurable} \right\}.$$

But the continuous functions are dense in $\{f \in L_1(Q) \mid |f| \le 1\}$, and if f_n converges to f in $L_1(Q)$, then, for any universally measurable g,

$$\int \mu(g) f_n(\mu) \, dQ(\mu) \to \int \mu(g) f(\mu) \, dQ(\mu)$$

uniformly over bounded sets of g's, i.e., the corresponding barycenters converge in norm: the barycenters of $\sigma(\text{NA}, C(S))$ continuous functions f with $|f| \le 1$ are normdense in B_Q. But, as seen above, those continuous functions can, by a further approximation, be assumed to be linear combinations of expressions $[\langle \mu, \varphi \rangle]^n$, $\varphi \in C(S)$, which define $\sigma(F, E)$-continuous functions on $\tilde{K}$: it follows that the barycenters corresponding to $\sigma(F, E)$-continuous functions f on $\tilde{K}$, with $|f| \le 1$, define a norm-dense subset of B_Q (subset because, as argued above, all those functions are measurable).

But, by the same arguments, the barycenters corresponding to those functions with $\tilde{Q}$ form a norm-dense subset of $B_{\tilde{Q}}$, and, by construction of $\tilde{Q}$, those barycenters are the same as with Q. Indeed, if f is $\sigma(F, E)$-continuous, $|f| \le 1$, and $\varphi \in E$, then $\langle \mu, \varphi \rangle f(\mu)$ is $\sigma(F, E)$-continuous, and thus has the same integral for Q and for $\tilde{Q}$.

Therefore B_Q and $B_{\tilde{Q}}$ have a common norm-dense subset, and since the norm topology on NA is the restriction of the norm topology on F, it follows that $B_Q = B_{\tilde{Q}}$. $\square$

Thus the best possible choice is to choose the compact S such that the given M-space itself is (isomorphic to) $C(S)$, and to look at its full dual $M(S)$. Obviously if we want the extreme points of the unit ball to be in some sense dense in the unit ball, we need at least that their convex hull be $\sigma(C(S), \text{NA})$-dense in the unit ball. But this is equivalent to ask that S be totally disconnected — indeed if S is totally disconnected, then this convex hull is even strongly dense, while if S is not, there exist at least two different points $x_1 \ne x_2$ such that every clopen set either contains both or none of both: indeed, otherwise the indicators of clopen sets would separate points, so that, by the Stone–Weierstrass theorem, their linear combinations would be dense in $C(S)$, which implies S totally disconnected. Let now F be the intersection of all clopen sets that contain x_1 and x_2: F is compact and perfect. Indeed, assume $z \in F$ is isolated in F: let O_1 (resp. O_2) be open neighborhoods of $F \setminus \{z\}$ (resp. $\{z\}$) such that $O_1 \cap O_2 = \emptyset$. By compactness, there exists a clopen set, say C, such that $F \subseteq C \subseteq O_1 \cup O_2$. But $C \cap O_1$ is open and $C \setminus O_2$ is closed, and both are equal: we have found a clopen set C such that $F \setminus \{z\} \subseteq C$, $z \notin C$: thus at least one of the points x_i is in C, therefore both, and thus $F \subseteq C$: F has to be perfect.

But then we know from Section 1 that F carries some non-atomic probability, and since no clopen set has a non-trivial intersection with F, this contradicts the $\sigma(C(S), \text{NA})$-density of the step functions:

Lemma 4.6. *Let S be compact. The unit ball of $C(S)$ is the $\sigma(C(S), \text{NA})$-closed convex hull of its extreme points iff S is totally disconnected.* $\square$

We are now in a situation where Lemmas 4.1–4.4 apply fully, using $E = C(S)$ and $F = \text{NA}$, where furthermore S is an S_0-space.

We could apply those results immediately to show that the extreme points of the unit ball are $\mathcal{T}$-dense in the unit ball, but we prefer to postpone this to the next section.

We want to finish this section by showing that the $\mathcal{T}$-topology on an M-space E is uniquely determined by E as a normed space — and further that it is independent of the particular norm that turns the ordered vector space E into an M-space.

Since E', both with the weak* topology and with the norm topology is uniquely defined in these terms, and since $\mathcal{T}$ can be defined using the class $\mathcal{K}_1$ of all weak* compact convex balanced subsets of NA, everything amounts to show that the subspace NA of E' is uniquely defined in those terms.

Lemma 4.7. (a) *The $\mathcal{T}$-topology on an M-space E is uniquely determined by E as a normed vector space. Further this definition is independent of the particular norm that turns the ordered vector space E into an M-space.*

(b) *The subspace NA of non-atomic elements of an L-space F is uniquely determined by F as a normed space. Further this definition is independent of the particular norm that turns the ordered space F into an L-space.*

Proof. As we have shown, (b) will imply (a), because equivalent M-space norms on E induce equivalent L-space norms on E'.

To prove (b), note that any element of F'' can be represented in a unique way as the barycenter of a positive measure μ_x of total mass $\|x\|$ on the extreme points of the unit ball (with the topology $\sigma(F'', F')$). This is because F' is isometric and lattice isomorphic to some space $C(X)$, with X compact, and obviously the extreme points of the unit ball of $M(X)$ are the measures $\pm \varepsilon_x, x \in X$.

Thus $\text{NA} = \{x \in F \ (\subseteq F'') \,|\, \mu_x \text{ is non-atomic}\}$ is a definition of NA that depends only on F as a normed space. And a characterisation of NA that depends only on E as an ordered space is well known ($\mu \geq 0$ is non-atomic if $\mu \geq \nu \geq 0$ implies $\nu = 0$ if ν is in an extreme ray of the positive cone).

This proves the lemma. $\square$

5. Measures on the tridual

From now on, we will systematically use the results of Section 1 and Section 3, mainly Lemmas 3.6 and 3.7, without reference.

Lemma 5.1. *Let S be compact. For any tight probability P with $\sigma(\mathrm{NA}, C(S))$-compact support on NA_1^+, there exists a tight probability $\tilde{P}$ with $\sigma(\mathrm{NA}'', \mathrm{NA}')$-compact support in the non-atomic elements of $\mathrm{NA}_1''^+$, such that the set $B_{\tilde{P}}$ in NA'' $(\sigma(\mathrm{NA}'', \mathrm{NA}'))$ equals B_P (under the canonical embedding of NA in NA'').*

Proof. P is carried by a set K of the form

$$K = \{\mu \in M(S) \,|\, \mu \geq 0, \langle \mu, 1 \rangle = 1, \forall n, \forall O \in \pi_n, \mu(O) \leq n^{-1}\}$$

where π_n denotes a sequence of finite coverings of S by open Baire sets. Let

$$\tilde{K} = \{\mu \in \mathrm{NA}'' \,|\, \mu \geq 0, \langle \mu, 1 \rangle \leq 1, \forall n, \forall O \in \pi_n, \mu(O) \leq n^{-1}\}$$

(where $\mu(O) = \sup\{\mu(f) \,|\, f \leq I(O), f \in C^+(S)\}$ by definition, and $C(S)$ is canonically identified with a subspace of NA').

Remark that NA' can be identified with some space $C(X)$, where X is Stonian. Further NA is then identified with those elements of $M(X)$ ($=\mathrm{NA}''$) that vanish on every subset of the first category in X. Also, the elements of NA, being non-atomic, have perfect supports, and since the union of those supports has to be dense in X, X is perfect.

Remark finally that the supports of elements μ of NA have to be clopen, since μ vanishes on all sets of the first category. For the same reason, if μ, ν are in NA, the restriction of ν to the support of μ is the part of ν absolutely continuous with respect to μ.

To avoid trivialities, we identify S with its perfect kernel (this amounts to identify with zero any functions in $C(S)$ that vanish identically on NA).

$C(S)$ is then canonically identified, under an order preserving isometry, with a subspace of $C(X)$. It is trivial to check that this isometry preserves the constant functions, and also the lattice operations — therefore it is induced (transposition) by a continuous mapping φ mapping X onto S.

As a first step, we want to show that the formula

$$\int \langle \mu, f \rangle g(\mu) \, d\tilde{P}(\mu) = \left[\int \bar{\mu} g(\mu) \, dP(\mu) \right](f)$$

defines $\tilde{P}$ as a positive linear functional of norm 1 on the space E generated by all functions on $\tilde{K}$ of the type $\langle \mu, f \rangle g(\mu)$, where $f \in C(X)$, g is $\sigma(M(X), C(S))$-continuous.

It is even sufficient to do this on a dense subspace of E (in the uniform topology on $\tilde{K}$) — and note that E contains the constants, because $\langle \mu, 1 \rangle = 1$ on $\tilde{K}$.

In order to have the signs more explicitly we approximate $\langle \mu, f \rangle$ uniformly by linear combinations of expressions $\mu(O)$, where O is clopen in X, and we approximate g uniformly by linear combinations of expressions $[\langle \mu, \psi \rangle]^n$, with $\psi \in C(S)$. Since $\psi = \psi' - \text{const.}$, with $\psi' \geq 1$, and since $\langle \mu, 1 \rangle = 1$ on $\tilde{K}$, we can even reduce ourselves to the case $\psi \geq 1$.

Thus we get for E expressions of the type

$$\sum_{i=1}^{k} a_i \mu(O_i) \mu^{n_i}(g_i) \quad (n_i \geq 0),$$

or, after rescaling the g_i's (since $\langle \mu, 1 \rangle = 1$, we can assume without loss $n_i \geq 1$),

$$F(\mu) = \sum_{i=1}^{k} \varepsilon_i \mu(O_i) \mu^{n_i}(g_i),$$

where $\varepsilon_i = \pm 1$, $n_i > 0$, $g_i > \delta$, $g_i \in C(S)$, O_i clopen in X.

We have to show that it is impossible to have at the same time $F(\mu) > \varepsilon > 0$ on $\tilde{K}$ and

$$\sum_{i=1}^{k} \varepsilon_i \left[\int \vec{\mu} \cdot \mu^{n_i}(g_i) \, dP(\mu) \right] (O_i) < -\varepsilon.$$

To further simplify notations, we can divide the whole expression by $\min(\varepsilon, \delta^{n_1}, \delta^{n_2}, \delta^{n_3}, \ldots)$ (multiplying the g_i's), to get $\varepsilon = 1$, $\delta = 1$.

Finally, note that all NA-measures $\int \vec{\mu} \cdot \mu^{n_i}(g_i) \, dP(\mu)$ are in $L_1(\nu)$, where $\nu = \int \vec{\mu} \, dP(\mu)$, and thus that their support is contained in the clopen support T of ν.

Thus the integral is not affected if O_i is changed outside of T: we can assume that, if $\varepsilon_i = 1$, $O_i \cup T = X$ and if $\varepsilon_i = -1$, $O_i \subseteq T$. But then, when $\varepsilon_i = 1$, we can write $\mu(O_i) = 1 - \mu(X \setminus O_i)$, and $X \setminus O_i$ is clopen in T, so we are reduced to the case where, when $\varepsilon_i = 1$, $\mu(O_i) = 1$, and otherwise $O_i \subseteq T$; to summarize:

$$F(\mu) = \sum_{i=1}^{k_1} \mu^{n_i}(g_i) - \sum_{j=1}^{k_2} \mu(O_j) \mu^{n_j}(g_j) > 1 \quad \text{on } \tilde{K},$$

$$\forall r: \quad g_r \in C(S), \ g_r > 1, \ n_r > 0,$$

$$O_r \text{ clopen in the support } T \text{ of } \nu = \int \vec{\mu} \, dP(\mu),$$

and

$$\int \left[\sum_{i=1}^{k_1} \mu^{n_i}(g_i) \right] dP(\mu) - \sum_{j=1}^{k_2} \left[\int \bar{\mu}\mu^{n_j}(g_j) \, dP(\mu) \right] (O_j) < -1.$$

Further, every set O_j can be identified with some indicator function in $L_\infty(\nu)$, and thus there exists an increasing sequence of compact sets K_n in S, that converges ν a.s. to O_j. We can also assume that each set K_n is the support of the restriction of ν to K_n. If we now look at the sets K_n in X (i.e., literally $\varphi^{-1}(K_n)$), they form an increasing sequence of compact sets, with $\nu(K_n) \to \nu(O_j)$. Let $\mathring{K}_n$ denote their (clopen) interior in $X : \nu(\mathring{K}_n) = \nu(K_n) \to \nu(O_j)$, thus $\nu(\mathring{K}_n \setminus O_j) = 0$, thus $\mathring{K}_n \cap T \subseteq O_j$. Also, since K_n is the support of $\nu|_{K_n}$ for the $C(S)$ topology, and $\nu|_{K_n} = \nu|_{\mathring{K}_n \cap T}$, we have that K_n is the closure of $\mathring{K}_n \cap T$ in the $C(S)$-topology.

Finally, our inequalities will remain valid if the sets O_j are replaced by sets $\mathring{K}_n \cap T$ for n sufficiently large.

Thus we can further assume that for all j, if we denote by $\bar{O}_j$ the closure of O_j in the $C(S)$-topology, and by $\mathring{\bar{O}}_j$ the interior of $\bar{O}_j$ in X, then

$$O_j = T \cap \mathring{\bar{O}}_j.$$

Since then $\nu(O_j) = \nu(\bar{O}_j)$ — and the same holds for all measures in $L_1(\nu)$ — our second inequality is equivalent to ($\bar{O}_j$ being a Borel set in the $C(S)$-topology),

$$\int \bar{F}(\mu) \, dP(\mu) < -1,$$

where

$$\bar{F}(\mu) = \sum_{i=1}^{k_1} \mu^{n_i}(g_i) - \sum_{j=1}^{k_2} \mu(\bar{O}_j)\mu^{n_j}(g_j).$$

Therefore, there exists a $\sigma(\mathrm{NA}, C(S))$-compact set $R \subseteq K$, of positive P-measure and such that R is the support of the restriction of P to R, satisfying

(1) $\bar{F}(\mu) < -1 \; \forall \mu \in R$;

(2) $\forall j$, there exists a decreasing sequence $f_{n,j} \in C(S), f_{n,j} \geq I(\bar{O}_j)$, such that $\mu(f_{n,j}) \to \mu(\bar{O}_j)$ uniformly on R.

Since $0 \leq \mu(f_{n,j}) - \mu(\bar{O}_j) \leq \varepsilon_n$ uniformly on R, the same inequality holds on the convex hull of R. Since further $\mu(\bar{O}_j)$ is uppersemicontinuous (for $\sigma(\mathrm{NA}, C(S))$), we still have

$$\mu(f_{n,j}) - \mu(\bar{O}_j) \leq \varepsilon_n \text{ on the } \sigma(\mathrm{NA}, C(S))\text{-compact convex hull } R^c \text{ of } R.$$

But any $\mu \in \mathrm{NA}$ vanishes on sets of the first category, so $\mu(\bar{O}_j) = \mu(\overset{\circ}{O}_j)$ on R^c. Finally, since $\bar{O}_j \backslash O_j$ is disjoint from the support of ν, we will have

$$\mu(f_{n,j}) - \mu(O_j) \leq \varepsilon_n \quad \text{uniformly on } R^c \cap L_1(\nu).$$

Since $F \geq 1 + \delta$ on this set, it follows that, if we pick n sufficiently large, and denote by ϕ the function obtained by replacing, in F, O_j by $f_{n,j}$, then $\phi > 1$ on $R^c \cap L_1(\nu)$.

Obviously ϕ is $\sigma(\mathrm{NA}, C(S))$-continuous. Also $\phi \leq \bar{F}$, therefore $\phi < -1$ on R.

Let now $\mu_0 \in R$, thus μ_0 is in the support of the restriction of P to R. Denote by V_α the decreasing net of closed neighborhoods of μ_0 in R and let

$$\bar{\mu}_\alpha = \frac{1}{P(V_\alpha)} \int_{V_\alpha} \bar{\mu} \, dP(\mu).$$

Obviously $\bar{\mu}_\alpha \in R^c \cap L_1(\nu)$, and $\bar{\mu}_\alpha \to \mu_0$. But by our inequalities we should have $\phi(\bar{\mu}_\alpha) > 1$, $\phi(\mu_0) < -1$, which contradicts the continuity of ϕ.

This proves our first step.

Thus $\tilde{P}$ can, by the Hahn–Banach theorem, be extended to a positive linear functional on $C(\tilde{K})$, i.e., to a tight positive measure on $\tilde{K}$. Since E contains the constants, $\tilde{P}$ is a tight probability with compact support on the non atomic elements of $(\mathrm{NA}'')_1^+$, such that $\forall f \in C(X), \forall g$, $\sigma(M(X), C(S))$-continuous,

$$\int \mu(f) g(\mu) \, d\tilde{P}(\mu) = \left[\int \bar{\mu} g(\mu) \, dP(\mu) \right](f).$$

Now we show that, for any probability $\tilde{P}$ with compact support on $(M(X)^+, \sigma(M(X), C(X)))$, whose barycenter $\bar{\mu} = \int \bar{\mu} \, d\tilde{P}(\mu)$ is in NA, the $\sigma(M(X), C(S))$-continuous functions form a dense subset of the unit ball of $L_\infty(\tilde{P})$.

Denote by T the (clopen) support of $\bar{\mu}$: we have $0 = \bar{\mu}(X \backslash T) = \int \mu(X \backslash T) \, d\tilde{P}(\mu)$, and, T being clopen, $\mu(X \backslash T)$ is $\sigma(M(X), C(X))$-continuous ≥ 0, and zero $\tilde{P}$ a.e., so it is zero on the support of $\tilde{P}$: any measure μ in the support of $\tilde{P}$ is carried by T.

Consider now any f in $C(X), f$ can be viewed as an element of $L_\infty(\bar{\mu})$ (this being the dual of $L_1(\bar{\mu})$). But the unit ball of $C(S)$ is dense in the unit ball of $L_\infty(\bar{\mu})$, in the sense that there exist $f_i \in C(S), \|f_i\| \leq 1$ such that f_i converges in $\bar{\mu}$-probability to f, or even (Egorov) $\bar{\mu}$-almost uniformly: let F be a S-compact set, such that $\bar{\mu}(F) \geq 1 - \varepsilon$, and such that the f_i's converge uniformly on F: then the interior $\overset{\circ}{F}$ of $F \cap T$ in X is clopen,

$\bar{\mu}(\mathring{F}) = \bar{\mu}(F) \geq 1 - \varepsilon$, and, on $\mathring{F}, f_i$ converges uniformly to f (by the continuity of f). But $\tilde{P}[\mu(T \backslash F) \geq \delta] \leq \bar{\mu}(T \backslash \mathring{F})/\delta \leq \varepsilon/\delta$. Therefore, for n large enough, $|f - f_n| < \delta$ on $\mathring{F}$, so that $|\mu(f) - \mu(f_n)| < \delta + \mu(T \backslash \mathring{F})$, thus $\tilde{P}[|\mu(f - f_n)|2\delta] \leq \varepsilon/\delta$: it follows that $\mu(f_n)$ converges to $\mu(f)$ in $\tilde{P}$-probability.

Remark now that the $\sigma(M(X), C(X))$-continuous functions are, as before, dense in the unit ball of $L_\infty(\tilde{P})$, and that by the Stone–Weierstrass theorem those can be approximated by polynomials in expressions $\mu(f), f \in C(X)$. Since those expressions can be approximated in $\tilde{P}$-probability by expressions $\mu(f), f \in C(S)$, and that polynomials in those last expressions are $\sigma(M(X), C(S))$-continuous, our assertion follows.

The lemma follows now, since we have constructed a probability $\tilde{P}$ having the required properties on NA″, and shown that B_P and $B_{\tilde{P}}$ have a common dense subset — the barycenters of the $\sigma(M(X), C(S))$-continuous functions. B_P and $B_{\tilde{P}}$ being closed, their equality follows. $\square$

From now on it will be more convenient to redefine $\mathcal{B}^0$ (cf. Corollary 4.1) using NA$^+$ instead of NA$_1^+$. Obviously this redefinition does not affect $\mathcal{B}_1$, neither the validity of any of our previous statements.

Definition. Let F be an L-space, F' its dual, F'' its second dual. F' being an M-space, the classes of subsets $\mathcal{B}_0$ and $\mathcal{B}_1$ in F'' are well defined — let us denote them by $\mathcal{B}_0''$, $\mathcal{B}_1''$.

Denote by $\mathcal{E}_0$ the class of those sets in $\mathcal{B}_0''$ which are included in F (canonically identified with a subspace of F'').

Denote by $\mathcal{E}$ the class of those (convex, closed, balanced) sets B in F, such that $\inf_{E \in \mathcal{E}_0} \sup_{x \in B} d(x, E) = 0$.

Remark that, by Lemma 4.7(b), the class $\mathcal{E}$ depends on F only as an ordered vector space, or only as a normed vector space.

A "band" (in Bourbaki's, 1969, terminology) in an L-space F is a closed subspace G such that $\mu \in G$, $\nu \in F$, $|\nu| \leq |\mu| \Rightarrow \nu \in G$.

The "orthogonal band" $G^\perp = \{\nu \in F \mid \forall \mu \in G, |\mu| \wedge |\nu| = 0\}$.

F is the direct sum of G and $G^\perp$, so that there exist projections (proj$_G$ and proj$_{G^\perp}$) on G and $G^\perp$, such that, for all $x \in F$, $x = \text{proj}_G(x) + \text{proj}_{G^\perp}(x)$, $\|x\| = \|\text{proj}_G(x)\| + \|\text{proj}_{G^\perp}(x)\|$.

Theorem 5.1. (i) *If $M(T)$ denotes the space of tight measures on a Hausdorff topological space T, then (defining $\mathcal{B}_0^{M(T)}$ for non-compact T as $\bigcup \{\mathcal{B}_0^{M(K)} \mid K \subseteq T, K \text{ compact}\}$):*

(a) *$\mathcal{B}_1^{M(T)} = \mathcal{E}^{M(T)}$. In particular $\mathcal{B}_1^F = \mathcal{E}^F$ whenever the L-space F is the dual of an M-space. In particular $\mathcal{B}_1^{F''} = \mathcal{E}^{F''}$.*

Denote also by U a Banach-algebra of bounded, universally measurable functions on T, containing all bounded continuous functions and endowed with the topology $\mathcal{T}$ of uniform convergence on the elements of $\mathscr{E}^{M(T)}$, and assume T universally measurable in some compact space (and thus in any compact space) — in other words, T is completely regular and any τ-smooth measure on T is tight. Then:

(b) *$\mathcal{T}$ is the strongest locally convex topology on U that coincides on bounded sets with the topology of convergence in measure for any tight measure on $M_{na}(T)$.*

Denote also by f an increasing, continuous function, with $f(0) = 0$. Then:

(c) *For any weakly compact set H of tight measures on the unit ball of $M_{na}(T)$, the set $\{x: \sup_{P \in H} \int f(|\langle x, y \rangle|)\, dP(y) \le 1\}$ is a neighborhood of 0. In particular,*

$$\{\text{barycenter}(P) \mid P \in H\} \in \mathscr{E}^{M(T)}.$$

If further $M(T)$ is the dual of the M-space U, i.e., T is compact and $U = C(T)$, then:

(d) *$\mathcal{T}$ is finer than — and coincides on bounded sets with — the vector topology for which 0 is in the closure of a set A iff 0 is in the closed convex hull of $\{f(|\langle x, \cdot \rangle|) \mid x \in A\}$ for the topology of uniform convergence on weak*-compact subsets of $M_{na}(T)$.*

(ii) (a) *For any band $G \subseteq F$,*

$$\mathscr{E}^G = \{\text{proj}_G(B) \mid B \in \mathscr{E}^F\} \subseteq \mathscr{E}^F.$$

In particular,

$$\mathscr{E}^F = \{\text{proj}_F(B) \mid B \in \mathscr{E}^{F''}\} \subseteq \mathscr{E}^{F''}.$$

(b) *If H denotes a weakly compact set of tight measures on the non-atomic elements of the unit ball of F'', then*

$$\{\text{proj}_F(\text{barycenter}(P)) \mid P \in H\} \in \mathscr{E}^F.$$

(c) (1) *If $B_i \in \mathscr{E}^F$, $\lambda_i \in R$, then $\lambda_1 B_1 + \lambda_2 B_2 \in \mathscr{E}^F$.*

(2) *If a closed, convex, balanced subset B of F satisfies*

$$\inf_{\tilde{B} \in \mathscr{E}^F} \sup_{x \in B} d(x, \tilde{B}) = 0,$$

then $B \in \mathscr{E}^F$.

(d) (1) $B \in \mathscr{E}^F$ iff there exists $B_P \in \mathscr{E}_0^F$ such that

$$\max_{x \in B} d(x, nB_P) \quad \left(= \max_{\|z\|_{F'} \le 1} (\|z\|_B - n\|z\|_{B_P}) \right) \quad converges \ to \ 0$$

(where $\|\cdot\|_{F'}$ denotes the usual norm in F', and for any $B \subseteq F$, $\|z\|_B = \sup_{x \in B} \langle z, x \rangle$; in particular, $\|z\|_{B_P} = \int |\langle z, \rho \rangle| dP(\rho))$; or equivalently, such that there exists a sequence $\lambda_n \to +\infty$ with $\sum_n nd(x, \lambda_n B_P) \le 1$ on B.

(2) For any $B_P \in \mathscr{E}_0^F$, the corresponding probability P has its support contained in the second dual of the vector space E_P spanned by B_P, i.e., the weak*-closure of E_P in F''.

(3) $\mathscr{E}^F = \bigcup_{\nu \in F} \mathscr{E}^{L_1(\nu)}$. Further, if $B \in \mathscr{E}^F$, then $B \in \mathscr{E}^{L_1(\nu)}$ where ν is the maximal element of a set B_P such as in (1), and $L_1(\nu)$ is the band generated by ν.

(e) (1) All compact (convex, balanced) sets of non atomic elements of F are in $\mathscr{E}^F$.

(2) Any set in $\mathscr{E}^F$ is a weakly compact set of non atomic elements.

Proof. (ii) (c) (1) is very easy: essentially do the same operations on the measures on the second dual that define the sets in $\mathscr{E}_0$, and use the triangle inequality for passing from the result for $\mathscr{E}_0$ to the result for $\mathscr{E}$.

(ii) (c) (2) follows immediately from the definition of $\mathscr{E}$ and will henceforth be used without reference.

(ii) (d) (1)

$$d(x, nB_P) = \inf_{y \in B_P} \|x - ny\| = \inf_{y \in B_P} \max_{\|z\|_{F'} \le 1} \langle x - ny, z \rangle$$

$$= \max_{\|z\|_{F'} \le 1} \inf_{y \in B_P} \langle x - ny, z \rangle$$

(by the max-min theorem), thus

$$d(x, nB_P) = \max_{\|z\|_{F'} \le 1} \left(\langle x, z \rangle - n \sup_{y \in B_P} \langle y, z \rangle \right).$$

But

$$\sup_{y \in B_P} \langle y, z \rangle = \sup_{|f| \le 1} \int \langle \rho, z \rangle f(\rho) \, dP(\rho) = \int |\langle \rho, z \rangle| \, dP(\rho) = \|z\|_{B_P}$$

(taking $f(\rho) = \operatorname{sign}(\langle \rho, z \rangle)$), so that

$$\max_{x \in B} d(x, nB_P) = \max_{\|z\|_{F'} \le 1} \max_{x \in B} (\langle x, z \rangle - n\|z\|_{B_P}) = \max_{\|z\|_{F'} \le 1} (\|z\|_B - n\|z\|_{B_P}).$$

It is also obvious that the uniform convergence to zero of $d(x, nB_P)$ is equivalent to the existence of a sequence $\lambda_n \to \infty$ such that $\sum_n nd(x, \lambda_n B_P) \leq 1$ on B.

Let finally $B_{P_n} \in \mathscr{E}_0^F$ be such that $d(x, B_{P_n})$ goes to zero uniformly on B. We have to find $B_P \in \mathscr{E}_0^F$ such that $B_{P_n} \subseteq \lambda_n B_P$ for λ_n sufficiently large. Let K_n be the support of P_n, $r_n = \max_{x \in K_n} \|x\|$. Let $\tilde{K}_n = (nr_n)^{-1} K_n : K = \{0\} \cup (\bigcup_n \tilde{K}_n)$ is compact in $(F'')^+$. Let $\tilde{P}_n$ be the image measure on $\tilde{K}_n$ (by the appropriate homothety) of $[2^n \|P_n\|]^{-1} P_n$, and let $P = \sum_n \tilde{P}_n : P$ is a tight probability with compact support K in $(F'')^+$, and obviously for λ_n sufficiently large, $B_{P_n} \subseteq \lambda_n B_P$.

This proves (ii) (d) (1).

For (ii) (d) (2) consider $\mu_0 \in \text{Supp}(P)$, and denote by O_α the decreasing net of open neighborhoods of μ_0: then $P(O_\alpha) > 0$, thus

$$\mu_\alpha = \frac{1}{P(O_\alpha)} \int_{O_\alpha} \vec{\nu} \, dP(\nu) \in E_p,$$

and obviously $\mu_\alpha \to \mu_0$.

(ii) (d) (1) implies that, if $B \in \mathscr{E}^F$, then $B \subseteq L_1(\nu)$, where ν is the maximal element of a set B_P such as in (d.1), and $L_1(\nu)$ is the band generated by the single element ν — this characterisation of subspaces $L_1(\nu)$ is very easy.

(ii) (d) (3) will therefore follow from (ii) (a).

(ii) (e) (1) follows from (ii) (c) because for any non-atomic $x \in F$, $\{x\} \in \mathscr{E}^F$, considering the unit mass at $\{x\}$.

(ii) (e) (2) If $B \in \mathscr{E}^F$, then by definition certainly $B \in B_1''$, thus, by Corollary 4.3, weakly compact in F''. But $B \subseteq F$, and thus weakly compact in F. To show that B consists only of non-atomic measures, it is sufficient to consider $B \in \mathscr{E}_0$ — the space of non-atomic measures is closed — i.e., $B \in B_0''$, $B \subseteq F$. $B \in \mathscr{B}_0''$ implies, by Corollary 3.2, that B consists of non-atomic elements of F'': the result follows now from the fact that points in F which are non-atomic in F'' are non-atomic in F — this follows for instance from the fact that F is a "band" in F'', or from the Stone representation; both of those will become clear in the following proof of (ii) (a).

We now prove (ii) (a): as remarked above, this will also terminate the proof of (ii) (d) (3), and further (ii) (b) will then be an immediate corollary of (i) (c), which implies that $\{\text{barycenter}(P) \mid P \in H\} \in \mathscr{E}^{F''}$, so that (ii) (b) follows then from the "in particular" clause in (ii) (a).

Thus (ii) will be fully proved, with the proviso that (ii) (b) cannot be used in the proof of (i) (c).

For (ii) (a) consider the Stone representation of F' as $C(X)$, F as the measures on X that vanish on all sets of the first category (X is Stonian).

Since F'' is the space of all measures on X, it is immediately obvious that F is a band in F'', so the "in particular" clause follows (F'' is also an L-space).

Thus we have to show that $G \in \mathscr{E}_0^G$ implies $B \in \mathscr{E}^F$, and that $B \in \mathscr{E}_0^F$ implies $\text{proj}_G(B) \in \mathscr{E}^G$ — the same result will immediately follow with $\mathscr{E}$ instead of $\mathscr{E}_0$, and this implies then (ii) (a).

Since G'' is a $\sigma(F'', F')$-closed subspace of F'', the probability P with compact support on G'' determined by $B \in \mathscr{E}_0^G$ is also a probability on F'', and obviously any Q with $|Q| \le P$ has the same barycenter in F'' as in G''. Thus $B \in \mathscr{B}_0^{F''}$ — but since $B \subseteq G \subseteq F$, it follows that $B \in \mathscr{E}^F$ — provided we show that P has a compact support of non-atomic elements in F''; i.e., the support of P being the same in G'' and in F'', we have to show that any non-atomic element of G'' is non-atomic in F''.

Remark that any $\mu \in F$ has a clopen support in X — indeed, the support is a compact set, and X being Stonian, its interior is clopen; since the boundary is of the first category, the interior is a closed set with full measure, and therefore contains the support. Now if $\mu \in G$, $L_1(\mu)$ is, by its definition as the band generated by μ, also contained in G. The set of all measures on the support S_μ of μ that vanish on sets of the first category is obviously a band; we will show that any such measure is absolutely continuous w.r.t. μ, so that, using the Radon–Nikodym theorem, this band is $L_1(\mu)$. Let thus A be a μ-negligible set contained in S_μ: there exists a decreasing sequence of open sets O_n in S_μ such that $A \subseteq O_n$, $|\mu|(O_n) \to 0$. But $\bar{O}_n$ is clopen, and $|\mu|(\bar{O}_n) = \mu(O_n)$: let $F = \bigcap_n \bar{O}_n$: F is a closed Baire set, $A \subseteq F \subseteq S_\mu$, and $|\mu|(F) = 0$. The interior of F is clopen and contained in S_μ; being of measure zero it must be empty by definition of S_μ. Thus F is of the first category: we have shown that any μ-negligible set in the support of μ is of the first category. Thus $L_1(\mu)$ is the set of all measures on S_μ that vanish on sets of the first category.

Let now $\mathring{S}_G = \bigcup_{\mu \in G} S_\mu$: $\mathring{S}_G$ is open, and any measure $\nu \in F$ carried by $\mathring{S}_G$ is in G. Indeed, $\exists K \subseteq \mathring{S}_G$, K compact and $|\nu|(X \setminus K) \le \varepsilon$. Any point in K is contained in some S_μ, and one can extract a finite covering S_{μ_i} from this open covering. Then $\sigma = \sum |\mu_i| \in G$, by definition of a band, and $K \subseteq S_\sigma \subseteq \mathring{S}_G$. Let σ_i be a sequence in G such that $S_{\sigma_i} \subseteq S_{\sigma_{i+1}}$, $|\nu|(X \setminus S_{\sigma_i}) < i^{-1}$. Let ν_i denote the restriction of ν to S_{σ_i}: we know from above that $\nu_i \in L_1(\sigma_i) \subseteq G$, and ν_i is norm-convergent to ν: G being closed, it follows that $\nu \in G$.

Let now S_G denote the closure of $\mathring{S}_G$: S_G is clopen, and $S_G \setminus \mathring{S}_G$ is negligible for any $\nu \in F$, so that G is the set of all measures in F carried by the clopen set S_G, which could be called the support of G. proj_G is therefore the restriction of any measure on X to S_G; and G'' is the set of all measures on S_G, and therefore a band in F''. Further, S_G being clopen, $\text{proj}_{G''}$ is weak*-continuous.

It follows now immediately that any non atomic element in G'' is non-atomic in F''.

There remains to show that $B_P \in \mathscr{E}_0^F$ implies $\text{proj}_G(B_P) \in \mathscr{E}_0^G$.

Since $\text{proj}_{G''}$ is weak*-continuous and maps positive, non-atomic measures to similar, if $\tilde{P}$ denotes the image measure of P by $\text{proj}_{G''}$, $\tilde{P}$ is a tight probability with compact support on the non atomic elements of $(G'')^+$, and if $\nu \in B_P$, i.e.,

$$\nu = \int \bar{\rho} f(\rho) \, dP(\rho), \, \tilde{\rho} = \text{proj}_{G''}(\rho),$$

then

$$\tilde{\nu} = \int \tilde{\rho} f(\rho) \, dP(\rho) = \int \tilde{\rho} E(f|\tilde{\rho}) \, dP(\rho) = \int \tilde{\rho} \tilde{f}(\tilde{\rho}) \, d\tilde{P}(\tilde{\rho}),$$

where $\tilde{f} = E(f|\tilde{\rho})$ is the conditional expectation of f given the σ-field generated by the mapping $\rho \to \tilde{\rho}$, where the measures on S_G are endowed with the Borel σ-field for the weak*-topology. Since $|\tilde{f}| \leq 1$, it follows that $\tilde{\nu} \in B_{\tilde{P}}$.

This finishes the proof of (ii).

Let us now turn to (i) (a). It is clear how the "in particular" clauses follow.

If $B \in \mathscr{B}_0^{M(K)}$, then by Lemma 5.1, $B \in \mathscr{E}^{M(K)}$ (even $\mathscr{E}_0^{M(K)}$), thus, since $M(K)$ is a band in $M(T)$, $B \in \mathscr{E}^{M(T)}$ (using (ii) (a)). Thus $\mathscr{B}_0^{M(T)} \subseteq \mathscr{E}^{M(T)}$, and therefore $\mathscr{B}_1^{M(T)} \subseteq \mathscr{E}^{M(T)}$ ((ii) (2)).

Consider now $B_P \in \mathscr{E}_0^{M(T)}$: by (ii) (d) (3), $B_P \in \mathscr{E}_0^{L_1'(\nu)}$, where ν is some tight probability on T.

By Proposition 3.1, the probability P with compact support on $(L'_\infty(\nu))^+$ is carried by a set $\{\rho \in (L'_\infty)^+ | \rho(A_n^i) \leq \varepsilon_n, \forall A_n^i \in \pi_n, \forall n\}$ where π_n is a sequence of ν-measurable partitions of T, and ε_n decreases to zero.

By Lusin's theorem, there exists a compact set $K \subseteq T$, such that $\forall i, \forall n, I(A_n^i)$ has a continuous restriction to K — i.e., A_n^i has a clopen restriction to K — and such that $\nu(K) \geq 1 - \varepsilon$.

Restricting ν to K determines a band in $L_1(\nu)$, and the restriction $B_{\tilde{P}}$ of B_P is at most ε-distant from the original B_P, where $\tilde{P}$ is as in the proof of (ii) (a) the image measure of P induced by the restriction mapping. Thus it is sufficient to consider $B_{\tilde{P}}$; i.e., we can assume that ν has compact support K, and that the π_n form a sequence of clopen partitions of K.

K being the support of ν, $C(K)$ can be identified with a subspace of $L_\infty(\nu)$, so that the dual $M(K)$ of $C(K)$ is canonically a quotient of $L'_\infty(\nu)$.

Let $\bar{P}$ be the image of P by the quotient mapping: obviously for any ρ in the support of $\bar{P}$, we still have $\rho(A_n^i) \le \varepsilon_n \ \forall A_n^i \in \pi_n, \ \forall n$, since $I(A_n^i) \in C(K)$, and therefore $\bar{P}$ still has compact support in $M_{\mathrm{na}}^+(K)$; using again Proposition 3.1. For any Q with $|Q| \le P$, obviously $|\bar{Q}| \le \bar{P}$.

Since $C(K) \subseteq L_\infty(\nu)$, the barycenter of $\bar{Q}$ (in $M(K)$, computed on $C(K)$) coincides on $C(K)$ with the barycenter of Q (in $L_1(\nu)$, computed on $L_\infty(\nu)$). But both being tight measures, they will therefore coincide on all Borel functions: $B_{\bar{P}} = B_P$, and this proves (i) (a).

Remark now that, to finish the proof of the theorem, it is sufficient to prove (i) (c). Indeed, (i) (b) will follow because (i) (c) implies that $\mathcal{T}$ is finer than the topology of convergence in measure for any tight measure on $M_{\mathrm{na}}(T)$, while (i) (a) and (the proof of) Lemma 4.4 imply that $\mathcal{T}$ is the strongest locally convex topology that coincides on bounded sets with the topology of convergence in measure for a very restricted class of tight measures on $M_{\mathrm{na}}(T)$. And (i) (d) will follow from (i) (c) by Lemma 4.1.

For (i) (c), remark first (the proof of) Lemma 4.2 shows that $\exists \tilde{f}$ increasing, convex, continuous, with $\tilde{f}(0) = 0$, such that the corresponding set defined with $\tilde{f}$ is smaller — and this is convex. Now, as remarked above, $\mathcal{T}$ is, by its definition, a maximal locally convex topology that coincides with its restriction to bounded sets, and on every bounded set there exists K such that $\tilde{f}(|\langle x, y \rangle|) \le K |\langle x, y \rangle|$ when x ranges in that bounded set and y in the unit ball of $M(T)$. So we have reduced the problem to the case where $f(z) = Kz$, i.e., to the "in particular" clause, or in other words, that $\sup_{P \in H} \int |\langle x, y \rangle| \, dP(y)$ is a continuous semi norm.

Now H being weakly compact, is uniformly integrable in some space $L_1(P_0)$, i.e., $\forall \varepsilon$ there exists a weak*-compact set K in the unit ball of $M_{\mathrm{na}}(T)$, and a number N such that any $P \in H$ is, in norm, ε-close to some measure $\tilde{P}$ with $|\tilde{P}| \le NP_{0|K}$. This means that — by the formula in (ii) (d) (1) for the distance between sets in terms of their seminors — it is sufficient to consider the case where $H = \{Q \,|\, |Q| \le NP_{0|K}\}$. This amounts to show that $\int |\langle x, y \rangle| \, dP(y)$ is a continuous semi norm for any tight probability P with weak*-compact support K in $M_{\mathrm{na}}(T)$.

Remark now that $M(T)$ is a band in the space $M(\beta T)$ of all measures on the Stone–Čech compactification of T, and K is still a weak*-compact set of non-atomic measures on βT. Thus $B_P \in \mathcal{B}_1^{M(\beta T)}$, by Corollary 4.1 (using $U_s = C(\beta T)$), and therefore $B_P \in \mathscr{E}^{M(\beta T)}$, by (i) (a). Since $M(T)$ is a band in $M(\beta T)$, it is therefore sufficient to show that $B_P \subseteq M(T)$, using (ii) (a).

Thus we have to show that, for any tight measure with weak*-compact support in $M_{\mathrm{na}}(T)$, its barycenter lies in $M_{\mathrm{na}}(T)$. Using the Hahn-decomposition of the measure, this is immediately reduced to the case of a probability measure. Next, using the measurability of the Hahn-decomposition in $M(\beta T)$ (Lemma 3.3), and the fact that it maps the band $M(T)$ to itself, the distributions of μ^+ and μ^- are tight probability measures on the unit ball of $M_{\mathrm{na}}^+(T)$: we can assume P is of this type. Therefore P is a norm-limit of probabilities with compact support in $M_{\mathrm{na}}^+(T)$. If a sequence of measures on a bounded set in $M(T)$ is norm convergent and has barycenters, then the limit also has a barycenter — the norm limit of the barycenter (this was also used implicitly above, when passing from general tight measures on the unit ball of $M(T)$ to such measures with compact support). It follows that we can assume P to be a probability with weak* compact support C in $M_{\mathrm{na}}^+(T)$. Denote by $\bar{\mu}$ the barycenter of P in $M(\beta T)$. If f_α denotes any net of bounded continuous functions decreasing pointwise to zero on T, then $\langle \rho, f_\alpha \rangle$ is a decreasing net of continuous functions on C decreasing pointwise to zero (because ρ is tight), and therefore uniformly to zero, so that $\bar{\mu}(f_\alpha) = \int \langle \rho, f \rangle \, dP(\rho)$ converges to zero: $\bar{\mu}$ is τ-smooth measure on T, and therefore, by the assumption on T, is tight.

This finishes the proof of the theorem. $\square$

Remark that we did not need the full force of the assumption that T is universally measurable in some compact set: what we basically need is that the closed convex hull of any weak*-compact set in $M(T)$ (or, what we showed to be equivalent: in $M_1^+(T)$) be weak*-compact. This is for instance also trivially verified as soon as Prohorov's tightness criterion for weak*-compactness holds.

We now want to show that the extreme points of the unit ball of $C(S)$ are dense in the unit ball simultaneously in terms of the $\mathcal{T}$-topology and in the exact sense of Theorem 2.2. We follow the notations of this theorem.

Theorem 5.2. *Let S be totally disconnected and weakly σ-Stonian. For any $B \in \mathscr{C}^{M(S)}$, and for any vector φ of non-atomic measures in $M(S)$, any $f \in C_d$ is in the closed (uniform topology) convex hull of the set*

$$V = \left\{ g \in E_d \ \middle| \ \varphi(g - f) = 0, \ \|g - f\|_B \left(= \sup_{\mu \in B} |\mu(g) - \mu(f)| \right) \le 1 \right\}$$

(where $|\cdot|$ denotes any norm on R^d).

Proof. By Lemmas 4.1–4.4, if we show that 0 is in the closed convex hull of $\{(\langle \rho, g - f \rangle)^2 \mid g \in E_d, \varphi(g - f) = 0\}$ for the topology of uniform convergence on compact sets of NA^+, we will know that the sets V are non empty.

For any compact set K in NA^+, there exists, by Proposition 3.1, a sequence of clopen partitions π_n of S, and a sequence ε_n decreasing to zero, such that $\forall n, \forall O \in \pi_n, \rho(O) \leq \varepsilon_n$ on this compact set.

Select now, using Theorem 2.2, on every $O \in \pi_n$ independently some $g \in E_d$ with $\varphi(g-f) = 0$ at random, by some lottery with finite support, such that $|E(g) - f| \leq \varepsilon$.

Then

$$E \|\langle \rho, g - Eg \rangle\|_2^2 = \sum_{O \in \pi_n} E \|\langle \rho, (g - Eg)I_O \rangle\|_2^2$$

$$\leq d\varepsilon_n \sum_{O \in \pi_n} \rho(O) = d\varepsilon_n \sup_{\rho \in K} \|\rho\|$$

(where $\|\cdot\|_2$ denotes Euclidean norm on R^d), and therefore

$$E \|\langle \rho, g - f \rangle\|_2^2 \leq d\varepsilon_n \sup_K \|\rho\| + \varepsilon^2 d \sup_K \|\rho\|^2 \leq \delta.$$

Thus V is non-empty.

If f was not in the closed convex hull of V, then we can use the same reasoning as in the corresponding part of Theorem 2.2 — use the Hahn-Banach theorem to get a separating functional, remove the non-atomic part of this functional into φ, approximate the atomic part by one with finite support, and then restrict ourselves to clopen sets to have a singleton as support (this restriction determines a band in $M(S)$). One gets in this way: $\exists \delta > 0, \exists (a_i)_{i=1}^d (\sum a_i = 0), \exists x_0 \in S$:

$$\sum a_i f_i(x_0) + \delta < \inf\{\sum a_i g_i(x_0) \mid g \in E_d, \varphi(g-f) = 0, \|g-f\|_B \leq 1\}.$$

Now B is a weakly compact set of non-atomic measures, so there exists a sufficiently small clopen neighborhood O of x_0 such that

$$\|(g_1 - g_2)I(O)\|_B \leq \tfrac{1}{2} \quad \forall g_1, g_2 \in C_d.$$

Choose now $g \in E_d$

– in the complement of O such that $\varphi(g-f) = 0$, $\|g-f\|_B \leq \tfrac{1}{2}$ (using the fact that we already proved that any such set V is $\neq \emptyset$);

– on O, such that $\varphi(g-f) = 0$, and $\sum a_i g_i(x_0) < \sum a_i f_i(x_0) + \delta$ (using Theorem 2.2).

This g gives a contradiction, which finishes the proof of the theorem.   □

Remarks. (1) The assumption that S is weakly σ-Stonian is only needed if $\varphi \neq 0$, because it is only needed in that case in Theorem 2.2. If $\varphi \neq 0$, nothing can be done if one does not have some assumptions like weakly σ-Stonian — already Lebesgue measure on the field of clopen subsets of $\{0, 1\}^\infty$ takes only dyadic values.

(2) Lemma 4.6 shows that one has to assume S totally disconnected if one wants approximation in any sense.

(3) Three results are crucially lacking here:

(a) How the class of sets $\mathscr{E}$ behaves when going to subspaces and to quotients — and not merely to direct summands as is done in Theorem 5.1. More specifically, since $\mathscr{E}^F$ depends on F only as an ordered vector space, or only as a normed space, one would like, if F and H denote two L-spaces, that

– if φ maps F continuously onto H, such that the open unit ball (resp. the positive cone) of H is the image of the open unit ball (resp. the positive cone) of F, then every set in $\mathscr{E}^H$ is the image of some set in $\mathscr{E}^F$;

– if similarly H is an appropriate subspace of F, every set in $\mathscr{E}^H$ is contained in some set in $\mathscr{E}^F$.

Such results would have immediate translations showing how the $\mathscr{T}$-topology behaves when going to quotients and to subspaces (for instance, already Theorem 5.1 immediately implies that if one makes the quotient of $C(S)$ by a band of "negligible functions", then the $\mathscr{T}$-topology on the quotient is the quotient of the $\mathscr{T}$-topology on $C(S)$).

(b) A direct characterisation of the sets in $\mathscr{E}$ (Corollary 2.4 shows that any attempt to look for compact sets for the topology of uniform convergence on any kind of $\sigma(C(S), \mathrm{NA})$-compact sets, i.e., anything like $\tau(\mathrm{NA}, C(S))$-compact sets, or on $\sigma(C(S), \mathrm{NA})$-Cauchy sequences would lead to all weakly compact subsets of NA, which is a much too large class).

This is of fundamental importance for applications to the Shapley value: one has to be able to recognise — or to check — directly if a given game is $\mathscr{T}$-continuous.

(c) Investigating whether in some sense the $\mathscr{T}$-topology is the best possible permitting Theorem 5.2.

The author was too unhappy with the length of what precedes to invest now more time and space in these questions.

6. Extensions of games

A game (in characteristic function form) is a real valued set function v defined for all sets (coalitions) in some algebra $\mathscr{A}$ of subsets of the player space Ω (usually, a σ-algebra), with $v(\emptyset) = 0$.

A first step in defining a Shapley-value is often to define an extension $\bar{v}$ of v to all measurable functions f with values in $[0, 1]$, where $\bar{v}(f)$ is intuitively thought of as representing the expectation of v of a random coalition, where "every player s is independently selected with probability $f(s)$ to be a member of this coalition".

For games with finitely many players, the above is the correct definition of the extension. For "non atomic games", the most performing procedure used up to now (Mertens, 1980) was (taking $\mathscr{A}$ a σ-field) to look at the increasing net of all finite sets of countably additive, non atomic measures on $\mathscr{A}$, and for every such set at all coalitions coinciding with f on this set. If v of those coalitions converged, this limit was called $v(f)$.

We exhibit here an extension procedure that includes the above, and works as well for atomic and non-atomic games, thereby permitting to extend the results of Mertens (1980) to include atomic games. This is the extension procedure used in Mertens (1988), where other examples of its use are given than games with atoms ("polynomial games").

We will also show that the improvement over Theorem 2.2 provided in Theorem 5.2 is useless in this connection, giving thereby a more precise, "quantitative" version of Theorem 5.2.

To take the best from Theorem 5.2, we will choose, among all coalitions that are close to f in the sense of Theorem 5.2, one at random such as to be on average uniformly close to f. And to do this independently for all players, we will apply this procedure independently over all elements of a finite partition, and go to the limit over all refinements of this partition.

To facilitate things, we represent $\mathscr{A}$ as the field of clopen subsets of some weakly σ-Stonian totally disconnected compact space S, and bounded measurable functions become then continuous functions. We define then

$$\tilde{\mathscr{F}} = \{\alpha = (\pi^\alpha, \varepsilon^\alpha, (\varphi_O^\alpha)_{O \in \pi^\alpha}, (B_O^\alpha)_{O \in \pi^\alpha}) \mid \pi^\alpha \text{ is a clopen partition of } S,$$
$$\varepsilon^\alpha > 0, \forall O \in \pi^\alpha \colon \varphi_O^\alpha \text{ is a finite set in } M_{\mathrm{na}}(O), B_O^\alpha \in \mathscr{C}^{M(O)}\}.$$

$\forall f \in C_d$ denote $f \cdot I(O)$ by f_O, and let

$$\mathscr{P}_{\alpha,f} = \{P \text{ probability with finite support on } E_d \mid \|E_P(\psi) - f\| \leq \varepsilon^\alpha,$$
$$\text{and } dP(\psi)\text{-a.s.}, \forall O \in \pi^\alpha, \varphi_O^\alpha(\psi - f) = 0, \|\psi - f\|_{B_O^\alpha} \leq 1, \text{ and}$$
$$\forall O' \in \pi^\alpha, O' \neq O \Rightarrow \psi_O \text{ and } \psi_{O'} \text{ are } (P)\text{-independent}\}.$$

Then $\mathscr{P}_{\alpha,f} \neq \emptyset$ by Theorem 5.2. Define also an order on $\tilde{\mathscr{F}}$ by $\alpha \leq \alpha' \cdot \equiv \cdot [\varepsilon^\alpha \geq \varepsilon^{\alpha'}, \pi^{\alpha'}$ is a refinement of π^α, the sets $\varphi_{O'}^{\alpha'}$ contain all restrictions to the elements of $\pi^{\alpha'}$ of all measures in the φ_O^α, and $\forall O' \in \pi^{\alpha'}, \exists x_{O'} \geq 0 \colon$ $\forall O \in \pi^\alpha, \sum_{O' \subseteq O} x_{O'} \leq 1, \sum_{O' \subseteq O} x_{O'} B_{O'}^{\alpha'} \supseteq B_O^\alpha]$.

Obviously, $\tilde{\mathscr{F}}$ is filtering increasing, and $\alpha' \geq \alpha$ implies $\mathscr{P}_{\alpha',f} \subseteq \mathscr{P}_{\alpha,f}$ so there is only one choice in this vein for the definition of the extension $\bar{v}$ at f (with $d = 1$): $\bar{v}(f)$ is the number defined by

$$\lim_{\tilde{\mathscr{F}}} \sup_{P \in \mathscr{P}_{\alpha,f}} |E_P(v(\psi)) - \bar{v}(f)| = 0.$$

Let now $\mathcal{F} = \{\alpha \in \tilde{\mathcal{F}} \mid \forall 0 \in \pi^{\alpha}, B_0^{\alpha} = \{0\}\}$. $\mathcal{F}$ is also filtering increasing, and the monotonicity of $\mathcal{P}$ on $\tilde{\mathcal{F}}$ holds a fortiori on $\mathcal{F}$. $\mathcal{P}_{\alpha,f} \neq \emptyset$ for $\alpha \in \mathcal{F}$ follows from Theorem 2.2. However, the proof of Theorem 5.2 shows that

$$\forall \alpha \in \tilde{\mathcal{F}}, \; \forall \delta > 0, \; \exists \alpha' \in \mathcal{F}: \; \forall f \in C_d, \; \forall P' \in \mathcal{P}_{\alpha',f}, \; \exists P \in \mathcal{P}_{\alpha,f}:$$

$$\|P - P'\| \leq \delta$$

(using the fact that, for product measures ΠP_i and ΠQ_i, we have $\|\Pi P_i - \Pi Q_i\| \leq \sum \|P_i - Q_i\|$).

Thus, at least as long as one is only interested in bounded games, there is no loss at all in using only the filter $\mathcal{F}$. And it would be extremely pathological indeed if there could arise some relevant loss for unbounded games.

Thus the extension can be defined simply in terms of the filter $\mathcal{F}$. It is obviously linear, positive, transforming monotonic games into monotonic games, and of norm 1 both in the supremum norm and in the variation norm — this last point because Theorem 2.2 applies in dimension $n > 1$, so that any increasing chain $0 = f_0 \leq f_1 \leq \cdots \leq f_n = 1$ is represented by a probability distribution on similar increasing chains of indicator functions.

Finally, the extension is invariant under all automorphisms of the algebra $\mathcal{F}$.

References

Aumann, R.J., Y. Katznelson, R. Radner, R. Rosenthal and B. Weiss (1983) 'Approximate purification of mixed strategies', *Mathematics of Operations Research*, 8(3):327.

Bourbaki, N. (1969) *Eléments de Mathématique, Livre VI*. Paris: Hermann.

Dvoretzky, A., A. Wild and J. Wolfowitz (1951) 'Relations among certain ranges of vector measures', *Pacific Journal of Mathematics*, 1:59-74.

Grothendieck, A. (1953) 'Sur les applications linéaires faiblement compactes d'espaces du type $C(K)$', *Canadian Journal of Mathematics*, 5:129-173.

Mertens, J.-F. (1980) 'Values and derivatives', *Mathematics of Operations Research*, 5(4):523-552.

Mertens, J.-F. (1988) 'The Shapley value in the non-differentiable case', *International Journal of Game Theory*, 17(1):1-65.

Phillips, R.S. (1940) 'On linear transformations', *Transactions of the American Mathematical Society*, 48:516-541.

PART II

ECONOMETRICS

Chapter 13

AN ECONOMETRIC APPROACH TO RATIONING AS A POLICY INSTRUMENT

Stephen M. GOLDFELD and Richard E. QUANDT

Princeton University, Princeton, NJ, USA

1. Introduction

Models of rationing behavior have a long tradition in the economics literature. In the last decade there has been a revival of interest in various aspects of the subject, both from theoretical and econometric points of view. Witness, for example, the now extensive literature on fix-price or temporary equilibrium models and on estimation and hypothesis testing in single and multimarket disequilibrium models.

In much of this work, rationing emerges as the result of some inherent rigidity, the source of which is not always made clear. There is, however, one strand of this literature in which rationing behavior emerges as an optimal strategy on the part of individual economic agents or policy makers. For example, Jaffee and Modigliani (1969) and Stiglitz and Weiss (1981) have studied the nature of optimal bank behavior which leads to credit rationing of loan customers. Similarly, Goldfeld, Jaffee and Quandt (1980) examined the circumstances under which it would be optimal for a policy maker such as a central bank to ration its "customers". The empirical work reported in that paper builds on earlier work in disequilibrium econometrics but, as the authors acknowledge, requires some strong, perhaps implausible, assumptions. The present paper seeks to put the econometrics of these types of rationing models on firmer grounds. As we shall see, this opens a wide

We are indebted to the National Science Foundation for support.

Economic Decision-Making: Games, Econometrics and Optimisation
Edited by J.J. Gabszewicz, J.-F. Richard and L.A. Wolsey
© *Elsevier Science Publishers B.V., 1990*

range of interesting econometric issues which may well have more general applicability.

The outline of the paper is as follows. Section 2 introduces a formal rationing model. Section 3 considers the econometric implementation of rationing models while some computational experience is described in Sections 4 and 5. The paper concludes with a brief summary and some suggestions for further research.

2. Rationing as an optimal policy

Our general motivation for rationing as an optimal policy can be seen by reference to Goldfeld, Jaffee and Quandt (1980) (henceforth GJQ). That paper considered a government financial authority which lends to the private financial institutions it regulates. The key element in this is the setting of an interest rate, x_t, which influences the demand for loans, y_t^d. The policy maker is also able to ration demand should it choose to do so. It picks an optimal policy consisting of x_t and a volume of loans extended, y_t, minimizing the loss function

$$L = (x_t - x_t^*)^2 + v_1(y_t - y_t^*)^2 + v_2(y_t - y_t^d)^2, \tag{2.1}$$

where x_t^* and y_t^* are desired values[1] and where the last term expresses the disutility of not satisfying demand (of course, y_t must be less than or equal to y_t^d).

We further posit

$$x_t^* = \alpha' z_{1t} + \varepsilon_{1t}, \tag{2.2}$$

$$y_t^* = \beta' z_{2t} + \varepsilon_{2t}, \tag{2.3}$$

$$y_t^d = \gamma_1 x_t + \gamma_2' z_{3t} + \varepsilon_{3t}. \tag{2.4}$$

We assume that x_t^* and y_t^* are known exactly to the policy maker. Equations (2.2) and (2.3) provide a model for those desired values where the stochastic terms reflect the inability of the outside econometrician to observe x_t^* and y_t^*. In contrast, the stochastic term ε_{3t} in (2.4) is unknown to the policy maker at the time it chooses x_t.[2] This suggests choosing an

---

[1] In terms of the GJQ model, x_t^* is related to the authority's own cost of funds, while y_t^* is the desired level of loans assumed to be a proxy for a desired level of housing activity financed by these loans. See Section 5.

[2] In GJQ the optimal strategy and subsequent econometric inplementation were based on the implausible assumption that the authority knows ε_{3t}.

optimal x_t by minimizing the expected loss, $E(L)$. We shall, in fact, do this below. However, for reasons which will be apparent when we consider issues of estimation, we first consider another approach.

A simplified approach. More particularly, we posit that the policy maker first chooses x_t and an "anticipated" value of y_t under the assumption that $\varepsilon_{3t} = 0$. That is, x_t and y_t are chosen to minimize (2.1) subject to (2.2)–(2.4) and the condition

$$y_t \le y_t^d. \tag{2.5}$$

Since, at this stage, ε_{3t} is assumed zero, (2.5) assumes that y_t does not exceed the expected level of borrowing, i.e., borrowers cannot be coerced, in an ex ante sense, to borrow more than they want. We further assume that after setting x_t, the policy maker learns the actual state of demand (i.e., in effect seeing the realization of ε_{3t}) and sets y_t in an optimal fashion, made precise below.

The solution to the policy maker's first-stage problem is determined by forming the Lagrangean

$$\bar{L} = (x - x^*)^2 + v_1(y - y^*)^2 + v_2(y - \gamma_1 x - \gamma_2' z_3)^2$$
$$+ \lambda(y - \gamma_1 x - \gamma_2' z_3), \tag{2.6}$$

where we have suppressed the time subscript. If we postulate that x and y are always positive, the following Kuhn–Tucker conditions are necessary and sufficient for the solution:

$$\frac{\partial \bar{L}}{\partial x} = 2(x - x^*) - 2v_2\gamma_1(y - \gamma_1 x - \gamma_2' z_3) - \lambda\gamma_1 = 0,$$

$$\frac{\partial \bar{L}}{\partial y} = 2v_1(y - y^*) + 2v_2(y - \gamma_1 x - \gamma_2' z_3) + \lambda = 0,$$

$$y \le y^d, \qquad (y^d - y)\lambda = 0.$$

Straightforward algebra yields the following solutions:

$$x = x_{\mathrm{I}} \equiv x^* + \frac{v_1\gamma_1(y^* - \gamma_2' z_3 - \gamma_1 x^*)}{1 + v_1\gamma_1^2} \quad \text{if } y^* \ge \gamma_1 x^* + \gamma_2' z_3, \tag{2.7}$$

$$x = x_{\mathrm{II}} \equiv x^* + \frac{\gamma_1 v_1 v_2(y^* - \gamma_2' z_3 - \gamma_1 x^*)}{v_1 + v_2 + \gamma_1^2 v_1 v_2} \quad \text{if } y^* < \gamma_1 x^* + \gamma_2' z_3. \tag{2.8}$$

Equation (2.7) corresponds to the case in which there is no anticipated rationing ($\lambda \ne 0$) while (2.8) is associated with anticipated rationing ($\lambda = 0$).[3]

---

[3] From (2.7) and (2.8), we see that when $y^* = \gamma_1 x^* + \gamma_2' z_3$, then $x_{\mathrm{I}} = x_{\mathrm{II}} = x^*$. To preserve space, we have not presented the two optimal solutions for y but, as the text suggests, when $\lambda \ne 0$ the anticipated y_{I} is $\gamma_1 x_{\mathrm{I}} + \gamma_2' x_3$.

The role of v_2 in the analysis is worthy of note. First, from (2.7) and (2.8) we see that whether there is anticipated rationing or not is independent of v_2, although the quantitative amount of anticipated rationing most certainly does depend on v_2.[4] In particular, rationing may take place even if $v_2 = 0$. When $v_2 = 0$, x_{11} becomes particularly simple, namely $x_{11} = x^*$, and the corresponding y is given by $y_{11} = y^*$.

Of course, as suggested earlier, we do not force the policy maker to stick with its anticipated y. Rather, after announcing x, the policy maker learns y^d and chooses an optimal y based on this information. With x set, this amounts to minimizing $v_1(y - y^*)^2 + v_2(y - y^d)^2$ subject to $y \le y^d$. Moreover, a bit of algebra reveals that this solution can be expressed compactly as[5]

$$y = \min\left(y^d, \frac{v_1 y^* + v_2 y^d}{v_1 + v_2}\right). \tag{2.9}$$

Equations (2.7), (2.8) and (2.9) completely characterize the optimal solution. We defer questions of estimation until the next section. Instead, we now develop the expected loss approach.

The expected loss approach. In the case just considered, the policy process was characterized by a first stage in which x and an anticipated y were chosen by ignoring the uncertainty associated with y^d. To account for this uncertainty requires minimizing $E(L)$ where, as before

$$L = (x - x^*)^2 + v_1(y - y^*)^2 + v_2(y - y^d)^2, \tag{2.1}$$

where y^d is given by eq. (2.4). If we assume ε_3 is normal with variance σ_3^2, then $y^d \sim N(\gamma_1 x + \gamma_2' z_3, \sigma_3^2)$. For use in what follows we denote this p.d.f. as $f(y^d)$, with the corresponding c.d.f. given by $F(y^d)$.

A final question arises as to the proper way to regard y in (2.1). If, in parallel with the previous setup, we regard y as chosen in a second stage after y^d is revealed, then y is given by the min-condition, (2.9). Hence at the time x is set, the policy authority should properly regard y as a random variable but explicitly recognize that the distribution of this variable is determined by its own future behavior. The optimal strategy is then to choose x to minimize $E(L)$ when L is given by (2.1), y^d by (2.4) and y by (2.9).

---

[4] It can be shown that anticipated rationing when $\lambda = 0$ is given by $v_1(\gamma_1 x^* + \gamma_2' z_3 - y^*)/(v_1 + v_2 + \gamma_1^2 v_2)$. By (2.8) this is positive, and decreasing in v_2.

[5] When $y = y^d$, the Lagrange multiplier which is non-negative is given by $2v_1(y^* - y)$, implying $y^* \ge y = y^d$. Then $y^* \ge y^d$ implies $(v_1 y^* + v_2 y^d)/(v_1 + v_2) \ge (v_1 y^d + v_2 y^d)/(v_1 + v_2) = y^d$. Hence (2.9) holds. For later use, we also note that when $y = y^d$ we have $y \le y^*$ and when $y = (v_1 y^* + v_2 y^d)/(v_1 + v_2) \le y^d$ we have $y^* \le y^d$ and hence $y \ge y^*$.

The actual derivation of this optimal strategy is somewhat involved and we shall just sketch a few steps. Taking expectations of (2.1) yields the following objective function to be minimized,

$$E(L) = (x - x^*)^2 + v_1[E(y) - y^*]^2 + v_1 \operatorname{var}(y) + v_2 E(y - y^d)^2. \qquad (2.10)$$

To evaluate (2.10) we need the mean and variance of y as well as $E(y - y^d)^2$. The first two of these require the p.d.f. of y while the last term can be most directly calculated from the p.d.f. of the variable $(y - y^d)$. From (2.9) and the algebra in footnote 5 we have that

$$y = \begin{cases} y^d & \text{if } y \le y^*, \\ \delta y^* + (1 - \delta) y^d & \text{if } y \ge y^*, \end{cases} \qquad (2.11)$$

where $\delta = v_1/(v_1 + v_2)$. From (2.11) we see that the p.d.f. of y, $h(y)$ has the following form

$$h(y) = \begin{cases} f(y), & -\infty \le y < y^*, \\ f\left(\dfrac{y - \delta y^*}{1 - \delta}\right)\left|\dfrac{1}{1 - \delta}\right|, & y^* \le y \le \infty, \end{cases} \qquad (2.12)$$

where $f(\ )$ is the p.d.f. of y^d.[6] From (2.12) and a bit of tedious manipulation one can derive $E(y)$ and $\operatorname{var}(y)$. For example, when expressed in terms of the standard normal p.d.f. ϕ (with corresponding c.d.f. Φ) we have

$$E(y) = \delta y^*(1 - \Phi(w)) + (\gamma_1 x + \gamma_2' z_3)(1 - \delta + \delta \Phi(w))$$
$$\qquad - \delta \sigma_3 \phi(w), \qquad (2.13)$$

$$w = (y^* - \gamma_1 x - \gamma_2' z_3)/\sigma_3. \qquad (2.14)$$

To evaluate $E(y - y^d)^2$ we note that

$$u = y - y^d = \begin{cases} 0 & \text{if } y \le y^*, \\ \delta(y^* - y^d) & \text{if } y \ge y^*, \end{cases}$$

so that the p.d.f. of u is given by

$$g(u) = \begin{cases} F(y^*) & \text{if } u = 0, \\ f(y^* - (u/\delta))(1/\delta) & \text{if } u < 0. \end{cases} \qquad (2.15)$$

---

[6] When $v_2 = 0$ and $\delta = 1$, the form of (2.12) simplifies because $y = \min(y^d, y^*)$ and the p.d.f. has a mass point at $y = y^*$. Thus, the second term in (2.12) reduces to $h(y) = 1 - F(y^*)$ when $y = y^*$ where $F(\ )$ is the c.d.f. of y^d.

Using the densities given in (2.12) and (2.15), we can compute $E(L|x)$ and differentiate this with respect to x to find the following first order condition:

$$H(x) \equiv (x - x^*) + \gamma_1 v_1 (\gamma_1 x + \gamma_2' z_3 - y^*) \left[\frac{v_2}{v_1 + v_2} + \frac{v_1}{v_1 + v_2} \, \Phi(w) \right]$$

$$- \gamma_1 v_1 \sigma_3 \phi(w) \left[\frac{v_1}{v_1 + v_2} \right] = 0. \tag{2.16}$$

Since both $\phi(w)$ and $\Phi(w)$ depend on x in a nonlinear way,[7] it is not possible to give an explicit algebraic solution for x. One can, of course, solve (2.16) numerically. Moreover, we can shed considerable light on the properties of the solution to (2.16).

Properties of the optimal strategies. We can readily establish that

$$H'(x) = 1 + v_1 \gamma_1^2 [1 + \delta(\Phi(w) - 1)]. \tag{2.17}$$

Since $H'(x)$ is therefore strictly positive we know that there is a unique solution to $H(x) = 0$.[8] Let us denote this by $\hat{x}$. A question naturally arises as to the relationship of $\hat{x}$ to the solution, call it $\tilde{x}$, given by the simplified approach summarized in (2.7) and (2.8). The nature of the relationship can most easily be seen by evaluating $H(x)$, from (2.16), at x_1, x_{11} given by (2.7) and (2.8). A bit of algebra reveals

$$H(x_1) = -\gamma_1 \sigma_3 v_1 \delta [\phi(w_1) - (1 - \Phi(w_1))w_1],$$

$$H(x_{11}) = -\gamma_1 \sigma_3 v_1 \delta [\phi(w_{11}) + \Phi(w_{11})w_{11}], \tag{2.18}$$

where from (2.14),

$$w_1 = (y^* - \gamma_1 x^* - \gamma_2' z_3) / \sigma_3 (1 + v_1 \gamma_1^2),$$

$$w_{11} = (v_1 + v_2)(y^* - \gamma_1 x^* - \gamma_2' z) / \sigma_3 (v_1 + v_2 + \gamma_1^2 v_1 v_2).$$

Intuitively, it should be the case that when σ_3^2 is small the solutions of $\hat{x}$ and $\tilde{x}$ should be quite close since $\tilde{x}$ should well approximate $\hat{x}$ when there is little uncertainty about demand. This intuition is confirmed by examining the limiting behavior of (2.18) as $\sigma_3^2 \to 0$. If $S = y^* - \gamma_1 x^* - \gamma_2' z_3 > 0$ then $\Phi(w_1) \to 1$ and $H(x_1) \to 0$. Alternatively, if $S < 0$, $\Phi(w_{11}) \to 0$. Comparing this with (2.7) and (2.8), we see that $\lim_{\sigma_3 \to 0} \hat{x} = \tilde{x}$.

Equation (2.18) can be used to shed further light on the relationship between $\hat{x}$ and $\tilde{x}$ for nontrivial values of σ_3^2. Using the standard properties

---

[7] For example, $\phi(w) = (1/\sqrt{2\pi}) \exp\{-((y^* - \gamma_1 x - \gamma_2' z_3)^2 / \sigma_3)/2\}$.

[8] We are here ignoring the possibility that $H(0) > 0$, which would imply a boundary solution of $x = 0$. For certain values of the parameters, e.g., $\delta = 1$ and $\gamma_1 > 0$, it can be shown that $H(0) < 0$, but in general the boundary solution needs to be ruled out by assumption.

of the normal distribution, both bracketed terms in (2.18) are positive. Hence, when $\gamma_1 < 0$, we see that $H(x_1)$ and $H(x_{11})$ are both positive. Since $H'(x) > 0$, we see that $\hat{x}$ must be less than both x_1 and x_{11}. We have thus established that $\hat{x} < \tilde{x}$. Thus, a policy maker who minimizes expected loss will, by choosing a lower value for x, be more likely to ration.[9] This result actually holds in more general sense, which we can see if we examine $d\hat{x}/d\sigma_3$. All the comparative statics qualitative results, under the assumption that $\gamma_1 < 0$, are summarized in Table 1, which also gives the qualitative effect of a change in each parameter on the quantity of expected rationing. The latter is defined as $E(y^d - y)$. (The relevant derivatives are given in Appendix 1).

The results are generally as expected. A decrease in x^* leads to a reduction in $\hat{x}$ but, since $d\hat{x}/dx^* < 1$, also corresponds to an increase in expected rationing. An increase in the target y, y^*, is accompanied by both a reduced $\hat{x}$ and diminished rationing. Increasing v_2, which raises the disutility from rationing, leads to a higher $\hat{x}$ and reduced rationing. Indeed, in the limit as v_2 gets arbitrarily large, we have that $E(y^d - y)$ tends to zero as $\hat{x}$ tends to x_1, the nonrationing certainty solution. An increase in v_1, the parameter affecting the disutility from deviating from y^*, in general has an uncertain sign. When $v_2 = 0$, raising v_1 unambiguously lowers $\hat{x}$ as would be expected. When $v_2 > 0$, however, the fact that lowering $\hat{x}$ raises $E(y^d)$ more than $E(y)$ serves to render ambiguous the overall effect. Finally, decreasing σ_3, the demand uncertainty, raises $\hat{x}$ and reduces expected rationing. This is in accord with the earlier comparison of $\hat{x}$ and $\tilde{x}$ as we have already seen that $\lim_{\sigma_3 \to 0} \hat{x} = \tilde{x}$.[10]

Table 1

P	$\dfrac{d\hat{x}}{dP}$	$\dfrac{dE(y^d - y)}{dP}$
x^*	$+$	$-$
y^*	$-$	$-$
v_1	$?$	$?$
v_2	$+$	$-$
σ_3	$-$	$+$

[9] This conclusion does not depend on the sign of γ_1. If $\gamma_1 > 0$ we would have $\hat{x} > \tilde{x}$ but demand would be higher at $\hat{x}$ and so rationing is still more likely. Since the assumption that $\gamma_1 < 0$ is more in keeping with our initial motivating example, we shall confine our attention to this case.

[10] It can be shown that for large σ_3 the expected loss solution is essentially linear in σ_3.

3. Econometric implementation

The previous section developed two related alternative models of policy-maker behavior. The second of these is perhaps more appealing but, as we shall see, presents econometric complications. The first model consists of eqs. (2.2)–(2.4) and (2.7)–(2.9). For convenience these are collected below in a slightly different form:

$$x^* = \alpha' z_1 + \varepsilon_1, \tag{3.1}$$

$$y^* = \beta' z_2 + \varepsilon_2, \tag{3.2}$$

$$x = \frac{\alpha' z_1 + v_1 \gamma_1 \beta' z_2 - v_1 \gamma_1 \gamma_2' z_3}{1 + v_1 \gamma_1^2} + \frac{\varepsilon_1 + v_1 \gamma_1 \varepsilon_2}{1 + v_1 \gamma_1^2}$$

$$\text{if } S = \beta' z_2 - \gamma_1 \alpha' z_1 - \gamma_2' z_3 + \varepsilon_2 - \gamma_1 \varepsilon_1 \geq 0, \tag{3.3}$$

$$x = \frac{(v_1 + v_2)\alpha' z_1 + \gamma_1 v_1 v_2 \beta' z_2 - \gamma_1 v_1 v_2 \gamma_2' z_3}{v_1 + v_2 + \gamma_1^2 v_1 v_2} + \frac{(v_1 + v_2)\varepsilon_1 + \gamma_1 v_1 v_2 \varepsilon_2}{v_1 + v_2 + \gamma_1^2 v_1 v_2}$$

$$\text{if } S < 0, \tag{3.4}$$

$$y^d = \gamma_1 x + \gamma_2' z_3 + \varepsilon_3, \tag{3.5}$$

$$y = \min\left(y^d, \frac{v_1 y^* + v_2 y^d}{v_1 + v_2} \right). \tag{3.6}$$

The only difference between this set of equations and those given earlier is that we have used (3.1) and (3.2) to rewrite (2.7) and (2.8) as (3.3) and (3.4). That is, we have explicitly introduced the stochastic terms and made apparent that the "switch condition" depends on the random variable S. The properties of S, in turn, depend on ε_1 and ε_2, which stem from our stochastic modeling of the behavior of the policy authority in the choice of its desired or target values for x and y.

We shall consider three alternative ways in which the parameters can be estimated, each of which applies the maximum likelihood method to some or all of the equations of the model. For this purpose, we shall assume that the ε_i are independently normal with variances σ_i^2.[11] The first approach consists of estimating the submodel consisting of (3.3) and (3.4). It can readily be seen that this submodel allows one to identify almost all the

---

[11] The most general derivation of the various likelihood functions would allow for a nonzero covariance between ε_1 and ε_2 but, given our previous discussion on timing aspects, would assume ε_3 independent of the other ε's if ε_3 is interpreted as a macro-shock. This assumption might have to be modified if demanders' behavior were assumed to be strategic.

parameters of interest in the full model.[12] Equations (3.3) and (3.4) constitute a version of a switching regression model to which one may apply the approach developed by Kiefer (1977). More particularly, (3.3) and (3.4) obviously constitute a model of the following form:

$$X_t = \begin{cases} B'_1 Z_t + u_{1t} & \text{if } S_t > 0, \\ B'_2 Z_t + u_{2t} & \text{otherwise,} \end{cases}$$

$$S_t = B'_3 Z_t + u_{3t}.$$

It can be shown that the p.d.f. of X_t is given by

$$g(X) = Pf_1 + (1 - P)f_2,$$

$$P = \Phi(B'_3 Z / \sigma_3),$$

$$f_1 = \sigma_1^{-1} P^{-1} \Phi\left[\frac{B'_3 Z / \sigma_3 + \rho_{13} r_1}{\sqrt{1 - \rho_{13}^2}}\right] \phi(r_1), \tag{3.7}$$

$$f_2 = \sigma_2^{-1}(1 - P)^{-1} \Phi\left[\frac{-B'_3 Z / \sigma_3 - \rho_{23} r_2}{\sqrt{1 - \rho_{23}^2}}\right] \phi(r_2),$$

$$r_j = (X - B'_j Z) / \sigma_j, \quad j = 1, 2,$$

and σ_j^2 and ρ_{ij} are variances and correlation coefficients for the u_j and where as before $\Phi(\ )$ and $\phi(\ )$ are the c.d.f. and p.d.f. of the standard normal, respectively. The product of terms in $g(X)$ then gives the relevant likelihood function. While maximization of this likelihood function yields most of the parameters of interest, these estimates are not fully efficient, since they ignore y.

A second set of estimates can be obtained from considering only eqs. (3.2), (3.5) and (3.6). Although this has the apparent structure of a simple disequilibrium model without a price equation, it is not a complete model, since x is also an endogenous variable. In particular, as can be seen from eqs. (2.7) and (2.8), x is not independent of y^*, unless $\varepsilon_2 \equiv 0$. This means that if x is regarded as exogenous in deriving the likelihood function, the resulting estimates will suffer from a type of endogenous policy bias. The quantitative importance of this, however, remains to be established.

We finally turn to the full model (3.1)-(3.6). We assume as before that ε_1, ε_2 and ε_3 are independent normal disturbance terms. We then perform a series of piecewise linear transformations, which take us from the joint

---

[12] One obvious exception is σ_3^2. In addition, if z_2 and z_3 share any common variables, including an intercept, their coefficients cannot be separately identified.

p.d.f. of $\{\varepsilon_1, \varepsilon_1, \varepsilon_3\}$ to the p.d.f. of $\{x, y\}$. The details of this derivation are in Appendix 2.

We now turn to the problem of estimating the expected loss model where x is implicitly given by

$$(x - x^*) + \gamma_1 v_1(\gamma_1 x + \gamma_2' z_3 - y^*)[1 - \delta + \delta \Phi(w)]$$
$$- \gamma_1 v_1 \sigma_3 \delta \phi(w) = 0, \tag{3.8}$$

and where $x^* = \alpha' z_1 + \varepsilon_1$, $y^* = \beta' z_2 + \varepsilon_2$ and $w = (y^* - \gamma_1 x - \gamma_2' z_3)/\sigma_3$. Estimation using (3.8) presents several problems, the least of which stems from the fact that (3.8) is only an implicit nonlinear equation. A more serious problem stems from the error structure of (3.8). While the x^* term introduces an additive error, y^* enters (3.8) in various nonlinear ways and the overall implied error structure is extremely complicated. It would thus appear that in the general case, the expected loss model is not easily estimable.

When $\varepsilon_2 \equiv 0$, however, we can derive the exact likelihood function for the observable variables, x and y. The joint density of x and y can be most easily obtained as the product of the conditional density of y given x and the marginal density of x. The former is just the density that results from the simple disequilibrium model ((3.2), (3.5) and (3.6)) since, as just noted, when $\varepsilon_2 \equiv 0$, x is independent of y^*. The marginal density of x follows straightforwardly from (3.8), given that $\varepsilon_1 \sim N(0, \sigma_1^2)$. The likelihood function thus derived will only be approximate for $\sigma_2 \neq 0$ and the consequences of this will be examined below. This difficulty also suggests the wisdom of trying other approximate ways to estimate the expected loss model.[13]

4. Some computational experience

We now describe some sampling experiments aimed at providing computational experience with rationing models. To minimize computational costs we have chosen a bare-bones specification with an intercept and one exogenous variable in each stochastic relationship. More specifically, the parameters appear as follows:

$$L = (x - x^*)^2 + v_1(y - y^*)^2 + v_2(y - y^d)^2,$$
$$x^* = \alpha_0 + \alpha_1 z_1 + \varepsilon_1,$$
$$y^* = \beta_0 + \beta_1 z_2 + \varepsilon_2,$$
$$y^d = \gamma_{20} + \gamma_{21} z_3 + \gamma_1 x + \varepsilon_3.$$

[13] For example, we have already seen that (3.8) collapses to the switch model given by (3.3) and (3.4) as σ_3^2 tends to zero so we could estimate the switch model with expected loss data. We should also note that estimation of (3.8) by itself does not permit the identification of all the parameters in (3.8).

There are nine basic parameters $(v_1, v_2, \alpha_0, \alpha_1, \beta_0, \beta_1, \gamma_{20}, \gamma_{21}, \gamma_1)$ and, given the assumption that the ε_i are independently normally distributed, three variances σ_i^2, $i = 1, 2, 3$.

The previous section outlined four methods for estimating the rationing model. We shall refer to these as Exploss (eqs. (3.2), (3.5), (3.6) and (3.8)), Switch (eqs. (3.3), (3.4)), Min (eqs. (3.2), (3.5) and (3.6)) and Full (eqs. (3.1)-(3.6)). While the Full and Exploss methods estimate all parameters, the remaining methods can only estimate some subset. For Switch the estimable parameters are $(v_1, v_2, \alpha_0, \alpha_1, \beta_1, \gamma_{21}, \gamma_1, \sigma_1^2, \sigma_2^2)$ while for Min they are $(\beta_0, \beta_1, \gamma_{20}, \gamma_{21}, \gamma_1, \sigma_2^2, \sigma_3^2)$. In addition, Min provides an estimate of $\delta = v_1/(v_1 + v_2)$.

The other details of the experiments are as follows. The z_i's were generated from the uniform distribution with ranges (0, 100), (0, 100) and (200, 400), or with ranges multiplied by 10. The parameter values were $v_1 = 4$, $v_2 = 2$, $\alpha_0 = 70$, $\alpha_1 = 1$, $\beta_1 = 0.5$, $\gamma_{20} = 60$, $\gamma_{21} = -0.25$, $\gamma_1 = 0.5$. For the small z range, $\beta_0 = 20$ while $\beta_0 = -655$ for the large z range. These values were chosen so that the mean of the switch variable, S, was zero. For all experiments $\sigma_1^2 = 250$ while the values of σ_2^2 and σ_3^2 were varied as indicated below. Finally, all experiments consisted of 50 replications and, except for one case, we dealt with sample sizes of size 40.

An overview of the sampling experiments is provided in Table 2.[14] There are six cases, I-VI, which come in pairs. In cases I, III and V the data are generated assuming that the policy maker follows the simplified approach of choosing x as if $\varepsilon_3 \equiv 0$, labeled "certainty" in Table 2. (In generating the y data, of course, ε_3 is drawn from the appropriate normal distribution.) In cases II, IV and VI the data are generated by assuming the policy maker

Table 2
Design of experiments

Case	σ_2^2	σ_3^2	z-range	Data generation
I	250	125	small	"certainty"
II	250	125	small	expected loss
III	250	2000	small	"certainty"
IV	250	2000	small	expected loss
V	250	500	big	"certainty"
VI	250	500	big	expected loss

[14] Some preliminary experiments examined the behavior of the Exploss method when $\sigma_2^2 = 0$. Judged by a variety of criteria, the method appeared to behave quite reasonably.

follows expected loss minimization. The range of the z's and σ_3 vary across the pairs. All four estimation methods are used in each case. In analyzing the results we shall mainly rely on a nonparametric statistic, the fraction of times one estimator is closer to the truth than another, although we shall also make occasional use of mean absolute deviations (MADs).

Table 3 reports the results of the average percentage win statistics for a bivariate comparison of methods across the various experiments.[15] For cases I, III and V, the simplified "certainty" cases, we anticipate that the Full method would be the most reliable estimating technique and this is borne out in the average percentage win statistics in Table 3. While, strictly speaking, the behavior across parameters is not independent, a rough measure of the standard error of this statistic is $2\frac{1}{2}$-3 percentage points. Given this, the superior performance of the Full method in cases I, III and V is statistically significant in most comparisons. Although not particularly designed for these cases, overall the Exploss method does better than the Min and Switch methods but less well than the Full method.

In cases II, IV and VI the data are generated by assuming the policymaker takes account of demand uncertainty so that the Exploss method should perform relatively better. This is generally borne out in Table 3 with the notable exception of the Full vs. Exploss in cases I and II. The relative performance of the four estimating methods can also be seen in Table 4 which reports the MADs for two cases, normalized so that the lowest entry in each row is unity.

Overall, the Full method is clearly best when it is appropriate while the Exploss method does relatively best when data are generated reflecting

Table 3
Average percentage win statistics*

	I	II	III	IV	V	VI
Exploss vs. Switch (7)	52.5	52.3	42.8	52.8	62.5	68.8
Exploss vs. Min (5)	60.3	61.7	58.0	63.3	47.3	48.3
Full vs. Exploss (9)	56.2	59.6	61.4	46.7	54.9	49.3
Full vs. Switch (7)	63.4	65.1	55.0	60.9	72.0	72.6
Full vs. Min (6)	71.7	72.7	64.7	65.0	53.2	51.8

* Entries give the average percentage of wins for the first-named method in each row. The number of parameters in each comparison is given in parentheses.

[15] As the Min method has relatively few parameters in common with Switch, this comparison is not presented. It should also be noted that the comparisons in Table 3 are restricted to nonvariance parameters.

Table 4
Relative MADs

	Case II				Case VI			
	Full	Exploss	Switch	Min	Full	Exploss	Switch	Min
v_1	1.9	1.0	15.8	—	1.0	1.1	2.5	—
v_2	1.0	5.7	20.1	—	1.0	1.2	2.3	—
α_0	1.2	1.5	1.0	—	1.2	1.0	1.6	—
α_1	1.0	2.3	2.1	—	1.2	1.0	1.7	—
β_0	1.0	1.3	—	3.2	1.0	1.1	—	1.1
β_1	1.0	1.2	1.6	5.8	1.0	1.0	2.5	1.3
γ_{20}	1.0	1.3	—	1.1	1.3	1.1	—	1.0
γ_{21}	1.0	1.5	3.0	2.9	1.0	1.0	2.3	1.1
γ_1	1.0	1.7	3.2	2.8	1.0	1.0	3.0	1.2
δ	1.0	1.8	2.6	1.8	1.0	1.1	1.6	1.8

demand uncertainty. At least for the range of parameters explored, the Full method also performs reasonably in this case.[16]

5. An application to "Central Banking"

This section reports on the application of the techniques developed to the issue, briefly noted in Section 2, of estimating the joint behavior of a financial authority and of the institutions that it regulates. More particularly, we examine the Federal Home Loan Bank Board (FHLBB) which provides loans to saving and loan associations (SLA) designed to stabilize housing and mortgage markets. In terms of eq. (2.1), y_t^d is the SLAs demand for such loans, x_t is the interest rate set by the FHLBB for such loans, and y_t is the realized quantity. The latter, in principle, reflects the balancing of rationing considerations and the desired values for x and y.

To make things specific, we posit that x_t^* depends on the cost of funds to the FHLBB (C) and the lagged loan rate, while y_t^* depends on variables related to the demand for housing.[17] The variables determining y_t^* are as follows: KD, the real stock of housing; VD, real household net worth; REP,

[16] In general, the Full method does least well for the intercept terms. It should also be noted that there is some mild evidence of a "policy bias" with the simple Min model. More particularly, for about two-thirds of all the parameter estimates the Min model had larger biases than the Full model.

[17] The lagged loan rate is meant to allow for the possibility that the FHLBB suffers a utility loss from changing the loan rate from period to period. For a more complete discussion of this issue and of the institutional details, see Goldfeld, Jaffee and Quandt (1980).

the inflow of deposit and mortgage payments to SLAs; H_{-1}, the lagged real value of housing starts. VD, REP and H_{-1} should influence housing activity positively and are therefore expected to yield negative coefficients in the y^* equation; the reverse is true for KD.

Finally, we need a specification for loan demand. We utilize the following variables: D88, unanticipated deposit inflows; CL4, a measure of mortgage commitments; M, the mortgage-deposit ratio at SLAs; and DUM, a dummy variable accounting for a special loan program offered by the FHLBB in 1970.[18] The various measures of mortgage loans or commitments made are expected to influence loan demand positively, while D88 and, of course, the rate on loans should yield negative coefficients.[19]

The first two columns of Table 5 report the results of estimating the model by the full method and the expected loss approach. The first two variables correspond to x_i^*, the next four to y_i^*, and the subsequent seven to the loan demand equation. Intercepts and variances were also estimated but to conserve space are not reported. Overall, the parameters in the first two columns are generally correctly signed and statistically significant. The one sign exception is the insignificant REP variable in the y^* equation. This equation presents some more general difficulties in that all the y^* parameters are insignificant with the Exploss method.

Overall, the parameters of y^* aside, the estimates from the two methods are both sensible and comparable. It is therefore of interest to use these to calculate various implied aspects of the underlying rationing behavior. For this purpose, we focus on the full method results. Perhaps the most interesting statistic is $E\{y_t^d \mid y_t\}$.[20] When this is computed, we find that $E\{y_t^d \mid y_t\} > y_t$ for each observation, suggesting that there is rationing in every period in our sample.[21] On the other hand, the actual amount of implied rationing is quite small, averaging 7.5 percent over the full sample. This, in turn, suggests the possibility that the data are well explained by some sort of equilibrium model.

---

[18] The same specification and variable names are used in Goldfeld, Jaffee and Quandt (1980). That paper also contains precise definitions of all the variables used in the present paper.

[19] The interest rate on loans is entered as the differential from the mortgage rate. Another measurement issue worth noting is that y is measured by the loan-deposit ratio and that a lagged dependent variable also appears in the demand equation.

[20] Calculation of this statistic is analogous to the computation of expected demand, given the observed quantity, in a supply-demand disequilibrium framework. For the relevant formulas, see Goldfeld and Quandt (1981).

[21] There is some evidence that when the observations are "one-sided", the sort of approach we are using may result in econometric difficulties. This may account for the behavior of the y^* estimates. See the discussion of the all-excess-demand issue in Quandt (1988).

The most natural equilibrium model, corresponding to our rationing models, is based on the loss function given by

$$L = (x - x^*)^2 + v_1(y^d - y^*)^2. \tag{5.1}$$

Under (5.1), the FHLBB still chooses x in the light of its desired values, x^* and y^*, but it assumes that the observed loan quantity is given by the demand function. Minimizing expected loss yields an interest-rate-setting equation given by

$$x = \frac{x^*}{1 + v_1\gamma_1^2} + \frac{v_1\gamma_1(y^* - \gamma_2'z_3)}{1 + v_1\gamma_1^2}, \tag{5.2}$$

which, given (2.2) and (2.3), can then be estimated jointly with the loan demand function. Joint estimation is desirable since the parameters of the demand function appear in (5.2). Results of this estimation appear in the third column of Table 5.

Formal comparisons of the equilibrium and rationing results are not readily available but an informal test suggests that the results are consistent with an equilibrium interpretation. In particular, we reestimated the rationing model by the full method imposing the restrictions on the first thirteen parameters given by the equilibrium estimates in Table 5. We thus estimated

Table 5
FHLBB results*

Variable	Full method		Exploss		Equilibrium	
	Estimate	t-stat.	Estimate	t-stat.	Estimate	t-stat.
C	0.285	8.61	0.295	8.47	0.236	6.92
x_{-1}	0.671	18.78	0.671	16.92	0.737	19.72
KD	0.449	3.87	2.613	1.17	0.426	4.14
VD	−0.087	3.95	−0.464	1.14	−0.005	2.47
REP	1.879	1.75	4.825	0.61	0.142	1.33
H_{-1}	−0.166	4.16	−0.881	1.25	−0.012	4.27
D88	−0.052	3.85	−0.043	3.01	−0.075	5.17
CL4	0.194	6.92	0.197	6.99	0.134	4.54
M_{-1}	0.054	3.35	0.052	3.11	−0.004	2.21
$M - M_{-1}$	0.565	16.22	0.566	16.46	0.478	12.30
DUM	1.109	9.56	1.104	9.63	1.141	8.35
x	−0.048	2.38	−0.017	1.34	−0.072	1.50
y_{-1}	0.916	33.45	0.907	29.35	1.002	41.14
v_1	0.071	7.98	0.034	6.12	1.540	1.48
v_2	9.814	9.39	21.605	1.22	—	—

* The sample period is quarterly 1958:1 to 1977:3.

eight free parameters, three intercepts, three variances, and v_1 and v_2. Using the resulting likelihood function value, in conjunction with the equilibrium value, we can construct a heuristic likelihood ratio test statistic of 11.26.[22] Since $\chi^2(13) = 22.36$, the results suggest that the equilibrium hypothesis can not be rejected. As before, we can also use the estimates to calculate $E\{y^d|y\}$ and we find that average percentage discrepancy between this and y is 0.3 percent.

On balance the data appear to be consistent with either a modest but systematic degree of rationing or a non-rationing interpretation. The latter interpretation also emerged in our earlier analysis of the data done from a different and slightly suspect approach. Nevertheless, in retrospect, the absence of a strong rationing effect is hardly a surprise.

6. Conclusions

This paper presents two types of rationing models that differ in their treatment of the underlying uncertainty. From a theoretical perspective the expected loss approach has the more appeal. Indeed, a number of interesting estensions of this model can be readily suggested. For one, it would be possible to extend the model to allow for more than one source of uncertainty. For example, we could allow for the possibility that the policy maker is uncertain both with respect to the strength of demand and in regards to the elasticity of demand with respect to its instrument (i.e., γ_1).[23] Still another related extension would be to adopt an explicit multiperiod setting where, perhaps, anticipations of rationing might be important.[24]

Appendix 1

The relevant expressions for the comparative statics of the expected loss

---

[22] See Portes, Quandt and Yeo (1988) for a discussion and similar application of this approach.

[23] See Goldfeld and Quandt (1986).

[24] Several potential areas of application of the extended expected loss model can be noted. One example stems from the work of Abel (1985) who analyzes inventory behavior in the face of stockouts, a setup that leads to min conditions. It also appears fruitful to apply the expected loss model to the multiperiod interest-rate setting behavior analyzed in Goldfeld and Jaffee (1970).

model referred to in the text are given below,

$$\frac{\mathrm{d}x}{\mathrm{d}x^*} = 1/H'(x), \qquad \frac{\mathrm{d}x}{\mathrm{d}y^*} = -v_1\gamma_1(1 - \delta + \delta\Phi)/H'(x),$$

$$\frac{\mathrm{d}x}{\mathrm{d}v_1} = -\gamma_1\sigma_3[\delta(2 - \delta)(w(1 - \Phi) - \phi) - w]/H'(x),$$

$$\frac{\mathrm{d}x}{\mathrm{d}v_2} = -\gamma_1\delta^2\sigma_3[w(\Phi - 1) + \phi]/H'(x), \qquad \frac{\mathrm{d}x}{\mathrm{d}\sigma_3} = v_1\gamma_1\delta\phi/H'(x).$$

To calculate the quantity of expected rationing, $E(y^{\mathrm{d}} - y)$, one can proceed directly from the p.d.f. of $y^{\mathrm{d}} - y$ or combine (4.13) and (4.16). The result is

$$R = E(y^{\mathrm{d}} - y) = \left(\frac{1 + v_1\gamma_1^2}{\gamma_1 v_1}\right)x + \gamma_2'z_3 - y^* - x^*/\gamma_1 v_1.$$

From this one can directly calculate the relevant derivatives. For example,

$$\frac{\mathrm{d}R}{\mathrm{d}x^*} = \gamma_1\delta(1 - \Phi)/H'(x), \qquad \frac{\mathrm{d}R}{\mathrm{d}y^*} = -\delta(1 - \Phi)/H'(x).$$

Appendix 2

It is convenient to write S in (3.3) as

$$S = y^* - \gamma_1 x^* - \gamma_2'z_3 = \bar{S} + \varepsilon_2 - \gamma_1\varepsilon_1, \tag{A.1}$$

where $\bar{S} \equiv \beta_2'z_2 - \gamma_1\alpha'z_1 - \gamma_2'z_3$. We now perform the sequence of transformations.

Step 1. Equations (3.1) and (A.1) define a linear transformation from $\{\varepsilon_1, \varepsilon_2, \varepsilon_3\}$ to $\{x^*, S, \varepsilon_3\}$ which now have a joint normal distribution.

Step 2. We next transform from $\{x^*, S, \varepsilon_3\}$ to $\{x, S, y^{\mathrm{d}}\}$. First note that from (3.3) and (3.4),

$$x = \begin{cases} x^* + \gamma_1 k_1 S & \text{if } S \geq 0, \\ x^* + \gamma_1 k_2 S & \text{if } S < 0, \end{cases} \tag{A.2}$$

where $k_1 = v_1/(1 + v_1\gamma_1^2)$, $k_2 = v_1 v_2/(v_1 + v_2 + \gamma_1^2 v_1 v_2)$. It follows immediately that the p.d.f. of x, S, y^{d} is

$$g(x, S, y^{\mathrm{d}}) = \begin{cases} f(x - \gamma_1 k_1 S, S, y^{\mathrm{d}}) & \text{if } S \geq 0, \\ f(x - \gamma_1 k_2 S, S, y^{\mathrm{d}}) & \text{if } S < 0. \end{cases} \tag{A.3}$$

Step 3. We next transform from (x, S, y^d) to (x, y^c, y^d) where y^c is the composite variable $y^c = \delta y^* + (1 - \delta) y^d$. By the definition of S and (A.2), we have

$$y^* = \begin{cases} S + \gamma_1(x - \gamma_1 k_1 S) + \gamma_2' z_3 & \text{if } S \geq 0, \\ S + \gamma_1(x - \gamma_1 k_2 S) + \gamma_2' z_3 & \text{if } S < 0, \end{cases}$$

and hence

$$y^c - (1 - \delta) y^d - \delta(\gamma_1 x + \gamma_2' z_3) = \begin{cases} \delta S(1 - \gamma_1^2 k_1) & \text{if } S \geq 0, \\ \delta S(1 - \gamma_1^2 k_2) & \text{if } S < 0. \end{cases} \tag{A.4}$$

From the definitions of k_1 and k_2 it follows immediately that $1 - \gamma_1^2 k_1 > 0$, $1 - \gamma_1^2 k_2 > 0$. It then follows that there is a one to one correspondence between the sign of S and the sign of $\tilde{S} = y^c - (1 - \delta) y^d - \delta(\gamma_1 x + \gamma_2' z_3)$. Solving (A.4), we have

$$S_i = [y^c - (1 - \delta) y^d - \delta(\gamma_1 x + \gamma_2' z_3)] / \delta(1 - \gamma_1^2 k_i), \tag{A.5}$$

where i indexes regimes and solution values and where $i = 1$ if $\tilde{S} \geq 0$ and $i = 2$ otherwise. Substituting (A.5) in (A.3) we obtain

$$\psi(x, y^c, y^d) = \begin{cases} \psi_1(x, y^c, y^d) = J_1 f(x - \gamma_1 k_1 S_1, S_1, y^d) & \text{if } \tilde{S} \geq 0, \\ \psi_2(x, y^c, y^d) = J_2 f(x - \gamma_1 k_2 S_2, S_2, y^d) & \text{if } \tilde{S} < 0, \end{cases} \tag{A.6}$$

where the regime classification conditions may be written equivalently in terms of S or $\tilde{S}$, and where $J_i = 1 / \delta(1 - \gamma_1^2 k_i)$ is the appropriate Jacobian of the transformation from (A.5).

The final step is to integrate out either y^c or y^d as required by the min condition. There are two cases to be considered: (i) $y^d < y^c$ and (ii) $y^d \geq y^c$. For $y^d < y^c$, $y = y^d$. In Figure 1 we represent a 45° line and the equation $\tilde{S} = 0$ (which has slope <1).

At the intersection of the 45° line and $\tilde{S} = 0$, $y^d = \gamma_1 x + \gamma_2' z_3$. The variable y^c must be integrated out for any value of y from the 45° line to infinity. If $y < \gamma_1 x + \gamma_2' z_3$, as at A_1, y^c has to be integrated out first from the 45° line to the line $\tilde{S} = 0$ using ψ_2 (because, from A_2 to A_3, $\tilde{S} < 0$) and then from A_3 to infinity using ψ_1 (because here $\tilde{S} > 0$). Denoting the value of y^c at A_3 by $\lim 1 = (1 - \delta) y + \delta(\gamma_1 x + \gamma_2' z_3)$, the appropriate piece of the density for this subcase is

$$\int_y^{\lim 1} \psi_2(x, y^c, y) \, dy^c + \int_{\lim 1}^{\infty} \psi_1(x, y^c, y) \, dy^c.$$

In the event that $y > \gamma_1 x + \gamma_2' z_3$, as at B_1, we must integrate out, using ψ_1, from B_3 to infinity.

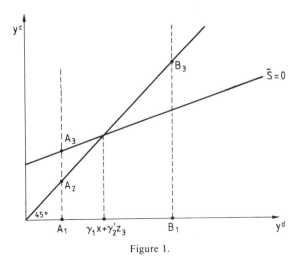

Figure 1.

A completely analogous argument applies when $y^d \geq y^c$. Defining $\lim 2 = [y - \delta(\gamma_1 x + \gamma_2' z_3)]/(1 - \delta)$ and combining the various pieces corresponding to whether y is smaller or larger than $\gamma_1 x + \gamma_2' z_3$, we obtain

$$
h(x, y) = \begin{cases}
h_1(x, y) = \displaystyle\int_y^\infty \psi_2(x, y, y^d)\,\mathrm{d}y^d + \int_y^{\lim 1} \psi_2(x, y^c, y)\,\mathrm{d}y^c \\[2mm]
\qquad + \displaystyle\int_{\lim 1}^\infty \psi_1(x, y^c, y)\,\mathrm{d}y^c \quad \text{if } y < \gamma_1 x + \gamma_2' z_3, \\[4mm]
h_2(x, y) = \displaystyle\int_y^\infty \psi_1(x, y^c, y)\,\mathrm{d}y^c + \int_{\lim 2}^\infty \psi_2(x, y, y^d)\,\mathrm{d}y^d \\[2mm]
\qquad + \displaystyle\int_y^{\lim 2} \psi_1(x, y, y^d)\,\mathrm{d}y^d \quad \text{if } y \geq \gamma_1 x + \gamma_2' z_3.
\end{cases}
\tag{A.7}
$$

The likelihood is then the product of terms $h_1(x, y)$ and $h_2(x, y)$ over appropriate observation indices that satisfy either $y_t < \gamma_1 x_t + \gamma_2' z_{3t}$ or $y_t \geq \gamma_1 x_t + \gamma_2' z_{3t}$.

References

Abel, A.B. (1985) 'Inventories, stock-outs and production smoothing', *Review of Economic Studies*, 52:283–293.

Goldfeld, S.M. and D.M. Jaffee (1970) 'The determinants of deposit-rate setting by savings and loan associations', Journal of Finance, 25:615-632.

Goldfeld, S.M., D.M. Jaffee and R.E. Quandt (1980) 'A model of FHLBB advances: Rationing or market clearing?', Review of Economics and Statistics, 62:339-347.

Goldfeld, S.M. and R.E. Quandt (1981) 'Single market disequilibrium models: Estimation and testing', Economic Studies Quarterly, 32:12-28.

Goldfeld, S.M. and R.E. Quandt (1986) 'Effects of multiple uncertainty on rationing', Economics Letters, 22:127-131.

Jaffee, D.M. and F. Modigliani (1969) 'A theory and test of credit rationing', American Economic Review, 59:850-872.

Kiefer, N.M. (1977) 'Models of switching, disequilibrium and endogenous change and the value of information', Report 7757, Center for Mathematical Studies in Business and Economics, University of Chicago, Chicago, IL.

Portes, R., R.E. Quandt and S. Yeo (1988) 'Tests of the chronic shortage hypothesis: The case of Poland', Review of Economics and Statistics, 70:288-295.

Quandt, R.E. (1982) 'Econometric disequilibrium models', Econometric Reviews, 1:1-63.

Quandt, R.E. (1988) The Econometrics of Disequilibrium Models. New York: Basil Blackwell.

Stiglitz, J.E. and A. Weiss (1981) 'Credit rationing in markets with imperfect information', American Economic Review, 71:393-410.

Chapter 14

EXPERIMENTAL DESIGN FOR DIRECT METERING OF RESIDENTIAL ELECTRICITY END-USES

Dennis J. AIGNER

University of California, Irvine, CA, USA

Peter SCHÖNFELD

Universität Bonn, Bonn, FR Germany

1. Introduction

"Conditional demand analysis (CDA)", as coined by Parti and Parti (1980), is a regression-based statistical technique for decomposing the total electricity consumption of a household into appliance-specific components. In its simplest form, consumption (annual, monthly, daily, or hourly) is regressed on a set of dummy variables indicating the ownership (or not) of major household electric appliances. There may be interaction terms as well to capture the weather-sensitivity of certain appliance loads such as air conditioning and space heating. The ability of the CDA method to estimate these appliance-specific components with any precision depends almost exclusively on whether the appliance ownership patterns among households are sufficiently heterogeneous. That every household owns a refrigerator or that households which own clothes washing machines tend to own electric clothes dryers as well, for example, mitigates against CDA's ability to

We are grateful to Nestor Arguea and Weiren Wang of the University of Southern California for able research assistance. Aigner's work was supported in part by the Electricity Commission of New South Wales (Australia). Schönfeld's work was supported in part by the University of Southern California and by the Deutsche Forschungsgemeinschaft, Sonderforschungs-bereich 303.

Economic Decision-Making: Games, Econometrics and Optimisation
Edited by J.J. Gabszewicz, J.-F. Richard and L.A. Wolsey
© *Elsevier Science Publishers B.V., 1990*

estimate those specific appliance contributions to total household consumption with accuracy.[1] In addition there is the problem of confusing ownership with utilization in the CDA model, something that is pursued by Dubin and McFadden (1984).

Not surprisingly, the augmentation of the CDA approach by additional sources of information has been the topic of further research. One such information source consists of "diaries" kept for usually short periods of time by sample households indicating when they use their appliances.[2] Another approach combines engineering data based on the technical operating characteristics of appliances and thermo-dynamic principles with the cross-section data on appliance ownership that underlies CDA. This was developed by Caves et al. (1985) for the Electric Power Research Institute. Finally, with the rapid development of solid-state metering devices it is now also economically feasible to consider the direct metering of specific appliances in order to reduce CDA estimation error. But, how large do the subsamples on which direct metering takes place have to be? This will depend, obviously, on the estimation method adopted to utilize the two sources of information and an objective function for purposes of characterizing the notion of precision of estimation in a multi-parameter context.

In this paper we report on our initial attempt to solve the problem of optimal experimental design for direct metering as a supplement to CDA. This takes place in the context of a two-appliance model. The basic theory of OLS and BLUE estimation is developed in the next section. Section 3 contains some implementation results, while Section 4 concludes with a discussion of extensions and directions for further research.

2. Methodology

2.1. OLS estimation

Consider the following simple CDA regression model,

$$
y = \alpha \begin{pmatrix} 1_1 \\ 1_2 \\ 1_3 \\ 1_4 \end{pmatrix} + \beta_1 \begin{pmatrix} 1_1 \\ 1_2 \\ 0_3 \\ 0_4 \end{pmatrix} + \beta_2 \begin{pmatrix} 1_1 \\ 0_2 \\ 1_3 \\ 0_4 \end{pmatrix} + \varepsilon,
\tag{1}
$$

---

[1] See Aigner et al. (1984) for more on this point.
[2] See Hill (1982) for an application of diary data to the estimation of residential end-use load profiles.

where y is an $n \times 1$ vector of cross-section observations on electricity consumption (annual, monthly, daily or hourly), ε is a corresponding vector of independent random errors with zero means and common variance σ_ε^2, α, β_1 and β_2 are the parameters to be estimated and 1_i and 0_i $(i = 1, \ldots, 4)$ are, respectively, column vectors of ones and zeros whose dimensions are defined as follows:

$\dim(1_1) = n_{11}$, the number of households that own both appliance #1 and appliance #2;

$\dim(1_2, 0_2) = n_{12}$, the number of households that own appliance #1 only;

$\dim(1_3, 0_3) = n_{21}$, the number of households that own appliance #2 only;

$\dim(1_4, 0_4) = n_{22}$, the number of households that own neither appliance.

Next, to begin suppose there are available m observations on β_1 directly, that is,

$$z = \beta_1 1_m + \eta, \tag{2}$$

where z is the $m \times 1$ vector of direct load observations on appliance #1 corresponding to the definition of y (i.e., annual, monthly, daily or hourly), 1_m is an $m \times 1$ vector of ones and η is an $m \times 1$ vector of independent random errors with zero means and common variance σ_η^2. As a working assumption we will also take η to be independent of ε. Thus, at the outset we treat the data underlying eq. (2) as if it came from a fresh sample. Obviously, in practice it will often be the case that direct metering will take place on a subsample of the households represented by eq. (1), in which event eq. (2) acts as a set of imperfect constraints on β_1. We return to this later.

Stacking (1) and (2) and forming the moment matrices required for least squares estimation, we have

$$X'X = \begin{pmatrix} n & n_{1.} & n_{.1} \\ n_{1.} & n_{1.} + m & n_{11} \\ n_{.1} & n_{11} & n_{.1} \end{pmatrix}$$

and

$$X'\begin{pmatrix} y \\ z \end{pmatrix} = \begin{pmatrix} \sum y_i \\ \sum_1 y_i + \sum z_j \\ \sum_2 y_i \end{pmatrix}.$$

where $n_{1.} = n_{11} + n_{12}$, $n_{.1} = n_{11} + n_{21}$, $\sum_1 y_i$ is the sum of elements of y over appliance #1 owners and $\sum_2 y_i$ is the sum of elements of y over appliance #2 owners.

Forming the OLS normal equations,

$$n\hat{\alpha} + n_1.\hat{\beta}_1 + n_{.1}\hat{\beta}_2 = \sum y_i,$$

$$n_1.\hat{\alpha} + (n_1. + m)\hat{\beta}_1 + n_{11}\hat{\beta}_2 = \sum_1 y_i + \sum z_j,$$

$$n_{.1}\hat{\alpha} + n_{11}\hat{\beta}_1 + n_{.1}\hat{\beta}_2 = \sum_2 y_i,$$

we can readily solve for $\hat{\alpha}$, $\hat{\beta}_1$ and $\hat{\beta}_2$. The results are as follows:

$$\hat{\alpha} = \bar{y}.. - \frac{n_1.}{n}\hat{\beta}_1 - \frac{n_{.1}}{n}\hat{\beta}_2,$$

$$\hat{\beta}_2 = \frac{n}{n_{.2}}(\bar{y}._1 - \bar{y}..), \tag{3}$$

$$\hat{\beta}_1 = \frac{n_2.}{n_1.n_2. + mn}\sum_1 y_i - \frac{n_1.}{n_1.n_2. + mn}\sum_1 y_i + \frac{n}{n_1.n_2. + mn}\sum z_j,$$

where $n_2. = n_{21} + n_{22} = n - n_1.$, $n_{.2} = n - n_{.1}$, and $\bar{\sum}_1 y_i$ is the sum of elements of y over the non-owners of appliance #1 (i.e., $\bar{\sum}_1 y_i = \sum y_i - \sum_1 y_i$). In forming these estimators we have, for case of computation, used the assumption $n_{11}/n_1. = n_{.1}/n$, which we refer to hereafter as "orthogonality" of design. It is relaxed below.

Now, computing the variance of $\hat{\beta}_1$, we get

$$V(\hat{\beta}_1) = \frac{1}{n}\left[p_{.1}\left(\frac{p_2.}{p_1.p_2. + m/n}\right)^2 + p_2.\left(\frac{p_1.}{p_1.p_2. + m/n}\right)^2 \right]\sigma_\varepsilon^2$$

$$+ \frac{1}{n}\left[\frac{m}{n}\left(\frac{1}{p_1.p_2. + m/n}\right)^2 \right]\sigma_\eta^2, \tag{4}$$

where $p_1. = n_1./n$ and $p_2. = n_2./n$. From this expression it is easy to determine how direct metering affects $V(\hat{\beta}_1)$:

$$\frac{\partial V(\hat{\beta}_1)}{\partial m} = \frac{1}{n^2(p_1.p_2. + m/n)^3}\left[\left(p_1.p_2. - \frac{m}{n}\right)\sigma_\eta^2 - 2p_1.p_2.\sigma_\varepsilon^2 \right], \tag{5}$$

which suggests that increases in m tend to decrease $V(\hat{\beta}_1)$ whenever $m/n \geq \frac{1}{4}$ or $2\sigma_\varepsilon^2 > \sigma_\eta^2$.

In deriving (3), we employed the orthogonality condition $n_{11}/n_1. = n_{.1}/n$. In reality, this condition can be dropped, in which event the OLS results appear as follows:

$$\hat{\alpha} = \bar{y}_{..} - p_{1.}\hat{\beta}_1 - p_{.1}\hat{\beta}_2,$$

$$\hat{\beta}_1 = [p_{.2}\bar{y}_{1.} - (p_{11.} - p_{.1})\bar{y}_{.1} - (1 - p_{11.})\bar{y}_{..} + p_{.2}\sum z_j/n_{1.}]/\Delta_1,$$

$$\hat{\beta}_2 = [(p_{1.} - p_{.11})\bar{y}_{1.} + (p_{2.} + m/n_{1.})\bar{y}_{.1} - (1 - p_{.11} + m/n_{.1})\bar{y}_{..}$$
$$+ (p_{1.} - p_{.11})\sum z_j/n_{1.}]/\Delta_1,$$

(6)

where

$$\Delta_1 = p_{.2}(p_{2.} + m/n_{1.}) - (p_{11.} - p_{.1})(p_{.11} - p_{1.}),$$

$$p_{1.} = n_{1.}/n, \quad p_{2.} = 1 - p_{1.}, \quad p_{.1} = n_{.1}/n, \quad p_{.2} = 1 - p_{.1},$$

$$p_{11.} = n_{11}/n_{1.}, \quad p_{.11} = n_{11}/n_{.1}.$$

The variance of $\hat{\beta}_1$ is easily computed to be

$$V(\hat{\beta}_1) = (K_1 + K_2 m)/\Delta_1^2,$$

where

$$K_1 = \left[\frac{p_{.2}^2}{n_{1.}} + \frac{(p_{11.} - p_{.1})^2}{n_{1.}} - \frac{(1 - p_{11.})^2}{n} - 2\frac{p_{.2}(p_{11.} - p_{.1})p_{11.}}{n_{.1}}\right]\sigma_\varepsilon^2,$$

$$K_2 = \frac{p_{.2}^2 \sigma_\eta^2}{n_{1.}^2}.$$

(7)

Paralleling (5),

$$\partial V(\hat{\beta}_1)/\partial m = \{K_2[p_{.2}p_{2.} - (p_{11.} - p_{.1})(p_{.11} - p_{1.})]$$
$$- 2K_1(p_{.2}/p_{1.}) - K_2(p_{.2}/p_{1.})m/n\}/\Delta_1^3.$$

(8)

If

$$\frac{m}{n} > \max\left\{\frac{p_{1.}}{p_{.2}}[(p_{11.} - p_{.1})(p_{.11} - p_{1.}) - p_{.2}p_{2.}],\right.$$

$$\left.\frac{p_{1.}}{p_{.2}}[p_{.2}p_{2.} - (p_{11.} - p_{.1})(p_{.11} - p_{1.})] - \frac{2K_1}{K_2}\right\}$$

then $\partial V(\hat{\beta}_1)/\partial m < 0$ and increasing m can decrease $V(\hat{\beta}_1)$.

The extension of these results to the case where there are direct metering observations on both appliances follows directly. Instead of (2) we now have

$$z_1 = \beta_1 1_{m1} + \eta_1 \quad \text{and} \quad z_2 = \beta_2 1_{m2} + \eta_2,$$

(9)

where (z_1, η_1) are of dimension $m_1 \times 1$ and (z_2, η_2) are of dimension $m_2 \times 1$. Otherwise the development follows that of eq. (2). The OLS normal equations are derived easily. They appear as

$$\hat{\alpha} = \bar{y}_{..} - p_{1.}\hat{\beta}_1 - p_{.1}\hat{\beta}_2,$$

$$\left(1 - \frac{n_{1.}}{n} + \frac{m_1}{n_{1.}}\right)\hat{\beta}_1 + \left(\frac{n_{11}}{n_{1.}} - \frac{n_{.1}}{n}\right)\hat{\beta}_2 = \bar{y}_{1.} - \bar{y}_{..} + \frac{1}{n_{1.}}\sum z_{1j}, \tag{10}$$

$$\left(\frac{n_{11}}{n_{.1}} - \frac{n_{1.}}{n}\right)\hat{\beta}_1 + \left(1 - \frac{n_{.1}}{n} + \frac{m_2}{n_{.1}}\right)\hat{\beta}_2 = \bar{y}_{.1} - \bar{y}_{..} + \frac{1}{n_{.1}}\sum z_{2j}.$$

Under "orthogonality" things simplify greatly.

To focus on the design aspects of the problem, we use the orthogonality assumption to generate $V(\hat{\beta}_1)$ and $V(\hat{\beta}_2)$ and adopt the "E-optimality" criterion after Keifer (1959). After some development we get

$$V(\hat{\beta}_1) + V(\hat{\beta}_2)$$

$$= \frac{1}{n}\left[p_{1.}\left(\frac{p_{2.}}{p_{1.}p_{2.} + m_1/n}\right)^2 + p_{2.}\left(\frac{p_{1.}}{p_{1.}p_{2.} + m_1/n}\right)^2\right.$$

$$\left. + p_{.1}\left(\frac{p_{.2}}{p_{.1}p_{.2} + m_2/n}\right)^2 + p_{.2}\left(\frac{p_{.1}}{p_{.1}p_{.2} + m_2/n}\right)^2\right]\sigma_\epsilon^2$$

$$+ \frac{1}{n}\left[\frac{m_1}{n}\left(\frac{1}{p_{1.}p_{2.} + m_1/n}\right)^2\sigma_{\eta_1}^2 + \frac{m_2}{n}\left(\frac{1}{p_{.1}p_{.2} + m_2/n}\right)^2\sigma_{\eta_2}^2\right]. \tag{11}$$

The optimal choices of m_1 and m_2 are those which minimize (11) subject to a cost constraint and non-negativity *given n*.

Relaxing the orthogonality condition, (11) becomes

$$V(\hat{\beta}_1) + V(\hat{\beta}_2)$$

$$= \left[\frac{(p_{11.} - p_{.1})^2}{n_{.1}}\sigma_1^2 + \frac{(p_{.2} + m_2/n_{.1})^2\sigma_1^2}{n_{1.}} - \left(1 - p_{11.} + \frac{m_2}{n_{.1}}\right)^2\frac{\sigma_1^2}{n}\right.$$

$$- 2\left(p_{.2} + \frac{m_2}{n_{.1}}\right)(p_{11.} - p_{.1})\frac{p_{11.}\sigma_1^2}{n_{.1}}$$

$$\left. + \left(p_{.2} + \frac{m_2}{n_{.1}}\right)^2\frac{m_1\sigma_2^2}{n_{1.}^2} + (p_{11.} - p_{.1})^2\frac{m_2\sigma_3^2}{n_{.1}^2}\right]\bigg/\Delta_1'^2$$

$$+ \left[\frac{(p_{.11} - p_{1.})^2}{n_{1.}}\sigma_1^2 + \frac{(p_{2.} + m_1/n_{1.})^2}{n_{.1}}\sigma_1^2 + \left(1 - p_{.11} + \frac{m_1}{n_{1.}}\right)^2\frac{\sigma_1^2}{n}\right.$$

$$- 2(p_{.11} - p_{1.})\left(p_{2.} + \frac{m_1}{n_{1.}}\right)\frac{p_{11.}\sigma_1^2}{n_{.1}}$$

$$\left. + (p_{.11} - p_{1.})^2\frac{m_1\sigma_2^2}{n_{1.}^2} + \left(p_{2.} + \frac{m_1}{n_{1.}}\right)^2\frac{m_2\sigma_3^2}{n_{.1}^2}\right]\bigg/\Delta_1'^2 \tag{12}$$

where

$$\Delta_1' = \left(p_{2.} + \frac{m_1}{n_{1.}} \right) \left(p_{.2} + \frac{m_2}{n_{.1}} \right) - (p_{.11} - p_{1.})(p_{11.} - p_{.1}),$$

$$\sigma_1^2 = V(\varepsilon_i), \quad i = 1, \ldots, n,$$

$$\sigma_2^2 = V(\eta_{1j}), \quad j = 1, \ldots, m_1,$$

$$\sigma_3^2 = V(\eta_{2k}), \quad k = 1, \ldots, m_2.$$

2.2. BLUE estimation

In order to derive the BLUE estimator, we use the generalized least squares method (GLS).

Stacking (1) and (2) together, the variance-covariance matrix of the error terms is

$$\Omega = \begin{pmatrix} \sigma_1^1 I_n & O_{nm} \\ O_{mn} & \sigma_2^2 I_m \end{pmatrix},$$

with corresponding moment matrices

$$X'\Omega^{-1}X = \begin{pmatrix} \sigma_1^{-2}n & \sigma_1^{-2}n_{1.} & \sigma_1^{-2}n_{.1} \\ \sigma_1^{-2}n_{1.} & \sigma_1^{-2}n_{1.} + \sigma_2^{-1}m & \sigma_1^{-2}n_{11} \\ \sigma_1^{-2}n_{.1} & \sigma_1^{-2}n_{11} & \sigma_1^{-2}n_{.1} \end{pmatrix}$$

and

$$X'\Omega^{-1}\begin{pmatrix} y \\ z \end{pmatrix} = \begin{pmatrix} \sigma_1^{-2}\sum y_i \\ \sigma_1^{-2}\sum_1 y_i + \sigma_2^{-2}\sum z_j \\ \sigma_1^{-2}\sum_2 y_i \end{pmatrix}.$$

Forming the GLS normal equations,

$$\sigma_1^{-2}n\hat{\alpha} + \sigma_1^{-2}n_{1.}\hat{\beta}_1 + \sigma_1^{-2}n_{.1}\hat{\beta}_2 = \sigma_1^{-2}\sum y_i,$$

$$\sigma_1^{-2}n_{1.}\hat{\alpha} + (\sigma_1^{-2}n_{1.} + \sigma_2^{-2}m)\hat{\beta}_1 + \sigma_1^{-2}n_{11}\hat{\beta}_2 = \sigma_1^{-2}\sum_1 y_i + \sigma_2^{-2}\sum z_j, \qquad (13)$$

$$\sigma_1^{-2}n_{.1}\hat{\alpha} + \sigma_1^{-2}n_{11}\hat{\beta}_1 + \sigma_1^{-2}n_{.1}\hat{\beta}_2 = \sigma_1^{-2}\sum_2 y_i.$$

Solving for α, $\hat{\beta}_1$ and $\hat{\beta}_2$ we get[3]

$$\hat{\alpha} = \bar{y}_{..} - p_{1.}\hat{\beta}_1 - p_{.1}\hat{\beta}_2,$$

$$\hat{\beta}_1 = [\, p_{.2}\bar{y}_{1.} - (p_{11.} - p_{.1})\bar{y}_{.1} - (1 - p_{11.})\bar{y}_{..} + p_{.2}(\sigma_1^2/\sigma_2^2)(\textstyle\sum z_j/n_{1.})]/\Delta_2,$$

$$\hat{\beta}_2 = \left[\, (p_{1.} - p_{.11})\bar{y}_{1.} + \left(p_{2.} + \frac{\sigma_1^2}{\sigma_2^2}\frac{m}{n_{1.}} \right)\bar{y}_{.1} - \left(1 - p_{.11} + \frac{\sigma_1^2 m}{\sigma_2^2 n_{1.}} \right)\bar{y}_{..} \right. \tag{14}$$

$$\left. + (p_{1.} - p_{.11})\frac{\sigma_1^2 \sum z_j}{\sigma_2^2 n_{1.}} \right] \Big/ \Delta_2,$$

where

$$\Delta_2 = p_{.2}\left(p_{2.} + \frac{\sigma_1^2 m}{\sigma_2^2 n_{1.}} \right) - (p_{11.} - p_{.1})(p_{.11} - p_{1.}).$$

Computing $V(\hat{\beta}_1)$ for comparison to (8),

$$V(\hat{\beta}_1) = (K_1' + K_2'm)/\Delta_2^2 \tag{15}$$

where

$$K_1' = \left[\frac{p_{.2}^2}{n_{1.}} + \frac{(p_{11.} - p_{.1})^2}{n_{.1}} - \frac{(1 - p_{11.})^2}{n} - \frac{2p_{.2}(p_{11.} - p_{.1})p_{11.}}{n_{.1}} \right]\sigma_1^2,$$

$$K_2' = \frac{p_{.2}^2}{n_{1.}^2}\frac{\sigma_1^4}{\sigma_2^2}.$$

Hence

$$\frac{\partial V(\hat{\beta}_1)}{\partial m} = \left\{ K_2'[\, p_{2.}p_{.2} - (p_{11.} - p_{.1})(p_{.11} - p_{1.})] \right.$$

$$\left. - K_1'\frac{2\sigma_1^2 p_{.2}}{\sigma_2^2 n_{1.}} - K_2'\frac{\sigma_1^2 p_{.2}}{\sigma_2^2 p_{1.}}\frac{m}{n} \right\} \Big/ \Delta_2^3. \tag{16}$$

Therefore if

$$\frac{m}{n} > \max\left\{ \frac{\sigma_2^2 p_{1.}}{\sigma_1^2 p_{.2}}[(p_{11.} - p_{.1})(p_{.11} - p_{1.}) - p_{.2}p_{2.})], \right.$$

$$\left. - \frac{\sigma_2^2 p_{1.}}{\sigma_1^2 p_{.2}}[(p_{11.} - p_{.1})(p_{.11} - p_{1.}) - p_{.2}p_{2.}] - 2\frac{K_1'}{K_2'} \right\}$$

then $\partial V(\hat{\beta}_1)/\partial m < 0$, which amounts to condition (8) *weighted* by σ_2^2/σ_1^2.

---

[3] Note that (14) comes down to (6) if we set $\sigma_1^2 = \sigma_2^2$.

Now in the case where there are two independent sets of direct metering observations the GLS normal equations are

$$\sigma_1^{-2} n\hat{\alpha} + \sigma_1^{-2} n_1 . \hat{\beta}_1 + \sigma_1^{-2} n_{.1} \hat{\beta}_2 = \sigma^{-2} \sum y_i,$$

$$\sigma_1^{-2} n_1 . \hat{\alpha} + (\sigma_1^{-2} n_1 . + \sigma_2^{-2} m_1) \hat{\beta}_1 + \sigma_1^{-2} n_{11} \hat{\beta}_2 = \sigma_1^{-2} \sum_1 y_i + \sigma_2^{-2} \sum z_{1j},$$

$$\sigma_1^{-2} n_{.1} \hat{\alpha} + \sigma_1^{-2} n_{11} \hat{\beta}_1 + (\sigma_1^{-2} n_{.1} + \sigma_3^{-2} m_2) \hat{\beta}_2 = \sigma_1^{-2} \sum_2 y_i + \sigma_3^{-2} \sum z_{2j},$$

or[4]

$$\hat{\alpha} = \bar{y}_{..} - p_1 . \hat{\beta}_1 - p_{.1} \hat{\beta}_2,$$

$$\left(1 - p_1 . + \frac{\sigma_1^2}{\sigma_2^2} \frac{m_1}{n_1 .}\right) \hat{\beta}_1 + (p_{11} . - p_{.1}) \hat{\beta}_2 = \bar{y}_1 . - \bar{y}_{..} + \frac{\sigma_1^2 \sum z_{1j}}{\sigma_2^2 n_1 .}, \qquad (17)$$

$$(p_{.11} - p_1 .) \hat{\beta}_1 + \left(1 - p_{.1} + \frac{\sigma_1^2 m_2}{\sigma_3^2 n_{.1}}\right) \hat{\beta}_2 = \bar{y}_{.1} - \bar{y}_{..} + \frac{\sigma_1^2 \sum z_{2j}}{\sigma_3^2 n_{.1}}.$$

Further development leads us to

$$V(\hat{\beta}_1) + V(\hat{\beta}_2)$$

$$= \left[\frac{(p_{11} . - p_{.1})^2}{n_{.1}} \sigma_1^2 + \left(p_{.2} + \frac{\sigma_1^2 m_2}{\sigma_3^2 n_{.1}}\right)^2 \frac{\sigma_1^2}{n_1 .} - \left(1 - p_{11} . + \frac{\sigma_1^2 m_2}{\sigma_3^2 n_{.1}}\right)^2 \frac{\sigma_1^2}{n}\right.$$

$$- 2\left(p_{.2} + \frac{\sigma_1^2 m_2}{\sigma_3^2 n_{.1}}\right)(p_{11} . - p_{.1}) \frac{\sigma_1^2 p_{11} .}{n_{.1}} + \left(p_{.2} + \frac{\sigma_1^2 m_2}{\sigma_3^2 n_{.1}}\right)^2 \frac{\sigma_1^4 m_1}{\sigma_2^2 n_1^2 .}$$

$$\left. + (p_{11} . - p_{.1})^2 \frac{\sigma_1^4 m_2}{\sigma_3^2 n_{.1}^2}\right] \Big/ \Delta_2'^2 \qquad (18)$$

$$+ \left[(p_{.11} - p_1 .)^2 \frac{\sigma_1^2}{n_1 .} + \left(p_2 . + \frac{\sigma_1^2 m_1}{\sigma_2^2 n_1 .}\right)^2 \frac{\sigma_1^2}{n_{.1}} - \left(1 - p_{.11} + \frac{\sigma_1^2 m_1}{\sigma_2^2 n_1 .}\right)^2 \frac{\sigma_1^2}{n}\right.$$

$$- 2\left(p_2 . + \frac{\sigma_1^2 m_1}{\sigma_2^2 n_1 .}\right)(p_{.11} - p_1 .) \frac{\sigma_1^2 p_{11} .}{n_{.1}} + \left(p_2 . + \frac{\sigma_1^2 m_1}{\sigma_2^2 n_1 .}\right)^2 \frac{\sigma_1^4 m_2}{\sigma_3^2 n_{.1}^2}$$

$$\left. + (p_{.11} - p_1 .)^2 \frac{\sigma_1^4 m_1}{\sigma_2^2 n_1^2 .}\right] \Big/ \Delta_2'^2$$

---

[4] Note that if we set $\sigma_1^2 = \sigma_2^2 = \sigma_3^2$ and $p_{11} . = p_{.1}$, (17) collapses to (10).

where

$$\Delta_2' = \left(p_{2\cdot} + \frac{\sigma_1^2 m_1}{\sigma_2^2 m_1} \right)\left(p_{\cdot 2} + \frac{\sigma_1^2 m_2}{\sigma_3^2 n_{\cdot 1}} \right) - (p_{\cdot 11} - p_{1\cdot})(p_{11\cdot} - p_{\cdot 1}).$$

Under the orthogonality condition, (18) can be simplified to[5]

$$V(\hat{\beta}_1) + V(\hat{\beta}_2) = \left(\frac{\sigma_1^2}{n_1} - \frac{\sigma_1^2}{n} + \frac{\sigma_1^4}{\sigma_2^2}\frac{m_1}{n_1^2} \right) \bigg/ \left(p_{2\cdot} + \frac{\sigma_1^2 m_1}{\sigma_2^2 n_1} \right)^2$$

$$+ \left(\frac{\sigma_1^2}{n_{\cdot 1}} - \frac{\sigma_1^2}{n} + \frac{\sigma_1^4}{\sigma_3^2}\frac{m_2}{n_{\cdot 1}^2} \right) \bigg/ \left(p_{\cdot 2} + \frac{\sigma_1^2 m_2}{\sigma_3^2 n_{\cdot 1}} \right)^2. \tag{19}$$

By minimizing $V(\hat{\beta}_1) + V(\hat{\beta}_2)$ subject to cost and nonnegativity constraints, we get optimal allocations of m_1 and m_2.

3. An illustration of OLS and GLS optimal designs

In order to implement the optimization problem thus described it is necessary to estimate σ_ε^2, $\sigma_{\eta_1}^2$ and $\sigma_{\eta_2}^2$, and to specify the per unit sampling costs associated with the direct metering of appliance #1 and appliance #2. Strictly speaking, $\sigma_{\eta_1}^2$ and $\sigma_{\eta_2}^2$ are variances of *observation errors* from direct metering and therefore are expected to be small. In order to illustrate the method, however, we have estimated them as the variance of total consumption for those customers owning *only* appliance #1 and appliance #2, respectively. σ_ε^2 is, of course, estimated as the residual variance in a regression of total consumption on an intercept term and dummy variables for appliance ownership à la eq. (1).

The sample we use for this purpose is the statistical control group from the Southern California Edison Company's residential time-of-use pricing experiment, as described in Lilland and Aigner (1984), consisting of 86 customers distributed over five strata defined by annual consumption. For these customers a full 12 months of summer data are available, "summer" being relevant owing to the choice of central air conditioning and electric range as the appliances to be studied.[6] For the purpose at hand we first averaged the data to get total consumption for a typical summer month and then produced the relevant variance estimates. These turned out to be $\hat{\sigma}_\varepsilon^2 = 164\,528\,\text{kWh}^2$, $\hat{\sigma}_{\eta_1}^2 = 311\,331\,\text{kWh}^2$ and $\hat{\sigma}_{\eta_2}^2 = 187\,997\,\text{kWh}^2$. As to the

---

[5] Note that if $\sigma_1^2 = \sigma_2^2$, (19) will be equivalent to (11). This is demonstrated in the Appendix.
[6] For the Edison Co., which serves customers in Southern California, the summer season is defined to be May through October. The data refer to the summers of 1979 and 1980.

required per unit sampling costs, we take them to be *equal,* a realistic assumption in this instance.

In Table 1 we illustrate the effects of the choice of starting values on the algorithm used to solve the problem:

$$\min_{(m_1,m_2)} \quad V(\hat{\beta}_1) + V(\hat{\beta}_2)$$

$$\text{subject to} \quad m_1, m_2 \geq 0, \qquad\qquad (20)$$

$$a_1 m_1 + a_2 m_2 \leq C,$$

for $a_1 = a_2 = 1$ and $C = 86$, and using (11) as the objective function.

From this we conclude that the objective function is globally well-behaved. This is further illustrated in Figure 1. In addition we have considered how the solution changes as a function of C. This is illustrated in Table 2, where we report as well the optimized values of $V(\hat{\beta}_1)$ and $V(\hat{\beta}_2)$ for use in the ultimate determination of the sample size required to augment CDA by direct metering. The proportion of observations devoted to metering appliance #1 (i.e., m_1^*/C) is a constant 56% independent of sample size. That is, the objective function is homogeneous of degree minus one in m_1 and m_2.

Because of the very large estimates of $\sigma_{\eta_1}^2$ and $\sigma_{\eta_2}^2$ used in this illustration the optimized values of $V(\hat{\beta}_1)$ and $V(\hat{\beta}_2)$ are not very useful for an analysis of required sample size. Nevertheless, it is instructive to at least consider how this information would be used: In the CDA work on this sample which produced $\hat{\sigma}_F^2$, the estimate of β_1 is 434 kWh. 50 direct metering observations, 27 of which would be devoted to appliance #1 will, according to Table 2, produce a standard error for $\hat{\beta}_1$ of $5506^{1/2} = 74.2$, or a 17% coefficient of variation. Increasing C to 100 drops this to 14%, and so on.

Table 1
Effects of starting values on solution values,
$m_1 + m_2 = n = 86$

Initial values		Solution values	
m_1	m_2	m_1^*	m_2^*
85	1	49	37
50	36	48	38
49	37	49	37
48	38	48	38
46	40	48	38
40	46	49	37
36	50	49	37
1	85	49	37

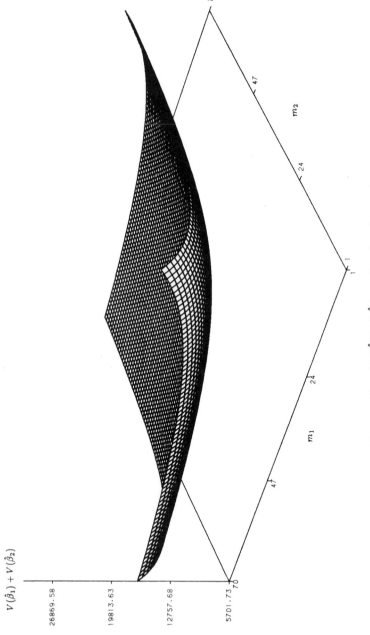

Figure 1. Plot of $V(\hat{\beta}_1)+V(\hat{\beta}_2)$ as a function of m_1 and m_2.

Table 2

Effects of direct metering sample size on solution values, for eq. (11):
OLS under orthogonality

C	m_1^*	m_2^*	m_1^*/C	$V^*(\hat{\beta}_1)$	$V^*(\hat{\beta}_2)$
50	27	23	0.54	5245	3988
86	48	38	0.56	3916	3027
100	56	44	0.56	3566	2761
120	67	53	0.56	3173	2439
140	79	61	0.56	2831	2210
200	112	88	0.56	2182	1678

Table 3

Effects of direct metering sample size on solution values for eq. (12):
OLS without orthogonality

C	m_1^*	m_2^*	m_1^*/C	$V^*(\hat{\beta}_1)$	$V^*(\hat{\beta}_2)$
50	27	23	0.54	5348	4062
86	48	38	0.56	3958	3058
100	56	44	0.56	3597	2784
120	67	53	0.56	3195	2455
140	78	62	0.56	2872	2196
200	112	88	0.56	2189	1683

In a similar fashion we have analyzed the behavior of solutions to the problems characterized by minimizing the objective functions (12), (18) and (19). These are reported in Tables 3–5.

In comparing these results, we note first that imposing "orthogonality" has little effect on the numerical solutions although it simplifies the functions to be optimized somewhat.[7] Going from OLS to GLS also yields only minor

Table 4

Effects of direct metering sample size on solution values for eq. (19):
GLS under orthogonality

C	m_1^*	m_2^*	m_1^*/C	$V^*(\hat{\beta}_1)$	$V^*(\hat{\beta}_2)$
50	25	25	0.50	4904	3809
86	45	41	0.52	3729	2877
100	53	47	0.53	3403	2635
120	64	56	0.53	3038	2339
140	76	64	0.54	2719	2128
200	109	91	0.55	2111	1630

[7] It is to be noted that "orthogonality" does not hold up well in the case at hand. $n_{11}/n_{1.} = 0.697$ while $n_{.1}/n = 0.547$.

Table 5
Effects of direct metering sample size on solution values for eq. (18):
GLS without orthogonality

C	m_1^*	m_2^*	m_1^*/C	$V^*(\hat{\beta}_1)$	$V^*(\hat{\beta}_2)$
50	25	25	0.50	5013	3876
86	45	41	0.52	3779	2905
100	53	47	0.53	3441	2657
120	64	56	0.53	3065	2355
140	76	64	0.54	2739	2139
200	109	91	0.55	2120	1635

improvements. This is probably because of the quite large values for the required variance components used in these illustrative calculations. Finally, while the OLS solutions exhibit homogeneity of degree minus one in m_1 and m_2, the GLS results do not. This aspect of the research needs to be explored fully.

4. Extension of the model

A more realistic CDA approach to electricity consumption may be based on a combined analysis-of-covariance and error components model. For each source of consumption — general consumption and specific consumption of selected appliances — the average level of demand is explained by fixed effects and concomitant variables according to household classification and objective factors while error components absorb the residual random variation. Thus if z_{i0} is general consumption and z_{ik} is specific consumption due to appliance k for observation i,

$$z_{i0} = \alpha'x(i) + \varepsilon_i, \qquad z_{ik} = \beta_k'x(i) + \eta_{ik}, \quad k \in [i], \tag{21}$$

where $x(i)$ is the vector of fixed effects and concomitant variables, $[i]$ is the ownership pattern pertinent to observation i, and ε_i, η_{ik} are the errors. Total consumption is

$$y_i = \left(\alpha + \sum_{k \in |i|} \beta_k\right)' x(i) + \varepsilon_i + \sum_{k \in |i|} \eta_{ik}, \tag{22}$$

and direct metering observations would have the form

$$z_{ik} = \beta_k'x(i) + \eta_{ik}. \tag{23}$$

We shall use i as the ownership pattern classifier. Thus, if there are n_i observations in ownership group i, (21) and (22) become

$$z_{i0} = X(i)\alpha + \varepsilon_i, \qquad z_{ik} = X(i)\beta_k + \eta_{ik}, \quad k \in [i], \tag{24}$$

$$y_i = X(i)\left(\alpha + \sum_{[i]} \beta_k\right) + \varepsilon_i + \sum_{[i]} \eta_{ik}, \tag{25}$$

where $\dim(z_{ij}) = \dim(y_i) = n_i$. Because of the various possibilities of choice for the level variables $x(i)$ and for the variance–covariance structure of the error components (24), (25) provide a most flexible framework for modelling end-use electricity demand. As mentioned above, identification and estimation of the parameters $\theta' = (\alpha', \beta'_1, \ldots, \beta'_k)$ requires appropriate diversification with respect to ownership patterns and level variables $x(i)$.

We shall analyze (25) for the case of $K = 2$ appliances and one level variable $x(i) \equiv 1$. There are $I = 4$ ownership groups, $i = 1, 2, 3, 4$. In fact,

$$\begin{aligned} y_1 &= 1_1\alpha + 1_1\beta_1 + 1_1\beta_2 + \varepsilon_1 + \eta_{11} + \eta_{12}, \\ y_2 &= 1_2\alpha + 1_2\beta_1 \qquad\quad + \varepsilon_2 + \eta_{21}, \\ y_3 &= 1_3\alpha \qquad\quad + 1_3\beta_2 + \varepsilon_3 \qquad\quad + \eta_{32}, \\ y_4 &= 1_4\alpha \qquad\qquad\quad + \varepsilon_4, \end{aligned} \tag{26}$$

where, again, $\dim(y_i) = n_i$ is the number of units (households). For the sake of simplicity we assume here that the error components are all uncorrelated,

$$\begin{aligned} &\Sigma(\varepsilon_i) = \sigma_0^2 I_{n_i}, \qquad \Sigma(\eta_{ik}) = \sigma_k^2 I_{n_i}, \\ &\Sigma(\varepsilon_i, \varepsilon_j) = 0, \quad i \neq j, \qquad \Sigma(\eta_{ik}, \eta_{jl}) = 0, \quad (i, k) \neq (j, l), \\ &\Sigma(\varepsilon_i, \eta_{jk}) = 0. \end{aligned} \tag{27}$$

Suppose that the σ_j^2's, $j = 0, 1, \ldots, K$, are known from a previous study. If we had the chance to allocate the n_i's subject to the cost constraint $\sum n_i = n$ we could optimize the design (26) by minimizing $\operatorname{tr} \Sigma(\tilde{\theta})$ with respect to n_1, n_2, n_3 and $n_4 = n - n_1 - n_2 - n_3$, where $\tilde{\theta}' = (\tilde{\alpha}', \tilde{\beta}'_1, \ldots, \tilde{\beta}'_K)$ is the GLS estimator of θ. In practice, of course, the n_i's are given by the cross section at our disposal. But a number of direct metering observations,

$$z_{ik\cdot m} = 1_{ik\cdot m}\beta_k + \eta_{ik\cdot m}, \tag{28}$$

where m indicates "direct metering" and $\dim(z_{ik\cdot m}) = m_{ik}$, might be chosen such that for the combined model (26), (28) $\operatorname{tr} \Sigma(\tilde{\theta})$ is minimized subject to a cost constraint $\sum_{i,k} c_{ik}m_{ik} \leq C$ thus bringing the combined model (26), (28) closer to the optimal "orthogonal" design. For this purpose observations (28) independent of (26) would be most helpful. In practice, however, the m_{ik}'s will be a subsample of the n_i's and the y_i's and $z_{ik\cdot m}$'s will be observed for the same units (households). In this situation a more elaborate notation is required since depending on the ownership group there can be a choice of metering one or more appliances at the same unit. A general notation is quite clumsy although the actual computations are no more complicated than in a K-way classification model.

In the two-way classification (26) notational conventions which differ from the general notation will be greatly simplifying. Let $z_{ik \cdot m}$, $\eta_{ik \cdot m}$ and m_{ik} be redefined, respectively, as z_{rs}, η_{rs} (dropping m), and m_{rs} where r characterizes the state of appliance $\#1$ and s the state of appliance $\#2$ as follows:

$r, s = 0$, non-ownership of appliance $\#1$, $\#2$;

$r, s = 1$, ownership of appliance $\#1$, $\#2$, but no direct metering;

$r, s = 2$, ownership of appliance $\#1$, $\#2$ and direct metering;

$r, s = *$, dummy 2, ownership of appliance $\#1$, $\#2$ and direct metering, but elsewhere.

Then any direct metering observation belongs to one of the following six mutually exclusive categories,

$$
\begin{aligned}
z_{2*} &= 1_{22}\beta_1 + \eta_{2*}, & m_{2*} &= \dim(z_{2*}) =: m_{22}, \\
z_{*2} &= 1_{22}\beta_2 + \eta_{*2}, & m_{*2} &= \dim(z_{*2}) = m_{22}, \\
z_{21} &= 1_{21}\beta_1 + \eta_{21}, & m_{21} &= \dim(z_{21}), \\
z_{12} &= 1_{12}\beta_2 + \eta_{12}, & m_{12} &= \dim(z_{12}), \\
z_{20} &= 1_{20}\beta_1 + \eta_{20}, & m_{20} &= \dim(z_{20}), \\
z_{02} &= 1_{02}\beta_2 + \eta_{02}, & m_{02} &= \dim(z_{02}).
\end{aligned}
\tag{29}
$$

The y_i's are partitioned accordingly,

$$
\begin{aligned}
y_1' &= (y_{22}', y_{21}', y_{12}', y_{11}'), & y_2' &= (y_{20}', y_{10}'), \\
y_3' &= (y_{02}', y_{01}'), & y_4' &= y_{00}',
\end{aligned}
\tag{30}
$$

where $y_{22} = y_{2*} = y_{*2}$ are synonymous and the household groups without direct metering have the sizes

$$
\begin{aligned}
m_{11} &= \dim(y_{11}) = n_1 - m_{12} - m_{21} - m_{22}, \\
m_{10} &= \dim(y_{10}) = n_2 - m_{20}, \\
m_{01} &= \dim(y_{01}) = n_3 - m_{02}, \\
m_{00} &= \dim(y_{00}) = n_4.
\end{aligned}
\tag{31}
$$

We now consider the joint regression model (26) and (29),

$$\begin{pmatrix} y \\ z \end{pmatrix} = X\theta + u, \tag{32}$$

where y and z are, respectively, the stacks of the y_i's in (26) and of the z_{rs}'s in (29), X and u are, respectively, the corresponding design matrix and disturbance vector, and $\theta = (\alpha, \beta_1, \beta_2)'$ are the regression coefficients. Note that the number of observations $N = \sum_{r,s} m_{rs}$ (sample size) differs from the number of units (households) $n = \sum_i n_i$. In fact,

$$N = m + n,$$

where

$$m := \dim(z) = 2m_{22} + m_{21} + m_{12} + m_{20} + m_{02} = m_{2.} + m_{.2}, \tag{33}$$

$$m_{r.} = m_{r0} + m_{r1} + m_{r2}, \qquad m_{.s} = m_{0s} + m_{1s} + m_{2s}.$$

Since y and z are assumed as being measured simultaneously at the same units an intraclass correlation is introduced in u which under (27) has a simple block-diagonal pattern, e.g.,

$$\Sigma \left\{ \begin{pmatrix} y_{22} \\ z_{2*} \\ z_{*2} \\ y_{20} \\ z_{20} \end{pmatrix} \right\} = \begin{pmatrix} (\sigma_0^2 + \sigma_1^2 + \sigma_2^2)I_{22} & \sigma_1^2 I_{22} & \sigma_2^2 I_{22} & 0 & 0 \\ \sigma_1^2 I_{22} & \sigma_1^2 I_{22} & 0 & 0 & 0 \\ \sigma_2^2 I_{22} & 0 & \sigma_2^2 I_{22} & 0 & 0 \\ 0 & 0 & 0 & (\sigma_0^2 + \sigma_1^2)I_{20} & \sigma_1^2 I_{20} \\ 0 & 0 & 0 & \sigma_1^2 I_{20} & \sigma_1^2 I_{20} \end{pmatrix}, \tag{34}$$

where $I_{rs} = I_{m_{rs}}$.

A nonsingular linear transformation applied to the model (32) clearly cannot change the Aitken estimator of θ. In general, however, it does affect the OLS estimator and, specifically, its precision. We shall here adopt a particular transformation of the design (32) by orthogonalizing all the observations (y', z') in the direct metering groups (diagonalizing their dispersion submatrices) which amounts to treating the direct metering observations as a set of "imperfect constraints" on the y regression. Although this transformation does not necessarily reduce the dispersion of the OLS estimator it helps to clarify the intrinsic structure of the GLS estimator. The "constrained" OLS estimator $\hat{\theta} = (\hat{\alpha}, \hat{\beta}_1, \hat{\beta}_2)'$ is given by the normal equations

$$(X_c' X_c)\hat{\theta} = X_c' \begin{pmatrix} y \\ z \end{pmatrix}_c, \tag{35}$$

where "c" denotes "constrained model", and the moments are the following
expressions (cf. (33)),

$$
X'_c X_c =
\begin{pmatrix}
[(m_{2.} - m_{21}) + (m_{.2} - m_{12}) + m_{00} - m_{22}] & & \\
+(m_{1.} - m_{11}) + (m_{.1} - m_{11}) + m_{11} & m_{1.} & m_{.1} \\
m_{1.} & m_{2.} + m_{1.} & m_{11} \\
m_{.1} & m_{11} & m_{.2} + m_{.1}
\end{pmatrix}
\tag{36}
$$

and

$$
X'_c \begin{pmatrix} y \\ z \end{pmatrix}_c =
\begin{pmatrix}
[(Y_{2.} - Y_{21}) + (Y_{.2} - Y_{12}) + Y_{00} - Y_{22}] \\
+(Y_{1.} - Y_{11}) + (Y_{.1} - Y_{11}) + Y_{11} \\
Z_{2.} + Y_{1.} \\
Z_{.2} + Y_{.1}
\end{pmatrix},
\tag{37}
$$

where

$$
Y_{rs} = 1'(y_{rs} - z_{rs}), \qquad Y_{r.} = Y_{r0} + Y_{r1} + Y_{r2}, \qquad Y_{.s} = Y_{0s} + Y_{1s} + Y_{2s},
$$

$$
Z_{2.} = 1'z_{20} + 1'z_{21} + 1'z_{22}, \qquad Z_{.2} = 1'z_{02} + 1'z_{12} + 1'z_{22}.
$$

Of course, z_{rs} is empty for $\max\{r, s\} \le 1$, and $z_{22} = z_{2*} + z_{*2}$.

The normal equations of the Aitken (GLS) estimator $\tilde{\theta} = (\tilde{\alpha}, \tilde{\beta}_1, \tilde{\beta}_2)'$ for
(32) or the equivalent "constrained model" are given by

$$
X'\Sigma^{-1}X\tilde{\theta} = X'\Sigma^{-1} \begin{pmatrix} y \\ z \end{pmatrix},
\tag{38}
$$

where

$$
X'\Sigma^{-1}X =
\begin{pmatrix}
a_0 + a_{01} + a_{02} + a_{012} & a_{01} + a_{012} & a_{02} + a_{012} \\
a_{01} + a_{012} & a_1 + a_{01} + a_{012} & a_{012} \\
a_{02} + a_{012} & a_{012} & a_2 + a_{02} + a_{012}
\end{pmatrix},
$$

$$
a_0 = \frac{1}{\sigma_0^2} [(m_{2.} - m_{21}) + (m_{.2} - m_{12}) + m_{00} - m_{22}],
$$

$$
a_1 = \frac{1}{\sigma_1^2} m_{2.}, \qquad a_2 = \frac{1}{\sigma_2^2} m_{.2},
\tag{39}
$$

$$
a_{01} = \frac{1}{\sigma_0^2 + \sigma_1^2} (m_{1.} - m_{11}), \qquad a_{02} = \frac{1}{\sigma_0^2 + \sigma_2^2} (m_{.1} - m_{11}),
$$

$$
a_{012} = \frac{1}{\sigma_0^2 + \sigma_1^2 + \sigma_2^2} m_{11},
$$

and

$$X'\Sigma^{-1}\begin{pmatrix} y \\ z \end{pmatrix} = \begin{pmatrix} b_0 + b_{01} + b_{02} + b_{012} \\ b_1 + b_{01} + b_{012} \\ b_2 + b_{02} + b_{012} \end{pmatrix},$$

$$b_0 = \frac{1}{\sigma_0^2}[(Y_{2.} - Y_{21}) + (Y_{.2} - Y_{12}) + Y_{00} - Y_{22}],$$

$$b_1 = \frac{1}{\sigma_1^2} Z_{2.}, \qquad b_2 = \frac{1}{\sigma_2^2} Z_{.2}, \tag{40}$$

$$b_{01} = \frac{1}{\sigma_0^2 + \sigma_1^2}(Y_{1.} - Y_{11}), \qquad b_{02} = \frac{1}{\sigma_0^2 + \sigma_2^2}(Y_{.1} - Y_{11}),$$

$$b_{012} = \frac{1}{\sigma_0^2 + \sigma_1^2 + \sigma_2^2} Y_{11}.$$

Optimal choice of the direct metering observations is obtained by solving either one of the constrained minimum problems,

$$\text{minimize} \quad \text{tr}\,\Sigma(\hat{\theta}) = \text{tr}[(X_c'X_c)^{-1}X_c'\Sigma_c X_c(X_c'X_c)^{-1}] \tag{41}$$

or

$$\text{minimize} \quad \text{tr}\,\Sigma(\tilde{\theta}) = \text{tr}[(X'\Sigma^{-1}X)^{-1}] \tag{42}$$

$$\text{subject to} \quad c_1(m_{20} + m_{02} + m_{12} + m_{21}) + c_2 m_{22} \le C,$$

$$m_{22} + m_{21} + m_{12} + m_{11} = n_1,$$

$$m_{20} + m_{10} = n_2, \tag{43}$$

$$m_{02} + m_{01} = n_3,$$

$$m_{00} = n_4.$$

Here we have assumed that the unit costs c_i of direct metering depend only on the number of appliances metered per unit. Since the traces (41), (42) are decreasing in the number m of z observations equality will obtain in the cost constraint (43). Thus, the decision variables are, e.g., m_{20}, m_{02}, m_{21}, m_{12}.

Full efficiency of the design will only be achieved under the criterion (42). This can be written as follows:

$$\text{tr}[(X'\Sigma^{-1}X)^{-1}]$$

$$= \frac{1}{D}[a_{012}(a_1 + a_2 + a_{01} + a_{02}) + (a_1 + a_2)(a_0 + a_{01} + a_{02} + a_{012})$$

$$+ (a_1 + a_{01})(a_2 + a_{02}) + (a_0 + a_{01})(a_{02} + a_{012})$$

$$+ (a_0 + a_{02})(a_{01} + a_{012})], \tag{44}$$

where

$$D = a_1 a_2 (a_0 + a_{01} + a_{02} + a_{012}) + a_0 a_1 (a_{02} + a_{012}) + a_0 a_2 (a_{01} + a_{012})$$
$$+ a_{01} a_{02} (a_0 + a_1 + a_2 + a_{012}) + a_{01} a_{012} (a_0 + a_1) + a_{02} a_{012} (a_0 + a_2).$$

To illustrate we consider the special case that there are only owners of both appliances and at most one appliance may be directly metered per household, i.e., $n_2 = n_3 = n_4 = 0$, $m_{22} = 0$, whence $m_{20} = m_{02} = m_{10} = m_{01} = m_{00} = 0$. Suppose that $c_1 = 1$ (c_2 is irrelevant) and that $C = m \leq n_1$ direct metering observations are feasible. Then $m = m_{21} + m_{12}$ or $m_{21} = m - m_{12}$ and $m_{11} = n_1 - m$. The decision variable is $m_{12} := x$. Here

$$a_0 = 0, \qquad a_1 = (m - x)/\sigma_1^2, \qquad a_2 = x/\sigma_2^2,$$

$$a_{012} = (n_1 - m)/(\sigma_0^2 + \sigma_1^2 + \sigma_2^2),$$

$$a_{01} = x/(\sigma_0^2 + \sigma_1^2), \qquad a_{02} = (m - x)/(\sigma_0^2 + \sigma_2^2).$$

Inserting these expressions in the generalized variance det $\Sigma(\tilde{\theta})$ gives

$$D = x(m - x)$$

$$\times \left[\frac{n_1 - m}{\sigma_0^2 + \sigma_1^2 + \sigma_2^2} \left(\frac{1}{\sigma_1^2} + \frac{1}{\sigma_0^2 + \sigma_2^2} \right) \left(\frac{1}{\sigma_2^2} + \frac{1}{\sigma_0^2 + \sigma_1^2} \right) \right.$$

$$\left. + \frac{x}{\sigma_2^2 (\sigma_0^2 + \sigma_1^2)} \left(\frac{1}{\sigma_1^2} + \frac{1}{\sigma_0^2 + \sigma_2^2} \right) + \frac{m - x}{\sigma_1^2 (\sigma_0^2 + \sigma_2^2)} \left(\frac{1}{\sigma_2^2} + \frac{1}{\sigma_0^2 + \sigma_1^2} \right) \right]$$

$$= \frac{\sigma_0^2 + \sigma_1^2 + \sigma_2^2}{\sigma_1^2 \sigma_2^2 (\sigma_0^2 + \sigma_1^2)(\sigma_0^2 + \sigma_2^2)} n_1 x(m - x). \tag{45}$$

Likewise the objective function becomes

$$\mathrm{tr}\, \Sigma(\tilde{\theta}) = \frac{1}{D} \left\{ \frac{2(n_1 - m)}{\sigma_0^2 + \sigma_1^2 + \sigma_2^2} \left[\left(\frac{1}{\sigma_2^2} + \frac{1}{\sigma_0^2 + \sigma_1^2} \right) x + \left(\frac{1}{\sigma_1^2} + \frac{1}{\sigma_0^2 + \sigma_2^2} \right) (m - x) \right] \right.$$

$$+ \frac{2}{(\sigma_0^2 + \sigma_1^2)(\sigma_0^2 + \sigma_2^2)} x(m - x) + \frac{2}{\sigma_2^2 (\sigma_0^2 + \sigma_1^2)} x^2$$

$$+ \frac{2}{\sigma_1^2 (\sigma_0^2 + \sigma_2^2)} (m - x)^2$$

$$\left. + \left(\frac{1}{\sigma_1^2} + \frac{1}{\sigma_0^2 + \sigma_2^2} \right) \left(\frac{1}{\sigma_2^2} + \frac{1}{\sigma_0^2 + \sigma_1^2} \right) x(m - x) \right\}. \tag{46}$$

Straightforward calculations lead to

$$
\operatorname{tr} \Sigma(\tilde{\theta}) = \frac{1}{n_1} \frac{\sigma_0^4 + \sigma_1^4 + \sigma_2^4}{\sigma_0^2 + \sigma_1^2 + \sigma_2^2} + \frac{2}{\sigma_0^2 + \sigma_1^2 + \sigma_2^2} \left[\frac{\sigma_2^2(\sigma_0^2 + \sigma_1^2)}{x} + \frac{\sigma_1^2(\sigma_0^2 + \sigma_2^2)}{m - x} \right],
$$

(47)

whence it is seen that tr $\Sigma(\tilde{\theta})$ has a unique minimum at (one of the integers bordering)

$$
x = m_{12} = \frac{1}{1 + \pi} m, \qquad m_{21} = \frac{\pi}{1 + \pi} m,
$$

(48)

where

$$
\pi = \sqrt{\frac{\sigma_1^2(\sigma_0^2 + \sigma_2^2)}{\sigma_2^2(\sigma_0^2 + \sigma_1^2)}}.
$$

Thus, if $\sigma_1^2 = \sigma_2^2$, we have $m_{12} = m_{21} = \frac{1}{2}m$, and if $\sigma_1^2 \neq \sigma_2^2$, there are more direct observations on the appliance with the larger consumption variance. It might also be noted that in the special case direct metering is required for parameter identifiability. This fact is reflected by (47) as tr $\Sigma(\tilde{\theta}) = \infty$ for $x = 0$, $x = m$, or $m = 0$. For consistency of $\tilde{\theta}$ one must have n_1, m_{12} and $m_{21} \to \infty$.

5. Final remarks

The results in this note are preliminary to and first steps of a more comprehensive analysis that considers direct metering observations as subsamples of the original cross section. This amounts to explicitly recognizing the correlation between the disturbances when the same households are used for purposes of direct metering. As to the numerical results, to our knowledge this is the first time such sample size calculations have been developed and illustrated, though some of the variance formulas appear in the empirical work of Fiebig et al. (1988) who analyze Australian data where CDA is supplemented by limited direct metering information.

Appendix

Proof of the equivalency between (19) under $\sigma_1^2 = \sigma_2^2 = \sigma_3^2$ and (11).

$$V(\hat{\beta}_1) + V(\hat{\beta}_2) = \left(\frac{\sigma_1^2}{n_{1\cdot}} - \frac{\sigma_1^2}{n} + \frac{\sigma_1^4}{\sigma_2^2}\frac{m_1\sigma_2^2}{n_{1\cdot}^2}\right) \Big/ \left(p_{2\cdot} + \frac{\sigma_1^2 m_1}{\sigma_2^2 n_{1\cdot}}\right)^2$$

$$+ \left(\frac{\sigma_1^2}{n_{\cdot 1}} - \frac{\sigma_1^2}{n} + \frac{\sigma_1^4}{\sigma_3^2}\frac{m_2\sigma_2^2}{n_{\cdot 1}^2}\right) \Big/ \left(p_{\cdot 2} + \frac{\sigma_1^2 m_2}{\sigma_3^2 n_{\cdot 1}}\right)^2. \qquad (19)$$

Now let

$$\sigma_1^2/\sigma_2^2 = \sigma_1^2/\sigma_3^2 = 1.$$

Then

$$\left(\frac{\sigma_1^2}{n_{1\cdot}} - \frac{\sigma_1^2}{n} + \frac{m_1\sigma_2^2}{n_{1\cdot}^2}\right) \Big/ \left(p_{2\cdot} + \frac{m_1}{n_{1\cdot}}\right)^2 + \left(\frac{\sigma_1^2}{n_{\cdot 1}} - \frac{\sigma_1^2}{n} + \frac{m_2\sigma_2^2}{n_{\cdot 1}^2}\right) \Big/ \left(p_{\cdot 2} + \frac{m_2}{n_{\cdot 1}}\right)^2$$

$$= \left[\frac{1}{n^2} n_{1\cdot}^2 \left(\frac{1}{n_{1\cdot}} - \frac{1}{n} + \frac{\sigma_2^2 m_1}{\sigma_1^2 n_{1\cdot}^2}\right)\sigma_1^2\right] \Big/ \frac{1}{n^2}(n_{1\cdot}\, p_{2\cdot} + m_1)^2$$

$$+ \left[\frac{1}{n^2} n_{\cdot 1}^2 \left(\frac{1}{n_{\cdot 1}} - \frac{1}{n} + \frac{\sigma_2^2 m_2}{\sigma_1^2 n_{\cdot 1}^2}\right)\sigma_1^2\right] \Big/ \frac{1}{n^2}(n_{\cdot 1}\, p_{\cdot 2} + m_2)^2$$

$$= \left[\frac{1}{n}\frac{n_{1\cdot}}{n}\left(1 - \frac{n_{1\cdot}}{n} + \frac{\sigma_2^2 m_1}{\sigma_1^2 n_{1\cdot}}\right)\sigma_1^2\right] \Big/ \left(p_{1\cdot}p_{2\cdot} + \frac{m_1}{n}\right)^2$$

$$+ \left[\frac{1}{n}\frac{n_{\cdot 1}}{n}\left(1 - \frac{n_{\cdot 1}}{n} + \frac{\sigma_2^2 m_2}{\sigma_1^2 n_{\cdot 1}}\right)\sigma_1^2\right] \Big/ \left(p_{\cdot 1}p_{\cdot 2} + \frac{m_2}{n}\right)^2$$

$$= \left[\frac{1}{n}p_{1\cdot}(1 - p_{1\cdot})\sigma_1^2\right] \Big/ \left(p_{1\cdot}p_{2\cdot} + \frac{m_1}{n}\right)^2$$

$$+ \left[\frac{1}{n}p_{\cdot 1}(1 - p_{\cdot 1})\sigma_1^2\right] \Big/ \left(p_{\cdot 1}p_{\cdot 2} + \frac{m_2}{n}\right)^2$$

$$+ \left[\frac{1}{n}p_{1\cdot}\frac{m_1}{n_{1\cdot}}\sigma_2^2\right] \Big/ \left(p_{1\cdot}p_{2\cdot} + \frac{m_1}{n}\right)^2 + \left[\frac{1}{n}p_{\cdot 1}\frac{m_2}{n_{\cdot 1}}\sigma_3^2\right] \Big/ \left(p_{\cdot 1}p_{\cdot 2} + \frac{m_2}{n}\right)^2$$

$$= \left[\frac{1}{n}p_{1\cdot}p_{2\cdot}\sigma_1^2\right] \Big/ \left(p_{1\cdot}p_{2\cdot} + \frac{m_1}{n}\right)^2 + \left[\frac{1}{n}(p_{\cdot 1}p_{\cdot 2})\sigma_1^2\right] \Big/ \left(p_{\cdot 1}p_{\cdot 2} + \frac{m_2}{n}\right)^2$$

$$+ \left[\frac{1}{n}\frac{m_1}{n}\sigma_2^2\right] \Big/ \left(p_{1\cdot}p_{2\cdot} + \frac{m_1}{n}\right)^2 + \left[\frac{1}{n}\frac{m_2}{n}\sigma_3^2\right] \Big/ \left(p_{\cdot 1}p_{\cdot 2} + \frac{m_2}{n}\right)^2$$

$$= (11).$$

References

Aigner, D.J., C. Sorooshian and P. Kerwin (1984) 'Conditional demand analysis for estimating residential end-use load profiles', *Energy Journal*, 5:81-97.

Caves, D.W., J.A. Herriges, K.A. Train and R.W. Windle (1985) 'A Bayesian approach to combining conditional demand and engineering models of end-use load curves', mimeo, Christensen Associates Inc., Madison, WI.

Dubin, J.A. and D.L. McFadden (1984) 'An econometric analysis of residential electric appliance holdings and consumption', *Econometrica*, 52:345-362.

Fiebig, D., R.A. Bartels and D.J. Aigner (1988) 'A random coefficient approach to the estimation of residential end-use load profiles', mimeo, University of Sydney, Australia.

Hill, D. (1982) 'The time-of-day demand for electricity by end-use: An analysis of Wisconsin data', Chapter 10 in: *Analysis of Residential Response to Time-of-Day Prices,* Report EA-2380, Electric Power Research Institute, Palo Alto, CA.

Keifer, J. (1959) 'Optimum experimental designs', *Journal of the Royal Statistical Society, Series B*, 21:272-304.

Lillard, L.A. and D.J. Aigner (1984) 'Time-of-day electricity consumption response to temperature and the ownership of air conditioning appliances', *Journal of Business and Economic Statistics*, 2:40-53.

Parti, M. and C. Parti (1980) 'The total and appliance-specific conditional demand for electricity in the household sector', *Bell Journal of Economics*, 11:309-321.

Chapter 15

ALLAIS CHARACTERISATION OF PREFERENCE STRUCTURES AND THE STRUCTURE OF DEMAND

Anton P. BARTEN

Center for Economic Research, Tilburg University, Tilburg, The Netherlands, and CORE, Université Catholique de Louvain, Louvain-la-Neuve, Belgium

1. Introduction

It is a postulate of empirical economics that model constants should be readily interpretable entities. The justification of this position is not so much their probable stability across different observation units. There is very little known about the true functional form of economic relations. A more important reason is the ability for formulate prior ideas about the sign and perhaps even about the size of coefficients to be estimated from the data. Such prior ideas may be based on introspection, casual observation or comparable empirical studies. Introspection, intuition, is usually in terms of relatively simple concepts.

In view of shortcomings of the data and specification errors in the models pure estimates are frequently not very reliable. The usual standard errors may only partly reflect their lack of precision. Prior information about the value of the coefficients is needed to form an opinion about the plausibility of the outcomes. This prior information more often than not is based on intuition. Apart from being used in an informal or formal test it can also be incorporated in the estimation procedure, for example, in a Bayesian approach.

In demand analysis, the concepts of complementarity, substitution and independence between commodities seem at first sight to be straightforward and close to intuition. If more of good x enhances the desirability of good y one speaks of complementarity. If more of x reduces the attractiveness

Economic Decision-Making: Games, Econometrics and Optimisation
Edited by J.J. Gabszewicz, J.-F. Richard and L.A. Wolsey

of y, goods x and y are said to be substitutes. The neutral position is that of independence. Examples are easy to find: wine and beer are substitutes, wine and cheese are complements, while wine and shoes, say, are mutually independent. Adjectives like strong and weak can be applied quite naturally to substitution and complementarity.

In view of the intuitive appeal of these notions one might have thought that they would be playing a major role in empirical demand analysis. This, however, is not the case. Even in the rare case that they are used it is not quite in accordance with the intuitive meaning just given. The least one can say is that there is a considerable degree of confusion. This leads Samuelson (1947) to consider the concept of complementarity (and substitution and independence) as being essentially unimportant, a statement which contrasts the one by Houthakker (1960), who considers the analysis of substitution and complementarity to be "one of the most cherished achievements of consumption theory".

It is clear that there is some need for a definition of complementarity and substitution that agrees well with intuition and at the same time can be useful for demand analysis. It is the contention of this paper that the mathematical expression given by Allais (1943) to characterise these concepts meets these requirements. At the same time it can be easily employed to identify groupwise interaction structures. Furthermore, a comparable formulation can be given to the effects of preference changing variables such as health or age.

The next section takes up two of the most commonly used expressions for complementarity and substitution and discusses their defects. This clears the way for the introduction of the Allais coefficients in Section 3. Section 4 shows how these Allais coefficients can be found back in a regular demand system, i.e., a system which explains the quantities demanded as a function of the budget and the prices. Section 5 does the same for an inverse demand system in which the prices are being explained and the quantities are given, next to the budget. The role of these coefficients to characterise separability structures of preferences is discussed in Section 6. The next section proposes a characterisation of the effects of other determinants than the budget, prices or quantities quite similar to the Allais one. A numerical example is next given to help forming an idea of the possibilities and limitations of the approach. Some concluding remarks end the paper.

2. Complementarity, substitution and independence

To set the stage for the discussion we will equip the consumer with an (at least) twice differentiable strongly quasi-concave utility function representing a well behaved preference order over the n-dimensional compact commodity space. Let this utility function be $u(q)$, with first-order derivatives $u_i(q)$, also known as the marginal utility of good i, and second-order derivatives $u_{ij}(q)$.

Associating the marginal utility u_i with desirability one can define complementarity by the positive sign of u_{ij}: the desirability of i increases if more of j is available. Substitution corresponds with a negative u_{ij} and independence with $u_{ij} = 0$. Unfortunately, the value of u_{ij} and its sign is not invariant under monotone increasing transformations of the utility function. Otherwise said, the sign of u_{ij} is not determined by the preference order but depends on a particular representation of the preference order. This sign can then obviously not be used to characterise the structure of preferences.

It is of some importance for what follows to derive the lack of invariance of u_{ij}. Let

$$v(q) = F(u(q)) \tag{2.1}$$

be a monotone increasing, i.e., order preserving, twice differentiable transformation of $u(q)$. Both $v(q)$ and $u(q)$ are equally valid representations of the same preference order. Hence,

$$F' = dv/du \tag{2.2}$$

is strictly positive. Correspondingly, one has

$$v_i(q) = \partial v(q)/\partial q = (dv/du)(\partial u(q)/\partial q_i) = F'u_i(q). \tag{2.3}$$

The marginal utilities change proportionally in the transition from $u(q)$ to $v(q)$ but they preserve their positive sign. Next let

$$F'' = dF'/du = d^2v/du^2 \tag{2.4}$$

be the second-order derivative of the transformation. Its sign depends on the nature of the transformation and does not depend on the preference order. One then has as the counterpart of u_{ij},

$$v_{ij}(q) = F'\partial u_i(q)/\partial q_j + F''u_i(q)u_j(q)$$
$$= F'u_{ij}(q) + F''u_i(q)u_j(q). \tag{2.5}$$

Given the positive nature of F' the first term has the same sign as $u_{ij}(q)$. The presence of F'' in the second term makes its sign dependent on the transformation. This then is also true for v_{ij}. The second-order derivatives are not adequate representations of interactions among goods in the preference order.

There is a strong tradition in demand analysis to work with invariant concepts only. Indeed, the utility function is not necessary to derive the main results of demand theory. Only properties of the preference order and of the budget set matter. Consequently, properties of the utility function that are not invariant do not play a role, are irrelevant. They do not leave a trace in observable demand behaviour. Once this was realised the use of (the sign of) the u_{ij} to characterise preference interactions was abandoned. A search was set in to find an invariant way to represent the notion of complementarity, substitution and independence.

The best known characterisation is the one attributed to Allen and Hicks. Let $f_i(m, p)$ be a regular demand function, explaining the quantity demanded of good i as a function of the total budget, m, and of the vector of all prices $p' = (p_i, \ldots, p_n)$. Next let

$$k_{ij} = [\partial f_i(m, p)/\partial p_j]_{u \text{ constant}} \tag{2.6}$$

be the income compensated price effect, also known as the Slutsky-effect. The negativity of demand implies $k_{jj} < 0$. Now, for $i \neq j$, a positive value of k_{ij} means that an increase in the price of j leads to an increase in the demand for i to substitute for the drop in the demand for j. Hence $k_{ij} > 0$ characterises substitution. If the drop in the demand for j, because of the increase in its price, entails also a drop in the demand for i, goods i and k move in a parallel fashion, are complements. Hence, $k_{ij} < 0$ is associated with complementarity. Clearly, $k_{ij} = 0$ is associated with independence.

There are several advantages to this choice. In principle, the k_{ij} can be easily measured. Complementarity and substitution are symmetric concepts in the sense that if i is a substitute for j, j is also a substitute for i, while the same holds for complementarity. The k_{ij} are also symmetric in i and j. The k_{ij} describe changes in the composition of demand bundles which occupy the same position in the preference order. They reflect the structure of the preference order. They are invariant.

There are certain disadvantages too. The adding up condition of demand states that $\sum_i p_i k_{ij} = 0$ while the homogeneity condition implies that $\sum_j k_{ij} p_j = 0$. Given the property that $k_{ii} < 0$ there must be a dominance of positive k_{ij} because prices are taken to be strictly positive. In the case of two commodities k_{12} is always positive irrespective of what intuition says about their mutual interaction. Houthakker (1960) considers the relative dominance of substitution a "minor blemish", precisely because it appears to contradict intuition. Another problem is the negativity of k_{ii}. Since a commodity is its own perfect substitute a positive value of k_{ii} would have been more natural. Furthermore, the adding-up condition and the homogeneity condition reflect the presence of an effective budget constraint. In fact, the k_{ij} only arise as the result of selecting the most preferred bundle on the frontier of the budget set. Intuitive notions about preference interactions are part of the theory of choice which is, to quote from Frisch (1959), "assumed to be independent of the particular organisational form of the market". Otherwise said the k_{ij} are not fundamental, not general enough to be used to characterise preference structures. Of course, they reflect such a preference structure but in an imperfect and possibly misleading way.

There have been other proposals for the characterisation of the interactions. With the exception of the Allais coefficients they share some of the disadvantages of the k_{ij}. We will meet one alternative, the sign of the elements of the Antonelli matrix, when discussing inverse demand in Section 5. However, it is appropriate to turn our attention now to the formulation of Allais.

3. The Allais coefficients

One way to derive the Allais coefficients is to start off from (2.5), rewritten here as

$$v_{ij} = F'u_{ij} + F''u_iu_j. \tag{3.1}$$

As noted when this expression was derived the sign of the second component was the source of the possible lack of correspondence in the sign of v_{ij} and u_{ij}. To handle this issue, first divide both sides of (3.1) by v_iv_j to obtain

$$\frac{v_{ij}}{v_iv_j} = \frac{F'u_{ij}}{F'u_iF'u_j} + \frac{F''u_iu_j}{F'u_iF'u_j} = \frac{u_{ij}}{F'u_iu_j} + \frac{F''}{F'}. \tag{3.2}$$

Use has been made of (2.3). The second component has been reduced to a constant independent of i and j. Next, take the difference between the left-hand side of (3.2) and v_{rs}/v_rv_s where r, s is another pair of commodities:

$$\frac{v_{ij}}{v_iv_j} - \frac{v_{rs}}{v_rv_s} = \frac{1}{F'}\left(\frac{u_{ij}}{u_iu_j} - \frac{u_{rs}}{u_ru_s}\right). \tag{3.3}$$

The sign of this difference is invariant. We would next like to get rid of the F'. For this purpose multiply both sides of (3.3) by $\sum_h v_hq_h = F'\sum_h u_hq_h > 0$

to obtain the Allais coefficients:

$$a_{ij} = \sum_h v_h q_h \left(\frac{v_{ij}}{v_i v_j} - \frac{v_{rs}}{v_r v_s} \right) = \sum_h u_h q_h \left(\frac{u_{ij}}{u_i u_j} - \frac{u_{rs}}{u_r u_s} \right). \tag{3.4}$$

The a_{ij} are clearly invariant. They are moreover free of units of measurement, as is not too difficult to verify.

The sign of the a_{ij} is determined already in (3.3). Note that the choice of r, s is free. Let it be some standard pair and define its interaction to be neutral. One may write

$$a_{ij} = \mu(q) u_{ij} / (u_i u_j) - \alpha(q) \tag{3.5}$$

with $\mu(q) = \sum_h u_h q_h$ and $\alpha(q) = \mu(q) u_{rs} / (u_r u_s)$. One also has

$$u_{ij} = u_i u_j a_{ij} / \mu(q) + \alpha(q) u_i u_j. \tag{3.6}$$

Consider a change in the marginal utility of good i:

$$du_i = \sum_j u_{ij} \, dq_j = (u_i / \mu(q)) \sum_j a_{ij} u_j \, dq_j + \alpha(q) u_i \sum_j u_j \, dq_j,$$

or in relative terms,

$$d \ln u_i = (1/\mu(q)) \sum_j a_{ij} (u_j q_j) \, d \ln q_j + \alpha(q) \, du$$

$$= \sum_j a_{ij} \nu_j \, d \ln q_j + \alpha(q) \, du \tag{3.7}$$

with $\nu_j = u_j q_j / \mu(q) = u_j q_j / (\sum_h u_h q_h) > 0$. Observe that $\sum \nu_k = 1$ and that the ν_j are invariant.

Expression (3.7) shows that the relative change in the marginal utility of good i can be decomposed in a part, $\alpha(q) \, du$, which is general and not invariant and a part which is invariant and specifically involves the i, j interactions. Here, the a_{ij} capture the impact of a (relative) change in q_j, weighted by ν_j or the relative desirability of j as represented by its marginal utility. It is then natural to associate positive a_{ij} with complementarity, negative a_{ij} with substitution and zero a_{ij} with independence. There is no formal objection against requiring a_{ii} to be negative.

The a_{ij} represent the type of interaction in terms of a difference from that of a standard pair. Changing the standard pair will change the a_{ij}. While the sign of the u_{ij} depends on the rather arbitrary choice of the utility indicator, the sign of the a_{ij} depends on the choice of the standard pair. It appears, however, to be easier to identify a neutral, independent, pair than to identify a particular utility indicator as the appropriate one.

Summing up, one may say that the a_{ij} can describe the interaction among commodities in the preference order in a way that comes close to one's intuition. When one says that cheese makes wine more attractive, it may be taken to mean that more of cheese makes wine more attractive than more of shoes and hence that cheese and wine are complements. An analogous statement can be made about beer and wine being more substitutable than shoes and wine. The choice of the standard pair is admittedly crucial but on first sight not too difficult.

As was mentioned earlier the a_{ij} are free of units of measurement. This still leaves their order of magnitude open. From (3.4) or (3.5) one can say very little about this. The a_{ij} can differ considerably from pair to pair or from the corresponding a_{ii} and a_{jj}. To make prior statements about weak or strong degrees of interaction in terms of values of the a_{ij} is then not too easily feasible. Allais introduces therefore the interaction *intensities* defined as

$$a_{ij}^* = a_{ij}/\sqrt{a_{ii}a_{jj}} \qquad (3.8)$$

where it is assumed that the a_{ii} are negative. Thus $a_{ii}^* = -1$, which charac-terises perfect substitution. It is then natural to require the a_{ij}^* to be on the interval $(-1, +1)$ with $+1$ representing perfect complementarity.

A word about the ν_j in (3.7). As already said the ν_j are invariant, positive and add up to one. The second law of Gossen defines the consumer equilibrium as the proportionality of the vector of marginal utilities, u_q, with that of prices:

$$u_q = \lambda p \qquad (3.9)$$

where λ is a positive factor of proportionality, interpretable as the marginal utility of the budget. If (3.9) holds $u_j q_j = \lambda p_j q_j$ and $\nu_j = p_j q_j/(\sum_h p_h q_h) = w_j$, the share of expenditure on j out of the total budget $m = \sum_h p_h q_h$. The ν_j obviously represents the willingness of the consumer to spend on commodity j. One can also say that ν_j expresses the importance of commodity j for the choice problem of the consumer.

One can organise the a_{ij} in an $n \times n$ matrix A. It follows from (3.5) that

$$A = \mu(q)\hat{u}_q^{-1} U \hat{u}_q^{-1} - \alpha(q)\iota\iota'. \qquad (3.10)$$

The use of ` over a vector indicates a diagonal matrix with the elements of the vector on the diagonal. This convention is also employed elsewhere in this paper. Since the axiom of desirability requires that all elements of u_q are strictly positive $\hat{u}_q^{-1}$ is defined. Here, and later on too, ι is a vector of all elements equal to one. The assumption of strong quasi-concavity of the utility function requires (see Barten and Böhm, 1982),

$$x'Ux < 0 \quad \text{for all } x \text{ such that } u'_q x = 0. \tag{3.11}$$

By defining $y = \dot{u}_q x$ one obtains

$$y'Ay = \mu(q)x'Ux - \alpha(q)(x'u_q)^2 \tag{3.12}$$

which is negative for all x such that $u'_q x = 0$ or, equivalently, for all y such that $\iota'y = 0$. Condition (3.11) implies that the rank of the matrix U is at least $n - 1$. Full rank of the Hessian matrix of the utility function cannot be guaranteed for all possible representations of the preference order. The strong quasi-concavity condition also requires A to be at least of rank $n - 1$, but the property of full rank of A is a property of the preference order. Its validity can be empirically verified, at least in principle. A further strengthening of the properties of A would be to require it to be negative definite.

4. Allais coefficients and the specification of a regular demand system

Basically, there are two types of demand systems. One, the *regular* system explains the quantities consumed, q, as a function of m, the budget and p, the prices. The other system explains the relative prices one is willing to pay for a given bundle of quantities and a fixed budget. This is the *inverse* demand system. Its specification is taken up in the next section. Here the focus will be on the regular demand system.

Starting off from (3.9) one has

$$\mathrm{d} \ln u_q = \mathrm{d} \ln p + (\mathrm{d} \ln \lambda)\iota. \tag{4.1}$$

It follows from (3.7) that

$$\mathrm{d} \ln u_q = A\dot{w} \, \mathrm{d} \ln q + (\alpha \, \mathrm{d}u)\iota \tag{4.2}$$

where use is made of $v_j = w_j$ and $\dot{w}$ is the diagonalisation of the vector of budget shares w. Combining (4.1) and (4.2) one obtains

$$A\dot{w} \, \mathrm{d} \ln q = (\mathrm{d} \ln \lambda - \alpha \, \mathrm{d}u)\iota + \mathrm{d} \ln p$$

or, assuming full rank of A,

$$\dot{w} \, \mathrm{d} \ln q = A^{-1}(\mathrm{d} \ln \lambda - \alpha \, \mathrm{d}u) + A^{-1} \, \mathrm{d} \ln p. \tag{4.3}$$

The quantities demanded have to satisfy the budget

$$p'q = m$$

which in differential logarithmic form can be written as

$$\text{d ln } m = w' \text{ d ln } q + w' \text{ d ln } p. \tag{4.4}$$

Since $w' \text{ d ln } q = \iota' \dot{w} \text{ d ln } q$, (4.3) and (4.4) can be combined to yield

$$\text{d ln } \lambda - \alpha \text{ d}u = (\iota' A^{-1} \iota)^{-1} [(\text{d ln } m - w' \text{ d ln } p) - \iota A^{-1} \text{ d ln } p)].$$

Using this result in (4.3) gives

$$\dot{w} \text{ d ln } q = A^{-1} \iota (\iota' A^{-1} \iota)^{-1} (\text{d ln } m - w' \text{ d ln } p)$$

$$+ [A^{-1} - A^{-1} \iota (\iota' A^{-1} \iota)^{-1} \iota' A^{-1}] \text{ d ln } p$$

$$= b(\text{d ln } m - w' \text{ d ln } p) + S \text{ d ln } p \tag{4.5}$$

with

$$b = A^{-1} \iota (\iota A^{-1} \iota)^{-1}, \tag{4.6}$$

$$S = A^{-1} - A^{-1} \iota (\iota A^{-1} \iota)^{-1} \iota A^{-1}. \tag{4.7}$$

System (4.5) with b and s constant is precisely the specification of a demand system proposed by Theil (1965). It later became known as the Rotterdam system.

The b_i are the marginal propensities to spend the budget on good i. As is easily seen from (4.6), $\iota' b = 1$. The matrix S is a simple transformation of K, the matrix of Slutsky coefficients k_{ij}, as given by (2.6),

$$S = (1/m)\dot{p}K\dot{p}. \tag{4.8}$$

It is clear that $s_{ij} = p_i k_{ij} p_j / m$ has the same sign as k_{ij}. Expression (4.7) provides the link between the Allais and the Hicks–Allen characterisation. This relation is not very straightforward, in the sense that there is no simple correspondence between the signs of the s_{ij} and the corresponding a_{ij}.

Equation (4.7) expresses S as a function of A. For practical purposes the inverse relation is of some interest. Estimation of (4.5) yields estimates of b and S which can be used to obtain values for A. These could be evaluated for their plausibility. In this indirect way the plausibility of the estimates for S and b can be analysed.

Let

$$\varphi = \iota' A^{-1} \iota. \tag{4.9}$$

Then

$$b = (\iota / \varphi) A^{-1} \iota \tag{4.10}$$

and

$$S = A^{-1} - \varphi bb' \tag{4.11}$$

which can also be written as

$$AS + \iota b' = I. \tag{4.12}$$

As is obvious from (4.9) through (4.11), $\iota'b = 1$ and $\iota'S = 0$. One can combine these results into the following expression:

$$\begin{pmatrix} A - (1/\varphi)\iota\iota' & \iota \\ \iota' & 0 \end{pmatrix} \begin{pmatrix} S & b \\ b' & 0 \end{pmatrix} = \begin{pmatrix} I & 0 \\ 0 & 1 \end{pmatrix}. \tag{4.13}$$

Let M be the $n \times n$ NW block of the inverse of the second matrix in (4.13). Then

$$A = M + (1/\varphi)\iota\iota'. \tag{4.14}$$

Here $1/\varphi$ is unknown. One may select its value in such a way that $a_{rs} = 0$. With e_r being the rth column of the identity matrix, then $(1/\varphi) = -e_r'Me_s$ and

$$A = M - e_r'Me_s\iota\iota'. \tag{4.15}$$

This expression is rather straightforward. One calculates M and subtracts from all its elements the value of $e_r'Me_s$. There is one degree of freedom which is used up by the determination of the standard pair. Otherwise said, given observed values for S and b, A cannot be determined unless one adds as an identifying restriction or normalisation that $a_{rs} = 0$. For that matter one may also choose for a_{rs} another value than zero. As a corollary to this statement one has that S and b are invariant for the choice of the standard pair and the value of that interaction.

5. Allais coefficients and the specification of an inverse demand system

Inverse demand systems explain the relative prices a consumer is willing to pay given his budget m and the quantities of the commodities. Inverse demand occurs, for example, in the case of quickly perishable goods like fresh vegetables and fresh fish, where the supply is basically fixed and the supplier is a price taker.

The dependent variable in inverse demand relations is usually taken to be the normalised price vector

$$\pi = (1/m)p. \tag{5.1}$$

Here π_i is the fraction of the budget paid for one unit of good i. Note that it follows from $p'q = m$ that $\pi'q = 1$. The consumer equilibrium (3.9) can be expressed in terms of π as

$$u_q = \lambda m \pi = \mu(q)\pi \tag{5.2}$$

or as

$$\pi = (1/\mu(q))u_q.$$

Take differentials

$$d\pi = (1/\mu(q))(-\pi u'_q \, dq + (I - \pi q') \, du_q)$$
$$= -\pi\pi' \, dq + (I - \pi q')(1/\mu(q))U \, dq.$$

A minor rearrangement yields the inverse demand system in differential form

$$d\pi = -(\pi - (I - \pi q')(1/\mu(q))Uq)\pi' \, dq$$
$$+ (I - \pi q')(1/\mu(q))U(I - q\pi') \, dq$$
$$= g\pi' \, dq + G \, dq \tag{5.3}$$

with

$$g = -\pi + (I - \pi q')(1/\mu(q))Uq \tag{5.4}$$

and

$$G = (I - \pi q')(1/\mu(q))U(I - q\pi') \, dq. \tag{5.5}$$

The change in prices is explained as the result from two shifts. The first one, $g\pi' \, dq$, is a scale effect. It represents the move from one indifference surface to the other. The second one, $G \, dq$, represents the move along an indifference surface (see Anderson, 1980).

The matrix G is known as the Antonelli matrix. It is the counterpart of the Slutsky matrix of regular demand systems. It also is a symmetric matrix and its diagonal elements are negative. Its rank is likewise $n - 1$.

The signs of the elements of G are sometimes also used to characterise interactions of the complementarity/substitution type. If goods i and j are substitutes more of good i reduces the price one is willing to pay for good j. Substitution means then $g_{ij} < 0$. A good being its own substitute corresponds then nicely with $g_{ii} < 0$. Complementarity corresponds with $g_{ij} > 0$: more of good i makes good j more attractive and increases the price one is willing to pay for it. However, complementarity will dominate. As is easily checked $Gq = 0$ and $q'G = 0$. With negative g_{ii} and positive q there must be at least one complementarity interaction even when intuition would consider all goods to be substitutes. This dominance of complementarity is of the same nature as the dominance of substitution in the case of the Allen–Hicks definition. The signs of the Antonelli coefficients are equally unsuitable as characterisations of preference interactions.

To establish the relation between the Allais matrix and the Antonelli matrix it is convenient to first transform the latter by multiplying its elements by $q_i q_j$:

$$H = \hat{q} G \hat{q} = (I - w\iota')(1/\mu(q))\hat{q} U \hat{q}(I - \iota w') \qquad (5.6)$$

and correspondingly to work with

$$h = \hat{q} g = -w + (I - w\iota')(1/\mu(q))\hat{q} U q. \qquad (5.7)$$

Note that use is made of $\hat{q}\pi = w$. Note also that $q'\pi = 1$. It follows from (3.10) and from (5.2) that

$$U = (1/\mu(q)[\hat{u}_q A \hat{u}_q - \alpha(q)u_q u_q']) = \mu(q)[\hat{\pi} A \hat{\pi} - \alpha(q)\pi\pi']. \qquad (5.8)$$

Inserting this result in (5.6) and (5.7) results in

$$H = (\hat{w} - ww')A(\hat{w} - ww'), \qquad (5.9)$$

$$h = -w + (\hat{w} - ww')Aw, \qquad (5.10)$$

which can also be expressed as

$$\begin{pmatrix} H & h \\ h' & 0 \end{pmatrix} = \begin{pmatrix} \hat{w} - ww' & -w \\ w' & 1 \end{pmatrix}$$
$$\times \begin{pmatrix} A - (2 + w'Aw)\iota\iota' & \iota \\ \iota' & 0 \end{pmatrix}\begin{pmatrix} \hat{w} - ww' & w \\ -w' & 1 \end{pmatrix} \qquad (5.11)$$

or equivalently as

$$\begin{pmatrix} A - (2 + w'Aw)\iota\iota' & \iota \\ \iota' & 0 \end{pmatrix} = \begin{pmatrix} \hat{w}^{-1} & \iota \\ -\iota' & 0 \end{pmatrix}\begin{pmatrix} H & h \\ h' & 0 \end{pmatrix}\begin{pmatrix} \hat{w}^{-1} & -\iota \\ \iota' & 0 \end{pmatrix}. \qquad (5.12)$$

As is evident from the last expression, given structures of H and h and values of w the Allais matrix is determined apart from an additive constant. By selecting a standard pair of goods r and s and assigning to the corresponding a_{rs} a value, zero, say, one can solve this lack of determination. The resulting values for the other a_{ij} can then be used to evaluate the extent to which the measured interaction corresponds with one's prior ideas.

Relation (5.11) is useful to trace the consequences of special structures of A for the specification of H. A particular type of special structure is the subject of the next section.

6. Separability of preferences

The separability of the structure of preferences is a source of restrictions on the Allais coefficients and hence on the demand function. Separability assumes a partition of the set of all n goods into N non-overlapping subsets of goods such that the preference order defined on a subset is independent of the consumption levels of goods not in the subset. Write

$$q' = (q'_A, q'_B, \ldots, q'_N) \tag{6.1}$$

for the partition of the quantity vector q into N subvectors. Let n_F be the number of goods in subset F and let S_F be the index set of the goods of subset F. Separability implies that the utility function can be written as

$$u(q) = z(u_A(q_A), u_B(q_B), \ldots, u_n(q_N)). \tag{6.2}$$

One has then

$$u_i(q) = \frac{\partial z}{\partial u_F} \frac{\partial u_F}{\partial q_i}, \quad i \in S_F, \tag{6.3}$$

and for $i \in S_F$, $j \in S_G$, $F \neq G$,

$$u_{ij} = \frac{\partial^2 z}{\partial u_F \partial u_G} \frac{\partial u_F}{\partial q_i} \frac{\partial u_G}{\partial q_j} = \zeta_{FG} u_i u_j \tag{6.4}$$

with

$$\zeta_{FG} = \frac{\partial^2 z}{\partial u_F \partial u_G} \bigg/ \left(\frac{\partial z}{\partial u_F} \frac{\partial z}{\partial u_G} \right). \tag{6.5}$$

Use (6.4) in (3.5) to obtain

$$a_{ij} = \mu(q)\zeta_{FG} - \alpha(q) = \tau_{FG} = \tau_{GF}. \tag{6.6}$$

All a_{ij} corresponding to $i \in S_F$ and $j \in S_G$, $F \neq G$, are equal and the value does not depend on the nature of i or j but on the characteristics of subsets F and G.

In the special case of strong separability or additive preferences (6.3) specialises to

$$u(q) = z\left(\sum_F u_F(q_F) \right). \tag{6.7}$$

Then $\partial z/\partial u_F$ is independent of F and $\partial^2 z/(\partial u_F \, du_G)$ is independent of F and G. Otherwise said ζ_{FG} is a constant, say ζ. Let the standard pair of goods, r and s, be also from different subsets. Then $a(q) = \mu(q)\zeta$ and according to (6.6) one has

$$a_{ij} = 0 \quad \text{or} \quad \tau_{FG} = 0, \qquad i \in S_F, \ j \in S_G, \ F \neq G. \tag{6.8}$$

The matrix A is then a block-diagonal matrix with the diagonal blocks corresponding to the various subsets.

An extreme case is that of complete preference independence, where each subset consists of one good only. Then

$$a_{ij} = 0 \quad \forall i, j, \ i \neq j, \tag{6.9}$$

and the matrix A is a diagonal matrix. Note that the a_{ij} are invariant under monotone transformations of $u(q)$. Complete preference independence is an ordinal property and not a cardinal one as Frisch (1959) once stated.

To trace the consequences of separability for demand it is useful to write

$$A = A_D + JTJ' \tag{6.10}$$

for the full matrix of Allais coefficients. Here A_D is a block diagonal matrix with A_F as a typical block. The typical element of A_F is a_{hi} with $h, i \in S_F$. It is assumed that A_F is nonsingular and thus that A_D is nonsingular. In (6.10) T is the $N \times N$ matrix of τ_{FG}. Its diagonal is zero. The $n \times N$ matrix J is defined by

$$J = \begin{pmatrix} j_A & 0 & \cdots & 0 \\ 0 & j_B & \cdots & 0 \\ \vdots & \vdots & \ddots & \vdots \\ 0 & 0 & \cdots & j_N \end{pmatrix} \tag{6.11}$$

where j_F is the n_F-vector of all elements equal to unity. Note that $J\iota_N = \iota_n$ where ι_N is the N-vector and ι_n is the n-vector of all elements equal to unity, respectively.

The case of strong separability corresponds to $T = 0$, that of commodity-wise strong separability to diagonal A_D and A.

The particular structure (6.10) for A finds its counterpart in one for S. Expression (4.7) gives S as a function of A^{-1}. On the basis of (6.10) one can write

$$A^{-1} = (A_D + JTJ')^{-1} = A_D^{-1} - R\hat{s}R' + RQ^{-1}R' \tag{6.12}$$

with

$$R = A_D^{-1} J (J' A_D^{-1} J)^{-1}, \qquad \hat{s} = J' A_D^{-1} J, \qquad Q = \hat{s}^{-1} + T.$$

Here $R\dot{s}R'$ is a block diagonal matrix of the same form as A_D or A_D^{-1}. The $n \times N$ matrix R is like J as defined by (6.11) with the j_F replaced by

$$r_F = A_F^{-1} j_F (j_F' A_F^{-1} j_F)^{-1}. \tag{6.13}$$

Clearly, $J'R = I$ and $\iota_n' R = \iota_N' J'R = \iota_N'$. The $N \times N$ matrix Q is the matrix T with the zero diagonal elements replaced by $(j_F' A_F^{-1} j_F)^{-1}$.

It follows from (6.12) that

$$A^{-1} \iota_n = A_D^{-1} \iota_n - R\dot{s}\iota_N + RQ^{-1}\iota_N$$
$$= A_D^{-1} \iota_n - A_D^{-1} \iota_n + RQ^{-1}\iota_N = RQ^{-1}\iota_N \tag{6.14}$$

while

$$\varphi = \iota_n' A^{-1} \iota_n = i_n' RQ^{-1}\iota_N = \iota_N' Q^{-1}\iota_N. \tag{6.15}$$

Using (6.12), (6.14) and (6.15) in (4.7) gives

$$S = A_D^{-1} - R\dot{s}R' + R[Q^{-1} - Q^{-1}\iota_N(\iota_N' Q^{-1}\iota_N)^{-1}\iota_N' Q^{-1}]R'.$$

Now $S_D = A_D^{-1} - R\dot{s}R'$ is a block diagonal matrix. Let

$$\Sigma = Q^{-1} - Q^{-1}\iota_N(\iota_N' Q^{-1}\iota_N)^{-1}Q^{-1}\iota_N' Q^{-1} \tag{6.16}$$

then

$$S = S_D + R\Sigma R' \tag{6.17}$$

which expresses clearly the formal similarity with (6.10). It is evident from (6.16) that Σ has the same relation to Q as S has to A. Given an estimate of Σ one can go back to Q and T to evaluate its proper meaning.

On the basis of (4.6), (6.14) and (6.15) one may write

$$b = RQ^{-1}\iota_N(\iota_N' Q^{-1}\iota_N)^{-1} = (1/\varphi)RQ^{-1}\iota_N.$$

Because of the special nature of R one has that

$$b_F = (1/\varphi)r_F e_F' Q^{-1}\iota_N, \tag{6.18}$$

i.e., b_F is proportional to r_F with $e_F' Q^{-1}\iota_N/\varphi$ as the factor of proportionality. b_F is an n_F-vector of marginal propensities to spend on the commodities of subset F out of the total budget m. Then β_F is the n_F-vector of the marginal propensities to spend on all goods of subset F together. It follows from (6.18) that

$$\beta_F = j_F' b_F = e_F' Q^{-1}\iota_N/\varphi \tag{6.19}$$

because (6.13) implies that $j_F' r_F = 1$. Consequently

$$b_F = \beta_F r_F$$

or

$$B = R\dot{\beta}$$

where B has the same structure as R and J with the b_F as the diagonal arrays. It cannot be guaranteed that all β_F are nonzero. Assuming this to be the case, however, one can express (6.17) also as

$$S = S_D + B\dot{\beta}^{-1}\Sigma\dot{\beta}^{-1}B' = S_D + B\Phi B'.$$ (6.20)

For a particular pair of goods i and j belonging to different subsets, F and G respectively, one has with $\varphi_{FG} = \sigma_{FG}/(\beta_F\beta_G)$,

$$s_{ij} = \varphi_{FG}b_ib_j$$ (6.21)

which is the usual representation of groupwise separable demand.

   Under strong separability $T = 0$. Then $Q = \dot{s}^{-1}$ and (6.16) simplifies to

$$\Sigma = \dot{s} - s(\iota's)^{-1}s'.$$

Here $\iota's = \varphi$. It follows from (6.19) that then $\beta_F = s_F/\varphi$ and $\beta = (1/\varphi)s$. Consequently

$$\Sigma = \varphi(\dot{\beta} - \beta\beta')$$

and

$$\Phi = \dot{\beta}^{-1}\Sigma\dot{\beta}^{-1} = \varphi(\dot{\beta}^{-1} - \iota_N\iota'_N).$$ (6.22)

This means that under strong separability the φ_{FG} in (6.21) becomes φ, i.e., independent of the nature of the subsets F and G.

   In the case of complete preference independence $s_{ij} = \varphi b_ib_j$ for all $i \neq j$.

   It is evident that specification (6.2) can be very useful for estimation. It can also be used in constructing commodity aggregates such that the interaction between the demand for the aggregates are characterised by the elements of the Φ matrix. These issues will not be pursued further here. We will rather turn to an extension of the Allais approach to the representation of the impact of other determinants than prices and the budget on demand.

7. Allais-type of coefficients for other determinants

The preference order may depend on factors that are in principle observable like age, health, sex, weather conditions, advertising and so on. In empirical research it is useful to be able to control for these, i.e., to include these factors in the explanation of demand. The changes in demand caused by variation in these other determinants have to fit in the budget. Their measurable impact on demand reflects this, causing a problem in evaluating the pure preference shifting effect of such other determinants. A way out of this dilemma is offered by an approach similar to that of the Allais coefficients.

Given the consumer equilibrium condition (3.9) the other determinants affect demand by way of their changing u_q, the vector of marginal utilities. Let x be the vector of quantifiable other determinants and let $u(q, x)$ be twice differentiable in x. One has for x_k being a typical element of the x vector:

$$\frac{\partial u_i}{\partial x_k} = \frac{\partial^2 u}{\partial q_i \, \partial x_k} \tag{7.1}$$

which like u_{ij} is not invariant under monotone increasing transformation of the utility function. Analogous to (3.1) one has for $v = F(u)$,

$$\frac{\partial v_i}{\partial x_k} = F' \frac{\partial^2 u}{\partial q_i \, \partial x_k} + F'' \frac{\partial u}{\partial q_i} \frac{\partial u}{\partial x_k}. \tag{7.2}$$

Analogy with (3.4) then leads to the following invariant interaction coefficient

$$e_{ik} = \kappa(q, x) \left(\frac{\partial u_i / \partial x_k}{u_i \, \partial u / \partial x_k} - \frac{\partial u_j / \partial x_k}{u_j \, \partial u / \partial x_k} \right) \tag{7.3}$$

where $\kappa(q, x) = \sum_g x_g \, \partial u / \partial x_g$ and j refers to a good j on which x_k has a "standard" type of impact, say a neutral one. The second term in (7.3) is taken to be a constant for all i. It is denoted by $\varepsilon_k(q, x)$.

One can use (7.3) to express (7.1) as

$$\partial u_i / \partial x_k = (u_i / k(q, x)) e_{ik} \, \partial u / \partial x_k + \varepsilon_k(q, x) u_i \, \partial u / \partial x_k. \tag{7.4}$$

For constant q and changing x one then has

$$du_i = \sum_k (\partial u_i / \partial x_k) \, dx_k$$

or

$$d \ln u_i = \sum_k e_{ik} \vartheta_k \, dx_k / x_k + \sum_k \varepsilon_k(q, x)(\partial u / \partial x_k) \, dx_k \tag{7.5}$$

with $\vartheta_k = x_k \, \partial / \partial x_k / \sum_g x_g \, \partial u / \partial x_g$. The ϑ_k represent the relative importance of x_k among all the x-variables. The last term in (7.5) is independent of i. The first term on the right-hand side shows the role of the e_{ik}. These coefficients measure the extent to which x_k specifically changes the desirability of good i in comparison to its impact on good j. The sign of e_{ik} indicates whether this desirability increases, stays the same or decreases.

The x_k can take on negative or zero values and to replace in (7.5), dx_k/x_k by d ln x is not in general permissible. Still we will use d ln x simply as a notational shorthand for dx_k/x_k. Then (7.5) can be rewritten as

$$\text{d ln } u_i = \sum_k e_{ik}\vartheta_k \text{ d ln } x_k + z \qquad (7.6)$$

with $z = \sum_k \varepsilon_k(q, x)(du/\partial x_k) \, dx_k$. Let E^* be a matrix with as typical element $e_{ik}\vartheta_k$. Then the vector expression of (7.6) reads as

$$\text{d ln } u_q = E^* \text{ d ln } x + z\iota. \qquad (7.7)$$

The impact on demand of the x variables can be easily traced. The impact on inverse demand is fairly straightforward. That on regular or direct demand is derived in what follows.

One starts off again from (4.1) but (4.2) now becomes

$$\text{d ln } u_q = A\dot{w} \text{ d ln } q + E^* \text{ d ln } x + (\alpha \, du_1 + z)\iota \qquad (7.8)$$

where du_1 refers to the change in utility associated with dq. Combining (7.8) with (4.1) gives

$$A\dot{w} \text{ d ln } q = (\text{d ln } \lambda - \alpha \, du_1 - z)\iota + \text{d ln } p - E^* \text{ d ln } x$$

or

$$\dot{w} \text{ d ln } q = A^{-1}\iota(\text{d ln } \lambda - \alpha \, du_i - z) + A^{-1} \text{ d ln } p - A^{-1}E^* \text{ d ln } x.$$

Using (4.4) results in a way analogous to (4.5) in

$$\dot{w} \text{ d ln } q = b(\text{d ln } m - w' \text{ d ln } p) + S \text{ d ln } p - SE^* \text{ d ln } x \qquad (7.9)$$

where b and S are defined by (4.6) and (4.7), respectively. The effect of the x variables is a rather complicated function of S and E^*. It is not such an easy matter to formulate prior ideas about that effect.

Let $Z = SE^*$ be in principle directly measurable. Can one retrieve E^* from that? Realising that $S\iota = 0$ and $b'\iota = 0$ one has

$$\begin{pmatrix} S & b \\ b' & 0 \end{pmatrix}\begin{pmatrix} (I - \iota b')E^* \\ 0 \end{pmatrix} = \begin{pmatrix} Z \\ 0 \end{pmatrix}.$$

Use (4.13) and the property that $\iota Z = 0$ to obtain

$$\begin{pmatrix} (I - \iota b')E^* \\ 0 \end{pmatrix} = \begin{pmatrix} A & \iota \\ \iota' & 0 \end{pmatrix}\begin{pmatrix} Z \\ 0 \end{pmatrix}$$

or

$$E^* = AZ + \iota b' E^*. \tag{7.10}$$

In scalar terms one has

$$e_i' E^* e_k = e_i' A Z e_k + b' E^* e_k.$$

Set $e_i' E^* e_k$ equal to zero. Then $b' E^* e_K = -e_j' A Z e_k$ and

$$e_i' E^* e_k = (e_i - e_j)' A Z e_k \tag{7.11}$$

is the final result.

Note that per additional x variable one has one degree of freedom which is fixed by the choice of the good with the standard response to x_k. Also note that it is possible to retrieve $e_{ik}\vartheta_k$ but not so easily e_{ik}. As is clear from (7.6) the $e_{ik}\vartheta_k$ are a kind of elasticities. Strictly speaking, the e_{ik} are analogous to the a_{ij} and the e_{ik}^* to the $a_{ij}w_j$.

8. A numerical example

To illustrate the relation between the Slutsky coefficients on the one hand and the Allais coefficients on the other hand we will use a set of s_{ij} and b_i values based on a regular Rotterdam demand system for food, Belgium, estimated with annual national accounts data for the period 1954–1984 (see Barten, 1987).

The original exercise covered nine food items. Some of these had very small budget shares. These have been integrated with each other in the case of Coffee and tea, Sugar and sweets and Other food which constitute here the category Other food, while Fish has been combined with Meat. The resulting six items are given in Table 1, together with their share in the budget, taken as an average over the sample period.

Table 1
Budget shares, estimated values of b_i and s_{ij} for food, Belgium, 1954–1984

Commodity	w_i	b_i	$s_{ij} \times 100$					
			1	2	3	4	5	6
1. Bread, pastry	0.12	0.03	−4.22					
2. Meat, fish	0.39	0.57	1.26	−11.48				
3. Dairy products	0.12	0.06	−0.81	3.32	−2.35			
4. Oils, fats	0.09	0.03	−0.28	0.94	−0.44	−1.10		
5. Vegetables, fruit	0.15	0.18	−0.10	5.01	0.00	0.45	−6.49	
6. Other food	0.13	0.14	4.15	0.95	2.80	0.43	1.12	−6.93

346   A.P. Barten

Table 1 gives the b_i. The budget elasticities can be calculated from b_i/w_i. It appears that Meat, fish and Vegetables, fruit are elastic. Other food has an elasticity of virtually one. The other three items are inelastic.

Table 1 also displays the s_{ij}. The S matrix is symmetric. Therefore only its lower triangular part is given. The row (and columns) of S add up to zero as can be verified. Of the 15 possible interactions 10 have a positive sign corresponding with substitution in the Hicks–Allen sense. Meat, fish is a substitute for all other items as is the case for Other food.

The s_{ij} values have been multiplied by 100 because of convenience of presentation. The estimated s_{ij} values tend to decrease with n, the number of commodities taken into account (here six), and with the degree of aggregation. Responses of demand to price changes tend then to be minor because of the absence of close substitutes.

It should be realised that the b_i and s_{ij} are point estimates with a varying but not overly high precision. This increases the need for a plausibility test. At the same time, though, our results as a representation of the actual state of affairs should be taken with the proverbial grain of salt.

The next step consists in constructing the matrix S bordered by the b vectors and with a zero in the SE corner, like it appears in (4.13). This matrix is inverted to yield the matrix $M = A - (1/\varphi)\iota\iota'$, which is given in Table 2. The small order of magnitude of the s_{ij} causes the m_{ij} to be fairly large in absolute value. Note that in Table 2 their values are divided by 10.

To construct the Allais coefficients from the m_{ij} one needs to select a standard pair. We took this to be 2. Meat, fish and 6. Other food, with $m_{2,6} = 4.47$. Subtracting this value from all elements of the matrix M yields the matrix of Allais coefficients given in Table 3. Here the minus sign indicates substitution, the plus sign complementarity. Of the 15 interactions 10 are substitutes, the same in number as in the case of the S matrix but

Table 2
Elements of matrix M

Commodity	$m_{ij}/10$					
	1	2	3	4	5	6
1. Bread, pastry	−5.49					
2. Meat, fish	0.45	−0.32				
3. Dairy products	2.45	−0.33	−5.56			
4. Oils, fats	0.00	0.21	2.36	−9.86		
5. Vegetables, fruit	0.21	0.12	0.43	−0.31	−1.17	
6. Other food	−2.89	0.45	1.61	−0.33	0.15	−2.84

Table 3
Allais coefficients

Commodity	$a_{ij}/10$					
	1	2	3	4	5	6
1. Bread, pastry	−5.94					
2. Meat, fish	0.01	−0.76				
3. Dairy products	2.00	−0.78	−6.01			
4. Oils, fats	−0.44	−0.24	1.91	−10.31		
5. Vegetables, fruit	−0.23	−0.33	−0.02	−0.75	−1.62	
6. Other food	−3.34	0	1.16	−0.78	−0.29	−3.29

there are differences in the pairs which are mutually substitutes or complements. Meat, fish is again a substitute of almost all other items. Other food is the exception, by construction. Other food is now a complement of Dairy products. This last item is a complement of Oils, fats, which is somewhat counterintuitive and of Bread, pastry, which makes sense. Vegetables, fruit appear to be a substitute of all other items.

The values of the a_{ij} are rather high. One can turn them into elasticities by multiplying the a_{ij} by w_j (see (4.2)). This does not help very much. The diagonal elasticities range from −9.3 for Oils, fats to −2.4 for Vegetables, fruits. A relatively high value of a_{ii} can be seen to reflect a high sensitivity of the preference order for good i. It would correspond with the nature of i as a basic need for necessity. In a relative sense, Meat, fish and Vegetables, fruit would then be more of a luxury. This is also reflected in these budget elasticities being larger than one.

Another way to analyse the resulting a_{ij} values is to express them in the form of interaction intensities, given in Table 4. It appears that only a very few interactions are of substance. Bread, pastry and Dairy products are rather strong complements which makes sense. Dairy products are also

Table 4
Allais interaction intensities a_{ij}^*

Commodity	1	2	3	4	5	6
1. Bread, pastry	−1					
2. Meat, fish	0.00	−1				
3. Dairy products	0.33	−0.36	−1			
4. Oils, fats	−0.06	−0.09	0.24	−1		
5. Vegetables, fruit	−0.08	−0.30	−0.01	−0.18	−1	
6. Other food	−0.75	0	0.26	−0.13	−0.13	−1

complementary to Oils, fats and Other food. The latter is highly substitutable by Bread, pastry, which is somewhat puzzling. Meat, fish is a rather strong substitute of Dairy products, another source of animal protein, and of Vegetables, fruit.

This example has demonstrated that one can retrieve Allais coefficients from estimates of S and b and that their relative values make sense in some cases and are difficult to understand in other cases. Their high absolute values may be due to a systematic underestimation of the elements of the matrix S. Since the matrix A is in a certain sense a generalised inverse of S, low values for the s_{ij} produce high values of the a_{ij} and vice versa. Further research is needed to clarify this issue.

9. Concluding remarks

The formal expression given by Allais to the notion of complementarity, substitution and independence is invariant under monotone increasing transformations of the utility function. In other words, it reflects properties of the preference order. At the same time it is rather close to one's intuition about these concepts.

The Allais coefficients are reflected in the coefficients of estimable regular or inverse demand systems. They can also be retrieved from estimates of these systems. These calculated values can be compared with prior ideas based on introspection. The plausibility of the estimates can then be judged. The Allais coefficients also reflect in a natural way the eventual separability of preferences. The effects of preference shifting variables can be given an interpretation similar to the Allais coefficients.

Until now most of the time only separability of preferences has been used to specify demand relations. It is of interest to take into account also other aspects of the preference order. The Allais coefficients provide a useful tool for this purpose.

References

Allais, M. (1943) 'Les données générales de l'économie pure', *Traité d'Economie Pure*. Paris: Imprimerie Nationale.
Anderson, R.W. (1980) 'Some theory of inverse demand for applied demand analysis', *European Economic Review*, 14:281–290.
Barten, A.P. (1987) *Models of the Rational Consumer*. Brussel: Vereniging voor Economie.
Barten, A.P. and V. Böhm (1982) 'Consumer theory', in: K.J. Arrow and M.D. Intriligator, eds., *Handbook of Mathematical Economics, Volume II*. Amsterdam: North-Holland.

Frisch, R. (1959) 'A complete scheme for computing all direct and cross demand elasticities in a model with many sectors', *Econometrica*, 27:177-196.

Houthakker, H.S. (1960) 'Additive preferences', *Econometrica*, 28:244-257.

Samuelson, P.A. (1947) *Foundations of Economic Analysis.* Cambridge, MA: Harvard University Press.

Theil, H. (1965) 'The information approach to demand analysis', *Econometrica*, 33:67-87.

Chapter 16

INVARIANCE ARGUMENTS IN BAYESIAN STATISTICS

Jean-Pierre FLORENS

GREMAQ, Université des Sciences Sociales, Toulouse, France

Michel MOUCHART

CORE and IAG, Université Catholique de Louvain, Louvain-la-Neuve, Belgium

Jean-Marie ROLIN

CORE and PROB, Université Catholique de Louvain, Louvain-la-Neuve, Belgium

1. Introduction

In this paper invariance arguments are shown to provide answers to various deep problems met in Bayesian methods. Let us first consider three such problems for which one or several difficulties are pointed out.

A first problem arises when dealing with so called "non-informative prior distributions". This concerns the possibility of specifying a distribution on the parameter space reflecting "prior ignorance" or "absence of prior information". A large body of literature has developed in this field. In most cases, it suggests the use of unbounded measures as prior specification and basically addresses two types of topics. One topic is concerned with the (mathematical) properties of such a device: existence of a posterior probability (see e.g., Mouchart, 1976), or modification of the properties of the Bayesian model with respect to the case where the prior specification is

Comments by J. Dutta and W. Härdle were instrumental in reorganizing the presentation of this paper and are gratefully acknowledged.

Economic Decision-Making: Games, Econometrics and Optimisation
Edited by J.J. Gabszewicz, J.-F. Richard and L.A. Wolsey
© *Elsevier Science Publishers B.V., 1990*

actually a probability measure, such as: "un-Bayesianities" (e.g., Dawid and Stone, 1972), "marginalization paradoxes" (e.g., Dawid, Stone and Zidek, 1973) or inadmissibility of the implied "Bayes solution" (e.g., Stein, 1956). This topic will not be pursued here. We rather consider the second one concerned with the construction of reasonable candidates for the label of such "non-informative" prior specification. Here again, two types of arguments may be distinguished: some are based on the idea of "minimizing a quantity of information" carried by the prior specification (e.g., Bernardo, 1979; Zellner, 1971); other ones are based on invariance. In this paper we shall deal only with those arguments based on invariance. On this topic further work may be found in Hartigan (1964, 1983), Lindley (1958) and Villegas (1971, 1972, 1977).

The second problem arises in the treatment of nuisance parameters and amounts to characterize Bayesian models such that the observation may be reduced by marginalization (often, on a suitable statistic) without losing information on the parameters of interest while retaining some robustness properties. In particular, attention is paid to the robustness with respect to modification of the prior distribution on the nuisance parameters. This problem also has a long history in statistical methods (see e.g., Barnard, 1963) and is solved, in a Bayesian framework, by two properties of conditional independence collectively known as a "mutual sufficiency" between a function of the parameter and a function of the observation. This property essentially means that the sampling distribution of the retained statistic depends only on the parameter of interest while the posterior distribution of the parameter of interest, given the full sample, actually depends on the retained statistic only. This property, investigated in more details in Florens, Mouchart and Rolin (1990a), to be referred as FMR, may be too general in the sense that it may require, for being checked, calculations that the requirement of robustness was precisely deemed to avoid. However invariance arguments will be shown to provide a characterization of mutual sufficiency without requiring an explicitation of heavy computations.

The last problem arises, in asymptotic theory, when looking for sufficient conditions providing the almost sure convergence of the posterior expectations of a given function of the parameters. When such conditions are satisfied, the involved function of the parameter is called an exactly estimable parameter. This concept has been more systematically analyzed in FMR. The difficulty, however, is to find an easily verifiable characterization of a large class of exactly estimable parameters. For example, in an i.i.d. experiment, (a priori) integrable functions of identified parameters are known to be exactly estimable; however intuitive this result is, its proof, in a Bayesian framework, is either confined to particular cases (e.g., De Groot, 1970, gives the proof in the finite case only) or relies on excessively involved arguments (see e.g., Hartigan, 1983). As a matter of fact this result is a particular case of a more general result involving three kinds of assumptions: identification, invariance (obtained in the i.i.d. case, through stationarity, i.e., invariance for the shift) and ergodicity (obtained, in the i.i.d. case, through independence). It should be noticed that the role of invariance is indeed crucial in the proof and that a proper treatment of invariance (rather than stationarity) also provides, for instance, adequate tools for handling incidental parameters.

Chapter 8 of FMR provides the basic tools to handle those problems in case where the prior specification is made through a probability measure rather than an unbounded measure. In this paper we extend those tools in order to be able to deal with unbounded measure, an inescapable issue when formalizing the concept of non-informative prior. This paper is however mainly expository, the technicalities being more developed in the companion paper (Florens, Mouchart and Rolin, 1990b).

Next section introduces the basic framework: invariant Bayesian experiments extended to the cases of unbounded prior measures. The next three sections handle the three problems sketched above. Section 3 deals with the elimination of nuisance parameters through arguments of maximal invariance leading to mutual sufficiency. Section 4 proposes a formalization of non-informativity by means of invariance arguments and Section 5 proposes an asymptotic analysis of the posterior expectations in an invariant case. The last section concludes the paper by a discussion of some examples.

2. Invariant Bayesian experiments

In this section we establish the useful notation to handle Bayesian experiments. Remember that in a sampling-theory framework, a *statistical experiment* may be described as a parametrized family of probabilities on a sample space, viz.:

$$\mathscr{E} = ((S, \mathscr{S}), P^a : a \in A) \tag{1}$$

where $(S, \mathscr{S})$ is the sample space, A is the parameter space and, for each $a \in A$, P^a is a probability measure on $(S, \mathscr{S})$, to be called a *sampling probability*. From a given statistical experiment, a *Bayesian Experiment* is built by introducing a *prior probability* μ on $(A, \mathscr{A})$ where $\mathscr{A}$ is specified in such a way that the mapping $a \mapsto P^a(X)$ is $\mathscr{A}$-measurable for any $X \in \mathscr{S}$. This measurability property ensures the existence of a unique probability measure Π on the product space $(A \times S, \mathcal{A} \otimes \mathcal{S})$ such that μ is its marginal probability on $(A, \mathcal{A})$ and P^a is a regular version of the conditional probability given $\mathcal{A}$. This will be expressed as

$$\Pi = \mu \otimes P^a, \tag{2}$$

$$\Pi(B \times T) = \int_B P^a(T)\mu(\mathrm{d}a), \quad B \in \mathcal{A}, \ T \in \mathcal{S}. \tag{3}$$

Under rather general conditions, Π accepts a dual decomposition into a marginal probability P on $(S, \mathcal{S})$, called a *predictive probability* and an indexed family of probabilities on $(A, \mathcal{A})$ viz., $\{\mu^s : s \in S\}$ constituting a regular version of the conditional probability given $\mathcal{S}$ and to be called *posterior probabilities*. Thus a (regular) Bayesian experiment may be described as:

$$\mathcal{E} = (A \times S, \mathcal{A} \otimes \mathcal{S}, \Pi = \mu \otimes P^a = P \otimes \mu^s). \tag{4}$$

In case where P^a and μ^s are respectively dominated by some suitable measure, we also write (4) in terms of densities,

$$\pi(a, s) = \mu(a)p(s \mid a) = p(s)\mu(a \mid s). \tag{5}$$

Note that we always stick to the following notational rule: Π for joint probabilities on $A \times S$, μ for probabilities on the parameter space and P for probabilities on the sample space, capital letters for probability measures and small letters for densities (except for μ, for which no confusion should arise).

Bayesian experiments may also be *extended* by considering σ-finite measures μ on $(A, \mathcal{A})$ rather than probability measures. In such cases, the primal construction (2)–(3) still defines unambiguously a unique σ-finite measure on the product space $A \times S$ but the dual decomposition in (4) requires more conditions for being justified. A natural such condition is that P, the trace of Π on $(S, \mathcal{S})$ i.e.,

$$P(X) = \int_A P^a(X)\mu(\mathrm{d}a), \quad X \in \mathcal{S}, \tag{6}$$

defines a σ-finite measure on $(S, \mathcal{S})$. In models dominated by Lebesgue measure, this may be interpreted as requiring that the predictive density

$$p(s) = \int p(s \mid a)\mu(a) \, \mathrm{d}a \tag{7}$$

is finite a.e., for the measure dominating P^a; one will recognize in (7) the denominator of the celebrated Bayes Theorem, used for the evaluation of the posterior density.

When the predictive measure is σ-finite on $(S, \mathscr{S})$, the posterior transition is well defined and has actually the same properties as a conditional probability. More details on this issue may be found in Mouchart (1976) or in Florens, Mouchart and Rolin (1990b).

In a sampling theory framework, an *invariant experiment* is defined by a set Φ of measurable transformations of the product space $A \times S$ such that, for any $\varphi \in \Phi$:

$$\varphi = (\varphi_A, \varphi_S), \qquad \varphi_A : A \to A, \quad \varphi_S : S \to S, \tag{8a}$$

$$P^a[\varphi_S^{-1}(X)] = P^{\varphi_A(a)}(X) \quad \forall X \in \mathscr{S}. \tag{8b}$$

In the sequel, for expository purposes, we only consider bijective transformations φ and therefore Φ is a group of transformations (with the composition of functions). We shall also assume that conditional probabilities are dominated by Lebesgue measure. In such a case, densities provide insightful formulae; in particular (8) may be rewritten as

$$p[\varphi_S^{-1}(s)|a] = p[s|\varphi_A(a)] \left| \frac{d\varphi_S^{-1}(s)}{ds} \right|^{-1} \tag{9}$$

or equivalently

$$p(s|a) = p[\varphi_S(s)|\varphi_A(a)] \left| \frac{d\varphi_S(s)}{ds} \right| \tag{10}$$

where $|\cdot|$ stands for the absolute value of the determinant of the matrix of partial derivatives.

An *invariant Bayesian experiment* is defined by endowing an invariant experiment with an invariant prior probability, i.e., a prior probability μ, satisfying

$$\mu[\varphi_A^{-1}(B)] = \mu(B) \quad \forall B \in \mathscr{A}, \; \forall \varphi \in \Phi.$$

The main properties of invariant Bayesian experiments along with some illustrative examples have been displayed in FMR (Chapter 8) but most of the applications detailed in FMR (Chapter 9) are confined to the case where, for any $\varphi \in \Phi$, φ_A is the identity on the parameter space so that any prior probability is invariant. This provides a suitable Bayesian approach to stationary processes (in the framework of shift invariance) but does not allow one to deal with more general types of invariant experiments. The main reason for that confinement was that when the parameter space is not compact, invariant prior probabilities fail to exist although there may exist σ-finite unbounded measures on the parameter space that enjoy the suitable invariance properties. In this paper and in a companion paper (Florens, Mouchart and Rolin, 1990b), we are consequently generalizing the exposition in FMR toward extended Bayesian experiments, i.e., Bayesian experiments constructed from a statistical experiment endowed with an unbounded σ-finite measure on the parameter space such that the implied predictive measure is σ-finite.

A *sampling invariant Bayesian experiment* is defined by endowing an invariant experiment with a prior (σ-finite) measure μ which, for the sake of coherence, must be *regular* for the set of transformations Φ in the following sense: for any $\varphi \in \Phi$, the image under φ_A of μ, i.e., $\mu \circ \varphi_A^{-1}$, must be σ-finite and absolutely continuous with respect to μ. This is equivalent to say that there exists a positive and finite density $g_\varphi(a)$ of $\mu \circ \varphi_A^{-1}$ with respect to μ, i.e.,

$$\mu[\varphi_A^{-1}(B)] = \int_B g_\varphi(a)\mu(da) \quad \forall B \in \mathcal{A}. \tag{11}$$

When μ is dominated by the Lebesgue measure, this may be rewritten in terms of density as

$$\mu[\varphi_A^{-1}(a)] = g_\varphi(a)\mu(a)\left|\frac{d\varphi_A^{-1}(a)}{da}\right|^{-1} \tag{12}$$

or equivalently

$$\mu(a) = g_\varphi[\varphi_A(a)]\mu[\varphi_A(a)]\left|\frac{d\varphi_A(a)}{da}\right|. \tag{13}$$

In order to obtain posterior invariance, i.e., the dual property to (8b), we have to consider a σ-finite measure μ *relatively invariant* with respect to φ_A for any $\varphi \in \Phi$, i.e., we suppose that there exists a function (to be called a module) $\delta : \Phi \to \mathbb{R}_0^+$ such that

$$\mu[\varphi_A^{-1}(B)] = \delta(\varphi)\mu(B) \quad \forall B \in \mathcal{A}, \ \forall \varphi \in \Phi. \tag{14}$$

This amounts to say that

$$g_\varphi(a) = \delta(\varphi) \quad \forall a \in A, \ \forall \varphi \in \Phi. \tag{15}$$

The density of such a relatively invariant prior measure must therefore satisfy the following functional equation

$$\mu(a) = \delta(\varphi)\mu[\varphi_A(a)]\left|\frac{d\varphi_A(a)}{da}\right|. \tag{16}$$

Indeed, it is shown in Florens, Mouchart and Rolin (1990b) that once such a relatively invariant prior measure has been found:
  (i) The joint measure Π is relatively invariant with the same module, i.e.,

$$\Pi[\varphi_A^{-1}(B) \times \varphi_S^{-1}(X)]$$
$$= \delta(\varphi)\Pi(B \times X) \quad \forall B \in \mathcal{A}, \ \forall X \in \mathcal{S}, \ \forall \varphi \in \Phi, \tag{17}$$

and we say that the Bayesian experiment is relatively invariant. Equivalently, in terms of density,

$$\pi(a, s) = \delta(\varphi)\pi[\varphi_A(a), \varphi_S(s)] \left| \frac{d\varphi_A(a)}{da} \right| \left| \frac{d\varphi_S(s)}{ds} \right|. \tag{18}$$

Once it has been verified that the implied predictive measure P is σ-finite on $\mathcal{S}$.
  (ii) The predictive measure is relatively invariant with the same module, i.e.,

$$P[\varphi_S^{-1}(X)] = \delta(\varphi)P[X] \quad \forall X \in \mathcal{S}, \ \forall \varphi \in \Phi. \tag{19}$$

Equivalently, in terms of density,

$$p(s) = \delta(\varphi)p[\varphi_S(s)] \left| \frac{d\varphi_S(s)}{ds} \right|. \tag{20}$$

  (iii) The posterior probability is conditionally invariant in the sense that

$$\mu^s[\varphi_A^{-1}(B)] = \mu^{\varphi_S(s)}[B] \quad \forall B \in \mathcal{A}, \ \forall \varphi \in \Phi, \tag{21}$$

and we say that the Bayesian experiment is a posteriori invariant. Equivalently, in terms of densities

$$\mu(a \mid s) = \mu[\varphi_A(a) \mid \varphi_S(s)] \left| \frac{d\varphi_A(a)}{da} \right|. \tag{22}$$

Remark. If $\delta(\varphi) = 1 \ \forall \varphi \in \Phi$, the prior measure is said to be invariant and the same is true for the predictive measure and the Bayesian experiment. Conversely, if $\delta(\varphi) \neq 1$ for some $\varphi \in \Phi$, the corresponding relatively invariant measure μ is necessarily unbounded and the corresponding Bayesian experiment is an extended one. Indeed, since $\varphi_A^{-1}(A) = A \ \forall \varphi \in \Phi$, it follows from (14), that $\mu(A) = \delta(\varphi)\mu(A)$ so that $\mu(A)$ is either 0 or ∞ once $\delta(\varphi) \neq 1$.

3. Maximal invariance and mutual sufficiency

In the (extended) sampling invariant Bayesian experiment

$$\mathscr{E} = (A \times S, \mathscr{A} \otimes \mathscr{S}, \Pi = \mu \otimes P^a, \Phi)$$

a measurable function $b : (A, \mathscr{A}) \to (B, \mathscr{B})$ is an *invariant parameter* if

$$b[\varphi_A(a)] = b(a) \quad \forall a \in A, \ \forall \varphi \in \Phi, \tag{23}$$

and a measurable function $t : (S, \mathscr{S}) \to (T, \mathscr{T})$ is an *invariant statistic* if

$$t[\varphi_S(s)] = t(s) \quad \forall s \in S, \ \forall \varphi \in \Phi. \tag{24}$$

An invariant parameter a^* is *maximal invariant* if any real invariant parameter is a function of it, i.e.,

$$\forall c : (A, \mathscr{A}) \to (\mathbb{R}, \mathscr{B}(\mathbb{R})) \ \text{such that} \ c[\varphi_A(a)] = c(a) \ \forall a \in A, \ \forall \varphi \in \Phi,$$

$$\exists d : (B, \mathscr{B}) \to (\mathbb{R}, \mathscr{B}(\mathbb{R})) \ \text{such that} \ c(a) = d[a^*(a)] \ \forall a \in A. \tag{25}$$

Similarly, an invariant statistic s^* is *maximal invariant* if any real invariant statistic is a function of it, i.e.,

$$\forall u : (S, \mathscr{S}) \to (\mathbb{R}, \mathscr{B}(\mathbb{R})) \ \text{such that} \ u[\varphi_S(s)] = u(s) \quad \forall s \in S, \ \forall \varphi \in \Phi,$$

$$\exists v : (T, \mathscr{T}) \to (\mathbb{R}, \mathscr{B}(\mathbb{R})) \ \text{such that} \ u(s) = v[s^*(s)] \ \forall s \in S. \tag{26}$$

We will suppose, in the sequel, that there exist both a maximal invariant parameter and a maximal invariant statistic.

It follows from the preceding section that, if t is an invariant statistic, its sampling distribution depends on a^* only. Such a property may be interpreted as a weakened version of stochastic independence between t and a conditionally on a^* and we will write such a property as

$$t \underset{w}{\perp\!\!\!\perp} a \,|\, a^*. \tag{27}$$

Indeed from (8b), we obtain

$$P^a[\varphi_S^{-1}\{t^{-1}(Y)\}] = P^{\varphi_A(a)}[t^{-1}(Y)] \quad \forall a \in A, \ \forall Y \in \mathscr{T}, \ \forall \varphi \in \Phi.$$

Therefore,

$$P^a[t^{-1}(Y)] = p^{\varphi_A(a)}[t^{-1}(Y)] \quad \forall a \in A, \ \forall Y \in \mathscr{T}, \ \forall \varphi \in \Phi,$$

i.e., $P^a[t^{-1}(Y)]$ is a real invariant parameter for all $Y \in \mathscr{T}$.

More generally, in a sampling invariant Bayesian experiment,

$$s^* \underset{w}{\perp\!\!\!\perp} a \,|\, a^*. \tag{28}$$

Now, if the prior measure is relatively invariant and if it has been verified that the implied predictive measure P is σ-finite on $\mathscr{S}$, we obtain conditional invariance of the posterior probability and by a similar argument, any invariant parameter b has a posterior distribution which depends on s^* only. More generally,

$$a^* \underset{w}{\perp\!\!\!\perp} s \,|\, s^*. \tag{29}$$

Conditions (28) and (29) define the *weak mutual sufficiency* of a^* and s^* and may be interpreted in the context of Barnard's sufficiency principle. Suppose that the parameter of interest is b and that some statistic t has the property that its sampling distribution depends on b only. It is then natural to ask whether t contains "all the sample information for the inference on b" or, alternatively, whether marginalization of the sample on t would lose no information for the inference on b. The concept of mutual sufficiency precisely provides a rigorous Bayesian justification for extracting the sample information from the sole "partial likelihood" derived from the sample distribution of t, i.e., $p(t\,|\,b)$. As shown above, the answer is positive if there exists a group of transformations, say Φ, that makes the (extended) Bayesian experiment relatively invariant and such that $b = a^*$ and $t = s^*$, i.e., are respectively the maximal invariant parameter and statistic.

Two particular cases may be of interest. Firstly, if in a sampling invariant Bayesian experiment, φ_A is surjective for any $\varphi \in \Phi$, i.e., the group Φ acts transitively on A, only the constant functions of the parameter are invariant, i.e., the maximal invariant parameter is trivial ($a^*(a) = b_0 \,\forall a \in A$). In this situation, the maximal invariant statistic is ancillary for any regular prior probability measure, i.e.,

$$a \perp\!\!\!\perp s^*. \tag{30}$$

This is then a tool for finding ancillary statistics. Secondly if in a sampling invariant Bayesian experiment, $\varphi_A(a) = a \,\forall a \in A, \,\forall \varphi \in \Phi$, all the functions of a are invariant, i.e., the maximal invariant parameter is the parameter ($a^* = a$). In this situation, any regular prior measure (and therefore probability) is invariant and the maximal invariant statistic s^* is sufficient, i.e.,

$$a \perp\!\!\!\perp s \,|\, s^*. \tag{31}$$

Note that this situation is met when dealing with stationary and exchange-able processes for which their distributions are invariant under the shift and the group of finite permutations respectively.

4. Non-informativity and invariance

The structure of transformations $\varphi = (\varphi_A, \varphi_S)$ as in (8a) is general enough to accommodate two important particular cases, viz., φ_A or φ_S being the identity on their respective domain of definition. Sampling invariance when φ_A is the identity on A is met, for instance, with exchangeable processes (i.e., invariant for the finite permutations of indices) or stationary processes (i.e., invariant for the shift); in that case, any measure on $(A, \mathscr{A})$ is invariant and, clearly, non-informativity is not the issue but sufficiency and asymptotic properties are especially relevant. Symmetrically, sampling invariance when φ_S is the identity on S refers to non-identified sampling processes: here the transformations φ_A represent observationally equivalent parameters in the sense that the sets $\Phi_a = \{\Phi_A(a) \,|\, \varphi \in \Phi\}$ represents parameters observationally equivalent to a, i.e., subsets of $\tilde{a}$, the equivalence class of a for the equivalence relation: $a \sim a' \Leftrightarrow P^a = P^{a'}$. In particular, when $\Phi_a = \tilde{a} \;\forall a \in A$, the maximal invariant parameters are the identified ones. In such a case, a relatively invariant prior measure is not desirable because it would typically lead to a non-σ-finite predictive measure and, consequently, to an undefined posterior distribution.

As mentioned earlier, invariant arguments are often invoked when for-malizing the concept of "non-informative" prior distributions. It is indeed natural to consider that saying that one has the same information on $a \in \mathbb{R}$ as on $a + \alpha$ for any $\alpha \in \mathbb{R}$ is a way of expressing an absence of information on a. More generally invariance of a distribution of parameter a may be viewed as a way of expressing ignorance about some aspect of parameter a. Indeed, suppose, for the sake of exposition, that a sampling model may be reparametrized in such a way that $a = (b, c)$ with $b = b(a)$ a maximal invariant parameter and c describing a "section" (in the sense: $\varphi_A(a) = \varphi_A(b, c) = (b, \varphi_C(c))$, $A = B \times C$ and $\{\varphi_C(c) \,|\, \varphi \in \Phi\} = C \;\forall c \in C$). A rela-tively invariant measure may then have the form (in terms of densities) $\mu(a) = \mu_1(b) \cdot \mu_2(c)$ where $\mu_2(c)$ is invariant (for φ_C) and $\mu_1(b)$ is arbitrary. Here a relatively invariant prior distribution expresses the idea that there is no information on c but the information on b is arbitrary. Thus a totally (resp., partially) non-informative prior distribution may be formalized as a relatively invariant measure such that all invariant functions of the parameter are constant, i.e., the maximal invariant parameter is trivial (resp., the maximal invariant parameter is not trivial). We like to stress that partial non-informativity would clearly not lead to uniqueness of prior specification. This feature may render the property of partial non-informativity attractive, namely, for the elimination of nuisance parameters as suggested in Section 3. This is particularly true when the nuisance parameters are incidental.

Formally, any group of transformations on A could be used for expressing (partial or total) non-informativity but, as mentioned above, the case $\varphi_S = i_S$ (the identity on S) is typically uninteresting; in other words φ_A is typically derived from a group of transformations φ_S on S that ensures the sampling invariance. The transformations φ_S may then be interpreted as modifications of the experimental conditions that leave unchanged the family of sampling probabilities. This suggests the following strategy when looking for non-informative prior distributions:

(i) Identify a family of transformations φ_S ensuring sampling invariance and endowed with a reasonable physical interpretation (such as, e.g., change of unit, of scales, rotations, etc.).

(ii) Derive the family of transformation φ_A and consider whether there exists (uniquely or not) an invariant prior measure endowed with a reasonable interpretation of non-informativity.

(iii) Check whether the implied predictive measure is σ-finite.

When these conditions are fulfilled, one has the insurance that the joint measure (on $A \times S$), the predictive measure and the posterior probabilities enjoyed suitable invariance properties; in particular, the posterior invariance may be interpreted as meaning that inference on a transformed parameter $\varphi_A(a)$ may be directly obtained from the inference on the untransformed parameter a after transforming the observations into $\varphi_S(s)$.

So far, the suggestion is to look for a prior measure invariant for a group of transformations (on A) derived from a sampling invariance. One could also consider alternative roads. In particular, for a given sampling invariance, it could be suggested that a suitable non-informative prior should be such that the implied predictive measure is (relatively) invariant for the group of transformations on the sample space. The question then arises whether this implies invariance of the prior measure. Results in Chapter 8 of FMR, characterizing invariance through stochastic independence with respect to a probabilization of the group of transformations make it reasonable to conjecture that under mild regularity conditions prior invariance would be necessary (and sufficient) for predictive invariance. Alternatively, for a given sampling invariance one could also suggest that a suitable non-informative prior measure should be such that the implied posterior distribution be also conditionally invariant; this again raises the question whether this requirement implies invariance of the prior measure. Results of FMR suggest that prior invariance would again be necessary (and sufficient) for posterior invariance but now under stronger regularity condition than for the previous conjecture.

5. Invariance in asymptotic experiment

In this section, we consider an invariant Bayesian experiment where the prior measure μ is a probability measure. This is typically the case in stationary and exchangeable processes where φ_A is the identity on A for any φ and S is the space of infinite sequences of observations.

Suppose now that Φ is ergodic on $\mathscr{S}$ given a; more explicitly,

$$P^a(X) \in \{0, 1\} \quad \forall a \in A, \ \forall X \in \mathscr{S} \text{ invariant.} \tag{32}$$

This would be the case, for instance, under a mixing condition such as

$$\lim_{n \to \infty} P^a(X \cap \varphi^{-n}(Y))$$

$$= P^a(X) \cdot P^a(Y) \quad \forall a \in A, \ \forall \varphi \in \Phi, \ \forall X, Y \in \mathscr{S}. \tag{33}$$

Suppose furthermore that Φ is such that the maximal invariant parameter a^* is identified. Under such conditions a basic result (see FMR, Chapter 8) is the following: any invariant parameter is exactly estimable, equivalently: the posterior expectation of any invariant function $f(a)$ is almost surely equal to the function itself. An example will be treated in Section 6.

6. Examples

In this section we briefly review some examples of invariant Bayesian experiments.

Example 1. *The Univariate Normal Model.* Let us consider an independent normal sampling with known variance,

$$(s_j \,|\, a) \sim \text{iN}(a, 1), \quad 1 \le j \le n, \qquad s = (s_1, \ldots, s_j, \ldots, s_n), \tag{34}$$

along with the group of translations,

$$\varphi_\alpha(a, s) = (\varphi_{\alpha,A}(a), \varphi_{\alpha,S}(s))$$
$$= (a + \alpha, s_1 + \alpha, \ldots, s_j + \alpha, \ldots, s_n + \alpha), \tag{35}$$

$$\Phi = \{\varphi_\alpha \colon \alpha \in \mathbb{R}\}. \tag{36}$$

Noticing that $(s_j + \alpha \,|\, a) \sim \text{iN}(a + \alpha, 1)$, we conclude that the sampling process is clearly conditionally invariant. Lebesgue measure provides an invariant prior measure (unique up to a multiplicative constant). The density of the joint measure may be written as

$$\pi(a, s) = (2\pi)^{-n/2} \exp -\frac{1}{2} \sum_j (s_j - a)^2$$

$$= (2\pi)^{-n/2} \exp -\frac{1}{2} \left\{ n(\bar{s} - a)^2 + \sum_j (s_j - \bar{s})^2 \right\} \tag{37}$$

where $\bar{s} = n^{-1} \sum_j s_j$. Thus Π is clearly invariant (with $\delta(\varphi_\alpha) = 1 \, \forall \alpha$). The predictive measure is σ-finite and invariant, indeed its density is

$$p(s) = \int_A \pi(a, s) \, da = (2\pi)^{-(n-1)/2} \exp -\frac{1}{2} \left\{ \sum_j (s_j - \bar{s})^2 + \ln n \right\} \tag{38}$$

and the posterior distribution is a conditionally invariant probability,

$$(a \,|\, s) \sim \text{N}(\bar{s}, 1/n). \tag{39}$$

In this case, the maximal invariant parameter a^* is trivial and any maximal invariant statistic such as $s^* = (s_2 - \bar{s}, \ldots, s_j - \bar{s}, \ldots, s_n - \bar{s})$ is clearly ancillary. This is a consequence of the mutual sufficiency argument dispelled in Section 3.

Example 2. *Mutual sufficiency in the Univariate Normal Model.* For the sake of exposition we first marginalize to the sufficient statistics an independent sampling from a normal distribution with both mean and variance unknown. Thus $s = (\bar{s}, v)$, $a = (\mu, \sigma^2)$ and

$$(\bar{s} \,|\, a) \sim \text{N}(\mu, n^{-1}\sigma^2), \tag{40}$$

$$(v \,|\, a) \sim \frac{\sigma^2}{n-1} \chi^2_{n-1}, \tag{41}$$

$$\bar{s} \perp\!\!\!\perp v \,|\, a. \tag{42}$$

As in Example 1, we consider the group of translations

$$\varphi_\alpha(a, s) = (\varphi_{\alpha,A}(a), \varphi_{\alpha,S}(s)) = (\mu + \alpha, \sigma^2, \bar{s} + \alpha, v), \tag{43}$$

$$\Phi = \{\varphi_\alpha \colon \alpha \in \mathbb{R}\}. \tag{44}$$

Here the coordinates σ^2 and v are not affected by the transformation φ_α. Clearly the sampling process is conditionally invariant. An invariant prior measure is built through the product of the Lebesgue measure on μ and an arbitrary measure on σ^2 provided only that the implied predictive measure is σ-finite, i.e., in case of continuous measure on σ^2 with density $f(\sigma^2)$,

$$p(\bar{s}, v) = \int p(\bar{s} \mid a)p(v \mid a)f(\sigma^2)\,\mathrm{d}a < \infty. \tag{45}$$

For *any* such $f(\sigma^2)$, σ^2 is a maximal invariant parameter and v is a maximal invariant statistic; therefore σ^2 and v are mutually sufficient:

$$\sigma^2 \perp\!\!\!\perp \bar{x} \mid v, \tag{46}$$

$$\mu \perp\!\!\!\perp v \mid \sigma^2, \tag{47}$$

and inference on σ^2 may rely on v rather than on $(\bar{s}, v)$ for whatever prior measure on σ^2 satisfying (45).

Example 3. *The Multivariate Regression Model.* Let us consider the following sampling model:

$$(y_j \mid B, \Sigma, z_1, \ldots, z_m) \sim \mathrm{iN}(B'z_j, \Sigma), \quad y_j \in \mathbb{R}^p, \ z_j \in \mathbb{R}^k, \ 1 \le j \le n. \tag{48}$$

Equivalently, $y_j = B'z_j + u_j$ with $(u_j \mid B, \Sigma, z_1, \ldots, z_n) \sim \mathrm{iN}(0, \Sigma)$. The objective of this example is the characterization of a class of relatively prior measures. We consider the following family:

$$\varphi_{M,N}(B, \Sigma, y_1, \ldots, y_n, z_1, \ldots, z_n)$$
$$= (MB' + N, M\Sigma M', My_1 + Nz_1, \ldots, My_n + Nz_n, z_1, \ldots, z_n) \tag{49}$$

and

$$\Phi = \{\varphi_{M,N} \mid M p \times p \text{ regular matrix}, \ N p \times k \text{ matrix}\}. \tag{50}$$

Let us remark that, in a conditional sampling model, the group naturally acts on the parameters and both on the "explained" variables and on the conditioning variables. The fact that the conditioning variables are invariant in these transformations is a special feature of this example but in order to preserve the conditional structure, the z_j's should not be combined with the parameters and the y_j's by the transformations.

The property

$$(My_j + Nz_j \mid B, \Sigma, z_1, \ldots, z_n) \sim \mathrm{iN}((MB' + N)z_j, M\Sigma M') \tag{51}$$

implies the conditional invariance of the sampling model. One has to look to a prior measure relatively invariant by the transformations $(B, \Sigma) \rightarrow (MB' + N, M\Sigma M')$. There exists — up to a multiplicative constant — a *unique* invariant measure (with module $\delta(\phi_{M,N}) = 1 \; \forall M, N$; see Nachbin, 1965), on the parameter space characterized by its density with respect to Lebesgue measure,

$$\mu(B, \Sigma) = |\Sigma|^{-(k+p+1)/2}. \tag{52}$$

Using such a prior, the predictive (σ-finite) measure is defined by the density

$$p(y_1, \ldots, y_n | z_1, \ldots, z_n) = K |Y'M_Z Y|^{-n/2} |Z'Z|^{1/2} \tag{53}$$

where K is an appropriate constant, Y and Z are the usual matrices collecting all the y_j's and the z_j's and $M_Z = I - Z(Z'Z)^{-1}Z'$. The posterior probability is well known to be (see Tiao and Zellner, 1964; Ando and Kauffman, 1965):

$$(B | \Sigma, Y, Z) \sim \text{MN}(\hat{B}, (Z'Z)^{-1} \otimes \Sigma), \tag{54}$$

$$(\Sigma | Y, Z) \sim \text{IW}(Y'M_Z Y, n), \tag{55}$$

where $\hat{B} = (Z'Z)^{-1}Z'Y$ and MN and IW denote the matrix normal and the inverted Whishart distribution respectively. This posterior is clearly conditionally invariant.

Let us remark that a smaller family of transformations would not characterize a unique invariant prior. It is clear that if $M = I_p$ any prior probability on Σ is invariant. If the group is restricted to the case $N = 0$ the unicity is not anymore guaranteed. Take for example $p = 1$ and $k = 2$. The transformation then becomes

$$(b_1, b_2, \sigma^2) \rightarrow (mb_1, mb_2, m^2\sigma^2) \tag{56}$$

and if f is a density on $\mathbb{R}$, any prior such that

$$\mu(b_1, b_2, \sigma^2) = f(b_1/b_2) \tag{57}$$

is invariant.

Instead of (52) one could consider a family of unbounded measure s indexed by ν with density

$$\mu(B, \Sigma) = |\Sigma|^{-(\nu+p+1)/2}. \tag{58}$$

For any $\nu \geq 0$, one obtains a relatively invariant measure (with a module function depending on ν, let $\delta_\nu(M, N)$. Zellner (1971) specified $\nu = 0$ on the basis of Jeffrey's invariance. Drèze (1976) (see also Drèze and Richard, 1983) suggested (52), i.e., $\nu = k$ for obtaining an invariant measure (i.e., $\delta_k(M, N) = 1$).

Example 4. *Stationary processes.* This example shows that an invariance argument may be used in asymptotic analysis of posterior expectations. The sample of the model is assumed to be an infinite sequence:

$$s = (s_n)_{n \geq 0} \tag{59}$$

on which operates the shift operator

$$\tau(s)_n = s_{n+1}. \tag{60}$$

If P^a are the sampling probabilities, P^a is stationary if and only if P^a is invariant by τ and then by $\tau^k = \tau \circ \tau^{k-1}$ for any k. In this case the Bayesian experiment associated to P^a is invariant by the family of transformations

$$\varphi_k(a, s) = (a, \tau^k(s)), \quad k \geq 0, \tag{61}$$

for any prior on A. For simplicity we assume that A is now provided with a prior probability.

Previous general results imply that the predictive probability is invariant, which here means that the predictive process is stationary, and that the posterior probability is conditionally invariant. This can be written as (see FMR, Chapter 9),

$$\mu^s(E) = \mu^{\tau^k(s)}(E) \quad \text{a.s.} \quad \forall k \text{ and } E. \tag{62}$$

Equivalently, the posterior probability is not affected by deleting the first k observations for any finite k.

In this example, the maximal invariant parameter is the parameter itself. A maximal invariant statistic cannot be exhibited but the maximal invariant σ-field is commonly used,

$$\mathscr{S}_I = \{X \in \mathscr{S} : \tau^{-1}(X) = X\} \tag{63}$$

and any invariant function is $\mathscr{S}_I$-measurable.

If the sampling process is ergodic (in particular if it is mixing or, more specifically, if it is independent), the sub-σ-field $\mathscr{S}_\tau$ is almost surely included in $\mathscr{A}$ and using the argument of Section 3 (and FMR, Chapter 4), it implies that $\mathscr{A} \subset \bar{\mathscr{S}}$ and that

$$E(f(a) | s_1, \ldots, s_n) \to f(a) \quad \Pi\text{-a.s.} \quad \text{as } n \to \infty \tag{64}$$

for any integrable function f of the parameter.

References

Ando, A. and G.M. Kaufman (1965) 'Bayesian Analysis of the independent multi-normal process, neither mean nor precision known', *Journal of the American Statistical Association*, 60:347–358.

Barnard, G.A. (1963) 'Some aspects of the fiducial argument', *Journal of the Royal Statistical Society*, 25:111-114.

Bernardo, J.M. (1979) 'Reference posterior distributions for Bayesian inferences' (with discussion), *Journal of the Royal Statistical Society, Series B*, 41:113-147.

Dawid, A.P. and M. Stone (1972) 'Un-Bayesian implications of improper Bayes inference in routine statistical problems', *Biometrika*, 59(2):369-375.

Dawid, A.P., M. Stone and J.V. Zidek (1973) 'Marginalization paradoxes in Bayesian and structural inference', *Journal of the Royal Statistical Society, Series B*, 35:189-233.

De Groot, M. (1970) *Optimal Statistical Decisions*. New York: McGraw-Hill.

Drèze, J.H. (1976) 'Bayesian limited information analysis of the simultaneous equations model', *Econometrica*, 44(5):1045-1075.

Drèze, J.H. and J.-F. Richard (1983) 'Bayesian analysis of simultaneous equations systems', in: Z. Griliches and M.D. Intriligator, eds., *Handbook of Econometrics, Volume 1*. Amsterdam: North-Holland, pp. 517-598.

Florens, J.-P. (1982) 'Expériences bayésiennes invariantes', *Annales de l'Institut Henri Poincaré*, 18:305-317.

Florens, J.-P., M. Mouchart and J.-M. Rolin (1990a) *Elements of Bayesian Statistics*. New York: Dekker.

Florens, J.-P., M. Mouchart and J.-M. Rolin, (1990b) 'Weak conditional independence and relative invariance in Bayesian statistics', Paper presented at the 10th Rencontre Franco-Belge de Statisticiens, held in Brussels, November 23-24, 1989.

Hartigan, J. (1964) 'Invariant prior distributions', *The Annals of Mathematical Statistics*, 35:836-845.

Hartigan, J. (1983) *Bayes Theory*. New York: Springer.

Lehman, E.L. (1959, 1986) *Testing Statistical Hypothesis*. New York: Wiley.

Lindley, D.V. (1958) 'Fiducial distribution and Bayes Theorem', *Journal of the Royal Statistical Society, Series B*, 17:102-107.

Mouchart, M. (1976) 'A note on Bayes theorem', *Statistica*, 36(2):349-357.

Nachbin, L. (1965) *The Haar Integral*. New York: Van Nostrand Reinhold.

Ruggiero, M. (1989) 'A Bayes semiparametric approach of some regression models', GREQE Working Paper, Université d'Aix-Marseille.

Stein, C. (1956) 'Inadmissibility of the usual estimator for the mean of a multivariate normal distribution', *Proceedings of the Third Berkeley Symposium 1*. Berkeley: University of California Press, pp. 197-206.

Tiao, G. and A. Zellner (1964) 'On the Bayes estimation of multivariate regression', *Journal of the Royal Statistical Society, Series B*, 26:277-285.

Villegas, C. (1971) 'On Haar priors', in: V.P. Godambe and D.A. Sproot, eds., *Foundations of Statistical Inference*. Toronto: Holt, Rinehart and Winston.

Villegas, C. (1972) 'Bayesian inference in linear relations', *Annals of Mathematical Statistics*, 43:1767-1791.

Villegras, C. (1977) 'On the representation of ignorance', *Journal of the American Statistical Association*, 72:653-654.

Weil, A. (1940) *Intégration dans les Groupes Topologiques et ses Applications*. Paris: Hermann.

Zellner, A. (1971) *An Introduction to Bayesian Inference in Econometrics*. New York: Wiley.

Chapter 17

A GENERAL THEORY OF CONDITIONAL PREVISION $P(X|Y)$ AND THE PROBLEM OF STATE-DEPENDENT PREFERENCES

Frank LAD

University of Canterbury, Christchurch, New Zealand

James M. DICKEY

University of Minnesota, Minneapolis, MN, USA

1. Introduction

Jacques Drèze throughout his distinguished career has been intrigued with decision problems involving "state dependent preferences", and their relevance to the construction of probability theory as a representation of personal uncertain knowledge (Drèze, 1958, 1987). This paper in his honor will outline the issues of state dependent preferences as they appear in a simple problem recently posed as a challenge to the operational subjective theory of coherent prevision. We will show how a resolution to the problem can be achieved by introducing a meaningful operational definition of a conditional prevision assertion denoted by $P(X|Y)$, where Y can be an arbitrary general quantity, not merely an event. We will set forth the basic mathematical requirements of coherent conditional prevision as a linear functional relative to the object quantity X, but as a non-linear functional relative to

This paper is offered in honor of Jacques Drèze, in recognition of his work on the most serious foundational questions in probability and decision theory. Our thanks to David Lane for pushing us to exemplify our operational definition of $P(X|Y)$ in a practical example, and to Jay Kadane for suggesting the currency exchange problem. Work by the second author was supported in part by the U.S. National Science Foundation, Grant No. DMS-8911548.

Economic Decision-Making: Games, Econometrics and Optimisation
Edited by J.J. Gabszewicz, J.-F. Richard and L.A. Wolsey
© *Elsevier Science Publishers B.V., 1990*

the conditioning quantity, Y. Philosophically, the resolution to the problem achieved through the definition of $P(X \mid Y)$ will highlight the importance of understanding the theory of coherent prevision as modulated by utility theory. It will also accentuate the recognition that *conditional* prevision is *not* necessarily related to a *temporal* sequence of learning based on accumulating information.

Although we will give precise definitions of concepts that are central to the specific arguments of our paper, we do presume some general familiarity with the ideas and notational style used in de Finetti's (1974, 1975) theory of coherent prevision. Especially relevant is his fundamental theorem of probability (1974, Section 3.10) which is explored at length in Lad, Dickey and Rahman (1990a,b). Our presentation here is organized as follows. Section 2 poses a problem regarding the unknown rate of currency exchange to be determined by trading in a market. The problem instantiates the issue of state dependent preferences in decision problems. Section 3 reviews the operational subjective characterization of conditional prevision, $P(X \mid E)$, conditioning on any event E, and proposes a formal generalization of the definition to include the meaningful status of an assertion $P(X \mid Y)$, when Y is an arbitrary quantity. Section 4 shows how recognition of the role of $P(X \mid Y)$ in the general theory of coherent prevision can resolve the puzzle posed in the currency exchange problem. Sections 5 and 6 contain philosophical discussions on two aspects of the theory of prevision that are highlighted in the resolution.

2. A simple problem of currency exchange

Consider the following simplified version of a currency exchange market in which pounds sterling can be exchanged for dollars. To keep the setup simple, suppose that there are three mutually exclusive and exhaustive possibilities. Define the partition $\{E_1, E_2, E_3\}$ with events

$$E_1 \equiv (\pounds 1 = \$1), \qquad E_2 \equiv (\pounds 1 = \$1.3) \quad \text{and} \quad E_3 \equiv (\pounds 1 = \$2).$$

Here the parenthetic expression $(\pounds 1 = \$1)$, for example, represents the number 1 if the public exchange rate offered by a specified bank on a specified day in the future is \$1 for £1, and represents the number 0 if not. Similar numerical meanings are ascribed to the events E_2 and E_3. Of course this setup could be embellished to greater realism, allowing all possible numerical values for the rate of exchange, and even buy-sell spreads. But these would only distract us from the point of the problem to be described here.

In de Finetti's theory, a "quantity" (sometimes called a "random quantity") is an operationally well-defined number, whose numerical value may be unknown at the time prevision assertions are made. As defined here, the quantities (events) E_1, E_2 and E_3 are unitless numbers, each equal to either 0 or 1, whose sum equals 1. Suppose you assert your probabilities as $P(E_1) = P(E_2) = P(E_3) = \frac{1}{3}$ on the basis of your asserted indifference to the prizes, $\$E_1 \sim \$E_2 \sim \$E_3$. (For example, $\$E_1$ pays you \$1 if E_1 occurs and \$0 if not.) This indifference is operationally identified by your willingness to exchange freely claims to $\$E_1$, $\$E_2$, $\$E_3$ and $\$\frac{1}{3}$.

Now an apparent problem arises if you consider in addition your willingness to exchange claims to fixed monetary prizes contingent on the values of E_i, but denominated in units of pounds rather than dollars. Could you also assert your probabilities for each of the three events as equal to $\frac{1}{3}$ by asserting your indifference among fixed contingent monetary prizes denominated in pounds, via the preference relation $£E_1 \sim £E_2 \sim £E_3$? Evidently, if you have settled on your indifference among the prizes denominated in dollars, as described in the paragraph above, you would *not* want to assert your indifference among the "same prizes" denominated in pounds. For while you would clearly regard as equivalent the values $£E_1 \sim \$E_1$, you would regard more highly the value $£E_2 \sim \$\frac{13}{10}E_2 > \$E_1$, and still more highly $£E_3 \sim \$\frac{2}{1}E_3 > \$\frac{13}{10}E_2 > \$E_1$. Your relative valuations among pound-denominated "fixed" payoffs apparently depend on the outcomes of the specified contingencies, E_1, E_2, E_3. The "fixed" £1 prizes associated with the contingencies are equivalent to different dollar denominated prizes, depending on the numerical value of the three continging events.

This is exactly the type of situation that generates the problem coined that of "state dependent preferences". You are indifferent between \$1 and £1 if $E_1 = 1$, but you prefer £1 to \$1 if $(E_2 + E_3) = 1$. The question it poses for probability theory is "how or why should you conclude in such a state of uncertainty that your probabilities for each of the three events equals $\frac{1}{3}$ on account of your equi-valuation of the three events denominated in dollars, when you would clearly not equi-value these very same events when denominated in pounds? The operational meaning of de Finetti's definition of "coherent prevision" would be undermined if the numerical value of a coherent prevision assertion depends on the arbitrary units in which the continging net gains would be denominated.

Anyone who has lived and has experienced the myriad changes of one's value orderings as one learns about states of affairs previously unknown and even unimagined, will recognize that, far from being merely a cute contrived problem, the general problem posed is a crucial one. Its satisfactory resolution is important for the operational subjective theory of probability, based as it is upon an operationally recognizable ordering of personal belief and value assertions. A variety of aspects of the problem, in specific and general form, are discussed in Kadane and Winkler (1988) and Schervish, Seidenfeld and Kadane (1989).

In the next section we defer briefly from the currency exchange problem in order to review the formal operational subjective definitions of conditional prevision, $P(X|E)$, and the related concept of a partitioned prevision, $P(X|\{H\})$, for a partition of events, denoted by $\{H\}$. In concluding the section we will propose an extended definition of conditional prevision to $P(X|Y)$, where Y may be an arbitrary quantity rather than merely an event.

3. A generalized concept of conditional prevision, allowing conditioning on a quantity rather than merely upon an event

Let us begin by reviewing de Finetti's operational definition of a conditional prevision assertion, and an associated quantity that can be defined in terms of such assertions.

Definition 3.1. Let X be any quantity, whose realm of possibilities is the set $\mathcal{R}(X) = \{x_1, \ldots, x_R\}$, and let E be any event, whose realm is $\mathcal{R}(E) = \{0, 1\}$. These two quantities may be logically related in any way. Minimally, $\mathcal{R}(X, E) \subseteq \mathcal{R}(X) \otimes \{0, 1\}$. Evidently, the product XE is also a quantity, which is necessarily logically related to X and E: $\mathcal{R}(X, E, XE) = \{(x, e, xe) | (x, e) \in \mathcal{R}(X, E)\} \subset \mathcal{R}(X, E) \otimes \mathcal{R}(XE)$. Your *conditional prevision for X given E*, denoted by $P(X|E)$, is a number you specify with the understanding that you are thereby asserting your willingness to engage any transaction that would yield you a net gain of the amount $s[XE - P(X|E)E]$, qualified only by the scale restriction that $|s[xe - P(X|E)e]| \le S$ for every pair of numbers $(e, xe) \in \mathcal{R}(E, XE)$. The symbol S denotes the scale of your maximum stake. Your specification of S constitutes your relegation of the transaction to yield "small scale" gains or losses.

The interpretation of such a transaction as a "called off bet" is well known. If $E = 1$, then your net gain from the transaction would equal $s[X - P(X|E)]$; but if $E = 0$, then your net gain would equal 0. Let us remind ourselves that coherency of prevision requires only the satisfaction of the condition that $P(XE) = P(X \mid E)P(E)$. We will not concern ourselves here with issues that founder on the possibility that $P(E) = 0$.

Let us consider briefly the denomination of units in which net gains are considered. In mathematical uses of Definition 3.1, the numbers denoted by the symbols X, E, x, e, s and S are generally understood to be unitless. In applied usage of the theory, the net-gain transaction units are often presumed for convenience to be one's own currency, either dollars, pounds, franks or yen, or whatever. But they could easily be thought of as oranges, or as kiwifruit, or as potatoes. Whatever be the units of gain in which one thinks for evaluating one's opinions about quantities according to Definition 3.1, they are generally submerged in the analysis of coherent opinions *per se*. But we will see in the next section how the explicit recognition of *units* is necessary in a problem such as the one of currency exchange, and more generally, in problems involving the feature of state dependent preferences.

Now we would like to generalize the operational definition of conditional prevision assertion to allow a meaningful assertion of a conditional prevision $P(X \mid Y)$ where Y need not merely be an event, but can be a general quantity with its own realm $\mathscr{R}(Y) = \{y_1, \ldots, y_S\} \neq \{0, 1\}$. So as to avoid confusion, let us begin by recognizing explicitly what we do *not* intend to mean by $P(X \mid Y)$.

In the common parlance of so-called "mathematical probability", the assertion that subjectivists call "prevision" is called "mathematical expectation". According to this formalism, by the conditional expectation expression $E(X \mid Y)$ is meant a function on $\mathscr{R}(Y)$ defined by the set of pairs

$$\{(y_1, E(X \mid Y = y_1)), (y_2, E(X \mid Y = y_2)), \ldots, (y_S, E(X \mid Y = y_S))\}.$$

Structurally, $E(X \mid Y)$ denotes a function on the space of possible values of the quantity Y.

In de Finetti's theory (1974), the technical apparatus that plays the role corresponding to $E(X \mid Y)$ is not what we will define as $P(X \mid Y)$, but it is another *quantity* which can be called a *partitioned prevision*. It is defined by de Finetti as follows.

Definition 3.2. Let $\{H\}$ represent a partition composed of the constituent events $H_1, H_2, \ldots, H_N$. And let X be any quantity for which you have assessed your conditional previsions $P(X \mid H_1), \ldots, P(X \mid H_N)$. Then your *partitioned prevision* for X given $\{H\}$, denoted by $P(X \mid \{H\})$ is defined as the sum

$$P(X \mid \{H\}) \equiv P(X \mid H_1)H_1 + P(X \mid H_2)H_2 + \cdots + P(X \mid H_N)H_N.$$

This is a *quantity* that equals your asserted prevision $P(X \mid H_1)$ if $H_1 = 1$, equals your $P(X \mid H_2)$ if $H_2 = 1, \ldots,$ and equals your asserted $P(E \mid H_N)$ if $H_N = 1$.

The linearity of coherent prevision requires that your prevision of your partitioned prevision of X given $\{H\}$ equal your unconditional prevision for X:

$$P[P(X \mid \{H\})] \equiv P\left[\sum_{i=1}^{N} P(X \mid H_i) H_i \right] = \sum_{i=1}^{N} P(X \mid H_i) P(H_i) = P(X).$$

This result is the operational subjective analogue of the result of formalist theory regarding conditional expectation that states $E_Y[E(X \mid Y)] = E(X)$. The relevant partition would be $\{Y\} = \{(Y = y_1), (Y = y_2), \ldots, (Y = y_S)\}$. Coherency requires that $P[P(X \mid \{Y\})] = P(X)$.

The extension we propose to the subjective notion of conditional previson to include the meaningful assertion of $P(X \mid Y)$ follows another tack. That is, we propose the following extension of Definition 3.1, merely replacing the conditioning event in the definition with a general quantity. Let us restate the definition in this form, and then comment on its meaning.

Definition 3.3. Let X and Y be any quantities, with realms $\mathcal{R}(X)$, and $\mathcal{R}(Y)$. These two quantities may be logically related in any way: $\mathcal{R}(X, Y) \subseteq \mathcal{R}(X) \otimes \mathcal{R}(Y)$. The product XY is also a quantity, which is necessarily logically related to X and Y: $\mathcal{R}(X, Y, XY) = \{(x, y, z) \mid (x, y) \in \mathcal{R}(X, Y)$ and $z = xy\} \subset \mathcal{R}(X, Y) \otimes \mathcal{R}(XY)$. Your *conditional prevision for X given Y*, denoted $P(X \mid Y)$, is the number you specify with the understanding that you are thereby asserting your willingness to engage any transaction that would yield you a net gain of the amount $s[XY - P(X \mid Y)Y]$ as long as $|s[xy - P(X \mid Y)y]| \leq S$ for every pair of numbers $(y, xy) \in \mathcal{R}(Y, XY)$. Again we denote by S the scale of your maximum stake.

Notice that we are defining $P(X \mid Y)$ as a single specified number, rather than as the unknown quantity, $P(X \mid \{Y\})$ (Definition 3.2), which was defined in terms of the several asserted conditional previsions $P(X \mid H_i)$. The interpretive meaning of $P(X \mid Y)$ according to this definition becomes clear by examining the quantity of your net gain associated with the transaction specified in the definition. We express your net gain as a function of the possible observation values of $X = x$, and $Y = y$:

$$\mathrm{NG}(x, y) = s[xy - P(X \mid Y)y] = s\{y[x - P(X \mid Y)]\}.$$

It is apparent that the direction of your net gain (that is, your net gain or your net loss) is determined by the algebraic sign of the difference $[x - P(X|Y)]$, but the scale of this "gain" is modulated by the unknown value of y. Expressed as an unknown quantity, your achieved net gain from the transaction of X for $P(X|Y)$ with the scale of the transaction contingent of the value of Y is

$$NG(X, Y) = s\{Y[X - P(X|Y)]\}.$$

Since your assertion of $P(X|Y)$ avows your willingness to engage such a transaction specified by either positive or negative valued scale factor s, coherency of your prevision requires that your $P[NG(X, Y)] = 0$. Finally then, the linearity of coherent prevision implies that your coherent prevision honor the equation $P[NG(X, Y)] = 0 = P(XY) - P(Y)P(X|Y)$, that is, $P(XY) = P(Y)P(X|Y)$.

It is easy to characterize the mathematical structure enjoyed by coherent conditional prevision assertions $P(X|Y)$ along with previsions for related quantities, $P(X)$, $P(Y)$, $P(XY)$ and $P(Y|X)$. We do so in the following theorem which is stated without proofs, though they are quite easy. Intriguing aspects of an extended theorem that are neglected here, allowing $P(Y) = 0$, are discussed in Lad (1989). Without further ado, let us note the following.

Theorem. *Let the symbols X_i and Y_i denote unknown quantities, while the symbols K_i denote specified constants. As long as none of the denominators that appear in the following statements equals 0, coherency among the previsions and the conditional previsions that appear in the following statements require that*

  (i) $P(X|K) = P(X)$ *and* $P(K|X) = P(K) = K$;

  (ii) $P(X|KY) = P(X|Y)$;

  (iii) $P[(K_1X_1 + K_2X_2)|Y] = K_1P(X_1|Y) + K_2P(X_2|Y)$;

  (iv) $P[X|(K_1Y_1 + K_2Y_2)] = \dfrac{K_1P(X|Y_1)P(Y_1) + K_2P(X|Y_2)P(Y_2)}{K_1P(Y_1) + K_2P(Y_2)}$;

  (v) *if* $\mathcal{R}(Y) = \{y_1, y_2, \ldots, y_S\}$, *then*

$$P(X|Y) = \frac{\sum_{i=1}^{S} P[X|(Y = y_i)]y_iP(Y = y_i)}{\sum_{i=1}^{S} y_iP(Y = y_i)}. \qquad \square$$

These results, which are simple to prove, will be used in the computational resolution of the currency problem in the next section. Having established an operationally identifiable meaning to the conditional prevision assertion

$P(X \mid Y)$, and having identified its coherence structure, let us return to the currency problem. We will examine how it is resolved by recognizing the role that can be played by the general conditional prevision assertion $P(X \mid Y)$ in the overall theory of prevision.

4. Using generalized conditional prevision $P(X \mid Y)$ to resolve the currency problem

Let us begin by supposing you do assert your $P(E_1) = P(E_2) = P(E_3) = \frac{1}{3}$, meaning thereby you assert your willingness to engage any transaction yielding you a net gain of

$$NG_S(E_1, E_2, E_3) = s_1[\$E_1 - \$\tfrac{1}{3}] + s_2[\$E_2 - \$\tfrac{1}{3}] + s_3[\$E_3 - \$\tfrac{1}{3}],$$

where this net gain (restricted only by small scale conditions on s_1, s_2 and s_3) is denominated explicitly in dollars. Coherency then requires your concomitant prevision assertion, $P[NG_S(E_1, E_2, E_3)] = 0$. We will deduce the numbers, denoted by p_1, p_2 and p_3, that you may assert for the similarly contingent transactions but denominated in pounds rather than dollars. We denote your net gain from such a transaction by

$$NG_£^*(E_1, E_2, E_3) = s_1[£E_1 - £p_1] + s_2[£E_2 - £p_2] + s_3[£E_3 - £p_3].$$

Now notice that in order to redenominate the net gain $NG_£^*$ in units of dollars, it would be necessary to multiply the unknown net gain by the unknown rate of exchange of dollars per pound, a quantity that we will denote by the symbol $(\$/£)$. Thus, the relation between the pound denominated quantity $NG_£^*(E_1, E_2, E_3)$ and an equivalent dollar denominated quantity, $NG_\$^*(E_1, E_2, E_3)$, would be

$$
\begin{aligned}
NG_\$^*(E_1, E_2, E_3) &= (\$/£)NG_£^*(E_1, E_2, E_3) \\
&= s_1(\$/£)[£E_1 - £p_1] + s_2(\$/£)[£E_2 - £p_2] \\
&\quad + s_3(\$/£)[£E_3 - £p_3] \\
&\neq NG_S(E_1, E_2, E_3).
\end{aligned}
\tag{1}
$$

Examining the second line of eq. (1), it is apparent that your assertion of numbers p_1, p_2 and p_3 that would signify your willingness to engage in any transactions yielding you $NG_\$^*(E_1, E_2, E_3)$, would amount to your assertion of the conditional previsions identified in Definition 3.3 as

$$p_1 = P[E_1 \mid (\$/£)], \qquad p_2 = P[E_2 \mid (\$/£)] \quad \text{and} \quad p_3 = P[E_3 \mid (\$/£)].$$

Notice that the conditioning quantity denoted by ($/£) is a quantity, but not an event, since the realm of possibilities for ($/£) is $\mathcal{R}(\$/£) = \{1, 1.3, 2\} \neq \{0, 1\}$.

Having recognized the numbers p_i as representing the conditional previsions $P[E_i \mid (\$/£)]$, we should be aware of the coherency requirement that as long as $P(\$/£) \neq 0$, the conditional prevision must satisfy

$$P[E_i \mid (\$/£)] = P[E_i(\$/£)] / P(\$/£).$$

We will use this result to compute the values of $P[E_i \mid (\$/£)]$ that cohere with the assertions $P(E_1) = P(E_2) = P(E_3) = \frac{1}{3}$.

Let us first note that, quite distinct from the net gain functions $\mathrm{NG}_\$^*(\cdot)$ and $\mathrm{NG}_£^*(\cdot)$, there is the net gain function you have presumably assessed to begin with, denoted by $\mathrm{NG}_\$(E_1, E_2, E_3)$. Such a net gain could also be appropriately redenominated in pounds by the product relation

$$\mathrm{NG}_£(E_1, E_2, E_3) = (£/\$)\mathrm{NG}_\$(E_1, E_2, E_3). \tag{2}$$

The pairs of net gain functions $[\mathrm{NG}_\$(\cdot), \mathrm{NG}_£(\cdot)]$ and $[\mathrm{NG}_\$^*(\cdot), \mathrm{NG}_£^*(\cdot)]$ that appear in eqs. (2) and (1), respectively, are quite distinct. The distinction is recognized explicitly in the following.

Your assertion of $P[\mathrm{NG}_\$(E_1, E_2, E_3)] = 0$, which presumably represents your initial assertions in this problem, does *not* imply, via coherency, that your $P[\mathrm{NG}_£(E_1, E_2, E_3)]$ is equal to 0. For the quantity $\mathrm{NG}_£(E_1, E_2, E_3)$ is defined as the *product* of the quantities $(£/\$)$ and $\mathrm{NG}_\$(E_1, E_2, E_3)$. As we will see, coherency restricts your assertion of $P[\mathrm{NG}_£(E_1, E_2, E_3)]$ to equal a number other than 0.

Finally, to complete the resolution of the currency exchange problem, let us list a column vector of all the quantities that are relevant for our consideration, and express the several linear relations among them that are accorded by their definitions. In the matrix equation shown in Figure 1, each column of the (17×3) matrix shows the value of the observed quantity vector that is associated with the corresponding constituent event of the partition $\{E_1, E_2, E_3\}$. Notice that the quantities denoted by $\mathrm{NG}_\$$, $\mathrm{NG}_£$, $\mathrm{NG}_£^*$ and $\mathrm{NG}_\$^*$ satisfy eqs. (4.1) and (4.2) in every outcome case. The final two quantities, denoted by \$ and £ will be defined and commented on in a later section. Let us first dispense with some easy computations, which identify the required asymmetry of prevision assertions evaluated on the basis of prizes denominated in terms of dollars and prizes denominated in terms of pounds.

On the basis of the linearity structure of the quantities in the matrix equation of Figure 1 and the well known linearity condition on coherent prevision, it is easy to deduce the following two groups of assertions that

$$
\begin{bmatrix}
E_1 \\
E_2 \\
E_3 \\
(\$/\pounds) \\
(\$/\pounds)E_1 \\
(\$/\pounds)E_2 \\
(\$/\pounds)E_3 \\
(\pounds/\$) \\
(\pounds/\$)E_1 \\
(\pounds/\$)E_2 \\
(\pounds/\$)E_3 \\
NG_\$(E_1, E_2, E_3) \\
NG_\pounds(E_1, E_2, E_3) \\
NG_\pounds^*(E_1, E_2, E_3) \\
NG_\$^*(E_1, E_2, E_3) \\
\$ \\
\pounds
\end{bmatrix}
=
\begin{bmatrix}
1 & 0 & 0 \\
0 & 1 & 0 \\
0 & 0 & 1 \\
1 & 1.3 & 2 \\
1 & 0 & 0 \\
0 & 1.3 & 0 \\
0 & 0 & 2 \\
1 & \frac{10}{13} & \frac{1}{2} \\
1 & 0 & 0 \\
0 & \frac{10}{13} & 0 \\
0 & 0 & \frac{1}{2} \\
s_1(\frac{2}{3})-(s_2+s_3)(\frac{1}{3}) & s_2(\frac{2}{3})-(s_1+s_3)(\frac{1}{3}) & s_3(\frac{2}{3})-(s_1+s_2)(\frac{1}{3}) \\
s_1(\frac{2}{3})-(s_2+s_3)(\frac{1}{3}) & s_2(\frac{20}{39})-(s_1+s_3)(\frac{10}{39}) & s_3(\frac{1}{3})-(s_1+s_2)(\frac{1}{6}) \\
s_1(1-p_1)-s_2p_2-s_3p_3 & s_2(1-p_2)-s_1p_1-s_3p_3 & s_3(1-p_3)-s_1p_1-s_2p_2 \\
s_1(1-p_1)-s_2p_2-s_3p_3 & s_2(1-p_2)(1.3)-(s_1p_1+s_3p_3)(1.3) & s_3(1-p_3)(2)-(s_1p_1+s_2p_2)(2) \\
1 & 1 & 1 \\
1 & 1.3 & 2
\end{bmatrix}
\begin{bmatrix}
E_1 \\
E_2 \\
E_3
\end{bmatrix}
$$

Figure 1.

cohere with the presumed assertions of $P(E_1) = P(E_2) = P(E_3) = \frac{1}{3}$:

$$P[E_1 | (\pounds/\$)] = P[E_1(\pounds/\$)]/P(\pounds/\$) = \tfrac{1}{3}/\tfrac{59}{78} = \tfrac{26}{59},$$

$$P[E_2 | (\pounds/\$)] = P[E_2(\pounds/\$)]/P(\pounds/\$) = \tfrac{10}{39}/\tfrac{59}{78} = \tfrac{20}{59},$$

$$P[E_3 | (\pounds/\$)] = P[E_3(\pounds/\$)]/P(\pounds/\$) = \tfrac{1}{6}/\tfrac{59}{78} = \tfrac{13}{59},$$

and

$$P[E_1 | (\$/\pounds)] = P[E_1(\$/\pounds)]/P(\$/\pounds) = \tfrac{1}{3}/\tfrac{43}{30} = \tfrac{10}{43},$$

$$P[E_2 | (\$/\pounds)] = P[E_2(\$/\pounds)]/P(\$/\pounds) = \tfrac{13}{30}/\tfrac{43}{30} = \tfrac{13}{43},$$

$$P[E_3 | (\$/\pounds)] = P[E_3(\$/\pounds)]/P(\$/\pounds) = \tfrac{2}{3}/\tfrac{43}{30} = \tfrac{20}{43}.$$

Both of these groups of conditional previsions are operationally meaningfully distinct from the original assertions $P(E_1) = P(E_2) = P(E_3) = \frac{1}{3}$. These presumed original prevision assertions represent the prices at which you are avowedly willing to exchange claims to the quantities E_i if the claims are denominated in dollars. If you bought one claim to each of these prizes, your net outlay would be $1 in return for a sure return of $1. The conditional previsions $P[E_i | (\pounds/\$)]$ represent your pound denominated prices for claims to quantities of E_i denominated in dollars, but then redenominated into units of pounds at the unknown exchange rate $(£/\$)$. The fact that the sum of your conditional previsions $\sum_{i=1}^{3} P[E_i \mid (£/\$)] = 1$, insures that if you bought one pound's worth of these three claims to a dollar for a net outlay of £1 at these specified prices, your sure return would equal £1. (Your net return would equal 0.) This "pound" might then be valued at $1 or $1.3 or $2, but it would still be one pound. This is exactly what happens to your pound if you do *not* use it to buy the three claims to $1, but merely hold it yourself.

Similarly, the conditional previsions $P[E_i \mid (\$/£)]$ represent your dollar-denominated prices for claims to quantities of E_i denominated in pounds, but translated back into units of dollars. Again, since the sum of your prices $\sum_{i=1}^{3} P[E_i \mid (\$/£)] = 1$, if you "bought" each of these three claims to a pound for a net outlay of $1, your sure return would equal $1.

Another point worth mentioning is that the coherent assertions of $P(E_1) = P(E_2) = P(E_3) = \frac{1}{3}$ imply that your $P[\mathrm{NG}_£^*(E_1, E_2, E_3)] = 0$ for *every* specification of scalars s_1, s_2 and s_3 if and only if the numbers denoted by p_1, p_2 and p_3 in the matrix equation are replaced by the cohering assertions $P[E_1 \mid (£/\$)]$, $P[E_2 \mid (£/\$)]$ and $P[E_3 \mid (£/\$)]$ that we have just computed. In fact, this is precisely what it would mean for these conditional previsions to cohere with your specified $P(E_i)$.

We have established the distinction between the operational meanings of the assertions we have denoted by $P(E_i)$, $P[E_i \mid (£/\$)]$ and $P[E_i \mid (\$/£)]$. This allows us to determine precisely the cohering prices that you must offer for the several types of prizes we have considered if you assert your $P(E_1) = P(E_2) = P(E_3) = \frac{1}{3}$ on the basis of your indifference to dollar denominated contingent prizes $\$E_1 \sim \$E_2 \sim \$E_3$. But the deepest question remains. Why should it be your valuations in terms of dollars that characterize the numerical values of your previsions? The answer is that it is *not* the units of *dollars* that are the basis for prevision, but general *utility units*, commonly referred to as *utils*, that are the universal base units of prevision. We will present this discussion in a section of its own.

5. On the denomination of prevision in units of utility

Suppose we press you on your avowed willingness to exchange $\$E_1$ for $\$E_2$ for $\$E_3$ for $\$\frac{1}{3}$. Why are you willing to do that? "Because $1 would buy an orange", you say. "And while the value of £1 might equal $1 or $1.3 or $2, an orange is an orange is an orange."

Now our simple exchange market caricature made no mention of oranges nor of their prices. But although the price of an orange today may be $1, there is nothing to insure that on the specified day in the future when the numerical values of E_1, E_2 and E_3 are determined, the price of an orange will still be $1. Should we not append to our currency problem an explicit recognition of the price of an orange in terms of dollars as an unknown quantity? What you apparently want to say is that you assert your value indifference

E_1 oranges $\sim E_2$ oranges $\sim E_3$ oranges.

Should we not then define your $P(E_1) = P(E_2) = P(E_3) = \frac{1}{3}$ in terms of your "orange denominated" indifference relations? In this case your previsions for "constant" orange denominated prizes redenominated into dollars should be represented explicitly as $P[E_1 | (\$/\text{orange})]$, $P[E_2 | (\$/\text{orange})]$ and $P[E_3 | (\$/\text{orange})]$.

Let us push our questioning still further. Perhaps between now and the day on which the numerical values of E_1, E_2 and E_3 are determined, the orange crop is damaged by freezing. So an orange is not an orange is not an orange. Where will the questioning end?

The substantive point that emerges from our analysis of the currency exchange problem is that prevision must be evaluated in terms of some "constant" units of net yield. In our discussion of the preceding sections, we have been arguing as if this unit of constant net yield were a dollar. But in reality, the temporal sequence of *exchange values* of dollars for pounds for oranges for potatoes is unknown. The sequential history of such exchange rates (prices) is, of course, the subject of an important branch of economic theory. It is the historical event registered in exchange markets.

The very first characteristic of coherent conditional prevision, $P(X | Y)$, that we noted in the theorem concluding Section 3 was that if X is a quantity and K is a specified constant, then coherency requires that $P(X | K) = P(X)$. But for any unknown general quantity, Y, there is no coherency restriction that $P(X | Y) = P(X)$. The "constant unit" of net yield that is central to the theory of coherent prevision is necessarily the constant utility unit, dubbed "the util". Suppose we denote it by U. In making any list of unknown quantities such as the one we enunciated in Section 4, we could always list the value of the constant util as one of the quantities. By its definition, its realm of possibility consists of the set whose exclusive member is the number 1. $\mathcal{R}(U) = \{1\}$. Formally, since it's realm has only one member, U is completely logically unrelated to every other quantity. That is, whatever be the realm of a quantity X, $\mathcal{R}(X)$, the realm of the vector (X, U) is $\mathcal{R}(X, U) =$

$\mathcal{R}(X) \otimes \mathcal{R}(U)$. It is in terms of this constant utility unit that net gains that define an individual's prevision must be defined. For whoever you are, and whatever way you might be uncertain about a quantity X, coherency of your prevision requires that you assert your $P(X) = P(X \mid U)$.

To solidify this awareness in the currency problem, we reexamine the vector of considered quantities and its realm matrix that we identified in the matrix eq. (3). The final two quantities in the vector were denoted as \$ and £. Notice that the realm of \$ is the set $\{1\}$. The "constant unit" of utility was characterized in our analysis of this problem as the dollar, and coherency required that your prevision assertions for E_1, E_2 and E_3 were specified in terms of $P(E_i) = P(E_i \mid \$)$. Whereas, coherency does not require that $P(E_i)$ equal $P(E_i \mid £)$.

On the basis of our explicit recognition now that the price of a util in dollars need not be constant over time, we must conclude that any full scale representation of a prevision elicitation problem must enshrine the util as the standard unit of net gains. Your prevision for any quantity is defined in terms of a util "unit": $P(X) = P(X \mid U)$.

This conclusion is not new. Rather, it was central to de Finetti's characterization of coherent prevision. Unfortunately, his discussions of the issue in his *Theory of Probability* (1974, Sections 2.9, 3.2 and 6.6) have not been widely studied. The mathematical basis for the utility modulation of the theory of prevision was laid by the important theorem on the characterization of associative generalized mean functions, studied simultaneously by Nagumo (1930), Kolmogorov (1930) and de Finetti (1931). The meaningful use of this theorem allowed de Finetti to conclude that the definition of prevision modulo utility, $P_U(X) = U^{-1}\{P[U(X)]\}$, is the unique definition of prevision that enjoys the associative property, which is the basis of conditional prevision. An excellent discussion of the relevance of this theorem to the axiomatic construction of subjective probability appears in the article of Daboni (1984).

Before we close, it would be well to capitalize on the insights afforded by the currency exchange problem by stressing the non-temporal meaning of a conditional prevision assertion that it illuminates.

6. On the non-temporal nature of conditional prevision

There is widespread confusion, particularly in some Bayesian statistical circles, that conditional probability statements have something to do with temporal learning or inferences that a person must make when learning from observations that previously had been unknown. The temporal learning interpretation is seriously examined in philosophical literature such as Levi (1978) and Kyburg (1980). The work of Goldstein (1985, 1986) did much to clarify the issue with regard to the operational meaning of conditional prevision. In de Finetti's view the coherency condition, $P(XE) = P(X|E)P(E)$, applies to three prevision values that are asserted at the same time. The assertion of $P(X|E)$ is an operationally meaningful act, even (and especially) before one learns whether $E = 1$ or $E = 0$. And obviously, both $P(X|E)$ and $P(X|\tilde{E})$ are meaningful assertions at the same time. Suppose you assert values for both of these conditional previsions. If then upon learning, say, that $E = 1$, you decide (in your new state of mind) to assert your $P(X)$ as equal to the same numerical value that you had previously asserted as your $P(X|E)$, this is a new and distinct assertion that you would be making. And it is in no way required by the condition of your coherency. Levi (1980) coined a word for such a further restriction — he termed it your "confirmational commitment" to $P(X|E)$. Lane and Sudderth (1984, 1985) deduce relevant theoretical consequences of such a commitment, and Lane (1987) provides illuminating discussion.

Labels aside, our technical construction in this paper of a meaningful assertion of uncertainty that you can make via a general conditional prevision $P(X|Y)$ accentuates the distinction between conditional prevision and sequential learning. It is evident that your assertion of $P(X|Y)$ amounts merely to an elicitation of a linear restriction on your simultaneous assertions of previsions for $P(X)$, $P(Y)$ and $P(XY)$, viz., $P(XY) = P(X|Y)P(Y) = P(Y|X)P(X)$. In abstract mathematical terms, our proposed definition of $P(X|Y)$ also completes the interpretation of the theory of prevision and conditional prevision as an inner product space, along lines described in Goldstein (1986).

References

Daboni, L. (1984) 'On the axiomatic treatment of the utility theory', *Metroeconomica*, 36:203–209.
Drèze, J.H. (1958) *Individual Decision Making Under Partially Controllable Uncertainty*, Ph.D. Thesis, Columbia University, New York.
Drèze, J.H. (1987) 'Decision theory with moral hazard and state-dependent preferences', CORE Discussion Paper 8545, Universite Catholique de Louvain, Louvain-la-Neuve.
Finetti, B. de (1931) 'Sul concetto di media', *Giornale Istituto Italiana degli Attuari*, 2:369–396.
Finetti, B. de (1974, 1975) *Theory of Probability*, Vols. 1 and 2. New York: Wiley.
Goldstein, M. (1985) 'Temporal coherence', in: J.M. Bernardo, M.H. DeGroot, D.V. Lindley and A.F.M. Smith, eds., *Bayesian Statistics 2*. Amsterdam: North-Holland; and Valencia: Valencia University Press.

Goldstein, M. (1986) 'Separating beliefs', in: P. Goel and A. Zellner, eds., *Bayesian Inference and Decision Techniques*. Amsterdam: North-Holland.

Kadane, J.B. and R.L. Winkler (1988) 'Separating probability elicitation from utilities', *Journal of the American Statistical Association*, 83:357-363.

Kolmogorov, A.N. (1930) 'Sur la notion de la moyenne', *Atti della Reale Accedemia Nazionale dei Lincei*, 12:388-391.

Kyburg, H. (1980) 'Conditionalization', *Journal of Philosophy*, 77:98-114.

Lad, F. (1989) 'Operational subjective statistical methods', photocopy draft edition, Department of Mathematics, University of Canterbury, Christchurch, New Zealand.

Lad, F., J.M. Dickey and M.A. Rahman (1990a) 'The fundamental theorem of prevision', *Statistica*, L(1):1-20, to appear.

Lad, F., J.M. Dickey and M.A. Rahman (1990b) 'Application of the fundamental theorem of prevision', manuscript, School of Statistics, University of Minnesota, Minneapolis, MN.

Lane, D.A. (1987) 'An epistemic justification of the law of total probability', *Bernoulli*, 1:155-167.

Lane, D.A. and W.D. Sudderth (1984) 'Coherent predictive inference', *Sankhyā Series A Part 2*, 46:166-185.

Lane, D.A. and W.D. Sudderth (1985) 'Coherent predictions are strategic', *Annals of Statistics*, 13:1244-1248.

Levi, I. (1978) 'Confirmational conditionalization', *Journal of Philosophy*, 75:730-737.

Levi, I. (1980) *The Enterprise of Knowledge*, Cambridge, MA: MIT Press.

Nagumo, M. (1930) 'Ueber eine Klasse der Mittelwerte', *Japanese Journal of Mathematics*, 7:71-79.

Schervish, M.J., T. Seidenfeld and J.B. Kadane (1990) 'State dependent utilities', *Journal of the American Statistical Association*, 85, to appear.

Chapter 18

BAYESIAN LIMITED INFORMATION ANALYSIS REVISITED

Luc BAUWENS

GREQE, Ecole des Hautes Etudes en Sciences Sociales, Marseille, France

Herman K. van DIJK

Erasmus University Rotterdam, Rotterdam, The Netherlands

1. Introduction

The econometric analysis of the laws of demand and supply makes, in many cases, use of the assumption that prices and quantities traded of economic commodities are *jointly* determined. Well known examples are the demand and supply for agricultural and financial commoditie. Econometric research is also directed towards the analysis of the *joint* dynamic behaviour of such variables as gross national product, investment, consumption, money supply, inflation, and unemployment. In particular, the secular and cyclical properties of these variables are of interest. The econometric study of market processes and of business cycle phenomena is, in this century, greatly advanced by the formulation of the *Simultaneous Equations Model (SEM)* (see Haavelmo, 1943).[1]

L. Bauwens acknowledges financial support from the Netherlands organisation for scientific research (NWO) for the preparation of this paper, which was started during a visit at Erasmus University in 1988. H.K. van Dijk acknowledges financial support from NWO and from GREQE/EHESS in 1989. The authors are indebted to Frank Kleibergen for research assistance and to Gerrit Draisma for assistance in preparing the figures.

[1] For a historical review and a critical evaluation of the role of the SEM we refer to Epstein (1987).

Economic Decision-Making: Games, Econometrics and Optimisation
Edited by J.J. Gabszewicz, J.-F. Richard and L.A. Wolsey
© *Elsevier Science Publishers B.V., 1990*

Given the specification of the SEM, estimation methods for its parameters were developed using the maximum likelihood and least squares principles. However, in an unpublished paper in 1962, Drèze argued that these classical estimation methods were inadequate in two respects. First, available information on parameters of interest is ignored. A classic example is the marginal propensity to consume, which is an unrestricted parameter in the simple Keynesian consumption function, while past experience and economic knowledge restricts it, for most countries, to a subinterval of the unit interval. Second, too much prior information is used in the sense that some variables are omitted from an equation without proper justification. For instance, the interest rate is deleted from the consumption function mentioned above. Thus, the interest elasticity of consumption is assumed to be zero in the long run. Starting from these limitations of classical estimation methods, Drèze made several contributions to the econometric analysis of the SEM from a Bayesian point of view.[2] A major result, contained in Drèze's 1976 *Econometrica* paper is the derivation of the functional form of the posterior density of the parameters of a single structural equation, which is analyzed from a limited information point of view (i.e., ignoring information on the parameters of the other structural equations).[3] This posterior density is proportional to a ratio of multivariate-t densities and is defined as the class of (1-1) *poly-t* densities (Dickey, 1968; Drèze, 1977; Zellner, 1971, p. 269).

In the present paper we reanalyze and extend some of the results obtained by Drèze. The organization of this paper is as follows. We start in Section 2 with an analysis of the exact form of the likelihood function of an underidentified SEM, in the structural parameter space. Using a two-step integration procedure we show that a uniform prior density on the structural parameters gives explosive behaviour of the marginal posterior densities of several parameters of an underidentified model. So, *noninformative priors may give sharp, albeit, pathological behaviour of posteriors.* For expository

---

[2] Drèze (1975, 1976), Drèze and Morales (1976) describe results on identification, limited information and full information estimation. An extensive survey is given by Drèze and Richard (1983).

[3] The reason for the focus on Bayesian limited information estimation was the difficulty of deriving computationally tractable and flexible results in the full information case. It is to some extent the same reason why, earlier, at the Cowles Commission, several researchers (e.g., Anderson, 1949) developed the limited information maximum likelihood estimator (LIML) as an alternative to the full information maximum likelihood estimator (FIML). We note that several computational procedures that are useful for Bayesian limited information analysis are given in Richard and Tompa (1980), Bauwens and Richard (1985) and Bauwens et al. (1981).

purposes, the integration steps are spelled out in detail since they are repeatedly used in the sequel of the paper.

In Section 3, we give a proof that, for a standard class of noninformative prior densities, the posterior density of the parameters of a single structural equation derived in a limited information framework, is a ratio-form poly-t density *if, and only if,* the prior degrees of freedom parameter has the value suggested by Drèze (1976). The noninformative priors that are discussed by Zellner (1971, p. 225) and Malinvaud (1978, p. 122) give different classes of posterior densities.

In Section 4 we discuss the approach where a single structural equation is completed with the unrestricted reduced form equations of the endogenous variables. This so-called *incomplete simultaneous equations model* has been used by, e.g., Hendry and Richard (1983), Richard (1984), Zellner (1971, Section 9.4), Drèze and Richard (1983, Sections 2 and 5) and Zellner, Bauwens and Van Dijk (1988). The advantage of this alternative approach is that it fits naturally to the field of modelling a single equation when one intends to investigate whether some explanatory variables are exogenous. We discuss several representations of the incomplete simultaneous equations model and show that the representation of Drèze and Richard and the representation of Zellner, Bauwens and Van Dijk are in a certain sense *dual* to each other. The duality follows from two different decompositions of the likelihood function. One may argue that the Drèze and Richard representation yields the Bayesian counterpart of the limited information maximum likelihood estimator or least variance ratio estimator and that the Zellner, Bauwens and Van Dijk representation yields the Bayesian counterpart of the instrumental variable estimator (in particular two-stage least squares and k-class).

In Section 5 we state the conditions under which the prior specification is invariant under the different representations of the model that are introduced in Section 4. Next, we derive the posterior densities of the equation system parameters for the different model representations. It is shown that Drèze and Richard (1983) use a conditional *matrix-t* density for the reduced form coefficients given a value of the structural coefficients and a marginal (1–1) poly-t density for the structural coefficients while Zellner, Bauwens and Van Dijk (1988) make use of a conditional *multivariate-t* density in the structural coefficients given a value of the reduced form coefficients and a so-called marginal (2–1) *poly-matrix-t* density in the reduced form coefficients. As a next step we discuss, briefly, in Section 6 how the different model representations of Section 4 and the distribution theoretic results of

Section 5 can be used for Bayesian inference on the validity of overidentifying restrictions and exogeneity assumptions. Some conclusions and suggestions for further work are given in Section 7. The appendices contain technical details and proofs.

2. The likelihood function of an underidentified simultaneous equations model

The complete SEM can be written in the structural form as

$$YB + Z\Gamma = U, \tag{2.1}$$

where Y is a $T \times m$ matrix of observations on m endogenous variables, Z is a $T \times k$ matrix of observations on k predetermined variables, and the data matrix $(Y \, Z)$ has full column rank. The matrix B is an $m \times m$ nonsingular matrix of unknown coefficients and Γ is a $k \times m$ matrix of unknown coefficients. U is a $T \times m$ matrix of unobserved disturbances. The T rows of U are assumed to be independent, each of them being normal with expectation zero and identical positive definite symmetric (PDS) covariance matrix Σ. The predetermined variables in Z that are not lagged values of variables in Y are assumed to be weakly exogenous (see Engle et al., 1983). At this stage, no restrictions are imposed on the matrices of parameters B, Γ and Σ (except for the PDS restriction). So, the model is underidentified. The reduced form of (2.1) is

$$Y = Z\Pi + V, \tag{2.2}$$

with Π and V given as

$$\Pi = -\Gamma B^{-1}, \qquad V = UB^{-1}. \tag{2.3}$$

It follows immediately from (2.1)-(2.3) that the SEM is an example of a nonlinear regression model in the sense that $E(Y|Z)$ is nonlinear in the parameters B and Γ, and also that given a particular value of B, the expected value of Y is linear in the parameter matrix Γ. So, given a value of B, one can make use of results from the statistical analysis of the multivariate linear regression model (see, e.g., Anderson, 1984, Chapter 8; Zellner, 1971, Chapter 8).

We study the functional form of the likelihood function of an underidentified SEM in the structural parameter space. Consider the likelihood function of (B, Γ, Σ) given the data matrix $D = (Y \, Z)$:

$$L(B, \Gamma, \Sigma \mid D) = (2\pi)^{mT/2} \|B\|^T |\Sigma|^{-T/2} \exp\{-\tfrac{1}{2} \operatorname{tr}[Q(B, \Gamma)\Sigma^{-1}]\}, \tag{2.4}$$

$$L(B, \Gamma, \Sigma \mid D) = L_c(\Sigma \mid B, \Gamma, D)L_m(B, \Gamma \mid D)$$
$$\downarrow$$
inverted Wishart step on Σ: equation (2.6)
$$\downarrow$$
$$L_m(B, \Gamma \mid D) = L_c(\Gamma \mid B, D)L_m(B \mid D)$$
$$\downarrow$$
complete squares on Γ: equations (2.7)-(2.9)
$$\downarrow$$
matrix-t step on Γ: equations (2.10)-(2.12)
$$\downarrow$$
$$L_m(B \mid D): \text{ equation (2.13)}$$

Figure 1. Marginalization of the likelihood function of (B, Γ, Σ). (One may interchange the order of integration and first integrate with respect to Γ by making use of the matrix normal distribution. As a next step one integrates with respect to Σ.)

where

$$Q(B, \Gamma) = (YB + Z\Gamma)'(YB + Z\Gamma). \tag{2.5}$$

For a derivation of (2.4) we refer to standard textbooks in econometrics, e.g., Zellner (1971, Chapter 9). One can marginalize (2.4) with respect to Σ and Γ as indicated in Figure 1.

The inverted Wishart step on Σ (loss of $m + 1$ degrees of freedom)

By making use of the definition of the inverted Wishart density function (Anderson, 1984, Chapter 7; Zellner, 1971, Appendix B.4) one can integrate (2.4) with respect to Σ as follows:

$$L_m(B, \Gamma \mid D) \propto \|B\|^T \int |\Sigma|^{-T/2} \exp\{-\tfrac{1}{2} \operatorname{tr}[Q(B, \Gamma)\Sigma^{-1}]\} \, d\Sigma$$
$$\propto \|B\|^T |Q(B, \Gamma)|^{-(T-m-1)/2} \tag{2.6}$$

under the conditions $|Q(B, \Gamma)| > 0$ and $T > 2m$. The proportionality signs indicate that the normalization factors of the likelihood and the inverted Wishart density, that do not depend on the parameters (B, Γ), have been deleted for notational convenience. The exponent $-(T - m - 1)/2$ indicates the loss of $m + 1$ degrees of freedom due to the marginalization with respect to Σ. If one conditions (2.4) on the maximum likelihood estimator $(YB + Z\Gamma)'(YB + Z\Gamma)/T$ for Σ, one obtains the same functional form as (2.5), except that the exponent is $-T/2$. This is the well-known concentrated likelihood function. We emphasize this difference between conditionalization and marginalization since it plays a major role in the sequel.

Complete squares on Γ

As a next step, we analyze the functional form of (2.6) by factorizing it as the product of a conditional function of Γ, given a value of B, and a function of B. Consider the matrix of sums of squares and cross-products $(YB + Z\Gamma)'(YB + Z\Gamma)$ and complete the squares in Γ, given a value of B. Then one obtains

$$(YB + Z\Gamma)'(YB + Z\Gamma) = B'\hat{\Omega}B + (\Gamma + \hat{\Pi}B)'Z'Z(\Gamma + \hat{\Pi}B), \qquad (2.7)$$

where $\hat{\Omega}$ is a function of the data only, given as

$$\hat{\Omega} = Y'M_zY, \qquad M_z = I_T - Z(Z'Z)^{-1}Z', \qquad (2.8)$$

and $\hat{\Pi}$ is a function of the data, given as

$$\hat{\Pi} = (Z'Z)^{-1}Z'Y. \qquad (2.9)$$

The matrix-t step on Γ (loss of k degrees of freedom)

We make use of the definition of the matrix-t density. (See, e.g., Drèze and Richard, 1983, p. 589; Zellner, 1971, Appendix B5; Dickey, 1967.) Given this definition and using equations (2.7)–(2.9), one can write (2.6) as

$$L_m(B, \Gamma \mid D) \propto |B'\hat{\Omega}B + (\Gamma + \hat{\Pi}B)'Z'Z(\Gamma + \hat{\Pi}B)|^{-(T-m-1)/2}$$
$$\times |B'\hat{\Omega}B|^{(T-m-k-1)/2}|B'B|^{(m+k+1)/2}. \qquad (2.10)$$

Note that we have used the equality $\|B\|^2 = |B'\hat{\Omega}B| \, |\hat{\Omega}|^{-1}$ and dropped the factor in $|\hat{\Omega}|$ in the second line. The first two factors on the right-hand side of (2.10) form a kernel of a matrix-t density in Γ. So, one can write

$$L_m(B, \Gamma \mid D) = L_c(\Gamma \mid B, D)L_m(B \mid D), \qquad (2.11)$$

where

$$L_c(\Gamma \mid B, D) \propto f_{MT}^{k \times m}(\Gamma \mid -\hat{\Pi}B, B'\hat{\Omega}B, Z'Z, T - m - k - 1), \qquad (2.12)$$

which is a conditional matrix-t density[4] under the usual conditions *and the condition* $0 < \|B\| < \infty$. So, one can write

$$L_m(B \mid D) = \int L_m(B, \Gamma \mid D) \, d\Gamma \propto |B'B|^{(m+k+1)/2}. \tag{2.13}$$

Clearly, if the elements of B are not restricted in an adequate way, the function (2.13), which can be interpreted as the marginal posterior density of B based on a uniform prior on all the parameters, is not integrable in $\mathbb{R}^{m \times m}$. This reflects simply the lack of identification of the structural parameters assumed at the beginning of this section. As a consequence, the marginal posterior density of Γ is in principle also not integrable. In practice, one could define (2.13) on a region of integration that is finite, e.g., the set $\{B \mid \varepsilon \le |B'B| \le M\}$, where ε is a small positive constant and M is a large finite constant. The results of the integrations of the functions (2.13) (or (2.12) times (2.13)), with respect to B may of course be sensitive with respect to the choice of ε and M, depending on the data.

In the maximum likelihood framework one substitutes $-\hat{\Pi}B$ for Γ in the likelihood function which is already concentrated with respect to Σ. Then one obtains

$$L_c(B \mid D) \propto \text{constant} \tag{2.13'}$$

as is well known since the structural form is not identified. The result that the likelihood function concentrated with respect to both Σ and Γ, i.e., (2.13)$'$, is flat, but that the marginal likelihood of B, given as (2.13), is not flat was implicit in Drèze (1976); see also Maddala (1976). A summary of the results on marginalization and conditionalization of the likelihood of an underidentified SEM is given in Table 1.

Table 1
Likelihood functions of equation system parameters B and Γ

	Marginal likelihood L_m	Conditional likelihood L_c
$L(B, \Gamma \mid D) \propto$	$\|B\|^T \mid Q(B, \Gamma)\|^{-(T-m-1)/2}$	$\|B\|^T \mid Q(B, \Gamma)\|^{-T/2}$
$L(B \mid D) \propto$	$\|B\|^{(m+k+1)/2}$	constant

---

[4] In this paper, we use the notation of Drèze and Richard (1983, Appendix A) for density functions: the subscripts of f are a mnemonic for the name of the density (e.g., MT for matrix-t), the superscripts indicate the dimension of the random variable the name of which is given as argument; then follow the parameters.

To get (2.10)–(2.13), we have implicitly used a truncated uniform prior density on the parameters (B, Γ, Σ). In order to show the effect of marginalization of Γ and Σ, one can introduce an extra positive parameter h through the following noninformative prior

$$p(B, \Gamma, \Sigma) \propto |\Sigma|^{-h/2}. \tag{2.14}$$

Then, after multiplication of (2.4) by (2.14), and after repetition of the steps from (2.4) to (2.12), one obtains the result that the posterior density of B, Γ and Σ can be decomposed as follows:

$$p(B, \Gamma, \Sigma \mid D) = p_c(\Sigma \mid B, \Gamma, D)p_c(\Gamma \mid B, D)p_m(B \mid D), \tag{2.15}$$

where

$$p_c(\Sigma \mid B, \Gamma, D) \propto f_{IW}^m(\Sigma \mid Q(B, \Gamma), T + h - m - 1), \tag{2.15a}$$

$$p_c(\Gamma \mid B, D) \propto f_{MT}^{k \times m}(\Gamma \mid -\hat{\Pi}B, B'\hat{\Omega}B, Z'Z, T + h - m - k - 1), \tag{2.15b}$$

$$p_m(B \mid D) \propto |B'B|^{-(h-m-k-1)/2}. \tag{2.15c}$$

A kernel of the conditional posterior density $p_c(\Gamma \mid B, D)$, equation (2.15b), is shown in Figure 2 for the case where $T = 15$, $h = m + k + 1$ with $m = 1$ and $k = 1$. Note that for this value of h the conditional density $p_c(\Gamma \mid B, D)$

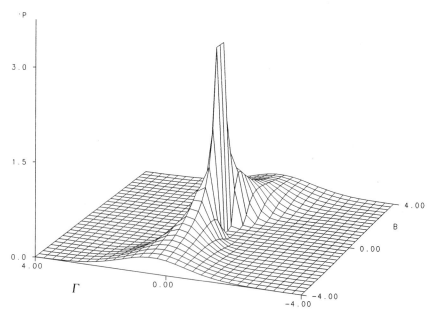

Figure 2. Kernel of $p(B, \Gamma \mid D)$ or $p_c(\Gamma \mid B, D)$ for $h = m + k + 1$ and $T = 15$.

and the joint density $p(B, \Gamma \mid D)$ are the same, since the marginal density $p_m(B \mid D)$ is uniform. The choice of the parameter values and the data is discussed in Appendix A. Clearly, the conditional densities become more concentrated when $B \to 0$ and have thick tails when B becomes large in absolute value. The conditional density is not defined for $B = 0$. Kernels of the marginal density $p_m(B \mid D)$ and of the joint density $p(B, \Gamma \mid D)$ are shown in Figure 3 and Figure 4, respectively, for different values of the degrees of freedom parameter h. One may distinguish three cases. If h is less than $m + k + 1$, one has a "polynomial" weighting function. See Figure 3, at the point $B = 0$, the function p_m is equal to 0, while it tends to ∞ in the areas where B tends to $\pm\infty$. If h is greater than $m + k + 1$, one has an "exponential" weighting function. See Figure 3, when B tends to 0, the function p_m tends to ∞, while it tends to 0 when B becomes large in absolute value. Finally, if $h = m + k + 1$, one has a flat weighting function. This is the value used by Drèze (1976). In practice, it appears a sensible strategy to experiment with a sequence of prior densities.

In order to illustrate further the difference between marginalization and conditionalization, one can work with the implied reduced form parameters

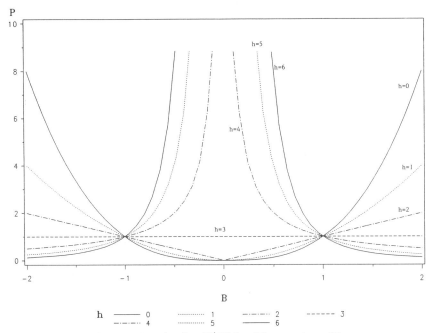

Figure 3. Kernels of $p_m(B \mid D)$ for different values of h.

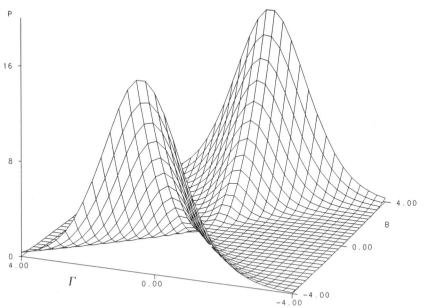

Figure 4a. Kernels of $p(B, \Gamma \mid D)$ for $h = 0$ and $T = 15$.

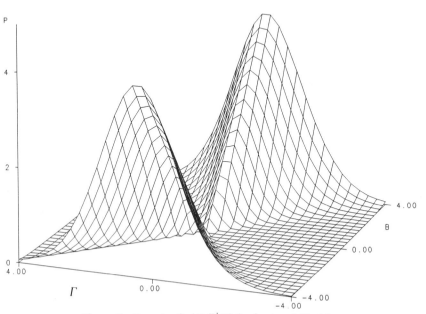

Figure 4b. Kernels of $p(B, \Gamma \mid D)$ for $h = 1$ and $T = 15$.

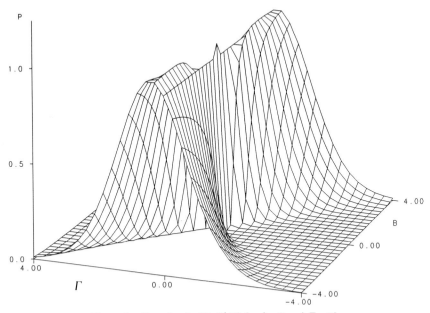

Figure 4c. Kernels of $p(B, \Gamma \mid D)$ for $h = 2$ and $T = 15$.

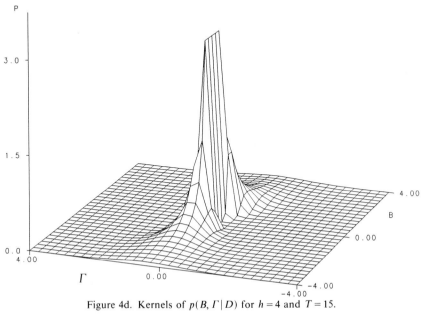

Figure 4d. Kernels of $p(B, \Gamma \mid D)$ for $h = 4$ and $T = 15$.

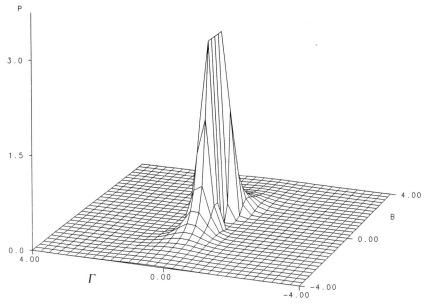

Figure 4e. Kernels of $p(B, \Gamma \mid D)$ for $h = 5$ and $T = 15$.

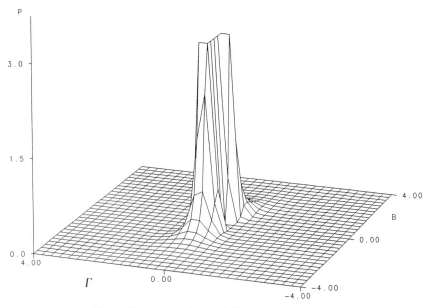

Figure 4f. Kernels of $p(B, \Gamma \mid D)$ for $h = 6$ and $T = 15$.

Π and Ω, where Ω is the PDS covariance matrix of each row of V, and is therefore related to the structural parameters by the relation

$$\Omega = B'^{-1}\Sigma B^{-1}. \tag{2.16}$$

As the transformation from (B, Γ, Σ) to (Π, Ω) is not one-to-one, we proceed as follows. First, perform the transformation of random variables that are elements of (B, Γ, Σ) to variables that are elements of (B, Π, Ω). The Jacobian determinant of this transformation is $\|B\|^{m+k+1}$ (see, e.g., Magnus and Neudecker, 1988, pp. 30–31 and Chapter 9). Second, marginalize the posterior density of (B, Π, Ω) with respect to B. In order to study the effect of this marginalization we transform the prior (2.14) to

$$p(B, \Pi, \Omega) \propto \|B\|^{m+k+1-h} \cdot |\Omega|^{-h/2}. \tag{2.17}$$

The likelihood function (2.4) can be rewritten as

$$L(B, \Pi, \Omega \mid D) \propto |\Omega|^{-T/2} \cdot \exp\{-\tfrac{1}{2}\mathrm{tr}[(Y - Z\Pi)'(Y - Z\Pi)\Omega^{-1}]\}. \tag{2.18}$$

The posterior density of (B, Π, Ω), which is proportional to the product of (2.17) and (2.18), can be marginalized with respect to Ω by using again the definition of the inverted Wishart density. Then one obtains

$$p(B, \Pi \mid D) \propto p_{\mathrm{u}}(\Pi \mid D) p_{\mathrm{m}}(B \mid D), \tag{2.19}$$

where

$$p_{\mathrm{u}}(\Pi \mid D) = f_{\mathrm{MT}}^{k \times m}(\Pi \mid \hat{\Pi}, \hat{\Omega}, Z'Z, T + h - m - k - 1) \tag{2.20}$$

is a matrix-t density with parameters that depend on the data and h but *that do not depend on B*, and

$$p_{\mathrm{m}}(B \mid D) \propto |B'B|^{(m+k+1-h)/2}, \tag{2.21}$$

which is equivalent to (2.13) if $h = 0$. Thus, we conclude that inference on Π is not sensitive to the truncation of $\|B\|$ to a finite range. However, as noted before, structural inference may be sensitive to the truncation of the range of $\|B\|$. In other words, the sample is informative on Π but not on B.

In the maximum likelihood framework, there is no Jacobian involved and there is no loss of degrees of freedom. That is, after concentrating (2.18) with respect to Ω, one obtains the concentrated likelihood function of Π, which is proportional to the same function as (2.20), except that $T + h - m - k - 1$ is replaced by T, and one obtains the "concentrated" likelihood of B, which is proportional to a constant; compare (2.13').

Summarizing, we have reviewed the implications of the lack of identification of the structural parameters of a SEM through marginalization and conditionalization of its likelihood function. Given the results (2.12), (2.13) and (2.15), there is a need for prior information, since a noninformative prior on the parameters of a nonidentified SEM may typically give an explosive behaviour of the posterior density in some directions of the parameter space while it is more regular in other directions. For work on informative prior densities in a full information framework we refer to, e.g., Zellner (1971), Drèze and Morales (1976), Bauwens (1984), Van Dijk (1984), Van Dijk (1987, and the references cited there, in particular, Kloek and Van Dijk, 1978; Van Dijk and Kloek, 1980). A survey is given by Drèze and Richard (1983).

3. Structural single equation analysis

Suppose one considers only prior information on the parameters of the first equation of (2.1), chosen without loss of generality, and no prior information on equations 2 to m. So, we have restricted matrices B, Γ, U, Σ, Π, V and Ω. In particular, we consider the case where (2.1) to (2.3) hold with B and Γ replaced by

$$B_r = \begin{pmatrix} 1 & \\ -\beta_1 & B_2 \\ 0 & \end{pmatrix}, \qquad \Gamma_r = \begin{pmatrix} -\gamma_1 & \\ & \Gamma_2 \\ 0 & \end{pmatrix}. \tag{3.1}$$

The submatrices B_2 and Γ_2 correspond to equations 2 to m and are unrestricted matrices of dimension $m \times (m-1)$ and $k \times (m-1)$, respectively. The first column of B has 1 as a first element by a normalization constraint, and the remaining $m-1$ elements have been partitioned into an $m_1 \times 1$ vector $-\beta_1$ of unrestricted parameters and an $m_0 \times 1$ vector of parameters, say β_0, restricted to 0. The first column of Γ_r has been partitioned into a $k_1 \times 1$ vector of unrestricted parameters $-\gamma_1$ and a $k_0 \times 1$ vector of parameters, say γ_0, restricted to 0. The zero restrictions in the first equation correspond to the exclusion of variables from it, usually for the purpose of identification. Let Y and Z be partitioned as

$$Y = (y_1 \quad Y_1 \quad Y_0), \qquad Z = (Z_1 \quad Z_0), \tag{3.2}$$

where y_1 is $T \times 1$, Y_1 is $T \times m_1$, Y_0 is $T \times m_0$, Z_1 is $T \times k_1$ and Z_0 is $T \times k_0$, while $1 + m_1 + m_0 = m$ and $k_1 + k_0 = k$. In summary, the system in structural form can be written as

$$y_1 = Y_1 \beta_1 + Z_1 \gamma_1 + u_1, \tag{3.3a}$$

$$YB_2 + Z\Gamma_2 = U_2. \tag{3.3b}$$

Note that u_1 is different from the first column of U in (2.1). The covariance matrix of the rows of the matrix $(u_1 \quad U_2)$ is denoted by Σ_r.

The likelihood function of the model has the same form as (2.4), but one makes use of the definitions of B_r and Γ_r given by (3.1). Suppose we keep the prior on Σ_r as given in (2.14), then one can write the posterior density $p(\beta_1, \gamma_1, B_2, \Gamma_2, \Sigma_r | D)$ in a straightforward way as

$$p(\beta_1, \gamma_1, B_2, \Gamma_2, \Sigma_r | D) \propto \|B_r\|^T |\Sigma_r|^{-(T+h)/2}$$

$$\times \exp\{-\tfrac{1}{2}\operatorname{tr}[(u_1 \quad U_2)'(u_1 \quad U_2)\Sigma_r^{-1}]\}, \qquad (3.4)$$

where $(u_1 \quad U_2)$ is restricted by (3.3a)–(3.3b).

In order to derive the marginal posterior density of the parameters of interest (β_1, γ_1), one has to integrate the join posterior with respect to Σ_r, Γ_2, and B_2. The integration with respect to Σ_r is done in the same way as in Section 2, equation (2.6), with the extra parameter h. The next step is to complete the squares on Γ_r as was done in Section 2, equations (2.7)–(2.9) for the case of Γ. Then one follows the steps given in (2.10)–(2.12), or in (2.15)–(2.15c). Finally, one obtains

$$p(\beta_1, \gamma_1, B_2, \Gamma_2 | D) \propto f_{\mathrm{RMT}}^{k \times m}(\Gamma_r | -\hat{\Pi}B_r, B_r'\hat{\Omega}B_r, Z'Z, T+h-m-k-1)$$

$$\times |B_r'B_r|^{(m+k+1-h)/2}. \qquad (3.5)$$

The mnemonic[5] RMT stands for a restricted (nonnormalized) matrix-t density in the sense that Γ_r is restricted as given in (3.1). We impose the condition $M \ge |B_r'\hat{\Omega}B_r| \ge \varepsilon$, with $\varepsilon > 0$ and $M < \infty$.

A next step is to integrate (3.5) with respect to Γ_2 by making use of properties of the matrix-t density. This involves some tedious derivations. A relatively easy procedure is the following. Assume that the restrictions on B_r and Γ_r are not yet imposed. We denote the first column of unrestricted elements of B by $\tilde{\beta}_1$ and the first column of unrestricted elements of Γ by $\tilde{\gamma}_1$. So, one can replace (3.1) by

$$B = (\tilde{\beta}_1, B_2), \qquad \Gamma = (\tilde{\gamma}_1, \Gamma_2). \qquad (3.1)'$$

If the restrictions of (3.1) are not imposed on (3.5), this density is a conditional matrix-t in Γ given a value of B (see (2.15b)). By making use of properties of the matrix-t density (see Zellner, 1971, Appendix B5; Drèze and Richard, 1983, p. 589), one can decompose the right-hand side of (3.5) in two factors. The first factor is a conditional matrix-t density of Γ_2 given a value of $\tilde{\gamma}_1$ (the unrestricted first column of Γ) and a value of B. The second factor is a marginal $k \times 1$ matrix-t density of $\tilde{\gamma}_1$, given a value of

---

[5] See footnote 4.

the first column of B, denoted by $\tilde{\beta}_1$. This latter density is defined as

$$p(\tilde{\gamma}_1|\tilde{\beta}_1, D) = f_{\mathrm{MT}}^{k\times 1}(\tilde{\gamma}_1|-\hat{\Pi}\tilde{\beta}_1, \tilde{\beta}_1'\hat{\Omega}\tilde{\beta}_1, Z'Z, T+h-2m-k) \qquad (3.6)$$

under the condition $M \geq \tilde{\beta}_1'\hat{\Omega}\tilde{\beta}_1 \geq \varepsilon$, with $\varepsilon > 0$ and $M < \infty$. We emphasize that the density (3.6) is *conditional on* $\tilde{\beta}_1$ *only, and not on* B_2, i.e. it is *conditionally independent* of B_2. Note that (3.6) can be interpreted as a multivariate-t density.

Integration of (3.5) with respect to Γ_2 gives a posterior density of $(\tilde{\beta}_1, \tilde{\gamma}_1, B_2)$ that is proportional to the right-hand side of (3.6) multiplied by the factor $|B'B|^{(m+k+1-h)/2}$ (compare (2.15b)–(2.15c) for the full information case). The factor $|B'B|^{(m+k+1-h)/2}$ can be deleted from (3.5) *if and only if* $h = m + k + 1$. Suppose that the prior on B_2 is uniform on a region of integration where $|B'B|$ is restricted to be finite. Using the definition of a matrix-t density, one can derive the marginal posterior density of $(\tilde{\beta}_1, \tilde{\gamma}_1)$ as

$$p(\tilde{\beta}_1, \tilde{\gamma}_1|D) \propto (\tilde{\beta}_1'\hat{\Omega}\tilde{\beta}_1)^{(T-m+1)/2}$$
$$\times[\tilde{\beta}_1'\hat{\Omega}\tilde{\beta}_1 + (\tilde{\gamma}_1 + \hat{\Pi}\tilde{\beta}_1)'Z'Z(\tilde{\gamma}_1 + \hat{\Pi}\tilde{\beta}_1)]^{-(T-m+k+1)/2}. \qquad (3.7)$$

We emphasize that the derivation of (3.7) does not depend on whether the restrictions on the first columns of B and Γ are imposed. That is, one may start with (3.4), with the restrictions imposed, and one can obtain the same functional form as given in (3.7) with $(\tilde{\beta}_1, \tilde{\gamma}_1)$ replaced by (β_1, γ_1) and with a proper adjustment of the data dependent matrices $\hat{\Omega}$, $\hat{\Pi}$, $Z'Z$, see below. However, the properties of the functional form of (3.7), in particular whether the function is integrable on a large region, depend on the restrictions. We distinguish two major cases.

First, suppose no restrictions are imposed. That is, equation (3.7) is maintained as it stands. The functional form of (3.7) has in this case the same properties as discussed in Section 2 for the full information case; compare equations (2.15)–(2.15c) with $h = m + k + 1$. The conditional multivariate-t density of $\tilde{\gamma}_1$ given a value of $\tilde{\beta}_1$ degenerates at $\tilde{\beta}_1 = 0$. Kernels of the joint posterior of $(\tilde{\beta}_1, \tilde{\gamma}_1)$ are given in Figure 5a for $T = 2$ and $T = 15$. Note that Figure 5a(ii) is the same as Figure 2. Further details on the choice of the parameter values and data are given in Appendix A.

As an intermediate case, consider the case where $\tilde{\beta}_1$ is replaced by the first column of B_r; see (3.1). Then one makes use of (2.8) and $\tilde{\beta}_1'\hat{\Omega}\tilde{\beta}_1$ in (3.7) is replaced by

$$(1 \;\; -\beta_1' \;\; 0')\hat{\Omega}\begin{pmatrix} 1 \\ -\beta_1 \\ 0 \end{pmatrix} = (y_1 - Y_1\beta_1)'M_z(y_1 - Y_1\beta_1), \qquad (3.8)$$

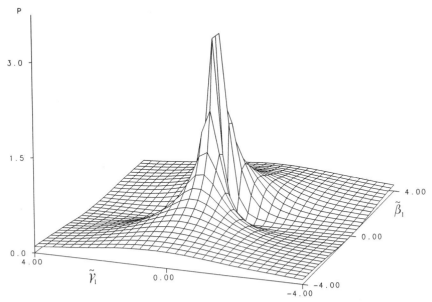

Figure 5a(i). Kernels of $p(\tilde{\beta}_1, \tilde{\gamma}_1 \mid D)$; no restrictions on parameters, $T = 2$.

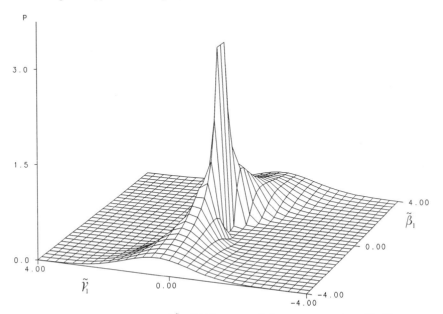

Figure 5a(ii). Kernels of $p(\tilde{\beta}_1, \tilde{\gamma}_1 \mid D)$; no restrictions on parameters, $T = 15$.

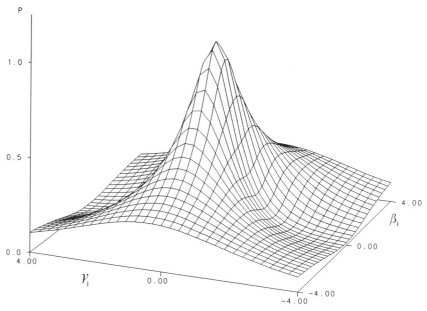

Figure 5b(i). Kernels of the (1–1) poly-t density $p(\beta_1, \gamma_1 | D)$, $T = 2$.

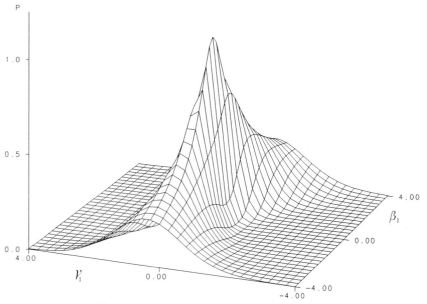

Figure 5b(ii). Kernels of the (1–1) poly-t density $p(\beta_1, \gamma_1 | D)$, $T = 15$.

where

$$M_Z = I - Z(Z'Z)^{-1}Z'. \tag{3.9}$$

Given the condition of full column rank of $(Y_1 \ Z)$ and given the normalization restriction that the first element of the vector $(1 \ -\beta'_1 \ 0')$ is equal to one, the right hand side of (3.8) is positive everywhere in the region of integration. The functional form of $p(\beta_1, \tilde{\gamma}_1 | D)$ is such that no degeneracy occurs as β_1 tends to zero.

Second, consider the case where the first columns of both B_r and Γ_r, given in (3.1), are substituted in (3.7) for the unrestricted vectors $\tilde{\beta}_1$ and $\tilde{\gamma}_1$. We make use of

$$\tilde{\beta}'_1 \hat{\Omega} \tilde{\beta}_1 + (\tilde{\gamma}_1 + \hat{\Pi}\tilde{\beta}_1)' Z'Z(\tilde{\gamma}_1 + \hat{\Pi}\tilde{\beta}_1) = (Y\tilde{\beta}_1 + Z\tilde{\gamma}_1)'(Y\tilde{\beta}_1 + Z\tilde{\gamma}_1). \tag{3.10}$$

Imposing the restrictions implies that (3.10) is replaced by $(y_1 - Y_1\beta_1 - Z_1\gamma_1)'(y_1 - Y_1\beta_1 - Z_1\gamma_1)$. If one completes the squares on β_1 and γ_1 one obtains

$$(y_1 - Y_1\beta_1 - Z_1\gamma_1)'(y_1 - Y_1\beta_1 - Z_1\gamma_1)$$

$$= s_1^2 + \begin{pmatrix} \beta_1 - \hat{\beta}_1 \\ \gamma_1 - \hat{\gamma}_1 \end{pmatrix}' \begin{pmatrix} Y'_1 Y_1 & Y'_1 Z_1 \\ Z'_1 Y_1 & Z'_1 Z_1 \end{pmatrix} \begin{pmatrix} \beta_1 - \hat{\beta}_1 \\ \gamma_1 - \hat{\gamma}_1 \end{pmatrix}, \tag{3.11}$$

where

$$\begin{pmatrix} \hat{\beta}_1 \\ \hat{\gamma}_1 \end{pmatrix} = \begin{pmatrix} Y'_1 Y_1 & Y'_1 Z_1 \\ Z'_1 Y_1 & Z'_1 Z_1 \end{pmatrix}^{-1} \begin{pmatrix} Y'_1 y_1 \\ Z'_1 y_1 \end{pmatrix}, \tag{3.12}$$

$$s_1^2 = (y_1 - Y_1\hat{\beta}_1 - Z_1\hat{\gamma}_1)'(y_1 - Y_1\hat{\beta}_1 - Z_1\hat{\gamma}_1).$$

In a similar way one may complete the squares on β_1 in (3.8). Then one obtains

$$(y_1 - Y_1\beta_1)'M_Z(y_1 - Y_1\beta_1) = s_2^2 + (\beta_1 - \beta_1^*)'Y'_1 M_Z Y_1(\beta_1 - \beta_1^*), \tag{3.13}$$

where

$$\beta_1^* = (Y'_1 M_Z Y_1)^{-1} Y'_1 M_Z y_1, \quad s_2^2 = (y_1 - Y_1\beta_1^*)'M_Z(y_1 - Y_1\beta_1^*). \tag{3.14}$$

Using the definition of a multivariate-t density one can write (3.7) as

$$p(\beta_1, \gamma_1 | D)$$

$$\propto \frac{\left[s_1^2 + \begin{pmatrix} \beta_1 - \hat{\beta}_1 \\ \gamma_1 - \hat{\gamma}_1 \end{pmatrix}' \begin{pmatrix} Y'_1 Y_1 & Y'_1 Z_1 \\ Z'_1 Y_1 & Z'_1 Z_1 \end{pmatrix} \begin{pmatrix} \beta_1 - \hat{\beta}_1 \\ \gamma_1 - \hat{\gamma}_1 \end{pmatrix} \right]^{-(\nu_1 + m_1 + k_1)/2}}{[s_2^2 + (\beta_1 - \beta_1^*)'Y'_1 M_Z Y_1(\beta_1 - \beta_1^*)]^{-(\nu_2 + m_1)/2}}, \tag{3.15}$$

where

$$\nu_1 = T - m - m_1 + k - k_1 + 1, \quad \nu_2 = T - m - m_1 + 1.$$

The right hand side of (3.15) is a ratio of multivariate-t kernels and is defined as a (1-1) poly-t density function.

We emphasize that this density is integrable if $k - k_1 > m_1$, which is the order condition for identification. This can be seen as follows. The tail behaviour of the marginal multivariate-t density of β_1 in the numerator depends on the degrees of freedom parameter which is equal to $T - m - m_1 + k - k_1 + 1$. In the denominator one has a quadratic form in β_1 raised to the power $-\frac{1}{2}(T - m + 1)$. The tail behaviour of the ratio of the two quadratic forms in β_1 depends on whether the difference in the exponents $T - m - m_1 + k - k_1 + 1$ and $T - m + 1$ is positive. This condition is equal to the order condition for identification $k - k_1 > m_1$. More details are given in Drèze (1976) or Dickey (1968). In Figure 5b we show a simple case of a (1-1) poly-t density with parameter values that are specified in Appendix A. We emphasize that the (1-1) poly-t density can have many different shapes than the one shown in Figure 5b, in particular, bimodality may occur.

We summarize this section in the following theorem.

Theorem 1. *Given the model* (3.1) *and the standard assumptions of a SEM, and given the class of noninformative priors defined in* (2.14), *the posterior density of the parameters of interest* (β_1, γ_1) *of a single structural equation is a* (1-1) *poly-t density, defined in* (3.15) *under the following conditions*:
   (i) *The order condition for identification is satisfied*: $k - k_1 > m_1$;
   (ii) *The prior degrees of freedom parameter h is given as $h = m + k + 1$*;
   (iii) $|B_r' B_r|$ *is finite.* $\square$

We end this section with some remarks.

First, we have not used the rank condition for identification but only the order condition. So uniform priors on a model that is underidentified may give sharp posteriors, see Maddala (1976). Note that we impose the condition that $|B_r' B_r|$ is finite. The sensitivity of the posterior results for this condition has to be investigated for each case. This remains an area for further research.

Second, in this section we have analyzed a single restricted structural equation while the remaining structural equations are unrestricted. In the next section we study the case where a single structural equation is completed with a set of unrestricted reduced form equations of the endogenous variables that appear in the structural equations. This is the so-called *incomplete simultaneous equations model* (see, e.g., Richard, 1984; Hendry and Richard,

1983). The connection between these two models can be studied as follows. Consider the posterior $p(\beta_1, \gamma_1, B_2, \Gamma_2 | D)$, equation (3.5). First, one applies the transformation of variables from $(\beta_1, \gamma_1, B_2, \Gamma_2)$ to $(\beta_1, \gamma_1, B_2, \Pi_2)$, where Π_2 is the matrix of reduced form parameters of the equations 2 to m. Next, one integrates the posterior of $(\beta_1, \gamma_1, B_2, \Pi_2)$ with respect to B_2 and with respect to those elements of Π_2 that do correspond to endogenous variables, which are deleted from the first structural equation. Then one has a posterior density $p(\beta_1, \gamma_1, \Pi_1 | D)$. The parameters Π_1 are in this case the implied reduced form parameters that correspond to the endogenous variables that are included in the structural equation. We note that one needs a special value of the prior parameter h in order to obtain a posterior of $p(\beta_1, \gamma_1, \Pi_1 | D)$ that is equal to the posterior studied in the next section. Details of such a rather tedious exercise are left to the interested reader and are omitted here, partly for space consideration.

Third, one can derive the result of Theorem 1 also if the prior (2.14) is replaced by

$$p(\beta_1, \gamma_1, \beta_2, \Gamma_2, \Sigma_r) \propto \| B_r \|^\tau |\Sigma_r|^{-h/2} \tag{3.16}$$

and one imposes $\tau - h = m + k + 1$. The justification for this prior is not trivial, since the posterior tends to infinity if B_r tends to infinity. In the case of no restrictions on the structural form one may start with a noninformative prior on the reduced form parameters (Π, Ω) and obtain (3.16) through an enlargement of the parameter space to (Π, B, Ω) and a transformation of variables from (B, Π, Ω) to (B, Γ, Σ).

Fourth, our derivation of Theorem 1 is based on a sequence of integration steps spelled out above. For a different sequence of integration steps based on, a.o., a decomposition of the Wishard density we refer to Drèze (1976).

4. Three representations of the incomplete simultaneous equations model

Consider again the first structural equation of the model given in Section 3 (see (3.3a)),

$$y_1 = Y_1 \beta_1 + Z_1 \gamma_1 + u_1. \tag{4.1}$$

The unrestricted reduced form equations corresponding to the right-hand side variables of Y_1 can be written as

$$Y_1 = Z\Pi_1 + V_1 = Z_1 \Pi_{11} + Z_0 \Pi_{10} + V_1, \tag{4.2}$$

where $\Pi_1 = (\Pi'_{11} \; \Pi'_{10})'$ is a $k \times m_1$ matrix of parameters, Π_{11} and Π_{10} being $k_1 \times m_1$ and $k_0 \times m_1$, respectively, and V_1 is a $T \times m_1$ matrix of unobserved disturbances.

The model defined by equations (4.1) and (4.2) incorporates no reduced form equations for other variables than the endogenous variables Y_1 of the right-hand side of (4.1). This will be typically the case when one starts an investigation with (4.1) considered as a regression model (i.e., model y_1 conditionally on Y_1 and Z_1), and later questions the exogeneity status of a subset of variables (Y_1) and adds equations (4.2). This is referred to as *the incomplete simultaneous equations model* (see Richard, 1984; Hendry and Richard, 1983; Drèze and Richard, 1983; Zellner, Bauwens and Van Dijk, 1988).

We note that, if one starts with a structural single equation analysis, some variables of Y, say Y_0, do not appear in the structural equation of y_1, but the reduced form (4.2) does contain equations for the endogenous variables Y_0 that do not appear in (4.1). Further, the incomplete simultaneous equations model contains, usually, less predetermined variables than the structural single equation analysis. A model with extra reduced form equations and extra predetermined variables is relevant when limited information inference is considered as a way to simplify the computational problem of estimation of a structural form.

By substituting $Z\Pi_1 + V_1$ for Y_1 in (4.1), one obtains the restricted reduced form equation of y_1, which can be written as

$$y_1 = Z\pi_1 + v_1 = Z_1\pi_{11} + Z_0\pi_{10} + v_1, \tag{4.3a}$$

where $\pi_1 = (\pi'_{11}, \pi'_{10})'$ is a $k \times 1$ vector restricted by

$$\pi_{11} = \gamma_1 + \Pi_{11}\beta_1, \tag{4.3b}$$

$$\pi_{10} = \Pi_{10}\beta_1, \tag{4.3c}$$

and $v_1 = u + V_1\beta$. Thus, one can interpret (4.3a)–(4.3c) as a *nonlinear regression* model (see Zellner, 1971, Chapter 9). There are several other interpretations for the model (4.1)–(4.2), for instance, the *unobserved independent variables model* (see, e.g., Zellner, 1970; Zellner, Bauwens and Van Dijk, 1988).

We make use of the following notation. We write (4.1)–(4.2) in matrix notation as

$$Y^*L + Z(\gamma \ \Pi_1) = (u_1 \ V_1), \tag{4.1}'$$

where

$$Y^* = (y_1 \ Y_1), \qquad L = \begin{pmatrix} 1 & 0' \\ -\beta_1 & I_{m_1} \end{pmatrix}.$$

We assume that the rows of the $T \times (m_1 + 1)$ matrix $(u_1 \; V_1)$ are independently, identically and normally distributed, with expectation equal to zero and PDS covariance matrix Ω^*, given as

$$\Omega^* = \begin{pmatrix} \sigma^2 & \omega_1' \\ \omega_1 & \Omega_1 \end{pmatrix}.$$

The likelihood function can be written as

$L(\beta_1, \gamma_1, \Pi_1, \Omega^* | D)$

$\propto |\Omega^*|^{-T/2} \exp\{-\tfrac{1}{2} \operatorname{tr}[(u_1 \; V_1)'(u_1 \; V_1)\Omega^{*-1}]\}$ (4.4a)

$\propto p(Y^*L) = f_{\mathrm{MN}}^{T \times m}(Y^*L | Z(\gamma \; \Pi_1), \Omega^* \otimes I_T),$ (4.4b)

where $(u_1 \; V_1)$ is restricted as in (4.1)$'$, and $f_{\mathrm{MN}}(\;)$ denotes a matrix-normal density function as defined in Drèze and Richard (1983, Appendix A). In the sequel, (4.1) and (4.2) will be called *Representation I* of the incomplete simultaneous equations model. We shall now define two other representations from alternative parametrizations.

Representation II is defined by decomposing $p(Y^*L)$, the matrix-normal density of $Y^*L = (y_1 - Y_1\beta_1 \; Y_1)$, as

$$p(Y^*L) = p(Y_1 | y_1 - Y_1\beta_1)p(y_1 - Y_1\beta_1),$$ (4.5a)

where

$$p(y_1 - Y_1\beta_1) = f_{\mathrm{N}}^{T}(y_1 - Y_1\beta_1 | Z_1\gamma_1, \sigma^2 I_T)$$ (4.5b)

and

$$p(Y_1 | y_1 - Y_1\beta_1) = f_{\mathrm{MN}}^{T \times m_1}(Y_1 | Z\Pi_1 + (y_1 - Y_1\beta - Z_1\gamma_1)\delta', \Phi \otimes I_T),$$ (4.5c)

with

$$\delta = \sigma^{-2}\omega_1,$$ (4.5d)

$$\Phi = \Omega_1 - \omega_1\sigma^{-2}\omega_1'.$$ (4.5e)

In (4.5b), $f_{\mathrm{N}}(\;)$ denotes a multivariate normal density function. The parameters β_1, γ_1, Π_1, δ, σ^2 amd Φ are in one-to-one correspondence with those of Representation I (see 4.4a) and the likelihood function $L(\beta_1, \gamma_1, \sigma^2, \Pi_1, \delta, \Phi | D)$ is the product of (4.5b) and (4.5c). This way of parametrizing the incomplete simultaneous equations model has been used by Drèze and Richard (1983, Sections 2 and 5).

Representation III is defined by the dual decomposition

$$p(Y^*L) = p(y_1 - Y_1\beta_1 | Y_1)p(Y_1),$$ (4.6a)

where

$$p(y_1 - Y_1\beta_1 \mid Y_1) = f_N^T(y_1 - Y_1\beta_1 \mid Z_1\gamma_1 + (Y_1 - Z\Pi_1)\eta, \tau^2 I_T) \qquad (4.6b)$$

and

$$p(Y_1) = f_{MN}^{T \times m_1}(Y_1 \mid Z\Pi_1, \Omega_1 \otimes I_T), \qquad (4.6c)$$

with

$$\eta = \Omega_1^{-1}\omega_1, \qquad (4.6d)$$

$$\tau^2 = \sigma^2 - \omega_1'\Omega_1^{-1}\omega_1. \qquad (4.6e)$$

The likelihood function $L(\beta_1, \gamma_1, \eta, \tau^2, \Pi_1, \Omega_1 \mid D)$ is proportional to the product of (4.6b) and (4.6c). This way of parametrizing the model has been used by Zellner, Bauwens and Van Dijk (1988).

Both reparametrizations have the advantage of cutting explicitly the likelihood function (4.4a) of the original parametrization into the product of two factors. This proves to be useful for defining some classes of prior densities and for integrating analytically some (possibly) nuisance parameters in order to derive posterior densities of parameters of interest, as we shall see in the next section.

In regression form the three models are summarized in Table 2. In Representation II the structural disturbances are added as artificial regressors in the reduced form equation. In Representation III the reduced form disturbances are added as artificial regressors to the structural equation. This turns out to be useful if one analyzes exogeneity; see Engle (1984) and Section 6. Note that v_{1t}' denotes the tth row of V_1; e_{1t}' is the tth row of E_1; u_{1t} is the tth element of u_1; and ε_{1t} is the tth element of ε_1.

Table 2
Three representations of an incomplete simultaneous equations model

Representation	I	II	III
Structural form	$y_1 - Y_1\beta_1 - Z_1\gamma_1 = u_1$	u_1 remains	u_1 replaced by $(Y_1 - Z\Pi_1)\eta + \varepsilon_1$
Reduced form	$Y_1 - Z\Pi_1 = V_1$	V_1 replaced by $(y_1 - Y_1\gamma_1 - X_1\beta_1)\delta' + E_1$	V_1 remains
	$cov(u_{1t}, v_{1t}) = \omega_1$	$cov(u_{1t}, e_{1t}) = 0$	$cov(\varepsilon_{1t}, v_{1t}) = 0$

5. Prior and posterior densities for the incomplete simultaneous equations model

When one uses the incomplete simultaneous equations model, one is interested mainly in doing inference on the coefficients β_1 and γ_1 of the structural equation (4.1) and in predicting future values of y_1; for the latter purpose, it is necessary to do inference on π_1 and Π_1; see (4.1)–(4.3). In this section, we discuss several classes of prior densities that may prove to be useful in practice and derive the corresponding posterior densities of the parameters β_1, γ_1, Π_1, σ^2 and Ω_1. Inference on τ^2 and Φ is not discussed in this paper. Inference on ω_1, δ and η is briefly discussed in Section 6.

5.1. Prior densities

To remain in the spirit of limited information, we assume that prior information may be available on the structural parameters β_1 and γ_1 and assume prior densities that are noninformative on the other parameters. We review three cases:

    (i) noninformative prior densities on all structural parameters;
    (ii) natural-conjugate prior densities on either β_1, γ_1 and σ^2 or β_1, γ_1, η and τ^2 — natural-conjugate with respect to (4.5b) or (4.6b);
    (iii) independent Student prior densities on β_1, γ_1 and β_1, γ_1 and η.

Case (i). Non-informative prior densities

For Representation I, it is given by

$$p(\beta_1, \gamma_1, \Pi_1, \Omega^*) \propto |\Omega^*|^{-(\alpha_0 + m_1 + 2)/2}. \tag{5.1}$$

That is, the elements of β_1, γ_1 and Π_1 are distributed uniformly and independently of Ω^* which has a degenerate inverted Wishart distribution with α_0 degrees of freedom; Drèze (1976) proposes the value $\alpha_0 = k$ (the number of predetermined variables) by reference to an invariance argument that is specific to the underidentified simultaneous equations model and is reformulated by Drèze and Richard (1983, Section 5). Zellner (1971) proposes $\alpha_0 = 0$ by reference to Jeffreys' invariance principle applied to the reduced form.

    For Representation II, a noninformative prior can be defined as the product of a noninformative prior $p(\beta_1, \gamma_1, \sigma^2)$, defined with respect to (4.5b), and a noninformative prior $p(\Pi_1, \delta, \Phi | \beta_1, \gamma_1, \sigma^2)$, defined independently with respect to (4.5c). The two noninformative priors are defined as if the regression equations of Representation II in Table 2 are unrelated and one assumes that β_1 and γ_1 are known in the enlarged reduced form equation of Representation II. We write this prior as

$$p(\beta_1, \gamma_1, \sigma^2, \Pi_1, \delta, \Phi) \propto (\sigma^2)^{-(\mu_0+2)/2} |\Phi|^{-(\nu_0+m_1+1)/2}. \tag{5.2}$$

By setting $\mu_0 = 0$ and $\nu_0 = 0$, one applies Jeffreys' invariance principle to (4.1) and the enlarged reduced form equation of Representation II. By choosing $\mu_0 = m_1 + k_1$, the number of regressors of (4.1), and $\nu_0 = k + 1$, the number of regressors in the enlarged reduced form equation, one obtains degenerate limits of natural-conjugate densities. In (5.2), the elements of β_1, γ_1, Π_1 and δ are distributed uniformly and independently of σ^2 and Φ; σ^2 has a degenerate inverted-gamma density with μ_0 degrees of freedom and is independent of Φ, and the latter has a degenerate inverted-Wishart density with ν_0 degrees of freedom.

For Representation III a noninformative prior can be defined in the same was as for Representation II. This yields

$$p(\beta_1, \gamma_1, \eta, \tau^2, \Pi_1, \Omega_1) \propto (\tau^2)^{-(\kappa_0+2)/2} |\Omega_1|^{-(\lambda_0+m_1+1)/2}. \tag{5.3}$$

For Jeffreys' invariance principle, applied to the enlarged structural equation of Representation III where Π_1 is assumed to be known, one sets $\kappa_0 = 0$, and for (4.2), one sets $\lambda_0 = 0$. For degenerate limits of natural-conjugate densities, one sets $\kappa_0 = 2m_1 + k_1$ and $\lambda_0 = k$.

The noninformative priors (5.1) to (5.3) can differ since they are defined for different parametrizations; (5.2) and (5.3) have two parameters but (5.1) has only one. These priors can be made compatible under certain conditions.

Theorem 2. *The noninformative prior measures* (5.1), (5.2) *and* (5.3) *are identical if, and only if, their parameters* α_0, κ_0, λ_0, μ_0 *and* ν_0 *satisfy the following relations*:

$$\alpha_0 = \kappa_0 - m_1 = \lambda_0 + 1 = \mu_0 + m_1 = \nu_0 - 1. \tag{5.4}$$

Proof. The Jacobian of the transformation from the parameters of Representation I to those of Representation II is $(\sigma^2)^{m_1}$, and the Jacobian of the transformation of the parameters of Representation I to those of Representation III is $|\Omega_1|$. Since $|\Omega^*| = \sigma^2 |\Phi| = \tau^2 |\Omega_1|$, one can easily make transformations of random variables from (5.1) to the implied prior measures on the parameters of Representation II and Representation III, and then compare the exponents with those of (5.2) and (5.3) to get (5.4). □

Table 3
Prior values of degrees of freedom parameters

Parameters	Drèze's invariance $(\alpha_0 = k)$	Jeffreys' invariance $(\alpha_0 = 0)$
μ_0	$k - m_1$	$-m_1$
ν_0	$k + 1$	1
κ_0	$k + m_1$	m_1
λ_0	$k - 1$	-1

Notice that it is not possible to satisfy (5.4) and at the same time to choose both μ_0 and ν_0 (or κ_0 and λ_0) according to Jeffreys' invariance principle or so as to obtain degenerate limits of natural-conjugate prior densities. Table 3 gives the values of the prior parameters κ_0, λ_0, μ_0 and ν_0 that satisfy (5.4) for the values of α_0 that have been proposed by Drèze and Zellner.

We give two remarks on noninformative prior densities.

First, in the incomplete simultaneous equations model one can choose different values of the degrees of freedom parameter and obtain the (1-1) poly-*t* class of posterior densities; see Subsection 5.2, while in the structural single equation analysis of Section 3 one may take only one value of the degrees of freedom parameter for the derivation of the (1-1) poly-*t* density.

Another class of noninformative prior densities is one where the prior is taken as proportional to the information matrix. We leave it to the interested reader to work this out for the three model representations; see also Zellner, Bauwens and Van Dijk (1988).

Note: the reader not interested in informative prior densities can go directly to Subsection 5.2.

Case (ii). Partially natural-conjugate prior densities

They can be defined only in the parametrizations of Representations II and III; this is one advantage of these reparametrizations. In fact, (5.2) and (5.3) are limiting cases of these partially natural-conjugate prior densities for Representations II and III. The natural-conjugate prior densities that we shall define are "partial", in the sense that they are defined with respect to a part of the likelihood function, e.g., (4.5b) for β_1, γ_1 and σ^2 — not taking into account the occurrence of β_1 and γ_1 in the other part (4.5c) — and (4.5c) for Π_1, δ and Φ, assuming that β_1 and γ_1 are known; for the complete set of parameters, the product of the two partial natural-conjugate prior densities is therefore not natural-conjugate. However, because we assume that there is usually no prior information except on the parameters of the structural equation, we shall use the limiting degenerate form of the partial natural-conjugate prior densities that could be defined on the parameters Π_1, δ and Φ (Representation II) or Π_1 and Ω_1 (Representation III), i.e., the second factor that appear in the right-hand side of (5.2) or (5.3).

For Representation II, the prior is given by

$$p(\beta_1, \gamma_1, \sigma^2, \Pi_1, \delta, \Phi) \propto f_N' \left(\begin{bmatrix} \beta_1 \\ \gamma_1 \end{bmatrix} \middle| \theta_0, \sigma^2 M_0^{-1} \right)$$

$$\times f_{ig}(\sigma^2 | s_0^2, \mu_0) |\Phi|^{-(\nu_0 + m_1 + 1)/2}, \qquad (5.5)$$

where $f_{ig}(\ )$ denotes an inverted gamma density. From (5.5), one sees that conditionally on σ^2, β_1 and γ_1 are jointly normally distributed, with an expectation equal to θ_0 and a covariance matrix proportional to σ^2, and σ^2 is marginally distributed as an inverted gamma variable with μ_0 degrees of freedom and scale parameter s_0^2.

For Representation III, the prior is given by

$$p(\beta_1, \gamma_1, \eta, \tau^2, \Pi_1, \Omega_1) \propto f_N'' \left(\begin{bmatrix} \beta_1 \\ \gamma_1 \\ \eta \end{bmatrix} \middle| \begin{bmatrix} \theta_0 \\ \eta_0 \end{bmatrix}, \tau^2 G_0^{-1} \right)$$

$$\times f_{ig}(\tau^2 | \tau_0^2, \kappa_0) |\Omega_1|^{-(\lambda_0 + m_1 + 1)/2}, \qquad (5.6)$$

where $n = l + m_1 = 2m_1 + k_1$. Conditionally on τ^2, β_1, γ_1 and η are jointly normally distributed, with an expectation independent of τ^2 and a covariance matrix proportional to τ^2, and τ^2 is marginally distributed as an inverted-gamma variable with κ_0 degrees of freedom and scale parameter τ_0^2. To be noninformative on η, one has to fix the appropriate elements of G_0 to 0.

Notice that (5.5) and (5.6) can easily be defined so that the marginal prior distribution of θ (i.e., β_1 and γ_1) is identical since it is a multivariate-t distribution.

Case (iii). Independent multivariate-t densities

It is defined by taking the marginal prior density of β_1, γ_1 (and possibly η for Representation II) obtained from (5.5) or (5.6).

For representation I, we write it as

$$p(\beta_1, \gamma_1, \Pi_1, \Omega^*) \propto f_t' \left(\begin{bmatrix} \beta_1 \\ \gamma_1 \end{bmatrix} \middle| \theta_0, M_0, \zeta_0 \right) |\Omega^*|^{-(\alpha_0 + m + 2)/2}. \qquad (5.7)$$

That is, β_1 and γ_1 are distributed independently of the other parameters, according to a multivariate-t distribution with expectation equal to θ_0, covariance matrix equal to $\zeta_0 M_0^{-1}/(\zeta_0 - 2)$ (if $\zeta_0 > 2$), and ζ_0 degrees of freedom, and the other parameters have the same noninformative prior as in (5.1).

For Representation II, we define the prior as

$$p(\beta_1, \gamma_1, \sigma^2, \Pi_1, \delta, \Phi) \propto p(\beta_1, \gamma_1)(\sigma^2)^{-(\mu_0+2)/2}|\Phi|^{-(\nu_0+m_1+1)/2}, \qquad (5.8)$$

where $p(\beta_1, \gamma_1)$ is the multivariate-t density of (5.7); again, the prior on the other parameters is the same noninformative one as in (5.2).

For Representation III, the prior is

$$p(\beta_1, \gamma_1, \eta, \tau^2, \Pi_1, \Omega_1) \propto f_t^n \left(\begin{bmatrix} \beta_1 \\ \gamma_1 \\ \eta \end{bmatrix} \middle| \begin{bmatrix} \theta_0 \\ \eta_0 \end{bmatrix}, G_0, \zeta_0 \right)(\tau^2)^{-(\kappa_0+2)/2}$$

$$\times |\Omega_1|^{-(\lambda_0+m_1+1)/2}. \qquad (5.9)$$

That is, β_1, γ_1 and η have a joint multivariate-t distribution, but one can easily remain noninformative on η; the prior on the other parameters is the same as in (5.3). We assume that the marginal density of β_1, γ_1 from (5.9) is exactly the multivariate-t density that appears in (5.7), denoted $p(\beta_1, \gamma_1)$ in the sequel.

5.2. Posterior densities

In this subsection we present two theorems that define different classes of posterior densities of the parameters β_1, γ_1 and Π_1. We concentrate on posterior densities for the case of the noninformative prior densities of Subsection 5.1 and for the models of Section 4. The posterior results for the informative prior densities of Subsection 5.1 and the models of Section 4 are similar to the results for the noninformative prior densities. That is, the same classes of posterior densities can be derived, only the parameter values of these posteriors differ from the noninformative case. Due to space considerations we have omitted the posterior results for the informative prior densities.

In order to make the sequence of integration steps in the derivation of the posterior densities of β_1, γ_1 and Π_1 more transparent, two summaries of these steps are shown in Figures 6 and 7. Figure 6 gives the steps according to the specification of Representation I. Figure 7 gives the steps after the reparametrizations that define Representations II and III.

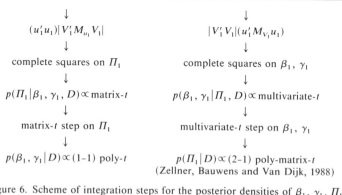

$p(\beta_1, \gamma_1, \Pi_1, \Omega^* | D)$ (equation (5.1) × equation (4.4a))

↓

inverted Wishart step on Ω^*

↓

$p(\beta_1, \gamma_1, \Pi_1 | D)$

↓

expand determinant $|(u_1 \ V_1)'(u_1 \ V_1)|$ as:

↓	↓
$(u_1'u_1)|V_1'M_{u_1}V_1|$	$|V_1'V_1|(u_1'M_{V_1}u_1)$
↓	↓
complete squares on Π_1	complete squares on β_1, γ_1
↓	↓
$p(\Pi_1|\beta_1, \gamma_1, D) \propto$ matrix-t	$p(\beta_1, \gamma_1|\Pi_1, D) \propto$ multivariate-t
↓	↓
matrix-t step on Π_1	multivariate-t step on β_1, γ_1
↓	↓
$p(\beta_1, \gamma_1|D) \propto$ (1-1) poly-t	$p(\Pi_1|D) \propto$ (2-1) poly-matrix-t
	(Zellner, Bauwens and Van Dijk, 1988)

Figure 6. Scheme of integration steps for the posterior densities of β_1, γ_1, Π_1.

We start in Figure 6 with the joint posterior of $(\beta_1, \gamma_1, \Pi_1, \Omega^*)$ for Model Representation I, i.e., the product of equations (5.1) and (4.4a). In a similar way as done in Sections 2 and 3, one can integrate this density with respect to Ω^* using the inverted Wishart density function. This yields

$$p(\beta_1, \gamma_1, \Pi_1 | D) \propto |(u_1 \ V_1)'(u_1 \ V_1)|^{-(T+\alpha_0)/2}. \qquad (5.10)$$

Note that the determinant in (5.10) is given as

$$|(u_1 \ V_1)'(u_1 \ V_1)|$$

$$= \begin{vmatrix} (y_1 - Y_1\beta_1 - Z_1\gamma_1)'(y_1 - Y_1\beta_1 - Z_1\gamma_1) & (y_1 - Y_1\beta_1 - Z_1\gamma_1)'(Y_1 - Z\Pi_1) \\ (Y_1 - Z\Pi_1)'(y_1 - Y_1\beta_1 - Z_1\gamma_1) & (Y_1 - Z\Pi_1)'(Y_1 - Z\Pi_1) \end{vmatrix}$$

and the projection matrices are defined as

$$M_{u_1} = I - u_1(u_1'u_1)^{-1}u_1', \qquad M_{V_1} = I - V_1(V_1'V_1)^{-1}V_1'.$$

The two equivalent ways to expand this determinant correspond to two ways to decompose the joint density $p(\beta_1, \gamma_1, \Pi_1 | D)$ into a conditional density and a marginal density. That is, the decomposition $p(\beta_1, \gamma_1, \Pi_1 | D) = p_c(\beta_1, \gamma_1 | \Pi_1, D)p_m(\Pi_1 | D)$ is used by Zellner, Bauwens and Van Dijk (1988) and the decomposition $p(\beta_1, \gamma_1, \Pi_1 | D) = p_c(\Pi_1 | \beta_1, \gamma_1, D)p_m(\beta_1, \gamma_1 | D)$ is similar to the derivation of Drèze and Richard (1983). We note that the poly-matrix-t class of densities that we derive in this paper was already mentioned as a possible class of densities by Dickey (1968). Due to space considerations we omit the detailed steps of the derivations.

A second approach to derive the posterior densities of β_1, γ_1 and Π_1 is to reparametrize the basic Representation I as done in Subsection 5.2 into the Representations II and III and to use the noninformative prior densities corresponding to these model representations. We summarize the different steps in Figure 7. An explicit proof is given in Appendix B and Appendix C.

The results of Figure 7 are summarized in the following two theorems.

parameter set $(\beta_1, \gamma_1, \Pi_1, \Omega^*)$

↓

REPARAMETRIZATION

↓

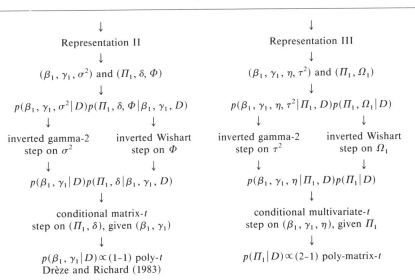

Representation II
↓
$(\beta_1, \gamma_1, \sigma^2)$ and (Π_1, δ, Φ)
↓
$p(\beta_1, \gamma_1, \sigma^2 | D)p(\Pi_1, \delta, \Phi | \beta_1, \gamma_1, D)$
↓   ↓
inverted gamma-2   inverted Wishart
step on σ^2 step on Φ
↓   ↓
$p(\beta_1, \gamma_1 | D)p(\Pi_1, \delta | \beta_1, \gamma_1, D)$
↓
conditional matrix-t
step on (Π_1, δ), given (β_1, γ_1)
↓
$p(\beta_1, \gamma_1 | D) \propto (1\text{-}1)$ poly-t
Drèze and Richard (1983)

Representation III
↓
$(\beta_1, \gamma_1, \eta, \tau^2)$ and (Π_1, Ω_1)
↓
$p(\beta_1, \gamma_1, \eta, \tau^2 | \Pi_1, D)p(\Pi_1, \Omega_1 | D)$
↓   ↓
inverted gamma-2   inverted Wishart
step on τ^2 step on Ω_1
↓   ↓
$p(\beta_1, \gamma_1, \eta | \Pi_1, D)p(\Pi_1 | D)$
↓
conditional multivariate-t
step on $(\beta_1, \gamma_1, \eta)$, given Π_1
↓
$p(\Pi_1 | D) \propto (2\text{-}1)$ poly-matrix-t

Figure 7. Reparametrizations and scheme of integration steps for posterior densities of β_1, γ_1, Π_1.

Theorem 3. *Given the class of noninformative prior densities of Theorem 2 and given Model Representation II, the marginal posterior density of the structural parameters (β_1, γ_1) is a $(1\text{-}1)$ poly-t density, and the conditional posterior density of Π_1 given a value of (β_1, γ_1), is a matrix-t density.*

The posterior of (β_1, γ_1) is defined, through its kernel,

$$p(\beta_1, \gamma_1 \mid D) \propto [(y_1 - Y_1\beta_1)'M_Z(y_1 - Y_1\beta_1)]^{(T+\alpha_0-m_1-k)/2}$$
$$\times [(y_1 - Y_1\beta_1 - Z_1\gamma_1)'(y_1 - Y_1\beta_1 - Z_1\gamma_1)]^{-(T+\alpha_0-m_1)/2}.$$

(5.11)

The density of Π_1 is defined as

$$p(\Pi_1 \mid \beta_1, \gamma_1, D)$$
$$= f_{\mathrm{MT}}^{k \times m_1}(\Pi_1 \mid \tilde{\Pi}_1, Y_1'\tilde{M}_{u_1}Y_1, Z'M_{u_1}Z, T + \alpha_0 - k),$$

(5.12)

where $\tilde{\Pi}_1 = (Z'M_{u_1}Z)^{-1}Z'M_{u_1}Y_1$ and

$$\tilde{M}_{u_1} = M_{u_1} - M_{u_1}Z(Z'M_{u_1}Z)^{-1}Z'M_{u_1}, \qquad M_{u_1} = I_T - u_1(u_1'u_1)^{-1}u_1'.$$

A proof of Theorem 3 is given in Appendices B and C. We note that $p(\beta_1, \gamma_1 \mid D)$ has the same functional form as given in Section 3, equation (3.15); compare equations (3.11)-(3.14). We remark that this method of derivation is, essentially, one followed by Drèze and Richard (1983).

Note that if one conditions $p(\Pi_1 \mid \beta_1, \gamma_1, D)$ on the limited information maximum likelihood estimator (LIML) of β_1, γ_1, then it can be shown that $\tilde{\Pi}_1$, the conditional posterior expectation of Π_1 is equal to the LIML estimator of Π_1.

The second theorem on posterior densities for β_1, γ_1 and Π_1 is based on Model Representation III. It is stated as follows.

Theorem 4. *Given the class of noninformative prior densities of Theorem 2 and given Model Representation III, the conditional posterior density of the structural parameters (β_1, γ_1), given a value of Π_1, is a multivariate-t density, and the marginal posterior density of Π_1 is a $(2\text{-}1)$ poly-matrix-t density.*

The density of (β_1, γ_1) is defined as

$$p(\beta_1, \gamma_1 \mid \Pi_1, D)$$
$$= f_t^{m_1+k_1}((\beta_1', \gamma_1')' \mid \hat{\theta}_1, (y_1'\tilde{M}_{V_1}y_1)^{-1}X'M_{V_1}X, T + \alpha_0 - m_1 - k_1),$$

(5.13)

where $X = (Y_1 \ Z_1)$ and

$$\hat{\theta}_1 = (X'M_{V_1}X)^{-1}X'M_{V_1}y_1, \qquad M_{V_1} = I_T - V_1(V_1'V_1)^{-1}V_1',$$
$$V_1 = Y_1 - Z\Pi_1, \qquad \tilde{M}_{V_1} = M_{V_1} - M_{V_1}X(X'M_{V_1}X)^{-1}X'M_{V_1}.$$

The density of Π_1 is defined through its kernel as

$$p(\Pi_1 \mid D) \propto \mid Y_1' \bar{M}_X Y_1 + (\Pi_1 - \bar{\Pi}_1)' Z' M_X Z (\Pi_1 - \bar{\Pi}_1) \mid^{(T + \alpha_0 - 1 - l)/2}$$

$$\times \mid Y_1' \tilde{M}_X^* Y_1 + (\Pi_1 - \Pi_1^*)' Z' M_X^* Z (\Pi_1 - \Pi_1^*) \mid^{-(T + \alpha_0 - l)/2}$$

$$\times \mid Y_1' M_Z Y_1 + (\Pi_1 - \hat{\Pi}_1)' Z' Z (\Pi_1 - \hat{\Pi}_1) \mid^{-(T + \alpha_0 - 1)/2}, \qquad (5.14)$$

where $l = m_1 + k_1$ and

$$\bar{M}_X = M_X - M_X Z (Z' M_X Z)^{-1} Z' M_X, \quad \bar{\Pi}_1 = (Z' M_X Z)^{-1} Z' M_X Y_1,$$

$$\tilde{M}_X^* = M_X^* - M_X^* Z (Z' M_X^* Z)^{-1} Z' M_X^*, \quad \Pi_1^* = (Z' M_X^* Z)^{-1} Z' M_X^* Y_1,$$

$$M_X^* = M_X - M_X y_1 (y_1' M_X y_1)^{-1} y_1' M_X, \quad \hat{\Pi}_1 = (Z' Z)^{-1} Z' Y_1. \qquad \square$$

A proof of Theorem 4 is omitted and left to the interested reader. It follows the similar steps as taken in Appendix B and C.

We end this section with two remarks.

First, one may extend Theorems 3 and 4 to the case where one has a conditional normal-inverted gamma-2 prior on the structural parameters and a locally uniform prior on the reduced form parameters. Similarly, one may use a multivariate-t prior on the structural parameters and be locally uniform on reduced form parameters. Details are omitted for space considerations.

Second, we have not stated explicitly the conditions that are sufficient for the existence of the integrals defined in the posterior distributions. These conditions are similar to the ones discussed in Section 3 and will be investigated explicitly in future work.

6. Remarks on Bayesian inference on exogeneity and overidentification

The posterior densities of β_1, γ_1 and Π_1 of Section 5 can be used for a diagnostic analysis of overidentifying restrictions and exogeneity restrictions. Of course, another approach is to specify prior odds and derive posterior odds for the restrictions mentioned above. However, some simple checks are the following.

The (1–1) poly-t density of (β_1, γ_1) (see (3.15) and Theorems 3 and 4) has as numerator the posterior density of the equation parameters of the standard linear model. Therefore, the variation in the denominator is an indication of the plausibility of exogeneity of the variables Y_1. If this function is constant, one may conclude that the variables Y_1 are exogenous.

A parametric analysis of exogeneity can be conducted in each of the three model representations. In Representation III one may investigate the posterior density of the parameter η. Algorithmic procedures for this purpose are given in Zellner, Bauwens and Van Dijk (1988). In Model Representation II one may analyze the posterior density of the parameter δ (see Lubrano, Pierce and Richard, 1986). In Model Representation I, one may investigate the posterior density of ω_1. In small samples, different results may emerge for the different representations. This is a topic for further research.

The validity of the overidentifying restrictions may be verified by comparing the (2-1) poly-matrix-t of Π_1 and the unrestricted matrix-t of Π_1.

One may also add variables to the structural equation and check how "close" the posterior density of its parameter is concentrated around zero.

Clearly, this is only a tentative list. More research in this area needs to be done. The use of a predictive approach is a worthwhile topic of research in this context.

7. Conclusions

We have reviewed Bayesian limited information analysis of the simultaneous equations model. Our results can be summarized as follows.

The marginal likelihood function of an underidentified SEM is not constant, but is explosive in some directions of the parameter space while it is more regular in other directions. Locally uniform priors are, therefore, not a suitable class of prior densities and there is a need for informative prior information.

Drèze's result that the parameters of a single structural equation have a (1-1) poly-t density holds under the condition that the prior degrees of freedom parameter has a particular value. It is of interest that in the incomplete simultaneous equations model one can derive the class of (1-1) poly-t densities for several different values of the degrees of freedom parameter.

One can show that the marginal posterior density of the implied reduced form parameters in the incomplete SEM is a so-called (2-1) poly-matrix-t density.

It appears that the different representations of the incomplete simultaneous equations model have each particular properties that are useful for the analysis of exogeneity and overidentification.

Clearly, the results are to be used in empirical studies. In applied work there is a need for diagnostic analysis on the plausibility of the prior assumptions. If one is interested in posterior results on the nuisance parameters such as the covariance matrix of the disturbances, one needs a decomposition of the inverted Wishart density along the lines discussed by Drèze (1976).

Appendix A

In this appendix we give some details on the Figures 2 to 5. First, we discuss the full information case; Figures 2 to 4. From (2.15b) and (2.15c) one can write the joint posterior density of (B, Γ) as

$$p(B, \Gamma \mid D) \propto |B'\hat{\Omega}B + (\Gamma + \hat{\Pi}B)'Z'Z(\Gamma + \hat{\Pi}B)|^{-(T+h-m-1)/2} |B'B|^{T/2}.$$

(A.1)

For Figures 2-4 we interpret B and Γ as scalars and take the data matrices $\hat{\Omega}$, $Z'Z$ and $\hat{\Pi}$ as $\hat{\Omega} = 1$, $Z'Z = 1$, $\hat{\Pi} = 0.10$. Further, $m = 1$ and $k = 1$. Then (A.1) becomes

$$p(B, \Gamma \mid D) \propto [B^2 + (\Gamma + 0.1B)^2]^{-(T+h-2)/2} (B^2)^{T/2}.$$

(A.2)

Clearly, if $h = 0$ or $h = 1$, the right-hand side of (A.2) tends to infinity when B tends to infinity. If $h > 2$ then (A.2) tends to infinity when B tends to zero. If $h = 2$, then one has the concentrated likelihood function that is only undefined when $B = 0$ and $\Gamma = 0$. Note that in the case of $h = 2$, the least upperbound for (A.2) in the point $(0, 0)$ is equal to one. One can rewrite (A.2) as

$$p(B, \Gamma \mid D) \propto \left[1 + \left(\frac{\Gamma + 0.1B}{B} \right)^2 \right]^{-(T+h-2)/2} |B|^{-1}(B^2)^{-(h-3)/2}.$$

(A.3)

Apart from the last factor, (A.3) is proportional to a conditional *univariate* t density of Γ given a value of B. A kernel of this conditional density is shown in Figure 2 for values of B in the interval $[-4, 4]$.

In the limited information case, Figure 5, we start with equation (3.7) and interpret $\tilde{\beta}_1$ and $\tilde{\gamma}_1$ as scalars. Further $m = 1$, $k = 1$, $\hat{\Omega} = 1$, $Z'Z = 1$, and $\hat{\Pi} = 0.1$. Then one has

$$p(\tilde{\beta}_1, \tilde{\gamma}_1 \mid D) \propto (\tilde{\beta}_1^2)^{T/2} [\tilde{\beta}_1^2 + (\tilde{\gamma}_1 + 0.1\tilde{\beta}_1)^2]^{-(T+1)/2}.$$

(A.4)

Clearly, this is the same function as (A.2) with $h = 3$. If one replaces $\tilde{\beta}_1$ by β_1 and $\tilde{\gamma}_1$ by γ_1, and if we impose on the right-hand side of (A.4) that $\tilde{\beta}_1^2 = (1 + \beta_1^2)$, then one has a kernel of a (1-1) poly-t density as shown in Figure 5.

Appendix B

Proof of Theorem 3.

- Model Representation II is given in Table 2 and repeated here for convenience with some new notation,

$$y_1 = (Y_1 \ Z_1)\begin{pmatrix} \beta_1 \\ \gamma_1 \end{pmatrix} + u_1 := X\theta + u_1, \tag{B.1}$$

$$Y_1 = (Z \ u_1)\begin{pmatrix} \Pi_1 \\ \delta' \end{pmatrix} + E := W\Delta + E. \tag{B.2}$$

Given the assumptions stated in Section 4, the likelihood function of this representation can be written as the product of (4.5b) and (4.5c),

$$L(\beta_1, \gamma_1, \sigma^2, \Pi_1, \delta, \Phi \mid D) = f_N^T(y_1 \mid Y_1\beta_1 + Z_1\gamma_1, \sigma^2 I_T)$$
$$\times f_{MN}^{T \times m}(Y_1 \mid Z\Pi_1 + u\delta', \Phi \otimes I_T). \tag{B.3}$$

- The prior density is given by (5.2) together with (5.4), i.e.,

$$p(\beta_1, \gamma_1, \sigma^2, \Pi_1, \delta_1, \Phi) \propto (\sigma^2)^{-(\alpha_0+2-m_1)/2} |\Phi|^{-(\alpha_0+2+m_1)/2}. \tag{B.4}$$

- Multiply $L(\cdot)$ with $p(\cdot)$; use the definition of the MN density function; and complete the squares on Δ. Then one obtains

$$p(\beta_1, \gamma_1, \sigma^2, \Pi_1, \delta, \Phi \mid D)$$
$$\propto (\sigma^2)^{-(\alpha_0+2-m_1)/2} f_N^T(y_1 \mid Y_1\beta_1 + Z_1\gamma_1, \sigma^2 I_T) |\Phi|^{-(T+\alpha_0+m_1+2)/2}$$
$$\times \exp\{-\tfrac{1}{2}\operatorname{tr} \Phi^{-1}[Y_1'M_W Y_1 + (\Delta - \hat{\Delta})'W'W(\Delta - \hat{\Delta})]\}, \tag{B.5}$$

where

$$M_W = I_T - W(W'W)^{-1}W' \text{ and } \hat{\Delta} = (W'W)^{-1}W'Y_1. \tag{B.6}$$

- From the definition of the MN and IW density functions, one recognizes in the formula above that

$$p(\Delta, \Phi \mid \beta_1, \gamma_1, \sigma^2, D)$$
$$= p(\Delta \mid \Phi, \beta_1, \gamma_1, \sigma^2, D)p(\Phi \mid \beta_1, \gamma_1, \sigma^2, D), \tag{B.7}$$

where

$$p(\Delta \mid \Phi, \beta_1, \gamma_1, \sigma^2, D) = f_{MN}^{(k+1) \times m_1}(\Delta \mid \hat{\Delta}, \Phi \otimes (W'W)^{-1}) \tag{B.8}$$

and

$$p(\Phi \mid \beta_1, \gamma_1, \sigma^2, D) = f_{IW}^{m_1}(\Phi \mid Y_1'M_W Y_1, T + \alpha_0 - k). \tag{B.9}$$

– Integrating the joint density (B.5) with respect to Δ and Φ gives

$$p(\beta_1, \gamma_1, \sigma^2 | D) \propto (\sigma^2)^{-(\alpha_0+2-m_1)/2} f_N^T(y_1 | Y_1\beta_1 + Z_1\gamma_1, \sigma^2 I_T)$$
$$\times |W'W|^{-m_1/2} |Y_1' M_W Y_1|^{-(T+\alpha_0-k)/2}. \quad (B.10)$$

The last two factors are the parts of the normalizing constants of the MN and IW conditional densities above, that depend on β_1 and γ_1. Then, we make use of

$$|W'W| = \begin{vmatrix} Z'Z & Z'u_1 \\ u_1'Z & u_1'u_1 \end{vmatrix} = |Z'Z|(u_1' M_Z u_1). \quad (B.12)$$

This follows from the usual expansion of determinants. Only $u_1' M_Z u_1$ depends on the parameters; furthermore

$$u_1' M_Z u_1 = (y_1 - Y_1\beta_1 - Z_1\gamma_1)' M_Z(y_1 - Y_1\beta - Z_1\gamma)$$
$$= (1 \; -\beta_1')' Y' M_Z Y(1 \; -\beta_1')', \quad (B.13)$$

where $Y = (y_1 \; Y_1)$ and $M_Z Z_1 = 0$. In addition

$$|Y_1' M_W Y_1| = |Y_1' Y_1| |W' M_{Y_1} W| |W' W|^{-1},$$

where $M_{Y_1} = I_T - Y_1(Y_1' Y_1)^{-1} Y_1'$, and

$$\begin{vmatrix} Y_1' Y_1 & Y_1' W \\ W'Y & W'W \end{vmatrix} = |Y_1' Y_1| |W' M_{Y_1} W| = |W'W| |Y_1' M_W Y_1|.$$

The determinant $|Y_1' Y_1|$ does not depend on the parameters, $|W'W|$ has already been analyzed, and $|W' M_{Y_1} W|$ does not depend on the parameters (see Appendix C).

– Collecting the factors depending on the parameters, using the definition of the normal density $f_N(\;)$, and completing squares in $\theta = (\beta_1' \; \gamma_1')'$

$$p(\beta_1, \gamma_1, \sigma^2 | D) \propto [(1 - \beta_1') Y' M_Z Y(1 - \beta_1')']^{(T+\alpha_0-m_1-k)/2}$$
$$\times (\sigma^2)^{-(T+\alpha_0-m_1+2)/2}$$
$$\times \exp\left\{ -\frac{1}{2\sigma^2} [y_1' M_X y_1 + (\theta - \hat{\theta})' X'X(\theta - \hat{\theta})] \right\}$$
$$(B.14)$$

($\hat{\theta} = (X'X)^{-1} X' y_1$ and M_X is the projection matrix of X). From the definition of the inverted gamma density (i.e., the one-dimensional IW density), one can then easily integrate out σ^2; the result is (5.11).

– To derive (5.12), we make use of the MN–IW conditional density of Δ, Φ. Notice that this density is in fact conditional on θ and not on σ^2; so we can drop σ^2 from the conditions.

The first step is to integrate out δ from $p(\Delta \mid \Phi, \theta, D)$ by standard properties of the normal density. This yields:

$$p(\Pi_1 \mid \Phi, \theta, D) = f_{MN}^{k \times m_1}(\Pi_1 \mid \tilde{\Pi}_1, \Phi \otimes (Z'M_{u_1}Z)^{-1}) \tag{B.15}$$

($\tilde{\Pi}_1$ is the submatrix of $\hat{\Delta}$ corresponding to Π_1 and is defined explicitly in Theorem 3, together with M_{u_1}).

The second and last step is to marginalize the latter density with respect to Φ. A well known property of the MN–IW density yields the result stated in (5.12) (see, e.g., Drèze and Richard, 1983, p. 589). $\square$

Appendix C

We show that $|W'M_{Y_1}W|$ does not depend on the parameters β_1 and γ_1. Consider

$$M_{Y_1}W = (M_{Y_1}Z \mid M_{Y_1}y_1 - M_{Y_1}Y_1\beta_1 - M_{Y_1}Z_1\gamma_1)$$
$$= (M_{Y_1}Z \mid M_{Y_1}(y_1 - Z_1\gamma_1)),$$

since $M_{Y_1}Y_1 = 0$. Hence

$$|W'M_{Y_1}W| = \begin{vmatrix} (y_1 - Z_1\gamma_1)'M_{Y_1}(y_1 - Z_1\gamma_1) & (y_1 - Z_1\gamma_1)'M_{Y_1}Z \\ Z'M_{Y_1}(y_1 - Z_1\gamma_1) & Z'M_{Y_1}Z \end{vmatrix}$$

$$= |Z'M_{Y_1}Z|$$
$$\times [(y_1 - Z_1\gamma_1)'M_{Y_1}(y_1 - Z_1\gamma_1)$$
$$- (y_1 - Z_1\gamma_1)'M_{Y_1}Z(Z'M_{Y_1}Z)^{-1}Z'M_{Y_1}(y_1 - Z_1\gamma_1)].$$

The first factor on the right-hand side depends only on the data. The second is equal to

$$y_1'M_{Y_1}y_1 - y_1'M_{Y_1}Z(Z'M_{Y_1}Z)^{-1}Z'M_{Y_1}y_1$$
$$+ \gamma_1'Z_1'M_{Y_1}Z_1\gamma_1 - \gamma_1'Z_1'M_{Y_1}Z(Z'M_{Y_1}Z)^{-1}Z'M_{Y_1}Z_1\gamma_1$$
$$- 2\gamma_1'Z_1'M_{Y_1}y_1 + 2\gamma_1'Z_1'M_{Y_1}Z(Z'M_{Y_1}Z)^{-1}Z'M_{Y_1}y_1$$
$$= y_1'M_{Y_1}y_1 - y_1'M_{Y_1}Z(Z'M_{Y_1}Z)^{-1}Z'M_{Y_1}y_1$$
$$+ \gamma'Z'M_{Y_1}Z\gamma - \gamma'Z'M_{Y_1}Z(Z'M_{Y_1}Z)^{-1}Z'M_{Y_1}Z\gamma$$
$$- 2\gamma'Z'M_{Y_1}y_1 + 2\gamma'Z'M_{Y_1}Z(Z'M_{Y_1}Z)^{-1}Z'M_{Y_1}y_1,$$

because $Z_1 \gamma_1 = Z\gamma$ upon defining $\gamma = \binom{\gamma_1}{0}$. So, the two terms in the second line cancel, and also the two terms on the last line, while the two terms on the first line depend only on data, and not on parameters.

References

Anderson, T.W. (1949) 'Estimation of the parameters of a single equation in a complete system of stochastic equations', *Annals of Mathematical Statistics*, 20:46-68.

Anderson, T.W. (1984) *An Introduction to Multivariate Statistical Analysis*. New York: Wiley.

Bauwens, L. (1984) *Bayesian Full Information Analysis of Simultaneous Equation Models using Integration by Monte Carlo*, Berlin: Springer.

Bauwens, L., J.-P. Bulteau, P. Gille, L. Longrée, M. Lubrano and H. Tompa (1981) 'Bayesian regression program (BRP) user's manual', CORE Computing Report 81-A-01.

Bauwens, L. and J.-F. Richard (1985) 'A 1-1 poly-*t* random variable generator with applications to Monte Carlo integration', *Journal of Econometrics*, 29:19-46.

Dickey, J.M. (1967) ''Matricvariate generalizations of the multivariate *t* distribution and the inverted multivariate *t* distribution', *Annals of Mathematical Statistics*, 38:511-518.

Dickey, J.M. (1968) 'Three multidimensional-integral identities with Bayesian applications', *Annals of Mathematical Statistics*, 39:1615-1628.

Dijk, H.K. van (1984) 'Posterior analysis of econometric models using Monte Carlo integration', Thesis, Erasmus University Rotterdam.

Dijk, H.K. van (1987) 'Some advances in Bayesian estimation methods using Monte Carlo integration', in: T.B. Fomby and G.F. Rhodes, eds., *Advances in Econometrics 6*. Connecticut: JAI Press, pp. 215-261.

Dijk, H.K. van and T. Kloek (1980) 'Further experience in Bayesian analysis using Monte Carlo integration', *Journal of Econometrics*, 14:307-328.

Drèze, J.H. (1962) 'The Bayesian approach to simultaneous equations estimation', ONR Research Memorandum 67, The Technological Institute, Northwestern University.

Drèze, J.H. (1975) 'Bayesian theory of identification in simultaneous equations models', in: S.E. Fienberg and A. Zellner, eds., *Studies in Bayesian Econometrics and Statistics*. Amsterdam: North-Holland.

Drèze, J.H. (1976) 'Bayesian limited information analysis of the simultaneous equations model', *Econometrica*, 44:1045-1075.

Drèze, J.H. (1977) 'Bayesian regression analysis using poly-*t* densities', *Journal of Econometrics*, 6:329-354.

Drèze, J.H. and J.-A. Morales (1976) 'Bayesian full information analysis of simultaneous equations', *Journal of the American Statistical Association*, 71:919-923.

Drèze, J.H. and J.-F. Richard (1983) 'Bayesian analysis of simultaneous equation systems', in: Z. Griliches and M.D. Intriligator, eds., *Handbook of Econometrics, Vol. 1*. Amsterdam: North-Holland.

Engle, R.F. (1984) 'Wald, likelihood ratio and Lagrange multiplier tests in econometrics', in: Z. Griliches and M.D. Intriligator, eds., *Handbook of Econometrics, Vol. 2*. Amsterdam: North-Holland.

Engle, R.F., D.F. Hendry and J.-F. Richard (1983) 'Exogeneity', *Econometrica*, 51:277-304.

Epstein, R.J. (1987) *A History of Econometrics*. Amsterdam: North-Holland.

Haavelmo, T. (1943) 'The statistical implications of a system of simultaneous equations', *Econometrica*, 11:1-12.

Hendry, D.F. and J.-F. Richard (1982) 'The econometric analysis of economic time series', *International Statistical Review*, 51:111-163.

Kloek, T. and H.K. van Dijk (1978) 'Bayesian estimates of equation systems parameters: an application of integration by Monte Carlo', *Econometrica*, 46:1-19.

Lubrano, M., R.G. Pierse and J.-F. Richard (1986) 'Stability of a UK money demand equation: A Bayesian approach to testing exogeneity', *Review of Economic Studies*, 53:603-634.

Maddala, G.S. (1986) 'Weak priors and sharp posteriors in simultaneous equation models', *Econometrica*, 44:345-351.

Magnus, J.R. and H. Neudecker (1988) *Matrix Differential Calculus with Applications in Statistics and Econometrics*. New York: Wiley.

Malinvaud, E. (1978) *Méthodes Statistiques de l'Économétrie*. Paris: Dunod.

Richard, J.-F. (1984) 'Classical and Bayesian inference in incomplete simultaneous equation models', in: D.F. Hendry and K.F. Wallis, eds., *Econometrics and Quantitative Economics*. Oxford: Basic Blackwell.

Richard, J.-F. and H. Tompa (1980) 'On the evaluation of poly-*t* density functions', *Journal of Econometrics*, 12:335-351.

Zellner, A. (1970) 'Estimation of regression relationships containing unobservable independent variables', *International Economic Review*, 11:441-454.

Zellner, A. (1971) *An Introduction to Bayesian inference in Econometrics*. New York: Wiley.

Zellner, A., L. Bauwens and H.K. van Dijk (1988) 'Bayesian specification analysis and estimation of simultaneous equation models using Monte Carlo integration', *Journal of Econometrics*, 38:39-72.

PART III

OPTIMISATION

Chapter 19

ELEMENTARY, CONSTRUCTIVE PROOFS OF THE THEOREMS OF FARKAS, MINKOWSKI AND WEYL

Roger J.-B. WETS

University of California, Davis, CA, USA

It usually comes as a surprise to the student of the theory of linear inequalities that Minkowski's, Weyl's and Farkas' Theorems require more than 3-line proofs. The proofs available in the literature (cf. for example, Goldman and Tucker, 1956) are elusively more complicated than seem warranted by the intrinsic simplicity of the assertions: finitely-generated convex cones are closed, finitely-generated convex sets are the intersections of a finite number of closed half-spaces. The proofs presented here are possibly still longer than one may wish for, but they are very elementary and *constructive*. The procedure they suggest combined with those for finding frames and lineality spaces of convex polyhedral cones (cf. Wets and Witzgall, 1967) has turned out to be as efficient as any known method for finding extremal elements of polyhedral sets (e.g., Motzkin et al., 1963). The proof-technique is, in flavor at least, similar to that of finding the facial structure of a polytope by adding a vector to an existing polyhedron discussed in Section 5.2 of Grünbaum (1967), as well as related to a number of procedures suggested in the literature for finding vertices of polytopes (see, Chernikova, 1965; Devroye, 1980; Swart, 1983). But either the development is "abstract" and would require some work before it could be implemented, or the description of the algorithmic procedures is rather involved and it is difficult to view them as "simple" proofs of these basic theorems.

Supported in part by grants of the National Science Foundation and the Royal Norwegian Council for Scientific and Industrial Research.

Economic Decision-Making: Games, Econometrics and Optimisation
Edited by J.J. Gabszewicz, J.-F. Richard and L.A. Wolsey
© *Elsevier Science Publishers B.V., 1990*

The *positive hull* of a finite collection $\{a_l \in \mathbb{R}^q, l = 1, \ldots, L\}$,

$$\text{pos}(a_1, \ldots, a_L) := \left\{ t \in \mathbb{R}^q \,\middle|\, t = \sum_{l=1}^{L} a_l \lambda_l, \lambda_l \geq 0, \text{ for } l = 1, \ldots, L \right\},$$

is the convex cone generated by these points.

Theorem 1 (Weyl). $\text{pos}(a_1, \ldots, a_L)$ *is the intersection of a finite number of half-spaces whose bounding hyperplanes pass through the origin.*

Proof. Set $a_0 = 0$. We show that if $\text{pos}(a_0, \ldots, a_{\nu-1})$ is the intersection of a finite number of half-spaces, then so is $\text{pos}(a_0, \ldots, a_\nu)$ with $1 \leq \nu \leq L$. Certainly $\text{pos}(a_0)$ is the intersection of a finite number of half-spaces, since

$$\text{pos}(a_0) = \{0\} = \{t \mid t_j \leq 0, j = 1, \ldots, q; -t_j \leq 0, j = 1, \ldots, q\}.$$

Now suppose that for some finite index set $J^{\nu-1}$,

$$\text{pos}(a_0, a_1, \ldots, a_{\nu-1}) = \{t \mid d_j \cdot t \leq 0, j \in J^{\nu-1}\}.$$

For $j \in J^{\nu-1}$, let $\alpha_j = d_j \cdot a_\nu$ and define

$$J_0 := \{j \mid \alpha_j = 0\}, \qquad J_- = \{j \mid \alpha_j < 0\}, \qquad J_+ := \{j \mid \alpha_j > 0\},$$

and for all $i \in J_+, j \in J_-$, let

$$d_{(i,j)} := d_i - (\alpha_i/\alpha_j)d_j.$$

The claim is that

$$\text{pos}(a_0, \ldots, a_\nu) = \{t \mid d_j \cdot t \leq 0, j \in J_0 \cup J_-; d_{(ij)} \cdot t \leq 0, i \in J_+, j \in J_-\},$$

and this would prove the theorem, since J_-, J_0 and J_+ are finite. Since for $l = 0, \ldots, \nu$, a_l satisfies the inequalities $d_j \cdot t \leq 0, j \in J_0 \cup J_-$ and $d_{(ij)} \cdot t \leq 0, i \in J_+, j \in J_-$, and since these inequalities determine a convex cone, $\text{pos}(a_0, \ldots, a_\nu)$ is necessarily included in the intersection of the closed half-spaces determined by these inequalities. And thus, all that needs to be proved is the inclusion in the other direction. Suppose that

$$d_j \cdot \hat{t} \leq 0, \quad j \in J_0 \cup J_-, \tag{1}$$

$$d_{(i,j)} \cdot \hat{t} = d_i \hat{t} - (\alpha_i/\alpha_j)d_j \hat{t} \leq 0, \quad i \in J_+, j \in J_-. \tag{2}$$

It suffices to show that there exists $\mu \geq 0$ such that $\hat{t} - \mu a_\nu \in \text{pos}(a_0, \ldots, a_{\nu-1})$ since it would imply that $\hat{t} = \mu a_\nu + (t - \mu a_\nu) \in \text{pos}(a_\nu, \text{pos}(a_0, \ldots, a_{\nu-1})) = \text{pos}(a_0, \ldots, a_\nu)$. By the induction hypothesis, this is equivalent to showing that there exists $\mu \geq 0$ such that

$$d_j(\hat{t} - \mu a_\nu) = d_j \hat{t} - \mu \alpha_j \leq 0 \quad \text{for all } j \in J^{\nu-1},$$

and this will be the case if and only if the interval

$$\left[\sup_{j \in J^+} \alpha_j^{-1} d_j \hat{t}_j, \inf_{j \in J^-} \alpha_j^{-1} d_j \hat{t}_j\right]$$

is nonempty and the right end-point of this interval is at or to the right of 0; with the usual convention that $\sup = -\infty$ if J^+ is empty and $\inf = \infty$ if J^- is empty. But that is exactly what is guaranteed by the inequalities (2) and (1). □

Corollary 2 (Farkas' Lemma). *Let $a_1, \ldots, a_n$ and b be elements of $\mathbb{R}^q$. Then either the linear system $\sum_{j=1}^n a_j \cdot x_j = b, x_1 \geq 0, \ldots, x_n \geq 0$ has a solution or there exists $\pi \in \mathbb{R}^q$ such that $a_j \cdot \pi \leq 0$ for $j = 1, \ldots, n$ and $b \cdot \pi > 0$.*

Proof. The assertion is self-evident if we reformulate it in the following terms: either b satisfies the linear system of inequalities $d_i \cdot t \leq 0, i = 1, \ldots, I$ or it fails to satisfy at least one of those inequalities, where $\{d_i, i = 1, \ldots, I\}$ is a finite collection such that

$$\text{pos}(a_1, \ldots, a_n) = \{t: d_i \cdot t \leq 0, i = 1, \ldots, I\}. \qquad \square$$

Corollary 3 (Farkas' Theorem). $\text{pos}(a_1, \ldots, a_L)$ *is a closed convex cone.*

Proof. $\text{pos}(a_1, \ldots, a_L)$ is the intersection of closed half-spaces. □

Corollary 4 (Minkowski). *A convex polyhedral cone*

$$C = \{t \in \mathbb{R}^q \mid d_j \cdot t \leq 0, j = 1, \ldots, J\}$$

is the positive hull of a finite collection of points in $\mathbb{R}^q$.

Proof. We claim that for pol C, the *polar* of C, one has

$$\text{pol } C := \{v \in \mathbb{R}^q \mid v \cdot t \leq 0 \ \forall t \in C\}$$

$$= \text{pos}(d_1, \ldots, d_J)$$

$$= \{v \in \mathbb{R}^q \mid a_l \cdot v \leq 0, l = 1, \ldots, L\}$$

for some finite collection $\{a_1, \ldots, a_L\}$. The last identity follows from Theorem 1, if we can prove the second one. Because all d_j for $j = 1, \ldots, J$ satisfy the inequalities $d_j \cdot t \leq 0$ for all $t \in C$, and the set defined by these inequalities is a convex cone, clearly we must have pol $C \supset \text{pos}(d_1, \ldots, d_J)$. If $\hat{v} \in \text{pol } C \setminus \text{pos}(d_1, \ldots, d_J)$, then for some $a_l, a_l \cdot \hat{v} > 0$. This, and the fact that $\hat{v} \cdot t \leq 0$ for all $t \in C$ means that $a_l \notin C$, and in turn, this means that for some j, $d_j \cdot a_l > 0$ contradicting the possibility that

$$d_j \in \text{pos}(d_1, \ldots, d_J) = \{v \mid a_l \cdot v \leq 0, l = 1, \ldots, L\}.$$

To complete the proof it suffices to demonstrate that $\text{pol}(\text{pol } C) = \text{pos}(a_1, \ldots, a_L) = C$. Indeed, if $\hat{t} \in C$ then $v \cdot \hat{t} \leq 0$, for all $v \in \text{pol } C$ and hence $\hat{t} \in \text{pol pol } C$, i.e., $C \subset \text{pol pol } C$. The inclusion in the other direction is obtained by simply observing that if $\hat{t} \in \text{pol pol } C$, then $\hat{t} \in \text{pos}(a_1, \ldots, a_L) = \{t \mid v \cdot t \leq 0 \ \forall v \in \text{pol } C\}$. But all $d_j \in \text{pol } C$ and thus $d_j \cdot \hat{t} \leq 0$ for $j = 1, \ldots, J$, i.e., $\hat{t} \in C$. $\square$

We have chosen to give this proof via polarity to illustrate the fact that Weyl's Theorem contains, at least implicitly, a separation theorem for convex polyhedral cones. We could also have given a proof based on arguments that are "dual" to those used in the proof of Theorem 1: an induction on the number of hyperplanes starting with

$$\{t \mid 0 \cdot t \leq 0\} = \text{pos}(\pm u_j, j = 1, \ldots, q)$$

where u_j is a unit vector with 1 in the jth position. The algorithm that follows is based on such a proof.

We sketch a procedure for finding a representation in terms of supporting hyperplanes of $\text{pos}(a_1, \ldots, a_n)$. In most of the applications that I have encountered, $\text{pos}(a_1, \ldots, a_n)$ is not pointed, and if full advantage is taken of the fact that the lineality space is easy to identify (Wets and Witzgall, 1967), the work required to find the supports is substantially reduced if this information is used when initializing the procedure. Let L be the lineality space of $\text{pos}(a_1, \ldots, a_n)$, let $(b_1, \ldots, b_K)$ be a linear base for $L^\perp$, and suppose that $\{a_1', \ldots, a_N'\} \subset \{a_1, \ldots, a_n\}$ is a collection such that

$$\text{pos}((a_1', \ldots, a_N') \cup L) = \text{pos}(a_1, \ldots, a_n);$$

the choice of the $\{a_j', j \in N\}$ could be such that it is a minimal collection. More specifically, we could begin by finding the lineality space of $\text{pos}(a_1, \ldots, a_n)$, identify those vectors that belong to the lineality space and choose a maximal subcollection of independent vectors. These would be our vectors $(b_1, \ldots, b_K)$. Next, among the vectors $a_1, \ldots, a_n$ that do not lie in the lineality space, we could identify those that are not positive linear combinations of the others. These would be our vectors $(a_1', \ldots, a_N')$, for all of these calculations one can rely on the procedures detailed in Wets and Witzgall (1967). The algorithm was implemented in this way, but there could be more efficient variants.

Algorithm 5. Finding supports for $\text{pos}(a_1, \ldots, a_n)$.

Step 0. Set $J^0 := \{1, \ldots, K+1\}$, $\nu = 1$,
$$d_j := b_j, \ j = 1, \ldots, K, \ d_{K+1} := -\sum_{k=1}^{K} b_k.$$

Step 1. Let $\kappa_{\nu-1} = $ number of elements in $J^{\nu-1}$.
For $j \in J^{\nu-1}$, $\alpha_j := a_\nu \cdot d_j$,
$$J_- = \{j: \alpha_j < 0\}, \ J_0 := \{j: \alpha_j = 0\}, \ J_+ := \{j: \alpha_j > 0\},$$
$$J^\nu := J_0 \cup J_- \cup \{j > \kappa_{\nu-1}: \ d_j = d_{(l,k)}, \ l \in J_+, k \in J_-\},$$
where $d_{(l,k)} := d_l - (\alpha_l/\alpha_k)d_k$.
Set $\nu \leftarrow \nu + 1$ and repeat until $\nu = n + 1$.

Stop. $\text{pos}(a_1, \ldots, a_n) = \{t \mid d_j \cdot t \leq 0, j \in J^n\}$.

For completeness sake, we conclude by showing that these results apply equally well to convex polyhedral sets, not just to cones. This is a very easy corollary of the above, what is needed is to identify every polyhedral set in $\mathbb{R}^n$ with a polyhedral cone in $\mathbb{R}^{n+1}$. The *convex hull* of a set $S \subset \mathbb{R}^n$ is denoted by $\text{co } S$; if S is finite, say $S = \{x_1, \ldots, x_q, q \text{ finite}\}$, we simply write $\text{co}(x_1, \ldots, x_q)$ for $\text{co } S$.

Proposition 6. *A nonempty subset C of $\mathbb{R}^n$ is a convex polyhedron if and only if it is a finitely generated convex set, i.e., C is the intersection of a finite number of half-spaces if and only if for some finite r and s,*

$$C = \text{co}(c_1, \ldots, c_r) + \text{pos}(p_1, \ldots, p_s).$$

Proof. Let $C = \text{co}(c_1, \ldots, c_r) + \text{pos}(p_1, \ldots, p_s)$. Then

$$C = \left\{ x \,\middle|\, \binom{x}{1} = \sum_{j=1}^{r} \binom{c_j}{1}\lambda_j + \sum_{k=1}^{s} \binom{p_k}{0}\lambda_k', \lambda_j \geq 0, \lambda_k' \geq 0 \right\}$$

$$= \left\{ x \,\middle|\, \binom{x}{\theta} \in \text{pos}\left(\binom{c_j}{1}, j = 1, \ldots, r; \binom{p_k}{0} k = 1, \ldots, s\right), \theta = 1 \right\}$$

$$= \{x \mid a_i \cdot x + \gamma_i\theta \leq 0, \ i = 1, \ldots, m; \ \theta = 1\}$$

$$= \{x \mid a_i \cdot x \leq -\gamma_i, \ i = 1, \ldots, m\}$$

for some finite number m; we used Weyl's theorem to pass from the second to the third equality. For the proof in the other direction, let

$$P := \{x \mid a_i \cdot x \leq \gamma_i, \ i = 1, \ldots, m\}$$

$$= \{x \mid a_i \cdot x - \gamma_i\theta \leq 0, \ i = 1, \ldots, m; \ -\theta \leq 0; \ \theta = 1\}$$

$$= \left\{ x \,\middle|\, \binom{x}{\theta} \in \text{pos}\left(\binom{b_j}{\beta}, j = 1, \ldots, J\right); \theta = 1 \right\},$$

with the last equality following from Corollary 4. Because the $(b_j, \beta_j) \in \{(x, \theta) \mid -\theta \le 0\}$, we necessarily have that $\beta_j \ge 0$. Without loss of generality, we can assume that for all j, $\beta_j = 1$ or $\beta_j = 0$; if not simply multiply (b_j, β_j) by β_j^{-1} whenever $1 \ne \beta_j > 0$, this will have no effect on the set of possible positive combinations. With $J_1 = \{j \mid \beta_j = 1\}$ and $J_0 = \{j \mid \beta_j = 0\}$,

$$P = \mathrm{co}(b_j, j \in J_1) + \mathrm{pos}(b_j, j \in J_0);$$

note that the index set J_0 is never empty as follows from the constraint $-\theta \le 0$. □

References

Chernikova, N.V. (1965) 'Algorithm for finding a general formula for the nonnegative solutions of a system of linear inequalities', *U.S.S.R. Computational Mathematics and Mathematics Physics*, 5:228-233.

Devroye, L. (1980) 'A note on finding convex hulls via maximal vectors', *Information Processing Letters*, 10.

Goldman, A. and A.W. Tucker (1956) 'Polyhedral convex cones', in: H. Kuhn and A. Tucker, eds., *Linear Equalities and Related Systems*. Princeton, NJ: Princeton University Press, pp. 53-97.

Grünbaum, B. (1967) *Convex Polytopes*. New York: John Wiley.

Motzkin, T.S., H.G. Thompson and R.M. Thrall (1963) 'The double description method', in: *Contributions of the Theory of Games II*. Princeton, NJ: Princeton University Press, pp. 51-73.

Swart, G. (1983) 'Finding the convex hull facet by facet', Technical Report No. 83-04-01, Department of Computer Science, University of Washington, Seattle, WA.

Wets, R.J.-B. and C. Witzgall (1967) 'Algorithms for frames and lineality spaces of cones', *Journal of Research of the National Bureau of Standards*, 71B:1-7.

Chapter 20

LONG STEPS WITH THE LOGARITHMIC PENALTY BARRIER FUNCTION IN LINEAR PROGRAMMING

Cornelus ROOS

Delft University of Technology, Delft, The Netherlands

Jean-Philippe VIAL*

Université de Genève, Genève, Switzerland

1. Introduction

Shortly after the publication of the new interior point algorithm of Karmarkar (1984), Gill, Murray, Saunders, Tomlin and Wright (1986) pointed out the connection between this new method and the classical logarithmic barrier method. In particular the search directions of both methods were proved to be linear combinations of two vectors, the affine scaling direction of Dikin (1967) and the so-called centering direction. The linear combinations are not the same in the two methods. Thus, the two algorithms are not equivalent (see Vial, 1989). Karmarkar's algorithm is polynomial and it requires $O(nL)$ iterations. Global convergence only was established for the barrier method.

Renegar (1988) proposed a path-following method requiring only $O(\sqrt{n}L)$ iterations. His approach is based on a projected Newton method for a certain potential, similar to, but not identical with, Karmarkar's potential. Gonzaga (1989a) derived another path-following approach, based on the logarithmic barrier function. See also Golfarb and Liu (1988). Roos and

* This author completed this work under the support of the research grant #1 467 0 86 of the Fonds National Suisse de la Recherche Scientifique.

Economic Decision-Making: Games, Econometrics and Optimisation
Edited by J.J Gabszewicz, J.-F. Richard and L.A. Wolsey
© *Elsevier Science Publishers B.V., 1990*

Vial (1988) gave simplified convergence proofs for Gonzaga's algorithm. All these methods are polynomial of order $O(\sqrt{n}L)$ iterations. However, the merit of this complexity result is more theoretical than practical. Gonzaga's algorithm proceeds with successive reductions of the penalty parameter, each time followed by a (small) Newton step. The reduction factor depends on n, the number of variables in the problem. This factor becomes close to 1 as n becomes large. Therefore the number of steps, though of order $O(\sqrt{n}L)$, becomes far too large to leave any hope for an efficient implementation. The same holds for all path-following methods.

Roos and Vial (1988) pointed out that a reasonable implementation strategy would be to proceed with much larger reductions of the penalty barrier term than the theory would recommend. After each reduction, the penalty term is fixed and a series of projected Newton's steps with line search, or so-called long steps, are taken until the iterate returns to the vicinity of the trajectory of centers. This strategy is appealing. It corresponds to a natural implementation of the classical interior penalty method with the logarithmic barrier function. It was not clear whether or not it would be polynomial.

The aim of this paper is to prove that this implementation is indeed polynomial. We show that the number of reductions of the penalty parameter is $O(L)$. Each reduction is followed by a series of inner steps, aiming at getting close to the analytic center associated with the current value of the penalty parameter. We prove that there are at most $O(nL)$ inner steps in total. In terms of complexity of the operations, the inner steps constitute the bulk of the computational effort. Thus the overall algorithm is $O(nL)$ in the number of iterations. This result puts the classical barrier method on a par with the projective algorithm of Karmarkar.

While this paper was being typed, one of the authors attended a lecture by Gonzaga (1989b) at the CORS/TIMS/ORSA meeting in Vancouver (May 8–10, 1989), who presented also a long step algorithm, basically using the same ideas. The main difference seems to be in the choice of the reduction factor of the penalty parameter. Gonzaga's factor is of the type $1 - \rho/\sqrt{n}$, where ρ is some fixed number. His algorithm converges in $O(\sqrt{n}L)$ iterations. In our method, the number of iterations is $O(nL)$, but the reduction factor is fixed and independent of n. However it can be shown that by setting $\rho = (1 - \theta)\sqrt{n}$ Gonzaga's reduction factor becomes independent of n, while the number of iterations becomes of order $O(nL)$. Gonzaga's result is therefore stronger.

As far as notations are concerned, e shall denote the vector of all ones. Given an n-dimensional vector x we denote by X the $n \times n$ diagonal matrix whose diagonal entries are the coordinates x_j of x; x^T is the transpose of the vector x and the same notation holds for matrices. Finally $\|x\|$ denotes the l_2 norm and $\|x\|_\infty$ the l_∞ norm of x.

2. The algorithm

We consider the linear programming problem

$$\min\{c^T x: Ax = b, x \ge 0\}. \tag{1}$$

Here A is an $m \times n$ matrix, b and c are m- and n-dimensional vectors respectively; the n-dimensional vector x is the variable in which the minimization is done. Without loss of generality we assume that all the coefficients are integer. We shall denote by L the length of the input data of (1).

We make the standard assumption that the feasible set of (1) is bounded and has a nonempty relative interior. As usual we assume that an initial interior feasible point x^0 is at hand such that $x_j^0 \ge 2^{-L}$ for each $j = 1, \ldots, n$. We assume that z_L is a known lower bound. Without loss of generality we assume that $|z_L|$ is of order $O(2^L)$. Finally we denote by z^* the (unknown) optimal value of the problem.

In order to simplify the analysis we shall also assume that A has full rank, though this assumption is not essential.

We consider the logarithmic barrier function

$$f(x, \mu) := \frac{c^T x - z^*}{\mu} - \sum_{j=1}^n \ln x_j, \tag{2}$$

where μ is a positive parameter. Since z^* is an unknown value it is not possible to compute the values of f. However one can compute differences of values and derivatives. It is well known that f is strongly convex on the relative interior of the feasible set. It also takes infinite values on the boundary of the feasible set. Thus it achieves a minimum value at a unique point. The necessary and sufficient first order optimality conditions for the minimization of this barrier function are:

$$A^T u + s = c, \quad s \ge 0, \tag{3}$$

$$Ax = b, \quad x \ge 0, \tag{4}$$

$$Xs = \mu e, \tag{5}$$

where u and s are m- and n-dimensional vectors respectively.

The projected Newton direction Xq associated with f at x is determined by

$$q = -P_{\mathcal{N}(AX)}\left(\frac{Xc}{\mu} - e\right). \tag{6}$$

where $P_{\mathcal{N}(AX)}$ denotes the operator of the orthogonal projection on the null space $\mathcal{N}(AX)$ of the matrix AX. It is easy to check that

$$q = e - Xs/\mu \tag{7}$$

with

$$s = c - A^{\mathrm{T}}u \tag{8}$$

and

$$u = (AX^2A^{\mathrm{T}})^{-1}AX(Xc - \mu e). \tag{9}$$

Note that u and s correspond to dual and slack variables in the dual linear programming problem. Note also that if the constraint matrix A has not full rank, the vector u is no longer unique, but the vector $A^{\mathrm{T}}u$ in (8) is still unique. Therefore, the algorithm below remains uniquely defined in that case.

Long Step Algorithm.
  Input:
  x^0 is a given interior feasible point;
  z_{L} is a lower bound for the optimal value;
  t is an accuracy parameter, $t \in \mathbb{N}$.
  begin
    $\mu_0 = c^{\mathrm{T}}x^0 - z_{\mathrm{L}}; \ x := x^0; \ \mu := \mu_0;$
    while $\mu > 2^{-t}$ **do**
    begin (outer step)
      while $\|q\| \geq 1$ **do**
      begin (inner step)
        $\bar{\alpha} := \arg\min_{\alpha>0}\{f(x + \alpha Xq, \mu): x + \alpha Xq > 0\};$
        $x := x + \bar{\alpha}Xq;$
      end (end inner step)
      $\mu := \frac{1}{2}\mu;$
    end (end outer step)
  end.

Remark. The reduction factor of μ is arbitrary. The value of the factor $\frac{1}{2}$ can be replaced by any fixed value in the open interval $(0, 1)$ (independent of n).

3. Convergence analysis

In this section we shall prove that the algorithm converges in $O(nL)$ iterations. But we need first to state and prove a series of four lemmas.

Lemma 3.1. *If* $\|q\| \leq 1$ *then* $c^{\mathrm{T}}x - z^* \leq \mu(n + \sqrt{n})$.

Proof. Let s and u be defined as in (8) and (9). By the definition (7) of q we have

$$\left\| e - \frac{Xs}{\mu} \right\| \leq 1.$$

This implies $s \geq 0$. So u is dual feasible and hence $b^{\mathrm{T}}u \leq z^*$. On the other hand,

$$\left| e^{\mathrm{T}}\left(\frac{Xs}{\mu} - e \right) \right| \leq \|e\| \left\| \frac{Xs}{\mu} - e \right\| \leq \sqrt{n}$$

and

$$e^{\mathrm{T}}\left(\frac{Xs}{\mu} - e \right) = \frac{x^{\mathrm{T}}s}{\mu} - n = \frac{c^{\mathrm{T}}x - b^{\mathrm{T}}u}{\mu} - n \geq \frac{c^{\mathrm{T}}x - z^*}{\mu} - n.$$

Hence the result. $\quad\square$

Lemma 3.2. *If x is such that* $\|q\| \leq 1$ *and* $0 < \theta < 1$, *then*

$$f(x, \theta\mu) \leq f(x, \mu) + \frac{1 - \theta}{\theta}(n + \sqrt{n}).$$

Proof. Using the previous lemma the proof becomes straightforward:

$$f(x, \theta\mu) = \frac{c^{\mathrm{T}}x - z^*}{\theta\mu} - \sum_{j=1}^{n} \ln x_j$$

$$= \frac{1 - \theta}{\theta} \frac{c^{\mathrm{T}}x - z^*}{\mu} + \frac{c^{\mathrm{T}}x - z^*}{\mu} - \sum_{j=1}^{n} \ln x_j$$

$$\leq \frac{1 - \theta}{\theta}(n + \sqrt{n}) + f(x, \mu). \quad\square$$

Consider the case that a step of length α is taken from x along the direction Xq. We denote by Δf the change in the potential function. It readily follows that

$$-\Delta f = -\alpha \frac{c^T X q}{\mu} + \sum_{j=1}^{n} \ln(1 + \alpha q_j). \tag{10}$$

The following lemma is a stronger version due to de Ghellinck and Vial (1986) of a result of Karmarkar (1984).

Lemma 3.3. *Let* $\alpha = (1 + \|q\|_\infty)^{-1}$. *Then* $-\Delta f \geq \|q\| - \ln(1 + \|q\|)$.

Proof. For any $\lambda > -1$ one has

$$\ln(1 + \lambda) = \lambda - \sum_{k=2}^{\infty} (-1)^k \frac{\lambda^k}{k} \geq \lambda - \sum_{k=2}^{\infty} \frac{|\lambda|^k}{k}.$$

Since $\alpha(1 + \|q\|_\infty) = 1$, $\alpha q_j > -1$, $j = 1, \ldots, n$. So, replacing λ by αq_j in the inequality and summing over j, we obtain

$$\sum_{j=1}^{n} \ln(1 + \alpha q_j) \geq \alpha \sum_{j=1}^{n} q_j - \sum_{j=1}^{n} \sum_{k=2}^{\infty} \alpha^k \frac{|q_j|^k}{k}. \tag{11}$$

Since

$$|q_j| / \|q\|_\infty \leq 1,$$

one has, for $k \geq 2$,

$$|q_j|^k / \|q\|_\infty^k \leq q_j^2 / \|q\|_\infty^2.$$

Using this inequality in (11) and interchanging summations, we obtain

$$\sum_{j=1}^{n} \ln(1 + \alpha q_j) \geq \alpha e^T q - \frac{\|q\|^2}{\|q\|_\infty^2} \sum_{k=2}^{\infty} \alpha^k \frac{\|q\|_\infty^k}{k}$$

$$\geq \alpha e^T q + \frac{\|q\|^2}{\|q\|_\infty^2} \left[\alpha \|q\|_\infty - \sum_{k=1}^{\infty} \alpha^k \frac{\|q\|_\infty^k}{k} \right].$$

In view of (10),

$$-\Delta f \geq \alpha \left(e - \frac{Xc}{\mu} \right)^T q + \frac{\|q\|^2}{\|q\|_\infty^2} [\alpha \|q\|_\infty + \ln(1 - \alpha \|q\|_\infty)].$$

Since $q = -P_{N(AX)}(Xc/\mu - e)$, one has $(e - Xc/\mu)^T q = \|q\|^2$. Replacing α by its value yields

$$-\Delta f \geq \frac{\|q\|^2}{\|q\|_\infty^2} [\|q\|_\infty - \ln(1 + \|q\|_\infty)]. \tag{12}$$

One can check that the function $(\lambda - \ln(1 + \lambda))/\lambda^2$ is decreasing for $\lambda \ge 0$. Hence we can replace $\|q\|_\infty$ by $\|q\|$ in (12). This proves the lemma. $\square$

Lemma 3.4. *The algorithm stops after K outer iterations, where K is the smallest integer such that $K \ge t + \ln \mu_0$.*

Proof. Let $\{\mu_k\}$, $k = 1, \ldots, K$, be the sequence of values of μ at the successive outer iterations. Clearly $\mu_k = 2^{-k} \mu_0$. The algorithm stops after K outer iterations when $2^{-K} \mu_0 < 2^{-t}$. This implies the inequality in the lemma. $\square$

In order to guarantee that the interior solution at which the algorithm stops can be used to compute a basic feasible solution in polynomial time, it suffices to take $t = O(L)$, according to a standard perturbation lemma. Thus it follows that the algorithm requires $O(L)$ iterations when used to find an exact solution of the problem (1).

Theorem 3.1. *The Long Step Algorithm stops after at most*

$$4[(t + \ln \mu_0)(n + \sqrt{n}) + 1 + 2nL)]$$

inner iterations. The last generated point, when denoted as x, satisfies

$$c^T x - z^* \le 2^{-t}(n + \sqrt{n}).$$

Proof. Let us denote by x^k the iterate at the end of the kth outer step. Then, due to Lemma 3.2, with $\theta = \frac{1}{2}$,

$$f(x^k, \mu_k) \le n + \sqrt{n} + f(x^k, \mu_{k-1}).$$

From Lemma 3.3 we know that during each inner iteration the decrease Δf in the potential function satisfies

$$-\Delta f \ge \|q\| - \ln(1 + \|q\|).$$

Since the right-hand side expression is an increasing function of $\|q\|$, and since during each inner iteration $\|q\| \ge 1$ holds, we find $-\Delta f \ge 1 - \ln 2 > \frac{1}{4}$. So we may write

$$f(x^k, \mu_k) \le n + \sqrt{n} + f(x^{k-1}, \mu_{k-1}) - \tfrac{1}{4} p_k,$$

where p_k denotes the number of inner iterations in the kth outer iteration. Hence it follows that

$$f(x^k, \mu_k) \le k(n + \sqrt{n}) + f(x^0, \mu_0) - \tfrac{1}{4} \sum_{j=1}^{k} p_j.$$

Thus we obtain

$$\tfrac{1}{4} \sum_{j=1}^{K} p_j \le K(n+\sqrt{n}) + f(x^0, \mu_0) - f(x^K, \mu_K).$$

So, denoting the total number of inner iterations by N, we have

$$\tfrac{1}{4} N \le K(n+\sqrt{n}) + f(x^0, \mu_0) - f(x^K, \mu_K).$$

Now observe that due to the definition of μ_0, and our assumption on x_0,

$$f(x^0, \mu_0) = 1 - \sum_{j=1}^{n} \ln x_j^0 \le 1 + nL.$$

Further, since x^K is feasible to (1), it can be written as a convex combination of basic feasible solutions. The coordinates x_j of each basic feasible solution satisfy $x_j \le 2^L, j = 1, \ldots, n$. Therefore

$$\sum_{j=1}^{n} \ln x_j^K \le nL.$$

So, $c^T x^K - z^*$ being positive, we have

$$-f(x^K, \mu_K) = \sum_{j=1}^{n} \ln x_j^K - \frac{c^T x^K - z^*}{\mu_K} \le nL.$$

Substitution of the last estimates in the inequality for N gives

$$N \le 4[K(n+\sqrt{n}) + 1 + 2nL)].$$

Finally, using the upper bound for the number K of outer iterations, as given by Lemma 3.4, the first part of the theorem follows. The second part is immediate from Lemma 3.1. $\square$

Remark. If we reduce μ in each iteration with a factor θ, $0 < \theta < 1$, instead of the factor $\tfrac{1}{2}$, then in the last inequality of the above proof the term $K(n+\sqrt{n})$ has to be multiplied with $(1-\theta)/\theta$.

As observed earlier, for the exact solution of the problem our algorithm requires $O(L)$ outer iterations, due to $K = O(L)$. So the proof of the last theorem makes clear that the total number of inner iterations is $O(nL)$.

References

Dikin, I.I. (1967) 'Iterative solution of problems of linear and quadratic programming', *Doklady Akademiia Nauk SSSR*, 174:747-748. [English translation: *Soviet Mathematics Doklady*, 8:674-675.]

Ghellinck, G. de and J.-Ph. Vial (1986) 'A polynomial Newton method for linear programming', *Algorithmica*, 1:425-453.

Gill, P.E., W. Murray, M.A. Saunders, J.A. Tomlin and M.H. Wright (1986) 'On projected Newton barrier methods for linear programming and an equivalence to Karmarkar's projective method', *Mathematical Programming*, 36:183-209.

Goldfarb, D. and S. Liu (1988) 'An $O(n^3 L)$ primal interior point algorithm for convex quadratic programming', manuscript, Department of Industrial Engineering and Operations Research, Columbia University, New York.

Gonzaga, C. (1989a) 'An algorithm for solving linear programming in $O(n^3 L)$ operations', in: N. Megiddo, ed., *Progress in Mathematical Programming*. New York: Springer, pp. 1-28.

Gonzaga, C. (1989b) 'Large-step path-following algorithms for linear programming', paper presented at the CORS/TIMS/ORSA meeting in Vancouver, May 8-10, 1989.

Karmarkar, N. (1984) 'A new polynomial time algorithm for linear programming', *Combinatorica*, 4:373-395.

Renegar, J. (1988) 'A polynomial-time algorithm based on Newton's method for linear programming', *Mathematical Programming*, 40:59-93.

Roos, C. and J.-Ph. Vial (1988) 'A polynomial method of approximate centers for linear programming', Report 88-68, Faculty of Technical Mathematics and Informatics, Technische Universiteit Delft, The Netherlands; to appear in: *Mathematical Programming*.

Vial, J.-Ph. (1989) 'A unified approach to projective algorithms for linear programming', to appear in: *The Proceedings of the 5th French-German Conference on Optimization held at Varetz, France (October 1988)*.

Chapter 21

FORMULATIONS AND BOUNDS FOR THE STOCHASTIC CAPACITATED VEHICLE ROUTING PROBLEM WITH UNCERTAIN SUPPLIES

Gilbert LAPORTE

Ecole des Hautes Etudes Commerciales de Montréal, Montréal, Que., Canada

François LOUVEAUX

Facultés Universitaires Notre-Dame de la Paix, Namur, Belgium

1. Introduction

The classical *vehicle routing problem* (VRP) consists of optimally designing vehicle routes from a depot to a set of cities in such a way that

    (i) all vehicles start and end their journey at the depot;

    (ii) all cities are served once by exactly one vehicle but a vehicle route may include several cities;

    (iii) some side constraints on the routes are satisfied;

    (iv) the sum of vehicle utilization costs and of routing costs is minimized.

Capacity constraints are the most widely used side constraints. They can be defined differently according to whether vehicles make collections or deliveries (or both in some problems). In order to provide a simpler interpretation for the models developed in this paper, we express the capacity constraints in terms of *collections*. Each city has a non-negative

The authors are grateful to the Canadian Natural Sciences and Engineering Research Council (grant A4747) for its financial support. Thanks are also due to Drs. Cock Bastian from Erasmus University, Rotterdam and to René Séguin from the University of Montréal for their valuable comments.

Economic Decision-Making: Games, Econometrics and Optimisation
Edited by J.J. Gabszewicz, J.-F. Richard and L.A. Wolsey
© *Elsevier Science Publishers B.V.*, 1990

indivisible *supply* and all vehicles have the same capacity. Each city must be served by one vehicle whose capacity can never be exceeded. There exists an extensive literature on this and several other VRP variants. Recent comprehensive surveys can be found in Bodin et al. (1983), Christofides (1985) and Laporte and Nobert (1987). Several meaningful *stochastic models* can be constructed for VRPs. In such models a number of decisions must be taken without full information on the values taken by some data (e.g., supplies, travel costs, etc.). These decisions are called *first stage decisions*. At the beginning of the second stage, full information becomes available. It is then possible to take some corrective or *recourse* action if necessary. Such action generates extra costs which must be taken into account in the first stage. Surveys on stochastic programming include those of Kall (1982) and Wets (1983). Due to the inherent difficulty of solving stochastic programs with integer recourse, no exact algorithm can reasonably be designed for this class of problems. Approximate algorithms for the stochastic VRP have been provided by Tillman (1969), and Golden and Stewart (1978) in the case of a Poisson supply distribution and by Golden and Yee (1979) in the case of more general distributions. Stewart and Golden (1983) later extended and generalized this work. Dror and Trudeau (1986) studied the expected cost of a route and provided a new approximate algorithm. Other types of stochastic VRPs not directly related to this study have been treated by a variety of authors. Leipälä (1978) considered problems in which inter-city travelling costs are non-deterministic while Jaillet (1985) solved travelling salesman problems (TSPs), i.e., one-vehicle uncapacitated VRPs, in which cities are visited with a given probability. In this paper, we study the following stochastic VRP recourse model. The first stage or long term decisions are the design of *planned* vehicles routes. When collections actually take place (the second stage level of decisions), a *failure* occurs if the actual supply of a route exceeds the vehicle capacity. In this case, at some point(s) on the route, a *break* takes place: the vehicle must return to the depot and empty its load before resuming its journey. When no prior information on supplies exists, breaks and failures coincide. The model is also applicable when such an information is available: it is then possible to plan the breaks so as to minimize their costs. The range of recourse actions is clearly wider in this situation, and we will provide a model with such an extended recourse action. These formulations are given in Section 2. Given the intractability of the general recourse model, we then study related easier problems whose optimal solutions provide bounds on the optimal solution of the general model. These bounds are described in Section 3.

2. Formulations

2.1. Recourse models

The classical formulation of a recourse model is:

(RM)

$$\min z(x) = f(x) + Q(x)$$

subject to $\quad x \in X$

where $Q(x) = E_\xi Q(x, \xi(\omega))$ is the mathematical expectation of some recourse function, X some deterministic constraint set on the first-stage decision vector x and $f(x)$ is some known function of x. Any constraint on the recourse (or second-stage action) is implicitly defined in $Q(x, \xi(\omega))$. ξ is a random vector on some probability space (Ω, Ξ, P). In this paper, we consider a stochastic VRP, in which the first-stage decisions correspond to the choice of planned routes and the second-stage decisions to corrective action in case of failure. Note that the choice of having the tours planned in advance is obviously justified whenever supplies become known only when the vehicle visit actually takes place. It is our belief that in several cases it is also appropriate even if supplies are known at the beginning of the planning period. It is indeed very often desired that drivers should always be assigned the same tour on a routine basis, so that the planned tour is modified only when failure occurs.

2.2. Notation and basic assumptions

Let $N = \{1, \ldots, n\}$ be the set of all cities, and $N_0 = \{0\} \cup N$ where 0 corresponds to the depot. Let c be the travel cost vector (c_{ij}) where $i, j \in N_0$ and $i \neq j$. It is assumed throughout the paper that the triangle inequality is satisfied. Let ξ_i be the non-negative supply of city $i \in N$, $\xi = (\xi_1, \ldots, \xi_n)$ and D, the vehicle capacity. The ξ_i's are independent random variables of finite mean μ_i and finite variance σ_i^2. It is assumed that $P(\xi_i \neq 0) > 0$ and $P(\xi_i > D) = 0$ for all $i \in N$ and that for any non-empty subset S of N, the probability distribution of $\sum_{i \in S} \xi_i$ can be computed or approximated.

2.3. Stochastic VRP with early information

In the two-stage formulation of the stochastic VRP with early information, it is assumed that the supplies are known before the vehicles start their journey, for instance at the beginning of each day. This creates flexibility in the way a possible failure is dealt with, as will be described in the recourse function. Define

$$x_{ij} = \begin{cases} 1 & \text{if arc } (i,j) \text{ is used in the optimal solution,} \\ 0 & \text{otherwise,} \end{cases} \quad (i,j \in N_0, i \neq j).$$

Let x denote the vector (x_{ij}) where $i,j \in N_0$ and $i \neq j$. In the sequel, all summations are assumed to run over indices i or j such that $i \neq j$. Let m be the number of vehicles with unit cost h. The stochastic VRP is defined as follows.

(SVRP)

$$\min_{x,m} z(x) = cx + hm + Q(x) \tag{1}$$

subject to

$$\underline{m} \leq m \leq \bar{m}, \tag{2}$$

$$\sum_{i \in N} x_{i0} = \sum_{j \in N} x_{0j} = m, \tag{3}$$

$$\sum_{i \in N_0} x_{ij} = 1 \quad (j \in N), \tag{4}$$

$$\sum_{j \in N_0} x_{ij} = 1 \quad (i \in N), \tag{5}$$

$$\sum_{i \in S} \sum_{j \notin S} x_{ij} \geq 1 \quad (S \subseteq N, |S| \geq 2), \tag{6}$$

$$x_{ij} \in \{0, 1\} \quad (i,j \in N_0), \tag{7}$$

where $Q(x)$ is the recourse function defined below by (RF1) or (RF2). The first-stage deterministic constraints specify that the number of vehicles lies between given bounds (2), that m vehicles enter and leave the depot (3), and that every city is entered (4) and left (5) exactly once. Constraints (6) are the classical TSP connectivity constraints (Dantzig, Fulkerson and Johnson, 1954): they prohibit the formation of illegal subtours, i.e., of routes disconnected from the depot. Consider a planned vehicle route as the ordered sequence $L = (i_0, i_1, \ldots, i_T, i_0)$ where $i_0 = 0$, $i_t \in N$ for $t = 1, \ldots, T$ and all i_t's are different. To route L, corresponds a vector $x_L = (x_{i_t, i_{t+1}})$ having all its components equal to 1 and a travel cost vector $c_L = (c_{i_t, i_{t+1}})$, where $t = 0, \ldots, T$ and $i_{T+1} = i_0$. When the information on the supplies of L becomes available, it is then known whether the vehicle capacity is sufficient or not. In the latter case, a failure occurs on the route. At some point, the vehicle will have to return to the depot after loading at city i, empty its load and resume its collections starting at city j. Such an action defines a break on arc (i, j). To describe the recourse problem, let

z_{ij}^ξ = the commodity flow on arc (i, j) in state of the world ξ $(i, j \in N_0, i \neq j)$,

$$w_{ij}^\xi = \begin{cases} 1 & \text{if a break occurs on arc } (i, j) \text{ in state of the world } \xi, \\ 0 & \text{otherwise,} \end{cases}$$

$(i, j \in N, i \neq j)$.

Let z^ξ and w^ξ denote the vectors (z_{ij}^ξ) and (w_{ij}^ξ) respectively. The recourse problem is then defined by

(RF1)

$$Q(x) = E_\xi Q(x, \xi) \tag{8}$$

where

$$Q(x, \xi) = \min \sum_{i \in N} \sum_{j \in N} (c_{i0} + c_{0j} - c_{ij}) w_{ij}^\xi, \tag{9}$$

subject to

$$z_{ij}^\xi \leq D x_{ij} \quad (i, j \in N_0, \xi \in \Xi), \tag{10}$$

$$w_{ij}^\xi \leq x_{ij} \quad (i, j \in N, \xi \in \Xi), \tag{11}$$

$$\sum_{j \in N_0} z_{ij}^\xi - \sum_{j \in N_0} z_{ji}^\xi \geq \xi_i - 2D \sum_{j \in N} w_{ij}^\xi \quad (i \in N, \xi \in \Xi), \tag{12}$$

$$\sum_{j \in N_0} z_{ij}^\xi - \sum_{j \in N_0} z_{ji}^\xi \leq \xi_i \left(1 - \sum_{j \in N} w_{ij}^\xi\right) \quad (i \in N, \xi \in \Xi), \tag{13}$$

$$\sum_{j \in N_0} z_{ij}^\xi \leq (\xi_i + D) \left(1 - \sum_{j \in N} w_{ij}^\xi\right) \quad (i \in N, \xi \in \Xi), \tag{14}$$

$$\sum_{j \in N} z_{0j}^\xi = 0 \quad (\xi \in \Xi), \tag{15}$$

$$z^\xi \geq 0, \quad 0 \leq w^\xi \leq 1 \text{ and integer} \quad (\xi \in \Xi). \tag{16}$$

This model is inspired by the commodity flow formulation introduced by Gavish and Graves (1982) for the deterministic VRP. The new variables w_{ij}^ξ and constraints (11)–(14) relate to the description of the additional trips in case of failure. Constraints (10) require that flows are non-zero only on planned routes and are at most equal to the vehicle capacity. Constraints (11) specify that a break on arc (i, j) can only occur if arc (i, j) belongs to a planned route. If no breaks occurs at i (which means $w_{ij}^{\xi} = 0$ for all $j \in N$, $\xi \in \Xi$ given), then by (12) and (13), the flow leaving i is exactly equal to the flow entering i plus the amount collected at i. In this case, (14) is clearly satisfied. By (10), this situation can only occur if the flow leaving i is less than the vehicle capacity. If a break occurs on arc (i, j) for a given ξ, w_{ij}^{ξ} is equal to 1. Then, (12) and (13) are redundant and, by (10), (14) and (15), the flow arriving at j is zero. This corresponds to unloading the vehicle at the depot. Constraints (10)–(13), guarantee that, on a given route and for a given ξ, a break takes place on arc (i, j) whenever a failure occurs at city i. However, since breaks are planned optimally, they do not necessarily coincide with failures. There can in fact be more breaks than failures. Note also that, when breaks can take place independently of failures, constraints (13)–(15) can be dropped by adding an extra term to the objective function:

$$\varepsilon \sum_{i \in N} \sum_{j \in N_0} z_{ij}^{\xi}$$

with $\varepsilon > 0$ sufficiently small. In such a case, it would never pay to increase any z_{ij}^{ξ} above the level specified by (12). The value of ε can be chosen, for example, as the marginal fuel cost for extra load. On the other hand, if a break occurs on arc (i, j) only if a failure also occurs, then in addition to (10)–(16), an extra constraint of the following form is required:

$$D \sum_{j \in N} w_{ij}^{\xi} \leq \xi_i + \sum_{j \in N_0} z_{ij}^{\xi} \quad (i \in N_0, \xi \in \Xi).$$

2.4. Stochastic VRP with late information

In this formulation of the stochastic VRP, it is assumed that supplies become known only when the vehicle arrives at the cities. Then, if the vehicle is unable to load the supply of city i, it returns to the depot, empties its load, and resumes its tour from city i. In this case, a failure and a break occur simultaneously at city i and the penalty corresponds to a return trip to the depot. As compared with the previous model defined by (1)–(16), only (RF1) is modified. We introduce the new variables w_i^{ξ} where

$$w_i^{\xi} = \begin{cases} 1 & \text{if a return trip to the depot occurs at } i \text{ in state of the world } \xi, \\ 0 & \text{otherwise.} \end{cases}$$

Variables w_{ij}^{ξ}, defined in the previous paragraph, are maintained. They take care of the following situation: when, after loading at city i, the total load is exactly equal to the vehicle capacity D, then after unloading at the depot, the vehicle can proceed to city j, next on its planned tour. Such an event can occur with non-zero probability in problems having discrete supply distributions. The recourse model is then defined by

(RF2)

$$Q(x) = E_\xi Q(x, \xi) \tag{8}$$

and

$$Q(x, \xi) = \min \sum_{i \in N} (c_{i0} + c_{0i}) w_i^\xi + \sum_{i \in N} \sum_{j \in N} (c_{i0} + c_{0j} - c_{ij}) w_{ij}^\xi \tag{17}$$

subject to

$$z_{ij}^\xi \le D x_{ij} \quad (i, j \in N, \xi \in \Xi), \tag{18}$$

$$\sum_{j \in N_0} z_{ij}^\xi - \sum_{j \in N} z_{ji}^\xi \ge \xi_i - D w_i^\xi - 2D \sum_{j \in N} w_{ij}^\xi \quad (i \in N, \xi \in \Xi), \tag{19}$$

$$\sum_{j \in N_0} z_{ij}^\xi - \sum_{j \in N_0} z_{ji}^\xi \le \xi_i \left(1 - \sum_{j \in N} w_{ij}^\xi \right) \quad (i \in N, \xi \in \Xi), \tag{20}$$

$$\sum_{j \in N_0} z_{ij}^\xi \ge \xi_i \left(1 - \sum_{j \in N} w_{ij}^\xi \right) - D(1 - w_i^\xi) \quad (i \in N, \xi \in \Xi), \tag{21}$$

$$\sum_{j \in N_0} z_{ij}^\xi \le \xi_i \left(1 - \sum_{j \in N} w_{ij}^\xi \right) + D(1 - w_i^\xi) - D \sum_{j \in N} w_{ij}^\xi \quad (i \in N, \xi \in \Xi), \tag{22}$$

$$D\left(w_i^\xi + \sum_{j \in N} w_{ij}^\xi \right) \le \xi_i + \sum_{j \in N_0} z_{ji}^\xi \quad (i \in N, \xi \in \Xi), \tag{23}$$

$$\xi_i + \sum_{j \in N_0} z_{ji}^\xi \le D(1 + w_i^\xi) \quad (i \in N, \xi \in \Xi), \tag{24}$$

$$w_i^\xi + \sum_{j \in N} w_{ij}^\xi \le 1 \quad (i \in N, \xi \in \Xi), \tag{25}$$

$$w_{ij}^\xi \le x_{ij} \quad (i, j \in N, \xi \in \Xi), \tag{26}$$

$$\sum_{j \in N} z_{0j}^\xi = 0 \quad (\xi \in \Xi), \tag{27}$$

$$z^\xi \ge 0, \quad 0 \le w^\xi \le 1 \text{ and integer} \quad (\xi \in \Xi). \tag{28}$$

The interpretation of (RF2) is as follows: when after collection at city i, the vehicle load is strictly smaller than the vehicle capacity, by (23) variables w_i^ξ and w_{ij}^ξ are zero for all $j \in N$. Then, by (19) and (20), the flow leaving i is equal to the flow entering i plus the amount collected at i. The remaining constraints (18), (21)-(22), (24)-(28) are all satisfied. If it is not possible to load city i's supply, (i.e., if the incoming flow plus city i's supply strictly exceed the vehicle capacity), then by (24), $w_i^\xi = 1$ and by (25), $w_{ij}^\xi = 0$ for all $j \in N$. By (21) and (22), the vehicle load after the return trip is equal to ξ_i. Here, (18)-(20), (23) and (26)-(27) are automatically satisfied. Finally, if after collection at i the vehicle load coincides with its capacity, there are three ways in which (23)-(25) can theoretically be satisfied: firstly by $w_i^\xi = 0$ and $\sum_j w_{ij}^\xi = 0$, secondly by $w_i^\xi = 1$ and $\sum_j w_{ij}^\xi = 0$ and thirdly by $w_i^\xi = 0$ and $\sum_j w_{ij}^\xi = 1$. Note, however, that since c satisfies the triangle inequality, the first two cases will not occur unless 0, i and j are collinear. Note that, under a very mild assumption, formulation RF2 is such that illegal subtours cannot be generated.

Proposition 1. *Let* (SVRP-RF2) *be the relaxation of* (SVRP-RF2) *obtained by removing constraints* (6). *Assume that for any subset S of cities, there exists $\xi \in \Xi$ such that $P(\sum_{j \in S} \xi \neq D) > 0$. Then, no solution to* (SVRP-RF2) *contains illegal subtours.*

Proof. Let (x, m) and (z^ξ, w^ξ) for all $\xi \in \Xi$ be a solution to (SVRP-RF2). Corresponding to the x_{ij}'s equal to 1 is a set of tours of the form $L = (i_0, i_1, \ldots, i_T = i_0)$ with no component other than i_0 being repeated. Let $S = \{i_1, \ldots, i_T\}$. Suppose there exists a tour disconnected from the depot. By assumption, $P(\xi_i \neq 0) > 0$ for all $i \in N$; hence $P(\sum_{j \in S} \xi_j \neq 0) > 0$. Assume first that $P(0 < \sum_{j \in S} \xi_j \leq D) > 0$. Then, for those values of ξ, no failure occurs on the tour and by (23) and (24), optimal recourse decisions will be such that $w_j^\xi = 0$ for all $j \in S$ and $w_{ij}^\xi = 0$ for all $i, j \in S$. The argument by Gavish and Graves (1982) applies: summing up constraints (19) over all $j \in S$ yields $0 \geq \sum_{j \in S} \xi_j$, which is a contradiction. If $P(0 < \sum_{j \in S} \xi_j \leq D) = 0$, then $P(\sum_{j \in S} \xi_j > D) > 0$. Assume there are values of ξ such that one failure occurs at city k (k may in fact depend on ξ). By (23) and (24), any optimal solution to the recourse problem will be such that $w_k^\xi = 1$, $w_{kj}^\xi = 0$ and $w_j^\xi = 0$ ($j \in S, j \neq k$). Summing up constraints (21) for $i = k$ and constraints (19) for all $j \in S$, $j \neq k$ yields

$$z_{i_{t-1} i_t}^\xi = \sum_{i \in N_0} z_{ik}^\xi \geq \sum_{j \in S} \xi_j > D$$

which now contradicts constraint (18) applied to arc (i_{t-1}, i_t) and proves the proposition if there are values of ξ with one failure on that tour. A similar contradiction can be derived if the only non-zero values of $\sum_{j \in S} \xi_j$ correspond to tours with two failures, and so on. By assumption, for the given set S, these are the only possible breaks and failures for at least one ξ, since there exists $\xi \in \Xi$ having a non-zero probability such that the cumulative supply does not coincide with the vehicle capacity. $\square$

Note that the above assumption is very weak. For example, it is always satisfied if ξ is a continuous random variable, or if D is non-integer and all supplies are integers. Solving (SVRP) defined by (RF1) or (RF2) in a reasonable amount of computing time seems unrealistic. Firstly, because finding the recourse function $Q(x)$ represents a considerable task which can only be undertaken in cases where Ξ has a finite support of small cardinality. Secondly (and mainly), because $Q(x, \xi)$, the recourse function for a given ξ, is the optimal value of a mixed integer program which does not seem to possess any desirable analytical property. We therefore propose to solve two problems that directly relate to the stochastic VRP and provide bounds on its optimal value.

3. Bounds on the optimal solution of the stochastic VRP

Consider the stochastic VRP problem and its optimal value z^*:

(SVRP)

$$z^* = \min_{x,m}\{z(x) = cx + hm + Q(x)\} \tag{1}$$

subject to (3)–(7) and

$$\underline{m} \le m \le \bar{m} \tag{2}$$

where $Q(x)$ is defined by either (RF1) or (RF2).

3.1. Lower bound

To obtain a lower bound on z^*, we consider separately a lower bound on the optimal value v^* of the routing problem "minimize $v = cx$, subject to (2)–(7)", and on the value of the expected penalty $Q(x)$. Let v_m^* be the optimal objective value of $(m\text{-VRP})$, i.e., (VRP) defined with $h = 0$ and a fixed value of m, and by replacing every component ξ_i of the supply vector by the minimum value $\underline{\xi}_i$ it can take

$(m\text{-VRP})$

$$v_m^* = \min_x \{cx\}$$

subject to (3)–(5), (7) and

$$\sum_{i \in S} \sum_{j \notin S} x_{ij} \ge \max\left\{\left\lceil \sum_{i \in S} \underline{\xi}_i \Big/ D \right\rceil; 1\right\} \quad (S \subseteq N, |S| \ge 2) \tag{29}$$

where $\lceil x \rceil$ denotes the smallest integer greater than or equal to x.

Constraints (29) are the TSP connectivity constraints extended to the VRP (Laporte and Nobert, 1987). Their right-hand side represents a lower bound on the number of vehicles required to serve S and hence, on the number of trips from S to $N_0 - S$. In the model with late information, a lower bound Q_m on the recourse function can be obtained as follows. Define the minimal number of failures for a given ξ and a given m as

$$f_m(\xi) = \max \left\{ \left\lceil \sum_{i \in N} \xi_i \Big/ D \right\rceil - m; 0 \right\}. \qquad (30)$$

A lower bound $Q_m(\xi)$ on the penalty for a given ξ is then computed as the sum of the $f_m(\xi)$ least cost return trips. The required lower bound is the expectation over ξ:

$$Q_m = E_\xi Q_m(\xi). \qquad (31)$$

In the model with early information, $Q_m(\xi)$ is easily determined as the sum of the $f_m(\xi)$ least cost values of $c_{i0} + c_{0j} - c_{ij}$ where $i \neq j$ and all pairs (i, j) have different origins and different destinations.

Proposition 2. *Let* $b_1 = \min_{\underline{m} \leq m \leq \bar{m}} \{v_m^* + hm + Q_m\}$. *Then* b_1 *is a lower bound on* z^*, *the optimal solution value of* (SVRP).

Proof.

$$z^* = \min_{x,m} \{cx + hm + Q(x)\}$$

$$= \min_m \left[hm + \min_x \{cx + Q(x)\} \right]$$

$$\geq \min_m \left[hm + \min_x \{cx\} + \min_x Q(x) \right]$$

$$\geq \min_m [hm + v_m^* + Q_m] = b_1. \qquad \square$$

Determining b_1 unfortunately requires the solution of $(\bar{m} - \underline{m} + 1)$ deterministic VRPs with the value of m successively fixed at $\underline{m}, \dots, \bar{m}$. A simpler bound is provided by:

Proposition 3. *Let* $b_2 = v^* + \min_{\underline{m} \leq m \leq \bar{m}} \{hm + Q_m\}$. *Then* $b_2 \leq b_1 \leq z^*$.

Proof.

$$z^* \geq b_1 = \min_{\underline{m} \leq m \leq \bar{m}} \{v_m^* + hm + Q_m\}$$

$$\geq \min_{\underline{m} \leq m \leq \bar{m}} \{v_m^*\} + \min_{\underline{m} \leq m \leq \bar{m}} \{hm + Q_m\}$$

$$= v^* + \min_{\underline{m} \leq m \leq \bar{m}} \{hm + Q_m\} = b_2. \qquad \square$$

3.2. Upper bound

Define the bounded penalty model as:

(BPM)

$$\min_{x,m} z_2(x, m, \beta) = cx + hm \tag{32}$$

subject to (2)-(7) and

$$Q_L(x) \leq \beta c_L x_L \quad (\beta > 0, \text{ for all } L) \tag{33}$$

where c_L, x_L have already been defined in Section 2.3, $Q_L(x)$ is the expected penalty due to failure on route L and β a positive parameter. The value of $Q_L(x)$ is obtained by solving the recourse problem defined by (RF1) or (RF2) on the components of L. The computation of an upper bound on $Q_L(x)$ is also provided in Laporte, Louveaux and Mercure (1989). In addition, this reference contains the description of an exact algorithm for the late information bounded penalty model.

Proposition 4. *Let* (x_2^*, m_2^*) *be a feasible and optimal solution to* (BPM) *and let* $z_2^*(\beta) = z_2(x_2^*, m_2^*, \beta)$ *be the associated objective value. Then* $b_3 = \min_{\beta > 0} \{(1 + \beta) z_2^*(\beta) - \beta h m_2^*\}$ *is an upper bound on* z^*, *the optimal solution value of* (SVRP).

Proof. Let (x_2^*, m_2^*) be an optimal solution to (BPM). By (6), this solution does not contain any illegal subtour. Moreover, every city is visited once. Hence, (x_2^*, m_2^*) is a feasible first-stage solution to (SVRP). Therefore,

$$z^* \leq z(x_2^*, m_2^*) = cx_2^* + hm_2^* + Q(x_2^*) = z_2^*(\beta) + Q(x_2^*).$$

The solution vector (x_2^*) can be rewritten as $(x_{2,1}^*; \ldots; x_{2,m_2^*}^*)$ where $x_{2,L}^*$ is the vector associated with route L. By interchanging expectations and summations over L, we obtain

$$Q(x_2^*) = E_\xi Q(x_2^*, \xi) = E_\xi \sum_{L=1}^{m_2^*} Q_L(x_{2,L}^*, \xi)$$

$$= \sum_{L=1}^{m_2^*} E_\xi Q_L(x_{2,L}^*, \xi) = \sum_{L=1}^{m_2^*} Q_L(x_{2,L}^*).$$

By (33), it follows that

$$Q(x_2^*) \le \sum_{L=1}^{m_2^*} \beta c_L x_{2,L}^* = \beta c x_2^* = \beta(z_2^*(\beta) - h m_2^*).$$

Therefore,

$$z^* \le (1 + \beta) z_2^*(\beta) - \beta h m_2^*.$$

Since this relation holds for all positive values of β, the conclusion follows. □

4. Conclusion

The vehicle routing problem with uncertain supplies occurs in a variety of practical situations. Recourse models for this problem can be defined but are generally considered to be computationally intractable. In this paper, we have developed such a model, with two variants corresponding to the time at which information on random supplies becomes available. We then developed lower and upper bounds for the problem, based on the solution of related simpler VRPs. While these results do not immediately lend themselves to the development of exact algorithms for the problem, they shed some light on its structure and could serve as the basis for future research.

References

Bodin, L.D., B.L. Golden, A. Assad and M. Ball (1983) 'Routing and scheduling of vehicles and crews. The state of the art', *Computers and Operations Research*, 10:69-211.

Christofides, N. (1985) 'Vehicle routing', in: E.L. Lawler, J.K. Lenstra, A.H.G. Rinnooy Kan and D.B. Shmoys, eds., *The Traveling Salesman Problem, A Guided Tour of Combinatorial Optimization*. Chichester: Wiley, pp. 431-448.

Dantzig, G.B., R. Fulkerson and S.M. Johnson (1954) 'Solution of a large-scale traveling salesman problem', *Operations Research*, 2:393-410.

Dror, M. and P. Trudeau (1986) 'Stochastic vehicle routing with modified savings algorithm', *European Journal of Operational Research*, 23:228-235.

Gavish, B. and S.C. Graves (1982) 'Scheduling and Routing in Transportation and Distribution Systems: Formulations and New Relaxations', Working Paper, Graduate School of Management, University of Rochester, Rochester, NY.

Golden, B.L. and W.R. Stewart (1978) 'Vehicle routing with probabilistic demands', in: D. Hogben and D. Fife, eds., *Computer Science and Statistics: Tenth Annual Symposium on the Interface, NBS Special Publication 503*, pp. 252-259.

Golden, B.L. and J. Yee (1979) 'A framework for probabilistic vehicle routing', *AIIE Transactions*, 11:109-112.

Jaillet, P. (1985) 'Probabilistic Traveling Salesman Problems', Ph.D. Thesis, Massachusetts Institute of Technology, Cambridge, MA.

Kall, P. (1982) 'Stochastic programming', *European Journal of Operational Research*, 10:125-130.

Laporte, G., F. Louveaux and H. Mercure (1989) 'Models and exact solutions for a class of stochastic location-routing problems', *European Journal of Operational Research*, 39:71-78.

Laporte, G. and Y. Nobert (1987) 'Exact algorithms for the vehicle routing problem', in: S. Martello, G. Laporte, M. Minoux and C. Ribeiro, eds., *Surveys in Combinatorial Optimization, Annals of Discrete Mathematics*, 31. Amsterdam: North-Holland, pp. 147-184.

Leipälä, T. (1978) 'On the solutions of stochastic traveling salesman problems', *European Journal of Operational Research*, 2:291-297.

Stewart, W.R. and B.L. Golden (1983) 'Stochastic vehicle routing: A comprehensive approach', *European Journal of Operational Research*, 14:371-385.

Tillman, F. (1969) 'The multiple terminal delivery problem with probabilistic demands', *Transportation Science*, 3:192-204.

Wets, R.J.-B. (1983) 'Stochastic programming: solution techniques and approximation schemes', in: A. Bachem, M. Grötschel and B. Korte, eds., *Mathematical Programming: State-of-the-Art 1982*. Berlin: Springer, pp. 506-603.

Chapter 22

AN ASSIGNMENT PROBLEM WITH SIDE CONSTRAINTS: STRONG CUTTING PLANES AND SEPARATION

Ronny ABOUDI

University of Miami, Miami, FL, USA

George L. NEMHAUSER

Georgia Institute of Technology, Atlanta, GA, USA

Introduction

The subject of this paper is a *constrained assignment problem* which is the classical assignment problem

$$\max \sum_{i \in N} \sum_{j \in N} c_{ij} x_{ij},$$

$$\sum_{j \in N} x_{ij} = 1 \quad \text{for } i \in N = \{1, \ldots, n\}, \tag{1}$$

$$\sum_{i \in N} x_{ij} = 1 \quad \text{for } j \in N, \tag{2}$$

$$x_{ij} = 0 \text{ or } 1 \quad \text{for } i, j \in N, \tag{3}$$

with the additional constraints that variables with indices in specified subsets of $N \times N$ must be equal. In particular, let R_k for $k = 1, \ldots, m \leq \frac{1}{2}n$ be disjoint subsets of $N \times N$ with $|R_k| \geq 2$. The side constraints are if (i, j) and (i', j') are in R_k then $x_{ij} = x_{i'j'}$. When $|R_k| = 2$ for all k, by renaming the

This work was supported in part by the National Science Foundation under Grant Nos. ECS-8540898 and ECS-8719128.

Economic Decision-Making: Games, Econometrics and Optimisation
Edited by J.J. Gabszewicz, J.-F. Richard and L.A. Wolsey
© *Elsevier Science Publishers B.V., 1990*

variables the side constraints can be written as

$$x_{2k-1,2k-1} - x_{2k,2k} = 0 \quad \text{for } k = 1, \ldots, m. \tag{4}$$

We call $\{(2k-1, 2k-1), (2k, 2k)\}$ a *couple* and refer to the problem given by (1)-(4) as the *couple constrained assignment problem* (CCAP).

Our study of CCAP was motivated by the problem of evaluating the classroom capacity of a large university (see Aboudi, 1986). This application is discussed in Section 1.

CCAP is NP-hard (see Aboudi, 1986; Padberg and Sassano, 1984). A general scheme for solving it is by relaxation and branch-and-bound. Here there are the usual tradeoffs between the tightness of the relaxation and the computational effort needed to solve it. Tighter relaxations reduce the size of the enumeration tree. Four possible relaxations are:

(i) Drop the side constraints. The relaxation is an assignment problem and yields an upper bound on the objective value of $B(A)$.

(ii) Form a Lagrangian relaxation by incorporating the side constraints into the objective function. For fixed multipliers, the relaxation is an assignment problem. By solving the Lagrangian dual, we obtain the bound $B(LD) \leq B(A)$.

(iii) Drop the integrality constraints to obtain the linear programming relaxation and the corresponding bound $B(LP)$. Because the constraint matrix of an assignment problem is totally unimodular, $B(LP) = B(LD)$.

(iv) Strengthen the linear programming relaxation by adding additional linear inequalities that are satisfied by all integral feasible solutions. This linear program yields a bound of $B(SLP)$. By definition, $B(SLP) \leq B(LP)$. The additional linear inequalities may be included in the original formulation or added when the linear programming relaxation has a fractional optimal solution or both.

The virtue of strengthening the linear programming relaxation is the stronger bounds. However, the additional work in doing this can be justified only if these valid inequalities are "strong" in the sense that they may be active in a solution to a linear programming relaxation that either gives an optimal solution to the integer program or a bound that is close to the optimal value of the integer program. Thus the inequalities need to define facets or at least nonempty faces of the convex hull of integer solutions. Moreover, because the number of these inequalities may be extremely large, it may be necessary to add them to the linear programming relaxation sequentially. In this case, it is very important to have a fast algorithm for finding strong valid inequalities that are not satisfied by an optimal fractional solution.

Recently, this strong cutting-plane approach has been used successfully to solve several NP-hard problems (see, e.g., Crowder, Johnson and Padberg, 1983; Grötschel and Padberg, 1985; and Nemhauser and Wolsey, 1988, for an exposition of the approach). In some instances enumeration is eliminated altogether. But the important matter is to keep the enumeration from getting out of hand for difficult instances.

Here we investigate this approach for solving the constrained assignment problem. The heart of the research involves deriving strong valid inequalities (Section 2), and solving the separation problem of finding violated inequalities (Section 3). Some computational experience is reported in Section 4 and extensions are mentioned in Section 5.

Since our approach uses the structure provided by the side constraints (4), it cannot handle more general linear side constraints, as has been done, for example by Aggarwal (1985) and Mazzola and Neebe (1986).

1. Evaluating classroom capacity (Aboudi, 1986)

Because of increasing enrollments and the conversion of classrooms to research space, the administration was under pressure to include a large number of new classrooms in its building construction program. But the administration was not convinced that current space was being used efficiently. In fact, it was already clear that if the course-time schedule was modified by shifting enough courses from busy periods (e.g., 11AM) to slack periods (e.g., 8AM), the current space would be adequate. But since a substantial change in the schedule would create another set of administrative and political problems, the administration's first priority was to see if, under the existing time schedule, a more efficient procedure for allocating courses to rooms would suffice.

To model the room assignment problem, it is first necessary to determine a feasible set of rooms for each course and then to estimate a number c_{ij} that represents the utility of assigning course i to room j for each feasible (i, j) pair. The feasibility and utility depend on factors such as estimated enrollment of the course, the seating capacity and special features of the room, and the distance between the pair of buildings containing the classroom and the instructor's office.

Next, a day is divided into a disjoint set of scheduling periods denoted by $t = 1, \ldots, T$. A scheduling period must be small enough so that if two courses do not overlap in time, they do not appear in the same scheduling period. Generally, it suffices to segment a day into half-hour intervals. For each scheduling period there is an assignment problem of courses to rooms, and the problems in consecutive periods are linked by the constraints that a course which meets in consecutive periods must be assigned the same room in each period. These constraints are precisely of the form $x_{ij} = x_{i'j'}$ where i and i' correspond to the same course, and j and j' correspond to the same room in consecutive periods. Additional constraints of this type arise if all meetings of a course, i.e., those on different days, are required to be in the same room. Thus we can think of the course — room assignment problem for the whole day as a CCAP in which for each course there is a row for each period in which it meets, and for each room there are T columns, and if i and i' correspond to the same course in different periods and t and t' correspond to the same room in the above periods then (i, t) and (i', t') must be paired; furthermore rows of the form (i, t) must be paired with columns of the form (j, t).

A simple heuristic for obtaining a feasible solution involves solving T independent assignment problems. The idea is to consider the period t^* with the largest number of courses first. The solution for t^* is then used to fix the room assignments for the courses that meet in t^*. This means that if course i meets in periods $t^* - k_1, \ldots, t^*, \ldots, t^* + k_2$, then in each of these periods it is assigned the same room, namely the room it has been assigned to in period t^*. Next, the remaining assignments are made for the second busiest period, etc.

By using this heuristic, we were able to show that the perceived shortage of classrooms was false. However, had it been necessary to find an optimal or even a provably nearly optimal solution, the heuristic may have failed because all of the periods from 9–12AM appeared to be tightly constrained.

2. Strong valid inequalities

Let $S = \{x \in \mathbb{R}^{n^2} : x \text{ satisfies } (1)-(4)\}$, and let $\text{conv}(S)$ denote the convex hull of the points in S. For $\emptyset \subset I, J \subseteq N$, let

$$x(I, J) = \sum_{i \in I} \sum_{j \in J} x_{ij}.$$

To derive the inequalities, we use a simple and well-known property of solutions to the assignment problem.

Proposition 1. *Let* $\emptyset \subset I, J \subseteq N$ *with* $|I| + |J| = n + k$, $k \geq 1$. *If* x *is a feasible solution to the assignment problem, then* $x(I, J) \geq k$. $\quad\square$

Let

$$K = \{2r - 1: \{2r - 1, 2r\} \subseteq I \cap J, r \le m\}$$

and

$$\tilde{K} = \{2r - 1: \{2r - 1, 2r\} \subseteq (N \backslash I) \cap (N \backslash J), r \le m\}.$$

From Proposition 1, we obtain an upper bound on $\sum_{i \in K \cup \tilde{K}} x_{ii}$ on all feasible assignments that satisfy (4). The essential idea is that if $x(I, J)$ is small, then $x(N \backslash I, N \backslash J)$ must also be small to have assignments in the rows in I and the columns in J. But since $K \subseteq I \cap J$ and $\tilde{K} \subseteq (N \backslash I) \cap (N \backslash J)$, $\sum_{i \in K \cup \tilde{K}} (x_{ii} + x_{i+1,i+1})$ also must be small, and since $x_{ii} = x_{i+1,i+1}$ for $i \in K \cup \tilde{K}$, $\sum_{i \in K \cup \tilde{K}} x_{ii}$ is small as well.

Proposition 2. *Let* $\emptyset \subset I, J \subseteq N$ *with* $|I| + |J| = n - 1$ *and* $|\tilde{K}| \ge 1$. *The inequality*

$$\sum_{i \in K \cup \tilde{K}} x_{ii} - x(I, J) \le 0 \tag{SVI}$$

is valid for conv(S).

Proof. It suffices to show that SVI is satisfied by all $x \in S$. This is obvious for all $x \in S$ with $\sum_{i \in \tilde{K}} x_{ii} = 0$ since if $i \in K$ then $i \in I \cap J$, so that SVI is just the sum of nonnegativity constraints. So suppose $\sum_{i \in \tilde{K}} x_{ii} = p \ge 1$. Delete the $2p$ row constraints and the $2p$ column constraints for $(i, i+1)$ with $i \in \tilde{K}$ and $x_{ii} = 1$. Now we have an $(n - 2p) \times (n - 2p)$ assignment problem with $|I| + |J| = n - 1 = (n - 2p) + 2p - 1$. Hence from Proposition 1, if x satisfies (1)-(3), then $x(I, J) \ge 2p - 1$.

Since $K \subseteq I \cap J$, we have $\sum_{i \in K} (x_{ii} + x_{i+1,i+1}) \le x(I, J)$. Furthermore, since $x_{ii} = x_{i+1,i+1}$ for $i \in K$ and the x_{ii} are integers, we have

$$\sum_{i \in K} x_{ii} \le \lfloor \tfrac{1}{2} x(I, J) \rfloor = x(I, J) - \lceil \tfrac{1}{2} x(I, J) \rceil \le x(I, J) - p$$

or

$$x(I, J) - \sum_{i \in K} x_{ii} \ge p.$$

Thus

$$\sum_{i \in \tilde{K}} x_{ii} - \left(x(I, J) - \sum_{i \in K} x_{ii} \right) \le p - p = 0. \quad \square$$

Note that the number of SVI inequalities is an exponential function of n.

Theorem 3. *Each of the SVI inequalities defines a facet of* conv(S).   □

The proof is given in Aboudi (1986).

If there is only one side constraint ($m = 1$), then the SVI inequalities and nonnegativity are the only additional constraints that are needed.

Theorem 4. *When* $m = 1$, conv(S) $= \{x \in \mathbb{R}^{n^2}\!: x$ *satisfies* (1), (2) *and* (4), $x \geq 0$ *and all of the SVI inequalities*}.   □

The proof is given in Aboudi (1986).

Example 1. Let $n = 7$, $m = 3$ and $I = J = \{5, 6, 7\}$. Then $K = \{5\}$, $\tilde{K} = \{1, 3\}$ and SVI is

$$x_{11} + x_{33} + x_{55} - \sum_{i=5}^{7} \sum_{j=5}^{7} x_{ij} \leq 0.$$

To motivate a more general class of valid inequalities, consider the following example.

Example 2. Let $n = 5$, $m = 2$, and $I = J = \{3, 4\}$. Then $K = \{3\}$, $\tilde{K} = \{1\}$ and we obtain the SVI inequality

$$x_{11} - (x_{34} + x_{43} + x_{44}) \leq 0.$$

However, if $x_{11} = x_{44} = 1$, the side constraints yield $x_{22} = x_{33} = 1$ and then the assignments constraints yield $x_{55} = 1$. Thus x_{55} can replace x_{44} in the above inequality so that

$$x_{11} - (x_{34} + x_{43} + x_{55}) \leq 0$$

is valid. This inequality is not dominated by any SVI inequality nor does it dominate any SVI inequality.

To capture the idea conveyed in Example 2 we introduce generalized SVI inequalities denoted by SVI: t that are based on a family of sets (I_q, J_q) with $|I_q| + |J_q| = n + 1 - 2q$ for $q = 1, \ldots, t$. Let $D_0 = \emptyset$,

$$D_q = \bigcup_{j=1}^{q} (I_j \times J_j),$$

$$K_q = \{2r - 1\!: \{(2r - 1, 2r - 1), (2r, 2r)\} \subseteq (I_q \times J_q) \setminus D_{q-1}, r \leq m\}$$

and

$$\tilde{K}_q = \{2r - 1\!: \{2r - 1, 2r\} \subseteq (N \setminus I_q) \cap (N \setminus J_q), r \leq m\}.$$

Theorem 5. *Given* (I_q, J_q) *for* $q = 1, \ldots, t$ *as defined above with* $\emptyset \subset \tilde{K}_1 \subseteq \tilde{K}_2 \subseteq \cdots \subseteq \tilde{K}_t$, *the inequalities*

$$\sum_{i \in \tilde{K}_1} x_{ii} + \sum_{q=2}^{t} \sum_{i \in K_{q-1} \cap \tilde{K}_q} x_{ii} + \sum_{i \in \bigcup_{q=1}^{t} K_q} x_{i+1,i+1} - \sum_{(i,j) \in D_t} x_{ij} \leq 0 \qquad (\text{SVI}:t)$$

are valid for $\text{conv}(S)$. (*When* $t = 1$ *the second sum is defined to equal* 0.)

Before proving the theorem, we note that SVI:1 is identical to SVI with $I = I_1$, $J = J_1$, $\tilde{K} = \tilde{K}_1$, $K = K_1$ and $I \times J = D_1$. Also the inequality of Example 2 is an SVI:2 inequality with $I_1 = J_1 = \{3, 4\}$ and $I_2 = J_2 = \{5\}$ since $\tilde{K}_1 = \{1\}$, $K_1 = \{3\}$, $\tilde{K}_2 = \{1, 3\}$, $K_2 = \emptyset$ and $D_2 = \{(3, 3), (3, 4), (4, 3), (4, 4), (5, 5)\}$.

Proof of Theorem 5. We first show that all of the coefficients in SVI:t are 0, ± 1. To prove this it suffices to show that

$$(K_{r-1} \cap \tilde{K}_r) \cap (K_{s-1} \cap \tilde{K}_s) = \emptyset \quad \text{for } 2 \leq r < s \leq t. \qquad (5)$$

To prove (5), suppose $h \in K_{r-1} \cap \tilde{K}_r$. By hypothesis $\tilde{K}_q \supseteq \tilde{K}_r$ for all $q > r$. Hence $h \in \tilde{K}_{s-1}$. By definition, $K_{s-1} \cap \tilde{K}_{s-1} = \emptyset$. Hence $h \notin K_{s-1} \supseteq K_{s-1} \cap \tilde{K}_s$.

Furthermore, since

$$\left\{ (i, i), (i+1, i+1) : i \in \bigcup_{q=1}^{t} K_q \right\} \subseteq D_t,$$

terms in the second and third sums of SVI:t will be cancelled by terms in the fourth sum. Thus the only variables with positive coefficients in SVI:t are x_{ii} with $i \in \tilde{K}_1$.

Now we show that any $x \in S$ satisfies SVI:t. Let $p_1 = \sum_{i \in \tilde{K}_1} x_{ii}$ and $p_q = \sum_{i \in K_{q-1} \cap \tilde{K}_q} x_{ii}$ for $q = 2, \ldots, t$. Define ι by

$$\iota = \begin{cases} t & \text{if } p_1, \ldots, p_t > 0, \\ \min_{1 \leq q \leq t} \{q : p_q = 0\} - 1 & \text{otherwise.} \end{cases}$$

If $\iota = 0$, $p_1 = 0$ and the left-hand side of SVI:t is nonpositive, so x satisfies SVI:t.

Now suppose that $\iota > 0$. Let $A_\iota = \bigcup_{q=1}^{\iota} K_q$ and $B_q = K_{q-1} \cap \tilde{K}_q$. Rewrite SVI:$t$ as

$$\sum_{i \in \tilde{K}_1} x_{ii} + \sum_{q=2}^{\iota} \sum_{i \in B_q} x_{ii} + \sum_{i \in A_\iota} x_{i+1,i+1} - \sum_{(i,j) \in D_\iota} x_{ij}$$

$$+ \sum_{i \in B_{\iota+1}} x_{ii} + \sum_{q=\iota+2}^{t} \sum_{i \in B_q} x_{ii} + \sum_{i \in A_t \setminus A_\iota} x_{i+1,i+1} - \sum_{(i,j) \in D_t \setminus D_\iota} x_{ij} \leq 0.$$

If $\iota = t$, the last four terms are identically zero.

Suppose $1 \le \iota \le t - 1$. We claim that

$$\sum_{i \in B_{\iota+1}} x_{ii} + \sum_{q=\iota+2}^{t} \sum_{i \in B_q} x_{ii} + \sum_{i \in A_{\iota} \backslash A_{\iota}} x_{i+1,i+1} - \sum_{(i,j) \in D_{\iota} \backslash D_{\iota}} x_{ij} \le 0.$$

The claim follows since $\sum_{i \in B_{\iota+1}} x_{ii} = p_{\iota+1} = 0$ by the definition of ι, and by the definitions of D_q, K_q and $\tilde{K}_q$, terms in the second and third sums are cancelled by terms in the fourth sum. Thus the sum of the remaining terms is nonpositive.

So it suffices to show that

$$\sum_{i \in \tilde{K}_1} x_{ii} + \sum_{q=2}^{\iota} \sum_{i \in B_q} x_{ii} + \sum_{i \in A_{\iota}} x_{i+1,i+1} - \sum_{(i,j) \in D_{\iota}} x_{ij} \le 0. \tag{6}$$

The proof of (6) essentially parallels the proof of Proposition 2. Let $p = \sum_{q=1}^{\iota} p_q$. Now delete the $2p$ row constraints and the $2p$ column constraints for $(i, i+1)$ with $i \in \tilde{K}_1 \cup \bigcup_{q=2}^{\iota} B_q$ and $x_{ii} = 1$. This leaves an $(n-2p) \times (n-2p)$ assignment problem to which we apply Proposition 1. Note that all of the deleted rows and columns have indices in the sets $N \backslash I_{\iota}$ and $N \backslash J_{\iota}$.

We have $|I_{\iota}| + |J_{\iota}| = n + 1 - 2\iota = (n-2p) + 2p - 2\iota + 1$. Hence $x(I_{\iota}, J_{\iota}) \ge 2p - 2\iota + 1$. Since $I_{\iota} \times J_{\iota} \subseteq D_{\iota}$ and for $i \in \bigcup_{q=2}^{\iota} B_q$, (i, i), $(i+1, i+1) \in D_{\iota} \backslash (I_{\iota} \times J_{\iota})$, we have

$$\sum_{(i,j) \in D_{\iota}} x_{ij} \ge x(I_{\iota}, J_{\iota}) + \sum_{q=2}^{\iota} \sum_{i \in B_q} (x_{ii} + x_{i+1,i+1}).$$

Since

$$\sum_{q=2}^{\iota} \sum_{i \in B_q} (x_{ii} + x_{i+1,i+1}) = 2(p - p_1),$$

it follows that

$$\sum_{(i,j) \in D_{\iota}} x_{ij} \ge 2p - 2\iota + 1 + 2(p - p_1) = 4p - 2\iota - 2p_1 + 1.$$

Also since if $i \in A_{\iota}$ then (i, i), $(i+1, i+1) \in D_{\iota}$, we have

$$\sum_{i \in A_{\iota}} x_{i+1,i+1} \le \left\lfloor \frac{1}{2} \sum_{(i,j) \in D_{\iota}} x_{ij} \right\rfloor.$$

Now combining the last two inequalities yields

$$\sum_{(i,j)\in D_\iota} x_{ij} - \sum_{i\in A_\iota} x_{i+1,i+1} \geq \left\lceil \frac{4p-2\iota-2p_1+1}{2} \right\rceil = 2p - p_1 - \iota + 1.$$

Finally

$$\sum_{(i,j)\in D_\iota} x_{ij} - \sum_{i\in A_\iota} x_{i+1,i+1} - \sum_{i\in K_1} x_{ii} - \sum_{q=2}^{\iota}\sum_{i\in B_q} x_{ii} \geq p - p_1 - \iota + 1 \geq 0,$$

as

$$\sum_{i\in K_1} x_{ii} + \sum_{q=2}^{\iota}\sum_{i\in B_q} x_{ii} = p,$$

and $p - p_1 \geq \iota - 1$ since $p_q \geq 1$ for $q = 2, \ldots, \iota$ by the definition of ι. $\quad\square$

It can be shown that some of the SVI: t inequalities with $t > 1$ define facets, e.g. the inequality of Example 2. However, we have not yet characterized those SVI: t inequalities that define facets.

3. Separation

The first step in solving CCAP by a strong cutting plane algorithm is to solve its linear programming relaxation consisting of the constraints (1), (2), (4) and nonnegativity. If the solution is not integral, we search for a violated SVI inequality. If such an inequality is found, we add it to the LP relaxation and continue. If no such inequality is found we resort to branch-and-bound.

The success of a strong cutting plane algorithm depends crucially on having an efficient procedure for detecting violated inequalities. However, we do not know an efficient algorithm that is certain to find a violated SVI inequality when one exists. Hence, we use heuristics.

To motivate the separation heuristic that attempts to determine whether there is a violated SVI inequality and to produce one when there is a violation, we consider the class of valid inequalities

$$x_{2q-1,2q-1} - x(I, J) \leq 0, \tag{VI:q}$$

where $q \leq m$, $I, J \subseteq N' = N\backslash\{2q-1, 2q\}$ and $|I| + |J| = n - 1$. The VI: q

inequalities have $\tilde{K} = \{2q - 1\}$ for some $q \le m$ and $K = \emptyset$. Thus a VI:q inequality is an SVI inequality if both $I \cap J$ and $(N' \backslash I) \cap (N' \backslash J)$ contain no couples. Otherwise, it is dominated by an SVI inequality. Hence, if VI:q is violated, the unique SVI inequality determined by I and J is also violated.

We will give an efficient algorithm that determines if any VI:q inequality is violated by a given point y; and if at least one is, the algorithm determines that VI:q inequality which is most violated by y. It is then trivial to determine the corresponding SVI inequality violated by y. The procedure can be executed for $q = 1, \ldots, m$. The case where no VI:q inequality is violated is discussed later.

The separation problem for VI:q, denoted by SEP(q, y), is given $y \in \mathbb{R}_+^{n^2}$ that satisfies (1), (2) and (4), find $I, J \subseteq N' = N \backslash \{2q - 1, 2q\}$, $q \le m$, such that $|I| + |J| = n - 1$ and $y(I, J)$ is minimum.

SEP(q, y) can be solved as a parametric max-flow or min-cut problem on a graph with $2n - 2$ nodes as explained below. Let $G = (V, E)$ be a directed graph with $V = \{s, t\} \cup V_1 \cup V_2$ and $E = E_1 \cup E_2 \cup E_3$ where s is the source node, t is the sink node, $(V_1 \cup V_2, E_1)$ is a complete bipartite graph with $|V_1| = |V_2| = |N'| = n - 2$ and all arcs pointing from V_1 to V_2, $E_2 = \{(s, v_i): \text{for all } v_i \in V_1\}$, $E_3 = \{(v_j', t): \text{for all } v_j' \in V_2\}$. The capacity of $(v_i, v_j') \in E_1$ is y_{ij} and the capacity of every edge in $E_2 \cup E_3$ is w, $0 \le w \le 1$.

Let $z(w)$ equal the capacity of a minimum $s - t$ cut and let $(U_w, \bar{U}_w)$ be a partition of V that yields a minimum cut. Observe that $z(w)$ is a concave and nondecreasing, piecewise linear function of w of the form $z(w) = kw + \alpha$. In particular, there is an interval $[0, w^*]$, $0 \le w^* < 1$, such that for $w \in [0, w^*]$, $U_w = \{s\}$ and $z(w) = (n - 2)w$.

Theorem 6 (see Cunningham, 1985; Padberg and Wolsey, 1984; Aboudi, 1986). *Let* $w^0 = w^* + \varepsilon$ *where* ε *is positive and arbitrarily small and let* $V_1^0 = U_{w^0} \cap V_1$ *and* $V_2^0 = \bar{U}_{w^0} \cap V_2$. *Then* (I_q^0, J_q^0) *is an optimal solution to* SEP(q, y) *where* $I_q^0 = \{i: v_i \in V_1^0\}$ *and* $J_q^0 = \{j: v_j' \in V_2^0\}$. $\square$

Hence by solving the max flow problem on G parametrically as a function of w, we can solve SEP(q, y) efficiently (see Aboudi, 1986, for details). Given (I_q^0, J_q^0), we immediately extend the corresponding VI:q inequality to the unique SVI inequality specified by I_q^0 and J_q^0. This procedure is repeated for $q = 1, \ldots, m$ and all of the violated SVI inequalities determined in this manner are added to the linear programming relaxation. On the other hand, if no violated SVI inequalities are identified by this approach, we use elementary search heuristics to see if we can find other cuts that yield violated SVI inequalities. If none are found, we resort to branch-and-bound using the LP formulation with (1), (2), (4), nonnegativity and any cuts that have been added at previous steps.

Example 3. Let $n = 5$, $m = 2$ and

$$y = \begin{pmatrix} \frac{3}{4} & 0 & 0 & \frac{1}{4} & 0 \\ 0 & \frac{3}{4} & 0 & \frac{1}{4} & 0 \\ \frac{1}{4} & \frac{1}{4} & \frac{1}{4} & 0 & \frac{1}{4} \\ 0 & 0 & \frac{1}{2} & \frac{1}{4} & \frac{1}{4} \\ 0 & 0 & \frac{1}{4} & \frac{1}{4} & \frac{1}{2} \end{pmatrix}.$$

Then for $q = 1$, the VI : q inequality

$$x_{11} - \sum_{j=3}^{5} x_{3j} \leq 0$$

is violated by y. This can be established by showing that in the graph of Figure 1, the maximum flow for $w^* = \frac{1}{2}$ equals $\frac{3}{2}$. While for any $w > \frac{1}{2}$, the maximum flow is less than $3w$. In particular for $w^0 = w^* + \varepsilon$, a minimum $s - t$ cut is given by the edge set $\{(s, 4), (s, 5), (3, 3'), (3, 4'), (3, 5')\}$, which yields $I_q^0 = \{3\}$ and $J_q^0 = \{3, 4, 5\}$.

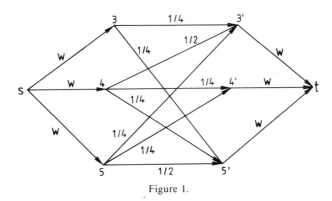

Figure 1.

4. Computational experience

We implemented a strong cutting plane algorithm that uses the separation procedure for SVI inequalities described in Section 3. The algorithm is coded in FORTRAN and is included as a user interface to LINDO. The details of the implementation are in Aboudi (1986). It is not interesting to test the algorithm on problems with purely random data because the probability of getting a fractional solution to the linear programming relaxation is small. This follows since if the solution to the linear programming relaxation is fractional at least one of the variables in a couple must be positive and the probability of a variable being positive in the linear programming relaxation is $O(n^{-1})$.

To ensure that some of the LP relaxations have fractional optimal solutions, it is necessary to correlate the cost coefficients of variables in a couple. One of the coefficients needs to be large and the other small. We generated problems with the coefficients c_{ij} uniformly distributed in $[a, b]$ except for

$$c_{ii} = \begin{cases} L & \text{for } i = 1, 3, \ldots, 2m-1, \\ 0 & \text{for } i = 2, 4, \ldots, 2m, \end{cases}$$

where L is strictly less than $2(a+b)$.

We compared our implementation of the strong cutting plane algorithm versus branch-and-bound on 50 problems where n ranged from 20 to 32 (from 400 to 1024 variables) and m, the number of side constraints, ranged from 6 to 10. The computational results are described in Tables 1–5. We report the value of the initial LP relaxation, the number of LP iterations to solve it, the number of times our separation routine was performed (major iterations), the total number of cuts added, the additional number of LP

Table 1
$n = 20$, $m = 6$, $[a, b] = [1, 40]$, $L = 77$

	LP Value	LP Itrs	Major Itrs	Cuts Added	Add'l Itrs	IP Value	Opt'l Found	Total Itrs	B&B Itrs
1	762.5	182	7	9	45	761	Yes	227	349
2	756.5	196	5	11	127	754	Yes	323	446
3	764.66	192	2	7	98	763	Yes	290	256
4	753	237	1	2	39	752	Yes	276	299
5	754	210	2	2	8	754	Yes	218	219
6	761.33	222	2	6	11	760	Yes	233	250
7	761.5	227	1	2	24	761	Yes	251	269
8	757.5	214	1	2	14	756	Yes	228	206
9	747	224	1	3	61	747	Yes	285	247
10	759	186	1	1	6	759	Yes	192	273
	Total							2523	2814

Table 2
$n = 23$, $m = 7$, $[a, b] = [1, 40]$, $L = 76$

	LP Value	LP Itrs	Major Itrs	Cuts Added	Add'l Itrs	LP Value	Opt'l Found	Total Itrs	B&B Itrs
1	880.5	275	1	2	36	880	Yes	311	318
2	875.33	222	1	3	20	875	Yes	242	410
3	875.66	227	3	9	131	875	Yes	358	567
4	875	256	1	3	43	874	Yes	299	422
5	880	233	2	3	44	880	Yes	277	283
6	866.25	226	3	9	135	865	Yes	261	405
7	864.66	293	5	11	177	864	Yes	474	394
8	865	208	1	1	10	865	Yes	218	332
9	868.5	313	1	1	5	868	Yes	318	314
10	883.66	305	4	5	57	882	No[a]	585[b]	453
	Total							3342	3898

[a] Solution was not found by the strong cutting plane algorithm. However, an upper bound of 883.25 was established.
[b] This includes strong cutting plane plus branch-and-bound.

iterations required to reoptimize after adding the cuts, the optimal value of the IP and whether the optimal solution was found without resorting to branch-and-bound. The last two columns of each table compare the performance of our algorithm to the branch-and-bound algorithm implemented in LINDO. The column labelled "Total Itrs" lists the total number of iterations

Table 3
$n = 25$, $m = 8$, $[a, b] = [1, 50]$, $L = 94$

	LP Value	LP Itrs	Major Itrs	Cuts Added	Add'l Itrs	IP Value	Opt'l Found	Total Itrs	B&B Itrs
1	1200.5	283	5	6	120	1198	Yes	403	315
2	1180.5	273	1	1	32	1179	Yes	305	735
3	1182	419	3	5	50	1181	Yes	469	479
4	1192.5	270	8	12	240	1191	Yes	510	622
5	1182.5	373	7	11	63	1182	Yes	436	452
6	1191.5	314	8	21	297	1189	Yes	611	469
7	1184	294	1	1	30	1184	Yes	324	322
8	1203.33	297	1	2	53	1203	Yes	350	490
9	1192.5	261	1	4	26	1192	Yes	287	406
10	1181.66	274	5	11	67	1180	No[a]	777[b]	708
	Total							4472	5196

[a] Solution was not found by the strong cutting plane algorithm. However, an upper bound of 1180 was established.
[b] This includes strong cutting plane plus branch-and-bound.

Table 4
$n = 30$, $m = 10$, $[a, b] = [1, 30]$, $L = 58$

	LP Value	LP Itrs	Major Itrs	Cuts Added	Add'l Itrs	IP Value	Opt'l Found	Total Itrs	B&B Itrs
1	869.25	394	1	5	86	869	Yes	480	682
2	872	405	1	1	5	872	Yes	410	422
3	870	391	1	1	90	869	Yes	481	591
4	874.4	401	9	21	223	874	Yes	624	1264
5	864.5	329	1	2	46	864	Yes	375	625
6	871.5	375	2	4	130	871	Yes	505	641
7	859	422	1	2	32	859	Yes	454	438
8	862.5	351	2	2	13	862	Yes	364	535
9	870.5	308	1	1	14	870	Yes	322	663
10	872.5	356	1	1	10	872	Yes	366	456
Total								4381	6318

required for our algorithm. The last column, labelled "B&B Itrs" lists the number of LP iterations of branch-and-bound.

Tables 1–5 demonstrate that on average our strong cutting plane algorithm required fewer LP iterations that standard branch-and-bound. One can also observe that only 3 out of the 50 problems required branch-and-bound to be invoked. That is, the overwhelming majority of the problems were solved to optimality by adding the facet-defining inequalities defined in Section 2.

Table 5
$n = 32$, $m = 6$, $[a, b] = [1, 50]$, $L = 97$

	LP Value	LP Itrs	Major Itrs	Cuts Added	Add'l Itrs	IP Value	Opt'l Found	Total Itrs	B&B Itrs
1	1552.5	391	2	4	36	1552	Yes	427	522
2	1559	337	1	1	18	1559	Yes	355	390
3	1537.75	442	1	2	41	1537	Yes	483	533
4	1552.33	389	1	2	26	1552	Yes	415	519
5	1543	355	6	10	103	1542	Yes	458	473
6	1531	397	4	4	27	1530	Yes	424	522
7	1547	461	7	12	168	1546	Yes	629	'588
8	1528.5	371	1	1	36	1527	Yes	407	724
9	1544	479	10	17	292	1543	Yes	771	663
10	1541	443	6	8	70	1540	No[a]	715[b]	562
Total								5084	5496

[a] Solution was not found by the strong cutting plane algorithm. However, an upper bound of 1540.2 was established.
[b] This includes strong cutting plane plus branch-and-bound.

5. Extensions

The valid inequalities given here can be generalized to accommodate somewhat more complicated models. These results are described in Aboudi (1986). For example, the SVI inequalities are easily extended to accommodate hypercouple side constraints of the form $x_{11} = \cdots = x_{pp}$ for any p with $2 \leq p \leq n$. The corresponding SVI inequalities are

$$\sum_{i \in K} x_{ii} + \sum_{i \in \tilde{K}} x_{ii} - x(I, J) \leq 0$$

with $I, J \subseteq N \backslash \{1, \ldots, p\}$ and $|I| + |J| = n - p + 1$.

It is also possible to modify the valid inequalities to accommodate the situation in which the subsets R_k for $k = 1, \ldots, m$ are not disjoint.

Finally, one can intepret the model studied here as a perfect matching problem on a bipartite graph with couple side constraints. Some generalizations of the SVI inequalities for perfect matching on general simple graphs with couple side constraints are also given in Aboudi (1986).

References

Aboudi, R. (1986) 'A constrained matching problem: A polyhedral approach', Ph.D. Thesis, School of Operations Research and Industrial Engineering, Cornell University, Ithaca, NY.

Aggarwal, V. (1985) 'A Lagrangean relaxation method for the constrained assignment problem', *Computers and Operations Research*, 12:97-106.

Crowder, H., E. Johnson and M. Padberg (1983) 'Solving large-scale zero-one linear programming problems', *Operations Research*, 31:803-834.

Cunningham, W. (1985) 'Optimal attack and reinforcement of a network', *Journal of the Association of Computing Machinery*, 32:549-561.

Grötschel, M. and M. Padberg (1985) 'Polyhedral computations', in: E.L. Lawler et al., eds., *The Traveling Salesman Problem*. New York: Wiley.

Mazzola, J.B. and A.W. Neebe (1986) 'Resource-constrained assignment scheduling', *Operations Research*, 34:560-572.

Nemhauser, G.L. and L.A. Wolsey (1988) *Integer and Combinatorial Optimization*. New York: Wiley.

Padberg, M. and A. Sassano (1984) 'Matching with Bonds: I', Consiglio Nazionale delle Richerche, Instituto di Analisi dei Sistemi ed Informatica, Rome, Italy.

Padberg, M. and L.A. Wolsey (1984) 'Fractional covers for forests and matching', *Mathematical Programming*, 29:1-14.

Chapter 23

FORMULATING SINGLE MACHINE SCHEDULING PROBLEMS WITH PRECEDENCE CONSTRAINTS

Laurence A. WOLSEY

CORE, Université Catholique de Louvain, Louvain-la-Neuve, Belgium

1. Introduction

Finding optimal solutions to single machine scheduling problems is a nontrivial task because, although it is often easy to find good feasible solutions (giving good upper bounds on the optimal value), it is very difficult to obtain tight lower bounds. This difficulty, plus recent successes in solving various combinatorial optimisation problems via integer or mixed integer programming, has encouraged various researchers to study the formulation of these problems as mixed integer programs. This note can thus be seen as a continuation of work started by Balas (1985), Dyer and Wolsey (1987), Peters (1988), Queyranne (1986), Queyranne and Wang (1988) and Wolsey (1985).

The particular problem we study here is the problem of finding the minimum sum of weighted start (or completion) times subject to precedence constraints. Formally the problem can be written as:

$$\min \sum_{j=1}^{n} w_j t_j,$$

$$t_j - t_i \geq p_i \quad \text{for } (i,j) \in F, \tag{1}$$

$$t_j - t_i \geq p_i \quad \text{or} \quad t_i - t_j \geq p_j \quad \text{for } (i,j) \in E,$$

Research supported by the Projet d'Action Concertée No. 87/92-106 of CORE.

Economic Decision-Making: Games, Econometrics and Optimisation
Edited by J.J. Gabszewicz, J.-F. Richard and L.A. Wolsey

where $w_j \geq 0$ is the weight associated with job j, $p_j > 0$ is its processing time, and t_j is a variable representing the start time of job j. F represents the ordered pairs of jobs for which job i must precede job j, written $i \to j$ (the precedence constraints), and E represents the other job pairs (i, j) with $i < j$ for which the order is to be determined.

We let T denote the set of feasible solutions $(t_1, \ldots, t_n)$ to (1). Other sets that it is natural to consider are the set T^m of minimal solutions in T given by

$$T^m = \left\{ t \colon t_j = \sum_{i=1}^{j-1} p_{\pi(i)}, \text{ where } \pi = (\pi(1) \cdots \pi(n)) \text{ is a feasible} \right.$$

$$\left. \text{permutation of the jobs} \vphantom{\sum_{i=1}^{j-1}} \right\}$$

and $T^+ = T^m \cup \mathbb{R}^n_+$. It is easy to see that $T \subseteq T^+$ as any point t in T defines a feasible permutation π. The example below shows that $T \subsetneq T^+$.

Example 1. Let $p_1 = 2$, $p_2 = 3$ and $p_3 = 4$, and suppose $\pi = (1, 2, 3)$ is a feasible sequence.

The corresponding point in T^m is $(t_1, t_2, t_3) = (0, 2, 5)$. The point $(1, 2, 5)$ is in T^+ as $(1, 2, 5) \geq (0, 2, 5)$, but is not in T as $t_2 - t_1 < p_1$.

When optimising in (1) with nonnegative weights, we will obtain the same result whether we solve over T^m, T or T^+, thus it is of interest to try to describe the convex hull of any of the three sets.

An alternative formulation approach is to explicitly represent the permutation π by using 0-1 variables δ_{ij}, where $\delta_{ij} = 1$ if i precedes j, and $\delta_{ij} = 0$ if j precedes i. Problem (1) can now be formulated as:

$$\min \sum_{j=1}^{n} w_j t_j, \tag{2}$$

$$t_j - t_i \geq p_i, \quad (i, j) \in F, \tag{3}$$

$$t_j - t_i \geq p_i - M(1 - \delta_{ij}), \quad (i, j) \in E \text{ or } (j, i) \in E, \tag{4}$$

$$\delta_{ij} + \delta_{ji} = 1, \quad (i, j) \in E, \tag{5}$$

$$\delta_{ij} = 1, \ \delta_{ji} = 0, \quad \text{for } (i, j) \in F, \tag{6}$$

$$\delta_{ij}, \delta_{ji} \in \{0, 1\} \quad \text{for } (i, j) \in E, \tag{7}$$

$$t \geq 0, \quad \delta \geq 0, \tag{8}$$

where $M = \sum_{i=1}^{n} p_i$. Note that if (t, δ) is feasible in (3)-(7), then $t \in T$.

In addition observe that any feasible solution (t, δ) will necessarily satisfy the "triangle inequalities"

$$\delta_{ij} + \delta_{jk} + \delta_{ki} \leq 2 \quad \text{for all } i, j, k, \; i \neq j \neq k. \tag{9}$$

On the other hand without the constraints (4) the δ_{ij} represent a feasible permutation if and only if δ satisfies (5)–(7) and (9).

As for many structured integer programs, the choice that arises is whether to look for a formulation involving only the t_j variables, or an "extended" formulation involving both t and δ variables. Both types of formulations have been studied for the case with no precedence constraints (Dyer and Wolsey, 1987; Queyranne, 1986; Wolsey, 1985).

Recently Queyranne and Wang (1988) proposed a set of valid inequalities for T involving just the t_j variables, and showed that this family completely describes conv(T) in the special case that the precedence graph is transitive "series-parallel". In addition they gave two other families of valid inequalities for the general case. Here we propose to examine the precedence constrained problem using the (t, δ) variables. This alternative approach has several potential advantages:

(i) with a small (polynomial) number of inequalities, we obtain a formulation as tight as the Queyranne and Wang formulation, which involves an exponential number of inequalities;

(ii) with a small number of inequalities, one does not need to describe a separation algorithm to generate one of the inequalities cutting off a given point t^*;

(iii) for general precedence constraints, the t-formulation is not a mixed integer linear program, and thus a special purpose branch and bound algorithm has to be built.

The obvious and important disadvantage is the increased number of variables δ_{ij} in the extended formulation.

In Section 2 we describe various valid inequalities for T^m, T or T^+ involving both the t and δ variables. We then show that all the inequalities involving only t_j variables derived by Queyranne and Wang (1988) can be obtained as nonnegative linear combinations of these (t, δ) inequalities. In Section 3 we look at various (t, δ) formulations based on these valid inequalities — in particular we obtain a relaxed formulation with O(n^2) constraints and variables that is tight when the precedence graph is transitive series-parallel, and a formulation with O(n^3) constraints that is at least as tight as the model using all the additional inequalities proposed by Queyranne and Wang.

In Section 4 we briefly introduce constraints that can be added to the formulations of Section 3 if deadlines or release date constraints are present.

2. Valid inequalities

Here we derive various valid inequalities in the (t, δ) space. The first family was proposed by Wolsey (1985) and shown to describe conv(T) in the absence of precedence constraints. Extensions can be found in Dyer and Wolsey (1987) and Queyranne (1986).

Proposition 1. *The constraints*

$$t_j = \sum_i p_i \delta_{ij} \tag{10}$$

and

$$t_j \geq \sum_i p_i \delta_{ij} \tag{11}$$

are valid for T^m and T^+ respectively. $\square$

Now we derive inequalities for T that make specific use of the precedence constraints $i \to j$ for $(i, j) \in F$. We let $S_i = \{k: (i, k) \in F\}$ denote the set of fixed successors of i, and $P_j = \{k: (k, j) \in F\}$ the set of fixed predecessors of j. The first inequality is obtained by subtracting the inequality (10) for t_i from the inequality (10) for t_j, and using the precedence relation.

Proposition 2. *If $(i, j) \in F$, the inequalities*

$$t_j - t_i \geq p_i + \sum_{k \in S_i \cap P_j} p_k + \sum_{k \in S_i \setminus P_j} p_k \delta_{kj} + \sum_{k \in P_j \setminus S_i} p_k \delta_{ik}$$
$$+ \sum_{k \in N \setminus (S_i \cup P_j)} p_k (\delta_{kj} - \delta_{ki}) \tag{12}$$

and

$$t_j - t_i \geq p_i + \sum_{k \in S_i \cap P_j} p_k + \sum_{k \in S_i \setminus P_j} p_k \delta_{kj} + \sum_{k \in P_j \setminus S_i} p_k \delta_{ik} \tag{13}$$

are valid for T.

Proof. The jobs processed during the time interval $[t_i, t_j]$ are job i, all the jobs $S_i \cap P_j$ that must be processed between i and j, plus all successors of i that are placed before j, plus all predecessors of j that are placed after i, plus all other jobs k that we place after i and before j. The validity of (13) follows from that of (12) as $(i, j) \in F$ and δ a feasible sequence implies that $\delta_{kj} \geq \delta_{ki}$. $\square$

For modelling purposes in more complicated problems with additional constraints, suppose we know that in a subset $\bar{T}$ of T, the maximum amount of idle time (time when no job is being processed) between t_j and t_i is α_{ji} when job j precedes job i. The following inequality, obtained from (12), is a possible replacement for the big-M inequality (4). For notational convenience we suppose $\delta_{jj} = 0$.

Proposition 3. *The inequality*

$$t_j - t_i \geq \sum_k p_k(\delta_{kj} - \delta_{ki}) - \alpha_{ji}\delta_{ji} \tag{14}$$

is valid for $\bar{T}$.

Proof. When $\delta_{ij} = 1$, this is precisely inequality (12) of Proposition 2. When $\delta_{ji} = 1$, $\delta_{kj} - \delta_{ki} = -1$ if k comes between j and i. Thus $-\sum_k p_k(\delta_{kj} - \delta_{ki})$ is the amount of time spent on processing jobs between t_j and t_i. α_{ji} is an upper bound on the idle time. Thus $t_i - t_j \leq -\sum_k p_k(\delta_{kj} - \delta_{ki}) + \alpha_{ji}$, which is precisely the inequality when $\delta_{ji} = 1$. $\square$

Now we consider the first two families of valid inequalities for T used by Queyranne and Wang (1988), namely

$$\sum_{i \in S} p_i t_i \geq \sum_{i < j, i \in S, j \in S} p_i p_j \quad \text{for } S \subseteq N \tag{15}$$

and

$$\left(\sum_{i \in N_1} p_i\right)\left(\sum_{i \in N_2} p_i t_i\right) - \left(\sum_{i \in N_2} p_i\right)\left(\sum_{i \in N_1} p_i t_i\right)$$

$$\geq \left(\sum_{i \in N_1} p_i\right)\left(\sum_{i < j, i, j \in N_2} p_i p_j\right) + \left(\sum_{i \in N_2} p_i\right)\left(\sum_{i < j, i, j \in N_1} p_i p_j + \sum_{i \in N_1} p_i^2\right), \tag{16}$$

where $N_1 \to N_2$, i.e., i precedes j for all $i \in N_1$ and $j \in N_2$, $N_1 \cap N_2 = \emptyset$, $N_1, N_2 \subseteq N$.

It is known and easily verified that (15) can be obtained as a convex combination of the inequalities (11), the equalities (5), and the nonnegativity of δ_{ij}. We show that the inequalities (16) can be derived in a similar manner.

Proposition 4. *The inequality* (16) *is dominated by a nonnegative combination of the constraints* (13) *and* (5).

Proof. Multiplying (13) by $p_i p_j$ for each $i \in N_1, j \in N_2$, dropping the term involving a sum over $S_i \cap P_j$, and summing gives

$$\sum_{i,j} p_i p_j t_j - \sum_{i,j} p_i p_j t_i \geq \sum_{i,j} p_i^2 p_j + \sum_{k \in N_1, i, j} p_i p_j p_k \delta_{ik} + \sum_{k \in N_2, i, j} p_i p_j p_k \delta_{kj}.$$

Rewriting we obtain

$$\left(\sum_{i \in N_1} p_i\right)\left(\sum_{j \in N_2} p_j t_j\right) - \left(\sum_{j \in N_2} p_j\right)\left(\sum_{i \in N_1} p_i t_i\right)$$

$$\geq \left(\sum_{j \in N_2} p_j\right)\left(\sum_{i \in N_1} p_i^2\right) + \left(\sum_{j \in N_2} p_j\right)\left(\sum_{i < k, i, k \in N_1} p_i p_k (\delta_{ki} + \delta_{ik})\right)$$

$$+ \left(\sum_{i \in N_1} p_i\right)\left(\sum_{j < k, j, k \in N_2} p_j p_k (\delta_{jk} + \delta_{kj})\right).$$

Now using (5), the claim follows. □

Queyranne and Wang (1988) also proposed two other families of valid inequalities for T when the precedence structure is locally of the form shown in Figure 1, where there exists a numbering of the nodes in N such that

$$\{(i, j) \in F: i, j \in \{1, 2, 3, 4\}\} = \{(1, 2), (3, 2), (3, 4)\}$$

and

$$Q \subseteq \{i \in N: (3, i) \in F \text{ and } (i, 2) \in F\}.$$

The inequalities they propose are

$$-\left(\sum_{i \in Q} p_i + p_1 + p_2 + p_4\right)\left(p_1 C_1 + p_3 C_3 + \sum_{i \in Q} p_i C_i\right)$$

$$+ \left[\left(p_1 + \sum_{i \in Q} p_i\right)\left(p_1 + p_2 + p_3 + p_4 + \sum_{i \in Q} p_i\right) + p_2 p_3\right] C_2 + p_3 p_4 C_4$$

$$\geq \left(p_1 + p_2 + p_4 + \sum_{i \in Q} p_i\right)$$

$$\times \left[p_1 p_2 + p_1 p_3 + p_2 p_3 + (p_1 + p_2 + p_3) \sum_{i \in Q} p_i + \sum_{i < j, i, j \in Q} p_i p_j\right] + p_3 p_4^2$$

$$\tag{17}$$

Figure 1.

and

$$-p_1 p_2 C_1 - \left[\left(p_4 + \sum_{i \in Q} p_i \right) (p_1 + p_2 + p_3 + p_4) + p_2 p_3 \right] C_3$$

$$+ (p_1 + p_3 + p_4) \left(p_2 C_2 + p_4 C_4 + \sum_{i \in Q} p_i C_i \right)$$

$$\geq \left(p_1 + p_3 + p_4 + \sum_{i \in Q} p_i \right)$$

$$\times \left[p_2^2 + p_4^2 + \sum_{i \in Q} p_i^2 + p_2 p_4 + (p_2 + p_4) \sum_{i \in Q} p_i + \sum_{i < j, i, j \in Q} p_i p_j \right] + p_1 p_2 p_3,$$

$$(18)$$

where $C_i = t_i + p_i$ is the completion time of job i.

Proposition 5. *The inequalities* (17) *and* (18) *are nonnegative linear combinations of the inequalities* (5), (6), (9) *and* (12). $\square$

For the proof, see Wolsey (1989).

3. Formulations

Here we use the valid inequalities developed in Section 2 to suggest various formulations for use in solving precedence constrained problems. We define several polyhedra in the (t, δ) space, the principal goal being to obtain linear programming formulations that solve the precedence-constrained scheduling problem in special cases, and in general give tight lower bounds for use in the branch and bound algorithm of a mathematical programming system.

Initially we consider valid formulations and relaxations for T^m. The first formulation is denoted Q_1, where

$$Q_1 = \{ (t, \delta) \in \mathbb{R}_+^n \times \mathbb{R}^{n(n-1)} : (t, \delta) \text{ satisfy } (5), (6), (10), (13) \},$$

and $P_1 = \text{proj}_t(Q_1)$ is its projection into the t-space.

3.1. Transitive series-parallel precedence graph

Transitive series-parallel precedence graphs are defined in Lawler (1978). Informally they are directed graphs that can be built up recursively starting

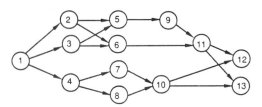

Figure 2. A transitive series parallel graph.

from a single node, either by putting two such graphs in *series* with directed arcs from the first to the second, or by putting two such graphs in *parallel*. An example of such a graph is shown in Figure 2.

Queyranne and Wang (1988) have shown the following very nice result.

Theorem 6. *If the precedence graph is transitive series-parallel, all nontrivial facets of* conv(T) *are of the form* (15) *or* (16) *for appropriately defined sets S, and* N_1, N_2, *respectively.* □

Based on our earlier propositions it follows that we obtain a compact formulation for such problems using the (t, δ) variables.

Theorem 7. *If the precedence graph is transitive series-parallel,* $P_1 = $ conv(T^m), *and the linear program:* min$\{wt: (t, \delta) \in Q_1\}$ *is tight.*

Proof. Using Proposition 4, all inequalities of the form (15) or (16) can be derived as a nonnegative combination of (5), (6), (11), (13) and $\delta_{ij} \geq 0$. These are precisely the constraints of Q_1 and thus the result follows from Theorem 6. □

We obtain a similar result if Q_1^* is the polyhedron obtained from Q_1 by replacing (10) by (11), and $P_1^* = \text{proj}_t(Q_1^*)$.

Corollary 8. $P_1^* = $ conv(T). □

3.2. The general case

As the linear program over Q_1 solves the scheduling problem over transitive series-parallel graphs, this also suggests that the formulation will give tight bounds in the general case. However observe that Q_1 is not necessarily a valid formulation without either the big-M inequalities (4), or the triangle inequalities (9) which guarantee that the δ-variables define a sequence. Thus to obtain a valid formulation we can take

$$Q_1^a = Q_1 \cap \{(t, \delta): (t, \delta) \text{ satisfies (4)}\}.$$

This formulation involves only $O(n^2)$ constraints and variables.

For the general case, Queyranne and Wang (1988) also proposed the families of inequalities (17) and (18). To obtain a comparable system consider the formulation Q_2, where

$$Q_2 = \{(t, \delta) \in \mathbb{R}^n \times \mathbb{R}_+^{n(n-1)}: (t, \delta) \text{ satisfy (5), (6), (9), (10)}\}.$$

Q_2 is at least as tight as Q_1 because (13) can be derived from the inequalities (6), (9) and (12) following the proof of Proposition 2, and (12) can be derived from (6) and (10). This formulation has been implicitly used by Potts (1985) in solving problems with up to 100 jobs using a special purpose algorithm based on Lagrangian relaxation.

Proposition 9. *All the inequalities* (15)–(18) *are valid inequalities for Q_2.*

Proof. The result follows from Propositions 4 and 5. □

Thus formulation Q_2 is as strong as formulation Q_1, and is as strong as the t-formulation consisting of all the inequalities proposed by Queyranne and Wang. However it has the disadvantage of having $O(n^3)$ constraints, which makes it an impossible formulation to use explicitly with a mathematical programming system, unless the triangle inequalities (9) are generated as cutting planes.

To terminate this section we consider one problem with $n = 30$ jobs, and consider the different bounds obtained from various linear programming relaxations (see Table 1). $(\bar{Q})$ indicates that the constraints (13) were only added for pairs $(i, j) \in F$ where i directly precedes j.

Table 1

Formulation	LP value	Size
Big-M [(2)–(6), (8)]	0	752×623
Big-M +(10)	107 321.6	782×623
$\bar{Q}_1$ [(5), (6), (8), (10), (13)]	113 137.2	239×623
Q_1 [(5), (6), (8), (10), (13)]	113 182.2	466×623
$\bar{Q}_1^a$ [(4)–(6), (8), (10), (13)]	113 138.1	832×623

The optimal solution of value 113 214 is found and proved optimal by branch and bound with 27, 13 and 29 nodes for formulations $\bar{Q}_1$, Q_1 and $\bar{Q}_1^a$ respectively. Similar results were obtained on other problems, though as remarked above applying branch and bound to formulations Q_1 and $\bar{Q}_1$ can lead to infeasible solutions. The general conclusion is that Q_1 or $\bar{Q}_1$ provide very effective tight lower bounds at a reasonable cost in terms of problem size. Q_2 provides an even better bound, but the $O(n^3)$ triangle constraints (9) must then be handled implicitly.

4. Release dates and deadlines

Here we briefly describe other inequalities that can be used for precedence-constrained problems with additional constraints such as deadlines and/or release dates. We let

$$T^d = T \cap \{t: t_i + p_i \le d_i \text{ for } i \in N\}$$

denote the set of feasible start times with deadlines, and

$$T^r = \{(t, t^*): t_i \ge r_i, t^* \ge t_i + p_i, \text{ for } i \in N, t \in T\}$$

denote the set of start times with release dates, where t^* denotes the completion time of all the jobs. When release dates are present, idle times may occur between jobs and the inequalities for T^m are no longer valid. The formulations Q_1^a or Q_1^b with (9) replaced by (10) are appropriate starting points as they are valid for T. An alternative using (13) in place of the big-M inequality (4) is to use a tightened-inequality derived from (12):

$$t_j - t_i \ge p_i + \sum_{k \in S_i \setminus P_j} p_k \delta_{kj} + \sum_{k \in P_j \setminus S_i} p_k \delta_{ik} - M' \delta_{ji} \quad \text{for } (i,j) \in E,$$

where M' is chosen appropriately. Now we indicate how to tighten or replace the above constraints using the deadlines or release dates. Let α^+ denote $\max\{\alpha, 0\}$.

4.1. Deadlines

We suppose that the jobs are ordered so that $d_1 \le d_2 \le \cdots \le d_n$.

Proposition 10. *Given* $j, k \in N$,

$$t_j + p_j + \sum_{\{i : i \le k, i \ne j\}} p_i \delta_{ji} + \sum_{\{i : i > k, i \ne j\}} [d_k - (d_i - p_i)]^+ \delta_{ji}$$
$$+ \sum_{Q_k} (p_i - [d_k - (d_i - p_i)]^+)(\delta_{ji} + \delta_{iq_i} - 1)$$
$$\le d_k + (d_j - d_k)^+ \delta_{kj}$$

is a valid inequality for T^d, *where* $Q_k \subseteq \{i : i > k\}$ *and* $q_i \in \{1, \ldots, k\}$.

Proof. If $d_j \le d_k$, the last term vanishes, $t_j \le d_k$ and all terms on the left after t_j must be carried out in the interval $[t_j, d_k]$. In particular, (i) job j takes time p_j, (ii) jobs i with deadline before d_k that are carried out after j take time p_i, (iii) jobs i with deadline after d_k but such that $p_i > d_i - d_k$ will use up part of the interval before d_k if they occur after j, and (iv) if the latter jobs also precede some job q_i whose deadline is before d_k, the total processing time p_i must fall in the interval $[t_j, d_k]$.

If $d_j > d_k$, and $\delta_{kj} = 0$, again $t_j \le d_k$ and the same argument holds. Finally if $d_j > d_k$ and $\delta_{kj} = 1$, all terms on the left must occur in the interval $[t_j, d_j]$. $\square$

Taking j to be a fictitious starting job with $t_j = 0$, $p_j = 0$, $d_j = 0$, and $\delta_{ji} = 1$ for all i, we obtain a corollary:

Corollary 11 (Peters, 1988).

$$\sum_{i \le k} p_i + \sum_{i > k} [d_k - (d_i - p_i)^+]^+ + \sum_{i > k} (p_i - [d_k - (d_i - p_i)^+]) \delta_{iq_i} \le d_k$$

is a valid inequality for T^d, *where* $q_i \in \{1, \ldots k\}$. $\square$

Similar inequalities can be obtained for release dates.

4.2. Release Dates

Here we assume $r_1 \le r_2 \le \cdots \le r_n$.

Proposition 12. *For* $k, j \in N$,

$$t_k \ge r_j + \sum_{i \ge j} p_i \delta_{ik} + \sum_{\substack{i < j \\ i \ne k}} (r_i + p_i - r_j)^+ \delta_{ik}$$

$$+ \sum_{i \in Q_j} [p_i - (r_i + p_i - r_j)^+](\delta_{ik} + \delta_{q_i,i} - 1) - (r_j - r_k)^+ \delta_{kj}$$

is a valid inequality for T^r, *where* $Q_j \subseteq \{i : i < j\}$ *and* $q_i \in \{j, j+1, \ldots, n\}$. $\square$

Analogous to Corollary 11, we obtain:

Corollary 13.

$$t^* \ge r_j + \sum_{i \ge j} p_i + \sum_{i < j} (r_i + p_i - r_j)^+ + \sum_{i < j} [p_i - (r_i + p_i - r_j)^+] \delta_{q_i,i}$$

is valid for T^r, *where* $q_i \in \{j, \ldots, n\}$. $\square$

Peters (1988) has used the inequalities of Corollary 12 to solve problems with deadlines (but no explicit precedence constraints) having up to 30 jobs. Dyer and Wolsey (1987) derived various other inequalities for T^r and compared the bounds given by different formulations.

The ultimate goal of this research is to obtain strong lower bounds for problems simultaneously involving several machines with precedence constraints, deadlines and release dates.

References

Balas, E. (1985) 'On the facial structure of scheduling polyhedra', *Mathematical Programming Study*, 24:179-218.

Dyer, M. and L.A. Wolsey (1987) 'Formulating the single machine sequencing problem with release dates as a mixed integer program', to appear in: *Discrete Applied Mathematics.*

Lawler, E.L. (1978) 'Sequencing jobs to minimize total weighted completion time subject to precedence constraints', *Annals of Discrete Mathematics*, 2:75-90.

Monma, C.L. and J.B. Sidney (1979) 'Sequencing with series-parallel precedence constraints', *Mathematics of Operations Research*, 4:215-224.

Peters, R. (1988) 'L'ordonnancement sur une machine avec des contraintes de délai', *Belgian Journal of Operations Research, Statistics and Computer Science*, 28:33-76.

Potts, C.N. (1985) 'A Lagrangean based branch and bound algorithm for single machine sequencing with precedence constraints to minimize total weighted completion time', *Management Science*, 31:1300-1311.

Queyranne, M. (1986) 'Structure of a single machine scheduling polyhedron', Working Paper, Faculty of Commerce and Business Administration, University of British Columbia, Vancouver, B.C.

Queyranne, M. and Y. Wang (1988) 'Single machine scheduling polyhedra with precedence constraints', Working Paper 88-MSC-017, Faculty of Commerce and Business Administration, University of British Columbia, Vancouver, B.C.

Wolsey, L.A. (1985) 'Mixed integer programming formulations for production planning and scheduling problems', Invited Talk at the 12th International Symposium on Mathematical Programming, MIT, Cambridge, August 1985.

Wolsey, L.A. (1989) 'Formulating single machine scheduling problems with precedence constraints', CORE Discussion Paper 8924, Université Catholique de Louvain, Louvain-la-Neuve, Belgium.

SUBJECT INDEX